Sensation and Perception

Sensation and Perception

THIRD EDITION

E. Bruce Goldstein

University of Pittsburgh

Wadsworth Publishing Company

Belmont, California

A Division of Wadsworth, Inc.

Psychology Editor: Kenneth King
Production Editor: Harold Humphrey
Managing Designer: Donna Davis
Print Buyer: Karen Hunt
Art Editor: Cathy Aydelott
Designer: Al Burkhardt
Copy Editor: Rene Lynch
Illustrators: Cyndie Clark-Huegel, John Foster, Wilma
Yeshke, Elizabeth Clark
Compositor: Graphic Typesetting Service
Cover Painting: Tony King, *Aesop 2*, 1977, acrylic on
canvas, 68 × 68 in. Reprinted by permission of O.K.
Harris Gallery, New York, New York
Cover Design: Donna Davis

Illustration credits appear at the end of the book.

Printed in the United States of America   34

    2   3   4   5   6   7   8   9   10——93 92 91 90 89

Library of Congress Cataloging-in-Publication Data

Goldstein, E. Bruce, 1941–
        Sensation and perception/E. Bruce Goldstein.—3rd
    ed.
            p.   cm.
        Bibliography: p.
        Includes indexes.
        ISBN 0-534-09672-7
        1. Senses and sensation.   2. Perception.   I. Title.
QP431.G64   1989   88-14198
152. 1—dc19   CIP

To Barbara

Brief Contents

Detailed Contents

C H A P T E R **3**

Basic Mechanisms of Vision   64

C H A P T E R **4**

Perceiving Color   108

CHAPTER **5**

Perceiving Brightness and Contrast   145

CHAPTER **6**

Perceiving Objects and Forms   188

CHAPTER 7

Perceiving Depth and Size   227

CHAPTER 8

Perceiving Movement and Events   274

CHAPTER 9

Perceptual Development   318

CHAPTER 10

Clinical Aspects of Vision   355

CHAPTER **11**

Hearing I: Psychophysics   382

CHAPTER **12**

Hearing II: Physiological Mechanisms   418

C H A P T E R *13*

Perceiving Speech   447

C H A P T E R *14*

The Cutaneous Senses   469

C H A P T E R *15*

The Chemical Senses   496

Boxes

Demonstrations

Preface

The book you are about to read is about research that asks questions like "How do our senses operate?" "What is the connection between nervous system activity and perception?" "How do people use information in the environment to perceive the environment?" What unfolds on these pages is a story about the many ingenious ways that have been used to answer these questions. About scientists collecting data ranging from the electrical firings of single nerve cells to people's descriptions of their experiences. About scientists proposing theoretical models to give meaning to this data. About research on topics ranging from molecular mechanisms to mental processes.

The diversity of the methods and theoretical approaches that have been used to answer questions about perception is reflected in this book by the description of research that studies perception at two levels of analysis: the physiological level, which focuses on relationships between stimuli and physiological processes (Figure a, below), and the psychophysical level, which focuses on relationships between stimuli and perception (Figure b). In addition, we pay considerable attention to the cross-talk between these levels that yields relationships between physiological processes and perception (Figure c).

The book's chapters are organized as follows: introduction to the field (Chapter 1); physiological principles (Chapter 2); introduction to vision (Chapter 3); vision (Chapters 4 through 10); hearing and speech (Chapters 11 through 13); the cuta-

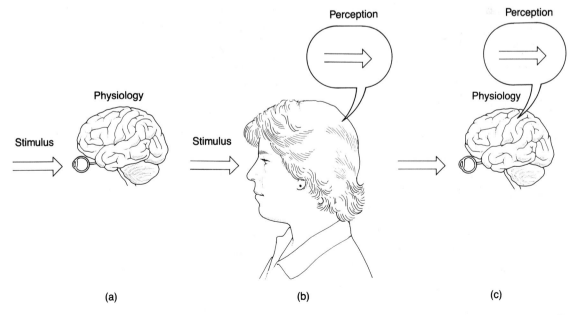

(a)   (b)   (c)

neous senses (Chapter 14); and the chemical senses (Chapter 15). Those familiar with the second edition will notice that most of the chapters have been rewritten and that Chapter 1 is entirely new. This new Chapter 1 replaces the description of psychophysical methods and signal detection that opened the second edition (now in Appendices A and B). The purposes of this new chapter are to transmit the excitement of the field of perception, to introduce some of the methods of perceptual research, and to make clear the idea that perception is best studied both at different levels of analysis and from different theoretical perspectives.

This book also stresses the idea that there are basic principles that hold across all of the senses. These principles are introduced in the first five chapters and are then illustrated throughout the rest of the book. For example, the chapter on the cutaneous senses (Chapter 14) highlights a number of these principles by its organization into sections that each state a specific parallel between vision and the cutaneous senses. This treatment reinforces the theme that there are basic principles that hold across all senses, while at the same time emphasizing the special properties of the cutaneous system.

In addition to an increased emphasis on basic principles and theoretical perspectives, this edition also includes two new features:

Demonstrations. "Student involvement" exercises integrated into the flow of the text so they will not be seen as "extras" that can be ignored.

Study questions. Questions keyed to page numbers in the text, specific enough to be helpful in studying for exams.

Features of the second edition that also appear in this edition are: end-of-chapter summary lists and glossary definitions, an extensive art program (expanded by over 200 new illustrations, most of them original drawings or photographs), interesting boxes (10 new ones, but 8 fewer boxes than the second edition since much of the previously boxed material has been integrated into the text), and extensive references (over 200 new ones, most from the 1980s).

There are also a large number of additions of content. Just a few of the topics that have been expanded from the second edition or are introduced for the first time here are: information processing by neural networks, "mapping" in neural structures, the role of extrastriate cortical areas in vision, spatial frequency effects in vision, hypothesis testing, "top down" processing, the information processing and computational approaches to form perception, the ecological approach to depth perception, event perception, vision and locomotion, the perception of music and complex tones, the theory of acoustic invariance in speech, and kinesthesis.

What will you know when you finish reading this book? You will know many of the facts about perception—about the structures of sensory systems, about how circuits of neurons influence perception, about how perception is controlled by sources of information in the environment. But I hope you will know more than just a list of facts. You will know that these facts add up to an understanding of how we experience the world around us. You will more fully appreciate the extraordinary complexity of the mechanisms responsible for this experience. You will know that there have been impressive recent advances in our knowledge of perception but that there is still much left to be discovered. But, most important of all, I hope that reading this book will make you more aware of how perception affects you personally. After all, perception is something you experience all the time, and the study of perception can enhance this experience. I've found that studying perception has made me more observant of my environment, more aware of my perceptions, and more appreciative of the miraculous process that transforms energy falling on receptors into the richness of experience. I hope reading this book has the same effect on you.

Pittsburgh, Pennsylvania
June 1988

Acknowledgements

It is a pleasure to write these acknowledgements, both because it is one of the last things I have to do before this project becomes a book, and because it gives me the opportunity to thank all of the people who have been so much help at various stages of this book's writing and production.

My first thanks go to Ken King, my editor, whose responsibility for this book's existence dates from the day we first met, in 1975, when he asked me how the sensation and perception books then available could be improved. I can't remember my answer, but I do remember saying that I had no intention of writing a sensation and perception book. I also remember that three months later Ken had convinced me to change my mind. Now, three editions later, I take this opportunity to say thanks, Ken, for talking me into it and a special thanks for the extraordinary support you have given me during the writing and production of this edition.

I would also like to thank some other people at Wadsworth for seeing the book through the production process. I thank Hal Humphrey for coordinating the production process with such good humor; Donna Davis for making sure the design of the book was "right," and for laughing at my jokes; and Cathy Aydelott for skillfully coordinating the complex art program. I thank Cyndie Clark Huegel, John Foster, Wilma Yeshke, and Elizabeth Clark, the artists whose contributions to this book can be seen in the many new figures that were created for this edition. I also thank Alison Cordray of the Pittsburgh Ballet Theater and Judith Davis of the Greenwich Workshop for graciously providing a number of beautiful pictures for Chapter 6 and the following people for providing scientific photographs: Irving Biederman, F. de Monasterio, Eleanor Gibson, Arthur Ginsburg, Mitchell Glickstein, David Hubel, Diane Kewley-Port, Charles Michael, and Vilaynur Ramachandran.

One of the most important parts of writing a textbook is getting feedback from colleagues who teach courses in sensation and perception and who are experts in various research areas. The following people provided invaluable feedback for this edition by commenting on single chapters, groups of chapters, and, in some cases, the book as a whole.

George J. Anderson
   University of Illinois–Champaign
Frank M. Bagrash
   California State–Fullerton
Irving Biederman
   University of Minnesota
Steve Burns
   Ohio State University
Carol Christensen
   Vassar College
J. Craig Clarke
   Pennsylvania State University
Richard Colker
   University of the District of Columbia
Velma Dobson
   University of Pittsburgh
Tobey Dye
   Loyola University
Robert Erickson
   Duke University

Phyllis Freeman
  SUNY at New Paltz

Howard Flock
  York University

Alan Gilchrist
  Rutgers University

Carl Granrud
  Carnegie-Mellon University

Donald Greenfield
  Eye Institute of New Jersey

Julian Hochberg
  Columbia University

Philip J. Kellman
  Swarthmore College

Diane Kewley-Port
  Indiana University

Donald Mitchell
  Dalhousie University

Roger Oesterreich
  SUNY at Albany

Alan Pantle
  Miami University

John Pittenger
  University of Arkansas at Little Rock

Dennis Proffitt
  University of Virginia

Vilaynur Ramachandran
  University of California–San Diego

James R. Sawusch
  SUNY at Buffalo

Earl D. Schubert
  Stanford University

Alan Searleman
  St. Lawrence University

Anne Treisman
  University of California–Berkeley

Brian A. Wandell
  Stanford University

Mike Wogalter
  University of Richmond

Finally, I thank Barbara Baker, to whom this book is dedicated, for her love, support and encouragement throughout this project.

About the Author

E. Bruce Goldstein is Associate Professor of Psychology at the University of Pittsburgh. He received his bachelor's degree in chemical engineering from Tufts University, his PhD in experimental psychology from Brown University and, before joining the faculty at the University of Pittsburgh, was a post-doctoral Research Fellow in the biology department at Harvard University. Dr. Goldstein has published numerous papers in visual physiology (Goldstein, 1967, 1978) and the psychophysics of visual perception (Goldstein, 1979, 1987, 1988). He teaches sensation and perception, introductory psychology, the psychology of gender, the psychology of film, and the psychology of art.

Note to the Student

As you read this book, you will encounter many facts about perception. You will also encounter two special features to help you learn these facts and to make them more meaningful to you.

One of these features, demonstrations or "mini-experiments," takes you beyond simply learning the facts of perception by engaging you in your own perceptual observations. These demonstrations are an integral part of the text, so be sure to read them. Better yet, however, *do* them. After all, since perception is something you *experience,* it is ridiculous to study it by just learning facts. Learning about perception firsthand by experiencing it should increase your understanding of the material and may also improve your ability to remember it.

Another feature, "Study Questions," is a list of questions to test your knowledge of what you have read. These questions, which you will find at the end of each chapter, are keyed to page numbers in the text, so you can find the answer on the page indicated.

Introduction to Perception

SOME QUESTIONS ABOUT PERCEPTION

On the first day of class I ask my students to write down a few of their questions about perception. Most people have no trouble doing this, and I usually receive questions ranging from the far out ("Is it true that blind people have a sixth sense that enables them to detect obstacles before they hit them?" "Are there any physiological mechanisms that explain ESP?") to their own experience ("Why does the eye still see the image of a spot of light after being exposed to a flashbulb?") to other people's experience ("Does everyone perceive things in the same way, or do some people perceive things differently than I do?" "What does a person who is color-blind see?") to physiology ("What mechanisms in the ear change mechanical energy into electrical energy?")

In this book we will discuss many of the questions that people ask before taking a course in perception. And we will also discuss many of the questions that people hardly ever ask before taking a course in perception, such as, "How do I perceive my friend Nancy?" or "Why doesn't the shape of

my desk appear to change as I walk past it?" People don't ask these questions because it is usually not obvious to them that there's a problem. You probably take seeing Nancy for granted. You may think that to see Nancy you only have to look at her, because it may not have occurred to you that seeing Nancy is the end result of a long, complex process. It may also not have occurred to you that the image your desk creates inside your eye changes drastically as you look at the desk from different vantage points, and that something must be happening to keep your perception of the desk from distorting each time you look at it from a new angle. One purpose of this book is to make you aware that much of what we take for granted in perception is really very complex and, in some cases, not well understood. You will see that perception does not just "happen."

WHAT ARE SENSATIONS AND PERCEPTIONS?

Since this book (and perhaps the course you're taking) is called Sensation *and* Perception, it seems logical to infer that **sensation** and **perception** are

F I G U R E 1 . 1 A face made up of "sensations." Each dot on this face represents an elementary "sensation." According to psychology circa 1900, all of these sensations add up to create our perception of the face.

two different things. And, in fact, historically, a distinction has been made between sensations and perceptions. Thomas Reid (1785), the philosopher who made the original distinction between sensations and perceptions, proposed that the crucial difference between them was that perceptions always refer to external objects, whereas sensations refer to experiences within a person that are not linked to external objects.

For example, smelling a rose, according to Reid, can involve both sensation *and* perception. Your experience is a *sensation* if you smell an odor without reference to the rose. "I smell sweetness" would, therefore, be a sensation. However, your experience is a *perception* if the odor is linked with the rose. "The rose smells sweet" would, therefore, be a perception.

Another example, following Reid's way of distinguishing between sensation and perception, would be to say that if we see the light of a star we are *sensing* a tiny point of brightness. But as soon as we see this point of brightness as linked to an actual object, such as the star, or even if we mistake it for a firefly, we are *perceiving* a star or a firefly.

This idea that perceptions always refer to external objects has played a role in some researchers' discussions of how infants perceive. It has been proposed, for example, that infants begin life experiencing only sensations and encounter perceptions only after they have had enough experience

with the world to link their sensations to the objects in the external world that produce them.

A different approach to distinguishing between sensation and perception was taken by the **structuralists,** a group of psychologists who, in the early 1900s, proposed that sensations are the elementary building blocks of perceptions. According to this idea, perceptions are created by the addition of numerous sensations, so each of the dots that make up the face in Figure 1.1 results in a sensation, and the sum of these sensations creates a perception— a "face," in this case. We will see later in this chapter that the structuralists' proposal that many sensations add together to form perceptions is not accepted today.

A practical problem with any distinction between sensations and perceptions is that in most everyday situations we *perceive* rather than just have sensations. For example, we usually interpret a flash of light as being generated by a light-emitting thing located in space, rather than being a disembodied sensation. Many psychologists, therefore, feel that, while it may be interesting to speculate about possible differences between sensations and perceptions, this distinction is not a very useful one. We take this point of view in this book, and will use the term *perception* to refer to all experiences caused by stimulation of the senses. From our point of view we *perceive* a single flash of light, or red, or a red Corvette. We will devote our energy not to trying to define perception, but to trying to understand how stimulation of the senses results in "redness," "automobiles," "sounds," "music," and all of the other experiences that are part of our awareness of the world around us.

WHY STUDY PERCEPTION?

Things that routinely happen every day do not capture our attention. Such is the case with perception. Along with breathing, it is one of our most routine activities, so we tend to take it for granted. But let's consider for a moment what life would be like without our senses. What would it be like to be without vision? or without hearing? or without touch? People missing just one of these senses are severely handicapped, although most learn to cope with their loss. But what if you were born lacking all three of these senses *plus* the ability to taste and smell? The effect would be shattering, because you would be isolated from everything in your environment. Consider for a moment what this would mean. If you survived infancy, would you ever become conscious of your isolation? Would you ever be able to develop language or the capacity to think? We can only speculate as to the answers to these questions, but one thing is certain—your experience would be barren and your very survival would be dependent on others.

The importance of the senses was recognized by the first psychologists, who reasoned that topics such as thinking, learning, memory, and emotion, all of which are central to the concerns of psychology, depend on receiving information about the outside world from our senses. Thus, research on the senses was of central importance in the work of most of the psychological laboratories that were being established in the United States and Europe at the end of the 19th and beginning of the 20th centuries, and many of the first psychologists were, therefore, perceptual psychologists.

Perception has interested researchers not only because of the central role it plays in all behaviors,

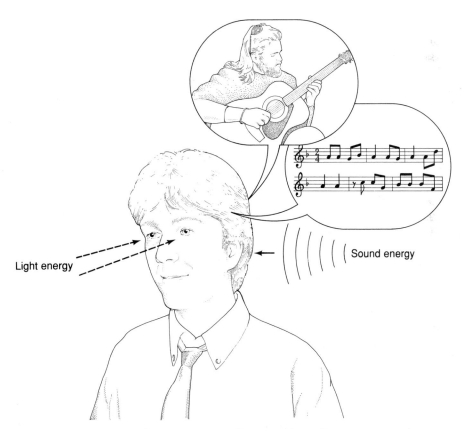

F I G U R E   1. 2   Light energy entering the eyes and sound energy entering the ears is turned into "vision" and "hearing," respectively. The environmental energy, indicated here by arrows and "sound waves," actually has a complex structure. Although "experience" is indicated by "experience balloons" emanating from the brain, the person's experience is located not in his brain but in the world around him. How environmental energy is transformed into perceptual experience is what this book is about.

but also because of its central role in the **mind-body problem,** one of the great unsolved scientific and philosophical problems of our time.

To understand the mind-body problem, consider the person in Figure 1.2. Light energy enters the person's eyes, sound energy (pressure changes in the air) enters the person's ears, and the person "sees" the light and "hears" the sound. But what causes these experiences of seeing and hearing? Most people answer this question by saying that we see and hear because of activity in the brain. But what is actually happening in the brain? Light does not reach the brain. Sound waves do not reach the brain. Instead, electrical signals carried in nerve fibers reach the brain, and it is these electrical signals that cause our experience of seeing and hearing. Therefore, perception, our *experience* of seeing the light or hearing the sound, results from a *physical process,* electrical signals in nerve fibers. The mind-body problem poses the question: How are these physical processes *transformed* into experience?

Bernita Rabinowitz, a student in my class, posed this question more eloquently in the following response to my request for questions about perception on the first day of class:

A human perceives a stimulus (a sound, a taste, etc.): This is explained by the electrical impulses sent to the brain. This is so incomprehensible, so amazing. How can one electrical impulse be perceived as the taste of a sour lemon, another impulse as a jumble of brilliant blues and greens and reds, and still another as bitter, cold wind? Can our whole complex range of sensations be explained by just the electrical impulses stimulating the brain? How can all of these varied and very concrete sensations—the ranges of perceptions of heat and cold, colors, sounds, fragrances and odors, tastes—be merely and so abstractly explained by differing electrical impulses?

One way to answer Bernita's question would be to try to explain how electrical impulses are *transformed* into perceptual experiences. If we could provide this explanation, we would have solved the mind-body problem. However, even the most brilliant scientist could not tell you how electrical signals in the brain (the body part of the mind-body problem) *become* perceptions (the mind part of the mind-body problem). The mind-body problem remains one of the great *unsolved* problems of our day.

Given their inability to determine *how* electrical signals become experience, scientists have done the next best thing and have searched for *relationships* between electrical signals and experience. Thus, we can tell Bernita that she sees reds, blues, and greens because of electrical activity in one area of her cortex and that she experiences the taste of lemon or a cold wind because of activity in other areas of her cortex. We can also tell her that her perception of red can be linked to a certain pattern of activity in one group of nerve cells in the visual system, whereas her perception of blue is caused by a particular pattern of activity in another group of nerve cells. A large portion of this book is about these relationships between physiological processes and experience.

Another question which has motivated people to study perception is, "What do animals perceive?" Perceptual research has shown that the perception of a rhesus monkey matches that of a human in many respects, but that most animals live in perceptual worlds that differ greatly from ours. Cats can't see small details as well as humans but can see large blurred forms better. Cats can see some colors, but not as many as humans. Dogs and many birds can hear sounds far beyond the range of human hearing, and bats sense their environment by a built-in sonar system.

Closely related to peoples' fascination with how animals perceive is their interest in how human infants perceive. Although the human infant was originally thought to possess few perceptual capacities, recent research has shown that infants can perceive much more than they were originally given credit for and that many of their perceptual abilities develop rapidly to close to adult levels during the first year of life.

While answering questions related to the mind-body problem and about the nature of animal and infant perception is a strong motivation to study perception, we also study it for more practical reasons. The study of perception has enabled us to begin to design devices to help blind people see and deaf people hear. We have learned how to precisely measure perceptual capacities so we can

B O X   1. 1   /   *Do You See What I See?*

Do you ever wonder whether you perceive things in the same way as everyone else? Most psychologists and philosophers feel it makes sense to assume that the general characteristics of most people's perceptions are the same. However, if you subscribed to a philosophical position called **radical skepticism,** you would believe that it is just as likely as not that other people perceive things very differently than you. The following statement, taken from a paper on the philosophy of perception, represents how a radical skeptic would view perception (Harman, 1974):

> You may not have the slightest reason to suppose that visual perception gives other people experiences that are anything like your visual experiences. Perhaps someone else has what would be for you auditory experiences. When he looks at the blue sky, it is like hearing middle C on the piano is for you. There seems to be no way to tell, since he would have been brought up to call that sort of experience the experience of blue. Indeed it is not clear that you have the slightest reason to suppose that others have anything you could recognize as experience. When others see things, their visual experience may be something you could not even imagine.
>
> But then is there any reason to suppose that others have experience at all? The suggestion is that, even if you could know that the people around you were made of flesh and blood, born of women, and nourished by food, they might for all you know be automatons, in the sense that behind their elaborate reactions to the environment there might be no experience.

But the suggestion is not merely that you do not *know* whether other people have any experience but also that you haven't the slightest reason to suppose they do.

Similarly, it might be suggested that you haven't the slightest reason to believe you are in the surroundings you suppose you are in, holding a book, reading an article on epistemology. It may look to you and feel as it would look and feel if you were in those surroundings, holding a book and reading an article. But various hypotheses could explain how things look and feel. You might be sound asleep and dreaming, or a playful brain surgeon might be giving you these experiences by stimulating your cortex in a special way. You might really be stretched out on a table in his laboratory with wires running into your head from a large computer. Perhaps you have always been on that table. Perhaps you are quite a different person from what you seem: you are a volunteer for a psychology experiment that involves having the experiences of someone of the opposite sex reading an article about epistemology in English, a language which in real life you do not understand. Or perhaps you do not even have a body. Maybe you were in an accident and all that could be saved was your brain which is kept alive in the laboratory. For your amusement you are being fed a tape from the twentieth century. Of course, that is to assume you have to have a brain in order to have experience; and that might be just part of the myth you are being given.

describe normal perception and, more important, so we can specify the perceptual losses that occur due to ageing, disease, or injury. We have applied our knowledge of perception to the acoustical design of concert halls and to the analysis of perfume fragrances. And our knowledge of perception has been

essential for understanding the perceptual demands encountered when driving cars, piloting airplanes, and making observations from inside space vehicles.

Understanding perception is also important for appreciating the perceptual experience called "art." A person visiting an art museum has made a decision to spend some time "perceiving" art, but for most people this perceptual experience is not aided by any knowledge of perception. Students who take my course, "The Psychology of Art," which relates our knowledge of perception to the process of perceiving pictures, see that an understanding of perception adds another dimension to their ability to "see" works of art.

So, the reasons to study perception range from a need to satisfy our intellectual curiosity about how the body works, to a need to develop practical solutions to perceptual problems, to the desire to better appreciate the perceptual aspects of art. But even if these reasons didn't exist, there is another reason for studying perception that is relevant to everyone reading this book. *Perception is something you experience all the time,* and the study of perception can enhance this experience. Studying perception will make you more aware of the environment around you and the processes that transform this environment into the experiences we call "perception."

The remainder of this chapter sets the stage for our study of perception by first looking at some of the ways perception can be studied and then describing some of the major theories of perception.

HOW CAN WE STUDY PERCEPTION?

Steps in the Perceptual Process

To begin to answer the question "How can we study perception?" let's consider the person in Figure 1.3 as he approaches a chair. To simplify our discussion, let's, for the moment, freeze this person in place and consider what is happening at a particular point in time. We begin our analysis of the perceptual process by dividing the process of perceiving the chair into the following seven steps:

1. Light hits the chair and is reflected into the person's eye.
2. An image of the chair is formed on the person's **retina,** a network of cells that line the back of his eye.

3. Electrical signals are generated by the **receptors,** structures designed to pick up energy from the environment and to change this environmental energy into electricity.
4. These electrical signals are transmitted from the receptors toward the brain by **neurons,** cells that are specialized for the transmission of electricity in the nervous system.
5. These electrical signals reach the brain.
6. These electrical signals are "processed" or "analyzed" by the brain.
7. The person perceives the chair.

These seven steps are a good starting point, but they don't do justice to the complexity of the perceptual process. First of all, static images (step 2) rarely occur. Both the perceiver's eyes and body are usually moving. Thus, if we could look at a person's retina, we would see images in constant motion. So when we unfreeze our person, allowing him to resume his approach to the chair, his movement creates movement on the retina, which sends new signals on their way to the brain, creating new perceptions to be experienced by the person. These new perceptions in turn create new possibilities for action, enabling the person to approach the chair and sit in it. So a more accurate view of the perceptual process includes two more steps:

8. The person reacts to his perception, usually by moving.
9. This movement changes the stimulus reaching the person, and the process continues.

Thus, while it is possible to break the perceptual process into a sequence of steps, as we have done above, it is more accurate to think of this process not as individual steps, but as a continuing process in which different processes are continuously occurring and, in some cases, affecting one another. Thus, as electrical signals reaching the brain create one moment's perception of the chair, new signals are being generated at the receptors to be sent toward the brain to create the next moment's perception, with the end result being a smooth, continuous perception of the chair as we move toward it.

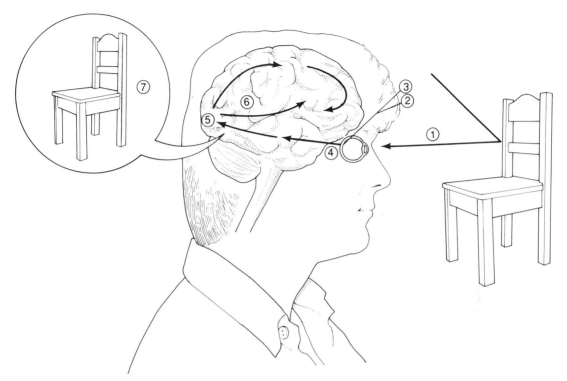

F I G U R E 1. 3 A very schematic picture of some of the steps in the perceptual process. Light bounces off of the chair (1) and into the person's eye, where it forms an image on the retina (2) and generates electrical impulses in the receptors (3). Nerve impulses travel along nerve fibers (4), reach the brain (5) where they are "processed" (6), and the perceiver sees the chair (7).

But, in addition to the above, we must also consider the role of cognitive processes such as thinking and memory. These cognitive processes are both an outcome of the perceptual process and a determinant of that process. Our perception of the chair may trigger thoughts about the chair, and our memories of chairs we have seen in the past may influence our perception of the chair. As we will see in this book, the process of perception involves an interaction between the information stimulating the receptors and information from our past experiences that is already within us.

How can we understand the process of perception? The answer to this question depends on whom you talk to, with different researchers focusing on different parts of the process. In the rest of this section we will look at a few of the approaches that have been used. We will see that some research takes a purely psychological approach, some takes a purely physiological approach, and some combines psychology and physiology. We will also see that most research, in order to simplify the problem of explaining perception, has dealt with the "frozen" observer of steps 1–7 above. But in addition we will see that some research does take the interaction between perception and action into account.

The Psychophysical Approach

Psychophysics is the study of the relationship between the physical stimulus and the observer's perceptual response to that stimulus.* Thus, psychophysics is the relationship between the beginning of the perceptual process (steps 1 and 2) and the end (step 7), leaving out the physiological steps in between. Although psychophysics skips over these physiological steps, psychophysical relationships often become the starting point for physiological investigations. Thus, as you read the following descriptions of psychophysical methods below, notice that many of the psychophysical results we will describe lead to physiological questions.

The phenomenological method.   One way to determine the relationship between the stimulus and perception is to ask the observer what he or she perceives. This is the **phenomenological method** of studying perception. This method is important because the first step in any area of perception research is describing the phenomenon to be studied. For example, in his studies on the colors of the spectrum in the 1660s, Isaac Newton's first step was to accurately describe the spectrum by assigning color names to its different wavelength bands. This step then opened the way for more quantitative investigations of the mechanisms of color vision, which still continue today.

A more recent example of the use of the phenomenological method is provided by Charles Tart's (1971) investigations of the psychological effects of marijuana. Tart constructed a questionnaire of over 200 statements, which described possible effects of marijuana and asked users to indicate how often each effect happened to them when they smoked marijuana. The results for one of the statements having to do with vision were as follows:

> Statement: "Things seen are seen more sharply in that their edges, contours, stand out more sharply against the background."

---

*The "classical" psychophysical *methods*, as developed by the early perceptual psychologists, emphasized the measurement of precise quantitative relationships between stimuli and perceptions. For example, a number of psychophysical procedures were designed to measure thresholds—the minimum amount of energy needed to detect a stimulus. *The psychophysical approach* as described here includes these methods as well as other, less quantitative techniques for determining relationships between stimuli and perceptions. More detailed descriptions of the "classical" psychophysical methods can be found in Appendix A.

Percent of users who experienced this effect:

Never	13
Rarely	13
Sometimes	31
Very Often	30
Usually	11

Thus, most people indicate that their vision is sharper when under the influence of marijuana.

The descriptions of the marijuana experience provided by Tart's questionnaire have led to additional quantitative research. For example, the report of sharper vision has led a number of researchers to test the **visual acuity** of people under the influence of marijuana. A visual acuity test measures the sharpness of vision by determining how much detail a person can detect. The most familiar kind of visual acuity test is the eye chart in your optometrist's or ophthalmologist's office.

The results of these visual acuity measurements have been surprising, however, because so far no one has been able to show that people under the influence of marijuana have better visual acuity than people not under the influence. This does not mean that results from the phenomenological method are wrong but rather that the phenomenological method and the standard acuity tests may be measuring different things. In this case the phenomenological method appears to have detected a perceptual effect that is difficult to measure with conventional techniques.

DEMONSTRATION

Modes of Color Appearance

In 1935 David Katz wrote a book called *The World of Colour*, in which he proposed that there are a number of different ways of perceiving colors that he called **modes of color appearance.** He distinguished these modes phenomenologically by simply noticing differences in their appearance. For example, he called two of them **surface color** and **film color.** We can appreciate some of the properties of these two modes of appearance by repeating some of Katz' phenomenological observations.

Distinguishing between surface and film modes. Surface mode: Look at a colored surface like a piece of paper, or the top of your desk. Where is the color located? (Katz' answers appear below.) Film mode: Punch a ¼-inch hole in a piece of cardboard or an index card and, holding the card 3–6 inches from you, view a surface from far enough away so you can't see the surface's texture. Be sure there is no glare on the surface. Where is the color located? Another way to see the film mode is to look at an area of clear sky, either with or without your peephole.

Katz' observations: The surface mode is located directly on the surface, and offers what Katz calls "visual resistance." The location of the film mode is uncertain, it has a spongy texture, and it can be penetrated.

Some characteristics of the film mode. While viewing the sky, make the following observations:

(a) Looking through your peephole viewer, how far away from the edge of the peephole does the surface of the sky appear?

(b) How does viewing the sky through a tube affect your perception of the sky's distance?

(c) Tilt your peephole viewer. What effect does this have on the apparent orientation of the sky's surface?

(d) Hold a card so that one edge is much closer to you than the other edge. Where is the sky located in relation to the near and far *corners* of the card?

Katz' observations: (a) The sky appears to be located at an indeterminate, but fairly close, distance from the edge of the peephole, and this distance changes little if the peephole's distance from you is changed. (b) The sky appears farther away when viewed through the tube. (c) The sky's orientation "tilts" when the peephole is tilted. (d) The part of the sky adjacent to the closer corner will appear nearer to you than the part of the sky adjacent to the farther corner, causing the impression of what Katz called an *arched* film color.

The phenomenological observations described above show that our perception of where a color is located in space depends on how we view the color. Katz' book provides many more phenomenological observations that show that seeing a color on a surface is only one of the ways in which we perceive color.

F I G U R E 1. 4 A scene with depth information. The fact that the person's body occludes the car indicates that she is in front of the car. The textured pattern of the bricks on the street provides another source of information for depth.

Identification of information sources in the environment. This approach asks the question: "What information in the environment contributes to our ability to perceive specific perceptual qualities?" We can illustrate this approach by considering how it has been applied to the perceptual quality of depth. For example, analysis of the environment pictured in Figure 1.4 reveals that there are a number of sources of information which indicate the relative distances of various objects in the scene. The fact that the person in the foreground covers up, or overlaps, part of the car tells us that the person is between us and the car. Based on this observation, we can suggest that **overlap** is a source of information for depth. We also notice that the texture of the street is coarse in the foreground and becomes finer and finer as distance increases. This change in texture, which creates what psychologists call a **texture gradient,** is another source of information for depth.

This approach to perception is similar to the phenomenological approach since it depends not on making precise measurements but on observation and description. Just as Newton's description of the spectrum led to later, more quantitative, studies relating wavelengths to color perception, so identification of information sources for depth has led to quantitative studies relating these sources of information to depth perception (Chapter 7).

Detection. How dim a light can you see? How faint a sound can you hear? These are questions about **detection,** and when asking these questions we are asking about **absolute thresholds**—the smallest amount of energy needed to detect a stimulus. Measurement of absolute thresholds has shown that we can detect lights containing as few as 7 quanta, where a **quantum** is the smallest possible unit of light energy. (The light bulb in your desk lamp emits tens of billions of quanta every second.) We can also detect odors produced by chemicals that have concentrations as low as 1 part chemical per trillion parts of air, and other animals, most notably dogs, have even lower thresholds for detecting odors. These low absolute thresholds, in defining the exquisite sensitivity of our senses, challenge the physiologist to explain how these biological systems can accomplish such impressive feats of detection.

We are often interested not in measuring absolute thresholds but in measuring **relative thresholds.** In measuring a relative threshold, we aren't interested in determining the exact number of light quanta or odor molecules necessary to detect a stimulus. Instead we are interested in determining how two or more thresholds compare to one another. For example, we might determine that our threshold for tasting a sugar solution is 5 times higher when we have a cold than when we don't have a cold. Or that our threshold for seeing green light is 10 times lower than our threshold for seeing blue light. (That is, 10 times less energy is needed to see a green light than to see a blue light.)

Let's look at an experiment in which we measure relative thresholds by determining the thresholds for seeing lights of different wavelengths. **Wavelength** is a property of light that is related to the fact that light energy travels in waves, much like the waves that are generated by dropping a pebble into a pool of water. The distance between the peaks of these light waves is the wavelength, and the wavelength of visible light is from about 360 nm (nm = nanometer = 10^{-7} cm) to about 760 nm. Color Plate 1.1, which shows the **visible spectrum,** indicates that the color of light changes with its wavelength, with short-wavelength light appearing blue, medium-wavelength light appearing green or yellow, and long-wavelength light appearing orange or red. We will have more to say about the relationship between color and wavelength in Chapter 4, but for now we will focus on measuring the relative threshold of light at different wavelengths.

To determine the threshold for seeing light as a function of wavelength, we present lights of different wavelengths, first 420 nm, then 440 nm, and so on, until we have traversed the entire visible spectrum. At each wavelength we determine the threshold for seeing the light using psychophysical methods designed for this purpose. These methods, described in Appendix A, specify precise, controlled ways for presenting stimuli to determine the minimum amount of light necessary for detection at each wavelength. The result of this series of threshold measurements is the curve in Figure 1.5, which shows that the threshold for seeing light is lowest in the middle of the spectrum; that is, less light is needed to see wavelengths in the middle of the spectrum than to see wavelengths at either the short- or long-wavelength ends of the spectrum.

Threshold is often changed to **sensitivity** by the formula, sensitivity = 1/threshold, and if we do this our relative threshold curve of Figure 1.5 becomes the relative sensitivity curve of Figure 1.6, which is called a **spectral sensitivity curve.** Throughout this book we will refer both to thresholds and to sensitivities, so it is important to

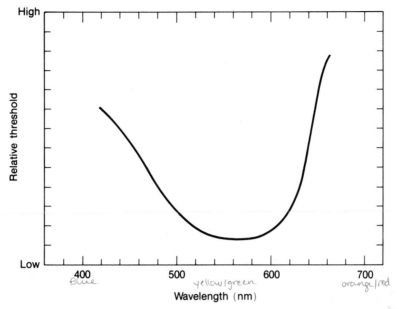

F I G U R E 1. 5 The threshold for seeing a light versus wavelength. (Adapted from Wald, 1964.)

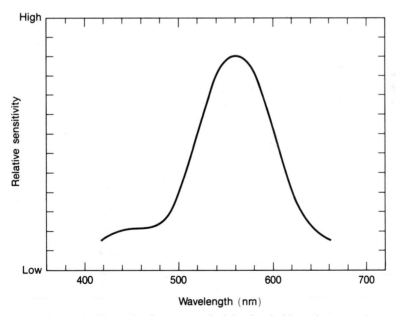

F I G U R E 1. 6 If we take the reciprocal of the thresholds in the curve above (reciprocal = 1/threshold), the curve turns over and becomes a plot of sensitivity versus wavelength, commonly known as a spectral sensitivity curve. (Adapted from Wald, 1964.)

remember that these terms are directly related to one another. Thus, the statements "her threshold for seeing the light is low" and "her sensitivity to the light is high" are equivalent.

Both the relative threshold curve of Figure 1.5 and the spectral sensitivity curve of Figure 1.6 show that the eye is most sensitive in the middle of the spectrum. Why is this so? In Chapter 3 we will see how these measurements of our ability to detect light of different wavelengths can be explained in terms of light-absorbing chemicals in the visual receptors. Thus, our determination of the spectral sensitivity curve is an important step in identifying a physiological mechanism responsible for vision.

Matching. In a **matching** experiment a subject usually adjusts two stimuli so they appear identical. Some of the most important insights into how we perceive colors have been achieved from the results of color-matching experiments in which a subject is presented with a disc illuminated with one wavelength and is asked to adjust the intensities of three other superimposed wavelengths on another disc (Figure 1.7), until both discs appear to be the same color. The fact that subjects can do this raises a question: How can two discs of light that are *physically different*—one containing just one wavelength and the other containing a mixture of three wavelengths—appear to be exactly the same color? As we will see in Chapter 4, the answer to this question is central to our understanding of color vision.

FIGURE 1.7 A color-matching experiment. The left disc, containing light of wavelength = 520 nm, remains constant. The amount of each of three wavelengths, 450, 500, and 620 nm, in the right disc is adjusted by the subject until the color of this disc looks exactly the same as the color of the left disc. When this match is made, the two discs are *perceptually the same*, even though they are *physically different* (they contain different wavelengths).

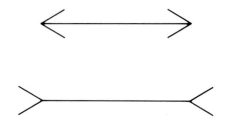

FIGURE 1.8 The Muller-Lyer illusion. Both lines are the same length (measure them), but appear different.

DEMONSTRATION

Measuring the Muller-Lyer Illusion

As you read this book you will become aware that the world is full of **illusions**—situations in which what our senses tell us does not match physical reality. One of the most well-known illusions is the **Muller-Lyer illusion** in Figure 1.8, in which the top line appears longer than the bottom one, even though they are exactly the same length (measure them).

How large is this illusion? One way to answer this question is to use the matching procedure. To do this, create a "standard" stimulus by drawing a line 30 mm long on an index card and adding outward-going fins as in the bottom Muller-Lyer figure. Then, on separate cards, create "comparison stimuli" by drawing 28, 30, 32, 34, 36, 38, and 40 mm lines with inward-going fins as in the top figure. Then ask your subject to pick the comparison stimulus that most closely matches the length of the standard stimulus. The difference between the lengths of the standard and comparison stimuli that match defines the size of the illusion, which usually ranges from 10 to 30 percent. Try running this matching procedure on a number of people to see how variable this illusion is for different people. Also try answering this question: Is the size of the illusion affected by the subject's knowledge of the illusion? Show the subject that the lines in Figure 1.8 are actually the same size, and then redetermine the size of the illusion.

Scaling. If I double the intensity of a light, will it appear twice as bright? If I add two teaspoons of instant coffee to a cup of boiling water, will the resulting coffee taste twice as strong as my usual one-teaspoon brew? Questions like these, about how the *magnitude of experience* is related to the *physical intensity of the stimulus,* are important because these questions explore the nature of our experience in the intensity ranges we encounter every day. Since we usually see objects in illuminations that are far above threshold and we brew our coffee so its taste is far above what we can just detect, it is as important to know how our senses operate at these above-threshold intensities as it is to know how they operate at, or near, threshold.

One of the techniques used to determine the relation between the magnitude of our experience and stimulus intensity is called **magnitude estimation.** This technique, developed by S. S. Stevens (1957), is simple: The experimenter first presents a "standard" stimulus to the subject—for example, a light of moderate intensity—and assigns it a value of, say, 10. Then lights of different intensities are presented, and the subject is asked to assign a number to each light that is propor-

tional to the brightness of the light. If the light appears twice as bright as the standard, it gets a 20, half as bright, a 5, and so on. Thus, each light intensity has a brightness assigned to it by the subject.

By obtaining brightness estimates for each intensity we can plot curves like the one in Figure 1.9, which show the relationship between intensity and brightness. This function, which rises rapidly at first and then levels off, shows that there is not a 1 to 1 relationship between intensity and brightness (see Box 1.2). That is, doubling the intensity does not double perceived brightness. Doubling the intensity causes only a small change in perceived brightness, particularly at higher intensities. This result is called **response compression.** As intensity is increased, brightness increases, but not as rapidly as intensity. To double the brightness it is necessary to multiply the intensity by about nine. A similar situation occurs for hearing. To double the loudness of a tone, we need to increase the energy in the tone by about 10, another example of response compression. But not all senses result in response compression. For example, the relationship between the intensity of an electric shock

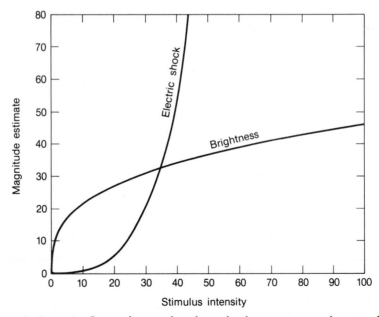

F I G U R E 1. 9 Curves showing the relationship between perceived magnitude and stimulus intensity for electric shock and brightness. (Adapted from Stevens, 1962.)

B O X   1 . 2   /   *The Physical and the Perceptual*

One of the messages of this book is that there is not always a 1 to 1 correspondence between *physical properties* of stimuli and our *perceptual response* to these stimuli. Familiar examples of this lack of correspondence are provided by visual illusions like the Muller-Lyer illusion in Figure 1.8 and the **Wundt-Hering illusion** below. Although the physical stimulus in the Wundt-Hering illusion contains two straight, parallel lines, we see these lines as being curved. It is, therefore, important to distinguish between the physical stimulus and our perceptual response to the stimulus.

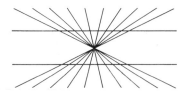

The importance of distinguishing between the physical stimulus and our perceptual response to

it is especially important when we consider the terms "intensity" and "brightness" that we use to describe the magnitude estimation experiments discussed in this section. Although "intensity" refers to a *physical property* of the stimulus and "brightness" refers to the person's *perceptual response* to the stimulus, these terms are often confused.

We can illustrate the difference between these terms by determining the intensity and brightness of the light produced by a small flashlight under two different conditions: (1) inside a dark basement, and (2) outside on a sunny day. When we measure flashlight's intensity with a light meter that records the amount of light energy, we find that the flashlight's intensity is the same whether it is in the basement or outside. Brightness, however, is a different story. In the dark basement, the flashlight appears very bright—its light brightly illuminates the basement, making it easy to see things that, without the light, are not visible. However, outside in the sunny backyard the light from the flashlight appears very dim—we

---

and the sensation produced by that shock, shown by the rapidly upward-sloping curve in Figure 1.9, illustrates **response expansion:** Doubling the shock intensity more than doubles the sensation. Although the curves relating stimulus intensity and perceived magnitude differ for different senses, these curves all follow the same mathematical function. We discuss this property in Appendix A.

Changing the environment. One of the most effective ways to determine the characteristics of the senses is to determine how changing the environment affects our perceptions. One example of this procedure is **dark adaptation,** in which the illumination is changed from light to dark and the person's threshold to a small flashing light is measured as a function of time in the dark. This deter-

mination, which uses the *detection* procedure, shows that the person's sensitivity increases in two distinct stages over a period of 20–30 minutes after the light is turned off (Figure 1.10). In Chapter 3 we will see that this psychophysical result occurs because of the existence of two different types of visual receptors.

D E M O N S T R A T I O N

Spending Some Time in Your Closet

You can demonstrate to yourself the time course of dark adaptation by finding a dark place and making some observations as you dark adapt. A closet is a good place to do this, because it is possible to regulate the intensity of light inside the closet by

can, in fact, hardly even see the light.

Thus, a *constant intensity* can result in *different brightnesses*. Intensity and brightness are not, therefore, the same thing. To measure intensity we measure the effect of the stimulus on a measuring instrument such as a light meter; to measure brightness we measure the effect of the

stimulus on a person. It is important to keep in mind that the response of the measuring instrument and the response of the person are rarely the same—a fact that is illustrated by the results of our magnitude estimation experiment (Figure 1.9), which show that doubling a light's intensity causes only a small change in its brightness.

Flashlight intensity = constant

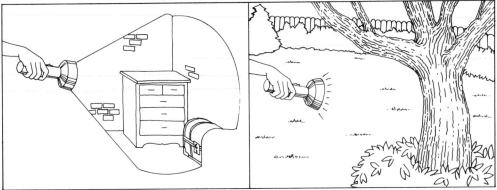

Flashlight brightness = high   Flashlight brightness = low

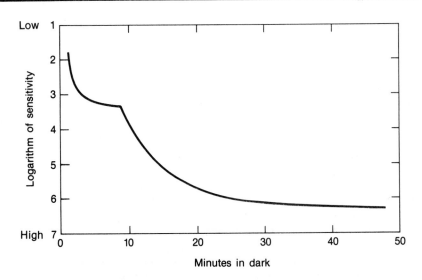

FIGURE 1. 10 Dark adaptation curve. Note that the sensitivity scale is upside down, so the curve above indicates that sensitivity is increasing with time in the dark. (From Chapanis, 1947.)

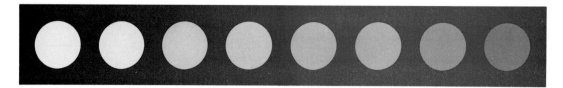

F I G U R E   1. 11

opening or closing the door. The idea is to create an environment in which there is dim light (no light at all, as in a darkroom with the safelight out, is too dark).

Bring this book into the closet, opened to this page. Close the closet door all the way so it is very dark, and then open it slowly until you can just barely make out the white circle on the far left of Figure 1.11.

Your task is simple. Just sit in the dark and become aware that your sensitivity is increasing by noting how the previously invisible circles to the right in Figure 1.11 slowly become visible over a period of about 20 minutes, and how once a circle becomes visible it gets easier to see as time passes.

If you stare directly at the circles they may fade, so move your eyes around every so often. Also, the circles will be easier to see if you don't look directly at them. Look slightly above the circles.

This demonstration demands patience, but remember that to become a Buddhist monk you have to sit motionless in front of the temple door for two days! Sitting in a closet for 20 minutes is easy compared to that. As you sit there, also notice that other objects in the closet slowly become visible, but be careful not to look directly at the light coming through the door, because that will slow the process of dark adaptation.

Another way to use the method of changing the environment to determine the characteristics of the senses is to expose a person to a stimulus for a brief period of time—usually a few minutes or less—and see how this exposure affects the person's perception.

Selective Adaptation to Colors and Tilted Bars

You can demonstrate how a brief exposure to one stimulus can affect perception by closing your right eye and looking at the red patch in Color Plate 1.2. Be sure the red patch is brightly illuminated, and after looking at it with your left eye for about a minute, observe it while blinking back and forth between your left and right eyes. The difference you see poses a question for further investigation: Why does the patch look more washed out when you look at it with your left eye?

Now look at the tilted lines on the left of Figure 1.12. Avoid looking at one place for too long by moving your eyes to different places in the pattern. After about 60 seconds, shift your gaze to the pattern on the right and observe the orientation of the bars. These bars, which are actually vertical, are usually perceived to tilt slightly after you observe the bars on the left.

 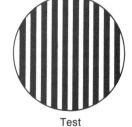

Inspection   Test

F I G U R E 1. 12 Stimuli for measuring the tilt aftereffect. Stare at the inspection pattern on the left for about 60 seconds, and then transfer your gaze to the test lines on the right. If you see the test lines as tilted, you are experiencing the tilt aftereffect.

This perceptual result poses the question: What happened during our 1-minute observation of the inspection bars to cause the test bars to tilt?

Both of the experiments you have just done are examples of **selective adaptation** experiments. The adaptation was *selective* because you observed just one color or just one orientation. As we will see in Chapters 4 and 7, when we discuss these effects further, the results of these experiments give us important insights into how the visual system operates.

Identification. Perception is not only influenced by the properties of the sense organs and the physical properties of the stimuli reaching the receptors, but it is also influenced by the subject's past history and experience with the world.

DEMONSTRATION

Identifying a Stimulus

After looking at the drawing above (Figure 1.13), close your eyes, turn to page 19 (the page just under this one), and open and shut your eyes rapidly to briefly expose the picture in Figure 1.17. Decide what the picture was and then open your eyes and read the explanation below it.

Did you identify Figure 1.17 as a rat (or a mouse)? If you did, you were influenced by the clearly rat- or mouse-like figure you observed initially. But people who first observe Figure 1.18 on page 21 usually identify Figure 1.17 as a man. (Try this demonstration on some other people.) The **rat–man demonstration** shows how the stimulus' meaning and the subject's expectations can influence our perceptions.

Later in this chapter, when we describe the cognitive approach to perception, we will look at another example of how the identification procedure can be used to demonstrate the effect of a person's past experiences on perception.

It should be clear from our discussion above

FIGURE 1.13 Look at this drawing first, then close your eyes, turn the page, so you are looking at the same place on the page directly under this one. Then open and shut your eyes rapidly. (Adapted from Bugelski & Alampay, 1961.)

that there are a large number of different methods of studying perception from a psychophysical point of view. In all of our examples we were looking at the relationship between the stimulus (steps 1 and 2 of the "process of perception") and perception (step 7). But we can also look at the physiological processes in steps 3–6 that intervene between the stimulus and perception.

Perception and Physiology

There are two ways of studying the physiological processes related to perception: (1) "Pure" physiology experiments, in which the major goal is to determine the properties of a physiological system without direct reference to perception, and (2) experiments which look for connections between physiology and perception. As we will see below, both kinds of experiments provide information about the senses, but the most useful approach for our purposes is the second one. Our purpose here will be to present a few examples of experiments done using each approach, leaving the details of physiological procedures to Chapters 2 and 3.

"Pure" physiology. Some researchers focus primarily on physiology, with little concern for the connections between physiology and perception. Such research might focus on the anatomy of a sensory system by tracing the routes that nerve fibers follow as they travel through the nervous system. Or other research might determine how the receptors that pick up energy from the envi-

F I G U R E 1. 14   David Hubel (left) and Torsten Wiesel (right), who won the 1981 Nobel prize in physiology and medicine for their research on the physiology of vision. The results of their research, which we will describe in Chapters 2, 3, 7, and 9, form the basis for much of our knowledge of visual physiology.

ronment transform this energy into electrical signals. These and other "pure" physiology studies, which provide information that helps us understand the physiological operation of the senses, have one thing in common: They do not deal *directly* with perception. Describing how a nerve cell functions may tell us something about the nerve cell, but it tells us nothing about perception, because the nerve cell doesn't perceive. Only people, or animals, can tell us about perception, because they are the ones who do the perceiving. It is, therefore, crucial that we not only study the properties of the nerve cell but that we try to relate these properties to perception.

Relating physiology to perception.   The most powerful way to relate physiology and perception is to look for relationships between physiological and behavioral data collected from the same organism. For example, David Hubel and Torston Wiesel (1962), two researchers who won the Nobel Prize in physiology and medicine in 1981, monitored the electrical activity of nerve cells in the cat's visual cortex (Figure 1.15) and found **orientation-selective cells** that respond best to bars of light oriented in a particular direction. Thus, a particular cell might respond best to a vertically oriented bar and another cell to a bar oriented at a 45-degree angle (Figure 1.16).

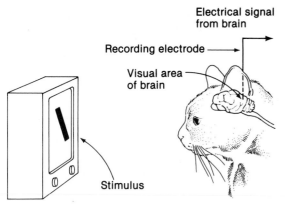

FIGURE 1. 15 Recording electrical signals from the visual cortex of an anesthetized cat. The bar-shaped stimulus on the screen causes nerve cells in the cortex to fire, and a recording electrode picks up the signals generated by one of these nerve cells.

FIGURE 1. 17 Did you see a "rat" or a "man"? Looking at the more rat-like picture in Figure 1.13 increased the chances that you would see this one as a rat. But if you had first seen the man version (Figure 1.18), you would have been more likely to perceive Figure 1.17 as a man. (From Bugelski & Alampay, 1961.)

FIGURE 1. 16 Bar stimuli for testing the response of an orientation-selective cell. These stimuli can be stationary, as on the right, or moving, as on the left.

Gary Blasdel and coworkers (1977) demonstrated a link between these orientation-selective cells and perception by rearing kittens from birth in an environment consisting only of vertical lines and then testing them both behaviorally and physiologically. The behavioral tests showed that these kittens could see vertical lines easily but could not see horizontal lines. The physiological tests showed that these kittens had many cells that responded to vertical lines but no cells that responded to hor-

izontal lines. This parallel between the results of the behavioral and physiological tests supports the idea that these orientation-selective nerve cells are, in fact, related to perception. Throughout this book we will make the point that the results of physiological experiments must be combined with the results of behavioral tests for the physiological results to have meaning for perception.

These links between physiology and perception are often determined entirely in animals, as in the experiments described above. But, often, the results of a physiological experiment on animals are compared to the results of a psychophysical experiment on humans. For example, we will see in Chapter 4 that some cells in the monkey's visual system respond in opposite ways to different colors. Such a cell might respond with an increase in nerve firing to blue light and a decrease to yellow; or with an increase to red light and a decrease to green. These cells have been called **opponent cells** because of the opposite, or opponent, nature of their response to different colors.

DEMONSTRATION

A Psychophysical Demonstration of Opponency

Look at the pattern of squares in Color Plate 1.3, keeping your eye fixed steadily at the center of the pattern for about 60 seconds. Then look at a white piece of paper and observe the resulting **after-image.** (Blink to bring the afterimage back, if necessary.) As you view it, compare the colors of the squares in the afterimage to the colors of the squares in the pattern. When you do this, you may notice an effect similar to those reported for the monkey's nerve cells—the blue square causes a yellow afterimage, the red square, a green afterimage. Just as the responses to blue and yellow are paired in a monkey's nerve cells, the responses to these colors are also paired in the afterimages. In Chapter 4 we will argue that there is a direct connection between the physiology of opponent cells and our perception of color.

Although most of our knowledge of the link between physiology and perception comes from comparing the results of physiological experiments on animals to psychophysical experiments on humans, it has sometimes been possible to make both physiological and psychophysical measurements on humans. For example, remember the dark adaptation experiment, which showed that vision becomes more sensitive as you spend more time in the dark?

What is responsible for this increase in sensitivity? Researchers have been able to link the increase in sensitivity during dark adaptation to an increase in the concentration of **visual pigment,** a chemical in the receptors that decreases in concentration in the light and increases in concentration in the dark. How is this relationship between sensitivity and visual pigment concentration determined? In Chapter 3 we will describe a technique that enables us to continuously monitor the amount of visual pigment in the human eye during dark adaptation.

It should be clear from our discussion so far that we have a large number of techniques at our disposal for studying the various steps in the process of perception. What you have just read are "Previews of Coming Attractions," because in the chapters that follow you will encounter these techniques and results again as we discuss them in more detail.

Descriptions, Mechanisms, and Levels of Explanation in Perception

We began our discussion of psychophysical and physiological methods by asking the question, "How can we understand the steps in the perceptual process?" We answered this question by describing a number of methods for the study of perception. It is important to realize, however, that, no matter which methods we use, we need to answer the following two questions if we are to truly understand perception.

1. What are the phenomena of perception?
2. What causes these phenomena to occur?

The first question requires a *description* of the various perceptual phenomena. The answer to this question includes descriptions of everyday experiences, such as "The rainbow has bands of different colors," "Some grades of sandpaper feel rough and some feel smooth," or "After I enter a dark room, my eyes slowly adjust to the dark." The answer also includes the results of laboratory experiments in which these experiences are measured more precisely or are linked to physical dimensions of the stimulus. For example, "Each band of colors of the rainbow contains light from a different part of the spectrum," or "Increasing the coarseness of a surface makes the surface feel rougher," or "When the illumination is changed from light to dark, a person's sensitivity to light increases in two stages, as shown in Figure 1.10." These descriptions, which are obtained through psychophysical experiments, are an important first step in trying to understand the process of perception, because they define the phenomena we want to explain.

Once the phenomena of perception are described, we can then ask our second question: "What *causes* these phenomena?" To answer this question, we need to understand all of the steps in the perceptual process. Just knowing the relationship between the stimulus and perception, or just knowing about how neurons transmit electrical energy from the receptors to the brain, won't do. We need to be able to understand perception *at all levels* of the perceptual process. David Marr (1982) expresses this thought when he says that

. . . trying to understand perception by studying only neurons is like trying to understand bird flight by studying only feathers (p. 27).

And Marr makes a similar point in the following example:

Think, for example, of the international network of airline reservation computers, which performs the task of assigning flights for millions of passengers all over the world. To understand this system it is not enough to know how a modern computer works. One also has to understand a little about what aircraft are and what they do; about geography, time zones, fares, exchange rates, and connections; and something about politics, diets, and the various other aspects of human nature that happen to be relevant to this particular task (p. 5).

What Marr is suggesting in these two examples is that to truly understand a system we need to analyze it at a number of different *levels*. In this book we will follow Marr's advice by looking at perception both at the *level of stimuli* and at the *level of physiology*.

We study perception at the **level of stimuli** by explaining perception in terms of the stimuli that control it. For example, we can study depth perception by specifying the stimuli in the environment that enable us to see depth. These stimuli include the overlap and texture gradients illustrated in Figure 1.4. In this book we will often describe perception at the level of stimuli. For example, we will show that our perception of depth depends on a number of different sources of information in the environment; we will show that our perception of visual illusions depends on some of the same stimuli that determine our perception of depth; and we will show that our ability to perceive speech depends on certain characteristics of sound signals.

We study perception at the **level of physiology** by explaining perception in terms of the physiological processes that control it. For example, the question "What is the mechanism of color perception?" can be answered by describing the way cells in the visual system respond to different wavelengths of light. Throughout this book, we will describe perception at the level of physiology by showing how the firing of neurons is related to perception.

F I G U R E 1. 18 Man version of the rat-man stimulus. (Adapted from Bugelski & Alampay, 1961.)

Having distinguished between these two levels of explanation, let's return to our psychophysical and physiological methods. Since psychophysics is concerned with the relationship between stimuli and perception, psychophysical methods are used to study perception at the level of stimuli. But we will see that psychophysics also plays an important role in studying perception at the level of physiology, because psychophysical methods have often been used to *predict* physiological mechanisms. For example, the psychophysical observation that looking at a red light causes a green afterimage led to the prediction of physiological processes that respond in opposite ways to red and green lights. Although this prediction was not taken seriously at the time it was proposed in the 1800s, it was confirmed many years later with the development of techniques for recording electrical signals from cells in the visual system.

As you read this book, you will begin to appreciate the richness of the field of perception. You will see that we can think of perception as being caused both by stimuli in the environment and by the firing of neurons in the nervous system. And you will see that these two levels of study do not operate independently of one another—that there is a good deal of "cross-talk" between them.

THE ROLE OF THEORIES IN PERCEPTION

Most perceptual theories focus on a small area within the larger field of perception. Thus, there are the-

FIGURE 1. 19 Max Wertheimer (1880–1943), whose experiments and theoretical writings stimulated the founding of the Gestalt school of psychology.

ories of color vision, theories of pitch perception, theories of visual illusions, and theories of form perception. This subdivision of the field into smaller areas, each serviced by one or more theories, is typical of the situation in science in general. It would, after all, be unreasonable to expect one theory to explain every known disease or to explain all biological or physical phenomena.

While there is no one THEORY OF PERCEPTION, a number of theories have been proposed which define ways of approaching perception and which specify the things that are important to pay attention to as we study perception. We will describe the most important of these perceptual theories or, perhaps more accurately, perceptual *approaches*, below. We will focus on approaches to studying form perception, since this is the area which

has attracted the most attention of perceptual theorists.

Structuralism

Perceptual psychology in the early years of the 20th century was dominated by the structuralists. Perceptions, according to the structuralists, are the result of the addition of many elementary sensations. The importance of this approach, which we described at the beginning of this chapter, is mainly historical, since the view that perceptions are made up of many sensations is not accepted today. But the structuralists' ideas did stimulate the birth of Gestalt psychology, an approach to perception that still flourishes today.

The Gestalt Approach

Gestalt psychology was born as a reaction to the structuralists' idea that perceptions are built up of many sensations. Max Wertheimer, one of the founders of Gestalt psychology (Figure 1.19), proposed the following argument against structuralism. Consider the situation diagrammed in Figure 1.20. A light on the left is flashed on and off, followed by 50 msec (50/1,000 sec) of darkness; then the line on the right is flashed on and off. This sequence of flash-darkness-flash causes a phenomenon called **apparent movement**—the perception of movement from left to right through the dark space separating the two flashed lights. How, asked Wertheimer, is it possible to explain our perception of a line moving through the dark empty space in terms of sensations? Since there is no stim-

(a)
Flash line
on left

(b)
50 msec of
darkness

(c)
Flash line
on right

(d)
Perception:
movement
from left
to right

FIGURE 1. 20 Wertheimer's experiment in movement perception.

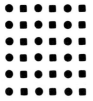

FIGURE 1.21 The perception of this figure as vertical columns illustrates the law of similarity.

ulation whatsoever in that space, there are no sensations present to provide an explanation. With this demonstration, Gestalt psychology replaced structuralism, and the phrase "The whole is different from the sum of its parts" became the battle cry of the Gestalt psychologists.

The Gestalt approach to explaining how we perceive form has centered on **laws of organization,** which are based on the idea that properties of the stimulus determine **perceptual grouping.** For example, the **law of similarity** states that *similar things tend to be grouped together.* According to the law of similarity, we perceive Figure 1.21 as columns of circles alternating with columns of squares, because the similar shapes appear to be grouped together. Similarly, the darkened circles group to create a perception of a "2" in Figure 1.22 because of their similar darkness.

The Constructive Approach

Constructivism, while not rejecting the Gestalt psychologists' ideas, proposes that to explain perception we must consider not only how properties of the *stimuli* influence perceptual grouping but also the active role of the *observer* as he or she takes in information provided by the stimuli. The constructivist approach proposes that perceptions are *constructed* by the observer from perceptual "data" obtained during active observation of the stimulus, with the interpretation of this data sometimes aided by the observer's knowledge of the environment and past experiences in perceiving.

A leading proponent of the constructivist approach, Julian Hochberg (Figure 1.23), places great emphasis on the role of eye movements in

FIGURE 1.23 Julian Hochberg (b1923), professor of psychology at Columbia University, is one of the leading proponents of the constructivist approach to perception.

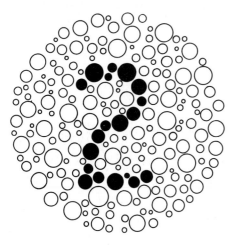

FIGURE 1.22 Grouping determined by similarity of lightness. The light circles form one group and the dark circles form another group.

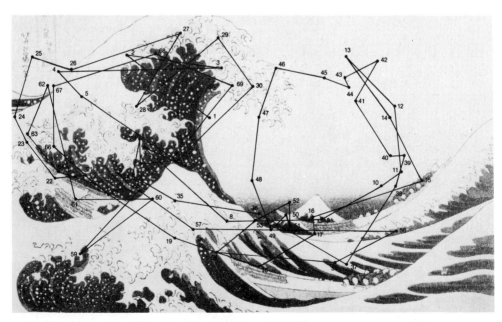

FIGURE 1. 24 A picture of The Wave by Hokusai Katsushika (1760–1850) that was presented to observers by Buswell (1935) in his study of eye movements. The record below indicates the pattern of fixations and eye movements made by an observer viewing this picture. (Also see Yarbus, 1967.)

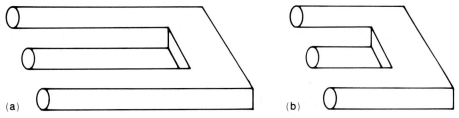

F I G U R E 1. 25   (a) An impossible object. Since we cannot attend to the entire object at once, we need to compare the parts of the object before we realize that it is impossible. (b) It is easier to see that this smaller object is impossible because we don't have to distribute our attention over such a large area.

perception, pointing out that as a person looks at a scene he or she takes in information by a series of **fixations**—in which the eye pauses 1–3 times every second to examine part of the stimulus— and **eye movements,** which propel the eye from one fixation to the next. This is shown in Figure 1.24, a record of the fixations and eye movements made by a subject observing Hokusai Katsushika's picture *The Wave.*

These eye movements are necessary for us to see all of the details of the scene, because a single fixation would reveal only the details near where we are looking. According to Hochberg (1970) these eye movements also have another purpose: The information they take in about different parts of the scene is used to create a "mental map" of the scene by a process of "piecing together" or "integration." The idea that we create a mental map from the information taken in by eye movements is supported by our response to objects like the one in Figure 1.25. When we first look at this object it appears to be a reasonable three-pronged shape. We become aware that it is actually an **impossible object,** one that could not exist in the three-dimensional world, only after we attempt to create a mental map of this object by comparing the information taken in as we fixate different parts of the object.

Hochberg's approach, with its emphasis on eye movements, is just one example of the constructivist approach. Later in this book we will describe other researchers' approaches to constructivism. We will see, however, that they all have in common the idea that our perceptions are the result of an active construction process in which information is combined, or processed, by the observer's mind. This view of perception is the one most compatible with the physiological approach, because the basic assumption behind the physiological approach is that our perceptions are *constructed* from the information contained in nerve impulses.

The Ecological Approach

The founder of the **ecological approach to perception** was J. J. Gibson (1979) (Figure 1.26), who objected to traditional perception experiments in which an observer looks at stimuli while sitting in one place. Gibson felt that, since we are usually moving through the environment, we should study perception in natural settings and should consider the stimulation an observer encounters as he or she moves through the environment. This concern for considering environmental stimuli has led psychologists practicing the ecological approach to focus on studying displays such as the texture gradients in Figures 1.4 and 1.28.

The ecological approach also rejects the constructivists' idea that our perceptions are the result of a constructive process in which information is combined in the observer's mind. According to ecological psychologists, there is enough information present in the environment to make mental calculations unnecessary. To understand the difference between the constructive and ecological approaches, let's consider how each approach would deal with the problem of size perception.

FIGURE 1.26 J. J. Gibson (1904–1979), who was professor of psychology at Cornell University for many years, published three books and many papers that have formed the basis of the ecological approach to visual perception.

A constructivist might argue that since the size of an object's image on our retina depends on its distance from us, our perception of that object's size must somehow involve a "taking into account" of its distance. Thus, as the observer in Figure 1.27 moves away from the cylinder, its image on the retina becomes smaller, so the observer needs to take its greater distance into account to accurately perceive its size.

An ecological psychologist, on the other hand, would argue that taking distance into account isn't necessary, because there is enough information in the environment to enable us to perceive size without considering distance. For example, the fact that the cylinder covers one unit of "texture" on the ground, no matter what the observer's distance (Figure 1.28), provides enough information to indicate its size without the need for a "taking into account" of its distance.

The Cognitive Approach

The **cognitive approach to perception** focuses on how perception is affected by the meaning of a stimulus, and by the subject's expectations. One example of this approach is the rat–man demonstration of Figures 1.13, 1.17, and 1.18. Another example is provided by Steven Palmer's (1975) experiment, in which he used the *identification* pro-

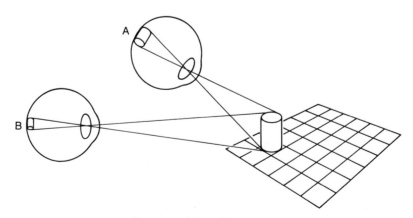

FIGURE 1.27 An observer, indicated by a single eyeball, looking at a cylinder on a checkerboard pattern from two different positions. The cylinder's image on the retina is larger when the observer is close (position A) that when the observer is far (position B).

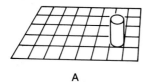
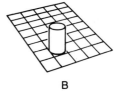

A   B

F I G U R E 1. 28 What the observer in Figure 1.27 sees from positions A and B. Although moving from A to B decreases the size of the cylinder in the field of view and changes the angle of view, the cylinder covers 1 unit of the texture gradient in both situations.

cedure, as follows: Palmer first presented a context scene such as the one on the left of Figure 1.29 and then briefly flashed one of the target pictures on the right. When Palmer asked subjects to identify the object in the target picture, they correctly identified an object like the loaf of bread, which is appropriate to the kitchen scene, 80 percent of the time, but correctly identified the mailbox or drum, two objects that don't fit into the scene, only 40 percent of the time. The subjects' ability to identify the object was affected by their expectations of what things are likely to be found in kitchens.

Experiments like this one add a cognitive dimension to our study of perception. **Cognition,** the study of mental activity, is a rich field that extends beyond perception to areas like memory, problem solving, and reasoning. But we will see

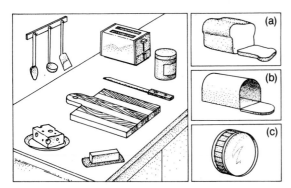

F I G U R E 1. 29 Stimuli used in Palmer's (1975) experiment. The scene at the left is presented first, and the observer is then asked to identify one of the objects on the right.

that these cognitions have an important role to play in perception, as well.

THE PLAN OF THIS BOOK

The goal of this book is to help you to understand the entire process of perception, from reception of the stimulus to the physiological processes triggered by the stimulus to perception of the stimulus. To accomplish this goal, we will look at perception on two different levels:

1. The psychophysical level: studying the relationship between stimuli and perception, and
2. The physiological level: studying the relationship between stimuli and the neural response.

And, most important, we will combine these two levels of analysis by looking at the relationship between neural responses and perception (Figure 1.30).

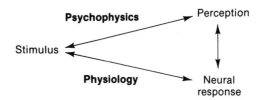

F I G U R E 1. 30 The relationships studied in this book. On the psychophysical level, we study the relationship between stimuli and perception. On the physiological level, we study the relationship between stimuli and the response of neurons. We combine these two levels of analysis by looking at the relationship between neural responses and perception.

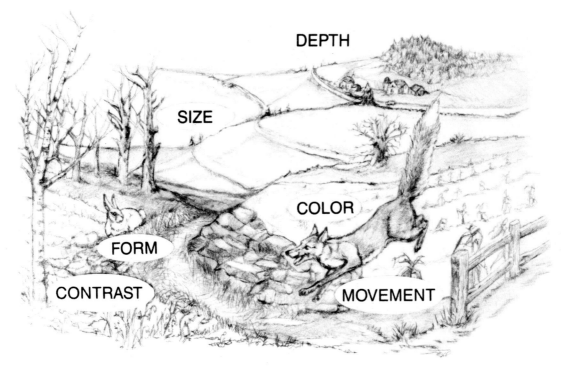

F I G U R E 1. 31 A scene showing some of the perceptual qualities to be described in the chapters that follow. *Color:* The red of the fox. *Contrast:* The difference in lightness between the black and white areas in the birch tree's bark. *Form:* The shape of the rabbit. *Depth:* The distance of faraway objects. *Size:* The height of the tree. *Movement:* The forward motion of the leaping fox. Since everything we see in this scene possesses each of these qualities (with the exception of the stationary parts of the scene, which have no movement), there are countless other examples of each of these qualities within this scene. To understand perception we must, therefore, understand how we perceive each of these qualities. After devoting Chapters 2 and 3 to establishing some physiological principles, we will dedicate Chapters 4–8 to describing what we know about our perception of these qualities.

We have seen that there are a number of methods available for studying perception at each of these levels and that cross-talk between the psychophysical and physiological levels is necessary if we are to relate physiological findings to perception. We have also referred to the fact that physiological mechanisms have sometimes been proposed based on psychophysical results. It is important to realize, however, that psychophysics is not simply a tool to be used in the service of physiology. Research at the psychophysical level of perception is of value in itself, since one of the most important tasks of the perceptual psychologist is to determine the connections between stimuli in the environment and our experiences.

To accomplish our goal, we will, throughout this book, describe both psychophysical and physiological research on perception and the connections between them, where such connections exist. We begin this process by introducing basic principles of sensory physiology in Chapter 2 and basic principles of vision in Chapter 3. These two chapters set the stage for the rest of the book, and especially for the five chapters that follow on visual perception. These chapters describe the qualities of "Color" (Chapter 4); "Brightness and Contrast" (Chapter 5); "Form" (Chapter 6); "Depth and Size" (Chapter 7); and "Movement and Events" (Chapter 8) (Figure 1.31).

These five chapters are followed by two more chapters on vision: "Perceptual Development" (Chapter 9), which describes psychophysical studies of visual development in humans and physiological studies of visual development in animals; and "Clinical Applications of Vision" (Chapter 10), which describes how various disorders can degrade vision.

The remaining five chapters are "Hearing" (Chapters 11 and 12); "Perceiving Speech" (Chapter 13); "The Cutaneous Senses"—touch, temperature, and pain (Chapter 14); and "The Chemical Senses"—smell and taste (Chapter 15).

As you read this book, you will, in each chapter, be introduced to new facts about perception. But you will also begin to notice that certain theories and principles repeat themselves. Although "heat and cold, colors, sounds, fragrances, and odors," to quote from Bernita's question at the beginning of the chapter, are vastly different experiences, they are all determined by the same nervous system and they all add together to create a single perceptual world. It is no wonder, therefore, that the diversity of perception is built on a foundation of similar principles. The first step in discovering these principles is to introduce some basic facts about the nervous system and its role in perception.

Summary

1. Philosophers and early psychologists drew a distinction between "sensation" and "perception." In this book, we will not distinguish between them; we will use the term "perception" to refer to experiences caused by stimulation of the senses.
2. Among the reasons for studying perception are (a) its relation to the mind-body problem, (b) interest in how animals and infants perceive, (c) practical applications of perception, and (d) the relevance of perception to everyday experience.
3. Perception can be broken down into a number of steps, beginning with the stimulus reaching the person's receptors and ending with perception. This process includes the effects of the person's reactions and cognitions.
4. The psychophysical approach to the study of perception involves the determination of the relationship between the physical stimulus and the person's perceptual response to that stimulus. The psychophysical approach yields a variety of kinds of information, using the following methods:
   (a) Phenomenological—describing perceptions. Examples: Tart's marijuana questionnaire; Katz' modes of color appearance.
   (b) Identification of information sources in the environment. Examples: depth information; texture gradients.
   (c) Detection—measuring thresholds. Example: the spectral sensitivity curve.
   (d) Matching—adjusting two stimuli until they appear identical. Examples: color matching; Muller-Lyer illusion.
   (e) Scaling—magnitude estimation of above threshold stimuli. Example: determining the relationship between light intensity and brightness.
   (f) Changing the environment—how do environmental manipulations affect perception? Examples: dark adaptation; selective adaptation to tilts and colors.
   (g) Identification—naming or recognizing a stimulus. Example: rat–man demonstration.
5. The physiological approach to the study of perception involves the study of the inner workings of perceptual systems. "Pure" physiology experiments study physiological processes without direct reference to perception. Experiments that look for connections between physiology and perception are more useful for studying perception. Examples: orientation-selective cells; opponent colors.
6. Two questions we need to answer to understand perception are (a) What are the phenomena of perception? and (b) What causes these phenomena to occur? To answer the first question we describe perceptual phenomena, based on psychophysical procedures. To answer the second question we study perception at both the level of stimuli—explaining perception in terms of the *stimuli* that control it—and at the level of physiology—explaining percep-

tion in terms of the *physiological processes* that control it. These two levels interact; for example, explanations at the level of stimuli have led to the proposal of mechanisms that operate at the level of physiology.

7. There are a number of theories that define ways of approaching perception. Among the most important theoretical approaches are (a) Structuralism: Perception is created from elementary sensations. (b) Gestalt: This theory replaced structuralism with the idea that the whole is different from the sum of its parts. (c) Constructivism: Perceptions are constructed by the observer from perceptual data obtained during active observation. (d) Ecological: It is important to consider environmental stimuli and the moving observer. (e) Cognitive: Perception

can be affected by the meaning of the stimuli and by the subject's expectations.

Boxes

1. According to a philosophical position called radical skepticism, it is just as likely as not that other people perceive things differently than you do. However, most psychologists assume that the general characteristics of most people's perceptions are the same.
2. It is important to distinguish between the physical properties of a stimulus and the perceptual response to that stimulus. For example, the intensity of a light is a physical property, whereas the light's brightness is a perceptual response.

Study Questions

1. How did the philosopher Thomas Reid distinguish between sensations and perceptions? What is the relationship between sensations and perceptions, according to the structuralists? (2)
2. When did the study of perception begin in psychological laboratories? (3)
3. What is the mind-body problem? (4)
4. List four reasons for studying perception. (4)
5. What are the nine steps in the perceptual process? (6)
6. What is psychophysics? (8)
7. What is the phenomenological method? Describe the work of Tart and Katz. (8)
8. What are some of the central concepts associated with "identification of information sources in the environment?" (9)
9. Describe the method of detection. What is an absolute threshold? A relative threshold? What is the relationship between threshold and sensitivity? Describe how the method of detection is used to determine a spectral sensitivity curve. (10)
10. Describe the method of matching and how it can be used to measure the magnitude of an illusion. (12)
11. Describe scaling, using the method of magnitude estimation. (13)
12. What is response compression? response expansion? (13)
13. Give three specific examples of how "changing the environment" can provide information about the senses. (14)
14. Describe your observations while dark adapting in

the closet. What do these observations prove? (14)
15. What is a selective adaptation experiment? (16)
16. Describe how the "identification" procedure has been used to show that perception is affected by past experience. (17)
17. What is a "pure" physiology experiment and what does it tell us about perception? (17)
18. Give examples of experiments that demonstrate connections between physiology and perception. (18)
19. What are the two basic questions we must answer to understand the perception flow diagram? (20)
20. Describe the levels at which we can specify the mechanisms of perception. (20)
21. What is structuralism and why was it abandoned? (22)
22. Describe the basic ideas of the Gestalt approach to perception. (22)
23. What is the constructivist approach? How are impossible objects used to illustrate one of the principles of constructivism? (23)
24. Describe the ecological approach to perception. (25)
25. Describe the cognitive approach to perception. (26)

Boxes

1. Describe the philosophical position of radical skepticism. How do perceptual psychologists deal with this philosophical position? (5)
2. What is the difference between intensity and brightness? Use these two terms in a description of a magnitude estimation experiment. (14)

Glossary

Absolute threshold. The minimum stimulus energy necessary for an observer to detect the stimulus. (10)

Afterimage. An image that is perceived after the original source of stimulation is removed. A visual afterimage usually occurs after fixating on a high-contrast stimulus for 30–60 seconds. (20)

Apparent movement. An illusion of movement that occurs between two objects separated in space when the objects are flashed on and off, one after another, separated by a time interval of about 50–100 msecs. (22)

Cognition. Mental activity. (27)

Cognitive approach. The approach to perception that focuses on how perception is affected by mental processing, stimulus meaning, and the subject's knowledge and expectations. (26)

Constructivism. The approach to perception that proposes that perceptions are constructed by the observer from perceptual "data" obtained during active observation of the stimulus. (23)

Dark adaptation. The process of adapting to the dark. The increase in sensitivity that occurs as a function of time in the dark. (14)

Detection. A procedure in which the subject's task is to determine whether a hard-to-detect stimulus is present. This stimulus can be near threshold or can be partially obscured by other stimuli. (10)

Ecological approach. The approach to perception that emphasizes studying perception as it occurs in natural settings, particularly emphasizing the role of observer movement. (25)

Eye movements. Movements of the eyes that occur as an observer views a stimulus. Voluntary eye movements are rapid movements of the eyes that last 10–80 msecs and are separated by fixations. (25)

Film color. One of the ways of experiencing color. According to Katz, the location of film color is uncertain, as when we see the color of the sky. (8)

Fixations. Pauses made by the eye as an observer views a stimulus. During these pauses, which can last fractions of a second or more, the observer takes in information about the stimulus. (25)

Gestalt psychology. A school of psychology that has focused on developing principles of perceptual organization, proposing that "the whole is different from the sum of its parts." (22)

Illusion. A situation in which an observer's perception of a stimulus does not correspond to the physical properties of the stimulus. For example, in the Muller-Lyer illusion, two lines of equal length are perceived to be different lengths. (12)

Impossible object. An "object" that can be represented by a two-dimensional picture but cannot exist in three-dimensional space. (25)

Laws of organization. A number of rules developed by the Gestalt psychologists that describe how small elements are grouped into larger configurations. (23)

Level of physiology. As used in this book, this refers to explanations of perceptual processes based on the relationship between physiological processes and perception. Related to this is the study of "pure" physiology, in which physiological processes of sensory systems are studied but are not directly related to perception. (21)

Level of stimuli. Investigations of perceptual processes, or explanations of perceptual processes, based on the relationships between stimulus conditions and perception. (21)

Magnitude estimation. A psychophysical method in which the subject assigns numbers to a stimulus that are proportional to the stimulus' subjective magnitude. (13)

Matching. A procedure in which the subject's task is to adjust two stimuli so they match on some dimension. An example of matching is adjusting the proportions of a number of mixed wavelengths so the mixture matches the color of another wavelength. (12)

Mind-body problem. The problem of how physical processes such as nerve impulses cause mental processes such as perceptual experience. (4)

Modes of color appearance. A term used by Katz to refer to the fact that there are a number of ways of perceiving colors. Film color and surface color are two modes of color experience. (8)

Muller-Lyer illusion. An illusion consisting of two lines of equal length, which appear to be different lengths because of the addition of "fins" to the ends of the lines. (12)

Neuron. A cell in the nervous system that generates and transmits electrical impulses. (6)

Opponent cells. Neurons that increase their firing to wavelengths in one part of the spectrum and decrease their firing to wavelengths in another part of the spectrum. (19)

Orientation-selective cells. Neurons that fire best to a stimulus presented in a specific orientation. (8)

Overlap. A source of information for depth. If object A covers object B, then object A is seen as being in front of object B. (9)

Perception. Experiences caused by stimulation of the senses. (1)

Perceptual grouping. The process of grouping or organizing small elements into larger configurations. (23)

Phenomenological method. A method in which the subject describes his or her perceptions (or "experience"). (8)

Psychophysics. Traditionally, this term refers to a number of methods for the quantitative measurement of thresholds (see Appendix A), but it is used more broadly in this book to refer to an approach to perception in which the relationship between properties of the stimulus and the subject's experience is determined. (7)

Quantum. The smallest possible packet of light energy. (10)

Radical skepticism A philosophical position which states that it is just as likely as not that other people perceive things very differently than you do. (5)

Rat–man demonstration. The demonstration in which presentation of a "rat-like" or "man-like" picture influences an observer's perception of a second picture, which can be interpreted either as a rat or as a man. (17)

Receptor. A sensory receptor is a neuron sensitive to environmental energy that changes this energy into electrical signals in the nervous system. (6)

Relative threshold. The amount of stimulus energy that can just be detected, expressed relative to another threshold. For example: "The amount of energy needed to detect a 500 nm light is twice as high as the amount of energy needed to detect a 540 nm light." (10)

Response compression. When doubling the physical intensity of a stimulus less than doubles the subjective magnitude of the stimulus. (13)

Response expansion. When doubling the stimulus intensity more than doubles the perceived magnitude of the stimulus. (14)

Retina. A complex network of cells that covers the inside back of the eye. These cells include the receptors, which generate an electrical signal in response to light. (6)

Selective adaptation. Selectively adapting a person or animal to one stimulus and then assessing the effect of this adaptation by testing with a wider range of stimuli. For example, adapting with vertical bars and then testing a person's sensitivity to bars of all orientations. (17)

Sensation. As defined by the structuralists, sensations are the elementary experiences that combine to form perceptions. According to the philosopher Thomas Reid, sensations refer to experiences within a person that are not linked to external objects. (1)

Sensitivity. 1.0 divided by the stimulus intensity necessary for a subject to detect a stimulus. The lower the stimulus intensity needed to detect a stimulus, the higher the sensitivity. (10)

Similarity, law of. A Gestalt law that states that similar things appear to be grouped together. (23)

Spectral sensitivity curve. The function relating a subject's sensitivity to light to the wavelength of the light. (10)

Structuralism. The approach to psychology, prominent in the late 19th and early 20th centuries, that postulated that perceptions result from the summation of many elementary sensations. (2)

Surface color. One of the ways of experiencing color. According to Katz, surface color is located directly on a surface. (8)

Texture gradient. The pattern formed by a regularly textured surface that extends away from the observer. The elements in a texture gradient appear smaller as distance from the observer increases. (10)

Visible spectrum. The range of wavelengths in the electromagnetic spectrum, from about 350–700 nm, which we can see. (10)

Visual acuity. The ability to resolve small details. (8)

Visual pigment. A light-sensitive molecule contained in the visual receptors. The reaction of this molecule to light results in the generation of an electrical response in the receptors. (20)

Wavelength. For light energy, the distance between one peak of a light wave and the next peak. (10)

Wundt-Hering illusion. An illusion in which straight lines that are superimposed over radiating oblique lines appear curved. (14)

CHAPTER **2**

The Nervous System
Electrical Signals in Neurons
Neural Circuits
The Sensory Code
The Mind-Body Problem Revisited
Studying the Neural Code

The Physiological Bases of Perception

Light enters your eyes. Pressure is applied to your skin. But before you see the light or feel the pressure, the nervous system must transform the light and pressure into electrical signals, this electricity must reach the brain, and the brain must have some way of determining what the signals mean. How is this process accomplished? In this chapter we will deal with questions like this one by looking at the physiological processes that control our perceptions. To do this we need to describe the structure of the nervous system and the properties of the electrical signals that travel in the nervous system.

THE NERVOUS SYSTEM

The nervous system is a communication system that transforms environmental energy into electrical energy and then transmits this electrical energy from one part of the body to another. This process begins when energy from the environment reaches the sensory receptors.

Sensory Receptors

The primary job of the receptors is to carry out the process of **transduction**—the transformation of environmental energy into electrical energy. The receptors for each sense are specialized to transduce a specific kind of environmental energy. Visual receptors, such as the one in Figure 2.1, contain light-sensitive chemicals called **visual pigments** that generate an electrical response to light. The receptors for touch and hearing are specialized to receive mechanical energy. Touching the skin transmits pressure through the skin, which deforms touch receptors such as the one shown in Figure 2.2. Sound vibrations travel through the air and into the ear, eventually bending tiny hair cells located deep inside the ear (Figure 2.3). Although we know that pushing on touch receptors or bending hair cells generates electrical responses, the exact mechanisms that cause these electrical responses are not known.

The receptors for smell and taste are specialized to receive chemical energy. Chemicals stimulate the small cilia that are receptors for smell

33

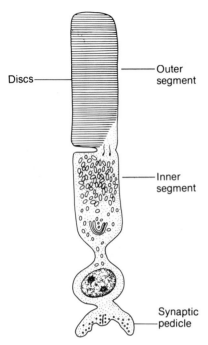

Discs—

Outer segment

Inner segment

Synaptic pedicle

FIGURE 2. 1 A visual receptor. The outer segment of the receptor contains a light-sensitive chemical called visual pigment.

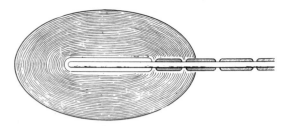

FIGURE 2. 2 A touch receptor that generates electrical signals in response to pressure. (From Lowenstein, 1960.)

(Figure 2.4) and the taste buds that are the receptors for taste (Figure 2.5), and this stimulation generates electrical signals in the receptors. In all of these cases, environmental energy is transformed into electrical energy by the receptors. The next step is to transmit this electrical energy toward the brain.

Transmission of Signals to the Brain

Strings of neurons. Signals are transmitted in the nervous system by cells called **neurons.** Receptors, such as the one on the left in Figure 2.6, are specialized neurons that transform environmental energy into electrical energy. A typical neuron, shown on the right in Figure 2.6, consists of a structure called a **cell body,** which receives electrical signals, and a **nerve fiber** (or **nerve axon**), which transmits these signals.

A typical sensory system, shown in Figure 2.7,

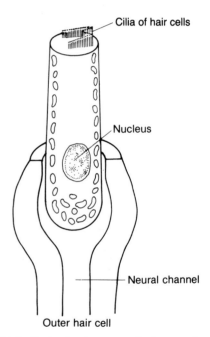

Cilia of hair cells

Nucleus

Neural channel

Outer hair cell

FIGURE 2. 3 A receptor for hearing that generates electrical signals when the cilia are bent by sound vibrations. (Adapted from Gulick, 1971.)

is a string of neurons reaching from a receptor to the brain. In this example, a pressure-sensitive receptor in the skin transmits an electrical signal along its nerve fiber to a **synapse** in the spinal cord. The synapse, shown in more detail in Figure 2.8, is a space between the end of one neuron's nerve

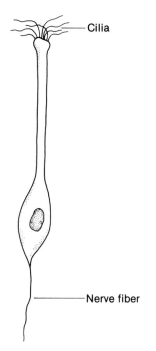

FIGURE 2. 4 A receptor for smell that generates electrical signals when airborne chemicals contact the cilia.

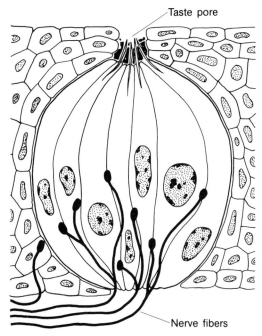

FIGURE 2. 5 A taste bud. Chemicals entering the taste pore generate an electrical signal in the taste bud. (Adapted from Murray & Murray, 1970.)

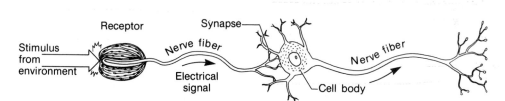

FIGURE 2. 6 A stimulus from the environment causes a receptor to generate an electrical signal that travels to the end of the receptor's nerve fiber. The cell body of the next neuron receives the signals from the nerve fiber and generates a new electrical signal, which is transmitted down the cell body's nerve fiber.

fiber (in this case, the receptor's nerve fiber) and the cell body of the next neuron (in this case, a neuron in the spinal cord). In order to travel up the spinal cord, the electrical signal must cross the synapse by causing structures called **synaptic vesicles** to release a **chemical transmitter,** which in turn generates a new electrical signal in the cell body of the neuron in the spinal cord. This chemical jump of the signal across the synapse makes it possible for signals to travel long distances along a string of many neurons.

It is important to note that nerve fibers are

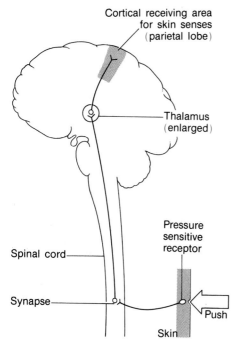

Cortical receiving area for skin senses (parietal lobe)

Thalamus (enlarged)

Pressure sensitive receptor

Spinal cord

Synapse

Push

Skin

F I G U R E 2. 7 A typical sensory system. The electrical signal that originates in the receptor is transmitted along a string of neurons toward the brain.

Electrical signal from receptor

Chemical transmitter being released

Cell body of neuron in spinal cord

Synaptic vesicles

New electrical signal

F I G U R E 2. 8 A close-up of the first synapse in Figure 2.7. The electrical signal from the receptor stimulates the synaptic vesicles, causing them to release a chemical transmitter. The chemical transmitter bridges the gap between the end of the receptor's nerve fiber and the cell body of the neuron in the spinal cord, and generates an electrical signal in the neuron.

usually grouped together to form a **nerve**—a bundle of many nerve fibers. This occurs in the system we are now considering and in other sensory systems as well. For example, about one million *nerve fibers* from the eye travel together to form the optic nerve.

Continuing its journey toward the brain, our nerve fiber from the skin travels up the spinal cord to synapse in a structure called the **thalamus** and then travels from the thalamus to the **cortical receiving area** for the sense of touch. Let's consider the thalamus and the cortical receiving areas in more detail.

The thalamus. The thalamus can be thought of as a switching station for the senses, because it is here that neurons from all the senses, except smell, synapse on their way to the brain. This synapsing of many neurons in the same area takes place throughout the nervous system, and the areas where

these groups of synapses occur are called **nuclei.** The thalamus, which is a nucleus itself, is made up of many smaller nuclei, each one serving a different sense.

Cortical receiving areas. After synapsing in the appropriate nucleus in the thalamus, the nerve fibers for each sense travel to the appropriate receiving area in the cortex, shown in Figure 2.9. In this figure we see that the cortical receiving area for touch is located at the top of the cortex in the **parietal lobe;** for vision, at the back of the cortex in the **occipital lobe;** and for hearing, on the side of the cortex in the **temporal lobe.** To help you remember which lobe goes with which sense, use the "T.O.P. Rule." T = **T**emporal for **T**ones (hearing), O = **O**ccipital for **O**bjects (seeing), and P = **P**arietal for **P**ressure (touch). A cortical area for smell has recently been located on the under-

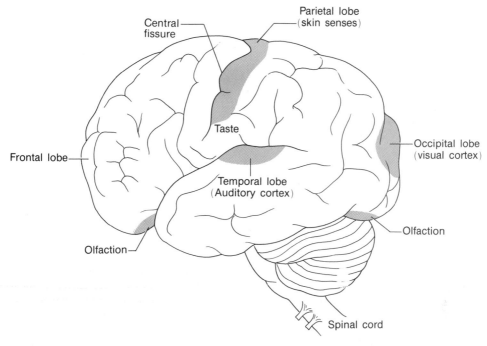

F I G U R E   2. 9   The human brain, showing the location of the primary receiving areas for the senses.

side of the frontal lobe, but the location of the area for taste is still not precisely known.

Somewhere in the brain, perhaps in the cortical receiving areas, perhaps elsewhere, the electrical signals result in perception. In our example, electrical signals reaching the parietal lobe from the skin cause us to perceive pressure. It is important to realize that you feel pressure on your skin when the electrical signals reach the brain; it is not necessary for the electrical signal to travel back to the skin, as I've found some people mistakenly believe. When electrical signals travel from the brain back toward the skin, the purpose is usually to stimulate muscles. Thus, if you wanted to react to someone touching your skin by touching them back, electrical signals would travel from your brain to the muscles in your arm and hand, causing your arm and hand to move. In general, perception is caused by signals that travel toward the brain while muscle movement is caused by signals that travel away from the brain.

ELECTRICAL SIGNALS IN NEURONS

"Wet" Signals in the Nervous System

Now that we have seen how electrical signals are transmitted from the receptors along nerve fibers to the brain, let's take a closer look at the nature of these electrical signals. When you think of electrical signals, you probably think about the electricity that travels in electrical wiring. These signals can be called "dry signals" because they are transmitted through strands of dry metal wire, and, in fact, we learn at an early age that electricity and water don't mix. However, the electrical signals that travel in nerve fibers can be called "wet signals" because they are transmitted through nerve fibers that are literally underwater.

This underwater travel is accomplished by the flow of charged molecules called **ions.** Ions occur when larger molecules are dissolved in water. For

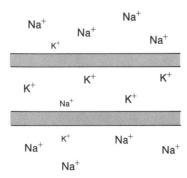

F I G U R E 2. 10 Cross section of a nerve fiber, showing the high concentration of sodium outside the fiber and potassium inside the fiber. Other ions, such as negatively charged chlorine, are not shown.

example, when sodium chloride (NaC1, or more familiarly, table salt) is dissolved in water, the salt molecule breaks into positively charged sodium (Na +) and negatively charged chlorine (C1 −). There are many Na + and C1 − ions in the water surrounding nerve fibers, and there are many potassium (K +) ions in the water inside nerve fibers (Figure 2.10). As we will see, the sodium and potassium ions are responsible for generating the nerve impulse.

To understand what happens when a nerve impulse travels down the fiber, let's assume that we can observe the sodium and potassium ions and at the same time measure the electrical charge inside the fiber. We measure this electrical charge with **microelectrodes,** small shafts of metal or glass with tip diameters of about 1/1,000 cm—small enough to record electrical signals from a single nerve fiber. We position a **recording electrode** inside the nerve fiber and a **null electrode** outside the nerve fiber, as shown in Figure 2.11, and note the difference in charge between them. We are now ready to observe what happens when a nerve impulse travels down the fiber.

The nerve impulse is caused by the flow of sodium into the fiber and potassium out of the fiber. This flow is triggered by changes in the fiber's **permeability** to sodium and potassium. Permeabil-

ity, a property of the membrane which forms the wall of the nerve fiber, refers to the ease with which a molecule can pass through the membrane. Before the nerve impulse occurs, the membrane's permeability to sodium and potassium is low, so there is little flow of these molecules across the membrane and the difference in the charge between the inside and outside of the nerve fiber is a constant—70 mV (Figure 2.11a). The nerve impulse begins when the membrane suddenly becomes permeable to sodium, causing this positively charged ion to rush into the fiber. Since sodium has a positive charge, our recording electrode records an *increase* in positive charge inside the nerve fiber, as shown in Figure 2.11(b). After sodium flows into the fiber for about 1/2,000 second, the membrane's permeability to sodium decreases and its permeability to potassium increases, and potassium flows out of the nerve fiber. Since potassium has a positive charge, our electrode records a decrease in positive charge inside the fiber until the charge returns to its original level, as shown in Figure 2.11c.

This process, sodium flowing in for 1/2,000 second, followed by potassium flowing out for 1/2,000 second, creates a positive charge inside the fiber that, from our vantage point at one place on the fiber, lasts only 1/1,000 second. However, this rapid change in the fiber's charge occurs not just at one place on the fiber but travels down the fiber to create our "wet" electrical signal, the **nerve impulse.** Nerve impulses, therefore, are traveling positive charges created by the flow of charged molecules called ions across the walls of the fiber. Let's now take a look at some of the basic properties of these nerve impulses.

Basic Properties of Nerve Impulses

To illustrate some basic properties of nerve impulses, let's look at the records in Figure 2.12, which show the response of a nerve fiber to pressure on the skin. The most obvious thing about these records is that each nerve impulse appears as a sharp spike. This occurs because we have compressed the time scale, as compared to that of Figure 2.11, so that we can display a number of nerve impulses.

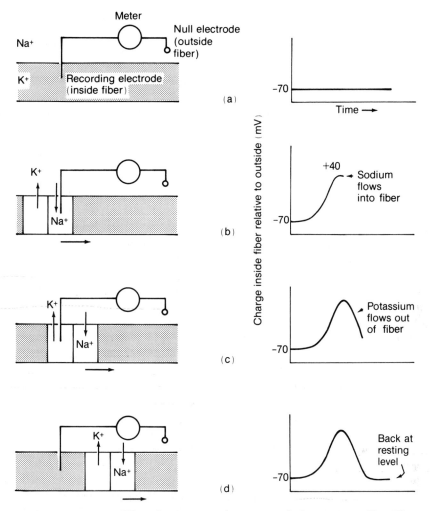

FIGURE 2.11   Effect of a nerve impulse as it travels down a nerve fiber. The recording setup is shown on the left, and the difference in charge between the inside and outside of the fiber is shown on the right. As long as the fiber is at rest, there is a difference in charge of −70 mV between the inside and the outside of the fiber, as shown in (a). In (b), (c), and (d), we see what happens as a nerve impulse travels down the fiber. The flow of sodium into the fiber and potassium out of the fiber is shown on the left, and the resulting change in the charge measured by the electrodes is shown on the right.

The three records in Figure 2.12 represent the fiber's response to three intensities of stimulation. Figure 2.12(a) shows how the fiber responds to gentle pressure applied to the skin, while Figures 2.12(b) and (c) show how the response changes as the pressure is increased. Comparing these three records leads to an important conclusion: Changing the stimulus intensity does not affect the *size* of the nerve impulses but does affect the *rate* of nerve firing.

It is important to realize, however, that, although increasing the stimulus intensity can

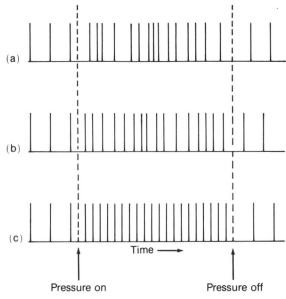

(a)

(b)

(c)

Time ⟶

Pressure on   Pressure off

F I G U R E 2. 12   Response of a nerve fiber from the skin to (a) soft, (b) medium, and (c) strong pressure applied to the fiber's receptor. Increasing the stimulus strength increases both the rate and regularity of nerve firing in this fiber.

increase the rate of nerve firing, there is an upper limit to the number of nerve impulses per second that can be conducted down a nerve fiber. This limit occurs because a neuron takes about 1 millisecond (1 msec = 1/1,000 sec) to recover from conducting a nerve impulse before it can conduct another one. This interval is called the **refractory period** of the fiber, and it sets the upper limit to the firing rate at about 500–800 impulses per second.

Another important property of nerve firing is illustrated by the beginning of each of the records of Figure 2.12. Notice that some nerve impulses occur even before the pressure stimulus is applied. In fact, many nerve fibers fire without any stimuli from the environment; this firing is called **spontaneous activity.** Although you may wonder why a nerve fiber would be designed to fire in the absence of outside stimulation, we will see later that this spontaneous activity plays an important role in determining our perceptions.

Jumping the Synapse: Excitation and Inhibition

Once a nerve impulse is generated at one end of a fiber, it travels down the entire length of the fiber without stopping or changing its size. However, this ability to travel the fiber's entire length does not, in itself, guarantee that a signal from the pressure receptor in your skin will reach the parietal lobe of your brain, because on its journey toward the brain, the nerve impulse must traverse a number of synapses. We saw in Figure 2.8 that when a nerve impulse reaches the synapse at the end of a neuron, the transmitter in the synaptic vesicles is released onto the cell body of the next neuron, causing an electrical response in that neuron. This electrical response can be either **excitatory or inhibitory,** depending on the type of transmitter and the nature of the cell body's membrane. **Excitation** increases the rate of nerve firing, whereas **inhibition** decreases the rate of nerve firing.

A neuron usually receives many excitatory and inhibitory inputs, with some neurons in the brain receiving inputs from as many as a thousand other neurons! Figure 2.13 shows how the generation of nerve impulses depends on the interplay of the excitatory (E) and inhibitory (I) stimulation converging on the cell. When the neuron receives excitatory input, the rate of firing increases above the spontaneous level, as shown in Figure 2.13(a); but as the amount of inhibition relative to excitation increases [(b) through (e)], the firing rate decreases. In (d) and (e), the inhibition is so strong that the rate of nerve firing is decreased to below the level of spontaneous activity.

NEURAL CIRCUITS

Introduction to Neural Circuits

In describing the basic structure of a sensory system, we saw that strings of neurons are connected by synapses. These strings of neurons and their synapses make it possible for nerve impulses to travel

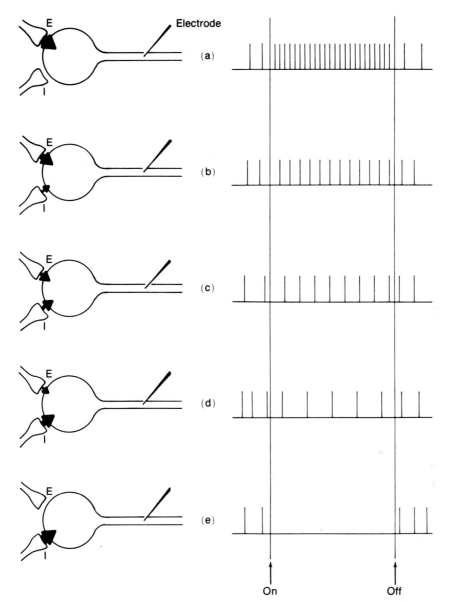

F I G U R E 2. 13 Effect of excitatory and inhibitory input on the firing rate of a neuron. The amount of excitatory and inhibitory input to the neuron is indicated by the size of the arrows at the synapse. The responses recorded by the electrode are indicated by the records on the right.

over long distances, but they also serve another purpose. Synapses are used by the nervous system to "process" electrical signals as they travel from the receptors to the brain. The electrical signals generated in the receptors are processed by the network of nerve fibers, or **neural circuits,** through which the signals travel. To illustrate how this processing works, we will compare the responses of three different neural circuits to the same stimulus.

We begin with a simple neural circuit and then

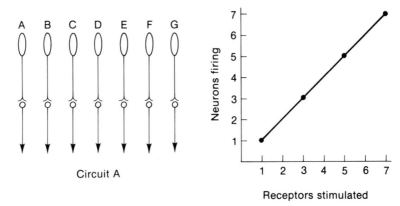

F I G U R E 2. 14   A linear circuit (left) and the response generated as we increase the number of receptors stimulated (right). See text for details.

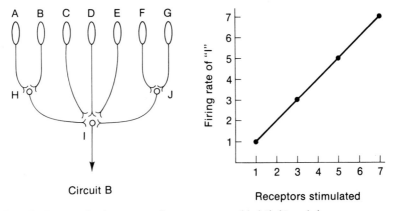

F I G U R E 2. 15   A circuit with convergence added (left) and the response generated as we increase the number of receptors stimulated (right). See text for details.

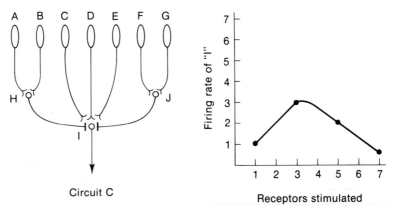

F I G U R E 2. 16   A circuit with both convergence and inhibition (left) and the response generated as we increase the number of receptors stimulated (right). See text for details.

increase the complexity of this circuit in two stages, noting how this increased complexity affects the circuit's response to the stimulus. In these circuits we represent receptors by ellipses ($\bigcirc$), cell bodies by circles ($\bigcirc$), nerve fibers by straight lines (—), excitatory synapses by Y's ($\prec$), and inhibitory synapses by T's ($\dashv$). For this example we will assume that the receptors respond to light, although the principles we will establish hold for any form of stimulation.

First, let's consider circuit A in Figure 2.14. This circuit is called a **linear circuit** because the signal generated by each receptor travels straight to the next neuron with no other neurons involved. Also, all of the synapses in this circuit are excitatory.

We will stimulate the circuit by first illuminating receptor D with a spot of light. We then change this spot into a bar of light by adding light so it covers (1) receptors C, D, and E, then (2) receptors B, C, D, E, and F, and, finally, (3) receptors A, B, C, D, E, F, and G. We will measure the response of the circuit by noting how many of the neurons are firing, and we plot this response in the graph to the right of the circuit. When we do this, we find that increasing the length of the line increases the number of neurons that are firing.

We now increase the complexity of the circuit by adding **convergence,** as shown in circuit B in Figure 2.15. Convergence occurs when two or more neurons synapse onto a single neuron. Thus, in this circuit, receptors A and B converge onto neuron H; C, D, and E converge onto I; F and G converge onto J; and H and J converge onto I. As in circuit A, all of the synapses are excitatory, but the addition of convergence creates cells that collect information from a number of other cells. We will focus our attention on cell I which, because of convergence, collects information from all of the receptors, and we will monitor the firing rate of this cell as we increase the length of our stimulating light, just as we did for circuit A.

Increasing the length of the stimulus increases the firing rate of cell I. This occurs because stimulating more receptors increases the amount of excitatory transmitter released onto cell I. Thus, we can measure the output of circuit B by monitoring the firing rate of a single neuron, rather than

counting the number of neurons firing, as was necessary for circuit A.

We now increase the circuit's complexity further by adding two inhibitory synapses to create circuit C, in which neurons H and J inhibit neuron I (Figure 2.16). Now consider what happens as we increase the number of receptors stimulated. The spot of light stimulates receptor D which, through its excitatory connection, increases the firing rate of neuron I. Extending the illumination to include receptors C and E adds the output of two more excitatory synapses to I and increases its firing further. So far, this circuit is behaving similarly to circuits A and B. However, when the illumination is extended further to include receptors B and F, something different happens: Receptors B and F stimulate H and J which, in turn, inhibit neuron I, decreasing its firing rate. Increasing the size of the stimulus further to cover receptors A and G increases the inhibition and again decreases the response of I.

Neuron I, therefore, responds best to a line of a particular length. Neuron I responds in this way because of how the neurons converging onto it process the information imaged on the receptors. These neurons are, therefore, not only *transmitting* electrical signals, but are also *processing* them by means of convergence and inhibition.

Neural Processing: Introduction to Receptive Fields

At the beginning of this chapter we saw that one of the first steps in the process of perception is the transformation by the receptors of environmental energy into electrical energy. We now see that another step in the process of perception is another transformation: the shaping of these electrical signals so that they more efficiently transmit information about the stimulus. This second transformation is accomplished by neural processing of the kind we introduced in circuit C, above. In this circuit, neural processing creates a neuron that responds best to a line centered on neuron D that is a particular length. A high firing rate in that neuron, therefore, might signal "medium-length line." We will see, as we continue our discussion of

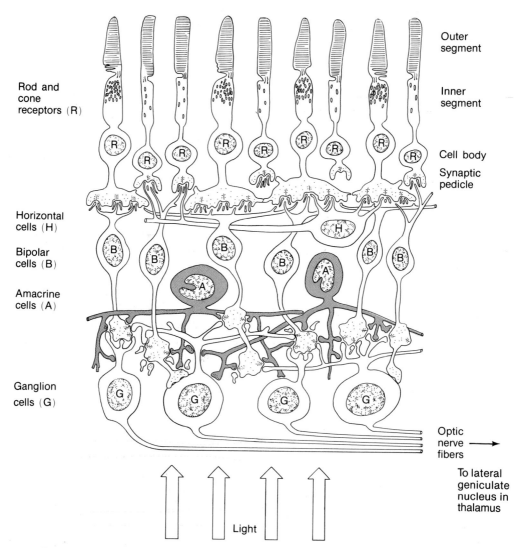

Outer
segment

Inner
segment

Rod and
cone
receptors (R)

Cell body

Synaptic
pedicle

Horizontal
cells (H)

Bipolar
cells (B)

Amacrine
cells (A)

Ganglion
cells (G)

Optic
nerve
fibers

To lateral
geniculate
nucleus in
thalamus

Light

F I G U R E 2. 17   Cross section of the primate retina. Processing occurs in the neural circuits of the retina, largely because of inhibition which is transmitted laterally by the horizontal and amacrine cells. (Adapted from Dowling & Boycott, 1966.)

neural processing, that the brain cannot determine the length of a line by monitoring the activity of only a single neuron, but creating neurons like I in circuit C is an important first step in transforming the information falling onto the receptors into a form that can more easily be used by the brain.

Let's now move from hypothetical circuits like the ones in Figure 2.16 to actual circuits in a sensory system. Figure 2.17 and Color Plate 2.1 show

such a circuit—the neurons of the retina. The retina, the layer of cells which covers the inside of the back of the eyeball, contains the two basic mechanisms of neural processing—convergence and inhibition. We can see the convergence by following the pathway that begins with the receptors. The receptors (R) synapse with **bipolar cells** (B), which then synapse with **ganglion cells** (G). The nerve fibers of the ganglion cells leave the back of

B O X 2.1 / *Intracellular and Extracellular Recording*

There are two ways to record the electrical signals of nerve cells. The electrode can be inserted into the cell **(intracellular recording),** or it can be positioned just outside the cell **(extracellular recording).** By far the more widely used of the two—and the one used in most of the studies described in this book—is extracellular recording, because it is much easier than intracellular recording. Intracellular recording is important, however, because it enables us to directly measure what is happening inside a cell.

The major difficulty with intracellular recording is that, because most nerve cells are very small, inserting electrodes into them is difficult. One solution to this problem is to find large cells, as A. L. Hodgkin and A. F. Huxley (1939) did in their studies of the giant squid axon. The giant squid axon measures almost 1 mm in diameter, making it possible to insert the recording electrode lengthwise into the axon, as shown in the left figure below.

In addition to making it possible to observe directly what is happening inside a cell, intracellular recording also makes possible the identification of the specific cell being studied. This is particularly important in the retina, in which many different kinds of cells exist next to each other. The cell's location in the retina can be determined at the end of an experiment, by injecting a dye into the cell through the electrode. Dyes have been developed that diffuse throughout the cell and result in pictures like the right one, below (Kaneko, 1970). We can tell from the shape of the dye-marker and location in the retina that this is an amacrine cell (see Figure 2.17).

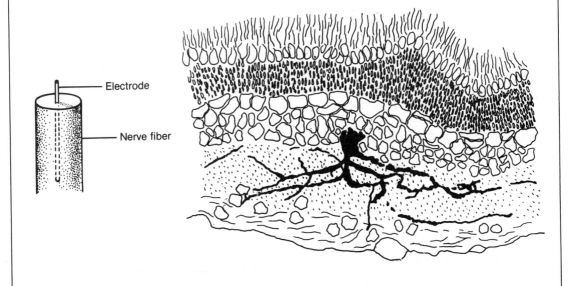

Electrode

Nerve fiber

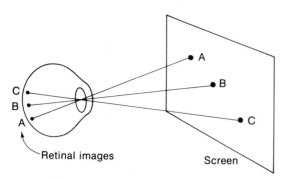

F I G U R E 2. 18 For every point on the screen, on which we present stimuli, there is a corresponding point on the retina.

the eye in the optic nerve to transmit the signals generated by the retina toward the brain.

In the picture of the retina in Figure 2.17, 9 receptors converge onto 6 bipolar cells, which converge onto 4 ganglion cells. In actuality, the convergence is much greater than this, since in each human retina 126,000,000 receptors converge onto 1,000,000 ganglion cells. Thus, on the average, every ganglion cell receives signals originating from 126 receptors.

In addition to the receptors, bipolar cells, and ganglion cells, there are also two other major types of cells in the retina: **horizontal cells,** which transmit signals *across* the retina, enabling different receptors or bipolar cells to communicate with each other, and **amacrine cells,** which also transmit signals across the retina, enabling different bipolar or ganglion cells to communicate with each other. Much of the inhibition in the retina is caused by these horizontal and amacrine cells.

We can measure the results of the retina's convergence and inhibition by placing an electrode near the nerve fiber of a ganglion cell (see Box 2.1) and determining how that cell responds to stimulation of the receptors. In practice, many experiments like this have been done with cats and monkeys, using a setup like the one shown in Figure 1.15, in which our stimuli are presented on a screen at which the animal (a cat, in this case) is looking. Since the cat's eye is kept stationary, presenting our stimuli on the screen is equivalent to shining lights on different places on the cat's retina, because for each point on the screen, there is a corresponding point on the cat's retina (Figure 2.18).

When we present our spot of light at different places on the screen, we find that stimulating anywhere in area A causes no change in the activity of our neuron (Figure 2.19a). Note that this neuron has some spontaneous activity and that presenting our stimulus to area A has no effect on the neuron's rate of firing. Eventually, however, we

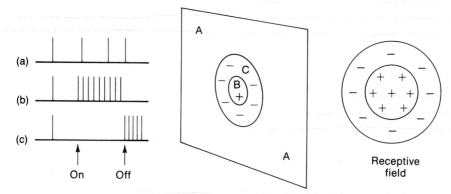

F I G U R E 2. 19 Response of a ganglion cell in the cat's retina to stimulation (a) outside the cell's receptive field (area A on the screen to the right), (b) inside the excitatory area of the cell's receptive field (area B), and (c) inside the inhibitory area of the cell's receptive field (area C). The excitatory center–inhibitory surround receptive field is shown on the far right without the screen.

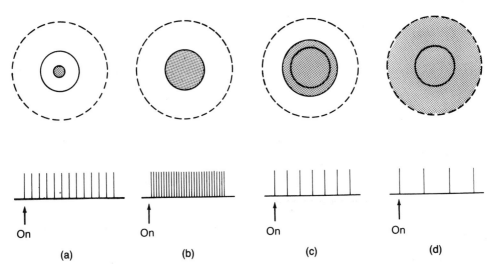

F I G U R E   2. 20   Response of an excitatory center–inhibitory surround receptive field. The area stimulated with light is indicated by the shading, and the response to the stimulus is indicated by the records below each receptive field. As the stimulus size increases inside the excitatory region of the receptive field in (a) and (b), the response increases. As the stimulus increases further so it covers the inhibitory region of the receptive field, the response decreases. This cell responds best to stimulation the size of the receptive field center. (Adapted from Hubel & Wiesel, 1961.)

stimulate area B and observe an **excitatory** or **on response,** an increase in the neuron's firing rate when the light is turned on. We mark this area with +'s to indicate that the response to stimulation of this area is excitatory. We also find that stimulating anywhere in area C causes an **inhibitory response,** a decrease in nerve firing when the stimulus is turned on, plus an **off response,** a burst of firing when the stimulus is turned off. We mark this area with −'s to indicate that responses to stimulation of this area are inhibitory. Areas B and C, taken together, are called the **receptive field** of the neuron: *the region of the retina which, when stimulated, influences the firing rate of the neuron.*

The receptive field in Figure 2.19 is called a **center-surround receptive field** because it responds one way to stimulation of the center area and another way to stimulation of the area surrounding this center area. This particular receptive field is an **excitatory center–inhibitory surround** receptive field, and there are also **inhibitory center–excitatory surround** receptive fields.

The fact that the center and surround of the receptive field result in opposite types of responses causes an effect called **center-surround antagonism.** This effect is illustrated in Figure 2.20, which shows what happens as we increase the size of a spot of light presented to the cell's receptive field. A small spot, presented to the excitatory center of the receptive field, causes a small increase in the rate of nerve firing (a), and increasing the light's size so it covers the entire center of the receptive field increases the cell's response, as shown in (b).

However, center-surround antagonism comes into play when we increase the size of the light further, so it begins to cover the inhibitory area, as in (c) and (d). Stimulation of the inhibitory surround counteracts the center's excitatory response, causing a decrease in the cell's firing rate. Thus, this cell responds best to a spot of light that is the size of the receptive field center.

The behavior of this cell is similar to the behavior of cell I in circuit C of Figure 2.16, since firing first increases in response to initial increases

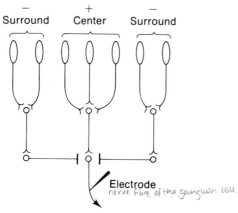

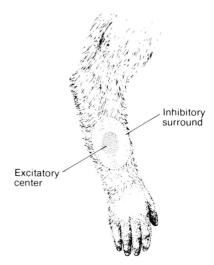

F I G U R E   2. 21 A neural circuit that would result in a center-surround receptive field. Signals from the surround receptors reach the cell from which we are recording via an inhibitory synapse, while signals from the center receptors reach this cell via an excitatory synapse. Thus, stimulation of the center receptors increases the firing rate recorded by our electrode, and stimulation of the surround receptors decreases the firing rate.

F I G U R E   2. 22 Excitatory center–inhibitory surround receptive field on the skin of the monkey's arm.

in stimulus size but then decreases when the stimulus becomes large enough to cause inhibitory responses in the circuit. The circuit in Figure 2.21 is similar to circuit C, but we have added an additional layer of cells to make it more similar to the retina. While still vastly oversimplified compared to the retina's actual circuitry, Figure 2.21 illustrates the convergence and inhibition which, in the retina, produce center-surround receptive fields.

Center-surround receptive fields are not limited to the visual system. Figure 2.22 shows an excitatory center–inhibitory surround receptive field of a neuron in the monkey's thalamus that receives signals from receptors in the skin of the monkey's arm.

It is not surprising that senses as different as vision and touch have similar receptive fields, because although the experiences of seeing and feeling a touch are very different, both vision and touch have receptors that define *surfaces* on which we can locate stimuli. Just as we can flash light on different locations on the surface of the retina, we can touch different locations on the surface of the

skin. This similarity, and the fact that similar principles of neural processing hold throughout the nervous system, creates similar receptive fields in these two very different senses.

Touch and vision also have something else in common: As neural processing continues along the pathway from the receptors toward the cortex, neurons become more and more specialized in the type of stimuli to which they respond. We will see that this is true for touch in Chapter 14, when we encounter cortical neurons that fire only to stimuli that move across the skin in certain directions. And there are neurons in the visual cortex called **complex cells** that also respond only when stimuli move across the retina in certain directions. We will wait until Chapter 3 to describe these directionally sensitive complex cells, but right now let's look at a cortical neuron called a **simple cell** that is the product of an earlier stage of neural processing in the cortex.

Simple cortical cells are the product of the neural processing that has occurred within the retina, along the pathway from the retina to the brain,

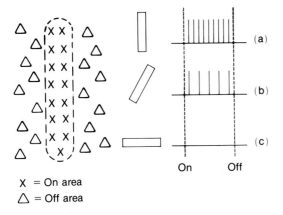

X = On area

△ = Off area

F I G U R E 2. 23 The receptive field of a simple cortical cell. This cell responds best to a vertical bar of light that covers the on area of the receptive field (a), and responds less well as the bar is tilted so that it covers the off area (b and c). (Adapted from Hubel & Wiesel, 1959.)

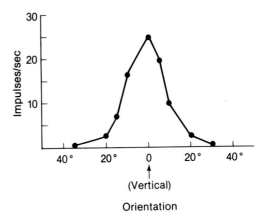

F I G U R E 2. 24 An orientation tuning curve of a simple cortical cell. This cell responds best to a vertical bar (orientation = 0) and responds less well as the bar is tilted in either direction.

and within the brain itself. Since simple cells are among the first we encounter after entering the visual receiving area of the cortex, they represent an early stage of neural processing *within the brain* (that's why they are called *simple* cortical cells).

Figure 2.23 shows the receptive field of such a cell. This receptive field is similar to the center-surround receptive field of the cell in Figure 2.19 because it is divided into excitatory and inhibitory areas, but it is different because these areas are arranged side by side rather than in the center-surround configuration. The receptive field of a simple cortical cell is arranged so that this cell responds best to a bar of light oriented in a particular direction. A large response results when the bar is oriented along the length of the receptive field, as in (a); a smaller response results when the bar is tilted, as in (b); and no response results when the bar is perpendicular to the orientation of the receptive field, as in (c) (Hubel & Wiesel, 1959).

This preference of simple cells for bars with particular orientations is shown graphically in Figure 2.24. This **tuning curve,** determined by measuring the responses of a simple cell to bars of light with different orientations, shows that this cell responds with 25 nerve impulses per second to a

vertically oriented bar. The cell's response decreases, however, as the bar is tilted away from the vertical, until a bar that is tilted 20 degrees from the vertical elicits only a small response. While this particular simple cell responds best to a bar with a vertical orientation, other simple cells respond best to bars with horizontal or diagonal orientations.

The fact that neural processing can create neurons that respond to specific stimulus properties raises an interesting possibility: Perhaps the brain interprets what the electrical signals in the nervous system mean by monitoring the firing of these highly specific cells. For example, imagine that there are cells that respond only when a spoon-shaped stimulus oriented at a 45-degree angle is presented to the retina, or that there are cells that respond only to a specific shade of green. If that were the case, firing of these cells would provide a signal to the brain indicating "spoon-shaped stimulus at a 45-degree angle" or "light green."

We will see in the next section, however, that although there are neurons that respond best to specific stimulus properties, these neurons alone cannot completely explain how the brain makes associations between electrical signals and these properties.

BOX 2.2 / *Seeing without a Retina: Electrical Stimulation of the Visual Cortex*

In normal vision, electrical signals generated in the retina are transmitted along nerve fibers; when these signals reach the visual cortex, we see. However, more than 100,000 people in the United States and Canada are totally blind, usually due to defects in the retina or optic nerve that prevent electrical signals from being generated in the retina or from being transmitted by the optic nerve to the visual cortex. William Dobelle and a team of researchers have developed plans for a visual **prosthesis:** an artificial eye that can produce vision in the blind by sending electrical signals to the visual cortex. One proposed system, shown in the figure on the left, consists of a subminiature television camera mounted in a glass eye. The TV camera picks up an image from the environment and converts it into a pattern of electrical signals that is transmitted to a tiny computer mounted in a pair of dummy glasses. After being processed by the computer, these signals stimulate an array of electrodes placed on the surface of the visual cortex, causing the person to see an image corresponding to the original image received by the TV camera.

Although the system shown in the figure on the left does not yet exist, some totally blind volunteers have had an array of 64 electrodes im-

planted on their visual cortex. A drawing of this array, based on an X-ray, is shown on the right. Wires from the electrodes pass through a small opening in the skull, at the back of the head, and then wind beneath the scalp in an S-shaped loop, before coming through the skin and terminating in a connector attached to the skull with special bone screws. Initial testing indicates that stimulation of the cortex by a single electrode causes the observer to perceive a **phosphene**—a small glowing spot of light that appears to be located at about arm's length. Stimulation of a number of electrodes causes a number of phosphenes to be seen as a pattern. For example, Craig, a 35-year-old government employee blinded 15 years earlier in an automobile accident, was able to see letters, geometrical shapes, and simple patterns in response to various patterns of stimulation of his electrode array. When a TV camera was connected to the system, Craig could also detect white horizontal and vertical lines on a dark background.

These initial results are promising, although many problems must be solved before a visual prosthesis becomes available. For example, phosphenes are not always seen in the position corresponding to the position of the electrode on the cortex. Adjacent electrodes may produce

---

THE SENSORY CODE

Now that we understand some of the basic principles of neural functioning, we are ready to return to the sequence of steps in the perceptual process (page 6). Since environmental energy is changed into electrical signals by the nervous system, our perception is based, not on direct contact with the environment, but on the brain's contact with electrical signals that *represent* the environment. We can think of these electrical signals as forming a **sensory code** that signals various properties of the environment to the brain. The idea that the nerve impulses form a code raises the **problem of sensory coding:** *How do electrical signals in the nervous system represent properties of the environment?*

The answer to the problem of sensory coding is one of the central themes of this book, and as you read the chapters that follow, we will return to this question again and again. We will ask how different colors—red, blue, green, and yellow—

phosphenes that are spaced far apart in the visual field, and adjacent phosphenes are sometimes produced by widely spaced electrodes. Additionally, some phosphenes are too bright and obscure others, and phosphenes often flicker, even in response to continuous electrical stimulation. The next step is the development of a 512-electrode stimulation system that would transmit complicated information rapidly enough so that the prosthesis could be used by a person as he or she walks through the environment (Dobelle et al., 1974, 1976; Dobelle, 1977).

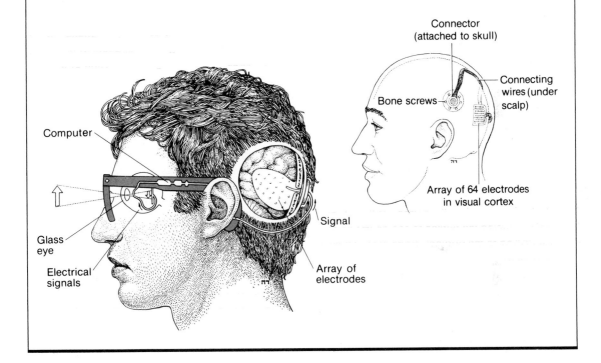

are represented by electrical signals in the nervous system. We will ask how the high pitch of the piccolo and the low pitch of the bassoon are represented by electrical signals in the nervous system. And we will ask how the different qualities we feel on the skin—coldness, heat, touch, and pain—are represented by electrical signals in the nervous system. These questions, and many more, are the topics of the chapters that follow. In the remainder of this chapter we will define some of the basic principles that will guide our search for the answers to these questions. We begin by considering how the brain distinguishes between the different senses based on nerve impulses.

The Code for Quality Across the Senses

One of the most basic distinctions the brain makes is among the different senses. How does the brain differentiate between seeing a light and hearing a sound, or between the taste of a lemon and the smell of perfume on the basis of nerve impulses?

Johannes Muller proposed an answer to this question in 1842 that has come to be known as the **doctrine of specific nerve energies.** This doctrine states that (1) the brain receives information about the environment by means of signals from the sensory nerves, and (2) the brain distinguishes among different senses by monitoring the activity in the different sensory nerves. So, activity in the optic nerve signals "light," the auditory nerve, "sound," and so on. Soon after Muller's doctrine was proposed, other investigators found that each of these nerves goes to a different area of the cortex, as shown in Figure 2.9, thereby making the code for quality across the senses simple: The sense that is stimulated is signaled by the location at which the electrical signals reach the brain.

The Code for Quality Within a Sense

But what signals different qualities *within* a sense? What is it about the nerve impulses reaching the brain that signals red, blue, green, or yellow for the sense of vision or salty, sweet, bitter, or sour for the sense of taste? What *information* is contained in nerve impulses that signals these different qualities?

To begin to answer this question, let's return to our observation that neural processing can endow neurons with the property of responding best to certain stimuli, and our suggestion that the firing of such neurons might signal the presence of specific aspects of the environment. The idea that the responses of specifically tuned neurons can provide

the sensory code is called **specificity theory.** Let's look at this idea in more detail.

Specificity theory. The basic idea behind specificity theory is that there are specifically tuned neurons that provide information about specific qualities in the environment. There are two ways of creating such neurons. One way is by neural processing, in which convergence, excitation, and inhibition combine to create neurons like simple cells in the visual cortex that respond best to lines of a specific orientation.

Another way of creating specifically tuned neurons is through receiving inputs from receptors that are tuned to respond only to specific stimuli. For example, a neuron that receives its input from a visual receptor that fires only when illuminated with a specific wavelength of light would, itself, be tuned to that wavelength.

To evaluate specificity theory, let's consider the possibility that there are receptors tuned to single wavelengths, as shown in Figure 2.25. Since our perception of color is closely linked to wavelength (see the visible spectrum, Color Plate 1.1), receptors that respond selectively to single wavelengths could potentially signal the hundreds of different colors we can perceive. (We will see in Chapter 4 that we see many different shades in addition to "basic" colors like blue, green, yellow, orange, and red. Consider, for example, the hundreds of different sample "chips" available at most paint stores.)

The idea of hundreds of color receptors, one for each color, encounters problems, however, when we consider that we can see a wide range of colors even in a spot of light so small that it covers only a few receptors on the retina. Clearly, hundreds of narrowly tuned receptors cannot explain the range of colors we perceive.

Specificity theory encounters similar problems when we consider the almost limitless number of different forms we can perceive. Robert Erickson (1984) has calculated that 10^{11} possible figures can be produced with just half a dozen lines of differing location, length, orientation, and color. Thus, there are simply too many colors and forms, and also tastes and smells, for our perceptions to be explained

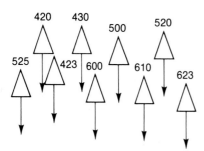

F I G U R E   2. 25   A hypothetical array of visual receptors, each tuned to respond only to light of a single wavelength.

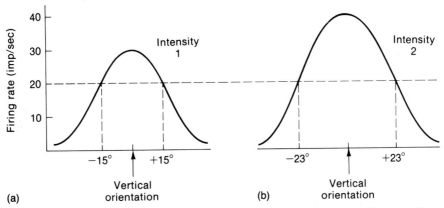

F I G U R E 2. 26   Orientation tuning curves for a single neuron. (a) The curve for a low intensity light. The dashed lines indicate that at this intensity the neuron fires at 20 impulses per second to orientations of − 15° and + 15°. (b) The neuron's response to a higher-intensity light. The dashed lines indicate that at this intensity the neuron fires at 20 impulses per second to orientations of − 23° and + 23°. Because the cell's firing rate is influenced by stimulus intensity, firing rate does not unambiguously indicate stimulus orientation.

in terms of neurons that fire only to specific perceptual qualities.

There is another argument against specificity theory: The highly specific neurons required by this theory simply do not exist. Although most neurons do respond *best* to a particular type of stimulus, they also respond to other stimuli. Consider, for example, simple cortical cells. The tuning curve for one of these cells, in Figure 2.26(a), shows that the cell responds best to a vertically oriented stimulus, but that the cell also responds to stimuli within ± 25 degrees of vertical. In addition, the response rate of this cell is influenced by stimulus intensity, as shown by the tuning curve in Figure 2.26(b). This tuning curve indicates that increasing the intensity increases the cell's response to all orientations, so orientations that elicit a poor response at the lower intensity can elicit a good response at the higher intensity.

These two properties of tuning curves—(1) that they respond to a range of stimuli and (2) that their firing is influenced by stimulus intensity— mean that a given rate of firing cannot unambiguously indicate orientation. For example, we can see from the curves in Figure 2.26 that a rate of 20 impulses per second could be due to a line with (1) an orientation of − 15 degrees at intensity 1,

(2) an orientation of + 15 degrees at intensity 1,
(3) an orientation of − 23 degrees at intensity 2 or
(4) an orientation of + 23 degrees at intensity 2.

We will see in Chapter 4 that a similar situation exists for color vision. Although there are receptors that are tuned to respond best to a particular wavelength of light (see page 118), these receptors also respond to other wavelengths and are influenced by stimulus intensity. Just as was the case for simple cortical cells, therefore, the firing rate of one of these cells cannot unambiguously indicate the wavelength of light. Thus, specificity theory is not the answer to the problem of sensory coding.* The answer appears, instead, to be closer to across-fiber-pattern theory.

Across-fiber-pattern theory. The **across-fiber-pattern theory** states that different qualities are signaled to the brain by the *pattern* of activity across a large number of neurons. Looking at the tuning curves for three different simple cortical cells in Figure 2.27(a), we see how an across-fiber-pattern might work for perceiving orientation. Neuron 1 responds *best* to lines oriented at 30 degrees, neu-

---

* We will see in Chapter 15, however, that taste quality may be signaled by a specificity code.

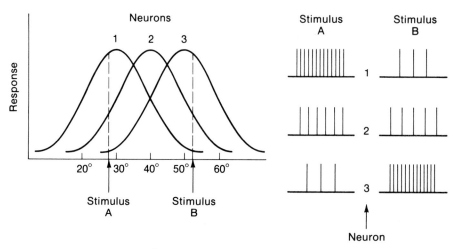

F I G U R E   2. 27   Left: Orientation tuning curves for three simple cells. Right: Records which indicate responses of each neuron to stimulus A (a line oriented at 28 degrees) and stimulus B (a line oriented at 52 degrees). These records show that stimula A and B generate different patterns of response across these three neurons (see Figure 2.28).

ron 2 to lines oriented at 40 degrees, and neuron 3 to lines oriented at 50 degrees.

Let's consider how each of these three neurons would respond to two different stimuli—stimulus A, a line oriented at 28 degrees, and stimulus B, a line oriented at 52 degrees. The records on the right of Figure 2.27 show how neurons 1, 2, and 3 respond to stimulus A. Neuron 1 responds best since stimulus A's orientation is close to this neu-

ron's best orientation. Neuron 2 responds less well, and neuron 3 responds hardly at all. Figure 2.28 shows that these same three neurons respond differently to stimulus B, with neuron 3 now responding most strongly, neuron 2 less well, and neuron 1 hardly at all.

Thus, the brain can differentiate between stimuli A and B by registering the *pattern* of firing across a number of neurons. This pattern, depicted in Figure 2.28, is a strong candidate for a potential code because it is unaffected, or affected only slightly, by changes in stimulus intensity. Increasing the intensity of stimuli A or B increases the firing rate of all three neurons but leaves their *patterns* of response to the two stimuli (1 > 2 > 3 for A and 3 > 2 > 1 for B) unchanged.

Further evidence for across-fiber-pattern theory is provided by an experiment in the sense of taste by Robert Erickson (1963, 1984). Erickson presented a number of different taste stimuli to a rat's tongue and recorded the response from the chorda tympani, a nerve that carries nerve fibers from the tongue toward the brain. Figure 2.29 shows how 13 nerve fibers respond to ammonium chloride (NH_4Cl), potassium chloride (KCl), and sodium chloride ($NaCl$). The solid and dashed lines show that the across-fiber pattern of these 13 neu-

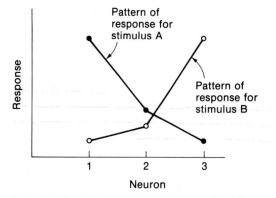

F I G U R E   2. 28   Graph showing the differing patterns of response of the three neurons in Figure 2.27 to stimuli A and B.,

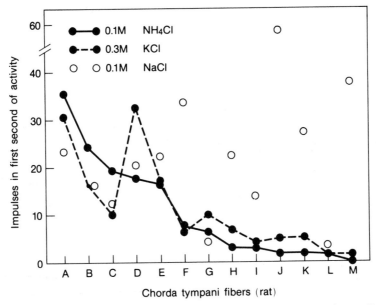

F I G U R E 2. 29 Across-fiber patterns of response to three salts in the rat. Each letter on the horizontal axis indicates a different single fiber. For each fiber the responses to three stimuli are plotted. (From Erickson, 1963.)

rons to ammonium chloride and potassium chloride are similar to each other but are different from the pattern for sodium chloride, indicated by the open circles.

Erickson reasoned that if the rat's perception of taste quality depends on the across-fiber pattern, then two substances with similar across-fiber patterns should taste similar. Thus, the electrophysiological results would predict that ammonium chloride and potassium chloride should taste similar and that both should taste different from sodium chloride. To test this hypothesis, Erickson shocked rats for drinking potassium chloride and then gave them a choice between ammonium chloride and sodium chloride. If potassium chloride and ammonium chloride taste similar, the rats should avoid the ammonium chloride when given a choice, and this is exactly what they did. And when the rats were shocked for drinking ammonium chloride, they then avoided the potassium chloride, as predicted by the electrophysiological results.

Erickson's results show that nerve fibers in the rat's chorda tympani are not highly specific; most fibers respond to many substances. His results also show that each substance has its own "signature" in the form of an across-fiber pattern of nerve firing, and this signature is correlated with the taste of the substance.

The Code for Subjective Magnitude

Our discussion of sensory coding has, so far, focused on how neurons signal different qualities; that is, how the neurons signal *what* the stimulus is. Another question posed by the problem of sensory coding is "What is the code for the subjective *magnitude* of a stimulus?" That is, how do neurons signal *how much* stimulus there is?

To try to answer this question, let's first consider what happens to nerve impulses when we increase the intensity of a stimulus. In Figure 2.12 we saw that increasing stimulus intensity increases the rate of nerve firing. This result, combined with the fact that increasing stimulus intensity also increases the **subjective magnitude** of that stimulus (increasing the intensity of a light usually causes it to appear brighter; increasing the intensity of a tone usually causes it to sound louder), suggests that the rate of nerve firing may be the code for magnitude. But before jumping to this conclusion, we should see whether nerve firing and subjective magnitude increase in the same way as we increase stimulus intensity. If they do, we would be on firmer ground when suggesting that the rate of nerve firing may be the code for subjective magnitude.

Before we consider some of the physiological evidence on this point, we need to return to the magnitude estimation procedure we described on page 13 of Chapter 1. Remember that magnitude estimation is the procedure developed by S. S. Stevens that enables us to determine functions like the ones in Figure 1.9 that relate a person's estimates of subjective magnitude to stimulus intensity. One of Stevens' major accomplishments was to show that plotting the *logarithm* of these magnitude estimates versus the *logarithm* of stimulus intensity changes the magnitude estimation curves for all the senses to straight lines, as in Figure 2.30. This is what we meant when we said in Chapter 1

that all magnitude estimation curves follow the same mathematical function. Stevens found that the function relating magnitude estimation to stimulus intensity can be described by the equation $P = KS^n$. Perceived magnitude, P, equals a constant, K, times the stimulus intensity, S, raised to an exponent, n, where n is the *slope* of the function relating magnitude estimation judgments to stimulus intensity on a log-log plot. This function is called a **power function,** because the stimulus intensity, S, is raised to a power, n.

The beauty of this equation and the straight-line functions that result is that it enables us to describe the relationship between subjective magnitude and stimulus intensity in terms of a single number, n, the exponent of the power function (or the slope of the line relating log magnitude estimate to log stimulus intensity), and knowing the slope, n, tells us something very important about each sense.

A slope of less than 1.0 indicates **response compression** like that observed for brightness (see page 13, Chapter 1). That is, doubling stimulus intensity does not double subjective magnitude. An exponent greater than 1.0 indicates **response expansion,** like that observed for shock. Doubling stimulus intensity more than doubles subjective magnitude. And an exponent of 1.0 indicates a **linear function.** Doubling stimulus intensity doubles subjective magnitude.

The fact that we can describe the relationship between subjective magnitude and stimulus intensity in terms of the exponent of a power function or, to put it another way, in terms of the slope of a line, enables us to deal more easily with the problem of sensory coding of magnitude. Most researchers have approached this problem by measuring the relationship between the rate of nerve firing and stimulus intensity and comparing this function to the one determined when measuring the relationship between subjective magnitude and stimulus intensity. If the physiological and psychophysical functions have the same slope, this is taken as evidence that the rate of nerve firing is the code for subjective magnitude (Figure 2.31).

Let's now look at some of the experiments that have compared physiology and magnitude estimates.

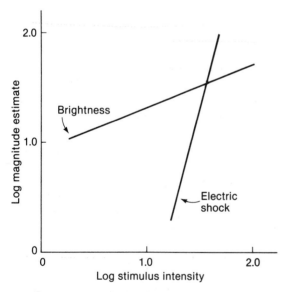

F I G U R E 2. 30 The two curves from Figure 1.9 plotted on log-log coordinates. Taking the logarithm of the magnitude estimates and the logarithm of the stimulus intensity turns the curves into straight lines. This straight-line relationship between log magnitude estimate and log stimulus intensity occurs for all of the senses. (Adapted from Stevens, 1962.)

One of the earliest, and most elegant, comparisons of physiology and magnitude estimates is an experiment done by Gerhard Werner and Vernon Mountcastle (1965) in which they determined the relationship between the rate of nerve firing and stimulus intensity for a pressure-sensitive neuron in the monkey's skin. They used a small plunger to push on a touch receptor called an Iggo corpuscle, which is located close enough to the surface of the monkey's skin to be seen with a microscope. By observing the corpuscle with a microscope as it was being pushed, they were able to measure the indentation of the receptor and to determine the function relating the rate of nerve firing and the amount of receptor indentation. When they did this, they found that nerve firing followed a power law with a slope of 0.5, exactly the same slope as that found when humans are asked to estimate the magnitude of pressure applied to their skin.

This correspondence between nerve firing in the monkey and magnitude estimates made by humans supports the idea that the rate of nerve firing may be the code for subjective magnitude. However, rather than comparing electrophysiological data from monkeys with psychophysical data from humans, it would be better to have both psychophysical and electrophysiological results for the human. These data have been provided by G. Borg and a team of investigators (1967), who recorded

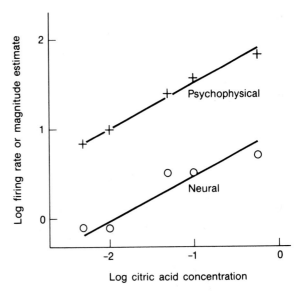

FIGURE 2. 32 Psychophysical and neural responses to citric acid. That these two functions have the same slope argues that the increase in the taste intensity experienced by subjects, as the concentration of the citric acid is increased, may be caused by the increased rate of nerve firing, which also occurs as the concentration of citric acid is increased. (From Borg, Diamant, Strom, & Zotterman, 1967.)

from the chorda tympani nerve in five patients undergoing middle ear operations. (The chorda tympani, which carries nerve fibers from the front of the tongue, passes through the middle ear on its way toward the thalamus.)

Borg used a large electrode to record the chorda tympani's response to solutions of citric acid, sucrose, and sodium chloride flowing over the tongue. He compared these neural responses with the patient's magnitude estimates of taste intensity determined two days before their operations. One patient's psychophysical and electrophysiological responses to citric acid are shown in Figure 2.32. When subjective magnitude is plotted versus citric acid concentration on a log-log scale, the psychophysical and electrophysiological functions are parallel, each with a slope of 0.5. These results, and similar results on some of Borg's other patients, support the idea that there is a close connection between the rate of nerve firing and subjective magnitude.

Although the two experiments described

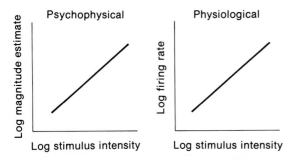

FIGURE 2. 31 Left: A hypothetical function relating log magnitude estimates and log stimulus intensity. Right: A hypothetical function relating log firing rate and log stimulus intensity. Two such functions with the same slope supports the idea that firing rate may be the code for subjective magnitude.

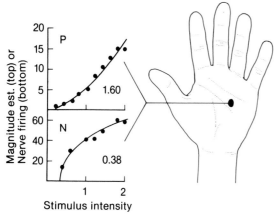

F I G U R E   2. 33 Neural and psychophysical functions for a touch stimulus presented to the hand. The neural function was determined by a technique called microneurography, which makes it possible to record from single nerve fibers in awake humans. After the receptive field of a single nerve fiber, indicated by the dot, was located, the relationship between the rate of nerve firing and the pressure of a touch stimulus was determined. The resulting function, indicated by the curve marked N, has an exponent of 0.38. The psychophysical function was determined by asking the subject to estimate the magnitude of a touch stimulus presented to the center of the cell's receptive field. The resulting function, marked P, has an exponent of 1.60. To appreciate the difference between these curves, note that doubling the stimulus intensity from 1 to 2 does not double the neural response (it changes from 40 to 60) but more than triples the psychophysical response (it changes from 5 to about 17). (From Knibestol & Vallbo, 1976.)

above, and a number of others (Franzen & Lindblom, 1976; Vallbo & Johansson, 1976), provide evidence that subjective magnitude is signaled by the rate of nerve firing, the correspondence between firing rate and subjective magnitude is not always so good. For example, using a technique called **microneurography,** developed by Swedish investigators A. B. Vallbo and K. E. Hagbarth (1967), we can record from a single nerve fiber in a person's hand that responds to a touch stimulus, and we can compare the firing rate of this nerve fiber to the person's magnitude estimates of the touch stimulus.

Figure 2.33, which shows the results of such an experiment, indicates that the relationship between nerve firing and stimulus intensity is not the same as the relationship between the person's magnitude estimates and stimulus intensity. The nerve fiber's response to the touch increases with an exponent of 0.38 (response compression), whereas the subjective magnitude of the touch increases with an exponent of 1.60 (response expansion). Thus, while the rate of nerve firing probably helps to signal the subjective magnitude of the stimulus, some other properties of nerve firing may also be involved in signaling stimulus magnitude.

What other information about stimulus magnitude might be contained in the nerve impulses? Look back at Figure 2.12. Note that increasing the stimulus intensity not only increases the firing rate but also changes the **temporal pattern,** or *timing,* of nerve impulses. At low intensities the time between successive nerve impulses is quite variable, whereas at high intensities it becomes fairly constant. Increasing the intensity often increases the regularity of nerve firing, and information such as this may signal the magnitude of the stimulus, with more regular nerve firing signaling higher stimulus intensities.

THE MIND-BODY PROBLEM REVISITED

Having introduced some of the basic principles of neural processing, let's now briefly return to the mind-body problem, which we introduced early in the first chapter. Remember that the mind-body problem poses the following question: How are physical processes in the body transformed into subjective experience? Given our knowledge of neural functioning, we now know more specifically what the properties of these physical processes are. The physical process that leads to subjective experience is electrical activity in single neurons and in large populations of neurons. We also know that this electrical activity is caused at the molecular level by the flow of sodium and potassium ions across the nerve membrane. So, in molecular terms, we can state that a particular perception is caused by a particular pattern of sodium and potassium flow in a population of neurons.

Knowing these facts about the nature of the physical processes in the brain, we can now restate the mind-body problem in more precise terms: How do patterns of sodium and potassium flowing across membranes become perceptions? Stating it in such concrete terms—referring to sodium and potassium flow rather than simply "physical processes"—puts the extreme difficulty of solving this problem into perspective. What experiment can we do to begin to understand how tens of thousands of ions moving across a membrane can become our experience of seeing a tree? The answer to this question is the same one we gave in Chapter 1: We do not know which experiments we might do to just begin to answer the mind-body problem. Thus, in the remainder of this book we will focus not on the mind-body problem, which we don't even know how to deal with, but instead will focus on studying the neural code, which we are at least beginning to understand.

STUDYING THE NEURAL CODE

As we study the neural code, one of our major goals is to identify information carried by the firing of neurons that the brain uses in the cause of perception. It is important to realize, however, that just because we are able to record a particular response with our electrodes does not tell us how, or even *whether*, the information recorded by our electrodes is actually used by the brain. For example, electrode recordings have shown that the firing of simple cells in the visual cortex contains information about the orientation of lines. But how is this information used by the brain to determine perception? There are a number of possible answers to this question. The firing of simple cells could (a) be irrelevant for perception, (b) be responsible for our perception of line orientation, or (c) represent an early stage of neural processing in the cortex which, when carried further, eventually does lead to perception.

The point is that in studying the physiological bases of perception, we are faced with two basic questions:

1. What information is present in the responses of specific neurons and in the responses of populations of neurons?
2. Is this information used by the brain, and, if so, how is it used?

It is important to keep these two questions in mind and to realize that identifying information in the brain is just the first step in unraveling the mystery of how physiological processes result in perception. You will see, as you read this book, that we know quite a bit about the first question but are just beginning to be able to suggest answers to the second one.

Summary

1. The nervous system is a communication system that transforms environmental energy into electrical energy and then transmits this electrical energy from one part of the body to another.
2. Receptors are neurons that convert environmental energy into electrical energy, a process called transduction. Receptors for each sense are specialized to respond to a specific kind of environmental energy.
3. A sensory system consists of a series of neurons that synapse at various nuclei on the way to the brain. Fibers from all sensory systems synapse in the thalamus, from which nerve fibers travel to the cortical receiving areas for each sense. The visual receiving area is in the occipital lobe, the auditory area is in the temporal lobe, and the area for the skin senses is in the parietal lobe of the cortex.
4. Electrical signals in neurons are "wet" signals, caused by the flow of charged molecules called ions. The nerve impulse is caused by sodium rushing into the fiber followed by potassium rushing out.
5. Increasing the intensity of a stimulus changes the rate of nerve firing but does not affect the size of

the nerve impulses. There is an upper limit to the rate of nerve firing because of a refractory period that occurs after the transmission of each nerve impulse.

6. Many nerve fibers fire without environmental stimulation. This spontaneous firing is called spontaneous activity.

7. The transmission of nerve impulses from one neuron to another depends on the interplay of excitatory and inhibitory signals at the synapse.

8. Neural circuits "process" electrical signals as they travel from the receptors toward the brain. This processing, which makes use of convergence and inhibition, can create neurons that respond to specific properties of the stimulus.

9. The retina contains five basic types of cells: receptors, bipolar cells, ganglion cells, horizontal cells, and amacrine cells. The horizontal and amacrine cells transmit electrical signals laterally across the retina.

10. The receptive field of a neuron in the visual system is the region of the retina which, when stimulated, influences the firing of the neuron.

11. Center-surround receptive fields have excitatory centers and inhibitory surrounds or inhibitory centers and excitatory surrounds. The opposite responses from the center and surround cause center-surround antagonism. Center-surround receptive fields are found not only in the visual system but also in the cutaneous (touch) system.

12. Simple cortical neurons are divided into excitatory and inhibitory areas arranged side by side and respond best to bars of a particular orientation.

13. The problem of sensory coding is: "How do electrical signals in the nervous system represent properties of the environment?"

14. The sensory code for quality across the senses is the location of the electrical signals reaching the brain.

15. The specificity theory of sensory coding states that different qualities within a sense are signaled to the brain by activity in specific nerve fibers. Arguments against specificity theory are (a) the large number of different qualities, (b) the absence of highly specific neurons, and (c) the fact that the firing of neurons is influenced not only by quality but also by stimulus intensity.

16. The across-fiber-pattern theory of sensory coding states that different qualities within a sense are signaled to the brain by the pattern of activity across a large number of neurons. There are a number of senses that use this type of coding.

17. The sensory code for subjective magnitude is probably the frequency of nerve firing, but some other property of nerve firing, such as the temporal pattern, may also be involved.

18. The mind-body problem, stated in physiological terms, is: "How do patterns of sodium and potassium flowing across membranes become perceptions?" We don't know how to solve this problem but can study the neural code.

19. In studying the neural code it is important to remember that identifying information in the nervous system is just the first step in determining how physiological processes result in perception. The second, and more difficult, step is to determine whether this information is used by the brain and, if so, how it is used.

Boxes

1. In intracellular recording, an electrode is inserted inside a nerve fiber. In extracellular recording, an electrode is positioned just outside the nerve fiber.

2. Experimental visual prostheses have been developed in which electrical stimulation of the visual cortex generates phosphenes that enable blind people to see crude shapes.

Study Questions

1. What is the major function of the receptors? (33)

2. Define: neuron, nerve fiber, synapse, chemical transmitter, thalamus, cortical receiving areas. Know which area goes with which sense. (34)

3. Stimulating a receptor in the hand triggers a sequence of nerve impulses that eventually results in a perception that the hand has been touched, and perhaps results in movement of the hand. At what point in this sequence of nerve impulses does perception occur? (37)

4. Define: "wet signals," "dry signals," recording electrode, null electrode, permeability. (37)

5. What is the most abundant substance outside of the nerve fiber? Inside of the fiber? What happens to these substances when the fiber is stimulated? How does the flow of these substances affect the charge inside the fiber? Be sure you understand Figure 2.11. (38)

6. Understand the basic properties of nerve impulses. How does changing the stimulus intensity affect the

size of nerve impulses? The rate of nerve firing? What is the refractory period? How does it affect the upper limit to nerve firing? What is spontaneous activity? (38)

7. Understand how excitation and inhibition interact to affect nerve firing (Figure 2.13). (40)

8. What are the basic differences between the circuits in Figures 2.14–2.16? What are the roles of convergence and inhibition in the circuits of Figures 2.15 and 2.16? (43)

9. What are the five basic cell types in the retina? Which cell does each of the five types synapse with? (44)

10. What is a receptive field? (47)

11. How does the response of a center-surround receptive field change as the diameter of a stimulus spot is increased (Figure 2.20)? What is center-surround antagonism? (47)

12. Draw a neural circuit that would result in a center-surround receptive field. (48)

13. Give a nonvisual example of a center-surround receptive field. (48)

14. What is a simple cortical cell? What does the tuning curve of a simple cortical cell tell us? (48)

15. What is the problem of sensory coding? (50)

16. What is the "doctrine of specific nerve energies"? (52)

17. What is specificity theory? What are three arguments against specificity theory? What do we mean when we say that a given rate of firing in an ori-entation selective neuron cannot unambiguously indicate orientation? (52)

18. What is across-fiber-pattern theory? Be sure you understand the principle behind Figure 2.28 and Erickson's experiment that supports pattern theory (Figure 2.29). (53)

19. What is subjective magnitude? What is the point of plotting the results of psychophysical magnitude estimate experiments on logarithmic scales? What is a power function and what does its slope tell us? (55)

20. What is the neural code for the magnitude of a stimulus? Describe three experiments relevant to this question. (55)

21. State the mind-body problem in molecular terms. (58)

22. What are the three possible answers to the question "How is the information in neuron firing used to determine perception?" (59)

Boxes

1. Define: intracellular recording, extracellular recording. What is one advantage of intracellular recording? (45)

2. Describe a system that causes blind people to see by stimulating their visual cortex. What is a phosphene? What are some problems with this system? (50)

Glossary

Across-fiber-pattern theory. The theory that sensory quality is signaled by the pattern of nerve activity across a large number of nerve fibers. (53)

Amacrine cell. A neuron that transmits signals laterally in the retina. Amacrine cells synapse with bipolar cells and ganglion cells. (46)

Bipolar cell. A neuron that is stimulated by the visual receptors and sends electrical signals to the retinal ganglion cells. (44)

Cell body. The part of a neuron that receives stimulation from other neurons. (34)

Center-surround antagonism. The competition between the center and surround regions of a center-surround receptive field. (47)

Center-surround receptive field. A receptive field that consists of a roughly circular excitatory area surrounded by an inhibitory area, or a circular inhibitory center surrounded by an excitatory area. (47)

Chemical transmitter. A chemical, released at the syn-apse by one neuron, that either excites or inhibits another neuron. (35)

Complex cell. A neuron in the visual cortex which responds best to moving bars with a particular orientation. (48)

Convergence. When many neurons synapse onto fewer neurons. (43)

Cortical receiving area. The area in the cortex that receives electrical signals from one sense. For example, the cortical receiving area for vision is in the occipital lobe of the cortex. (36)

Doctrine of specific nerve energies. States that the brain receives environmental information from sensory nerves and that the brain distinguishes between the different senses by monitoring the activity in these sensory nerves. (52)

Excitation. A condition that facilitates the generation of nerve impulses. (40)

Excitatory center–inhibitory surround receptive field.

A center-surround receptive field in which stimulation of the center area causes an excitatory response and stimulation of the surround causes an inhibitory response. (47)

Excitatory response. Response of a nerve fiber in which the firing rate increases. (40, 47)

Extracellular recording. Recording from a cell with the tip of the electrode just outside the cell. (45)

Ganglion cell. A neuron in the retina that receives inputs from bipolar and amacrine cells. The axons of the ganglion cells are the fibers that travel toward the brain in the optic nerve. (49)

Horizontal cell. A neuron that transmits signals laterally across the retina. Horizontal cells synapse with receptors and bipolar cells. (46)

Inhibition. A condition that decreases the likelihood that nerve impulses will be generated. (40)

Inhibitory center–excitatory surround receptive field. A center-surround receptive field in which stimulation of the center causes an inhibitory response and stimulation of the surround causes an excitatory response. (47)

Inhibitory response. Response of a nerve fiber in which the firing rate decreases. (40, 47)

Intracellular recording. Recording from a cell with the tip of the electrode inside the cell. (45)

Ions. Charged molecules found floating in the water that surrounds nerve fibers. (37)

Linear circuit. A circuit in which one neuron synapses with another, with no convergence. (43)

Linear function. A function relating the logarithm of subjective magnitude (magnitude estimate) to the logarithm of stimulus intensity that has a slope of 1.0. (56)

Microelectrode. A thin piece of wire or glass that is small enough to record electrical signals from single nerve fibers. (38)

Microneurography. A technique which makes it possible to record from single nerve fibers in the skin that respond to touch stimuli in the awake human. (58)

Nerve. A group of nerve fibers traveling together. (36)

Nerve axon. See nerve fiber.

Nerve fiber. In most sensory neurons the nerve fiber is the long part of the neuron that transmits electrical impulses from one point to another. (34)

Nerve impulse. A rapid change in electrical potential that travels down a nerve fiber. (38)

Neural circuit. A number of neurons that are connected by synapses. (40)

Neuron. A cell in the nervous system that generates and transmits electrical impulses. (34)

Nuclei. Small areas in the nervous system at which many synapses occur. (36)

Null electrode. One of a pair of electrodes used to record nerve activity. The null electrode is positioned in a neutral area so that it is unaffected by nerve activity. (38)

Occipital lobe. A lobe at the back of the cortex that is the site of the cortical receiving area for vision. (36)

Off response. The response of a nerve fiber in which there is an increase in the firing rate when the stimulus is turned off. (47)

On response. The response of a nerve fiber in which there is an increase in the firing rate when the stimulus is turned on. Same as excitatory response. (47)

Parietal lobe. A lobe at the top of the cortex that is the site of the cortical receiving area for touch. (36)

Permeability. A property of a membrane that refers to the ability of molecules to pass through the membrane. If the permeability to a molecule is high, the molecule can easily pass through the membrane. (38)

Phosphene. A small glowing spot of light. (50)

Power function. A mathematical function of the form $P = KS^n$, where P is perceived magnitude, K is a constant, S is the stimulus intensity, and n is an exponent. (56)

Problem of sensory coding. The problem of determining how characteristics of nerve impulses represent properties of the environment. (50)

Prosthesis. A artificial device which substitutes for a missing part of the body. (50)

Receptive field. A neuron's receptive field is the area on the receptor surface (the retina, in the case of vision) that, when stimulated, affects the firing of that neuron. (47)

Recording electrode. A small shaft of metal or glass which, when connected to appropriate electronic equipment, records electrical activity from nerves or nerve fibers. (38)

Refractory period. A time period of about 1/1,000 second that a nerve fiber needs to recover from conducting a nerve impulse. No new nerve impulses can be generated in the fiber until the refractory period is over. (40)

Response compression. When doubling the physical intensity of a stimulus less than doubles the subjective magnitude of the stimulus. (56)

Response expansion. When doubling the physical intensity of a stimulus more than doubles the subjective magnitude of the stimulus. (56)

Sensory code. Electrical signals in the nervous system form a code that represents properties of stimuli in the environment. (50)

Simple cell. A neuron in the visual cortex that responds best to bars of a particular orientation. (48)

Specificity theory. The theory that different qualities are signaled to the brain by the activity in specific nerve fibers that fire only to that quality. (52)

Spontaneous activity. Nerve firing that occurs in the absence of environmental stimulation. (40)

Subjective magnitude. The magnitude of a person's sensory experience. (55)

Synapse. A small space between the end of one neuron and the cell body of another neuron. (34)

Synaptic vesicles. Small packets of chemicals located on one side of the synapse. When stimulated by a nerve impulse these chemicals are released onto the cell body on the other side of the synapse. (35)

Temporal lobe. A lobe on the side of the cortex that is the site of the cortical receiving area for hearing. (36)

Temporal pattern. The timing of nerve impulses. For example, two sequences of nerve impulses, one in which the time between successive impulses is regular and one in which the time between impulses varies, would have different temporal patterns. (58)

Thalamus. A nucleus in the brain where neurons from all of the senses, except smell, synapse on their way to their cortical receiving areas. (36)

Transduction. In the senses, the transformation of environmental energy into electrical energy. (33)

Tuning curve. For cells in the visual cortex, the function that relates the cell's firing rate to the orientation of the stimulus. (49)

Visual pigment. A light-sensitive molecule contained in the visual receptors. The reaction of this molecule to light results in the generation of an electrical signal in the receptor. (33)

C H A P T E R 3

Basic Mechanisms of Vision

Vision begins with light, but before we see this light, it must be transformed into electrical energy by the receptors of the eye, and this electrical energy must travel a long and complex path from the receptors to the visual cortex and beyond. In the last chapter, we began our description of this process, focusing on the idea that the electrical signals generated by the receptors are processed by neural circuits as they transmit these signals from their beginning point in the receptors to their destinations in the brain. We now continue our description of this process by describing in more detail some of the basic facts about the physiology of vision that we will need as we continue our study of vision in the chapters that follow.

Our plan in this chapter is first to describe the different types of stimuli that are used to study vision and then to describe how the visual system's structure and physiology are related to visual perception.

THE STIMULI FOR VISION

Visible light, the band of electromagnetic energy with wavelengths between 360 and 700 nm, is the stimulus for vision. We can perceive light by looking directly at a light source that emits these wavelengths, such as the sun or a light bulb. Most of the light we perceive, however, is reflected into our eyes from objects in the environment, with this reflection providing information about the nature of these objects (Figure 3.1).

Distal Stimuli, Proximal Stimuli, and Visual Angle

The stimulus in Figure 3.1 is typical of the kinds of stimuli we see every day. To deal with these

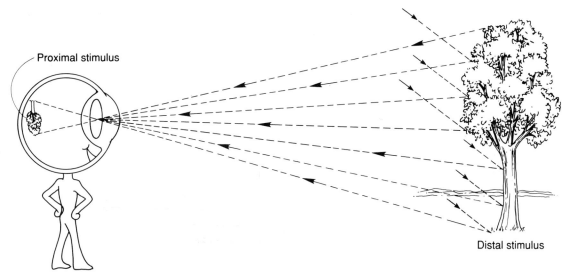

Proximal stimulus

Distal stimulus

F I G U R E 3. 1 An "eyeball heavy" person looking at a tree. The person sees the tree only because light is reflected from it into the person's eye. We can specify the tree stimulus in two ways: (1) as a distal stimulus, in which we specify the dimensions of the tree and its location in the environment; (2) as a proximal stimulus, in which we specify the size and location of the tree on the person's retina.

stimuli, we need to be able to specify their characteristics. We will describe two different ways of specifying perceptual stimuli by considering the person observing the tree in Figure 3.1. One way is to say that "the subject is viewing a 4-meter-tall tree from a distance of 7 meters." When we do this we are treating the tree as a **distal stimulus**—a stimulus located at a distance from the observer. We are specifying the tree's **physical size** (4 meters) and **physical distance** (7 meters), the values we determine when we measure the size of the tree and its distance from the observer.

We can, however, also consider the stimulus in a different way by specifying the size of the stimulus on the surface of the retina. When we do this, we are considering the tree as a **proximal stimulus**—a stimulus located on the observer's receptors—and rather than specify physical size, we specify **retinal size**—the size of the image the stimulus casts on the retina. We can, therefore, say that the tree in Figure 3.1 has a retinal size of 0.5 mm. Usually, however, rather than specifying the proximal stimulus in terms of mm on the retina, we

specify it in terms of a measure called **visual angle.** This way of specifying the stimulus is very common, and we will use it frequently in this book, so it is important to understand what we mean when we say, "The visual angle of the stimulus is 1 degree."

Figure 3.2(a) shows how to determine visual angle, this time using a person as a stimulus instead of a tree. We extend one line from the nodal point of the observer's eye (a point near the center of the lens) to the top of the object and another line from the nodal point to the bottom of the object. The visual angle is the angle between those two lines. From this definition, we can see that the visual angle depends on the physical size of the object. Thus, the large man has a larger visual angle than the small man. It is, however, extremely important to realize that visual angle depends not only on the object's physical size, but also on its distance from the observer. Thus, as we can see from Figure 3.2(b) and (c), moving the small man farther decreases the visual angle. Visual angle is, therefore, determined by both an object's physical size *and* its distance from the observer.

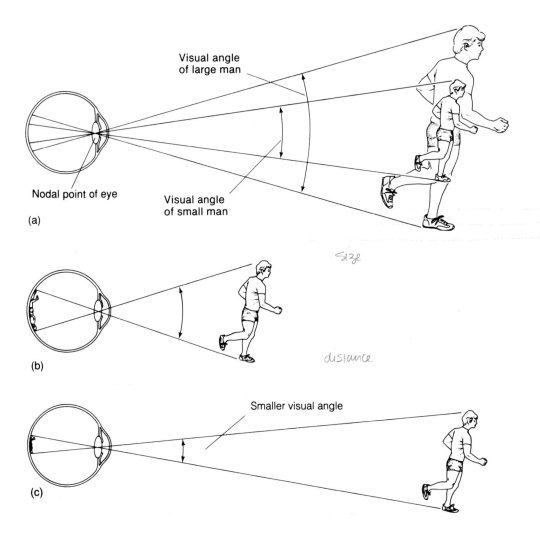

Visual angle
of large man

Nodal point of eye

Visual angle
of small man

(a)

size

(b)

distance

Smaller visual angle

(c)

F I G U R E 3. 2   (a) To determine the visual angle of any object, extend lines from
the nodal point of the eye to the top and bottom of the object, in this case a man. If two
objects are the same distance from the observer, the one that is larger will have a larger visual
angle. Thus, the larger man has a larger visual angle than the smaller man. As the man in
(b) walks away, his visual angle gets smaller, as shown in (c). Thus, if two objects are the
same physical size, the one that is closer has a larger visual angle.

DEMONSTRATION

Visual Angle and Size in the Field of View

An advantage of specifying size in terms of visual angle is that it tells us how large an object is in our field of view. To get a feel for how this works, look at your fingernail from a distance of 3 inches. When you do this, your fingernail has a visual angle of about 10 degrees (assuming your fingernail measures about ½ inch from top to bottom). Now move your fingernail to 24 inches distant (about arm's length for most people). It now has a visual angle of about 1 degree and takes up a much smaller portion of your field of view. (Note: One degree of visual angle equals about 0.4 mm on the surface of the adult human retina.)

Now place an object with a physical height of about 3 inches about 2 feet away on your desk, and then, closing one eye, position your fingernail so it is just to the side of the object and its height matches the object's height in your field of view. When you do this, both your fingernail and the object will have the same visual angle. For a 3-inch-high object at 2 feet your fingernail will be about 3 inches from your eye, and the visual angle for both the object and your fingernail will be about 10 degrees. Since visual angle is determined by both an object's physical size and its distance from the observer, two objects can have very different physical sizes but the same visual angle, and when their visual angle is the same, they cover the same area in your field of view.

Now that you know that the visual angle of your ½-inch-high fingernail at 24 inches is about 1 degree (more exactly, it is 1.2 degrees), you can use your fingernail as a measuring device to determine the visual angles of much larger but farther away objects, such as the moon. Try this, before looking up the answer at the bottom of page 68.

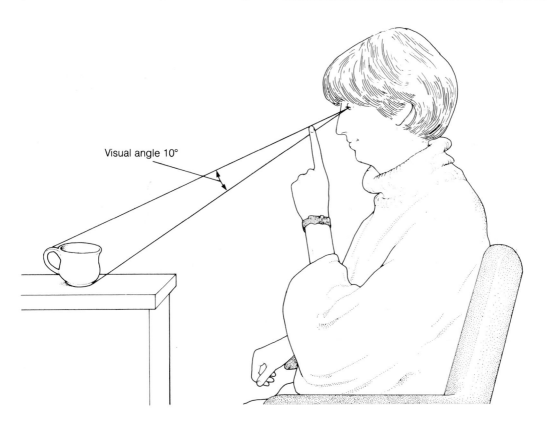

Visual angle 10°

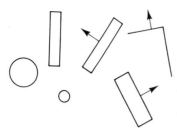

F I G U R E 3. 3 Geometrical stimuli of the type used in many experiments. The stimuli shown here include stationary circles and lines, moving lines, and a moving "corner."

F I G U R E 3. 4 These two gratings illustrate the effect of spatial frequency on contrast. When viewed from a distance of about 2 feet, the high-spatial-frequency grating on the right appears to have less contrast than the low-spatial-frequency grating on the left. (From Blakemore & Sutton, 1969.)

Now that we have described the distal and proximal methods of specifying the stimulus, let's describe some of the most common stimuli and the types of experiments in which these stimuli would be used.

Geometrical Stimuli

Visual stimuli come in all shapes and sizes, but the most basic and most widely used are simple geometrical stimuli like those in Figure 3.3. As we will see in this chapter, a common use for these types of stimuli is mapping receptive fields of neurons in the visual cortex. The simplest of these stimuli is the "spot." It has been used not only to map receptive fields but as a favorite way of presenting the

Answer: 0.5 degrees.

stimulus in experiments which ask questions such as "What is the threshold intensity for seeing light?" and "What color is this light?"

Grating Stimuli and Spatial Frequency

The two displays of alternating black and white bars in Figure 3.4, which are called **gratings,** differ in **spatial frequency,** the number of repeating patterns per unit distance, where one repeating pattern is one black bar plus one white bar. Since the grating on the right has more repeating patterns than the one on the left, we would say that this grating has a higher spatial frequency than the one on the left.

Spatial frequency as a way of specifying a visual stimulus is important because the spatial frequency of a stimulus can affect our perception of its various qualities. For example, although the black lines of both gratings in Figure 3.4 are printed from the same ink, the bars in the grating on the right don't look as dark as the bars in the grating on the left, when viewed from a distance of about 2 feet. As we will see in Chapter 5, when we describe grating stimuli in more detail, the spatial frequency of a stimulus can affect our perception of its lightness or darkness.

When we describe spatial frequency and its effect on perception in more detail in Chapter 5, we will see that spatial frequency is important not only for understanding how we perceive gratings but also for understanding how we perceive scenes like those we encounter in the environment. We will see that every visual stimulus contains both high and low spatial frequency components, with high spatial frequencies associated with small, detailed parts of the scene, and low spatial frequencies associated with larger, less-detailed parts of the scene (Figure 3.5).

Ecological Stimuli

Spots, bars, and gratings, the types of stimuli we have discussed so far, bear little resemblance to the kind of stimuli we encounter in the real world. In addition, the way subjects view these stimuli in perception experiments bears little resemblance to

F I G U R E 3. 5 (left) Photograph of a scene; (middle) the scene with low frequency components emphasized; and (right) the scene with high spatial frequency components emphasized. (Pictures courtesy of Arthur Ginsburg.)

the way we view stimuli in the real world. Whereas we usually view the environment as we move through it, subjects typically view stimuli like spots, bars, and gratings with their eyes held as stationary as possible and as they sit in a fixed position with their heads constrained in a chin rest (Figure 3.6), to ensure that the stimuli are presented to a specific area of the retina.

J. J. Gibson, the founder of the ecological approach to the study of perception (see p. 25, Chapter 1), thought that it made more sense to specify visual stimuli in a way that was more closely related to the way we perceive the real world. To do this, he introduced the concept of the **ambient optic array.**

To understand this concept, let's consider the stimulation reaching the person in Figure 3.7. This person perceives the objects, surfaces, and textures in the scene because of the way the light rays reaching the person are *structured* by these objects, surfaces, and textures. This structure, which is extremely complex because there are rays converging on the person from every part of the environment, is the ambient optic array.

The importance of the ambient optic array lies not in the structure it defines at any point in time but in the way it changes as the observer moves. According to Gibson, these changes determine perception. This approach to describing the visual stimulus differs from the other approaches

F I G U R E 3. 6 A person in a psychophysical experiment. The person's head is stabilized by a chin rest in this experiment.

we have discussed in a number of ways. For example: (1) The appropriate stimuli for perceptual research, according to the ecological approach, are stimuli that carry information about the environment. (2) The effect of the observer's movement is of central importance. The optic array as seen from a particular viewpoint is much less important than the *changes* that occur in the optic array as

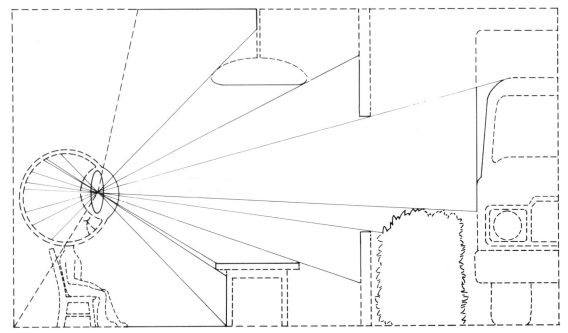

F I G U R E 3 . 7 As we pointed out in Figure 3.1, everything we see reflects light into our eyes. Here we carry this idea a step further by showing that the objects we see give *structure* to the light reaching the person's eyes. Surfaces visible to our observer are indicated by solid lines, invisible surfaces by dashed lines. Each of the visible surfaces structures the pattern of light entering the observer's eye. This structured light is the ambient optic array.

an observer moves. For example, an ecological psychologist would focus on how parts of the optic array flow past a moving observer.

As we discuss visual perception in the chapters that follow, we will be describing each of the three types of stimuli introduced above in more detail, with grating stimuli and spatial frequency more fully described in Chapter 5 ("Brightness and Contrast"), and ecological stimuli more fully described in Chapter 6 ("Objects and Forms"), Chapter 7 ("Depth and Size"), and Chapter 8 ("Movement and Events"). Most of the research we will discuss in this chapter uses geometrical stimuli like the ones in Figure 3.3.

Now that we have introduced some of the basic visual stimuli, we are ready to look at the structure and functioning of the visual system on which these stimuli act.

FOCUSING LIGHT ONTO THE RETINA

First Steps in the Visual Process

As light enters the eye, the process of vision begins. The first step is the focusing of light by the **cornea** and **lens** onto the receptors of the retina. We saw in Figure 2.17 that the retina is a complex network of neurons, and in Figure 3.8 we can see how the retina lines the back of the eye. One thing we can't see in these figures, but which is shown in Figure 3.9, is that the retinal receptors are facing "backwards," away from the light, so that before the light reaches them, it must pass through the ganglion, amacrine, bipolar, and horizontal cells.

Why do the receptors face away from the light? The reason lies in a layer of cells called the **pigment epithelium.** This layer, which is a deep black color,

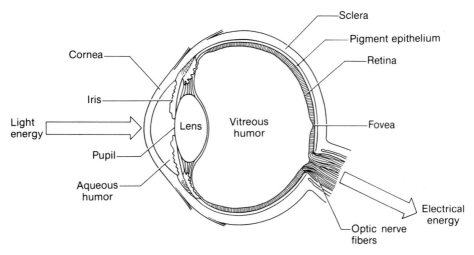

F I G U R E 3. 8 A cross section of the human eye. Structures we will be referring to in this chapter are the focusing elements (the lens and cornea), the retina, which contains the receptors for vision as well as other neurons, the pigment epithelium, a layer containing nutrients and enzymes, upon which the retina rests, and the optic nerve, which contains the optic nerve fibers that transmit electrical energy out of the retina. The small depression in the retina, which is called the fovea, contains only cone receptors. The rest of the retina, which is called the peripheral retina, contains both rod and cone receptors.

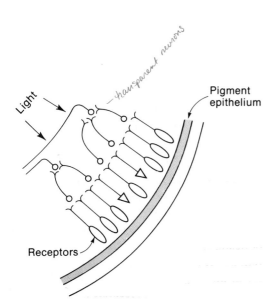

F I G U R E 3. 9 Close-up of the retina showing how the receptors face away from the light so the light must pass through the other retinal neurons before reaching the receptors. Since these neurons are transparent they do not prevent the light from reaching the receptors.

contains nutrients and chemicals called enzymes that are vital to the receptors' functioning. We will consider what these enzymes do later in this chapter, but for now suffice it to say that the receptors face backwards so they can be in close contact with the pigment epithelium. Backwards-facing receptors pose little problem for vision, however, since the light easily passes through the other cells, which are transparent, and reaches the receptors. Let's consider how the light is focused onto the receptors.

Focusing Light onto the Receptors

Focusing parallel light. The eye focuses light with its two focusing elements, the cornea and the lens, which, if everything is working properly, bring light entering the eye to a sharp focus on the retina.

To understand how these focusing elements work, let's first consider what happens when we look at a small spot of light located more than 20 feet away. Coming from this distance, light rays that reach the eye are essentially parallel, as in Figure 3.10(a), and these parallel rays are brought

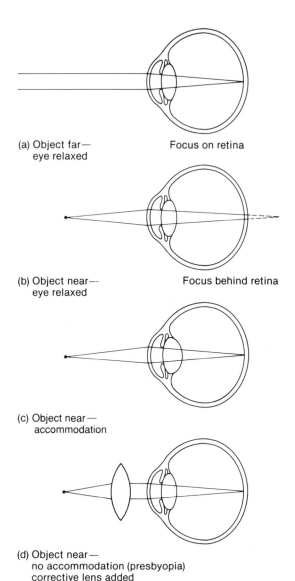

(a) Object far—
    eye relaxed   Focus on retina

(b) Object near—
    eye relaxed   Focus behind retina

(c) Object near—
    accommodation

(d) Object near—
    no accommodation (presbyopia)
    corrective lens added

F I G U R E   3. 10   Focusing of light rays by the normal eye. (a) Parallel rays, from a spot of light greater than 20 feet away, are focused onto the retina. (b) When the spot of light is moved closer to the eye, the rays are no longer parallel, and the focus point of the light is pushed back behind the retina. (c) Accommodation, indicated by the fatter lens in this picture, pushes the focus point forward onto the retina. (d) If the ability to accommodate is decreased, as in the presbyopic eye, a corrective lens is needed to bring light to a focus on the retina.

to a focus on the retina. If, however, we move our spot closer to the eye, the rays are no longer parallel, as in Figure 3.10(b), and the point at which light comes to a focus moves to behind the retina. Of course, the light never comes to a focus in this situation because it is stopped by the retina, and if things remain in this state, both the image on the retina and our vision will be out of focus.

Focusing nonparallel light: accommodation. Fortunately, the eye can increase the **focusing power** of the lens to bring the image formed by nonparallel rays of light into focus on the retina. This increase in focusing power is accomplished by a process called **accommodation,** in which tightening the ciliary muscles at the front of the eye increases the curvature of the lens so that it gets fatter, as in Figure 3.10(c). This increased curvature bends the light rays leaving the lens more sharply and moves the focus point forward, resulting in a sharp image on the retina, and, therefore, sharp vision. The beauty of accommodation is that it happens automatically: The eye constantly adjusts the lens's focusing power to keep the image on the retina sharp as we look at objects located at different distances.

D E M O N S T R A T I O N

Becoming Aware of What Is in Focus

Because accommodation is done unconsciously, the constant change in the focusing power of the lens, which allows us to see clearly at different distances, is not something people are normally aware of. In fact, this unconscious focusing process works so efficiently that most people assume that everything, near and far, is always in focus. You can demonstrate to yourself that this is not so by closing one eye, looking at a faraway object (at least 20 feet distant), and then, while still looking at the far object, moving a pencil toward you while noticing the pencil point. (Don't focus on the point, just "notice" it.) As the pencil gets closer, you should notice that the point becomes blurred and is seen double. When the pencil is about 12 inches away, focus on the point. It is now seen sharply, but the faraway object you were focusing on before is blurred.

Now, bring the pencil even closer until you can no longer see the point sharply no matter how hard you try. Notice the strain in your eyes as you try unsuccessfully to bring the point into focus.

Your exercises in focusing show that accommodation enables you to bring both near and far objects into focus, but that they are not in focus at the same time. You also saw that accommodation has its limits. The distance at which you could no longer see the pencil clearly, even though you were straining to accommodate, is called the **near point,** the point at which your lens can no longer adjust to bring close objects into focus. As illustrated in Figure 3.11, the location of the near point depends on a person's age. The near point for most 20-year-olds is at about 10 cm, but this increases to 14 cm by age 30, 22 cm at 40, and 100 cm at 60. The reason for this loss in the ability to accommodate at close distances is that the lens hardens with age and the ciliary muscles, which control accommodation, become weaker. These changes make it more difficult for the lens to change its shape for vision at close range. Though this gradual decrease in accommodative ability poses little problem for most people before the age of 45, at around 45 years of age the ability to accommodate begins to decrease rapidly, and the near point moves beyond a comfortable reading distance. This decreased ability to accommodate (with the resulting increase in the distance of the near point) is called **presbyopia,** or "old eye."

Presbyopia affects everyone, no matter how good their eyesight when they are young, because it is a normal consequence of ageing. This means that all people eventually experience difficulty in reading, when their inability to accommodate makes it impossible for them to focus at a comfortable reading distance—about 12–18 inches. The solution to this problem is a corrective lens that adds the necessary focusing power to bring light to a focus on the retina, as shown in Figure 3.10(d). Many people also need corrective lenses because they are either nearsighted or farsighted. We will discuss these and many other visual problems in Chapter 10 (Clinical Aspects of Vision).

THE OVERALL PLAN OF THE VISUAL SYSTEM

We are already familiar with the retina, the first neural network through which electrical signals generated in the receptors pass on their way to the brain. Let's now look at the overall plan of the visual system and then look in more detail at each of its components.

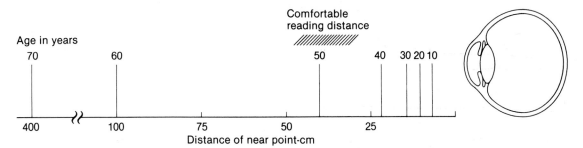

F I G U R E 3. 11 Near point as a function of age. The distance of the near point in centimeters is indicated on the scale at the bottom, and various ages are indicated by the vertical lines. Objects closer than the near point cannot be brought into focus by accommodation. Thus, as age increases, the ability to focus on nearby objects becomes poorer and poorer; eventually, past the age of about 50, reading becomes impossible without corrective lenses.

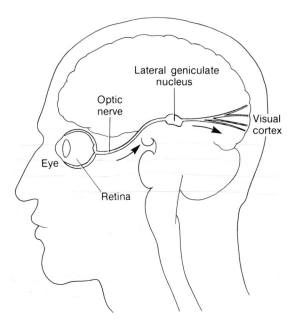

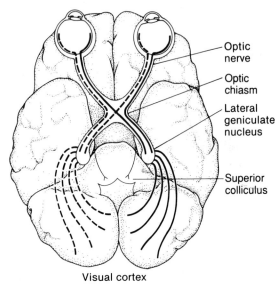

FIGURE 3. 12 A side view of the visual system, showing the three major sites along the primary visual pathway where processing takes place: the retina, the lateral geniculate nucleus (LGN), and the visual receiving area of the cortex.

FIGURE 3. 13 The visual system seen from underneath the brain, showing how some of the nerve fibers from the retina cross over to the opposite side of the brain at the optic chiasm. A small proportion of optic nerve fibers goes to the superior colliculus. Most go to the lateral geniculate nucleus and then to the visual receiving area in the occipital lobe of the cortex.

Two views of the overall plan of the visual system are shown in Figures 3.12 and 3.13. Most of the nerve fibers leaving the retina in the optic nerve travel in the **primary visual pathway,** which takes them from the retina to the **lateral geniculate nucleus (LGN)** in the thalamus, and then to the **visual receiving area** in the occipital lobe of the cortex. The visual receiving area is also called the **striate cortex,** because when it is sliced it has a striped appearance. A small percentage of the nerve fibers leaving the retina travel to the **superior colliculus,** a structure which is important in controlling eye movements.

We will focus our attention on the primary visual pathway and will deal with the following questions:

1. What are the structural properties of the retina, LGN, and cortex?
2. How do neurons in the primary pathway respond to stimulation of the retina?

3. What is the relationship between physiology (both structural properties and neural responses) and perception?

We will answer these questions by starting with the receptors for vision, the rods and cones, and then we will follow the visual pathway from the receptors to the LGN and then to the visual cortex. Our major goals are to describe the functioning of these structures, and, when possible, to establish links between this functioning and perception.

THE RECEPTORS FOR VISION: THE RODS AND CONES

Structure and Distribution

If you were able to look directly down onto the receptors, you would see the **mosaic of receptors** shown in Figure 3.14 and Color Plate 3.1. This

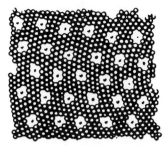

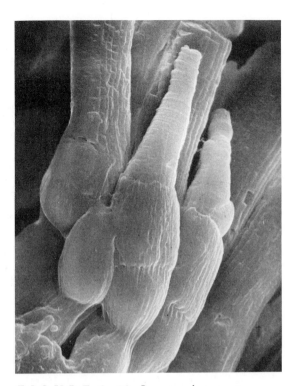

F I G U R E 3. 14   The "mosaic" of receptors. This is a view looking down on the human retina, showing the tops of the rod and cone receptor outer segments. The rods are more numerous and, in this particular area of peripheral retina, are more densely packed than the cones. The space around each cone is created by the large cone inner segment, near the base of the receptor, that is fatter in cones than in rods (see Figure 2.17). This drawing shows the thinner tips of the rod and cone outer segments. (Drawing from Schultze, 1866.)

F I G U R E 3. 16   Scanning electron micrograph showing the rod and cone outer segments. The rod outer segment on the left is so large that it extends out of the picture, but the cylindrical shape of the rods and the tapered shape of the cones can be clearly seen in this picture. (Lewis, Zeevi, & Werblin, 1969.)

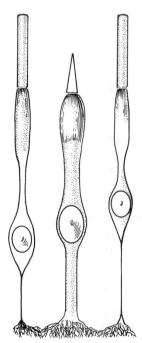

mosaic is the surface on which the image is focused by the cornea and lens.

If we look at the receptors from the side, we can differentiate two different types on the basis of their outward appearance. One type, the **rods,** are longer and rod shaped, whereas the other type, the **cones,** are much shorter and cone shaped, as shown both in an 1872 drawing by Max Schultze, who first described these two receptor types (Figure 3.15), and in the modern scanning electron micrograph of Figure 3.16. (Also see Figures 2.1, 2.17, and Color Plate 2.1 for additional depictions of the receptors.)*

These rods and cones are not, however, evenly distributed in the retina. There is one area in the

F I G U R E 3. 15   Drawing of the rod and cone receptors made in 1872 by Max Schultze, which clearly shows the differences in the shapes of the rod and cone outer segments.

---

* The cones in the fovea (see below) are, however, more elongated than the rest of the cones in the retina.

●   +

FIGURE 3. 17

retina, the **fovea** (see Figure 3.8), which contains only cones. The fovea is located directly on the line of sight, so any time we look directly at an object, its image falls on the fovea. The fovea is small, however, so only objects with a visual angle of about 0.5 degree or less have an image that falls completely on the fovea.

There are about 6 million cones in the retina, but since the fovea is so small, only a small fraction of these cones are found in this cone-rich area. Most of the cones are in the **peripheral retina,** the area that surrounds the fovea. Even though most of the cones are in the peripheral retina, they are outnumbered by the rods by about a 20 to 1 ratio, since all 120 million rods in the retina are in the periphery.

The retina is, therefore, a blanket of receptors, covering almost the entire back of the eye. The one place on the back of the eye that is not covered with receptors is the place where the optic nerve leaves the eye. This is called the **blind spot,** because light imaged there is not seen.

DEMONSTRATION

"Seeing" the Blind Spot

You can demonstrate the existence of the blind spot to yourself by closing your right eye and, with the cross above lined up with your left eye, looking at the cross while moving the book (or yourself) slowly back and forth. When the book is about a foot from your eye the circle disappears. At this point, the image of the circle falls on the blind spot.

Why aren't we usually aware of the blind spot? There are a number of reasons. First, we usually use two eyes, so when an image falls on the blind spot of one eye, it falls on the receptors of the other. But this explanation doesn't really answer the question, because we usually aren't aware of the blind spot, even when we look with only one

eye. One reason we aren't aware of it, even with one-eyed vision, is that the blind spot is located off to the side of our visual field, which means, as we will see in this chapter, that we don't see it in sharp focus. Because it isn't in sharp focus and because we don't know exactly where to look for it (as opposed to the demonstration, in which we know that the circle will disappear), the blind spot is hard to detect.

But perhaps the most important reason that we don't see the blind spot is that some as yet poorly understood mechanism "fills in" the place where the image disappears. Think about what happened when the spot above disappeared. The place where the spot used to be wasn't replaced by a "hole" or by "nothingness"; it was filled in by the white page. If the spot had been surrounded by a pattern, then the pattern would have filled in the area where the spot had been (try this by drawing your own stimulus).

Dark Adaptation

We are interested in rods and cones not only because they look different but because they have different properties. It is these properties that led von Kris to propose the **duplicity theory of vision** in 1896. This theory states that the retina is made up of two types of receptors that not only look different but also have different properties and operate under different conditions. The remainder of this section on the eye and retina will be devoted to describing both the physiological and the perceptual differences between the rods and cones. We begin by showing how the rods and cones function differently during the process of **dark adaptation,** the increase in sensitivity that occurs when the illumination changes from light to darkness.

You are familiar with dark adaptation from your own experience: When the illumination is changed from light to darkness, you find it difficult to see anything at first, but as you spend more time in the dark, your sensitivity increases and you can eventually see things that at first seemed shrouded in darkness (remember "Spending Some Time in the Closet" from Chapter 1).

Although it is obvious that your sensitivity increases as you spend more time in the dark, it is not obvious that this increase takes place in two distinct stages, an initial rapid stage and a later slower stage. In this section, we will describe three experiments to show that the initial rapid stage is due to the cones and the second slower stage is due to the rods. In our first experiment, we will describe how to measure a **dark adaptation curve** which shows the two-stage process of dark adaptation. In our second experiment, we will describe how to measure the dark adaptation of the cones alone; and in our third experiment, we will describe how to measure the dark adaptation of the rods alone. Finally, we will show how the different adaptation rates of the rods and cones can be explained by the properties of chemicals in the receptors called visual pigments.

Experiment #1: Determining a two-stage dark adaptation curve. In all of our dark adaptation experiments we ask our observer to adjust the intensity of a small flashing test light so he can just barely see it. In the first experiment, our observer looks at a display like the one in Figure 3.18. The observer looks at the small fixation point while paying attention to the flashing test light. Since the observer is looking directly at the fixation point, the point's image falls on the fovea while the image of the test light falls in the periphery. Thus, the test light stimulates both rods and cones, and any adaptation measured with this test light should reflect the activity of both the rod and cone receptors.

The usual procedure in a dark adaptation experiment is to first expose a person to a fairly intense light, a process called **light adaptation,** and

as the observer is exposed to this adapting light, we determine his sensitivity to the test light by asking him to adjust its intensity until it can just barely be seen. The resulting sensitivity is labeled **light adapted sensitivity** in Figure 3.19.

After determining the light adapted sensitivity, we begin the process of dark adaptation by turning out the adapting light. This causes the test light to appear much brighter, and the observer therefore decreases its intensity until he can again just barely see it. As dark adaptation progresses, the light again begins to appear brighter and the observer therefore decreases its intensity further. The solid line of Figure 3.19 shows the dark adaptation curve measured during 28 minutes in the dark. (Note that the sensitivity axis of this graph is reversed, so downward movement of the curve indicates an *increase* in sensitivity.)

The observer's sensitivity increases in two phases. It first increases for about 3–4 minutes after the light is extinguished and then levels off; then, after about 7–10 minutes, the sensitivity increases again and continues to do so for another 20–30 minutes. In this experiment, the sensitivity at the end of dark adaptation, labeled **dark adapted sensitivity,** is about 100,000 times greater than the light adapted sensitivity measured prior to dark adaptation.

Experiment #2: Measuring cone adaptation. To measure the adaptation of the cones, we repeat the first experiment but have the observer look directly at the test light, which is small enough that its entire image falls on the all-cone fovea; the resulting dark adaptation curve, indicated by the dashed curve in Figure 3.19, therefore reflects only the activity of the cones. This curve matches the initial phase of our original dark adaptation curve but does not include the second phase. Does this mean that the second phase is due to the rods? We can show that the answer to this question is "yes" by doing another experiment.

Experiment #3: Measuring rod adaptation. We know that the curve of Figure 3.19 is due only to cone adaptation because our test light was imaged on the all-cone fovea. To measure a pure rod dark

Fixation point ✕   ◯ Test light

F I G U R E   3. 18 Fixation and test lights used in experiment to measure the dark adaptation curve.

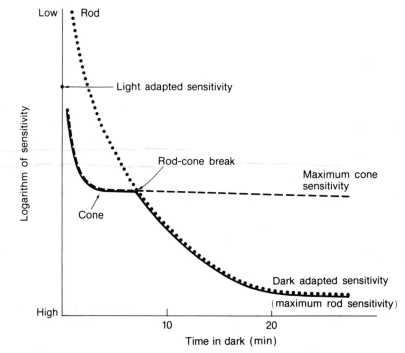

FIGURE 3. 19 Dark adaptation curves. There are actually three curves shown in this figure. The solid line shows the two-stage dark adaptation curve measured in experiment #1, with a cone branch at the beginning and a rod branch at the end. The dashed line shows the cone adaptation curve measured in experiment #2. The solid and dashed curves actually begin at the point marked "light adapted sensitivity," but there is a slight delay between the time the lights are turned off and measurement of the curve begins. The dotted line shows the rod adaptation curve measured in experiment #3. Note that as these curves go down, sensitivity *increases*.

adaptation curve, we must change to a different observer. The reason for this is that no area of our "normal" observer's retina contains *only* rods (the fovea contains only cones and the periphery contains rods *and* cones). Thus, in our third experiment, we measure dark adaptation in a **rod monochromat,** a person who has a retina that, because of a genetic defect, contains *only* rods.

The dark adaptation curve of a rod monochromat is shown by the dotted curve in Figure 3.19 (Rushton, 1961). As soon as the adaptation light is extinguished, the rods begin to gain sensitivity and continue to do so until reaching their final dark adapted level in about 30 minutes. The fact that the rods begin dark adapting immediately after the light is extinguished means that they are adapting during the cone phase of a normal per-

son's dark adaptation curve; however, we don't see this rod adaptation because the cones are more sensitive than the rods at the beginning of dark adaptation. We see rod adaptation only after the rods have become more sensitive than the cones, at the **rod-cone break** (Figure 3.19), about seven minutes after the beginning of dark adaptation.

In addition to showing that the rods are responsible for the second phase of the dark adaptation curve and that they begin adapting immediately after the adapting light is extinguished, the rod monochromat's dark adaptation curve also shows the much slower adaptation of the rods compared to the cones. The rods take 20–30 minutes to achieve their maximum sensitivity, compared to only 3–4 minutes for the cones. We will now show that these differences in the rate of adaptation can

F I G U R E 3. 20 Model of a visual pigment molecule. The longer horizontal part of the molecule is the protein opsin. The smaller part on top of the opsin is the light-sensitive retinal. In the actual molecule, the opsin is considerably longer compared to the opsin than shown here. (Left) shows the molecule's shape before the retinal absorbs light, and (right) shows its shape after the retinal absorbs light. This change in shape is one of the steps that accompanies generation of an electrical response in the receptor.

be traced to differences in properties of chemicals inside the rods and cones called visual pigments.

Visual pigment regeneration. **Visual pigments** are the chemicals in the receptors that transform light energy into electrical energy. A model of the visual pigment molecule is shown in Figure 3.20. This molecule consists of two parts, a long protein called **opsin,** and a much smaller light-sensitive component called **retinal** (short for *retinaldehyde*). When light is absorbed by the retinal part of the visual pigment molecule, it changes shape (right photo), triggering a series of steps that results in generation of an electrical signal in the receptor.

Following this change in shape, the retinal part of the molecule breaks away from the opsin. This process is called **pigment bleaching** because, as the two parts of the molecule separate, the retina changes from its original red color to orange, then to yellow, and finally becomes transparent, as shown in Color Plate 3.2. Before this bleached molecule can again change light energy into electrical energy, the pieces of molecule must reunite. This process, which is called **pigment regeneration,** depends on enzymes contained in the pigment epithelium, the black layer located just in back of the receptors. (The receptor's need to be close to these enzymes is why the receptors face backwards toward the pigment epithelium.)

Since the visual pigment changes from dark to light as it bleaches and from light back to dark as it regenerates, we can measure the concentration of pigment in the eye by determining how much light the pigment absorbs. To understand how this is done, look at Figure 3.21. A dim measuring beam with a constant intensity is projected into the eye. This beam passes through the retina, hits the back of the eye, and is reflected. On its way through the retina and back out, much of the

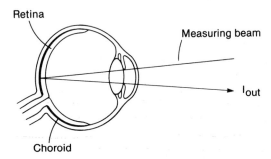

F I G U R E 3. 21 The principle underlying retinal densitometry. When visual pigment is exposed to light, the visual pigment molecules in the retina get lighter, causing them to absorb less of the measuring beam and increasing the amount of light reflected from the eye (I_{out}). As the molecules regenerate in the dark, they get darker, absorb more light, and decrease the amount of light reflected from the eye.

beam's light is absorbed by visual pigment in the receptors, by other structures in the retina, and by the black pigment epithelium in back of the retina. Some light survives this absorption, however, and a beam with intensity I_{out} is reflected from the eye.

Now consider what happens when we bleach the visual pigment by exposing the eye to light. Bleaching turns the pigment molecules from dark to light. As more pigment molecules bleach, the pigment in the receptors gets lighter and, therefore, absorbs less of our measuring beam. Since less light is being absorbed by the pigment, the intensity of the light reflected from the eye, I_{out}, increases. Therefore, by measuring I_{out} we can determine how much pigment has been bleached. Conversely, if after bleaching we allow the visual pigment to regenerate in the dark, the pigment gets darker and the intensity of the reflected beam, I_{out}, decreases.

William Rushton (1961) used the above procedure, which is called **retinal densitometry,** to measure the concentration of cone and rod pigment during dark adaptation. He determined the rate of cone pigment regeneration by shining his measuring beam onto the fovea of a normal observer, and he determined the rate of rod pigment regeneration by shining his measuring beam onto the retina of a rod monochromat. His results show that cone pigment takes 6 minutes to completely regenerate, while rod pigment takes over 30 minutes. Rushton also measured psychophysical dark adaptation curves in both observers and found that the rate of cone dark adaptation matched the rate of cone pigment regeneration, and the rate of rod dark adaptation matched the rate of rod pigment regeneration.

Thus, Rushton's results support the ideas that visual pigment regeneration is responsible for the increased sensitivity that occurs during dark adaptation and that rods are slow to adapt because rod pigment is slow to regenerate. So, the next time you turn out the lights in your bedroom, remember that both the rod and cone visual pigments begin regenerating immediately. The resulting increases in pigment concentration cause the increased sensitivity that enables you, 10 minutes later, to detect the light coming in under the door, and 20 minutes later to detect dimly illuminated objects that were completely invisible when you turned out the light. In the next section, we will see that in addition to determining the time course of rod and cone dark adaptation, visual pigments also determine your ability to detect different wavelengths of light.

Spectral Sensitivity

How sensitive are you to different wavelengths in the visible spectrum? The answer to this question is contained in spectral sensitivity curves, like the one in Figure 1.6 that defines the relationship between visual sensitivity and the wavelength of light. We will now show that there are actually two spectral sensitivity curves, one for cone vision and one for rod vision.

To determine the spectral sensitivity curve for cone vision we use the procedure described in Chapter 1 (p. 10), determining a person's sensitivity to test lights of wavelengths across the spectrum, while shining our test light on the fovea so it stimulates only cone receptors. When we do this we get the dashed curve in Figure 3.22, which is called the **cone spectral sensitivity curve.**

To measure the spectral sensitivity curve for rod vision, we dark adapt the eye and present test lights to the peripheral retina. If the eye is dark adapted, presentation of threshold flashes result in a **rod spectral sensitivity curve** (solid curve, Figure 3.22). This curve shows that the rods are more sensitive to short-wavelength light than are the cones, with the rods most sensitive to light of 500 nm and the cones most sensitive to light of 560 nm. This difference in the sensitivity of the rods and cones to different wavelengths means that as our vision shifts from our cones to our rods during dark adaptation, we should become relatively more sensitive to short-wavelength light, that is, light nearer the blue end of the spectrum.

We can illustrate this sensitivity shift by doing dark adaptation experiments using colored test flashes. Figure 3.23 shows dark adaptation curves determined by presenting either red or blue test flashes to the peripheral retina. You can see that the color of the test flash makes a big difference in

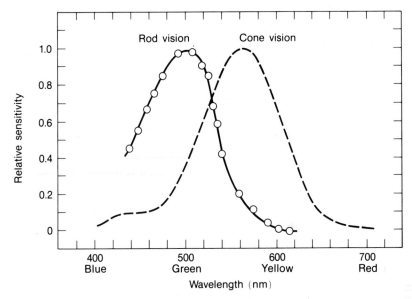

F I G U R E 3. 22 Spectral sensitivity curves for rod vision and cone vision. The maximum sensitivities of these two curves have been set equal to 1.0. However, as we saw in Figure 3.4, the relative sensitivities of the rods and cones depend on the conditions of adaptation, with the cones more sensitive in the light and the rods more sensitive in the dark. The circles plotted on top of the rod curve represent the absorption spectrum for the rod visual pigment. (From Wald & Brown, 1958; Wald, 1964.)

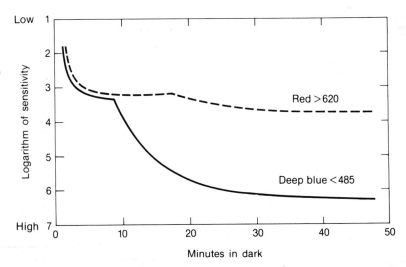

F I G U R E 3. 23 Dark adaptation curves measured with long-wavelength (red) and short-wavelength (deep blue) test flashes. The red curve has only a small rod branch because the rods are relatively insensitive to red light. (From Chapanis, 1947.)

the dark adaptation curve. Sensitivity measured with a red test flash, which contains only wavelengths above 620 nm, shows just a small increase after the rod-cone break, while sensitivity measured with a deep blue test flash, which contains only wavelengths shorter than 485 nm, shows a large increase following the rod-cone break. Thus, when rod vision takes over from cone vision during dark adaptation, our sensitivity to short wavelengths increases more than our sensitivity to long wavelengths.

DEMONSTRATION

Spending Some More Time in The Closet

You can demonstrate the shift from cone to rod vision to yourself by returning to the closet (see "Spending Some Time in Your Closet," p. 14, Chapter 1) and making the following observations.

1. Before entering the closet, dark adapt one eye by closing it for about 10 minutes. This should take place in the light so that your opened eye stays light adapted while your closed eye is dark adapting.

2. After completing step 1, enter the closet, and with the door open, observe Color Plate 3.3 with your light adapted eye and compare the brightness of the blue and red flowers. When viewed with your light adapted eye under daylight illumination, the two flowers should appear approximately equal in brightness.

3. Close the door so that the closet is completely dark. Close your light adapted eye and open your dark adapted eye.

4. Slowly crack open the door until enough light is present for you to just see the flowers with your dark adapted eye. If you have kept the light intensity low enough, you will be seeing with your rods, and the flowers should appear grey rather than red and blue (since we perceive in black and white with our rods and in color with our cones, as we will see in Chapter 4). It is important to notice that the flowers' relative brightness should now be different than when you viewed them with your light adapted eye. The flower on the left should now appear slightly brighter than the flower on the right. (If you have forgotten how the flowers looked to your light adapted eye, close your dark adapted

eye, open the door, and observe the flowers with your light adapted eye again.)

The increases in the brightness of the blue flower compared to the red one occurs because the rods are more sensitive to short-wavelength light than the cones. This shift from long-wavelength to short-wavelength sensitivity is called the **Purkinje shift,** after Johann Purkinje, who described this effect in 1825.

While your eye is dark adapted, continue your observations in the closet as follows:

5. Look at Color Plate 3.3 with your light adapted eye under bright illumination (be sure not to open your dark adapted eye in bright illumination). Slowly close the door until you can no longer see the flowers and switch from your light adapted to your dark adapted eye. The flowers will become visible again because of the greater sensitivity of your dark adapted eye.

6. Look at the words in the book under bright illumination with your light adapted eye. Then slowly close the door until the illumination is very dim but still bright enough so that you can read the words. Since you are using your cones, reading is possible, even if the illumination is low. Now close the door, switch to your dark adapted eye, and slowly open the door until you can just tell that there are letters and words on the page. Try reading the words. Since you are now using your rods, you will find reading very difficult or impossible, even though you can see the page and make out the fuzzy outlines of the words. You can't read very easily with your rods because the rods see details poorly, as we will see later in our discussion of the rods and cones.

Pigment absorption spectra. The difference we have described between the rod and cone spectral sensitivity curves can be explained by differences in the **absorption spectra** of the rod and cone visual pigments. An absorption spectrum is a plot of the amount of light absorbed by a visual pigment versus the wavelength of the light. George Wald, who won the 1967 Nobel Prize for his research on visual pigments, determined the absorption spectrum of human rod pigment by chemically extracting the pigment from retinas obtained from eyes donated to medical research (Wald & Brown, 1958). The resulting solution contains primarily rod pigment, since the rods contain about 99 percent of the visual pigment in the human retina. (Remember that there are 20 times more rods than cones in the retina and that the cones are much smaller than the rods.)

When Wald and Brown measured the amount of light absorbed by the pigment solution at wavelengths across the visible spectrum, they obtained the absorption spectrum plotted as open circles in Figure 3.22. The match between the pigment absorption spectrum and the rod spectral sensitivity curve indicates that the spectral sensitivity of rod vision is due to the absorption of light by the rod visual pigment.

How does the spectral sensitivity curve for cone vision compare to the absorption spectrum of cone visual pigment? To answer this question we need to solve a difficult problem: How can we measure the absorption spectrum of cone pigment if 99 percent of the pigment that we chemically extract from the retina is rod pigment? The solution to this problem was provided by the development of a technique called **microspectropho-**

tometry. In microspectrophotometry, rather than shining a beam of light through a solution of visual pigment that has been chemically extracted from millions of receptors, we shine a beam of light through the pigment while it is still inside an individual receptor. This is difficult to do because cones are very small, but Brown and Wald (1964) successfully designed an optical system that could focus a beam of light through a single cone receptor, enabling them to measure the absorption spectrum of the visual pigment inside this receptor.

Figure 3.24 shows Wald and Brown's (1965) measurements using the microspectrophotometry procedure. There are three curves because there are three different cone pigments, each contained in its own receptor. The **short-wavelength pigment** absorbs light best at about 435 nm, the **medium-wavelength pigment** absorbs light best at about 535 nm, and the **long-wavelength pigment** absorbs light best at about 565 nm. More recent measurements (Bowmaker & Dartnall, 1983) place the maximum absorption of the three pigments at 419 nm, 531 nm, and 558 nm.

How do we get from short-, medium-, and long-wavelength cone pigments that absorb at 419, 531, and 558 nm to a psychophysical spectral sen-

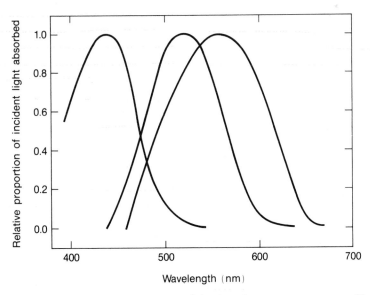

F I G U R E 3. 24 Absorption spectra of the three human cone pigments. (From Wald & Brown, 1965.)

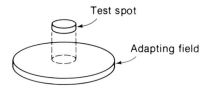

Test spot

Adapting field

F I G U R E   3. 25   Stimulus arrangement for Stiles' two-color threshold method. The small test spot is superimposed on the larger adapting field. The wavelength of the adapting field is kept constant, and the wavelength of the test spot is changed to measure the spectral sensitivity at wavelengths across the spectrum.

sitivity curve that peaks at 560 nm? Apparently these three cone pigments combine to result in the spectral sensitivity curve. This was demonstrated by comparing the pigment absorption spectra to spectral sensitivity curves determined using the **two-color threshold method** introduced by W. S. Stiles (1953). In this method, the spectral sensitivity curve is measured by determining the sensitivity to test lights presented on top of an **adapting field** (Figure 3.25).

The purpose of the adapting field is to bleach away two of the cone pigments and spare one. For example, an adapting field containing long-wavelength light bleaches the medium and long-wavelength pigments and leaves the short-wavelength pigment. Each spectral sensitivity curve Stiles obtained using this method matched the absorption spectra of the unbleached cone pigment, supporting the idea that the spectral sensitivity curve of the cones is due to the combined action of the three cone pigments (Bowmaker & Dartnall, 1980).

By looking at dark adaptation and spectral sensitivity, we have demonstrated that the visual pigments play an important role in shaping our perceptions. We have also shown, in Chapter 2, that neural processing plays a large role in shaping our perceptions. We will now return to the latter idea by showing how the sensitivities of rods and cones are affected by the connections between the receptors and other neurons in the retina.

Sensitivity and Neural Wiring

We now move from showing how properties of the receptors' visual pigments influence perception, to showing how the way the receptors are connected to other neurons influences perception. We will see that the signals generated by the rods and cones travel in different types of neural circuits, and that these differences affect perception.

One of the basic differences between rod and cone "wiring" is their **convergence**—the degree to which a number of receptors send their signals to a single neuron. When we consider that there are 120 million rods and 6 million cones in the retina and that the signals from these millions of receptors converge onto the 1 million ganglion cells that carry signals out of the retina in the optic nerve, it is clear that the signals from many rods and many cones must converge onto far fewer ganglion cells. It is also clear from these numbers that rods converge much more than cones, with each ganglion cell receiving signals from an average of about 120 rods but from only about 6 cones. This difference between rod and cone convergence becomes even greater when we consider foveal cones, many of which have "private lines" to ganglion cells, with each ganglion cell receiving signals from only one cone—a complete lack of convergence.

How does the difference in rod and cone convergence affect perception? Let's consider how convergence affects our sensitivity to light by doing some hypothetical experiments. We already know from our dark adaptation experiments that the dark adapted rods are much more sensitive than the dark adapted cones. To understand how neural wiring contributes to this greater sensitivity, let's consider the two circuits in Figure 3.26. We show five rod receptors converging onto one ganglion cell and five cone receptors each synapsing on its own ganglion cell. We have left out the bipolar, horizontal, and amacrine cells in these circuits for simplicity, but the conclusions we reach from our experiments will not be affected by these omissions.

In our first experiment we ask the question "How intense must a stimulus be to cause the rod and cone ganglion cells to fire?" To answer this

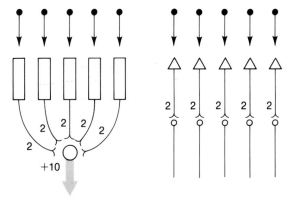

Response   No response

F I G U R E 3. 26 The wiring of the rods (left) and cones (right). The arrow above each receptor represents a "spot" of light that stimulates the receptor. The numbers represent the number of response units generated by the rods and cones in response to a spot intensity of 2.0. At this intensity the rod ganglion cell receives 10 units of excitation and fires, but each cone ganglion cell receives only 2 units and, therefore, does not fire. Thus, the rods' greater spatial summation enables them to cause ganglion cell firing at lower stimulus intensities than the cones'.

question, let's assume that we can present small spots of light to individual rods and cones. (Although it isn't possible to do this in the human retina, let's assume that it is, for the purposes of our experiment.) We will also make the following additional assumptions:

1. 1 unit of light intensity causes 1 unit of response in a receptor.
2. A ganglion cell must receive 10 "response units" to fire.
3. When a ganglion cell fires, we see.

We begin our experiment by presenting spots of light with intensity = 1.0 to each of our receptors. In this situation, the rod ganglion cell receives 5 response units, 1 from each of the 5 receptors, and each of the cone ganglion cells receives 1.0 response units, 1 from each receptor. Thus, when intensity = 1.0, neither the rod nor the cone ganglion cells fire. If, however, we increase the inten-

sity to 2.0, the rod ganglion cell receives 2.0 response units from each of its 5 receptors for a total of 10 response units. We have, therefore, reached threshold for the rods' ganglion cell, it fires, and we see the light. Meanwhile, at the same intensity, the cones' ganglion cells are still far below threshold, each receiving only 2 response units. We must increase the intensity to 10.0 to cause the cones' ganglion cells to fire.

The results of this experiment demonstrate that one reason for the rods' high sensitivity compared to the cones' is due to the rods' greater **spatial summation**—many rods summate, or add up, their responses by feeding into the same ganglion cell. The cones, on the other hand, summate less, because only one or a few cones feed into a single ganglion cell.

Although spatial summation accounts for much of the rods' superior sensitivity, the rods also have other properties which contribute to their high sensitivity. For one thing, the rods are larger than the cones and therefore a rod receptor absorbs more light than a cone receptor. In addition, individual rods generate larger electrical responses than individual cones (Barlow & Mollon, 1982).

Acuity and Neural Wiring

The reason it is often difficult to pick your friend's face out of a crowd immediately is that to recognize a face, you must look directly at it. Only all-cone foveal vision enables you to detect small details, so only the particular face at which you are looking is seen in enough detail to be recognized, while the rest of the faces in the crowd fall on the rod-rich peripheral retina and can't be recognized. You find your friend only after you move your eyes to bring the image of his or her face onto your foveas.

D E M O N S T R A T I O N

Foveal vs. Peripheral Acuity

You can demonstrate the superiority of foveal vision over peripheral vision by looking at the X below and, without moving your eyes, seeing how many letters you can see to the left. If you do this without

---

B O X   3. 1.   /   *Diurnal and Nocturnal Vision*

The human eye contains both cones and rods, which enable us to see well in the brightness of the day and in the dimness of the night. However, many animals have eyes that contain only cones or predominantly rods,* and these animals can therefore see well only during the day or only at night. Lizards, ground squirrels, chipmunks, and prairie dogs have day, or **diurnal vision;** flying squirrels, rats, and a small mammal called the bush baby have night, or **nocturnal vision.** The all-cone retinas of the diurnal animals give them the good acuity they need to catch the small animals and insects they eat, whereas the rod-dominated retinas of the nocturnal animals give them the good sensitivity they need to see well in the dark.

Good acuity for diurnal animals and good sensitivity for nocturnal animals are also achieved by other means in addition to cones and rods. Diurnal animals achieve good acuity

*It has proven very difficult to find animals that have *only* rods. For example, although the rat has such a large proportion of rods that it's difficult to find the cones, there is a low level of cone functioning in the rat's retina.

by having large eyes, so the image on the retina can be big and cover many cones. Thus, birds, which achieve good acuity with their cone-dominated retinas, further increase their acuity with huge eyes that take up most of the space in their head. The eyes of many birds are so large that they actually touch each other, making it possible to stimulate one eye by shining light through the wall of the other (Levine, 1955)!

Nocturnal animals achieve greater sensitivity by means of large lenses and corneas that help collect light. The eye of the opossum, a nocturnal animal, is shown on the left below. Compare the large lens and cornea of this eye to the much smaller lens and cornea of the diurnal ground squirrel eye, shown on the right (Tansley, 1965). Another means of increasing sensitivity is a reflecting surface called the **tapetum,** located behind the retinas of some nocturnal animals. The tapetum increases the amount of light hitting the receptors, by reflecting light back through the retina. The glow you see when you shine light into a cat's eye is light reflected from the cat's tapetum.

---

cheating (no fair moving your eyes!), you will find that you can read only a few letters. Because of the low visual acuity of the rods, you cannot read letters that are imaged very far into the periphery.

D P H C N R L A Z I F W N S M Q P J K D **X**

Visual acuity can be measured in a number of ways, one of which is to determine how far apart two dots have to be before a space can be seen between them. This is done by presenting a pair of closely spaced dots and asking whether there are one or two dots. Acuity can also be measured by determining how large the elements of a checkerboard or grating pattern must be so the pattern can

be detected. The letters of the Snellen chart and the Landolt rings, in Figure 3.27, are perhaps the most familiar ways of measuring acuity. The observer's task is to identify the Snellen letter or to indicate the location of the gap in the Landolt rings. We will discuss this method of determining acuity in Chapter 10, "Clinical Aspects of Vision."

We can measure the differences between rod and cone visual acuity by comparing a person's ability to detect test patterns in the fovea and in the periphery (as in the demonstration above) or by measuring how acuity changes during dark adaptation. When we do this we find that visual acuity drops (that is, details must be larger in order to be seen) as we move from fovea to periphery and as vision changes from cone to rod function during

If a nocturnal animal wants to venture out into the daylight, it must have a way to protect its sensitive eyes. This protection is accomplished in some nocturnal animals by a pupil that becomes a vertical slit when it contracts in response to light. A slit pupil protects the retina against light better than a round pupil, because it can close all the way; whereas a round pupil can never close completely. Thus, an animal that is active at night can sun itself on a rock during the day, with its sensitive eyes protected by its completely closed pupil. Tansley (1965) points out, however, that truly nocturnal animals have rounded pupils, because they never venture into the bright daylight and therefore don't need to protect their retinas from the light.

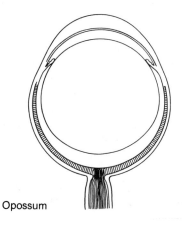

Opossum

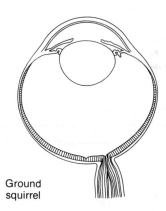

Ground squirrel

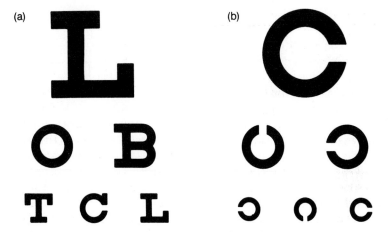

(a)   (b)

F I G U R E 3. 27   Snellen letters (a) and Landolt rings (b) used to test visual acuity. We will discuss acuity testing in more detail in Chapter 10. (From Riggs, 1965b.)

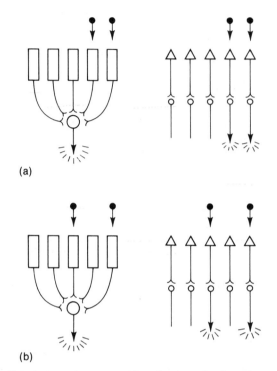

(a)

(b)

F I G U R E 3. 28 Neural circuits for the rods (left) and cones (right). The receptors are being stimulated by two spots of light. See text for details.

dark adaptation. Thus, although rod vision is much more sensitive to light than cone vision, it is much less able to detect small details than is cone vision.

To understand how differences in rod and cone wiring can explain the cones' greater acuity, let's do another hypothetical experiment, this time stimulating the circuits in Figure 3.28 with two spots of light, each with an intensity of 10. The question we ask in this experiment is "Under what conditions can we tell that there are two separate spots of light?" We begin by presenting the two spots next to each other, as in Figure 3.28(a). When we do this, the rod ganglion cell fires and the two adjacent cone ganglion cells fire. The firing of the single rod provides no hint that two spots were presented, and the firing of two adjacent cones could have been caused by a single large spot. However, when we spread the two spots apart as in Figure 3.28(b), the output of the cones signals two spots, because there is a silent cell between the two

that are firing, but the output of the rods still provides no information that would enable us to say that there are two spots. Thus, the rods' convergence decreases its ability to resolve details.

In addition to neural wiring, a factor responsible for the cones' greater acuity is their small size (which you may remember decreases their *sensitivity*), which enables them to be packed more closely together than the rods. In fact, birds such as hawks and falcons can resolve finer details than humans because their cones are packed more closely in the retina (Fox, Lehmkuhle, & Westendorf, 1976).

THE GANGLION CELLS

As we move away from the receptors and toward the brain, our major concern will be to answer the question: What kinds of information are carried by neurons at different levels of the visual system? We will do this by determining how neurons in different places in the visual system respond to stimulation of the retina. We began answering this question in the last chapter when we introduced the concept of a neuron's **receptive field**—the region on the receptor surface (in this case, the retina) which, when stimulated, influences the firing rate of the neuron. We saw that retinal ganglion cells have center-surround receptive fields like the one in Figure 3.29. Illumination of the excitatory center of the receptive field causes an increase in nerve firing, and illumination of the inhibitory surround causes a decrease in firing as long as the light is on and a burst of firing (the off response) when the light is turned off.

One of the first properties that researchers

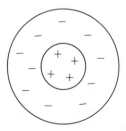

F I G U R E 3. 29 Excitatory-center, inhibitory-surround receptive field.

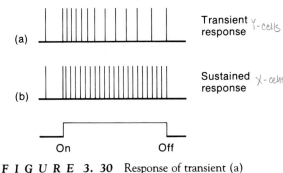

F I G U R E 3. 30 Response of transient (a) and sustained (b) ganglion cells. The onset and offset of the light is shown below the responses.

T A B L E 3. 1 / *Properties of X- and Y-Cells.*

Property	X	Y
Response	Sustained	Transient
Center-surr. antagonism?	Yes	No
Receptive field distribution	Most near fovea	Evenly distributed
Response to movement		Better
Speed of nerve transmission		Faster
Proposed function	Detail and pattern perception	Motion perception

noted as they studied the receptive fields of these ganglion cells is the *center-surround antagonism* we described in Chapter 2—the fact that simultaneous stimulation of both excitatory and inhibitory areas causes little or no response (Figure 2.20). But then researchers noticed that some ganglion cells continued to respond even when both their center and surround regions were illuminated. This observation would, by itself, not have been considered particularly significant if it weren't for another observation: These same ganglion cells also respond differently than other ganglion cells to stimulation of just their excitatory area.

When the excitatory area of one of these cell's receptive fields is illuminated, the cell responds as in Figure 3.30(a)—a burst of firing when the light is turned on, followed by a decrease in firing as the light remains on. This response, which is called a **transient response,** is different from the response of the other kind of ganglion cell, shown in Figure 3.29(b), a **sustained response** of continued firing as long as the excitatory area of the receptive field is illuminated.

Researchers called cells with the sustained response **X-cells** and cells with the transient response **Y-cells** and then proceeded to discover even more differences between them. Two important differences between X and Y cells are the location of their receptive fields and the type of stimuli they prefer. The receptive fields of Y-cells are distributed fairly evenly across the whole retina, whereas the receptive fields of X-cells are concentrated in and

around the fovea, the all-cone, high-acuity area of the retina. Also, Y-cells respond much better to rapidly moving objects than do X-cells, and the nerve fibers of Y-cells transmit nerve impulses faster than the nerve fibers of X-cells.

Taken together, these differences between X- and Y-cells, summarized in Table 3.1, have led some researchers to suggest that X-cells may be responsible for our perception of *pattern* and fine detail (remember that X-cells are concentrated near the fovea) and that Y-cells may be responsible for our perception of *motion* (remember that Y-cells respond well to rapidly moving stimuli and their fibers conduct nerve impulses rapidly). Perhaps, these researchers suggest, Y-cells signal the presence of a rapidly moving object as it enters your field of view, and X-cells signal the details of that object once you have moved your eyes to look directly at it (Woodhouse & Barlow, 1982).

Not all researchers agree with the idea that X-cells are responsible for pattern perception and Y-cells for motion perception (see Lennie, 1980), but there is no question that these X- and Y-cells do have different properties, and just as rods and cones result in different perceptions, it seems likely that X- and Y-cells also result in different perceptions.

THE LATERAL GENICULATE NUCLEUS

The lateral geniculate nucleus (LGN) is the first place that ganglion cells in the primary visual pathway synapse. The receptive field properties of LGN cells are similar to those of ganglion cells, having a center-surround configuration, and most LGN cells can also be classified as either X- or Y-cells. Many neurons in the LGN play an important role in color vision, as we will see in Chapter 4, but for now let's look, not at the properties of individual neurons, but at the way these neurons are *organized* within the LGN. We will focus on this organization, because it introduces an important principle: *Neurons in the visual system, and in other sensory systems as well, are arranged within three-dimensional structures on the basis of specific properties of these neurons.*

What does this statement mean? First, let's consider a basic geometrical fact about the visual system. The mosaic of retinal receptors forms a two-dimensional surface, and the responses generated when light stimulates these receptors travel in the optic nerve to the LGN, which is a three-dimensional structure (Figure 3.31). Thus, we need to ask how the information which is initially imaged on the flat retinal surface is organized within the three-dimensional structure of the LGN.

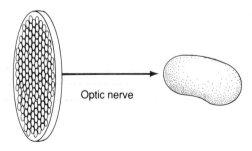

Retinal surface (2-D)   LGN (3-D)

F I G U R E 3. 31 Neurons from the two-dimensional retinal surface travel to the three-dimensional lateral geniculate nucleus. This poses the following problem: How is the information from the two-dimensional surface of the retina organized inside the three-dimensional volume of the LGN?

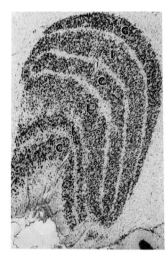

F I G U R E 3. 32 Cross section of the lateral geniculate nucleus. This is what the LGN looks like when treated with a stain that darkens the cell bodies of the LGN neurons. This darkening shows that there are six layers of cell bodies, each separated by a light band. Layers 1, 4, and 6, marked C, receive input from the contralateral eye, and layers 2, 3, and 5, marked I, receive input from the ipsilateral eye. See text for details. (From Livingstone & Hubel, 1988.)

To answer this question, we need to look at the internal structure of the LGN. When we do this, by cutting the LGN in half and looking at it in cross section (Figure 3.32), we see that it is organized into six layers.

We will show how information from the retina is organized within these six layers by determining the locations of the receptive fields of a few neurons in the LGN. First, we record from neurons A, B, C, and D in layer 6 (Figure 3.33), and determine the retinal location of the receptive fields of each of these neurons. (Remember that no matter where our electrode is, receptive fields are *always* on the retina.) When we do this, we find that neurons that are next to each other in the LGN have receptive fields that are next to each other on the retina so that there is a *map* of the retina in layer 6 of the LGN. This is called a **topographic map** because of the match between the locations relative to one another of the receptive fields on the retina and the locations relative to one another

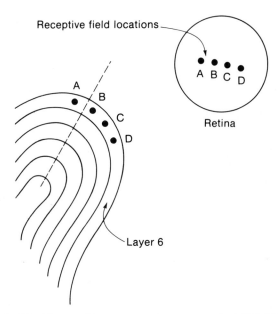

F I G U R E 3. 33   Topographic mapping of neurons in the LGN. The neurons at A, B, C, and D in layer 6 of the LGN have receptive fields located at positions A, B, C, and D on the retina. The receptive fields of neurons encountered along an electrode track perpendicular to the surface of the LGN (dashed line) all have approximately the same location on the retina.

of neurons in the LGN. This topographical mapping of the receptor surface within a three-dimensional structure is a common feature not only of other structures in the visual system (we will see that similar maps exist in the cortex) but also of most of the other sensory systems.

Having determined that layer 6 contains a topographic map of the retina, let's now look at the other layers. When we do this, we find that these layers also contain topographic maps and that the maps in the other layers are lined up with one another. In other words, if we lower an electrode through the LGN along the track indicated by the dashed line in Figure 3.33, we find that the neurons encountered along that track all have receptive fields in the same location on the retina. Thus, 1 million ganglion cell fibers from each eye travel to the LGN in the two optic nerves, and once these fibers reach the LGN, each one finds its place near other fibers that left from the same place on the retina.

In addition to being organized topographi-cally, neurons in the LGN are organized in terms of the left and right eyes. Each layer receives input from only one eye, with layers 2, 3, and 5 receiving input from the **ipsilateral eye** and layers 1, 4, and 6 receiving input from the **contralateral eye.** To understand what we mean by *ipsilateral* and *contra-lateral*, we need to realize that the LGN, like many structures in the body, is found on both the left and right sides of the brain (see Figure 3.13). For a particular LGN, the ipsilateral eye is the eye on the same side of the brain and the contralateral eye is the one on the opposite side of the brain. Thus, layers 2, 3, and 5 of the LGN in the left hemisphere of the brain receive inputs from the left eye and layers 1, 4, and 6 receive inputs from the right eye.

THE VISUAL CORTEX

Nerve fibers reaching the cortex from the layers of the LGN also encounter layers in the cortex. The visual cortex, seen in cross section in Figure 3.34,

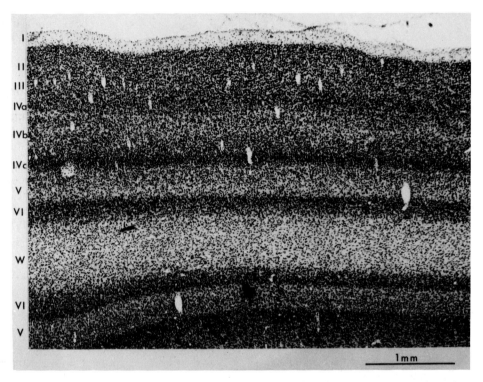

F I G U R E 3. 34 The layers of the visual cortex. Fibers from the LGN enter from the bottom through the "white matter" (W) below layer VI and synapse in layer IVc. (From Hubel & Wiesel, 1977.)

consists of six layers which contain approximately 100 million cells within a thickness of about 2 mm. Fibers from the LGN arrive at layer IVc of the cortex and from there signals are sent to layers above and below this layer. Unlike the LGN, in which neurons from each eye send their signals to different layers, neurons from both eyes send their signals to all layers of the cortex.

If we record from neurons at the place where LGN fibers enter layer IV, we find that the receptive fields of these neurons have center-surround receptive fields. This makes sense, because these fibers have come directly from the LGN neurons which have center-surround receptive fields. But if we record from cells in the other layers, things become more interesting, because it is in these layers that we encounter cells with new types of receptive fields.

Receptive Fields of Cortical Cells

Simple cortical cells. We have already seen, in Chapter 2, that simple cortical cells have receptive fields in which the excitatory and inhibitory regions are arranged side by side (Figure 2.23) and which respond best to bars of a specific orientation (Figure 2.24).

Complex cortical cells. Like simple cells, complex cells respond best to bars of a particular orientation. Unlike simple cells, complex cells don't respond to small spots of light or to stationary stimuli. Most complex cells respond when a correctly oriented *bar* of light *moves* across the entire receptive field. Further, many complex cells respond best to a particular *direction* of movement (Figure 3.35).

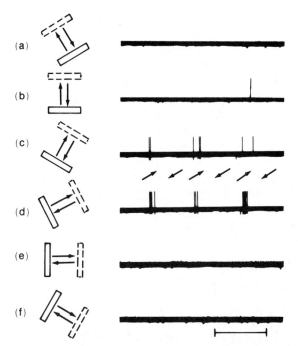

turn the stimulus into a bar by extending its length, as in Figure 3.36(e), the cell no longer fires (Hubel & Wiesel, 1965a).

Cortical Cells as Feature Detectors

We have now come a long way from the receptors to the cortex, and we have seen that the information processing that occurs between the receptors and the cortex results in cortical neurons that fire in response to specific features of the stimulus. For this reason, these neurons are often called **feature detectors.** Table 3.2, which summarizes the properties of the major types of cells in the visual system, makes clear an important fact about neurons in the visual system: As we travel farther from the retina, it takes more specific stimuli to cause a cell to fire. Retinal ganglion cells respond to just

FIGURE 3. 35 Response of a complex cell recorded from the visual cortex of the cat. The stimulus bar is moved back and forth across the receptive field. The records on the right indicate that the cell fires only when the bar is moved in a specific direction. The cell does not respond when the bar is oriented as in (a), (b), (e), and (f). A slight response occurs in (c). The best response occurs in (d), but even when the bar is at this optimal orientation, a response occurs only when the bar is moved from left to right as indicated by the arrows above the records. No response occurs when the bar moves from right to left. The horizontal bar in the lower right represents 1 second. (From Hubel & Wiesel, 1959.)

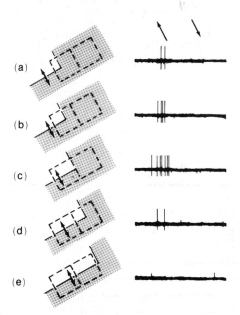

FIGURE 3. 36 Response of a hypercomplex (or end-stopped) cell recorded from the visual cortex of the cat. This cell responds best to a light corner moving up; there is no response when the corner moves down. Note that as the corner is made longer as we progress from (a) to (b) to (c), the cell's firing rate increases, but that when the length is then increased further, as in (d) and (e), the firing rate decreases. (From Hubel & Wiesel, 1965a.)

Hypercomplex or end-stopped cortical cells. Hypercomplex cells fire only to moving lines of a specific length or to moving corners or angles. The cell in Figure 3.36 responds best to a corner that is moving upward across the receptive field, as shown in record (c). While the length of the stimulus does not affect the complex cell in Figure 3.35, the hypercomplex cell will not fire if the stimulus is too long. Because of this property, hypercomplex cells are also referred to as **end-stopped cells.** If we try to

TABLE 3.2

Cell	Characteristics
Optic nerve fiber (ganglion cell)	Center-surround receptive field. Responds best to small spots but will also respond to other stimuli.
Lateral geniculate	Center-surround receptive field. Very similar to the receptive field of an optic nerve fiber.
Simple cortical	"On" and "off" areas arranged side by side. Responds best to bars of a particular orientation.
Complex cortical	Will not respond to small spots. Responds best to movement of a correctly oriented bar across the receptive field. Many cells respond best to a particular direction of movement.
Hypercomplex (end-stopped) cortical	Will not respond to small spots. Responds to corners, angles, or bars of a particular length moving in a particular direction.

about any stimulus, whereas hypercomplex cells respond only to bars of a certain length moving in a particular direction.

This property of responding only to specific stimuli is even more pronounced in some neurons found in areas of the cortex outside the visual receiving area. For example, Figure 3.37 shows the response of a neuron in the temporal lobe of the monkey that responds better to faces than to any other stimulus (Bruce, Desimone, & Gross, 1981).

What role do cortical feature detectors play in perception? Do we perceive forms based on the firing of these neurons? While it is possible that there are neurons specialized to signal biologically significant stimuli like faces, it is unlikely that our perception of forms in general is based on the firing of individual feature detectors. As we pointed out in Chapter 2 (page 52), there are simply too many different forms.

It is, however, reasonable to suggest that orientation-selective neurons may play a role in the perception of simple stimuli such as lines of a particular orientation. Evidence to support this idea comes from the results of psychophysical **selective adaptation** experiments (see Chapter 1, p. 16). In these experiments we determine an observer's **contrast sensitivity** to gratings like the ones in Figure 3.38. We do this by determining the smallest intensity difference between the light and dark bars at which she can just barely see the bars. This intensity difference, which is the threshold for seeing

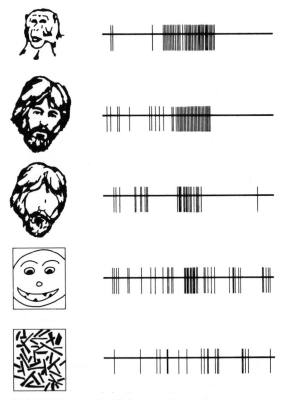

FIGURE 3.37 Responses of a neuron in the monkey's temporal lobe to various stimuli. This neuron responds best to a full face, as shown by its response to monkey and human faces in the top two records. Removing the eyes or presenting a caricature of a face reduces the response, and this neuron does not respond to a random arrangement of lines. (From Bruce, Desimone, & Gross, 1981.)

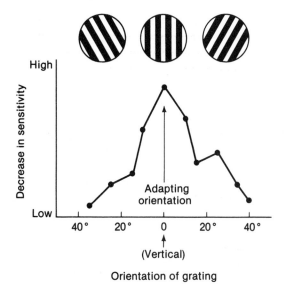

F I G U R E 3. 38 The effects of selective adaptation to a vertical grating on an observer's contrast sensitivity. This curve shows that adapting to the vertical grating causes a large decrease in the observer's ability to detect the vertical grating when it is presented again, but that this adaptation has less effect on gratings that are tilted to either side of the vertical. Gratings tilted more than about 35 degrees from the vertical are essentially unaffected by adaptation to the vertical grating.

the grating, is then converted to contrast sensitivity by dividing it into 1.0 (see Chapter 1, page 10).

We determine the contrast sensitivity for gratings of a number of different orientations and then have the observer look at one grating (say, the vertically oriented one) for about a minute. This is the selective adaptation part of the experiment. After she adapts to the vertical grating, we then remeasure her contrast sensitivity to all of the gratings. When we do this, we find that her sensitivity to the vertical grating has decreased; that is, before she can see the vertical grating, we must increase the difference in intensity between the light and dark bars. Her sensitivity to the other gratings has also decreased, though not as much as to the vertical grating. This result is shown by the curve in Figure 3.38. If this curve looks familiar, it's because

it is very similar to the electrophysiological tuning curve for a simple cortical cell shown in Figure 2.24.

Why should the psychophysical curve look similar to the electrophysiological tuning curve? Perhaps adaptation to the vertical grating stimulates neurons that respond best to vertical lines, the stimulation fatigues these neurons, and this fatigue makes it harder to see vertical orientations. Therefore, our psychophysical curve shows the greatest decrease in sensitivity for the vertical orientation and drops off for other orientations, just as does the electrophysiological tuning curve.

Although the results of selective adaptation experiments suggest that orientation-selective neurons do play a role in human perception, we cannot explain our perception of complex forms solely on the basis of these neurons. Hubel and Wiesel, and many other investigators who study neurons in the visual cortex, are the first to state that these relatively simple feature detectors cannot resolve the complexities of everyday perception. Before you can perceive a chair or your friend Nancy, the simple forms represented by feature detectors must somehow be combined into the complex forms that you see every day, and we do not yet know how this is accomplished.

The Organization of the Visual Cortex

One thing that is clear from our description of the properties of cortical neurons is that a substantial amount of neural processing occurs in the cortex. Neurons outside the cortex respond equally well to most orientations, whereas most neurons within the cortex respond selectively to specific orientations, to movement, and to the direction of movement.

The sophisticated responses of cortical neurons are accompanied by a sophisticated organization. Rather than simply describing this organization, we will show how it was discovered by David Hubel and Torsten Wiesel (see Figure 1.16), who received the 1981 Nobel Prize for their descriptions of the properties of simple, complex, and hyper-

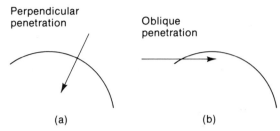

Perpendicular penetration

Oblique penetration

(a)   (b)

F I G U R E 3. 39   Perpendicular and oblique electrode penetrations of the cortex.

complex cells and for the work we will now describe.

Hubel and Wiesel's primary goal in these experiments was to describe how neurons with common characteristics are organized in the cortex. To do this they penetrated the cortex with electrodes oriented either *perpendicularly* to the cortical surface, as in Figure 3.39(a), or *obliquely* to the cortical surface, as in Figure 3.39(b). As they penetrated the cortex, they stopped at closely

spaced intervals and determined the properties of neurons along the electrode track. The first question they asked was, "Where on the retina are the receptive fields of these neurons located?"

Location columns and retinal maps in the cortex. When Hubel and Wiesel lowered an electrode perpendicularly to the surface of a monkey's cortex, they found that the neurons along this track had receptive fields either on top of each other or very close together on the retina, as shown in Figure 3.40(a). The cortex is therefore organized into location columns, with the neurons within a location column having their receptive fields at the same location on the retina.

When Hubel and Wiesel penetrated the cortex obliquely and recorded from neurons separated by 1 mm along the electrode track, they found that the receptive fields were systematically displaced, with neurons close to each other along the electrode track having receptive fields close to each other on the retina, as shown in Figure 3.40(b).

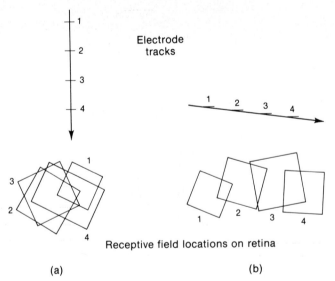

Electrode tracks

Receptive field locations on retina

(a)   (b)

F I G U R E 3. 40   (a) When an electrode penetrates the cortex perpendicularly, the receptive fields of neurons encountered along this track overlap. The receptive field recorded at each numbered position along the electrode track is indicated by a correspondingly numbered square. (b) When the electrode penetrates obliquely, the receptive fields of neurons recorded from the numbered positions along the track are displaced, as indicated by the numbered receptive fields, with neurons near each other in the cortex having receptive fields near each other on the retina.

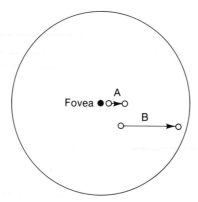

FIGURE 3. 41 How receptive field location changes when recording from 2 neurons separated by 1 mm on the cortex. Arrow A shows the small shift in receptive field location that occurs for two cortical neurons that receive inputs from an area of retina on or near the fovea. Arrow B shows the larger shift in location that occurs when the two cortical neurons receive inputs from a more peripheral area of the retina.

Thus, as in the LGN, there is a topographic map of the retina on the cortex.

As Hubel and Wiesel determined receptive field locations of neurons along the oblique track, they measured how far apart the receptive fields moved on the retina every time they advanced their electrode 1 mm. When they did this they found that their results depended on the electrode's location in the cortex. When recording from an area of cortex that received input from receptors near the fovea, moving the electrode 1 mm across the cortex caused only a small shift in the location of receptive fields, as shown by arrow "A" in Figure 3.41. If, however, they were recording from an area that received input from a more peripheral area of the retina, moving the electrode 1 mm caused a much larger shift in the location of receptive fields, as shown by arrow "B" in Figure 3.41. Thus, the same distance on the cortex represents a small distance on the retina near the fovea and a larger distance on the retina in the periphery.

We can appreciate the importance of this result by looking at the relationship between distance on the cortex and distance on the retina in another way. Figure 3.42 shows that a small retinal area near the fovea is allotted more space on the cortex than the same-sized retinal area in the periphery. This effect is called the **magnification factor** since

the foveal representation on the cortex is *magnified* compared to the periphery.

We can understand why this magnification factor occurs by considering how neurons are packed in the retina and in the cortex. In the retina, the foveal receptors are packed very closely together, whereas peripheral receptors are much more widely spaced. These differences in the packing of the receptors are mirrored by the ganglion cells that receive signals from these receptors, with the gan-

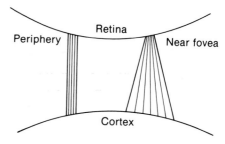

FIGURE 3. 42 The relationship between area on the retina and area on the cortex. In this illustration, two equal-sized areas on the retina are served by different-sized areas on the cortex, with the area near the fovea being alotted more space than the area in the periphery. (Based on data from Hubel & Wiesel, 1974.)

glion cells serving the foveal receptors being much more densely packed than the ganglion cells serving the peripheral receptors (Stone, 1965). However, when we look at how cortical neurons are packed, we find that the density of these neurons remains constant across the visual cortex. Consider what this means: since a small area of fovea sends many more ganglion cells to the cortex than the same area of peripheral retina, the foveal input requires more space on the cortex. This results in the magnification factor—more cortical space is allotted to parts of the retina that send more densely packed inputs to the cortex.

The importance of the magnified representation of the fovea on the cortex for our purposes is that it is related to perception. The areas of the retina with high receptor densities, high ganglion cell densities, and more space on the cortex are the areas with the highest acuity. As we know from our discussion of the rods and cones earlier in this chapter, the fovea is the part of the retina we use for high-acuity tasks such as reading this book or picking your friend's face out of a crowd. We now see that this high acuity is achieved not only because of the way the cones are wired in the retina but also because of the large amount of cortical space devoted to the fovea. In Chapter 14, when we discuss touch, we will see that an analogous situation occurs for the skin. Areas on the skin such as the fingertips that are capable of resolving fine details are allotted more space on the cortex than areas such as the back that are less sensitive to details.

Orientation columns in the cortex. In the process of discovering simple, complex, and hypercomplex cells in the cortex, Hubel and Wiesel observed an interesting phenomenon. When they lowered their electrode so that its path was perpendicular to the surface of the cortex, as shown in Figure 3.43, they encountered all three types of cells—simple, complex, and hypercomplex—but the cells had something in common: Their preferred orientations were the same. Thus, all cells encountered along the electrode track at A in Figure 3.43 respond best to horizontal lines, whereas all those along electrode track B respond best to lines oriented at about 45

degrees. Thus originated the idea that the cortex is organized into **orientation columns,** with each column containing cells that respond best to a particular orientation.

The finding that cells with the same orientation preference are organized into columns is consistent with Hubel and Wiesel's proposal that complex cells are constructed from inputs from a number of simple cells with the same preferred orientation, and hypercomplex cells are constructed from a number of complex cells with the same preferred orientation. If this idea is correct, grouping cells with similar preferred orientations together would make the construction process much easier.

This columnar organization of the cortex, which Hubel and Wiesel discovered while doing electrophysiological experiments, has been confirmed by means of an anatomical technique, called the **2-deoxyglucose technique.** This technique is based on the following facts:

1. Brain cells depend on glucose as a source of metabolic energy.
2. Cells that are more active use more glucose.
3. 2-Deoxyglucose (2-DG) can masquerade as

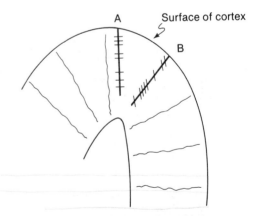

F I G U R E 3. 43 Electrophysiological evidence for orientation columns in the visual cortex. A microelectrode oriented perpendicular to the surface of the cortex will encounter simple, complex, and hypercomplex cells along its path, but all of these cells will have the same preferred stimulus orientation (indicated by the lines cutting across each electrode track).

glucose (if injected into an animal, it is taken up by active cells as glucose is).

4. After 2-DG is taken up by the cell, it begins to be metabolized, but the resultant metabolite can't cross the membrane of the cell's wall and so accumulates inside the cell.

These properties of 2-DG enabled Hubel, Wiesel, and Michael Stryker (1978) to do the following experiment: After injecting radioactively labeled 2-DG into a monkey, they stimulated the monkey's visual system by moving black and white vertical stripes back and forth in front of the animal for 45 minutes. This stripe movement increases activity in cells that prefer vertical orientations, causing them to increase their takeup of radioactive 2-DG. After this stimulation the monkey was sacrificed, and when its brain was examined, Hubel, Wiesel, and Stryker found that the cortex contained the regularly spaced narrow bands of radioactivity shown in Figure 3.44. These narrow bands, which were caused by the high activity of cells that respond best to vertical stripes, showed anatomically what had previously been demonstrated electrophysiologically: The visual cortex is made up of columns that contain cells with the same preferred orientation.

In addition to demonstrating that the visual cortex is made up of columns of cells with the same preferred orientation, Hubel and Wiesel showed that adjacent columns have similar, but slightly different, orientations. They showed this by moving an electrode through the cortex obliquely, so the electrode cut across orientation columns. As they did this they found that the neurons' preferred orientations changed in an orderly fashion and that for every millimeter they moved across the cortex they encountered cells that respond to the entire 180-degree range of orientations.

Ocular dominance columns in the cortex. In addition to being organized for the location of their receptive fields on the retina and for their preferred orientation, neurons in the cortex are also organized in terms of the eye to which they respond best. About 80 percent of the neurons in the cortex respond to stimulation of both the left and right eyes. However, most cells respond *better* to one eye than to the other. This preferential response to one

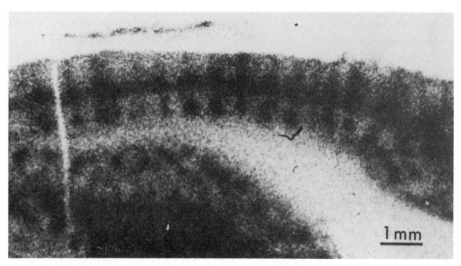

F I G U R E 3. 44 Magnified picture of a slice of visual cortex that has taken up radioactive 2-DG as described in the text. The dark vertical bands, produced by the radioactive 2-DG, are orientation columns. The dark horizontal band is layer 4 of the cortex. Neurons in this layer receive inputs from the LGN and respond to all orientations. (From Hubel, Wiesel, & Stryker, 1978.)

eye is called **ocular dominance,** and cells with the same ocular dominance are organized into **ocular dominance columns** in the cortex.

Hubel and Wiesel observed these columns during their oblique penetrations of the cortex. They found that a given area of cortex usually contained cells that all responded best to one of the eyes, but when the electrode was moved about 0.25–0.50 mm, the dominance pattern changed to the other eye. Thus, the cortex consists of a series of columns which alternate in ocular dominance in an L-R-L-R pattern.

Hypercolumns. We have seen that the visual cortex is organized into columns in terms of three different properties of the stimulus:

1. Its location on the retina: Cortical neurons serving the same retinal location are found in columns about 1 mm wide.
2. Its orientation on the retina: Cortical neurons responding to the same orientation are found in columns, which are arranged so all possible orientations are included within 1 mm of cortex.
3. Its presentation to the left or right eye Cortical neurons that respond best to each eye are located in 0.25–0.50-mm-wide columns.

One of the things that may strike you about the summary above is the similarity of the sizes of the three types of columns. Location columns are about 1 mm wide, orientation columns are about 1 mm wide, and the left and right eye dominance columns together are about 1 mm wide. What this means, according to Hubel and Wiesel, is that a 1.0 mm block of cortex can serve as a **processing module** for a particular area of the retina. This processing module, which Hubel and Wiesel call a **hypercolumn,** is shown schematically in Figure 3.45.

The cortex is made up of thousands of these hypercolumns, each one serving a small area of the retina. (Remember that there is a topographic map of the retina on the cortex.) Thus, if we present a bar of light oriented at a 45-degree angle to a small area of the retina of the left eye, we will activate neurons in the hypercolumn serving that area of the retina, and within that hypercolumn, neurons

will respond in the left ocular dominance column and in the 45-degree orientation column, as shown in Figure 3.45. If we make this bar longer, we will activate more hypercolumns and more neurons in the left ocular dominance columns and 45-degree orientation columns.

One thing is clear from Hubel and Wiesel's work on cortical organization. The information that specifies "long-bar-shape" is translated into a pattern of cortical stimulation that differs greatly from the long-bar-shape of the stimulus. But this should not surprise us if we remember our discussion of the sensory code on page 50 of Chapter 2. In that discussion, we stated that perception is based

not on direct contact with the environment, but on the brain's contact with electrical signals that *represent the environment.* We can think of these electrical signals as forming a *code* that signals various properties of the environment to the brain.

Thus, the cortical representation of a stimulus presented to the retina does not have to *resemble* the stimulus, it just has to contain information that *represents* the stimulus. A long bar on the retina is represented not by a bar on the cortex but by the firings of many neurons in different cortical columns.

THE COMPLEXITIES OF PERCEPTION

It should be clear from our description of the basic mechanisms of vision that, as we stated in Chapter 1, "perception does not just happen." It should also be clear that perception cannot be explained in terms of pictures formed on the retina or on the cortex. The neural basis of perception is built on complex wiring that creates specialized neurons organized into thousands of modules, each of which process information falling on a small area of the retina.

But as impressive as this feat of neural wiring and organization is, it represents only a small beginning toward our understanding of perception. The discoveries of feature detectors and columnar organization raise as many questions as they answer. Consider, for example, that we see complete coherent scenes. The information from many cortical

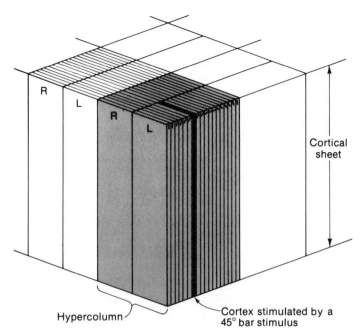

F I G U R E 3. 45 A very diagrammatic picture of a hypercolumn. A hypercolumn consists of a left and right ocular dominance column that receives inputs from the same location on the retina. Within each ocular dominance column is a complete set of orientation columns. When a bar of a particular orientation is presented to the area of retina served by a particular hypercolumn, the orientation column in that hypercolumn is activated. The activation that occurs in response to a bar oriented at 45 degrees presented to the left eye is indicated in this picture by the darkened 45-degree orientation column in the left ocular dominance columns.

modules must, somewhere in the cortex, be combined, or coordinated, to result in our coherent perception. And consider the types of things we see when we perceive. Leaves fluttering in the trees, automobiles driving down the street, the Grand Canyon. How can our perception of these things and the countless other things in our environment be explained by "feature detectors" that respond best to very simple straight-line stimuli?

As if these questions weren't difficult enough, remember that our emphasis in this chapter has been on how the visual system determines *what* an object is. But another problem we solve easily every day is determining *where* an object is. We can appreciate the complexity of this problem by considering a simple fact: As we look at different things by orienting our head, eyes, and bodies, the image

of a particular object moves all over the retina. Yet, if the object is stationary, we perceive it as occupying a particular unchanging position in space. Clearly, the answer to the question "How do we determine where an object is?" is more complex than simply "by where its image falls on the retina."

To make things even more interesting, the way we interpret our perceptions is influenced by our memories and expectations. Consider, for example, the stimulus in Figure 3.46. Are the objects under the arrow letters or numbers? Well, it depends. Most people identify the top object as a "B" since it is in a letter context but identify the bottom object as a "13" since it is in a number context. Yet they are both the same physical stimuli, which we would assume are causing identical responses in our feature detectors. Clearly, something more than

A B C
12 B 14

F I G U R E 3. 46 Our interpretation of the object under the arrow is affected by the letters or numbers surrounding it.

feature detectors is involved in creating our differing responses to this stimulus.

All of these complexities could cause us to wonder whether we will ever be able to understand anything as complex as perception. But it is these complexities that make perception interesting. Thousands of researchers in many different laboratories are working on solving the problems posed by the complexities of perception. And although there is much that remains to be understood, we have come a long way in a relatively short period of time. Before the 1950s, we had only a rudimentary understanding of how neurons in the visual system operated and had no conception of the exquisite organization of the visual cortex. Thus, our present state of knowledge represents a tremendous advance in our understanding of both the physiological and psychophysical bases of perception, within a relatively short period of time. It seems reasonable to expect, therefore, that the coming years will bring us much closer to reaching our goal of being able to explain perception at both the level of stimuli and the level of physiology.

In the next five chapters we will focus on specific perceptual qualities, beginning with our perception of color, then brightness and contrast, form, depth and size, and movement. As we consider these perceptual qualities, we will return to many of the physiological principles established in this chapter. But we will also rely heavily on psychophysics, both for its contribution to our understanding of perception at the level of stimuli and for the answers that psychophysics brings to our understanding of perception at the level of physiology.

Summary

1. When we specify a distal stimulus, we specify properties of the stimulus such as its size and distance. When we specify a proximal stimulus, we specify the properties of its image on the retina.
2. An important characteristic used to specify proximal stimuli is the visual angle. Visual angle is the angle determined by extending lines from the nodal point of the observer's eye to the top and bottom (or left and right sides) of a visual stimulus.
3. Simple geometrical stimuli are the most basic and widely used stimuli in perception research.
4. Alternating dark and light bars, which are called gratings, are used as stimuli in some perceptual experiments. The spatial frequency of the grating is the number of repeating patterns (one dark bar and one light bar) per unit distance.
5. Ecological stimuli are produced by the structuring of light by objects and surfaces in the environment into the ambient optic array. The ecological approach to perception postulates that the major source of information for perception is the changes that occur in the ambient optic array as the observer moves through the environment.
6. As light enters the eye it is focused onto the retinal receptors by the cornea and lens. If this focusing system is working properly, parallel, or nearly parallel, rays of light from a distant light source are focused onto the retina. Moving a point light source closer to the eye so that its rays become nonparallel moves the focus point back so the image is no longer in focus on the retina.
7. The focusing power of the lens can be increased by accommodation, which moves the focus point forward to achieve a sharp image on the retina by causing the light rays leaving the lens to bend more sharply. The limit of accommodation is specified by the near point, the distance at which the lens can no longer adjust to bring near objects into focus. The increase in the near point with age is called presbyopia.

8. The fibers in the primary visual pathway travel from the retina to the lateral geniculate nucleus (LGN) to the visual receiving area in the occipital lobe of the cortex. Some fibers travel to the superior colliculus.

9. The receptors for vision are the rods and the cones. Duplicity theory states that the rods and cones have different properties. Some differences between the rods and cones are:

Property	Cones	Rods
shape of outer segment	conelike	rodlike
number	6 million/retina	120 million/retina
distribution	fovea and periphery	periphery only
dark adaptation	fast	slow
spectral sensitivity	most sensitive at 560 nm	most sensitive at 500 nm
dark adapted sensitivity	lower	higher
acuity	high	low

10. The place where the optic nerve leaves the back of the eye is called the blind spot. We are usually not aware of the blind spot because of a mechanism that "fills in" the place where the image disappears.

11. Visual pigments, the chemicals in the receptors that transform light energy into electrical energy, are bleached by light and regenerate in the dark. Measurement of the rate of pigment regeneration using a procedure called retinal densitometry shows that the cones dark adapt faster than the rods because cone visual pigment regenerates faster than rod visual pigment during dark adaptation.

12. Cones are more sensitive to long-wavelength light and rods to short-wavelength light. The shift from long-wave to short-wave sensitivity during dark adaptation is called the Purkinje shift.

13. The special sensitivity curve of the rods is determined by the absorption of light by the rod pigment, rhodopsin (λ max = 500 nm), and the spectral sensitivity curve of the cones is determined by the absorption of light by the three cone pigments (λ max = 420, 535, and 565 nm).

14. The greater dark adapted sensitivity of the rod system compared to the cone system is due to the greater spatial summation of the rods.

15. One reason for the greater acuity of the cones is that fewer cones than rods converge onto each bipolar or ganglion cell.

16. There are two types of retinal ganglion cells, X-cells that have a sustained response and Y-cells that have a transient response. It has been proposed that X-cells are responsible for detail and pattern perception and Y-cells are responsible for motion perception.

17. The lateral geniculate nucleus is organized into layers, each one receiving inputs from only one eye. There is a topographic map of the retina within each layer.

18. There are simple, complex, and hypercomplex neurons in the visual receiving area. Simple cortical cells respond best to bars of a particular orientation, complex cells respond best to bars of a particular orientation that are moving in a specific direction, and hypercomplex (or end-stopped) cells respond best to bars of a specific length and orientation moving in a specific direction.

19. Cortical neurons are called feature detectors because they respond to specific features of stimuli. The results of psychophysical selective adaptation experiments support the idea that orientation-selective cortical neurons may play a role in human perception.

20. Neurons in columns perpendicular to the surface of the visual cortex have receptive fields that are close together on the retina. These columns are, therefore, called location columns.

21. The magnification factor refers to the fact that more space on the cortex is devoted to the fovea than to the same area of peripheral retina.

22. Neurons in columns perpendicular to the surface of the visual cortex all have the same preferred orientation. These columns are, therefore, called orientation columns.

23. Neurons in columns perpendicular to the surface of the visual cortex respond best to one of the eyes. These columns are, therefore, called ocular dominance columns.

24. A hypercolumn is a processing module that contains location columns for a particular area of cortex, orientation columns for all possible orientations, and left and right eye ocular dominance columns. The cortex contains thousands of hypercolumns, each of which processes information from a small area of the retina.

Boxes

1. Our retina is a duplex retina, which contains both rods and cones. Some animals, however, have retinas that contain only cones or predominantly rods, and these animals, therefore, can see well only during the day or only at night.

Study Questions

1. Describe distal stimulus, proximal stimulus, visual angle. Be sure you understand how visual angle is measured and how it is possible that two objects with different physical sizes can have the same visual angle. (65)

2. What are the three most common types of visual stimuli? (68)

3. What is a grating? spatial frequency? Why is spatial frequency important? (68)

4. Why did Gibson reject the idea of using geometrical stimuli? What is the optic array and under what conditions does it best transmit information about perception? (69)

5. Why does the retina face "backwards"? (70)

6. How are the rays of light from a spot of light more than 20 feet from the eye focused on the retina of a normal eye? What happens when we move the spot of light closer than 20 feet? (71)

7. How does accommodation change the focusing power of the eye to keep the image on the retina sharp as we look at objects at different distances? What is the near point? (72)

8. How does the ability to accommodate change as we get older? What is presbyopia? What is the treatment for presbyopia? (73)

9. What are the three main structures in the primary visual pathway? (74)

10. How are the rods and cones distributed on the retina? (76)

11. What is the blind spot? Why aren't we usually aware of it? (76)

12. What is dark adaptation? How is a dark adaptation experiment carried out? What is light adapted sensitivity? Dark adapted sensitivity? (76)

13. Plot the dark adaptation curves that result from the following experiments: (77)
    (a) The observer looks at a fixation light while paying attention to a test light in the peripheral retina.
    (b) The observer looks directly at a small test light.
    (c) The observer is a rod monochromat.

14. What do the results of the experiments in 13, above, tell us about the dark adaptation curve? What is happening to the sensitivity of the rods during the cone branch of the dark adaptation curve? (78)

15. What is a visual pigment? What happens to a visual pigment when it absorbs light? When it remains in the dark after absorbing light? (79)

16. What is retinal densitometry? What do the results of retinal densitometry experiments tell us about the relationship between rod and cone visual pigment regeneration and the rate of dark adaptation? (80)

17. How do we determine the spectral sensitivity curve for cone vision? For rod vision? Compare the rod and cone spectral sensitivity curves. In which region of the spectrum are the rods most sensitive? The cones? (80)

18. How do the differences in the sensitivity of rods and cones to different wavelengths affect dark adaptation curves measured with short and long wavelengths? (80)

19. What is the Purkinje shift? How is it explained by the rod and cone spectral sensitivity curves? (82)

20. What is an absorption spectrum? What is the relationship between the rod absorption spectrum and spectral sensitivity? (82)

21. What is microspectrophotometry? What are the three cone pigments? (83)

22. What does the two-color threshold method tell us about the cone spectral sensitivity curve? (84)

23. How do the convergence and spatial summation of rods and cones differ? How do these differences affect the sensitivity of the rod and cone systems? (85)

24. Compare rod and cone visual acuity. How is visual acuity measured? (85)

25. How does spatial summation explain the differences between rod and cone acuity? (88)

26. What are the differences between X and Y ganglion cells? How do they respond, how are they distributed in the retina, and what are their proposed functions? (89)

27. Describe the layered structure of the LGN. Does each layer receive information from one eye or from both eyes? (90)

28. Describe the topographic maps of the retina in the LGN. (90)

29. Describe the receptive fields of neurons at the places where LGN fibers enter layer 4 of the cortex. (92)

30. Describe the properties of simple, complex, and hypercomplex cells. (92)

31. What is a feature detector? How do the properties of feature detectors change as we record from neurons farther from the retina? (93)

32. Describe a selective adaptation experiment. What do the results of such an experiment tell us about the possible role of orientation-selective neurons in human perception? (94)

33. If we lower an electrode perpendicular to the surface of the cortex and record the locations of each neuron's receptive field, what will we find? What happens if we repeat this procedure but insert the electrode so it is not oriented perpendicular to the cortical surface? (96)

34. What is the magnification factor? How does it follow from the densities of foveal and peripheral

receptors and the density of neurons in the cortex? What is the functional significance of the magnification factor? (97)

35. What is an orientation column? Describe the electrophysiological method and the anatomical method for detecting these columns. How do the orientations represented in adjacent columns compare? (98)
36. What is an ocular dominance column? (99)
37. What is a hypercolumn? What does it mean to say that a hypercolumn is a "processing module"? (100)

38. Give an example to illustrate the idea that the cortical representation of a stimulus doesn't have to resemble the stimulus. (101)
39. What does the "B/13" stimulus in Figure 3.46 illustrate? (101)

Box

1. Describe the characteristics of the eyes of animals with diurnal and nocturnal vision. (86)

Glossary

Absorption spectrum. A plot of the amount of light absorbed by a visual pigment versus the wavelength of light. (See Figure 3.4.) (82)

Accommodation. The eye's ability to bring objects located at different distances into focus by changing the shape of the lens. (72)

Adapting field. A field of light presented to adapt the receptors. (84)

Ambient optic array. The way the light of the environment is structured by the presence of objects, surfaces, and textures. (69)

Blind spot. The place where the optic nerve leaves the back of the eye, causing a small area to be without visual receptors. (76)

Complex cell. A neuron in the visual cortex that responds best to moving bars with a particular orientation. (92)

Cones. Cone-shaped receptors in the retina that are primarily responsible for vision in high levels of illumination, and for color vision and detail vision. (75)

Cone spectral sensitivity curve. A graph showing the cone system's sensitivity as a function of wavelength. (80)

Contralateral eye. The eye on the opposite side of the head from the structure to which the eye sends inputs. (91)

Contrast sensitivity. Sensitivity to the difference in the light intensities in two adjacent areas. Contrast sensitivity is usually measured by taking the reciprocal of the minimum intensity difference between two bars of a grating necessary to see the bars. (94)

Convergence. When many neurons synapse onto fewer neurons. (84)

Cornea. The transparent focusing element of the eye that is the first structure through which light passes as it enters the eye. (70)

Dark adaptation. Visual adaptation that occurs in the dark, in which the sensitivity to light increases. (76)

Dark adaptation curve. The function that traces the time course of the increase in visual sensitivity that occurs during dark adaptation. (77)

Dark adapted sensitivity. The sensitivity of the dark adapted eye. (77)

2-Deoxyglucose technique. A anatomical technique that has made it possible to visualize the orientation columns in the visual cortex. (98)

Distal stimulus. Stimulus located at a distance from the observer. (65)

Diurnal vision. Vision specialized to function during the day. (86)

Duplicity theory of vision. The idea that the rod and cone receptors in the retina operate under different conditions and have different properties. (76)

End-stopped cell. See hypercomplex cell. (93)

Feature detector. A neuron that responds selectively to a specific feature of the stimulus. (93)

Focusing power. The degree to which a structure such as the lens or cornea bends light. The greater the focusing power, the more the light passing through that structure is bent. (72)

Fovea. A small area in the retina that contains only cone receptors. (76)

Grating. A stimulus pattern consisting of alternating light and dark bars. (68)

Hypercolumn. A column of cortex about 1 mm on a side, which contains a location column for a particular area of retina, left and right ocular dominance columns, and a complete set of orientation columns. A hypercolumn can be thought of as a processing module for a particular location on the retina. (100)

Hypercomplex cell. A neuron in the visual cortex that

responds best to corners moving in a particular direction or bars of a specific length moving in a particular direction. (93)

Ipsilateral eye. The eye on the same side of the head of the structure to which the eye sends inputs. (91)

Lateral geniculate nucleus (LGN). The nucleus in the thalamus that receives nerve fibers from the optic nerve and sends fibers to the cortical receiving area for vision. (74)

Lens. The transparent focusing element of the eye through which light passes after passing through the cornea and the aqueous humor. (70)

Light adaptation. Visual adaptation that occurs in the light in which the sensitivity to light decreases. (77)

Light adapted sensitivity. The sensitivity of the light adapted eye. (77)

Location column. A column in the visual cortex that contains neurons with the same receptive field locations on the retina. (96)

Long-wavelength pigment. Cone visual pigment that absorbs light maximally in the long-wavelength end of the spectrum. In humans, this pigment absorbs maximally at 558 nm. (83)

Magnification factor. A small area on the retina in or near the fovea receives more space on the cortex than the same area of peripheral retina. (97)

Medium-wavelength pigment. Cone visual pigment that absorbs light maximally in the middle of the spectrum. In humans, this pigment absorbs maximally at 531 nm. (83)

Microspectrophotometry. A procedure for determining pigment absorption spectra that involves shining light through single receptors or through small numbers of receptors. (83)

Mosaic of receptors. The pattern of the rods and cones as seen looking down on the retina. (74)

Near point. The distance at which the lens can no longer accommodate to bring close objects into focus. Objects nearer than the near point can only be brought into focus by using corrective lenses. (73)

Nocturnal vision. Vision specialized to function at night. (86)

Ocular dominance. Preferential response of a neuron to one eye. (100)

Ocular dominance column. A column in the visual cortex that contains neurons with the same ocular dominance. (100)

Opsin. The protein part of the visual pigment molecule, to which the light-sensitive retinal molecule is attached. (79)

Optic array. See ambient optic array.

Orientation column. A column in the visual cortex that contains neurons with the same orientation preference. (98)

Peripheral retina. All of the retina except the fovea and a small area surrounding the fovea. (76)

Physical distance. The distance of an object from the eye. (65)

Physical size. The size of an object. (65)

Pigment bleaching. When a visual pigment molecule absorbs light, a bleaching process begins in which the molecule changes shape and the color of the rod visual pigment changes from red to transparent. Sometime early in this process, visual transduction takes place. (79)

Pigment epithelium. The layer on which the retina rests. The pigment epithelium contains enzymes that are necessary for pigment regeneration. (70)

Pigment regeneration. The reconstruction of the visual pigment molecule from its bleached state to its original unbleached state. (79)

Presbyopia ("old eye"). Inability of the eye to accommodate due to the hardening of the lens and weakening of the ciliary muscles, which occurs as people get older. (73)

Primary visual pathway. The pathway from the retina to the lateral geniculate nucleus to the visual receiving area in the cortex. (74)

Processing module. Used in this chapter to refer to hypercolumns, each of which processes information from a small area of the retina. (100)

Proximal stimulus. The stimulus located on the observer's receptors. (65)

Purkinje shift. The shift from cone spectral sensitivity to rod spectral sensitivity that takes place during dark adaptation. (82)

Receptive field. A neuron's receptive field is the area on the receptor surface (the retina, in the case of vision) that, when stimulated, influences the firing rate of that neuron. (88)

Retinal. The light-sensitive part of the visual pigment molecule. (79)

Retinal densitometry. A procedure for measuring the concentration of visual pigment in the living eye that involves projecting a dim beam of light into the eye and measuring the fraction of this beam that is reflected back out of the eye. (80)

Retinal size. The size of an image on the retina. (65)

Rod-cone break. The point on the dark adaptation curve at which vision shifts from cone vision to rod vision. (78)

Rod monochromat. A person who has a retina in which the only functioning receptors are rods. (78)

Rods. Rod-shaped receptors in the retina that are primarily responsible for vision in low levels of illumination. The rod system is extremely sensitive in the dark but cannot resolve fine details. (75)

Rod spectral sensitivity curve. A graph showing the rod system's sensitivity to light as a function of the light's wavelength. (80)

Selective adaptation. Selectively adapting a person or animal to one stimulus and then assessing the effect of this adaptation by testing with a wide range of stimuli. For example, adapting with vertical bars and then testing a person's sensitivity to bars of all orientations. (94)

Short-wavelength pigment. Cone visual pigment that absorbs maximally at short wavelengths. In the human, this pigment absorbs maximally at 419 nm. (83)

Simple cortical cell. A neuron in the visual cortex that responds best to bars of a particular orientation. (92)

Spatial frequency. In a grating stimulus, spatial frequency refers to the frequency with which the grating repeats itself per degree of visual angle. For more natural stimuli, high spatial frequencies are associated with fine details, and low spatial frequencies are associated with grosser features. (68)

Spatial summation. When the effect of stimulation is summated, or added, over a large area. (85)

Striate cortex. The visual receiving area of the cortex located in the occipital lobe. (74)

Superior colliculus. A structure at the base of the brain that is important in controlling eye movement. A small proportion of the nerve fibers in the optic nerve synapse in the superior colliculus. (74)

Sustained response. The continuous firing that occurs in X-cells in response to continued illumination. (89)

Tapetum. A reflecting surface located behind the retina in some animals. (86)

Topographic map. A map in which there is a spatial correspondence between two structures. For example, there is a topographic map of the retina on the cortex in which each point of the retina corresponds to a point on the cortex. (90)

Transient response. The burst of firing that occurs in Y-cells in response to the onset of illumination. (89)

Two-color threshold method. A method used by Stiles in which thresholds to different wavelengths are measured with a test flash that is superimposed on an adapting field. (84)

Visual angle. The visual angle of an object is the angle between two lines that extend from the observer's eye, one to one end of the object and the second to the other end of the object. An object's visual angle is always determined relative to an observer; therefore, an object's visual angle changes as the distance between the object and the observer changes. (65)

Visual pigments. Light-sensitive chemicals found inside the rod and cone outer segments. (79)

Visual receiving area. The area in the occipital lobe, also called the striate cortex, that receives inputs from the lateral geniculate nucleus. (74)

X-cells. Ganglion cells that respond with a sustained response. In addition, these cells have other properties, listed in Table 3.1, that differentiate them from Y-cells. (89)

Y-cells. Ganglion cells that respond with a transient response. In addition, these cells have other properties, listed in Table 3.1, that differentiate them from X-cells. (89)

CHAPTER 4

Perceiving Color

PERCEPTUAL QUESTIONS AND PERCEPTUAL PRINCIPLES

This book began by describing some of the questions students ask about perception on the first day of class. Since that opening discussion we have asked a number of questions ourselves. In Chapter 1 we posed the following two questions that we need to answer to understand perception:

1. What are the phenomena of perception?
2. What causes these phenomena to occur?

In Chapter 2, as we described the basic principles of sensory physiology, we posed two further questions that we need to answer to understand the physiology of perception:

1. What information is present in single neurons and in populations of neurons?
2. Is this information used by the brain, and, if so, how?

In Chapter 3, as we introduced some basic principles of vision, we posed some additional questions:

1. What is the structure of the visual system?
2. How do neurons respond to stimulation of the receptors?
3. What is the relationship between physiology (both structure and neural response) and perception?

In Chapters 1–3 we both posed these questions and began answering them. Why do we repeat them here? Because we will be answering these same questions, or variations of them, throughout this book. Despite the differences among qualities as diverse as color, depth, pitch, and taste, we will, as we study these qualities, see that there are general principles that hold across qualities and senses. We introduced this idea of general principles in Chapter 1 (p. 29) when we pointed out that since all of our perceptions are determined by the same nervous system, " . . . the diversity of perception is built on a foundation of similar principles." We will, therefore, open this chapter and the next one by stating some principles that are illustrated by the material in these chapters.

Given the number of different visual qualities to choose from, why have we decided to begin with color? Color is one of the most obvious and pervasive of the perceptual qualities. We interact with color whenever we note the color of a traffic light, when we pick clothes that are color coordinated, or when we enjoy the colors of a painting. Color also has a survival function. Some animals use protective coloration to hide from predators, and color indicates the degree of ripeness or spoilage of many foods. Yet a person who is completely color-blind is not as severely handicapped as someone who, for example, has lost the ability to identify forms or to see movement. We pick color to begin our discussion of specific qualities not because it is obvious in our environment or because of its importance for survival but because it provides a model system. This system not only illustrates many of the principles we have established in the first three chapters but also enables us to establish a number of new principles that can be applied to the other qualities we will study in the chapters to come. We begin by listing the basic principles that are emphasized in this chapter.

1. Perception is a private experience. Our radical skeptic in Box 1.1 posed the proposition that "you may not have the slightest reason to suppose that visual perception gives other people experiences that are anything like your visual experiences." In the process of asking "What is color?" we will consider this idea further.

2. We can explain perception at different levels. In Chapter 1 we introduced the idea that perception can be explained at the level of stimuli or at the level of physiology. This idea of explanations at different levels is beautifully illustrated by the history of research on color vision, which has been marked by important discoveries using both psychophysical and physiological methods.

3. Physiological mechanisms can be deduced from psychophysical observations. Color vision provides the classic example of psychophysics predicting physiology. We will see that the two physiological theories of color vision that are accepted today were conceived in psychophysics laboratories over a century ago.

4. Perception is shaped by neural processing. Our discussion of this principle in Chapter 3 focused on how the different properties of the rods and cones lead to differing perceptions. We will now focus our attention on how processing by three different types of cone receptors causes our experience of color.

5. Perception can remain constant in the face of changing stimulation. Here we introduce for the first time the idea that our perception may remain the same even when the stimulation entering our eyes changes.

We will encounter each of these principles in this chapter. We begin by asking, "What is color?", a question that begins with some definitions of color and leads us to ask how we can describe our experience of seeing color.

WHAT IS "COLOR"?

Definitions of Color

One approach to defining **color** is in terms of **spectral composition**—the wavelengths that are contained in the light stimulus. (Read page 10 of Chapter 1 to review wavelength, if necessary.) Gunter Wyszecki (1986) approaches color in this way by defining it as follows: *If two fields seen against the same background have the same shape, texture, and exposure duration but have different spectral compositions, then the difference we perceive between them is a difference in color.* We will, later in this chapter, look in more detail at specifically how color depends on spectral composition.

Another approach to defining color is in terms

of example. The *Report on Color Terminology* of the British Colour Group (1948) uses this approach to define color as *a property of material objects, including sources of light, by which they are visually distinguished as possessing the qualities of redness, greenness, brownness, whiteness, greyness, etc.*

Notice that this definition includes "whiteness" and "greyness" as examples. White, grey, and black are **achromatic colors,** and "blue," "red," and "green" are **chromatic colors.** In this chapter we will focus on chromatic color, leaving achromatic color for the next chapter. Another term for chromatic color is **hue,** but this term is rarely used in everyday language. We usually say "the color of the fire engine is red" rather than "the hue (or chromatic color) of the fire engine is red." We will, therefore, use the word "color" to mean "chromatic color" or "hue" throughout the rest of this chapter.

Color as a Private Experience

If a friend who is completely color-blind asked you to describe the experience of "color," what would you say? Stop for a moment, and think. When you consider your response, you can appreciate the difficulty of describing this experience without using examples of the experience itself. For example, Webster's (1956) definition describes color as "a quality of visible phenomena, distinct from form and from light and shade, such as the red of blood." Notice that the example of "red" is crucial to this definition of color. If we try looking up a specific color such as "blue," we find the following definition: "Any of several colors whose hue is or resembles that of the zenith of the clear sky; any color in that portion of the color spectrum lying between green and violet (reddish blue)." Again the dictionary resorts to an example, defining "blue" in terms of the color of the sky or its relationship to other colors in the spectrum.

If the only way we can describe color is by examples, it is impossible to make someone who is color-blind understand what it is like to experience color. If you tell someone who is completely color-blind and sees only in shades of grey that blue is the color of the sky, you tell the person that you experience something called "blue" when you look

at the sky, but you don't convey the *quality* of that experience. A similar situation exists for color-deficient people who see some colors but not as many as a person with normal color vision. If such a person says that the sky looks blue, does he or she see the same blue as you? Probably not. The color-deficient person might, in fact, be perceiving a color which you call "green," but which he or she has learned to call "blue," since blue is the generally accepted name for the color of the sky. These examples illustrate our first principle: *Perception is a private experience.* We can't share the essence of experiencing "blue" with someone who has never perceived "blue" or with someone who may perceive blue differently than we do.

This privateness of perception holds not only for color but for all other subjective experiences as well. Thus, just as we can't share the essence of experiencing "blue" with someone who has never experienced "blue," we also can't share the essence of being touched or tickled, or smelling a rose, or tasting an apple, or hearing music, with someone who has never experienced these things.

What does the private experience of color mean for people with normal color vision? It may mean that despite our assumptions to the contrary, different people with normal color vision may actually perceive colors differently. Experiments in which people are asked to name colors suggest that we may differ in what we see, just as we differ in height, weight, reaction time, or any other measurable characteristic. For example, let's consider the results of an experiment in which observers were shown a visible spectrum (like the one in Color Plate 1.1) and were asked to indicate which part of the spectrum appeared to be the purest orange, the purest yellow, the purest green, and so on (Chapanis, 1965). Individual observers can make these judgments very reliably (that is, observers repeat their judgments accurately), but large differences exist between observers. One observer might say that the purest green is a 500 nm light while another says that the purest green is a 505 nm light. Or if asked to name the colors of particular wavelengths, one observer might say that a 560 nm light looks yellowish green while another says that the same wavelength looks greenish yellow. Do these observers perceive colors differently? Maybe or maybe not. The results indicate that either the observers perceive colors differently *or* they perceive them in the same way but give them different names.

Thus, although these color-naming experiments suggest that people with normal color vision may experience colors differently, the privateness of such experience makes it impossible to know whether this is so. In the remainder of this discussion we will, therefore, ignore the possibility that people may differ somewhat in how they perceive colors. Instead, we will assume that observers with normal color vision perceive colors in approximately the same way, and we will devote our attention to describing some of the properties of color.

How Many Colors Can We See?

The above question can be answered in a number of different ways. One approach is to start at one end of the visible spectrum (see Color Plate 1.1) and slowly increase the wavelength until the observer indicates that he or she can discriminate a difference in color. When we do this, we find that observers can discriminate about 150 steps between 380 and 700 nm. We can, however, multiply these 150 discriminable colors in two ways. (1) We can vary the intensity of each step. Changing the intensity usually changes the brightness of the color (although we will see in Chapter 5 that increasing intensity does not *always* increase brightness). (2) We can vary the **saturation** of each step. If we start with a 640 nm light, which appears red, and then add white to it, we say that the resulting pink color is less saturated than the original red. Saturation is inversely related to the amount of whiteness in a color—that is, the more saturated a color, the less whiteness it contains. Taking into account that each of the 150 discriminable colors can have many values of brightness and saturation, one investigator calculated that we can discriminate over 7 million different colors!

Another approach to determining the number of colors we can see is to ask how many color names there are. The worlds of advertising, paint manufacturing, and cosmetics expose us to such names as crushed strawberry, azure blue, Kelly green,

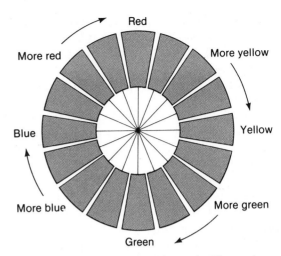

F I G U R E 4. 1 The color circle. This circle, shown in color in Color Plate 4.1, arranges colors by placing perceptually similar colors next to each other. When we do this, we find that the colors can be arranged in a circle. The four pure (or unique) colors are found at 12, 3, 6, and 9 o'clock on the circle.

and Chinese red. Although the ingenious names invented to describe different shades of paint, lipstick, floor tile, and fabric may not be as high as 7 million, it is still impressively high. One compilation, published by the National Bureau of Standards, lists 7,500 different color names (Judd & Kelly, 1965).

Obviously, 7 million or even 7,500 are far too many colors for us to deal with, so color scientists prefer to deal with just a few basic colors. The smallest list of basic colors has been proposed by Leo Hurvich (1981), who states that we can describe all the colors we can discriminate by using only six terms and their combinations. These terms are red, yellow, green, and blue for the chromatic colors and black and white for the achromatic colors.

Though many schemes have been proposed to describe the relationships between different colors, perhaps the most straightforward of these schemes is the color circle, shown in Figure 4.1 and Color Plate 4.1. To create a color circle, we arrange colors so that each is perceptually similar to the one next to it. Thus, as we move around the circle we see the colors change gradually from one to the next, and since they are arranged in a circle we eventually get back to where we started.

Hurvich (1981) describes the experience of moving around the circle in this way: If we start with red at 12 o'clock and move clockwise around the circle, the colors become increasingly yellowish, passing through various shades of orange, until we reach pure yellow at 3 o'clock. We call this pure yellow because it contains no trace of the red we just left or of the green we approach as we move further around the circle. As we continue, colors become greener, until we reach a pure green at 6 o'clock. After green, blue becomes stronger until we reach a pure blue at 9 o'clock, and then the blue turns to violet as red begins to reappear, until we arrive back at pure red at the top of the circle. Though we encounter many different colors as we travel around the circle, we can see from this way of organizing them that all chromatic colors can be considered to consist of various proportions of the four basic colors: red, yellow, green, and blue.

Now that we have established the existence of a multitude of different colors and have identified the four basic ones, we are ready to begin explaining how our perception of these colors comes about. In the process of doing this, our second principle, that *we can explain perception at different levels,* will come into play, because we will be considering both psychophysical and physiological approaches to the study of color perception. We begin by asking a basic question: What *physical property* of light is connected to our experience of color? The answer begins in Isaac Newton's room at Cambridge University in 1704.

COLOR AND WAVELENGTH

In his room at Cambridge University, Isaac Newton (later *Sir* Isaac Newton) placed a prism so that sunlight shining through a hole in the shutter of his window entered the prism. He observed that the sunlight became transformed by its passage through the prism into a spectrum of colors like the one in Color Plate 1.1. When Newton recombined the spectral colors with a lens, he reclaimed the sunlight with which he started. On the basis of this and other experiments, Newton concluded that sunlight is made up of each of the spectral colors. Later work showed that these spectral colors differed in wavelength, with wavelengths between about 400 and 450 nm appearing violet; 450–500 nm, blue; 500–570, green; 570–590, yellow; 590–620, orange; and 620–700, red. Thus, knowing

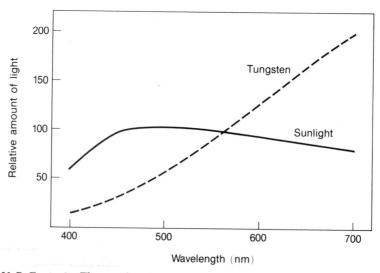

F I G U R E 4. 2 The wavelength distribution of sunlight and of light from a tungsten light bulb. (Based on data from Judd, MacAdam, & Wyszecki, 1964; Wyszecki & Stiles, 1967.)

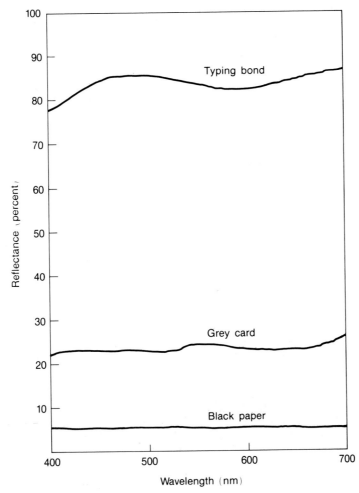

FIGURE 4. 3 Reflectance curves for surfaces that appear white, grey, and black. (Adapted from Clulow, 1972.)

the wavelength of a light gives us a good idea of its color.

In our everyday experience, however, we are rarely exposed to single wavelengths. Light sources that illuminate the objects in our environment give off many different wavelengths, and the objects reflect many wavelengths into our eyes. Let's first describe the wavelengths given off by our three main sources of light: the sun, light bulbs, and fluorescent lights.

Figure 4.2 is a graph of the **wavelength distributions** of sunlight and "tungsten" light. The wavelength distribution for sunlight is relatively flat, indicating that sunlight contains an approxi- mately equal intensity of each wavelength across the spectrum. Such light is called **white light.** The wavelength distribution of light given off by fluorescent bulbs (not shown here) is approximately white, although the wavelengths emitted by a fluorescent bulb depend on the gases inside the bulb. (Bulbs made by different companies may contain different gases and so have different wavelength distributions.) The wavelength distribution for the light emitted by conventional light bulbs, called **tungsten light** after the bulb's tungsten filament, contains much more intensity at long wavelengths than at short wavelengths, as indicated by the dashed line in Figure 4.2.

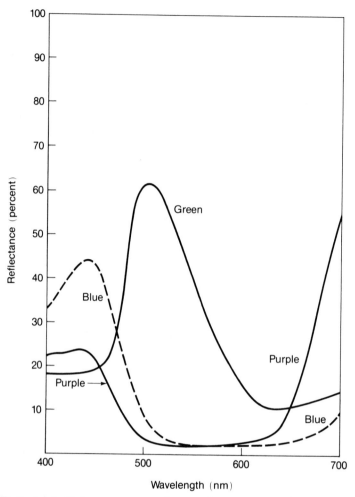

Reflectance (percent)

Wavelength (nm)

F I G U R E 4. 4 Reflectance curves of some colored pigments. Knowing which wavelengths are reflected by a pigment enables us to roughly predict the pigment's color by consulting Table 4.1 on page 115. Try this for these pigments and for the foods in Figure 4.5. (Adapted from Clulow, 1972.)

Light from sources such as the sun or light bulbs can reach our eyes directly if we look at the light sources (not recommended in the case of the sun!), but most of the light we see is reflected from objects in the environment. To understand why objects have different colors, we must look at the **reflectance curves** of the <u>objects themselves.</u> Reflectance curves for some pigments and common objects are shown in Figures 4.3, 4.4, and 4.5. These curves show the percentage of light of each wavelength which is reflected by these pigments or objects when they are illuminated by white light.

(Later in this chapter, we will consider the effect of illuminating objects with light that is not white.) Notice that each pigment or object reflects a wide band of wavelengths. <u>As indicated in Figure 4.3,</u> <u>white paper reflects equally all wavelengths from</u> <u>400 to 700 nm.</u> This equal reflection of all wavelengths in the spectrum makes sense if we remember Newton's experiment, which showed that white light is made up of all visible wavelengths. A grey card and black paper also equally reflect all wavelengths but less of each wavelength than the white paper: <u>The grey card reflects about 23 percent of</u>

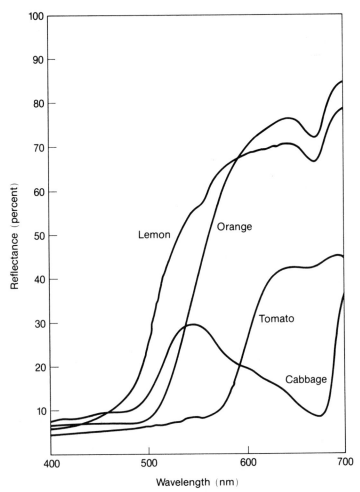

F I G U R E 4. 5 Reflectance curves of some common foods. (Adapted from Clulow, 1972.)

each wavelength, the black paper only about 5 percent.

The objects with the reflectance curves in Figures 4.4 and 4.5 do not, however, reflect all wavelengths equally. They reflect some wavelengths but absorb others. This property, which is called **selective reflection,** is shared by all objects that have a hue, or chromatic color, and the reflectance curves show that the region of the spectrum reflected determines the object's color. The relationship between the color perceived and the wavelengths reflected is indicated in Table 4.1.

The objects we have talked about so far reflect some wavelengths and absorb the rest, but what

T A B L E 4.1 / *Relationship between Wavelengths Reflected and Color Perceived*

Wavelengths Reflected	Perceived Color
Short	Blue
Medium	Green
Long	Red
Long and Medium	Yellow
Long and a Little Medium	Orange
Long and Short	Purple
Long, Medium, and Short	White

B O X   4. 1   /   *Why Is the Sky Blue?*

Why is the sky blue? We can answer this question by considering what happens to the sun's light on its way into the earth's atmosphere. Sunlight entering the atmosphere encounters many small particles, which scatter the light. When these particles are small in relation to the wavelength of the light, a condition known as **Rayleigh scattering** occurs (named after Lord Rayleigh, who first described the effect and who also won the Nobel Prize for discovering argon), and the scattering is *inversely* proportional to the fourth power of the wavelength of the light. This inverse proportionality means that short wavelengths are scattered *more* than long wavelengths, with the result shown in the figure to the left below. The scattered short-wavelength light

gives the sky its blue color. Long-wavelength light is not scattered as much, and most of it is transmitted directly through the atmosphere to the observer, making direct sunlight appear yellow.

Rayleigh scattering also explains why the setting (and rising) sun looks red. In this case, illustrated in the right figure, the light from the setting sun travels a greater distance through the atmosphere than it does at noon, and this increases the amount of short and medium wavelengths that are scattered. By the time the light reaches the observer, only the longest wavelengths remain, and the sun therefore appears red.

The physics of light scattering also helps us understand why mist appears white. This occurs because the particles in mist are large compared to the wavelength of light and do not scatter short wavelengths preferentially, as in Rayleigh scattering. With all wavelengths scattered equally, we perceive a misty white (Riggs, 1965a; Ross, 1974).

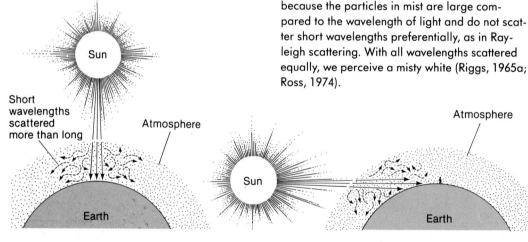

---

about translucent things, such as liquids, plastics, and glasses? The relationship between wavelengths and color shown here also holds for these objects, except that they *transmit* rather than reflect light, and if they selectively transmit certain wavelengths, they appear colored. For example, cranberry juice selectively transmits long-wavelength light and appears red, while limeade selectively

transmits medium-wavelength light and appears green.

Establishing the connection between color and wavelength is the first step in understanding the mechanisms underlying color perception. But to get at these mechanisms, we need to go beyond describing the relationship between wavelength and color. The first experiments that did go beyond describing this relationship have led to hypotheses concerning the physiological mechanisms of color vision. That these experiments were not physiological experiments but <u>psychophysical experiments that resulted in physiological hypotheses leads us to our third principle</u>: *Physiological mechanisms can be deduced from psychophysical observations.* In a paper reviewing recent research on the physiology of color vision, Peter Lennie (1984) describes this situation as follows:

Color vision has attracted scientific attention for at least 250 years, though it was not until the nineteenth century that we began to understand it properly. Since then, physicists and psychologists have provided very precise descriptions of the phenomena of color vision and in many cases have also formulated physiological hypotheses to help explain them. Until recently physiologists contributed rather little to the emerging story, for they lacked the techniques to study the mechanisms pointed to by the psychologists. However, physiological advances of the last 20 years have provided much new information on the mechanisms of color vision. (p. 243)

Let's now look at these psychophysical descriptions of the phenomena of color vision and at the physiological theories that were proposed based on these descriptions.

PSYCHOPHYSICAL RESEARCH ON COLOR PERCEPTION

Color Matching and the Trichromatic Hypothesis

In a **color-matching** experiment, observers are asked to match the color of one light by mixing together three wavelengths. For example, as shown in Figure 4.6, the observer might be asked to match the color of a 500 nm light presented in the test field by mixing together 420 nm, 560 nm, and 640 nm lights in the comparison field. Observers with normal color vision can do this and, in fact, <u>can match any wavelength in the test field by mixing these three wavelengths</u> in the appropriate proportions. (Any three wavelengths can be used in the comparison field, as long as we can't match any one of them by mixing the other two.) Observers cannot,

Test   Comparison

F I G U R E 4. 6 Test and comparison fields used in a color-matching experiment. In this experiment, a 500 nm light is being matched by mixing lights of 420 nm, 560 nm, and 640 nm.

however, match all test wavelengths if they are provided with only *two* other wavelengths. For example, <u>if we were given only the 420 nm and 640 nm lights to mix, we would be unable to match certain colors.</u>

Based on the fact that at least three wavelengths are needed to match any wavelength in the test field, Thomas Young (1802) proposed the **trichromatic theory of color vision.** This theory, which was later championed by Hermann von Helmholtz (1852) (see Figure 4.7), and so is also called the

F I G U R E 4. 7 Hermann von Helmholtz (1821–1894), who championed the trichromatic theory of color vision.

Young-Helmholtz theory, states that color vision depends on three receptor mechanisms, each with different spectral sensitivities.

According to this theory, light of a particular wavelength stimulates the three mechanisms to different degrees, and the ratio of activity in the three mechanisms results in the perception of a color. Each color is, therefore, coded in the nervous system by its own ratio of activity in the three receptor mechanisms, an arrangement you may recognize from Chapter 2 as across-fiber coding.

We can see how this coding works by referring to the response curves for the three mechanisms in Figure 4.8. We will call these three mechanisms the short-wave mechanism (S), the medium-wave mechanism (M), and the long-wave mechanism (L) to refer to the regions of the spectrum to which they are most sensitive. With these three curves we can determine the response of the three mechanisms to any wavelength. So, presentation of a 500 nm light results in a response of 1.3 from the S mechanism, 9.0 from the M mechanism, and 6.0 from the L mechanism. According to trichromatic theory, this 1.3 to 9.0 to 6.0 ratio of activity signals the perception of a particular color, in this case the green of a 500 nm light.

If color perception is based on the ratios of activity of three receptor mechanisms, we should be able to determine which colors will be perceived if we know the response of each of the receptor mechanisms. Figure 4.9 shows the relationship between the responses of the three receptors and our perception of color. In this figure, the responses in the S, M, and L receptors are indicated by the size of the receptors. For example, blue is signaled by a large response in the S receptor, a smaller response in the M receptor, and an even smaller response in the L receptor. Yellow is signaled by small response in the S receptor and large, approximately equal responses in the M and L receptors.

This theory of color vision enables us to predict which colors should result when we combine lights of different colors. For example, if we project a spot of red light onto a spot of green light, what color should result? The patterns of receptor activity in Figure 4.9 show that a green light causes a

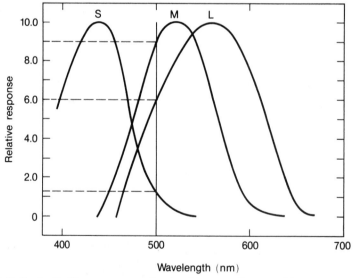

F I G U R E 4. 8 Response curves for the short-, medium-, and long-wave mechanisms proposed by trichromatic theory. These curves, which are identical to the absorption spectra of the three cone pigments shown in Figure 3.24, enable us to determine the relative response of each mechanism to light of any wavelength. In the example shown here, the response of each mechanism to a 500 nm light is determined by drawing a line up from 500 nm and noting where this line intersects each curve. (Curves from Wald & Brown, 1965.)

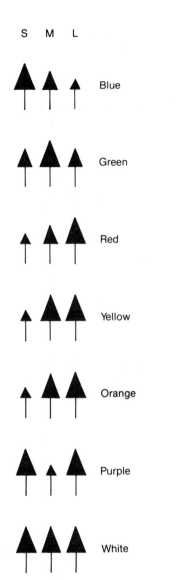

F I G U R E   4. 9   Patterns of firing of the three types of cones to different colors.

light causes activity in the S receptors, and yellow light causes activity in the M and L receptors. Thus, combining both lights should stimulate all three receptors equally and we should perceive white. (If you are surprised by this result because you have learned that blue and yellow make green, see Box 4.2 for an explanation.)

Having seen how three receptor mechanisms can signal different wavelengths and, therefore, different colors, let's consider, in more detail, what is happening when our observer matches the 500 nm light of Figure 4.6 with a mixture of 420 nm, 560 nm, and 640 nm lights.

When our observer matches one wavelength with a mixture of three other wavelengths, he is perceiving two *physically different stimuli* as being *identical.* We can understand why two physically different stimuli can look identical by considering what we would observe if we could monitor the response of the receptors to the 500 nm test field and to the 420 nm + 580 nm + 640 nm comparison field. On the left of Figure 4.10 we see that the 500 nm light causes a ratio of activity of 1.3 to 9.0 to 6.0 in the S, M, and L receptors (remember that we determined this from Figure 4.8). On the right of Figure 4.10, we see that the mixture

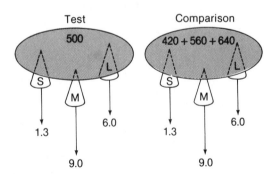

F I G U R E   4. 10   If we could simultaneously monitor the responses of the short-, medium-, and long-wave cones to the test field, which contains the 500 nm light, and to the comparison field, which contains the mixture of 420 nm, 560 nm, and 640 nm lights that perceptually match the 500 nm test light, we would find no difference in the responses of the two sets of receptors. Since the responses to the two fields are identical, they will be perceptually indistinguishable.

large response in the M receptor and a red light causes a large response in the L receptor. Together, therefore, they should result in a large response in the M and L receptors and a much smaller response in the S receptors. This is the pattern for yellow, which we do, in fact, see when red and green lights are mixed.

Let's pose another color mixing problem: What happens when we mix blue and yellow lights? Blue

---

BOX 4.2 / *When Does Blue Plus Yellow Equal Green?*

It may have surprised you to read on page 119 that a blue light plus a yellow light stimulate all the cones equally and result in the perception of white. How can this be? Most people think that mixing blue with yellow results in green. In fact, these people are right, but they are talking about mixing paints rather than mixing lights. Let's consider what happens when we mix blue and yellow paints compared to what happens when we mix blue and yellow lights.

Mixing paints is called **subtractive color mixture.** To understand how subtractive color mixture causes blue and yellow to equal green, let's first consider what happens to white light that illuminates blue and yellow paint. White light is made up of all the wavelengths of the visible spectrum: the wavelengths that cause us to see blue, green, yellow, orange, and red. When the white light hits the blue paint, some of these wavelengths are absorbed (or subtracted) and some are reflected. As you can see from the figure, blue paint absorbs wavelengths associated with yellow, orange, red, and some of the green, and reflects blue and a little green. Yellow paint absorbs blue, orange, red, and some of the green, and reflects yellow and a little green.

What happens when we mix these two paints together? When they are mixed, both paints still absorb the same colors they absorbed when alone. This means that the mixture of blue and yellow paints will absorb *all* the blue (since yellow paint absorbs blue when alone), *some* of the green (blue and yellow paints both absorb some green when alone), *all* the yellow (absorbed by blue when alone), and *all* the orange and red (absorbed by both blue and yellow when alone). After all this absorbing, what's left? The only color that remains is the green reflected by both blue and yellow. (Remember that these paints don't absorb all the green.) *The only colors reflected from a mixture of paints are the colors reflected by both paints in common.* Since green is the only color reflected by *both* the blue and yellow paints, it is the only color reflected from the mixture, and we therefore perceive green.

The only reason that our blue and yellow mixture resulted in green was that there was a little green in each of the paints. What if our blue paint reflected only blue and our yellow paint reflected only yellow? These paints would have no colors reflected in common, so mixing them would result in little or no reflection across the spectrum, and, therefore, the mixture would appear black. It is rare, however, to find paints that reflect light in only one region of the spectrum. Most paints, like our original blue and

---

of three wavelengths also causes the same ratio of activity in the three types of receptors. Since the two physically different stimuli have identical physiological effects, the two lights appear identical.

Two lights such as this, which have different wavelength distributions but are perceptually identical, are called **metamers,** and what we have described above is the basic principle of metamers: *Two lights with different wavelength distributions appear the same color if they stimulate the S, M, and L receptors in the same ratios.*

We have seen that, according to trichromatic theory, color vision is based on three types of receptors with different sensitivities. But what would our perception be like if we had only one type of receptor? We can answer this question by considering how a single type of receptor would respond to light of different wavelengths. This receptor, with the response curve shown in Figure 4.11, responds best to light of 500 nm and, therefore, for a given light intensity, fires most strongly to a 500 nm light. Thus, if we present 500 nm and 550 nm lights of

yellow, reflect a broad band of wavelengths, encompassing at least two colors. If paints didn't reflect a range of wavelengths, then many of the **color mixing** effects that painters take for granted would not occur.

Let's compare the subtractive process, which occurs when mixing paints, to the additive process, which occurs when mixing lights. Mixing lights is called **additive color mixture,** because all the wavelengths contained in each light still reach the eye when the lights are superimposed. Consider what happens when we look at blue and yellow lights that have been superimposed on a white projection screen. The short wavelengths of the blue light are reflected from the screen into our eyes, and the medium and long wavelengths of the yellow light are also reflected from the screen into our eyes. The

result? Short, medium, and long wavelengths reach our eyes and we perceive white.

We can appreciate the difference between mixing paints and mixing lights by considering that every time we add a light to some existing light, we *add to* the amount of light reflected from the screen into the observer's eye. However, every time we add an additional glob of paint to a mixture of paints, we *subtract from* the amount of light reflected from the mixture into the eye. This opposite nature of additive and subtractive color mixture is perhaps best illustrated by comparing the color that results from mixing blue, green, and red lights to the color that results from mixing blue, green, and red paints. Mixing the lights results in white, while mixing the paints results in black.

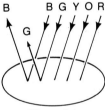

Blue paint

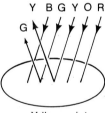

Yellow paint

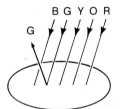

Blue paint + yellow paint

the same intensity, this receptor fires more strongly to the 500 nm light.

The greater firing to the 500 nm light does not mean, however, that we can rely on the output of this receptor to tell us whether a 500 or 550 nm light is present. To understand why this is so, consider what happens if we stimulate this receptor with a high-intensity 550 nm light and a low-intensity 500 nm light. When we do this, the receptor fires more to 550 nm than to 500 nm. We cannot, therefore, distinguish between different

wavelengths based on the output of a single receptor; when we describe different types of color-blindness, we will see that people with only one type of receptor confuse different wavelengths.

Now let's consider what happens when there are two receptor mechanisms as in Figure 4.12. Adding the second mechanism enables the nervous system to signal wavelength on the basis of the ratio of activity in the two receptors. For example, a 500 nm light causes a large response in receptor 1 and a small response in receptor 2, whereas

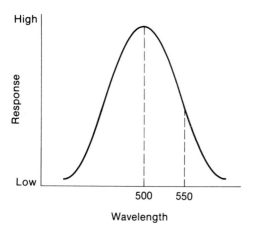

F I G U R E 4. 11 Response curve for a single receptor type. The intersections of the dashed lines with the curve indicate that, *for a given intensity,* this receptor will fire more strongly to a 500 nm light than to a 550 nm light. We could, however, generate a larger response to the 550 nm light by increasing its intensity.

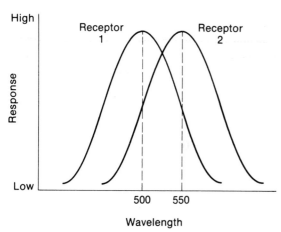

F I G U R E 4. 12 Response curves for two receptor mechanisms. The response of each mechanism to a given wavelength can be determined by noting where a vertical line originating at that wavelength intersects the response curve. In this example we can see that a 500 nm light causes a larger response in receptor 1 than in receptor 2 and that a 550 nm light causes a larger response in receptor 2 than in receptor 1. Increasing the intensity of either wavelength will increase the response generated in each mechanism but won't affect the sizes of the response in the two mechanisms relative to one another.

a 550 nm light causes a large response in receptor 2 and a smaller response in receptor 1. Thus, two receptors with different response curves are able to signal the presence of different wavelengths, and we will see below that people with two receptor mechanisms can, in fact, perceive colors, although not as well as people with three receptor mechanisms.

The way Young and Helmholtz reasoned from the psychophysical result that a minimum of 3 wavelengths are needed to match any wavelength in the spectrum to the conclusion that color vision is based on three receptor mechanisms shows how psychophysics can predict physiology. (Because, as we will soon see, their physiological prediction was correct.) However, before we consider the physiological data that supports the Young-Helmholtz theory, let's look at another example of how psychophysics can predict physiology, this one provided by Ewald Hering's phenomenological approach to the study of color vision.

Phenomenological Observations and the Opponent-Process Hypothesis

Ewald Hering (1878) (Figure 4.13) was an astute observer of the phenomenology of color vision. (See page 8 of Chapter 1 to review the phenomenological method.) Let's first make our own phenomenological observations and then consider the theory that Hering proposed based on similar observations.

D E M O N S T R A T I O N

Afterimages and Simultaneous Contrast

Cut out a ½-inch square of white or grey paper and place it in the center of the green square in Color Plate 1.3. Cover the other squares with white paper and stare at the center of the ½-inch square for 60 seconds. Then look at a white background and observe the **afterimage.** (Blink to bring back the afterimage if it fades.) What color is the outside area of the afterimage? What color is the small square in the center?

When you make these observations, you will probably notice that green and red are paired: The afterimage corresponding to the green area of the

FIGURE 4. 13 Ewald Hering (1834–1918), who proposed the opponent-process theory of color vision.

TABLE 4.2 / *Afterimages*

Original Square	Color of Outside Afterimage	Color of Inside Afterimage
Green ——————— Red		Green
Red	Green	Red
Blue	Yellow	Blue
Yellow —————— Blue		Yellow

the result. Table 4.2, which indicates the usual results of these observations, shows a clear pairing of red and green, and of blue and yellow.

DEMONSTRATION

Visualizing Colors

We can illustrate the pairing of red and green and blue and yellow in another way by trying to visualize certain colors. Start by visualizing the color red. Attach this color to a specific object such as a fire engine if that makes your visualizing easier. Now do the same thing for blue. Visualizing basic colors like blue and red is easy, but now try to visualize mixtures such as bluish green; reddish yellow; yellowish blue; and reddish green. You were probably able to visualize a bluish green or a reddish yellow, but found it difficult (or impossible) to visualize a reddish green or a bluish yellow.

original square is red. You will probably also notice that green and red are paired in another way: Inside the red afterimage, in the place corresponding to the white area inside the original square, is a green afterimage. This afterimage is due to **simultaneous contrast,** an effect that occurs when surrounding an area with a color changes the appearance of the surrounded area. In this case, the red afterimage surrounds a white area, and the white area becomes green. Another demonstration of simultaneous contrast is shown in Color Plate 4.2, a pattern created by the artist Josef Albers. Although both X's are printed from the same ink and therefore reflect exactly the same wavelengths of light, the X on the top looks yellow, but the one on the bottom looks grey or violet. (Convince yourself that these two X's are, in fact, printed from the same ink, by looking at the place where they meet.)

Repeat your observations on the red, blue, and yellow squares in Color Plate 1.3 and notice

The above observations, all of which demonstrate a linkage between red and green and between blue and yellow, led Hering to propose that red and green are paired and that blue and yellow are paired. He also observed that people who are color-blind to red are also blind to green, and people who can't see blue also can't see yellow.

This pairing of blue and yellow and of red and green led Hering to propose the **opponent-process theory of color vision** in 1878 (Hering, 1878/1964; Hering, 1905/1964). The basic idea underlying

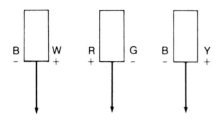

F I G U R E 4. 14   The three opponent mechanisms proposed by Hering.

Hering's theory is shown in Figure 4.14. He proposed three mechanisms, each of which responds in opposite ways to different intensities or wavelengths of light. The Black (−)-White (+) mechanism responds positively to white light and negatively to the absence of light. Red (+)-Green (−) responds positively to red and negatively to green, and Blue (−)-Yellow (+) responds negatively to blue and positively to yellow. According to Hering, these positive and negative responses represent the buildup and breakdown of chemicals in the retina: White, yellow, and red cause a reaction that results in a buildup of the chemical; black, blue, and green cause a reaction that results in a breakdown of the chemical.

Quantitative Measurements of Opponency

The psychophysical evidence on which Hering based opponent-process theory is *qualitative* in nature since there are no numbers associated with observations like "looking at green causes a red afterimage." But 75 years after Hering proposed his theory, Leo Hurvich and Dorthea Jameson (1957) put the psychophysics of opponent-process theory on firm quantitative ground by determining the strengths of the blue, yellow, red, and green components of the blue-yellow and red-green mechanisms for wavelengths across the visible spectrum.

Let's first consider how Hurvich and Jameson determined the strength of the blue mechanism, beginning at 430 nm. The blue mechanism obviously has substantial strength at 430 nm because a 430 nm light looks violet (reddish blue). But how can we put a number on the amount of "blueness" in a

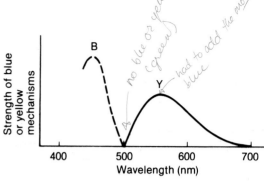

F I G U R E 4. 15   Strength of the blue and yellow mechanisms across the spectrum. Note that at no wavelength do blue and yellow occur together, and that, at 500 nm, the strengths of both mechanisms are zero, indicating that a 500 nm light (which appears green) contains no traces of blue or yellow. (From Hurvich & Jameson, 1957.)

430 nm light? Hurvich and Jameson reasoned that since yellow is the opposite of blue and therefore cancels it, they could determine the amount of blueness in a 430 nm light by adding yellow light until it canceled all perception of blueness. When they did this, adding more and more yellow to the 430 nm light, the violet became increasingly desaturated and eventually lost all of its blueness. After measuring how much yellow it took to eliminate all blueness at 430 nm, Hurvich and Jameson made similar measurements at other wavelengths and obtained the dashed curve in Figure 4.15, which shows that the strength of the blue mechanism reaches a maximum at 440 nm and then decreases, until at 500 nm its strength is zero. This means that 500 nm light, which looks green, does not appear blue at all. (See the spectrum in Color Plate 1.1.)

We determine the strength of the yellow mechanism by increasing the wavelength above 500 nm. When we do this, we start to see yellows: a yellowish-green, a greenish yellow, a bright yellow, and then a reddish yellow. To measure the amount of yellowness above 500 nm, Hurvich and Jameson added blue to these wavelengths until it eliminated all perception of yellowness. The result is the solid curve in Figure 4.15. The yellow mechanism responds to lights between 500 and 700 nm, with its maximum response at about 550 nm.

Figure 4.16 shows the results of similar exper-

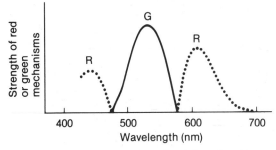

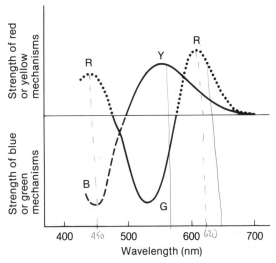

F I G U R E 4. 16 Strength of the red and green mechanisms across the spectrum. Note that at no wavelength do red and green occur together and at 475 nm and 580 nm the strengths of both the red and green mechanisms are zero, indicating that neither a 475 nm light (which appears blue) nor a 580 nm light (which appears yellow) contains any traces of red or green. (From Hurvich & Jameson, 1957.)

iments in which Hurvich and Jameson measured the strengths of the red and green mechanisms. For the red mechanism, they determined how much green light was needed to cancel the perception of redness at each wavelength, and for the green mechanism, they determined how much red light was needed to cancel the perception of greenness at each wavelength. The results for the red mechanism (the dotted curve), which show considerable strength not only at long wavelengths (where we would expect it), but also at short wavelengths, far from the red end of the spectrum, might seem surprising. The red mechanism's strength at short wavelengths becomes less surprising, however, if we remember that short-wavelength light looks violet (the color at about 10 o'clock on the color circle of Color Plate 4.1), which is a reddish blue. The curve for the green mechanism (the solid line in Figure 4.16) indicates that this mechanism responds to wavelengths between about 490 nm and 580 nm, with its maximum response at about 525 nm.

Figure 4.17 plots the results of Figures 4.15 and 4.16 on the same graph. In this figure, the blue and green curves have been inverted to emphasize the fact that blue (plotted as negative in the figure) opposes yellow (plotted as positive) and that green (negative) opposes red (positive).

F I G U R E 4. 17 The curves of Figures 4.15 and 4.16 plotted together, with the blue and green curves inverted to indicate the opponent nature of the blue-yellow and red-green pairs. (From Hurvich & Jameson, 1957.)

These curves could just as well be reversed, with blue and green positive and red and yellow negative.

We can use the curves in Figure 4.17 to determine the amount of each color present at any wavelength in the spectrum. For example, these curves show that at 450 nm both the blue and red mechanisms are activated and at 620 nm both the red and yellow mechanisms are activated.

We can also use these curves to explain how colors mix to form other colors. For example, consider red plus green. According to the opponent curves, a green light of, say, 560 nm activates the green and yellow mechanisms and a red light of, say, 630 nm activates the red and yellow mechanisms. As shown in Figure 4.18, the result of these activations is a canceling of the red and green responses, leaving only the yellow response—hence our perception of yellow. Remember that according to trichromatic theory, mixing green and red results in yellow because this combination equally stimulates the middle- and long-wave receptors to signal yellow, as indicated in Figure 4.9.

We have seen that the opponent-process and trichromatic mechanisms were proposed based on

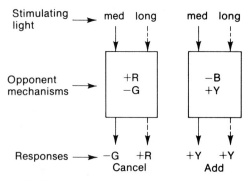

F I G U R E   4. 18   How opponent process theory would explain the fact that green plus red lights are perceived as yellow when superimposed. Left: The +R−G mechanism responds to green (medium-wavelength) and red (long-wavelength) light by generating a (−) response to the green and a (+) response to the red. These opposing responses cancel, leaving no response. Right: The −B+Y mechanism responds to both the medium- and long-wavelength lights by activating the Y part of the −B+Y mechanism. Since this yellow response is the only response generated by the opponent mechanisms, we see yellow.

psychophysical observations made in the 1800s. We are now going to move ahead to the 1950s and 1960s to look at physiological research that supports these theories and shows that color vision is based on the simultaneous operation of both the trichromatic and opponent mechanisms.

PHYSIOLOGICAL RESEARCH ON COLOR PERCEPTION

Let's first consider the physiological evidence for trichromatic theory.

Receptors, Pigments, and the Trichromatic Hypothesis

The central hypothesis of trichromatic theory, that there are three receptor mechanisms with different spectral sensitivities, was confirmed physiologically when the absorption spectra of human cone pigments were measured using the technique of microspectrophotometry (see page 83) (Brown &

Wald, 1964). Microspectrophotometry, which enabled researchers to measure the absorption spectra of visual pigments inside single cone receptors, showed that there are three types of cone receptors—a short-wave receptor, which absorbs light best at 419 nm, a medium-wave receptor, which absorbs best at 531 nm, and a long-wave receptor which absorbs best at 558 nm (Dartnall, Bowmaker, & Mollon, 1983).

Once the absorption spectra of these three cone types was determined, researchers found that the three types of cones differ in both their relative numbers and in their distribution in the retina. The baboon retina which, like the human retina, has three types of cones, contains 54 percent medium-wave cones, 38 percent long-wave cones, and 13 percent short-wave cones (Marc & Sperling, 1977). Of particular interest is the relatively small proportion of short-wave cones in the fovea, with these cones accounting for just 3–4 percent of the foveal receptors. This lower proportion of short-wave cones has a number of perceptual consequences, as described in Box 4.3.

Opponent Cells in the Retina and LGN

Although Hering's opponent-process theory was supported by numerous psychophysical observations, only recently has it been taken as seriously as trichromatic theory. One reason for its slow acceptance was that people couldn't imagine a physiological process that could result in either the buildup or the breakdown of a chemical substance. This poor acceptance of opponent-process theory is illustrated by the amount of coverage given the theory in Yves LeGrand's 1957 book *Light, Color and Vision*, a standard reference on vision. Though 25 pages are devoted to trichromatic theory, opponent-process theory is dealt with in less than a page.

It wasn't until solid physiological evidence became available that opponent-process theory began to gain equal footing with trichromatic theory. This evidence took the form not of chemicals that were either broken down or built up by different wavelengths, as Hering proposed, but by electrical signals that respond in opposite ways to

---

BOX 4. 3 / *What's Special about Blue?*

Short-wave cones (S-cones), which absorb light best in the area of the spectrum that appears blue, are in a distinct minority compared to the medium- and long-wave cones (M-cones and L-cones). The scarcity of the S-cones has a number of consequences for our perception of blue. One consequence of the fact that the S-cones are only 3–4 percent of the foveal receptors in the fovea is that a small patch of color that may look bluish-green when viewed off to the side loses its blueness when viewed within the fovea.

The small number of S-cones also affects visual acuity for blue. Remember that one reason cone acuity is better than rod acuity is that the close packing of the foveal cones creates the fine "grain" that is necessary to achieve sharp vision. This fine grain does not exist, however, for the relatively scarce S-cones and this results in low acuity for short-wavelength targets (Pokorney, Graham, & Lanson, 1968; Green, 1968).

If we move outside the fovea, we find that there are fewer S-cones than M- or L-cones in the peripheral retina also. This is illustrated in Color Plate 3.1, a picture of the mosaic of retinal receptors that shows the rods (small circles), M- and L-cones (large dark circles), and S-cones (large yellow circles) in a monkey's peripheral retina. The yellow marking that distinguishes the

S-cones from the M- and L-cones is caused by a fluorescent dye called Procion yellow which, when injected into the eye, fills the S-cones but not the others. F. de Monesterio, S. J. Scheir, and E. McCrane (1981), who took these pictures, hypothesize that the dye fills only the S-cones because these cones have more fragile membranes than the M- or L-cones.

Recent genetic research has uncovered yet another difference between the S-cones and the M- and L-cones. Jeremy Nathans, Darcy Thomas, and David Hogness (1986) have succeeded in isolating the genes that program the formation of both the rod and cone visual pigment molecules. Their results show that the genes for the M and L pigments are very similar to one another and are different from the gene for the S pigment and the gene for the rod pigment. This discovery led Nathans to conclude that the gene for the S-cone pigment and the rod pigment each evolved early, whereas the M and L pigments evolved much later from a common ancestor.

Our perception of blue, therefore, is served by short-wavelength receptors that are not only much rarer than the medium- and long-wavelength receptors but are also descended from an earlier and different genetic ancestor.

---

different wavelengths. The first evidence of this kind was provided by Gunnar Svaetichin (1956), who recorded a slow electrical response from cells in the fish retina. This electrical response, which he called the **S-potential,** had a property that supported the opponent-process theory: The S-potentials of many cells responded positively to light at one end of the spectrum and negatively to light at the other end of the spectrum. This is illustrated by the responses in Figure 4.19. The top record is

for a "red-green" cell that responds negatively at short wavelengths and positively at long wavelengths. The bottom record is for a "blue-yellow" cell that responds positively at short wavelengths and negatively at long wavelengths. Svaetichin also recorded red-green and blue-yellow cells in which the response direction was reversed from those shown here, while maintaining the opposing nature of the short- and long-wavelength responses.

A few years after Svaetichin's discovery of

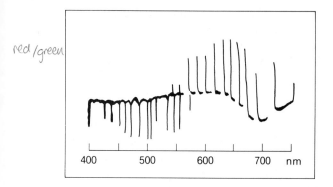

red/green

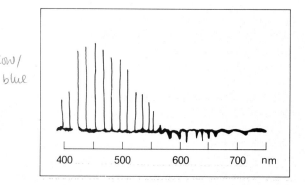

yellow/
blue

FIGURE 4. 19 S-potentials recorded from the fish retina. The vertical lines are the responses generated by test flashes; wavelengths are indicated on the horizontal scale. (From Svaetichin, 1956.)

opposing S-potentials, Russell DeValois (1960) showed that cells in the monkey's lateral geniculate nucleus (LGN) also have opponent properties. He found that certain cells in the LGN respond to light at one end of the spectrum with an increase in nerve firing, and to light at the other end of the spectrum with an inhibition of spontaneous activity. The firing of four such cells is shown in Figure 4.20. For each cell, spontaneous activity is indicated in the top record, and the responses to 450 nm (blue), 510 nm (green), 580 nm (yellow), and 660 nm (red) lights are shown in the other records. The B + Y − cell responds to the 450 nm light with an increase in firing and to the 580 nm light with an inhibition of spontaneous activity. The G + R − cell increases its firing to the 510 nm light and decreases its firing to the 660 nm light. The Y + B − and R + G − cells also show opponent responses, but they are inhibited by short wavelengths and are excited by long wavelengths. This demonstration of opponent properties in the LGN shows that the information in the slow retinal S-potentials is translated into the single-unit activity that is transmitted toward the brain.

The results of Svaetichin's and DeValois' experiments made believers out of researchers who had doubted the physiological reality of opponent-process theory, and opened the way for other

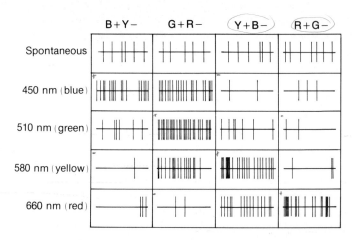

FIGURE 4. 20 Responses of opponent cells in the monkey's lateral geniculate nucleus. These cells respond in opposite ways to blue and yellow (B + Y − or Y + B −) or red and green (G + R − or R + G −). (From DeValois & Jacobs, 1968.)

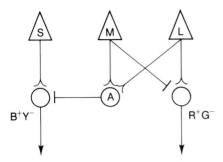

FIGURE 4.21 Neural circuit showing how the B–Y and R–G mechanisms can be created by excitatory and inhibitory inputs from the three cone receptors. See text for details.

researchers to determine the detailed properties of these **opponent cells.** Subsequent research has uncovered a number of different types of opponent cells (Derrington et al., 1983; DeValois & Jacobs, 1984), with most of these cells having one thing in common: They are excited by wavelengths at one end of the spectrum and inhibited by wavelengths at the other end of the spectrum.

The existence of these opponent cells raises two questions: (1) How are these cells created by neural processing? and (2) Why are these cells necessary for color vision? We will consider each of these questions in turn.

Figure 4.21 shows a neural circuit that creates opponent cells from the signals generated by the three types of cone receptors. To understand this circuit, let's first focus on the R+G− cell. This cell receives inhibitory input from the M cone and excitatory input from the L cone. Thus, light in the middle of the spectrum, which preferentially stimulates the M cone, will cause an inhibitory response in this cell. Similarly, light at the long-wave end of the spectrum, which preferentially stimulates the L cone, will cause an excitatory response in this cell. A R+G− cell, therefore, is constructed from opposing inputs from the M and L cones.

The B+Y− cell is slightly more complex because it receives an excitatory input from the S cone and an inhibitory input from cell A, which sums the inputs from the M and L cones. This arrangement makes sense if we remember that we

perceive yellow when both the M and L receptors are stimulated (p. 119). Thus, cell A, which receives inputs from both of these receptors, causes the "yellow" response of the B+Y− mechanism.

Although this diagram is greatly simplified, it illustrates the basic principles of the neural circuitry for color coding in the retina. The unique thing about this circuit compared to others we have considered up till now, is that its response is determined not only by the arrangement of inhibitory and excitatory synapses but also by the properties of the receptors that send signals to these synapses. We can think of the processing in this circuit as taking place in two stages: first, in the receptors, which respond with different patterns to different wavelengths, and then at the synapses, which process the signals received from the receptors.

Having described the circuit responsible for the opponent neurons, let's now consider our second question: Why are these neurons necessary? Doesn't the pattern of firing of the three cone receptors contain adequate information to signal which wavelength has been presented? The answer is yes. However let's consider what an opponent cell does with this information by looking at the opponent R+G− cell in Figure 4.21.

The R+G− opponent cell takes the *difference between* the responses of the L and M receptors by subtracting the inhibitory signal of the M receptor from the excitatory signal of the L receptor. When it does this, the M and L receptor responses shown in the upper left panel of Figure 4.22 are transformed into the opponent response of the R+G− cell shown in the lower left panel of the figure.

What does taking this difference accomplish? Let's look at how the receptors and the opponent cell respond to two nearby wavelengths, labeled 1 and 2 in Figure 4.22. The top right panel, which shows how the M and L receptors respond to those two wavelengths, indicates that there is information in these responses to signal the difference between wavelengths 1 and 2. When wavelength 1 is presented, receptor M responds more than receptor L, and when wavelength 2 is presented receptor L responds more than receptor M. The lower right panel of the figure shows how the oppo-

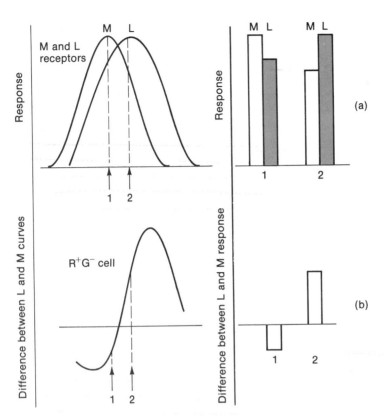

FIGURE 4.22 (a) Left: response curves for the M and L receptors. Right: bar graph indicating the size of the responses generated in the receptors by wavelengths 1 (left pair of bars) and 2 (right pair).
(b) Left: response of an R+G− cell that receives excitatory input from the L receptor and inhibitory input from the M receptor. Right: bar graph showing the opponent response of the R+G− cell to wavelengths 1 and 2. The response to 1 is inhibitory and the response to 2 is excitatory.

nent cell responds to the two wavelengths. The R+G− cell is inhibited by wavelength 1 and is excited by wavelength 2.

To compare these two ways of responding to wavelengths 1 and 2, ask yourself this question while looking at Figure 4.22: "Which information is simpler—the receptor information in the upper right panel, or the opponent information in the lower right panel?" Clearly, the opponent information in the lower panel is simpler, and this simplicity makes it easier to tell the difference between the neural responses generated by each of the wavelengths. One of the functions of opponent neurons is, therefore, to transform the neural information generated by the receptors into a simpler form that potentially enhances the visual system's ability to distinguish between different wavelengths.

Neural Processing and Perceptual Experience

Our next step in describing the physiology of color vision is to look at how color is coded in the cortex.

But before we do this, let's stop for a moment to consider our fourth principle, that *perception is shaped by neural processing.* We have seen that perceptual experience is both trichromatic (as measured by color-mixing experiments) and opponent (as observed phenomenologically). The idea that these different types of color experience are related to different physiological mechanisms is shown in Figure 4.23. At the beginning of the visual system, the receptor's properties determine our ability to match colors by mixing wavelengths. Later in the system, the properties of the opponent cells determine experiences such as the perception of after-images and simultaneous contrast. Thus, we do not have to deal with the problem facing early color vision researchers who had to choose between the competing trichromatic and opponent-process theories (with most choosing trichromatic theory). We now know that both the trichromatic and opponent mechanisms shape our perceptions. One operates at the receptors, the other at neurons further downstream, but *both* determine our experience of seeing color.

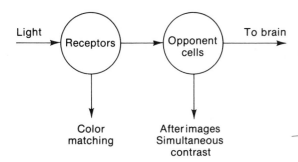

Light → Receptors → Opponent cells → To brain

Receptors → Color matching

Opponent cells → Afterimages Simultaneous contrast

F I G U R E 4. 23 Our experience of color vision is shaped by physiological mechanisms both in the receptors and in the opponent neurons. The existence of three different cone receptors is responsible for the fact that we need a minimum of three wavelengths to match any wavelength in the spectrum. The opponent cells are responsible for perceptual experiences such as afterimages and simultaneous contrast. Note that although the activity in the receptors and other neurons early in the visual system may shape our perception of color, color perception doesn't actually occur until the signals from these early neurons reach the brain.

We now continue our description of the opponent mechanisms by looking at how neurons in the visual cortex respond to different wavelengths of light.

Color Coding in the Striate Cortex Area 17

Most cells in the striate cortex—the primary visual receiving area—have opponent properties like those observed in cells in the LGN. Research on cortical cells has focused not only on how these cells respond to different wavelengths but also on (1) how these responses depend on stimulation of different areas of a cell's receptive field and (2) how cells responsive to color are organized in the cortex.

Many different types of opponent cells have been found in the striate cortex (see DeValois &

Jacobs, 1984; Michael, 1983; Zeki, 1977). We will focus on one type—the **double color-opponent cells**—both because they are common and because of their potential role in perception. The response of a double-opponent cell recorded from layer IVc of the monkey's cortex is shown in Figure 4.24 (Michael, 1978). (Remember from Chapter 3 that layer IVc contains center-surround cells that receive inputs from the lateral geniculate nucleus.) Reading down from the top of this figure, we see that this cell responds to stimulation of the center of its center-surround receptive field with a burst of firing to a red spot (a), and with an off response to a green spot (b). Thus the center of this cell's receptive field has an R + G − opponent response. If we now stimulate the receptive field's surround, we get an off response to red (c) and an on response to green (d), so the surround has an R − G + opponent response. Since the cell responds in an opponent fashion, but in opposite ways depending on whether the center or surround is stimulated, it is called a double color-opponent cell.

These double color-opponent cells are particularly significant, because they may play a role in the perception of simultaneous contrast. We can understand why this is so by considering how this cell responds to different stimuli. A situation in which there is no contrast, such as a small red disc on a red background, results in little or no response, since the response of the excitatory center (R +) is canceled by the response of the inhibitory surround (R −). Similarly, little or no response occurs to a green disc on a green background. However, a situation in which there is considerable contrast, such as a red disc on a green background, will cause this cell to fire vigorously, as shown in Figure 4.25, since the excitatory response of the surround (G +) adds to the excitatory response of the center (R +). Perceptually, surrounding red with green creates a large simultaneous contrast effect, causing the red to become much brighter and more saturated than if it were not surrounded by the green.

Margaret Livingstone and David Hubel (1984) have observed that these types of double-opponent cells (R + G − center/R − G + surround) are by far the most common types of color cells in the monkey, and they suggest that there may be a functional reason for this. Monkeys, in their natural habitat,

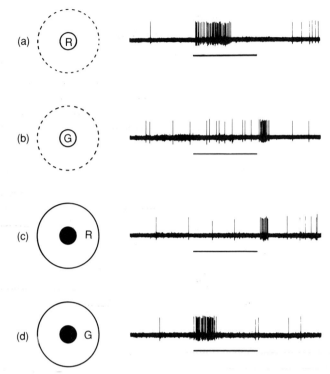

F I G U R E 4. 24 Response of a double-opponent cell in the monkey's cortex. This cell's center responds (a) with an increase in firing to red and (b) with an off response to green. The surround responds (c) with an off response to red and (d) with an increase in firing to green. (From Michael, 1978.)

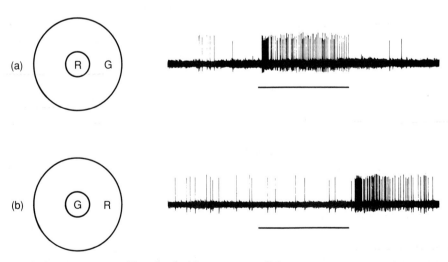

F I G U R E 4. 25 How the double-opponent cell from Figure 4.24 responds to simultaneous contrast. This cell responds with a large response (a) to red in the center and green in the surround or (b) to green in the center and red in the surround, but responds little when the entire receptive field is covered with red or with green. (From Michael, 1978.)

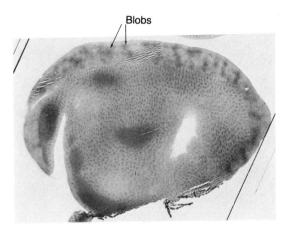
Blobs

FIGURE 4.26 Cross-section of the monkey's visual cortex, showing the blobs (dark areas). These blobs contain cells that respond to color but not to orientaton.

need to perceive brightly colored fruit, usually red or orange in color, on a green leafy background, exactly the kind of stimulus that elicits the maximum response from this type of double-opponent cell.

Livingstone and Hubel have also observed that these color-opponent cells are concentrated in areas they call **blobs,** so called because these areas show up as blob-like shapes when the cortex is treated with a special stain (Figure 4.26). These blobs, which appear to receive inputs from the opponent cells in layer IVc (Michael, 1986, 1987), contain cells that respond to colors but that do not respond to orientation, as do most other cells in the visual cortex. This segregation of color-sensitive cells within the blobs and orientation-sensitive cells outside the blobs has led Livingstone and Hubel to suggest that there are two parallel pathways in the visual cortex—blob pathways which are important for perceiving color, and nonblob pathways which are important for perceiving orientation and form. The idea that different functions are processed in separate pathways is one we will encounter again in Chapter 6 when we see that information for an object's location and identity is processed in separate pathways. (See Box 6.2 and Livingstone & Hubel, 1988.)

COLOR DEFICIENCY

Now that we have seen how color information is processed by the visual system, let's consider what happens when this processing is affected by a change in the physiology of the system. We will begin by describing the results of color-matching experiments on color-deficient people and will then consider the physiological mechanisms responsible for these results. The color-matching experiments that led to trichromatic theory showed that we can match any wavelength in the spectrum by mixing a minimum of three other wavelengths in appropriate proportions. We call a person who needs three wavelengths to match any other wavelength in the spectrum a **trichromat.** One difference between trichromats and people who are color deficient is the number of wavelengths they need to match any other wavelength in the spectrum. A **monochromat** can do this matching by adjusting the intensity of any other wavelength. Thus, a monochromat needs only one wavelength to match any color in the spectrum. A **dichromat** can match any wavelength by mixing two other wavelengths. Finally, an **anomalous trichromat** needs to mix three wavelengths to match any other, just as a normal trichromat does, but mixes these wavelengths in different proportions than a trichromat and is not as good at discriminating between wavelengths that are close together.

The results of these color-matching measurements provide an objective way of distinguishing between people with different types of color vision. But after distinguishing between these people based on their ability to match colors, we are still left with the question: What colors do they see? Remembering our discussion from the beginning of the chapter about color perception being a private experience, you know that one way *not* to answer this question would be to ask color-deficient observers what color they perceive at each wavelength across the spectrum. Just because a dichromat can say "this appears blue" does not necessarily mean that his or her experience is the same as a trichromat's experience of "blue."

How, then, can we tell what colors dichromats perceive? One way would be to locate a person with trichromatic vision in one eye and dichromatic vision in the other eye. Since both eyes are connected to the same brain, it would be possible for this person to look at a color with the dichromatic eye and then determine which color it corresponds to in the trichromatic eye. Luckily, such people do exist. They are called **unilateral dichromats** since they are dichromatic in just one eye. Although they are extremely rare, the few unilateral dichromats who have been tested have helped us determine the nature of a dichromat's color experience (Graham, Sperling, Hsia, & Coulson, 1961; Sloan & Wollach, 1948). Let's now look at the nature of this experience for monochromats and dichromats.

Monochromatism

This rare form of color blindness is usually hereditary and occurs in only about 10 people out of a million (LeGrand, 1957). Monochromats usually lack a functioning cone system; therefore, their vision has the characteristics of rod vision in both dim *and* bright lights. Monochromats see everything in shades of lightness (white, grey, and black) and can, therefore, be called color-*blind* (as opposed to dichromats, who see some chromatic colors and are therefore called color *deficient*).

In addition to a loss of color vision, monochromats have poor visual acuity and are so sensitive to bright lights that they often must protect their eyes with dark glasses during the day. The reason for this sensitivity to intense lights is that when rods, which are not designed to function in bright light, are the only functioning receptors, they become overloaded in strong illumination and cause a perception of glare.

Dichromatism

Dichromats experience some colors, though a lesser range than trichromats. There are three major forms of dichromatism—protanopia, deuteranopia, and tritanopia—all of which are hereditary and sex linked. We say that they are sex linked because

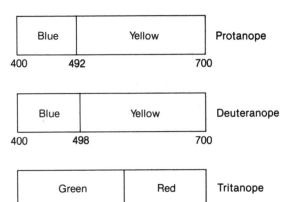

F I G U R E 4. 27   The color perceptions of the three kinds of dichromats. The number under the dividing line indicates the wavelength of the neutral point, the wavelength at which grey is perceived.

women can carry the gene for color deficiency without being color deficient themselves, and they pass the condition to their male offspring. Thus, as we will see below, many more men than women are dichromats.

Protanopia. **Protanopia,** which affects 1 percent of males and 0.02 percent of females, results in the perception of colors across the spectrum indicated in Figure 4.27. A protanope perceives short-wavelength light as blue, and as wavelength is increased the blue becomes less and less saturated until, at 492 nm, the protanope perceives grey. The wavelength at which the protanope perceives grey is called the **neutral point.** At wavelengths above the neutral point, the protanope perceives yellow, which becomes increasingly saturated as wavelength is increased, until at the long-wavelength end of the spectrum the protanope perceives a saturated yellow.

Deuteranopia. **Deuteranopia,** which affects about 1 percent of males and 0.01 percent of females, results in the perception of colors across the spectrum as shown in Figure 4.27. A deuteranope perceives blue at short wavelengths, yellow at long wavelengths, and has a neutral point at about 498 nm (Boynton, 1979).

Tritanopia. Tritanopia is very rare, affecting only about 0.002 percent of males and 0.001 percent of females. As indicated in Figure 4.27, a tritanope sees green at short wavelengths, red at long wavelengths, and has a neutral point at 570 nm (Boynton, 1972).

Physiological Mechanisms

What are the physiological mechanisms for color deficiency and color blindness? Most monochromats are color-blind because they have just one type of cone or no cones. Dichromats are color deficient because they are missing a visual pigment. William Rushton (1964), using his retinal densitometry technique (described in Chapter 3) to measure the visual pigments in protanopes and deuteranopes, found that the protanope is missing the long-wavelength cone pigment and the deuteranope is missing the medium-wavelength cone pigment. It has been difficult to measure the visual pigments of the tritanope, both because of the tritanope's rarity and because of the low concentration of the short-wavelength pigment, even in normal retinas, but it appears that the tritanope is missing the short-wavelength pigment.

That each form of color blindness corresponds to a missing visual pigment is consistent with trichromatic theory. Trichromatic theory would predict that a person with only two pigments would need only two wavelengths to match any other wavelength, which is, in fact, the case; however, other aspects of color blindness are consistent with opponent-process theory. First, the colors perceived by color-deficient observers correspond to the blue-yellow and red-green pairs of opponent-process theory (remember, this was one of the observations that led Hering to propose the theory). Second, if we compare the neutral points in Figure 4.27 to Hurvich and Jameson's psychophysical functions for trichromatic observers in Figure 4.17, we see that the neutral points for the deu-

teranope and protanope fall near 500 nm, the wavelength at which the strength of the blue-yellow mechanism is zero. We would predict this location of the neutral point if deuteranopes and protanopes are missing their red-green mechanism, since seeing with only the blue-yellow mechanism would result in no perception of color at 500 nm. Similarly, the neutral point for the tritanope falls near 580 nm, the wavelength at which the strength of the red-green mechanism is zero. Thus, if tritanopes are missing their blue-yellow mechanism, we would expect them to perceive grey at 580 nm.

COLOR VISION IN ANIMALS

Since color is a private experience, and we have no way of knowing for certain what other *peoples'* experience of color is like, it is unreasonable to expect that we can know what other *species'* experience of color is like. We can, however, show that some animals, such as fish, birds, and some monkeys, do have good color vision, and that other animals are either monochromats or dichromats.

How can we tell which animals have color vision and which don't? One way to tell is on the basis of an animal's normal behavior (Tansley, 1965). If color is a feature of one sex or is used in a species' mating or threat displays, it is likely that members of the species can perceive these colors. For example, that a territory-holding male robin attacks an intruder because of its red breast suggests that the robin has color vision. Similarly, it seems likely that peacocks have color vision, so the female can perceive the male's colorful plumage.

Another way to determine if an animal has color vision is to train it to respond to one hue and not to another. However, in these experiments it is important to be sure the animal is not making its judgments based on the fact that one light appears brighter than the other. Unfortunately, many experiments that claim to provide evidence for color vision in animals are simply demonstrations that the animal can discriminate between a bright light and a dim light. To ensure that brightness plays no role in making a discrimination, it is necessary to measure an animal's spectral sensitivity curve (see p. 10) and, based on this curve, to adjust stimuli of different wavelengths so they will appear equally bright to the animal. Using procedures such as this, it has been shown that the pigeon and chicken probably have trichromatic vision (Lashley, 1916; Hamilton & Coleman, 1933).

Another way to approach the question of whether an animal sees colors is to consider its physiology. If an animal has only one visual pigment, color vision is unlikely. If an animal has more than one visual pigment, this suggests, but does not guarantee, that color vision is present. The only way to prove that an animal has color vision is by testing the animal's behavioral response to different wavelengths, as described above.

A good example of a case in which both physiological and behavioral evidence indicate the presence of color vision is the fish. The fish has three cone pigments (Marks, 1965; Tomita Kaneko, Murakami, & Paulter, 1967), its retina generates opponent S-potentials (Svaetichin, 1956; see Figure 4.19), and behavioral experiments indicate that goldfish have trichromatic vision (Yager & Thorpe, 1970).

Most mammals have either no color vision or minimal color vision. Though cats were originally thought to be color-blind (Tansley, 1965), recent behavioral and electrophysiological results indicate that they may be dichromats (Mello & Peterson, 1964; Sechzer & Brown, 1964; Meyer & Anderson, 1965; Pearlman & Daw, 1970). Another mammal that may be a dichromat is the squirrel (Tansley, 1965; Michael, 1969), but it appears that the dog lacks color vision.

Monkeys have the best color vision among nonhuman primates. New World monkeys such as the *Cebus* are dichromats (Grether, 1939), whereas the squirrel monkey has vision that corresponds to a human anomalous trichromat (DeValois & Jacobs, 1968). The color vision of the Old World rhesus monkey is excellent, being nearly identical to the human's. This is supported by psychophysical experiments and by microspectrophotometry, which has isolated three cone pigments similar to the human's (Marks, Dobelle, & MacNichol, 1964; DeValois & Jacobs, 1968). Thus, the human and

rhesus monkey possess the best color vision of the mammals, and we must look to birds and fish to find comparable color vision in other species.

COLOR CONSTANCY

Our Perception of Color Depends on More than Wavelength

Our discussion so far has focused on the idea that wavelength is the major determinant of color perception. Although this is true, it is not the whole story. We can appreciate this when we consider what happens when we observe objects that are illuminated with lights of different wavelength distributions. For example, we first observe an object that appears blue outside when illuminated by sunlight. When illuminated by sunlight, which contains approximately equal energy at all wavelengths (solid curve in Figure 4.2), the object reflects mainly short wavelengths into our eyes. We then take that object indoors and illuminate it with tungsten light. Since tungsten light contains much more energy at long than at short wavelengths (dashed curve in Figure 4.2), our object now reflects more long-wavelength light than it did when outside, but it still appears blue.

Dorthea Jameson (1985) has calculated that the wavelengths reflected from a blue color chip illuminated by tungsten light can match the wavelengths reflected by a yellow color chip illuminated by sunlight. But even though changing the illumination on a blue chip from the sunlight of outdoors to the tungsten illumination of indoors greatly increases the amount of long wavelengths reflected from it, we perceive little or no change in the color of the chip. As Jameson puts it, "A blue bird would not be mistaken for a goldfinch if it were brought indoors." (p. 84).

This relative constancy of perceived color under different conditions of illumination is called **color constancy,** a phenomenon you can demonstrate to yourself by looking at one of the color illustrations in this book, first under the light of a light bulb and then under the daylight illumination coming in through your window. The differences you perceive between these two conditions are slight, even though much more long-wavelength light is reflected from the picture when illuminated by tungsten light.

Color constancy, therefore, illustrates our fifth principle: *Perception can remain constant in the face of changing stimulation.* In the chapters that follow, we will see that this principle also applies to other visual qualities.

It is important to note, however, that although our perception of colors does not change as much as we might expect under different conditions of illumination, some changes do take place. On a recent visit to the art museum, I noticed that one of my favorite paintings had been moved from a location where it received mostly natural light to one where it received much more artificial light. Its colors had not changed so much that I could really say that the blues had become greener or the greens yellower, but the painting somehow looked different than it did before. In fact, experiments have shown that fluorescent lighting alters our perception of colors (Helson, Judd, & Wilson, 1956), and many people have found, unhappily, that their new clothes which looked exactly right in the fluorescently lit store, have changed to a different color at home (Hurvich, 1981).

That our color perception does change a little when we change the illumination indicates that we usually experience not total but *approximate* color constancy. Though only approximate, however, color constancy is still an impressive phenomenon. An object's color is determined primarily by its reflectance curve—the *percentage* of light reflected from the object at each wavelength (Figure 4.4)— not by the actual *amount* of light that reaches the observer's eye at each wavelength.

What Causes Color Constancy?

Why does color constancy occur? A number of factors, including chromatic adaptation, the presence of the surroundings, and the observer's knowledge of the usual colors of objects, apparently work together to achieve this effect. Let's consider each of these factors.

Chromatic Adaptation. One of the most powerful mechanisms responsible for color constancy is chromatic adaptation, an effect you can experience for yourself.

DEMONSTRATION

Adapting to Red

Illuminate the red field of Color Plate 1.2 with a bright light from your desk lamp; then, with your left eye close to the page and your right eye closed, look at the field with your left eye for about 30–45 seconds. At the end of this time, look up and around, first with your left eye and then with your right. When you do this, all of the reds and oranges viewed with the left eye will look less saturated and less bright than those viewed with the right eye. You have changed your color perception by means of **chromatic adaptation.** Adaptation to the red light selectively affects your long-wavelength cone pigment, which decreases your sensitivity to red light.

We can understand how chromatic adaptation may contribute to color constancy by considering what happens when you walk into a room illuminated with tungsten light. The eye adapts to the long wavelengths which predominate in the tungsten light, and this chromatic adaptation decreases your eye's sensitivity to long wavelengths. This decreased sensitivity causes objects that normally appear yellow or red to appear less bright, thus compensating for the greater amount of long wavelength light in the room. The result is a negligible change in your perception of color.

If the above explanation of color constancy is valid, then the light in our tungsten-illuminated room should appear yellower if we do not adapt to it. You can test this idea by standing outside at night and observing the window of an illuminated room from a distance. Since you are not standing in the room, you are not adapted to its light; therefore, the light you see through the window looks yellower than when seen from inside the room.

Another way to look at the role of chromatic adaptation in color constancy is to ask how illumination would affect color perception if our eyes could *not* chromatically adapt. Let's consider how color film, which cannot adapt, reproduces colors under different illuminations. Color Plate 4.3 is a photograph of a desk illuminated by sunlight shining through a window. The colors in this photograph correspond to those you would see if you were standing in the room, because the desk was photographed with "daylight" film, which is designed to give correct color reproduction in daylight illumination. If, however, we wait until dark and then turn on our tungsten desk lamp, we get the photograph in Color Plate 4.4. The reddish color of the picture occurs because daylight film correctly reproduces colors in illumination that contains an equal amount of light at each wavelength, but tungsten illumination contains much more long-wavelength than short-wavelength light. Unlike the eye, the outdoor film can't adapt to the extra long wavelengths in the tungsten light, so the picture looks red. The different appearance of Color Plates 4.3 and 4.4 represent what we might experience under changing illuminations if our perception lacked color constancy. •

The surroundings. Color constancy is also affected by an object's surroundings.

D E M O N S T R A T I O N

Masking the Surroundings

We can illustrate the effect of the surroundings on color constancy by a simple demonstration. Illuminate the green quadrant of Color Plate 1.3 with tungsten light; then look at it through a small hole punched in a piece of paper, so that all you see through the hole is part of the green area. Now repeat this observation while illuminating the same area with daylight from your window. With the

---

• To compensate for the absence of color constancy in film, we use different types of film for different illuminations. To photograph at night under tungsten illumination, we use "tungsten" film, which is designed to correctly reproduce color in tungsten light. If we photograph outdoors with tungsten film, our pictures will appear blue. This occurs because the tungsten film is designed for tungsten illumination, which contains much less short-wavelength than long-wavelength light. The blueness in our picture results from the added short wavelengths contained in daylight illumination.

surroundings masked, most people perceive the green area to be slightly yellower under the tungsten light than under daylight. Color constancy works less well when we mask off the surroundings, although the reason for this is complicated and not totally understood.

Memory color. **Memory color** refers to the fact that an object's characteristic color influences our perception of that object's color; for example, making the object we know as a ripe tomato appear redder. This idea is supported by the results of an experiment done by John Delk and Samuel Fillenbaum (1965). They showed observers shapes like the ones in Figure 4.28, all of which were cut from the same sheet of orange-red cardboard. Shapes such as the heart and apple were characteristically red, while others, such as the bell and mushroom, were not. The observer's task was to match the color of each object with that of a background field, by adjusting the amount of redness in the background field. The result, in agreement with the idea of memory color, was that characteristically red objects, such as the heart and apple, were matched with a redder background field than were nonred objects, such as the bell and mushroom.

Memory color also occurs in afterimages. Charles White and David Montgomery (1976) had subjects view a picture of either (1) an American flag that had black stars on an orange background and black stripes alternating with green stripes, or

F I G U R E 4. 28 Some of the stimuli used in Delk and Fillenbaum's (1965) experiment on memory color. Although all of the stimuli were cut from the same orange-red paper, the apple and heart were judged to appear slightly redder than the mushroom and bell.

Wavelength (nm)

400

500

600

700

C O L O R   P L A T E   1.1 The visible spectrum. See pages 10, 111, and 112.

C O L O R   P L A T E   1.2 Field for selective adaptation demonstration. See page 137.

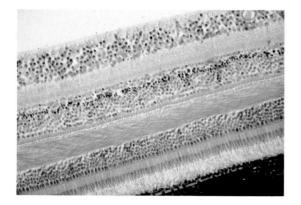

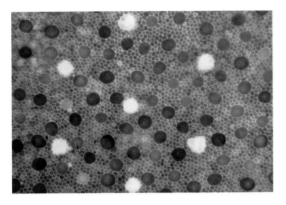

a

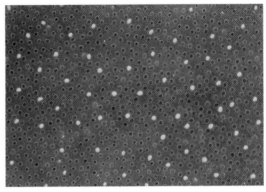

b

C O L O R P L A T E 3.1 (a and b) The "mosaic of receptors." Looking down on the rods and cones in an area of a monkey's peripheral retina. The more numerous small circles in (a) are the rods. The larger circles are the cones. The cones appear larger because the retina has been sliced across the receptor inner segments (see Figure 2.17), which are fatter in the cones than in the rods. A special dye which affects only the short-wavelength cones has stained them yellow. Note the regular repeating pattern of both the short-wavelength cones and the cones as a whole. The right picture shows a larger area of the same part of the retina. (Photographs from de Monasterio et al., 1981.)

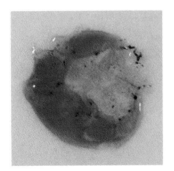
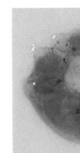
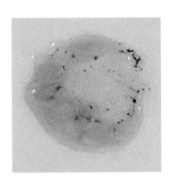

C O L O R P L A T E 3.2 How the color of a frog's retina changes as the visual pigment in the retina bleaches, as described on page 79. The left picture was taken immediately after the bleaching light was turned on, so little bleaching has occurred and the retina appears red. When the retina is placed on a flat surface, its edges bend over, causing a double layer of retina and a deeper red color around the edges. The black spots are small pieces of the pigment epithelium, the cell layer on which the retina rests when in the eye. The middle picture was taken after some bleaching so the retina is lighter red, and in the right picture, further bleaching results in a light orange appearance. When bleaching is completed, the orange fades and the retina becomes transparent. If this retina were still in the frog's eye, the transparent retina would regain its red color as the pigment regenerates in the dark; however, little regeneration occurs when the retina is dissected from the eye, as in these pictures.

retinal breaking away from opsin

COLOR PLATE 3.3
Red and blue flowers for the adaptation
demonstration described on page 82.

COLOR PLATE 4.1
The color circle. See pages 111–112.
From Hurvich (1981).

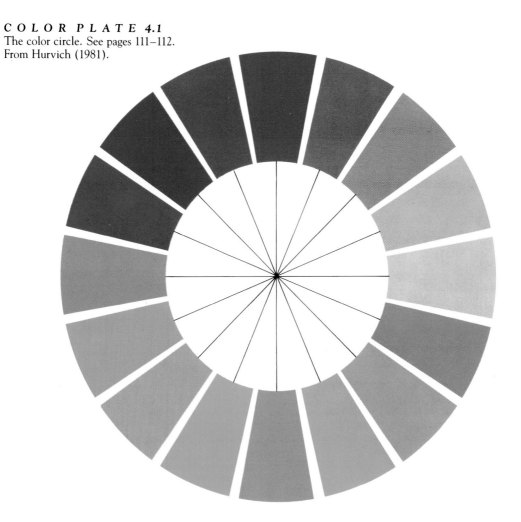

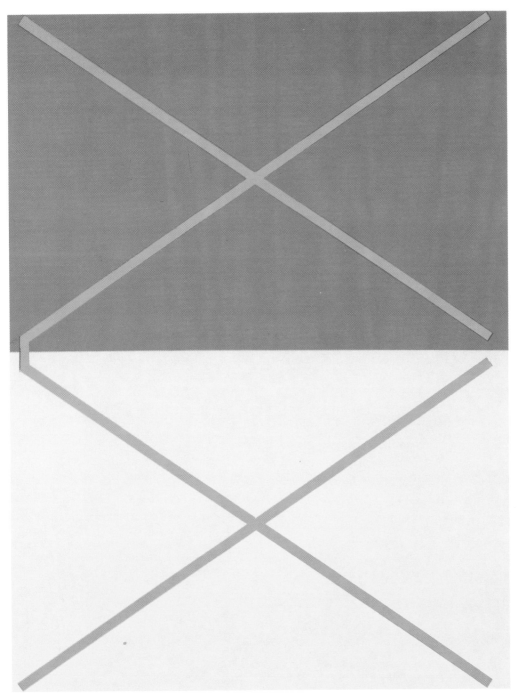

C O L O R   P L A T E   4.2   A simultaneous contrast demonstration by Joseph Albers (1975), an artist who often uses simultaneous contrast in his paintings. See page 123. Courtesy of Yale University Press.

C O L O R   P L A T E   4.3   A photograph taken with "daylight" film under daylight illumination provided by sunlight from a window on the left. The colors in this photograph correspond to an observer's perception of the scene. See page 138.

C O L O R   P L A T E   4.4   A photograph taken with "daylight" film under tungsten illumination provided by the desk lamp in the upper left of the photograph. The observer's perception of this scene is similar to that depicted in Color Plate 4.3 above, but since the film doesn't have color constancy, this photograph has an orange tint. See page 138.

C O L O R   P L A T E   5.1   It is difficult to tell from this photograph whether the branches sticking out are a lighter green than the other branches or if they are being illuminated by sunlight. See pages 183–184.

C O L O R   P L A T E   5.2   This branch reveals that the branches sticking out in Plate 5.1 are a lighter green than the rest of the branches.

C O L O R   P L A T E   5.3   The spreading effect described in Box 5.1 on page 153 (from Evans, 1948). Top: The red background is the same on the left and in the middle but appears different due to the "spreading effect" of the black and white lines. Bottom: The blue is physically the same all the way across but appears lighter in the middle due to the spreading effect.

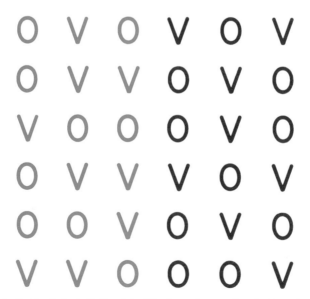

C O L O R   P L A T E   6.1   The boundary in this display, which is perceived immediately (it "pops out"), is caused by the difference in color on the two sides of the display. See page 214 for details.

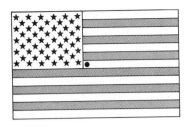

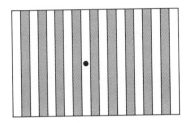

FIGURE 4. 29 Stimuli for White and Montgomery's (1976) experiment that showed that memory color occurs in afterimages. To generate red and white afterimages, observers viewed either the black and green striped American flag or the control pattern. See text for details.

(2) a picture of a control pattern of vertical black and green stripes (Figure 4.29). After viewing either the control pattern or the flag for 30 seconds, subjects saw an afterimage of either alternating red and white vertical stripes for the control pattern or the familiar red, white, and blue for the flag. The subject's task was to adjust a red test field to match the color of the red stripes in the afterimages. When they did this, they adjusted the test field to a redder red when the afterimage was generated by the stripes of the flag than when it was generated by the control stripes. Thus, our perception of the color of an afterimage can be affected by our prior knowledge of the object that the afterimage represents.

While memory color is a real effect, it is also a small one and plays only a minor role in color constancy, since objects without a characteristic color, such as a sweater or a piece of colored paper, also stay about the same color under changing illumination.

"THE RAYS ARE NOT COLOURED"

To end this chapter, let's consider the question, "What makes a tomato red?" This might at first seem like an easy question, because by taking into account what we know about color perception we might answer that a tomato looks red because it reflects long-wavelength light. And this answer is correct, as far as it goes. Long wavelengths *are* usually associated with "redness."

But let's push our question further by asking *why* long wavelengths look red? Why don't long wavelengths look blue? or green? Although specific colors are related to specific wavelengths, the connection between wavelength and the experience we call "color" is an arbitrary one. There is nothing intrinsically "red" about long wavelengths or "blue" about short wavelengths. In fact, the wavelengths that we perceive as having color are not themselves colored at all. Isaac Newton (1642–1727) made this observation in his book *Opticks*, when he said that

. . . .the Rays to speak properly are not coloured. In them there is nothing else than a certain Power and Disposition to stir up a Sensation of this or that Colour. . . . So Colours in the Object are nothing but a Disposition to reflect this or that sort of Rays more copiously than the rest. . . .

In other words, the colors that we see in response to different wavelengths are not *contained* in the wavelengths themselves but are *created* by our nervous system. The same can be said of other experiences, such as hearing, which is our response to pressure changes in the air. Why do we perceive rapid pressure changes as high pitched and slow changes as low pitched? Is there anything intrinsically "high pitched" about rapid pressure changes? Or consider the sense of smell. We perceive some substances as "sweet" and others as "rancid," but where is the "sweetness" or "rancidity" in the molecular structure of the substances that enter our nose? Again, the answer is that these perceptions are not in the molecular structure. They are created by our nervous system.

Our examples so far describe situations in which the nature of the experience elicited by a stimulus is arbitrary. There are, however, situations in which our experience is not arbitrary. Consider, for example, your perception of a penny and a quarter. The fact that we see both as round and the penny as smaller than the quarter is not arbitrary. We can determine the roundness or the size of the coins independently of our vision, by using a compass or a ruler, or with our sense of touch. In this situation we can compare our perception to the physical properties of the stimulus and can decide whether or not our perception is **veridical**—that is, whether it matches the actual physical stimulus. Thus, our perception of some qualities such as size, shape,

and depth can be tested against a physical object to determine whether or not it is veridical. However, other qualities, like color, pitch, taste, and smell, cannot be tested for veridicality. "Redness" cannot be measured with a physical measuring instrument because it is a creation of our visual system. In Newton's words, "The rays are not coloured."

The idea that color is a creation of our visual system adds another dimension to the idea that experience is shaped by physiology. What we are saying here is that experience is not only *shaped* by physiology but, in cases such as color vision, hearing, taste, and smell, the very *nature* of our experience is *created* by physiology.

Summary

1. The following principles are illustrated in this chapter:
   (a) Perception is a private experience.
   (b) We can explain perception at different levels.
   (c) Physiological mechanisms can be deduced from psychophysical observations.
   (d) Perception is shaped by neural processing.
   (e) Perception can remain constant in the face of changing stimulation.
2. It is difficult to define color without using examples, because the perception of color is a private experience.
3. There are chromatic colors (like red and blue) and achromatic colors (like white, grey, or black).
4. People with normal color vision may perceive colors differently from one another; however, since our perception of color is a private experience, it is impossible to tell whether or not this is so.
5. We can discriminate about 150 different steps between 380 and 700 nm. If we vary the intensity and the saturation of each step, we can discriminate over 7 million colors. One compilation lists over 7,500 different color names.
6. The color circle is based on four pure colors: red, yellow, green, and blue.
7. Our perception of color is closely linked to the wavelength of the light. The wavelengths that reach the eye are determined by the wavelength distributions of light sources such as the sun, light bulbs, and fluorescent lights, and by the reflectance curves of objects that reflect light from these sources.
8. Objects that selectively reflect some wavelengths but not others have chromatic color.

9. Observers with normal color vision can match any wavelength in a test field by mixing a minimum of three other wavelengths in various proportions. This finding led to the trichromatic, or Young-Helmholtz, theory of color vision, which states that color vision results from the action of three cone receptor mechanisms with different spectral sensitivities. Each color is signaled by a particular ratio of activity in the three receptor mechanisms.
10. Two lights that have different wavelength distributions but are perceptually identical are called metamers. Metamers look the same because they stimulate the short-, medium-, and long-wavelength receptors in the same ratios.
11. We need a minimum of two different receptor mechanisms to distinguish between different wavelengths and to perceive colors.
12. The idea that blue and yellow are opposites and red and green are opposites is supported by the fact that we can't see a bluish-yellow or a reddish-green and by the nature of simultaneous contrast, afterimages, and color blindness. These psychophysical observations led to the proposal of opponent-process theory, the idea that there are blue-yellow and red-green mechanisms in which blue and yellow have opposing properties and red and green have opposing properties.
13. Hurvich and Jameson's psychophysical measurements enable us to understand how opponent-process theory explains color mixing.
14. The three pigments of cone vision correspond to the three receptor mechanisms of trichromatic theory.
15. Opponent cells found in the retina and the lateral

geniculate nucleus provide physiological evidence for opponent-process theory.

16. Opponent cells transform the information from the receptors into a new form by taking the difference between the receptor responses. This step of neural processing sharpens the difference between responses generated by different wavelengths.

17. Color vision is best explained by a combination of trichromatic and opponent-process theories, with trichromatic theory explaining the operation of the receptors and opponent-process theory explaining the operation of neurons beyond the receptors.

18. Double color-opponent cells in the cortex provide a physiological explanation for color contrast. These cells are concentrated in areas called blobs. The double-opponent cells in these blobs respond to wavelength but not to orientation. This has led to the suggestion that there are two parallel pathways in the visual cortex—one for perceiving color and one for perceiving orientation.

19. Color-matching experiments indicate that there are three major kinds of color vision defects: anomalous trichromatism, dichromatism, and monochromatism.

20. There are three kinds of dichromats: protanopes, deuteranopes, and tritanopes. These dichromats are missing long-, medium-, and short-wavelength cones, respectively, and there is evidence that protanopes and deuteranopes are missing the red-green opponent mechanism and tritanopes are missing the blue-yellow mechanism.

21. Most animals are either monochromats or dichromats, although fish, birds, and some monkeys have trichromatic vision. Cats are probably dichromats and dogs appear to lack color vision.

22. Changing the illumination from sunlight to tungsten light causes little change in our perception of an object's color. This lack of color change with changing illumination is called color constancy. However, since our perception of color does change a little when we change the illumination, we usually experience not total but approximate color constancy.

23. Color constancy is caused by a combination of factors including chromatic adaptation, the presence of the surroundings, and memory color.

24. Although specific colors are related to specific wavelengths, the connection between wavelength and experience we call "color" is an arbitrary one, with the perception of color being a creation of our visual system. This is what Newton meant when he said that "The Rays . . . are not coloured."

Boxes

1. The sky appears blue because short wavelengths entering the atmosphere are scattered more than long wavelengths.

2. There are two ways of mixing colors. Mixing lights together results in additive color mixing, whereas mixing paints together results in subtractive color mixing.

3. The scarcity of the short-wavelength cones causes our acuity for blue to be low and causes a decrease in the perception of blue in the fovea. Recent genetic research shows that the gene that programs the formation of the short-wavelength pigment is descended from a different genetic ancestor than the genes for the formation of the medium- and long-wavelength pigments.

Study Questions

1. What is color? hue? chromatic color? achromatic color? (109)

2. What five principles of perception are illustrated in this chapter? (109)

3. Why is color often defined by giving examples? What problems are involved in making someone who is color-blind understand what it is like to experience color? (110)

4. What evidence suggests that people with normal color vision perceive the same stimuli as different colors? (110)

5. Is it possible to *prove* that there are differences in the way people with normal color vision experience colors? (111)

6. What is saturation? How many different colors can we discriminate? How many color names are there? What is the smallest list of basic colors? (111)

7. Describe the color circle. What does the color circle tell us? (111)

8. What is the connection between wavelength and color? Know the order of the colors one encounters when moving from short to long wavelengths. (112)

9. What is the wavelength distribution of sunlight? tungsten light? (113)

10. What are the reflectance curves for white, grey, and black papers, and for objects with chromatic color? (114)

11. What property is shared by all objects that have chromatic color? What is selective reflection? Know the connection between wavelength and color in Table 4.1. (115)

12. Describe a color-matching experiment. What are the results of these experiments on normal observ-

ers and what theory of color vision was proposed based on these results? (117)

13. What is the trichromatic theory of color vision? Be sure you understand how ratios are obtained in Figure 4.8. Also know the receptor firing patterns caused by each color (Figure 4.9) and how to predict the results of mixing lights of different colors. (117)

14. What are metamers? What is the physiological explanation for metamers? (120)

15. What is the minimum number of receptor types required for color vision? What is the reasoning behind your answer? (122)

16. What is the psychophysical evidence for opponent-process theory? (123)

17. Who proposed opponent-process theory? What is the basic idea behind opponent-process theory? (123)

18. How did Hurvich and Jameson measure the strength of the blue, yellow, red, and green mechanisms? Understand the graph in Figure 4.17, which shows the relative strengths of the different mechanisms at each wavelength. (124)

19. How does opponent-process theory explain the fact that mixing red and green results in yellow? (125)

20. What is the physiological evidence for the trichromatic and opponent-process theories? (126)

21. How can both trichromatic *and* opponent-process theories be correct? Describe the neural circuit that creates opponent responses based on input from three receptor mechanisms. (129)

22. What is the advantage of opponent neurons? (129)

23. Explain how trichromatic and opponent mechanisms both determine our experience. (130)

24. Describe the responses of double color-opponent cortical cells. What is the functional significance of these cells? What is the connection between these cells and blobs? (130)

25. What is a trichromat? An anomalous trichromat? A dichromat? A monochromat? How do these peo-

ple match colors in a color-matching experiment? (133)

26. Describe the color perceptions of deuteranopes, protanopes, and tritanopes. What is the neutral point? (134)

27. How were the color perceptions of 26, above, determined? (134)

28. What are the physiological mechanisms responsible for color blindness? Which visual pigment is missing in each form of color blindness? (135)

29. How can we tell if an animal has color vision? Which animals are trichromats? Dichromats? (135)

30. How does changing the illumination affect our perception of color? What is color constancy? Approximate color constancy? Describe how chromatic adaptation, the surroundings, and memory color contribute to color constancy. (136)

31. Taking a picture outside with indoor (tungsten) film makes the picture look too _____. (Understand why.) (138)

32. What does the statement "the rays are not coloured" mean? What do we mean when we say that our perception of color is a creation of our nervous system? (139)

33. What do we mean when we say that the nature of the experience elicited by a stimulus is arbitrary? Is this the case for all visual qualities? (140)

Boxes

1. Why does the sky appear blue? (116)

2. Understand how colors are created by mixing paints (subtractive color mixture). What is the difference between subtractive and additive mixture? If you are given the result of mixing two colors, you should be able to tell whether this result was due to additive or subtractive color mixture. (120)

3. Why do we say that blue is "special"? (127)

Glossary

Achromatic color. Colors without hue—white, black, and all the greys between these two extremes. (110)

Additive color mixture. Occurs when superimposing lights of different colors. (121)

Afterimage. An image that results after steady fixation on a high-contrast stimulus or brief exposure to a relatively bright stimulus such as a photographic flash. (122)

Anomalous trichromat. A person who needs to mix a minimum of three wavelengths to match any other wavelength in the spectrum, but mixes these wave-

lengths in different proportions than a trichromat. (133)

Blobs. Cells found in areas of the visual cortex that take up a stain that selectively colors areas which contain the enzyme cytochrome oxidase. Many of these cells have double color-opponent receptive fields. (133)

Chromatic adaptation. Adaptation of the eye to chromatic light. Chromatic adaptation is selective adaptation to wavelengths in a particular region of the visible spectrum. (137)

Chromatic color. Colors with hue. (110)

Color. A property of objects and lights by which they are said to possess qualities such as redness, greenness, whiteness, greyness, etc. (109)

Color constancy. Perception of an object's hue remains constant even when the wavelength distribution of the illumination is changed. Approximate color constancy means that our perception of hue usually changes a little when the illumination changes, though not as much as we might expect from the change in the wavelengths of light reaching the eye. (136)

Color deficiency. People with color deficiency (also called "color blindness") see fewer colors than people with normal color vision and need to mix fewer wavelengths to match any other wavelength in the spectrum. (133)

Color matching. A procedure in which observers are asked to match the color in one field by mixing two or more lights in another field. (117)

Color mixing. Combining two or more different colors to result in a new color. See additive color mixture and subtractive color mixture. (121)

Deuteranopia. A form of red-green color dichromatism caused by lack of the middle-wavelength cone pigment. (134)

Dichromat. A form of color deficiency. Dichromats can match any wavelength in the spectrum by mixing two other wavelengths. Deuteranopes, protanopes, and tritanopes are all dichromats. (133)

Double color-opponent cell. A cell with a center-surround receptive field that responds in an opponent manner to stimulation of the field's center with a reversed opponent response to stimulation of the surround. For example, if the center response is $R + G -$ the surround response will be $R - G +$. (130)

Hue. The experience of a chromatic color such as red, green, yellow and blue or combinations of these colors. (110)

Memory color. The idea that an object's characteristic color influences our perception of that object's color. (138)

Metamers. Two lights that have different wavelength distributions but are perceptually identical. (120)

Monochromat. A person who is completely color-blind and, therefore, sees everything as black, white, or shades of grey. A monochromat can match any color in the spectrum by adjusting the intensity of any other wavelength. (133)

Neutral point. The wavelength at which a dichromat perceives grey. (134)

Opponent cell. A neuron which has an excitatory response to wavelengths in one part of the spectrum and an inhibitory response to wavelengths in the other part of the spectrum. (129)

Opponent-process theory of color vision. This theory states that our perception of color is determined by the activity of two opponent mechanisms, a blue-yellow mechanism and a red-green mechanism. The responses of the two colors in each mechanism oppose each other, one resulting in an excitatory response and the other in an inhibitory response. (This theory also includes a black-white mechanism, which is concerned with the perception of brightness.) (123)

Protanopia. A form of red-green dichromatism caused by a lack of the long-wavelength cone pigment. (134)

Rayleigh scattering. Sunlight is scattered by small particles in the earth's atmosphere, with the amount of scatter being inversely proportional to the fourth power of the light's wavelength. This means that short-wavelength light is scattered more than long-wavelength light. (116)

Reflectance curve. The function relating the percent of light reflected from an object versus wavelength. See Figures 4.3, 4.4, and 4.5 for examples of reflectance curves. (114)

Saturation. The relative amount of whiteness in a chromatic color. The less whiteness a color contains the more saturated it is. (111)

Selective reflection. When an object reflects some wavelengths and absorbs others. (115)

Simultaneous contrast. Surrounding one color with another changes the appearance of the surrounded color. (123)

Spectral composition. The wavelengths that are contained in a light stimulus. (109)

S-potential. An electrical response with opponent properties that has been recorded from cells in the fish retina. (127)

Subtractive color mixture. Occurs when mixing together paints of different colors. (120)

Trichromat. A person with normal color vision. Trichromats can match any wavelength in the spectrum by mixing three other wavelengths in various proportions. (133)

Trichromatic theory of color vision. This theory postulates that our perception of color is determined by the ratio of activity in three cone receptor mechanisms with different spectral sensitivities. (117)

Tritanopia. A form of blue-yellow dichromatism thought to be caused by a lack of the short-wavelength cone pigment. (135)

Tungsten light. Light produced by a tungsten filament. Tungsten light has a wavelength distribution that has relatively more intensity at long wavelengths than at short wavelengths. (113)

Unilateral dichromat. A person who has dichromatic vision in one eye and trichromatic vision in the other eye. (134)

Veridical perception. Occurs when the perception of a stimulus's properties matches the physical properties of the stimulus. (140)

Wavelength distribution. The amount of energy in a light at each of the wavelengths in the spectrum. See Figure 4.2 for examples of wavelength distributions. (113)

White light. Light that contains an equal intensity of each of the visible wavelengths. (113)

Young-Helmholtz theory of color vision. See Trichromatic theory of color vision. (118)

CHAPTER 5

Perceiving Brightness and Contrast

When you look at the scene in Figure 5.1 you perceive different intensities of light reflected from the trees, the snow, the farmhouses, and the horse and buggy traveling down the road. If you didn't perceive these different intensities, you would have great difficulty perceiving these objects. It might help if the objects had different hues, but in the hueless black and white environment of our picture, our ability to see the different objects depends almost solely on our ability to perceive their different intensities. This perception of intensity, which we call **brightness,** is, therefore, of crucial importance to our ability to perceive different objects as separate from one another. Also crucial for our perception of objects is **contrast,** the perception of the *difference* in the intensity of two areas. Contrast is generally good in the scene of Figure 5.1, so we have little difficulty in differentiating one object from another. Low contrast, as might occur in a dense fog, would decrease our ability to see the individual objects in the scene.

In this chapter we will consider the factors that influence our perception of brightness and contrast. We will first consider some factors that are responsible for our perception of brightness, and

we will then focus more closely on contrast. As you read this chapter, you will notice examples illustrating many of the basic principles we established in the previous four chapters. In addition, we introduce two additional principles:

1. Perception is multiply determined. We saw in discussing color perception in the previous chapter that our perception of color is determined by wavelength plus a number of other factors. That perceptions are often determined by more than one factor is illustrated by the many things that determine our perception of brightness and contrast.

2. Presently, we can explain some perceptions physiologically but can't explain others. One of the major assumptions of this book is that all of our perceptions are determined by physiological mechanisms. Having said this, however, it is important to realize that *at our present state of knowledge* there are some things we can't explain physiologically. Thus, after showing how a simple neural circuit can explain some facts of brightness perception, we will show that this circuit cannot explain other facts of brightness perception.

145

F I G U R E 5. 1 *Winter Scene* 1982 by Clifton Page.

WHAT IS BRIGHTNESS?

We have defined brightness as the perception of the intensity of light reflected from a surface.* There are two things that affect the amount of light reflected from a surface: (1) the intensity of illumination falling on the surface, and (2) the **reflectance** of the surface, where reflectance is the *percentage* of the illumination that is reflected from the surface. We can illustrate how both the intensity of illumination falling on a surface and the reflectance of a surface can affect our perception

of brightness by looking at the board in Figure 5.2.

In Figure 5.2(a) a white board is evenly illuminated by a light directly overhead. The brightness is therefore the same across the whole board. But shielding the light from the back of the board, as in Figure 5.2(b), causes the front of the board to be more intensely illuminated. The front, therefore, reflects more light into our eyes than does the back and thus appears brighter. We can also change the amount of light reflected from different areas of the board by painting half of the board black, as in Figure 5.2(c). Now the front of the board again appears brighter than the back, because it reflects more light into our eyes than does the back. Thus, the brightness of different areas of the board can be changed by either changing the illumination on different parts of the board, or by changing the reflectance of different parts of the board. In

---

* Brightness also refers to our perception of intensities that occur when we look directly into a light source like the sun (not recommended) or a light bulb. However, since most of our perception involves looking at light that is reflected from the surfaces of objects, it is this perception we will emphasize here.

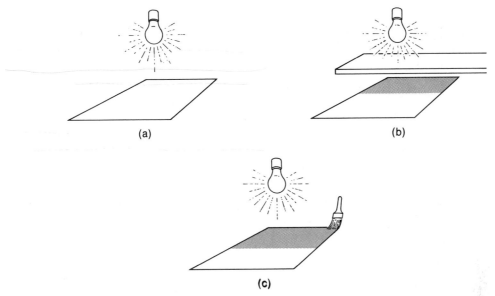

F I G U R E 5. 2   (a) An evenly illuminated white board (brightness the same across the board); (b) a shadowed white board (brightness greater in front); (c) a painted white board (brightness greater in front).

both cases we perceive a difference in brightness between the front and back of the board.

Though changing the board's illumination and changing its reflectance both affect our perception of brightness, the board usually *looks different* in the two cases. In Figure 5.2(b) we see a shadow on the board, and in Figure 5.2(c) we see black paint. When we change the board's reflectance by painting it, we are not only changing its brightness but we are also changing its lightness. **Lightness,** our perception of reflectance, is a special case of brightness perception that we will consider in more detail at the end of the chapter. For now, however, we will use the term brightness to refer to our perception of light intensity, whether caused by the illuminating intensity or the reflectance of a surface.

Our plan in this chapter is to extend our discussion of neural circuits in Chapters 2 to 4 by showing how our perception of brightness is influenced by the operation of neural circuits. Following this we will focus our attention on some of the factors that influence our perception of both brightness and contrast.

MACH BANDS: HOW A NEURAL CIRCUIT INFLUENCES BRIGHTNESS PERCEPTION AT BORDERS

We begin our consideration of brightness by describing some psychophysical observations that (1) describe an interesting perceptual effect that occurs near the border between two areas, and (2) lead to the proposal of a physiological mechanism to explain this perceptual effect.

In the 1870s the German scientist Ernst Mach made a number of observations that showed that our perception of the brightness of two areas does not always match the distribution of light intensities across these areas. Such an effect is shown in Figure 5.3, a series of stripes that appear different than their intensity distributions.

We can appreciate this difference between the intensity distributions of the stripes and our perception of the stripes by first measuring the intensity across the stripes in Figure 5.3 with a light meter. If we start at A and measure the amount of

(a)

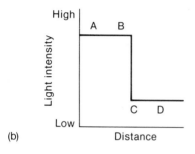

(b)

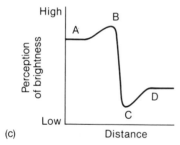

(c)

F I G U R E   5. 3   (a) Mach bands at a contour. Just to the left of the contour, near B, a faint light band can be perceived, and just to the right at C, a faint dark band can be perceived. (b) A plot showing the physical intensity distribution of the light, as measured with a light meter. (c) A plot showing the perceptual effect described in (a). The bump in the curve at B indicates the light Mach band, and the dip in the curve at C indicates the dark Mach band. Note that the bumps are not present in the physical intensity distribution.

light reflected by the stripes between A and D, we obtain the result shown in Figure 5.3(b). We see that the intensity distribution between A and B is flat; that is, the same amount of light is reflected across the entire distance between A and B. Then,

the intensity drops sharply at the border and stays at a constant lower level between C and D.

Although our light meter tells us that the intensities remain constant across the two stripes, we *perceive* something very different. At B there appears to be a band that is brighter than the rest of the left stripe, and at C there is a band that is darker than the rest of the right stripe. These bright and dark bands, which are called **Mach bands**, are represented graphically in Figure 5.3 (c).

D E M O N S T R A T I O N

Creating Mach Bands in Shadows

In Figure 5.3 we created Mach bands with grey stripes. You can also create Mach bands by casting a shadow, as shown in Figure 5.4. When you do this you will see a dark Mach band near the border of the shadow and a light Mach band on the other side of the border. The light Mach band is often harder to see than the dark band.

If the Mach bands we perceive do not exist in the intensity distribution, where do they come from? Mach's answer to this question was based on his observation that covering all but one of the stripes in a display like the one in Figure 5.3 eliminates the bands. If you try this for yourself, you will see that without the influence of the adjacent stripes, the remaining stripe appears the same all the way across, just like its intensity distribution.

Mach's observation that the bands vanish when the adjacent stripes are covered led him to propose a physiological mechanism to explain Mach bands. The light and dark bands must, according to Mach, be caused by "an organic reciprocal action of the retinal elements on one another" (1904, p. 218). Mach's hypothesis is that illumination of one area of the retina affects the response of receptors in another nearby area of the retina.

Mach's hypothesis is important both because it is correct and because it is an example of a physiological conclusion based on a psychophysical observation. In fact, the technical means for testing Mach's hypothesis, which he proposed in the

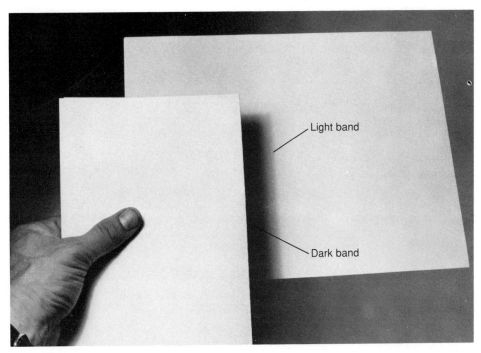

F I G U R E 5. 4   Shadow-casting technique for observing Mach bands. Illuminate a sheet of white paper with your desk lamp and then cast a shadow with another piece of paper.

late 1800s, did not become available until many years after Mach's death. In 1956, Kuffer Hartline, Henry Wagner, and Floyd Ratliff published a paper that demonstrated Mach's predicted "reciprocal action of retinal elements on one another," an effect they called lateral inhibition.

Lateral Inhibition

The creature in Figure 5.5, the horseshoe crab, or **Limulus,** was chosen for Hartline, Wagner, and Ratliff's experiment because of the structure of its eye. The *Limulus* eye is made up of hundreds of tiny ommatidia, with each **ommatidium** having a small lens on the eye's surface that is located directly over a single receptor. Since each lens and receptor is roughly the diameter of a pencil point, it is possible to illuminate and record from a single receptor without illuminating its neighboring receptors.

When Hartline, Wagner, and Ratliff recorded from the nerve fiber of receptor A, as shown in

Figure 5.6, they found that illumination of that receptor caused the large response shown in Figure 5.6(a). But when they added illumination to the three nearby receptors at B, the response of receptor A decreased, as shown in Figure 5.6(b). They also found that increasing the illumination of B further decreased A's response, as shown in Figure 5.6(c). Thus, illumination of the neighboring receptors *inhibited* the firing of receptor A. This inhibition is called **lateral inhibition** because it is transmitted laterally, across the retina, in a structure called the **lateral plexus.**

What does the result of the Hartline experiment on the *Limulus* have to do with the perception of Mach bands in humans? The answer to this question lies in the similarity between the lateral plexus of the *Limulus* and the horizontal and amacrine cells of the human retina. All of these structures transmit signals across the retina, thereby providing a pathway for transmitting inhibitory signals from one receptor to another.

F I G U R E 5. 5 A *Limulus*, also known as the horseshoe crab. Its large eyes are made up of hundreds of ommatidia, each containing a single receptor.

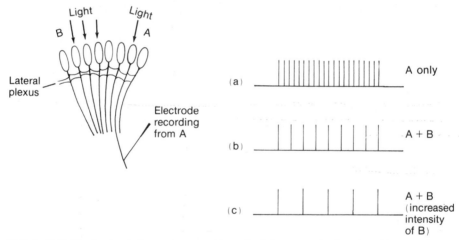

F I G U R E 5. 6 A demonstration of lateral inhibition in the *Limulus*. The records on the right show the response recorded by the electrode recording from the nerve fiber of receptor A when receptor A is stimulated and (a) no other receptors are stimulated, (b) the receptors at B are stimulated simultaneously, and (c) the receptors at B are stimulated at an increased intensity. (Adapted from Ratliff, 1965.)

A Neural Circuit for Mach Bands

The existence of this lateral system for transmitting inhibition across the retina enables us to construct a simple neural circuit that would result in the perception of Mach bands. Such a circuit is shown in Figure 5.7, which shows four receptors, each of which sends lateral inhibition to its neighbors on both sides. To show how this circuit could cause the perception of Mach bands, let's illuminate these receptors so A and B receive intense illumination and C and D receive dim illumination, analogous

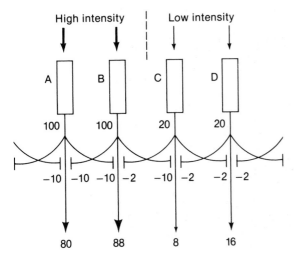

F I G U R E 5. 7 Four receptors that inhibit each other. If we know the initial output of each receptor and the amount of lateral inhibition, we can calculate the final output of the receptors. (See text for a description of this calculation.)

to the stimulus we would create by illuminating all four receptors and then casting a shadow on receptors C and D.

Let's assume that receptors A and B generate responses of "100" whereas C and D generate responses of "20," as shown in Figure 5.7. Thus, without inhibition A and B generate equal responses and C and D generate equal responses. We can show, however, by means of the following calculation, that lateral inhibition can modify the initial responses of these receptors to achieve a physiological effect that mimics the perception of Mach bands.

1. Start with the initial response of each cell, 100 for A and B and 20 for C and D.
2. Determine the amount of inhibition that each cell receives from its neighbor on each side. For the purposes of our calculation, we will assume that each cell sends inhibition to its neighbor equal to one-tenth of that cell's initial output. Thus, cells A and B will send $100 \times 0.1 = 10$ units of inhibition to their neighbors, and cells C and D will send $20 \times 0.1 = 2$ units of inhibition to their neighbors.

3. Determine the final output of each cell, where final output equals initial response minus inhibition. Remember that each cell receives inhibition from its neighbor on either side. (We assume here that receptor A receives 10 units of inhibition from an unseen receptor on its left and that D receives 2 units of inhibition from an unseen receptor on its right.) The calculation for each cell in Figure 5.7 is:
Cell A: Output = $100 - 10 - 10 = 80$
Cell B: Output = $100 - 10 - 2 = 88$
Cell C: Output = $20 - 10 - 2 = 8$
Cell D: Output = $20 - 2 - 2 = 16$

The graph of these responses in Figure 5.8 looks very similar to Figure 5.3(b). There is an increase in nerve firing on the light side of the border at B and a decrease on the dark side at C. The lateral inhibition in our circuit has, therefore, created "Mach bands" in the neural response. A circuit similar to this one, but of much greater complexity, is probably responsible for the Mach bands that we see.

This creation of Mach bands by lateral inhibition illustrates the point we made in the last chapter, that *perception is an outcome of processing by the nervous system.* As the nervous system processes the information from the environment, it often changes it so that what we perceive is not

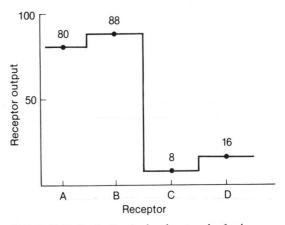

F I G U R E 5. 8 A plot showing the final receptor output calculated for the circuit of Figure 5.7. The bump at B and the dip at C correspond to the light and dark Mach bands, respectively.

High intensity: more inhibition   *Less intensity: Less inhibition*

F I G U R E 5. 9 Simultaneous contrast. The two center squares reflect the same amount of light into your eyes but, due to the simultaneous contrast effect, look different.

necessarily an exact copy of the energy in the environment.

Another demonstration of this principle, which also involves the perception of the brightness of two adjacent areas, is the simultaneous contrast effect.

D E M O N S T R A T I O N

Simultaneous Contrast

Punch two holes 2¼ inches apart in a card or piece of paper, place the two holes over the squares in Figure 5.9, and compare the brightness of the two squares as seen through the holes. You may be surprised to see that the two squares look the same when their backgrounds are masked by the paper, even though they look very different when the whole figure is visible.

The reason the two squares look the same when their backgrounds are masked is simple: They reflect the same amount of light into your eyes. They look different when the mask is removed because of the effect of their backgrounds, and this effect is probably due to lateral inhibition. According to this explanation, the light background on the left darkens our perception of its square because the receptors stimulated by this background send inhibition to the receptors stimulated by the square (Figure 5.10). The dark background on the right does not, however, have this darkening effect because the receptors stimulated by this background send little inhibition to the receptors stimulated by the square.

Although lateral inhibition plays an important role in determining our perception of brightness, it is not a complete explanation. For example, consider the simultaneous contrast demonstration. The light background on the left darkens our perception of its square, but lateral inhibition should be most powerful near the square's borders and should have little influence on our perception of the square's center. Yet we perceive

---

B O X 5. 1 / *The Spreading Effect*

Look at the top design in Color Plate 5.3. It appears to contain two fields of red, a dark field on the left and a lighter one in the center. However, in reality, both reds are physically the same. To see that the red is, in fact, the same across the picture, look very closely at the contour between the light and dark. If you concentrate your attention on the red background and ignore the black and white lines, you will see that the red is the same on either side of the contour. In fact, the contour that you see when you look at the picture as a whole vanishes.

The darkening of the red on the left side is due to the presence of the black lines, and the lightening of the red in the center is due to the white lines. It is as though the darkness of the black has spread, making the red on the left darker, and the lightness of the white has spread, making the red on the right lighter. Bezold, who described this effect in 1876, called it the **spreading effect,** and later workers have called this effect **assimilation.** Note that assimilation has an effect opposite to simultaneous contrast. In simultaneous contrast, adding a lighter ring around an area makes it appear darker. In assimilation, placing light lines inside a homogeneous field makes the field appear lighter.

Although you may think that assimilation is simply an obscure perceptual effect, it is, in fact, one of the basic principles that underlie our perception of pictures such as Mellan's engraving of *Samson and Delilah* below. Compare the shading on the light areas of Delilah's face to the shading of the background. The background looks darker than the light area on the face not because the background is shaded but because the background contains horizontal lines. The horizontal lines in the background function in the same way as the black lines in the color plate. The darkness of the lines in the background "spreads," making the spaces between the lines, which are actually as white as the face, appear darker.

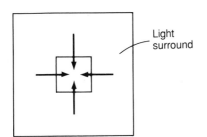

Light surround

F I G U R E 5. 10 The image cast on the retina by the left side of the simultaneous contrast demonstration of Figure 5.9. The light surround stimulates receptors surrounding the dark square and this stimulation sends lateral inhibition to the area stimulated by the square, as indicated by the arrows. This inhibition decreases the firing caused by the square and makes it appear darker.

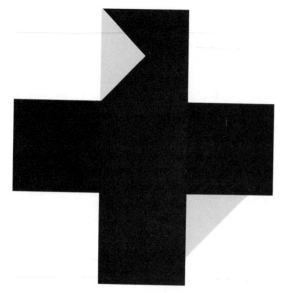

FIGURE 5. 11 The Wertheimer-Benary demonstration. The two grey triangles reflect the same amount of light, but the one in the upper part of the cross looks slightly lighter.

the entire square to be darkened equally. Our simple explanation based on lateral inhibition doesn't explain why this is so.

Another example of a phenomenon not explained by lateral inhibition is shown in Figure 5.11. Since both grey triangles are bounded on two sides by black and on one side by white, we would expect the amount of lateral inhibition coming from the areas surrounding the two triangles to be identical. However, most people see the triangle contained inside the body of the cross as lighter than the triangle between the two arms. Again, a simple explanation based on lateral inhibition doesn't explain this effect. These demonstrations, therefore, support the principle that there are some perceptions that we cannot presently explain physiologically.

In this section we have focused on how lateral inhibition influences our perception of brightness. In the next sections we will be more concerned with the things that influence our perception of contrast. We will see that contrast is affected by the nature of the contours between two areas, the spatial frequency of the stimulus, and the observer's state of adaptation.

WHAT IS CONTRAST?

Before we describe some of the factors that affect our perception of contrast we need to understand that contrast can be defined in two different ways. One way of defining contrast, which we have already stated in the opening of this chapter, is that contrast is the *perception* of the difference in the intensity of two areas. When we define contrast in this way we are referring to **perceptual contrast.** Contrast can also be defined as the difference in the intensity of two areas. Notice that this definition omits the term "perception" that appears in the first definition. When we define contrast in this way we are referring to **physical contrast.**

To illustrate these two ways of defining contrast, consider the two pictures in Figure 5.12. To measure the physical contrasts in these pictures we use a light meter to determine the intensities of light reflected from the light and dark areas of the picture. When we do this, we find that the difference between the amount of light reflected from the dark and the light areas is greater in the picture on the right than in the picture on the left. The right picture, therefore, has more physical contrast than the left picture.

We determine the perceptual contrast in these pictures by looking at them. When we do this we perceive more of a difference between the dark and light areas in the picture on the right than in the picture on the left. Thus, the right picture has more perceptual contrast than the left picture. In these pictures, therefore, there is a correspondence between physical contrast and perceptual contrast, with high physical contrast leading to high perceptual contrast.

Physical and perceptual contrast do not, however, always correspond to one another. Consider,

F I G U R E 5. 12   Two pictures that differ in contrast. The picture on the right has higher physical and perceptual contrast than the one on the left.

for example, the stripe containing A and B in Figure 5.3. When we measure the intensity across this stripe with a light meter we find that it is the same across the width of the stripe. That is, there is no physical contrast across the width of this stripe. Perceptual contrast, however, is a different story; we perceive a difference in intensity between the center of the stripe, the dark Mach band at A, and the light Mach band at B. There is, therefore, some perceptual contrast between these areas. Perceptual contrast can, therefore, exist in the absence of physical contrast.

In the next section we will describe an example of a situation in which there is physical contrast—two adjacent areas with different intensities—but no perceptual contrast—we perceive no intensity difference between these two areas.

Our major concern in the next sections will be with perceptual contrast, which we will refer to simply as "contrast." Remember, therefore, that when you read "contrast," *think* "perceptual contrast." When we are discussing physical contrast we will use the term "physical contrast."

Let's now begin our discussion by considering how the nature of contours affects contrast.

THE EFFECT OF CONTOURS ON CONTRAST PERCEPTION

Contour has been defined as the "narrow region which visually separates something from something else" (O'Brien, 1958). We are particularly interested in contours, not only because they help separate different areas but also because the sharpness of the contour determines how we perceive the contrast between areas on either side of it.

Fuzzy and Sharp Contours

If two areas reflect the same amount of light, but one has a fuzzy contour and the other a sharp contour, the one with the fuzzy contour will contrast less with its background. In fact, if the transition between an area and its background is very fuzzy, the contrast between them can vanish altogether.

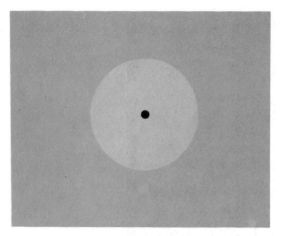 

FIGURE 5. 13   Discs with sharp and blurred contours. See text for viewing instructions.

DEMONSTRATION

Making a Disc Disappear

Stare at the center of the fuzzy-contoured disc on the right of Figure 5.13. If you keep your eyes very still for about 30 seconds, the disc will disappear. When this happens, the contrast between the disc and its background has vanished, since we no longer perceive a difference in brightness between the two areas. This is a good example of a situation in which there is physical contrast between two areas but no perceptual contrast. Now see if you can make the sharp-contoured disc on the left side vanish by staring at it in the same way. You will see that this is difficult or impossible to accomplish.

Why does the fuzzy disc fade while the sharp disc does not? The answer to this question lies in how the contours of the two discs stimulate the retinal receptors, and in the fact that even when you try to keep your eyes steady by looking at one point, your eyes "jiggle" or move, involuntarily.

DEMONSTRATION

The Jiggle of the Eyes

Look at the small black dot in the middle of Figure 5.14 for about 60 seconds and then look at the white dot. Even if you try very hard to look steadily

at the white dot, you will see an image of the grid pattern jiggling on top of the figure. This jiggle is due to **involuntary eye movements.**

Let's now consider what happens on the retina when you stare at the center of the sharp disc in Figure 5.13. As you stare at this disc, trying to keep your eyes completely steady, your eyes still move very slightly because of involuntary eye movements, which cause the image of the sharp disc to jiggle on your retina. The jiggling causes the contour of the disc to fall first on some receptors and then on others. The amount of light stimulating the receptors near the sharp contour is therefore constantly changing, and it is this change that keeps the disc visible.

Now let's consider the fuzzy disc. The image of this disc also jiggles on the retina. However, the jiggling of the fuzzy contour causes only slight changes in the amount of light stimulating the receptors near the contour. If you keep your eyes still enough, the small change in stimulation caused by movement of this fuzzy contour is not enough to maintain perception, and the disc fades from view.

Based on this reasoning, we can propose an explanation at the level of stimuli for why the fuzzy disc fades but the sharp one doesn't: *The visual system responds well to changing stimulation but responds*

F I G U R E 5. 14   Grid pattern for perceiving eye movements. See text for viewing instructions. (From Verheijen, 1961.)

poorly, or not at all, to constant stimulation. If this hypothesis is correct, then we would predict that stopping the sharp disc's contour from jiggling on the retina should cause the disc to fade from view. But how might we stop this jiggle? We could stop the eye from moving, but that is very difficult. A better way is to let the eye continue to move normally while causing the object at which it looks to move with the eye. If the eye moves 1 degree to the right and the object simultaneously moves 1 degree to the right, the object's image will not move on the retina. This technique is called the **stabilized image** technique because the image is stabilized on the retina.

Stabilizing the Image

One method of stabilizing the image on the retina is shown in Figure 5.15 (Pritchard, 1961). The observer wears a specially designed contact lens, attached to which is a small projector that projects the stimulus into the observer's eye. Every time the

eye moves, the projector system and stimulus move with it; therefore, the resulting image always stimulates the same retinal receptors.

The stabilized image technique helps us find out what happens to the sharp disc when its contour does not jiggle on the retina. When the stabilized disc is first presented, the observer sees it, but within about 3 seconds this disc completely fades from view. By stopping the sharp contour from stimulating new receptors, we eliminate perception of the disc, as predicted from our hypothesis that the visual system does not respond well to constant stimulation.

Since the stabilized disc fades because of a lack of change in the stimulation of receptors, we might wonder why the *center* of the sharp disc in Figure 5.13 didn't fade when we viewed it under normal (nonstabilized) conditions. You can understand why we might expect the center to fade, by considering what's happening to the receptors under the center of the disc. Although involuntary eye movements cause the disc's center to move along with the con-

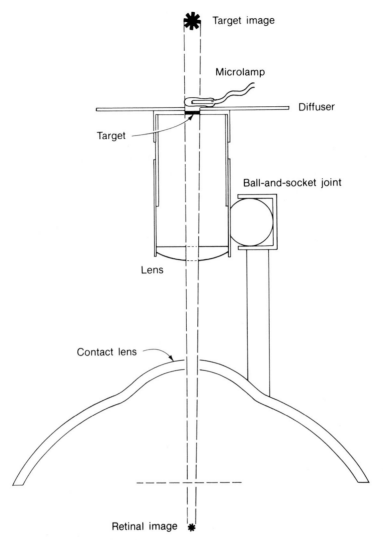

F I G U R E 5. 15 Stabilized image device used by Pritchard (1961). Since the contact lens and projector move every time the eye moves, the image projected into the eye always falls on the same point on the retina, as suggested at the bottom of the illustration. The entire optical system weighs only one quarter of a gram.

tours, this movement causes no change in the amount of light falling on the receptors under the center, because the center of the disc is homogeneous. Therefore, we might expect the center to fade like a stabilized image. However, it does not fade, apparently because the sharp contour that surrounds it is still present and jiggling around on the retina.

John Krauskopf (1963) showed that the pres-

ence of the sharp contour keeps the center of the disc from fading by having observers look at a stimulus display like the one in Figure 5.16. The inner disc was red and the outer ring green. Under normal viewing conditions, the observer perceived a red disc inside a green ring. But Krauskopf stabilized the contour between the two discs, while leaving the outer contour unstabilized. Thus, the outer contour of the green ring was jiggling on the

BOX 5. 2 / *The Ganzfeld, or, What Happens When You Wear Ping-Pong Balls on Your Eyes?*

One way to eliminate the movement of contours on the retina is to use the stabilized image technique. Another way is to eliminate the contours by having observers look into a homogeneous field called a **Ganzfeld.** Wolfgang Metzger (1930; described in Koffka, 1935) constructed one of the first Ganzfelds. He had observers sit facing a whitewashed wall that filled their entire field of view. They reported feeling as though they were looking into a fog with a filmy appearance like the sky.

Another way to achieve a Ganzfeld is to have the observer (your author, in this case) wear half a ping-pong ball over each eye (Hochberg, Triebel, & Seaman, 1951). In this situation, the observer perceives a fog like the fog Metzger's observers saw. But more interesting than this fog is the observer's perception when colored lights are projected onto the ping-pong balls. When this is done, some observers at first report seeing the colors, but after 3–6 minutes they say that the colors disappear completely. In most cases observers don't want to believe that the

lights are not being dimmed or turned off, even when the experimenter tells them that the colored lights are still present. The effect of a Ganzfeld is similar to the effect of a stabilized image: Elimination of moving contours eliminates the observer's perception of form and color (Cohen, 1957).

retina, as it would under normal viewing conditions, but the contour between the red and green areas was stabilized. The result was that the inner contour and the red disc vanished and was filled in by green. This dramatic demonstration shows that the jiggling of contours maintains our perception of the area *inside* those contours. We don't

FIGURE 5. 16 The stimulus display used by Krauskopf (1963). In the actual display, the inner disc was red and outer ring green. The contour between the two colors was stabilized so it remained stationary on the retina, but the outer contour was not stabilized, so it jiggled on the retina, as indicated by the arrows on the contour.

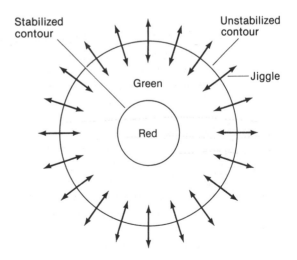

Stabilized contour

Unstabilized contour

Jiggle

Green

Red

know why the jiggling contours keep the inside area from fading, but there is no doubt that without sharp contours, contrast becomes poor or vanishes altogether.

Now that we have considered Mach bands and contours, let's consider the two basic questions about perception that we introduced in Chapter 1 (see p. 20) and that we will be asking throughout this book:

1. What are the phenomena of perception?
2. What causes these phenomena?

How have we dealt with these two questions so far? First, let's consider Mach bands. Mach answered the first question by describing what Mach bands are—the perception of a light band on one side of a border and a dark band on the other side. He then answered the second question in two ways. First, working at the level of stimuli, he suggested that Mach bands in one stripe are caused by the influence of adjacent stripes. Then, working at the level of physiology, he suggested that the bands are caused by the "reciprocal action of retinal elements." Many years later, after the development of electrophysiological recording techniques, Mach's proposed physiological mechanism was confirmed by physiologists.

Now let's consider the effect of contours on contrast. We answered the first question by establishing that contrast is maintained by sharp contours and vanishes if the contours are fuzzy or are stabilized on the retina. We answered the second question at the level of stimuli by showing that the visual system responds best to changing stimulation. This psychophysical observation is supported by the physiological observations that cortical neurons, like the complex and hypercomplex cells we described in Chapter 3, respond only to moving stimuli, and that many cells with simple and center-surround receptive fields respond best when stimuli are turned on or off.

Despite the physiological evidence that supports the idea that changing stimulation is important for maintaining vision, we still lack a complete physiological explanation of why stabilized images fade and how jiggling contours keep the center areas of nonstabilized stimuli (like the cen-

ter of our sharp disc) from fading. Thus, although we have been able to explain how contour affects contrast at the level of stimuli, we have not been able to fully explain these contour effects at the level of physiology.

THE EFFECT OF SPATIAL FREQUENCY ON CONTRAST PERCEPTION

Our perception of the contrast between two areas is affected not only by what happens at the border between the two areas but also by the spatial frequency of the stimulus. Remember, from Chapter 3, that spatial frequency, when applied to grating stimuli like the one in Figure 3.4, refers to the number of cycles per unit distance across the grating, where one cycle is a black bar and a white bar. When looking at the grating on the left of Figure 3.4 from a distance of about 2 feet, you will see that the contrast of this grating is higher than the contrast of the grating on the right. That is, the difference in the brightness of the black and white bars is more pronounced in the left grating. The difference in spatial frequency causes this difference in contrast.

We will begin our discussion of spatial frequency by measuring the relationship between spatial frequency and contrast for a wide range of spatial frequencies. But before measuring this relationship, we need to describe the grating stimulus in more detail.

The Grating Stimulus

To understand how gratings are used in research, we need to be able to describe them more precisely than "black and white bars." We specify the properties of gratings by specifying the grating's (1) waveform, (2) physical contrast, and (3) spatial frequency.

Waveform. The waveform of a grating refers to the shape of the grating's intensity distribution. Figure 5.17 shows two gratings and their intensity distributions. The intensity distribution for the

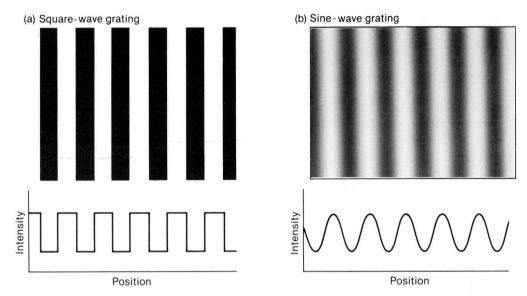

F I G U R E 5. 17 (a) Left: square-wave grating and its intensity distribution. (b) Right: sine-wave grating and its intensity distribution. The abrupt changes in intensity of the square-wave grating are seen as sharp contours, whereas the more gradual changes in intensity of the sine-wave grating are seen as fuzzy contours.

grating in Figure 5.17(a) shows that this grating's intensity abruptly alternates between high (for each white bar) and low (for each black bar). Since the distribution looks like a series of squares, this grating is called a **square-wave grating.** The intensity distribution for the grating in Figure 5.17(b) shows that this grating's intensity alternates more gradually between high and low. Since this distribution follows a mathematical function called a sine wave, this grating is called a **sine-wave grating.** There are also sawtooth-wave gratings, triangle-wave gratings, and many others, all named by the shape of their intensity distributions, but most research on the perception of contrast has used square-wave and sine-wave gratings.

Physical contrast. A grating's physical contrast is equal to its amplitude, A, divided by its mean intensity, M, which is indicated by the dashed line in Figure 5.18. Figure 5.18 shows two gratings with different physical contrasts. In Figure 5.18(a), the physical contrast is high, whereas in Figure 5.18(b), the physical contrast is lower.

Spatial frequency. We have defined spatial frequency as the number of cycles per unit distance across the grating. Thus, the grating in Figure 5.18 contains 3½ cycles, and since the grating is 2 inches wide, we could say that this grating has a spatial frequency of 3½ cycles per 2 inches, or 1¾ cycles per inch. However, spatial frequency is usually not specified in cycles per inch but in cycles per degree of visual angle. (If necessary, see page 65 of Chapter 3 to review the concept of visual angle.) The advantage of this method of specifying spatial frequency is that it tells us what is happening on the retina (Figure 5.19).

The Contrast Sensitivity Function

We saw in Figure 3.3 that the low-frequency grating (wide bars) has more contrast than the high-frequency grating (narrow bars). But these are just two gratings. What would be the result if we looked at others? Is the contrast of low-frequency gratings always higher than that of high-frequency gratings? To answer this question we must systematically

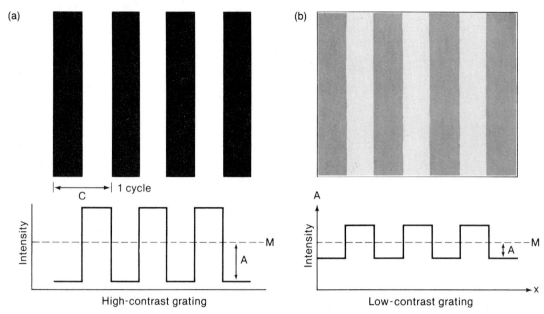

F I G U R E 5. 18 A high-contrast square-wave grating (left) and a low-contrast grating (right). Both gratings have the same mean intensity (M), indicated by the dashed line, but the grating on the left has a larger amplitude (A). The contrast of the gratings can be determined by dividing the amplitude of the grating by the mean intensity. The distance marked C, on the grating on the left, indicates the size of one cycle. Each of these gratings contains 3½ cycles.

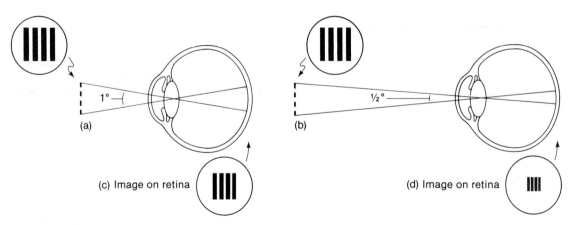

F I G U R E 5. 19 Viewing a grating at different distances changes its visual angle and, therefore, the size of its image on the retina. In (a) a 3½ cycle grating is viewed so that its visual angle is 1 degree. In (b) the same grating is viewed from twice as far so its visual angle is ½ degree. When the visual angle is 1 degree, the retinal image is larger (c) than when the visual angle is ½ degree (d).

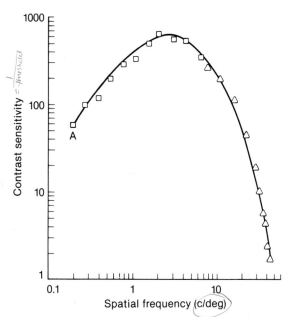

F I G U R E 5. 20 A contrast sensitivity function (CSF) for a sine-wave grating, as measured by Campbell and Robson (1968).

measure the contrast of gratings over a wide range of frequencies. We need to determine the **contrast sensitivity function (CSF).**

The contrast sensitivity function (CSF) is a plot of the physical contrast needed to see a grating versus the grating's spatial frequency. To measure the CSF, we start with a grating of very low frequency (wide bars) and with physical contrast so low that the grating cannot be seen—that is, it appears to be a homogeneous grey field. We then slowly increase the physical contrast of the grating until the observer reports that he or she can just barely see its bars. This level of physical contrast is called the *threshold* for seeing the bars. To plot the CSF, we convert the threshold into **contrast sensitivity,** by the relationship contrast sensitivity = 1/threshold, just as we did for the spectral sensitivity curves of Figure 1.6. The result of this determination is point A in Figure 5.20.

Next, we increase the grating's spatial frequency by narrowing the bars and then repeating the above procedure, determining how much physical contrast enables the observer to just barely see

the bars. If we continue this procedure using gratings with higher and higher spatial frequencies, we get the curve in Figure 5.20, which is the contrast sensitivity function for a sine-wave grating (Campbell & Robson, 1968). This CSF tells us that the visual system is most sensitive to sine-wave gratings with spatial frequencies of about 3 cycles per degree. (You may wonder why Campbell and Robson used sine-wave rather than square-wave gratings. They did this because sine-wave gratings can be mathematically analyzed by a technique called Fourier analysis that tells us some important things about the visual system. If you are interested in Fourier analysis, see Appendix D.)

The CSF in Figure 5.20 tells us that our ability to detect a grating depends on the grating's spatial frequency. What is the mechanism responsible for this relationship? One idea is that the contrast sensitivity function reflects the activity of a number of *detectors,* or **spatial frequency channels,** each of which are sensitive to a narrow range of spatial frequencies.

Spatial Frequency Channels in the Visual System. The idea of spatial frequency channels in the visual system that are sensitive to narrow ranges of spatial frequencies is supported by the results of a psychophysical procedure called **selective adaptation.** A typical selective adaptation experiment would be done as follows:

1. Determine the contrast sensitivity function (curve A in Figure 5.21).
2. Adapt a person by having him look at a 7.5-cycle/degree grating for 1–2 minutes.
3. Redetermine the contrast sensitivity function. The resulting CSF, curve B of Figure 5.21, shows a decreased sensitivity only in the frequency range around the adapting frequency of 7.5 cycles/degree. If we repeat this experiment with an adapting stimulus with a different spatial frequency, we would get the same result except that the CSF would be decreased in sensitivity only near the frequency of the new adapting stimulus.

The results of this selective adaptation exper-

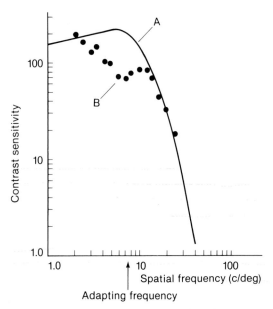

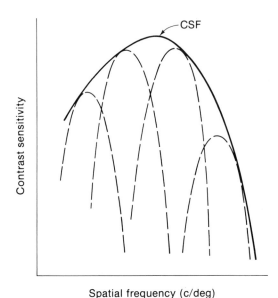

FIGURE 5.21 The results of a selective adaptation experiment. The solid curve (A) indicates the CSF determined prior to adaptation. The data points (curve B) indicate the CSF determined after adaptation to a 7½ cycle/degree grating. Note that the adaptation causes a maximum decrease in contrast sensitivity at a spatial frequency of 7½ cycles/degree. (From Blakemore & Campbell, 1968.)

FIGURE 5.22 The contrast sensitivity function (solid line) and some of its underlying channels (dashed lines). These channels, each of which is sensitive to a narrow range of frequencies, add together to create the CSF.

iment (and many other similar experiments) support the idea that the CSF is generated by the action of a number of channels like the ones in Figure 5.22, each of which are sensitive to a narrow range of spatial frequencies.

Many researchers believe it likely that these channels correspond to neurons in the cortex. According to this idea, the decrease in sensitivity observed in our selective adaptation experiment occurs when inspection of the adapting grating fatigues those neurons sensitive to a narrow range of frequencies around the adapting frequency. When we redetermine the CSF, the decreased responsiveness of these neurons decreases the sensitivity around the adapting frequency.

The hypothesis that selectively tuned neurons are responsible for the CSF is supported by L. Maffei and A. Fiorentini's (1973) experiments in which gratings with different spatial frequencies were

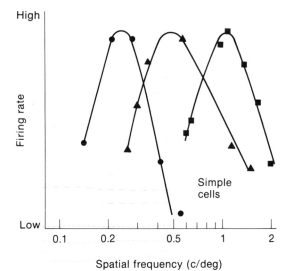

FIGURE 5.23 Tuning curves for three simple cortical cells to gratings moved across their receptive fields. These cells, each of which responds to gratings with a narrow range of frequencies, may correspond to the channels that underlie the broader CSF. (Adapted from Maffei & Fiorentini, 1973.)

moved across the receptive fields of simple cortical cells. Figure 5.23, which shows tuning curves for three simple cells, indicates that each cell responds best to a different spatial frequency and each cell is tuned to respond to a narrow range of frequencies, just as are the psychophysically determined channels of Figure 5.22. Perhaps these cells are the hypothesized spatial frequency channels.

DEMONSTRATION

Selective Adaptation of Size

Look at Figure 5.24 by moving your eyes back and forth along the horizontal line between the two gratings on the left, for about 60 seconds. This adapts you to the wide (low-frequency) bars above the line and to the narrow (high-frequency) bars below the line. After this adaptation, shift your gaze to the dot between the two gratings on the right and compare the spacing between the lines of the top and bottom gratings. The lines of the top gratings will probably appear more closely spaced than those of the bottom grating, even though the bars are actually the same size.

We can explain our perception of the gratings on the right of Figure 5.24 in terms of the adaptation of neurons that respond to a narrow range of spatial frequencies. To understand how this might work, let's first consider the response generated by the two gratings on the right *before* the adaptation. These gratings generate a large response in neurons that respond best to frequencies that match the gratings' frequency, indicated by bar M in Figure 5.25(a). These gratings also generate some response in neurons that respond best to lower (L) and higher (H) frequencies than the gratings.

When we adapt to the low-frequency grating (top left), neurons that respond best to low frequencies become fatigued. Then, when we shift our eyes to the grating on the right, we get the response shown in Figure 5.25(b); the neurons tuned to low frequencies respond less than before they were adapted. Similarly, when we adapt to the high-frequency grating (bottom left), neurons that respond best to high frequencies become fatigued. Then, when we shift our eyes to the grating on the right, we get the response shown in Figure 5.25(c); the neurons tuned to high frequencies respond less than before they were adapted.

Thus, adaptation to the gratings on the left

F I G U R E   5. 24   Gratings for size-adaptation experiment. See text for details.

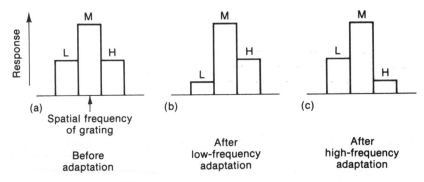

FIGURE 5. 25 How neurons that respond best to low (L), medium (M), and high (H) spatial frequencies respond to the gratings on the right of Figure 5.23, (a) before adaptation; (b) after adapting to the low-frequency grating; and (c) after adapting to the high-frequency grating. These changes in the pattern of firing caused by adaptation are accompanied by changes in our perception of the grating.

changes the pattern of firing caused by the two gratings on the right. After adaptation, the pattern of firing to the top-right grating is weighted toward high frequencies (and we, therefore, see the bars as thinner), whereas the pattern of firing to the bottom-right grating is weighted toward low frequencies (so we see the bars as thicker).

Contrast Sensitivity and Visual Acuity

Before the idea of spatial frequencies was introduced, most work on the resolving power of the visual system was limited to measuring visual acuity (see p. 85, Chapter 3). Most visual acuity experiments, however, study only a small portion of our ability to resolve details. To illustrate this, let's consider an experiment in which visual acuity is measured using a grating stimulus. When doing this, the experimenter usually asks what the finest grating is that a person can detect, and this detection task is usually carried out with a grating of high physical contrast made up of very fine (high spatial frequency) lines. Such an experiment measures the resolving power of the visual system only for stimuli with high physical contrasts and high spatial frequencies. Measuring visual acuity in this way is fine, as far as it goes. However, by focusing only on high physical contrast and high spatial frequency, this method ignores the wide range of spatial frequencies and physical contrasts found in

environmental stimuli. Seeing fine details (reading a book, threading a needle) involves high spatial frequencies, whereas seeing larger objects (a nearby car, a person's face, a whole person) involves low spatial frequencies. When you read a book under good lighting conditions, you are dealing with high spatial frequencies and high physical contrast, but when you try to find a seat in a dark movie theater without bumping into people, you are dealing with low spatial frequencies and low physical contrast.

The contrast sensitivity function helps us better understand how we perceive the wide range of stimuli we see every day. An experiment that compared the CSFs of a group of 73-year-old observers to the CSFs of a group of 18-year-old observers provides a good example of the application of spatial frequency analysis. When these two groups were given a standard visual acuity test, both showed essentially the same visual acuity. However, the CSFs of the two groups were a different story. Though the ability to see narrow (high-frequency) gratings was the same for both groups (as would be expected from their similar acuities), the older observers required three times more contrast to see the wide (low-frequency) gratings (Sekuler, Hutman, & Owsley, 1980). Sekuler et al. suggest that the older observers' insensitivity to low spatial frequencies may explain why older people often have difficulty recognizing faces and many other objects that require low spatial frequency information.

DEMONSTRATION

Spatial Frequencies in a Picture

Look at the picture in Figure 5.26 from a distance of about 3 or 4 feet, and notice the faint white border between the grey shadow on the right side of the container and the grey background. Now slowly move closer to the picture, while noticing this border. As you move closer, the border becomes less and less distinct, until when you are very close (6–12 inches) the border may even vanish!

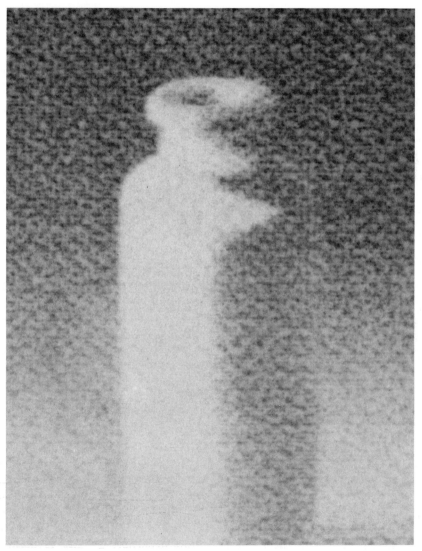

F I G U R E 5. 26 *Requiem* (detail), pastel and acrylic, by Tom McDonald, 1982. When viewed from a distance of about 3 feet, the low-contrast border on the upper right of the container is visible. However, by moving closer to the picture, you decrease the spatial frequency of the border, and if you move still closer, the border becomes less distinct and may even vanish.

The vanishing border in Figure 5.26 can't be explained in terms of visual acuity, because as you move closer, you should be able to see details better. However, we can understand why the border vanishes by considering what happens to its spatial frequency as you move closer. Moving closer increases the size of the border's image on your retina and, just as gratings with large bars have lower spatial frequencies than gratings with small bars, the border seen close up has a lower frequency than the border seen from far away. Since our sensitivity to contrast drops off at low spatial frequencies (see the CSF in Figure 5.20), moving closer causes us to lose our ability to detect the faint, low-contrast white border.

The spatial frequency approach, therefore, tells much more about a person's visual capabilities than simply measuring visual acuity. And, in addition, research inspired by the spatial frequency approach has suggested that neural channels sensitive to specific frequencies may play an important role in vision.

THE OBSERVER'S STATE OF ADAPTATION

Our perception of contrast depends not only on contours and spatial frequencies, but also on the observer's state of dark adaptation. To describe how our perception of contrast is influenced by adaptation, let's consider how it changes as we move between the bright backyard and the dim basement of Figure 5.27.

From Backyard to Basement

Suppose you decide to come inside from the bright, sunny backyard of Figure 5.27(a). As you enter the dimly lit basement, your perception corresponds to Figure 5.27(b) and you realize that not only is it darker in the basement than it is outside but you're also having a hard time making out the difference between the dryer and the mittens on top of it. There is a lack of contrast between them. However, as you stay in the basement, you notice that

it begins to seem less dark, that you can begin to see the mittens on the dryer, and that you can even begin to see the sink in the corner. This familiar process of *dark adaptation* that we described in Chapter 3 adjusts the visual system's sensitivity to match the lower light level in the basement, and after 5–10 minutes, you perceive the basement as in Figure 5.28(a).

A similar process occurs when you move from the basement to the backyard. At first you are blinded by the light and can see objects only faintly, as in Figure 5.28(b), but within a short time your eyes become adapted to the light, and you again see the backyard as in Figure 5.27(a).

Why is this adaptation process necessary? Why must we wait for our eyes to adjust their sensitivity before we can make out the objects in the backyard or the basement? To answer these questions, let's consider what is required of the visual system. We want (1) to be able to see in very dim and very bright light (that is, we want to have a very large **operating range**) and (2) to be able to tell the difference between two things that are very close together in intensity (that is, we want to have high sensitivity to small differences in *physical contrast*).

Our visual system meets both of these requirements. When we are dark adapted, we can see in the extremely low-light levels in a darkened room, and when we are light adapted, we can see in the extremely high-light levels of a bright day. Yet we can also detect the difference between two objects that differ in intensity by less than 1 percent. We can understand how the visual system does this by introducing the concept of operating curves.

Operating Curves

An **operating curve** describes the relationship between the intensity of a light and how bright that light appears. Figure 5.29 shows a curve that defines a large operating range. The operating range is the sloping portion of the curve from an intensity of about 100 to about 1 billion (10^9). Within this range, changing the intensity causes changes in the brightness of the stimulus. For example, if we increase the intensity from A to B, the brightness increases from A' to B'. Below 100 and above 10^9

(a)

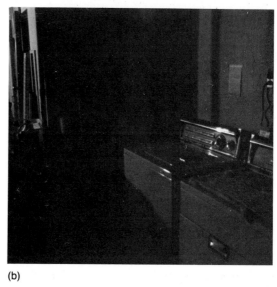

(b)

F I G U R E 5. 27 Left: a sunny backyard. Right: your perception immediately after entering the basement from the backyard.

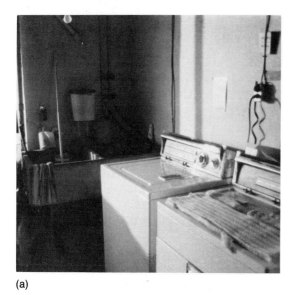

(a)

(b)

F I G U R E 5. 28 Left: your perception after adjusting to the dim light of the basement. Right: your perception immediately after entering the backyard from the basement.

the curve becomes horizontal, and changing the intensity does not affect the brightness. It might seem that this would be an ideal operating range for the visual system, because it is large enough to handle intensities ranging from the dimness of your basement to the brightness of your backyard. Unfortunately, there is a problem. To achieve this large operating range, we have sacrificed sensitivity to physical contrast. That is, we would have difficulty telling the difference between two intensi-

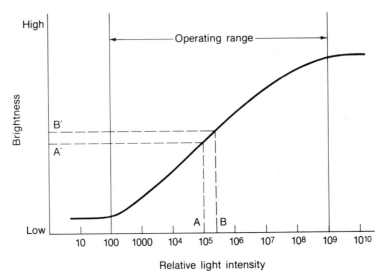

F I G U R E 5. 29 An operating curve that results in a large operating range but poor contrast sensitivity.

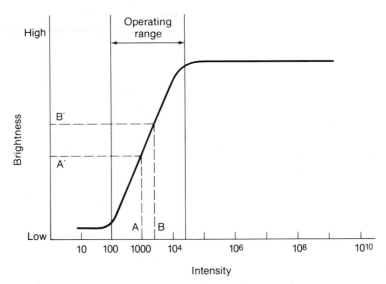

F I G U R E 5. 30 An operating curve that results in good contrast sensitivity but a small operating range.

ties that are close together, because a small intensity change causes only a very small change in the brightness.

For good sensitivity to physical contrast, our operating curve should look like the one in Figure 5.30. This curve represents good physical contrast sensitivity, because a small change in intensity causes

a large change in brightness. Increasing the intensity from A to B increases the brightness from A′ to B′, a larger change than for the operating curve of Figure 5.29. However, the problem with the curve in Figure 5.30 is that it represents a very narrow operating range. If this were the operating curve for your visual system, you could see only

BOX 5. 3 / *Contrast in Photographs*

The photographs of the bridge below are printed from the same negative, but the one on the left was printed on normal-contrast paper and the one on the right on high-contrast paper.

Like human vision, photographic papers have operating curves. The curves for the papers used to print these two photographs are shown below each.* The curve for the high-contrast paper indicates that all intensities lower than 10 give a white image and all intensities greater than 50 give a black image. Shades of grey occur only at intensities between 10 and 50. Thus, when the

*For photographic operating curves, increasing the amount of light presented to the paper *decreases* the brightness. For visual operating curves, increasing the amount of light presented to the observer *increases* the brightness.

photo is printed on high contrast paper, the gradations of shading in the face are lost and the picture appears mostly as blacks and whites, as in the photo on the right. Unless you wanted to lose the greys in a picture, you would probably not use high-contrast paper. You would, however, use it if you wanted to enhance the contrast of a scene having a small range of intensities such as might occur in a picture taken in a dimly lit room, or if you wanted to obtain a "graphic arts" effect as in the picture on the right.

The operating curve for the normal-contrast paper indicates that shades of grey occur at intensities between 10 and 250—a much larger operating range than the range of the high-contrast paper. Thus, in the photograph on the left we see the blacks and whites in the scene as well as the many shades of grey in between.

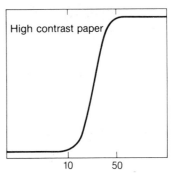

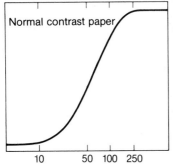

Black

Dark grey

Medium grey

Light grey

White

Normal contrast paper

10   50 100 250

High contrast paper

10   50

Total amount of light presented to paper

over a very small range of intensities. For example, if you could see well in the low intensities of your basement, you would be completely dazzled by the glare of your backyard.

How can the visual system achieve good physical contrast sensitivity *and* a large operating range? The visual system achieves this result by using a fairly narrow operating range, as in Figure 5.30, and by shifting this range to match the level of illumination. Figure 5.31 shows how this works. In dim light, the visual system operates according to curve A; when the light level is increased, the curve shifts to B, and when the level is further increased, the curve shifts to C. In other words, at a particular level of illumination, the visual system works within a fairly narrow operating range that is set to respond at that level of illumination. When the illumination is changed, the operating curve shifts to match the new level. This shifting of the curve is what is happening during light and dark adaptation. The price we pay to achieve good physical contrast sensitivity *and* a large operating range is that we must allow time for our visual system to adapt to the level of illumination.

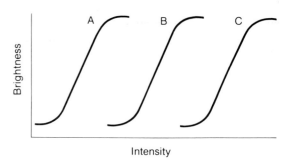

F I G U R E 5. 31 A family of operating curves that together cover a large operating range, but each has good contrast sensitivity.

A physiological demonstration of this shifting of operating curves is shown in Figure 5.32. These curves were obtained by recording from single neurons in the LGN of the cat. The receptive field of the neuron was located, and then the response to test flashes presented to the center of the receptive field was determined. Curve A shows that when the background illumination is dim, this cell oper-

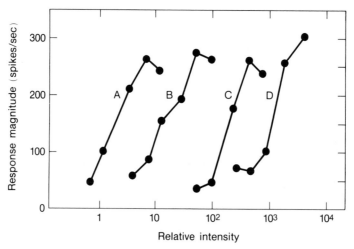

F I G U R E 5. 32 Operating curves determined by measuring the relationship between test flash intensity and the firing rate of neurons in the cat's LGN, at four different adapting levels. Curve A was determined by presenting test flashes to the dark adapted retina. Curves B, C, and D were determined by presenting test flashes in the presence of background lights of increasing intensities (B is the least intense; D is the most intense). (From Schweitzer-Tong, 1976.)

ates in the low intensity range; and when the background illumination is raised, the operating range shifts to higher intensities, as shown by curves B, C, and D. Thus, single nerve cells in the visual system have narrow operating curves that shift as the background intensity is changed.

LIGHTNESS CONSTANCY

We close this chapter by focusing our attention on the perception of lightness—the perception of a surface's reflectance, which we describe by the terms white, grey, or black. In general, surfaces with high reflectance (reflecting 80–90 percent of the illumination) look white, and surfaces with low reflectance (reflecting 0–10 percent) look black. Surfaces with intermediate reflectances look grey.

When we say that our perception of lightness depends on reflectance, we are saying that our perception of lightness depends on *a property of the surface*. This means that for a given surface, our perception of lightness should remain the same even if we change the illumination. That is, a surface that reflects 90 percent of the light should look

F I G U R E 5. 33 Grey scale.

white, whether it is illuminated by intense sunlight or by a dim desk lamp.

The fact that the lightness of a surface stays relatively constant when the amount of light is changed over a large range is called **lightness constancy**. One of the early experiments that demonstrated this effect was performed by Burzlaff in 1931.

Burzlaff's Lightness Constancy Experiment

The stimuli for Burzlaff's experiment were two sets of 48 squares, which covered the range of lightnesses shown in the grey scale of Figure 5.33, from extremely white to extremely black. He mounted one set of the squares in order, from white to black, on a large piece of cardboard, mounted the other set in random order on an identical piece of cardboard, and then presented the two sets of squares

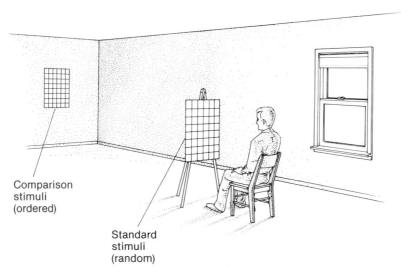

Comparison
stimuli
(ordered)

Standard
stimuli
(random)

F I G U R E 5. 34 Burzlaff's (1931) experiment. The observer's task was to judge whether each of the dimly lit comparison stimuli was lighter or darker than one of the brightly lit standard stimuli.

to the observer as shown in Figure 5.34. The ordered set was mounted on the dimly lit far wall of the room, whereas the random set was located with the observer near the window and was exposed to about 20 times more light than the squares on the wall.

The procedure of the experiment was as follows: One of the squares from the brightly illuminated set near the observer was designated the "standard." The experimenter then pointed to each of the dimly illuminated "comparison" squares on the far wall and asked the observer whether each comparison square was lighter than, darker than, or the same greyness as the standard. Using this procedure to determine which comparison square most closely matched the standard square, Burzlaff found that the comparison square that matched the standard square had about the same reflectance as the comparison square. For example, observers said that a comparison square with a reflectance of about 78 percent appeared to be the same greyness as a standard square with a reflectance of about 72 percent.

Let's consider what this result means. The observers matched two squares that were close in reflectance, even though the standard square was exposed to 20 times more illumination than the comparison square. The importance of this finding can be made more clear by calculating the *amount* of light reflected from each square. We can't calculate the actual amount of light reflected since we don't know how much light was coming through Burzlaff's window; however, since we know that there was about 20 times more light hitting the standard squares than the comparison squares, we can calculate the relative amount of light reflected by each square, as follows:

Relative amount of light reflected = reflectance × relative light intensity.

Comparison square = 78 × 1 = 78
Standard square   = 72 × 20 = 1,440

Thus, Burzlaff's observers said that two squares appeared to be the same shade of grey when one of them reflected 78 units of light and the other reflected 1,440 units of light. Therefore, the *percentage* of light reflected from an object into the

eye and not the *amount* determines our perception of lightness. Objects that look black, like the far right rectangle on the grey scale of Figure 5.33, reflect about 5 percent of the light falling on them into your eye. Objects that look grey reflect about 10–70 percent of the light (depending on the shade of grey), and objects that look white, like the far left rectangle in the grey scale, reflect 80–90 percent.

Lightness constancy means that we see the true properties of the object no matter what the illumination is. The white page of this book is seen as white in a dimly lit room or in bright sunlight, and the black print on the page is seen as black, no matter what the illumination. It's a good thing lightness constancy occurs, because, without it, the lightnesses of the objects around us would be constantly changing. Taking a piece of coal from inside to outside would change it from black to white! Without lightness constancy, it would become meaningless to say "this coal is black" or "this paper is white," because their lightnesses would change every time we changed the illumination.

DEMONSTRATION

Demonstrating Lightness Constancy to Yourself

You can do a crude lightness constancy experiment by illuminating a piece of white paper with your desk lamp and selecting the square on the grey scale of Figure 5.33 that appears to be the same whiteness. Without changing the illumination on your grey scale, turn off the lamp that illuminates the white paper, so now it is illuminated only by the general light level in your room. Repeat your lightness judgment. Even though you decreased the illumination substantially when you turned off the lamp, it is unlikely that your white paper became dark grey. Turning off the light changes the illumination while having little or no effect on lightness.

Another way to demonstrate lightness constancy is to again illuminate the paper and to cast a shadow by placing your hand between the lamp and the paper. The question here is, Does the paper appear to change color from white to dark grey in the area that is shadowed? If lightness constancy holds, your answer to this question will be "no."

A possible reaction to the above observations is, "I agree that the paper didn't change from white to dark grey when I turned off the light or cast a shadow on the paper, but it did *look different.*" There is no question that this is true, but it is important to realize that the difference you perceive is a difference not in lightness but in *brightness,* with the paper under high illumination appearing bright and the paper under low illumination appearing much less bright (remember that brightness is defined as our perception of *intensity*). Thus, as we change illumination, brightness changes, but lightness remains relatively constant. A piece of coal seen inside looks black (lightness) but appears dimly illuminated (brightness), whereas the same piece of coal seen outside still looks black (lightness remains constant) but appears brightly illuminated (brightness increases).

What is responsible for lightness constancy? The answer to this question involves a number of different factors, each of which helps us to perceive lightness accurately under differing conditions of illumination.

Lightness Constancy and Relationships

We already know from the simultaneous contrast demonstration of Figure 5.9 that an object's background can affect its brightness. In that figure two identical squares appeared different because they were on different backgrounds. Figure 5.35 illustrates the effect of an object's background in another way. In this case, the two squares are physically different but appear the same (or almost the same) because they are on different backgrounds. (To eliminate the effect of the backgrounds, view the small squares through two holes punched in a card, as you did for Figure 5.9.)

F I G U R E 5. 35 The two small squares reflect different amounts of light but appear close in lightness. To appreciate the actual physical difference between these squares, punch two holes 2¼ inches apart in a card and look at the two squares with the background masked.

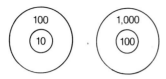

F I G U R E 5. 36 How simultaneous contrast can make two different discs appear identical. If light intensities were as indicated by the numbers in the outer rings and inner discs, the inner discs would appear identical because the ring-to-disc ratio is 10 to 1 in both cases. (Wallach, 1963.)

The principle behind this effect is called the **ratio principle** (Wallach, 1963; Jacobsen & Gilchrist, 1988). According to this principle, shown in Figure 5.36, two areas that reflect different amounts of light will look the same if the ratios of their intensities to the intensities of the surrounds are kept constant.

We can understand how the ratio principle helps explain lightness constancy by considering how you perceive the black letters on the pages of this book. The letters look black whether viewed under dim or intense illumination, because even if we change the illumination, the ratio of the light intensity reflected from the letters to the light intensity reflected from the paper remains the same (Figure 5.37).

An experiment by Gelb (1929) demonstrates the importance of relationships in the perception of lightness constancy. Figure 5.38, the setup for Gelb's experiment, shows a disc of low reflectance suspended in completely black surroundings. The key feature of this experiment was the presence of a hidden light that illuminated only the disc. When viewed from the observer's position, the disc, which would look black in your living room or outdoors, looked white. This result occurred because the only stimulus present, other than the disc, was the black background, which reflected only a small amount of light compared to the secretly illuminated disc. This perception of a black disc as white is consistent with the idea that relationships are important in determining lightness. But Gelb wasn't satisfied just to turn a black disc white; he also wanted to make it turn black again. He did this by placing a

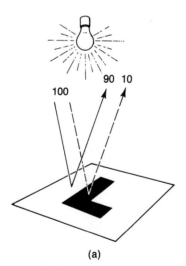

(a)

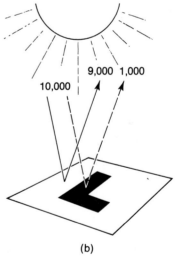

(b)

F I G U R E 5. 37 What happens to the amount of light reflected from a sheet of white paper and from a black letter (L) on the paper, when viewed (a) under low illumination in which the intensity equals 100, and (b) under high illumination in which the intensity equals 10,000. In both cases, the paper reflects 90 percent of the light and the letter reflects 10 percent, so that the ratio of the light intensities reflected from the paper and the letter remains at 9:1 under both levels of illumination.

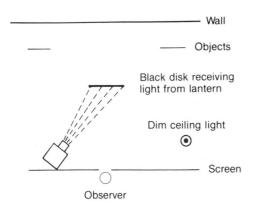

Wall

Objects

Black disk receiving light from lantern

Dim ceiling light

Screen

Observer

F I G U R E 5. 38 The setup of Gelb's concealed illumination experiment. The observer could not see the light on the left, which was projected only onto the black disc. The background, which is also black, was dimly illuminated by the ceiling light. (From Hochberg, 1971.)

small piece of white paper in front of the disc so that it became illuminated by the hidden light. As soon as the white paper was introduced, the disc turned black! This new relationship, with the white paper reflecting much more light than the disc, caused the disc to look dark.

Gelb's experiment shows that lightness constancy breaks down—an ordinarily black object can appear white—if the ordinarily black object has the highest intensity in the field. This effect occurs only under special conditions such as those used by Gelb: a hidden light and no other comparison objects in the field. As soon as a comparison object is placed in the light with the black disc, the relationship between the white paper and the disc reinstates the lightness constancy, and the disc becomes black.

Before we leave Gelb's experiment, let's ask another question: What effect does the observer's knowledge of the situation have on his or her perception? Once the white paper is presented, the observer becomes aware that the disc is really black. You might think that once the truth is known, the disc would always be perceived as black, but this is not the case. When the small piece of white paper is removed, the black disc turns white again, and no amount of knowledge will make it turn

black. Knowledge of the situation does not necessarily affect our perception.

Lightness Constancy in Shadows

When we say that a lump of coal remains black when we take it from inside to outside because the relationship between the coal and its surroundings remains constant, we are assuming that everything in the environment, both inside and outside, is illuminated evenly. But this is not always the case. You have only to look around to see that the world is illuminated unevenly, with areas of high and low illumination and, especially outside on a sunny day, with many shadows.

To appreciate the problem that shadows pose for perception, let's return to our board of Figure 5.2, which demonstrates two different ways to create contrast. In Figure 5.2(b) we created contrast by casting a shadow on the board, whereas in Figure 5.2(c) we created contrast by painting part of the board black. Although in both cases we have decreased the amount of light reflected from the board into our eyes, our perceptions of the board's lightness are very different. In (b) we perceive the back of the board to be in shadow but to have the same lightness ("white") as the front of the board. In (c) we perceive the back of the board to have a different lightness ("black") from the front of the board.

According to Alan Gilchrist and coworkers (1983), we perceive the boards in (b) and (c) differently by making a distinction between an **illumination edge,** an edge or contour in which the *illumination* on a surface changes, as in (b), and a **reflectance edge,** an edge in which the *reflectance* of a surface changes, as in (c). One way to look at the problem of lightness constancy in shadows is to assume that lightness constancy occurs in shadows because we somehow know that the shadow's edge is created by a change in illumination rather than by a change in reflectance. Thus, when you see shadows like the one in Figure 5.39 you do not assume that the shadowed grass is dark green and the grass in sunlight is light green. Instead, you assume that the shadowed and unshadowed areas

F I G U R E 5. 39

have the same lightness—that is, they are the same shade of green all over—but that less light falls on some areas than on others.

How do we tell the difference between an illumination edge and a reflectance edge? One way we do this is to notice the nature of the shadow's edge. Cast a shadow yourself and look at the edge between the shadowed and nonshadowed areas. You will see that the edge is fuzzy, as in Figure 5.40. This fuzzy area, which is called the shadow's **penumbra,** is responsible for much of the lightness constancy in shadows.

DEMONSTRATION

Covering the Penumbra

If the penumbra is responsible for lightness constancy, we should be able to decrease lightness constancy by eliminating the penumbra. This is exactly what Ewald Hering (1905) did in his ringed shadow experiment, which you can carry out yourself. Produce a shadow on a piece of white paper with a small object; then draw a dark border along the contour of the shadow, as in Figure 5.41. If this

F I G U R E 5. 40 A shape-sorting box and its shadow.

F I G U R E   5. 41   The same box and shadow as in Figure 5.39 with the shadow's penumbra covered by a black border.

border covers the penumbra, the shadowed area will change in appearance. Instead of looking like a shadow on a piece of white paper, it looks like a dark spot on the paper. Eliminating the penumbra decreases lightness constancy by causing us to perceive an illumination edge as a reflectance edge.

The penumbra tells us that a shadow is present, and once we know we are dealing with a shadow, we know that the illumination is changing, not the object's lightness. The penumbra helps us know that shadows are shadows. Another thing that identifies shadows is the shadow's shape. They are often shaped like trees, people, cars, and the other objects in the environment. It is unlikely that the pattern on the grass and building in Figure 5.39 could be anything but a shadow of a tree; therefore we interpret it that way. It is conceivable that the dark pattern on the house in Figure 5.42 could be due to a strange paint job, but it is much more likely, since it resembles the tree branches the art-

ist has included in the upper left corner, that the pattern results from a shadow rather than a change in lightness. We can be fooled, however, by paintings such as the one in Figure 5.43. In this case the painter fools us by painting a pattern that looks like a shadow. (Look at this picture closely. Where's the key?)

Lightness Constancy and Perceived Illumination

A number of experiments have shown that an observer's interpretation of how an object is illuminated affects his or her perception of the object's lightness.

D E M O N S T R A T I O N

The Mach Card Demonstration

To show how lightness is affected by the perception of the direction of illumination, we can carry out a demonstration originally proposed by Ernst Mach. To do this you need only a small card or piece of paper. Fold the card as shown in Figure 5.44, then orient it so that the left side is illuminated slightly less than the right (the light should be coming from the right). When viewed at about a 45-degree angle from above with two eyes, the two sides of the card look about the same lightness. That both sides look white, even though one is more intensely illuminated, is an example of lightness constancy. Now, close one eye and continue viewing the card. Eventually, your perception should "flip" so that the card appears to stand on end like an open book with the inside toward you, as in Figure 5.45. When this happens, something else also happens. The shadowed left side of the card gets much darker and the illuminated right side may even appear luminous. Lightness constancy has been eliminated—both sides of the card originally appeared white, but now one side appears dark and the other appears light.

We can explain the Mach card effect by considering how we register the illumination relative to the card. Before the card flips, we perceive the

F I G U R E 5. 42 *Corfu, Lights and Shadows* by John Singer Sargent. (Museum of Fine Arts, Boston.)

right side of the card as illuminated and the left side as in shadow. Our perceptual system apparently takes the illumination conditions into account and both sides of the card appear white. That is, lightness constancy is working. After the card flips, however, the apparent illumination conditions change. Now the shadowed left side appears to be facing toward the light and the illuminated right side appears to be facing away from the light. This creates the following problem for the perceptual system: Although the left side appears to be facing

F I G U R E 5. 43 *No. 277* (1968) by Jiro Takamatsu. Many people who look at this fail to notice that the "shadow" is being produced by an invisible key!

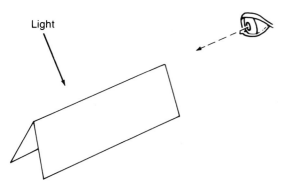

Light

F I G U R E 5. 44 How to view the Mach card.

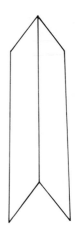

F I G U R E 5. 45 What the Mach card looks like when it perceptually "flips."

toward the light, only a small amount of light is reflected from that side. Similarly, although the right side appears to be facing *away from* the light, a large amount of light is reflected from that side. The perceptual system's solution: The left side must be made of a low-reflectance material and the right side of a high-reflectance material. Thus, the erroneous information about the flipped card's orientation relative to the light causes a breakdown in lightness constancy that causes the left side to appear dark and the right side to appear light.

D E M O N S T R A T I O N

Lightness at a Corner

You can use your folded card for another demonstration in which we eliminate lightness constancy. Stand the folded card on end so it resembles the outside corner of a room, and illuminate it so one side is illuminated and the other is in shadow. When you look at the corner, you can easily tell that both sides of the corner are white, but that the non-illuminated side is shadowed. Now punch a hole in another card and, with the hole near the corner of the folded card and your eye about a foot from the hole, view the corner through the hole. If, when viewing the corner in this way, you perceive the corner as a flat surface, your perception will change so the edge between the illuminated and shadowed sides of the corner changes from an illu-

mination edge to a reflectance edge. Eliminating our perception of depth at the corner eliminates lightness constancy.

Alan Gilchrist (1977) has performed an ingenious experiment to show that our perception of lightness can be affected by how we perceive an object's illumination. Gilchrist took a white card (which we will call the "test" card) and caused it to appear either white or dark grey by changing only the card's *apparent* position in space. His setup is shown in Figure 5.46. The observer looks through a peephole and sees three cards: a black card; the white test card attached to a doorway inside a dimly lit room; and another white card, attached to the far wall of a brightly lit room.

The key to this experiment is how the test card is perceived to be illuminated. In part 1 of the experiment, the cards are mounted as shown in Figure 5.46 and are perceived as shown in Figure 5.47(a). The test card and black card appear to be inside the dimly lit room, with the test card located in front. In part 2 of the experiment, the actual positioning of the cards is exactly the same, as shown in Figure 5.47(b), but the way the cards appear to overlap is changed so that the observer perceives

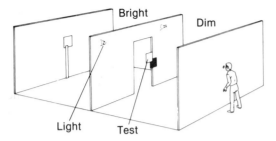

F I G U R E 5. 46 The setup used by Gilchrist (1977). The observer looks at the three cards through a peephole. Two of the cards are attached to the middle wall, and one is attached to the far wall. The intensities of light reflected from each card remain constant throughout the experiment. The test card and the card on the far wall are both made of white material, but the card on the far wall reflects much more light than the test card because it is illuminated by lights mounted on the middle wall.

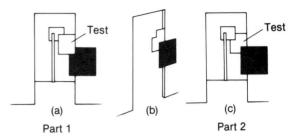

F I G U R E 5. 47 (a) What the observer sees in part 1 of Gilchrist's experiment. When the test card appears to be in front of the back card, it appears white. (b) The arrangement of the cards in part 2 of the experiment. The test card is now attached to the back of the black card, and its upper left corner is cut out so that it *appears* to be as in (c)—located in back of the card on the far wall—when viewed through the peephole. When the test card appears to be in back of the card on the far wall, it appears dark grey. Note that the test card's appearance changes, even though both the card's actual position in space and its illumination remain constant throughout the experiment.

the display as shown in Figure 5.47(c). The test card now appears to be in back of the white card on the far wall of the brightly lit room. It is important to remember that in both parts of the experiment the *actual* position of the test card is always the same. What changes is the *apparent* position of the test card.

The observer's task in Gilchrist's experiment was to judge the lightness of the test card. The observer did this by matching the test card to one of a series of papers ranging from black (given a value of 2.0) to white (given a value of 9.5). In part 1 of the experiment, the average lightness, as judged by a number of observers, was 9.0, just slightly less white than the whitest paper available. This makes sense, since the test card is made of white paper and reflects much more light than the black card next to it.

The key result of Gilchrist's experiment is that when the apparent position of the test card changes to the far room, as in Figure 5.47(c), the average lightness of this card decreases to 3.5, a dark grey. Why did the lightness of the test card change? Because it appears to be illuminated by the same light as the white card on the back wall but reflects much less light. The perceptual system's solution: The test card must have a low reflectance and so

is perceived as a dark grey. Remember, however, that the real reason the test card reflects less light is that it is actually in the dimly lit near room. This explanation may sound familiar because it is similar to the one we proposed to explain the results of the Mach card demonstration.

Gilchrist's experiment shows that our perception of the way an object is illuminated can influence our perception of lightness. This result is, however, not simply an interesting demonstration of how the perceived illumination affects lightness perception. Both Gilchrist's result and the results of the Mach card demonstration are relevant to our discussion on page 152 about the physiological mechanisms for our perception of lightness. We pointed out that, although lateral inhibition can explain our perception of Mach bands (Figure 5.3) and our perception of the simultaneous contrast effect (Figure 5.9), it cannot explain the different lightnesses of the two grey triangles in Figure 5.11.

In that discussion, we said that we would encounter more situations in which lateral inhibition alone can't explain our perceptions, and the Mach card demonstration and Gilchrist's results are two such situations. Consider what happens to the

Mach card's image on the retina when it flips from one orientation to another. Since the card never actually moves, the perceptual flip is not accompanied by any change in the pattern of light and dark on the retina. Because lateral inhibition depends solely on the pattern on the retina, it cannot explain the change in lightness seen in the Mach card demonstration. Similarly, in Gilchrist's experiment, a very small change in the pattern of light and dark on the retina (see Figure 5.47) is accompanied by a large change in the appearance of the test card, which cannot be explained by lateral inhibition.

So, while we can provide physiological explanations for some things, we are still unable to explain many perceptual phenomena in terms of physiology. Though we can explain simultaneous contrast in terms of lateral inhibition, we have no physiological explanation for why the Mach card and Gilchrist's test card change their appearance. This, of course, does not mean that physiological explanations do not exist. They do exist—we just haven't discovered them yet.

UNCOVERING THE COMPLEXITIES OF PERCEPTION

In this chapter, we have seen how the complexities of our perception of brightness, contrast, and lightness have been uncovered by laboratory experiments that are specifically designed to tease out mechanisms that may not be obvious from our everyday experience. Thus, when Alan Gilchrist constructs an environment (Figure 5.46) that fools us into thinking an object is in a far room illuminated with a bright light when, in actuality, it is in a near room illuminated by a dim light, he creates a situation that rarely occurs in real life. But the result of this contrived stimulus is a greater understanding of how our perception of illumination affects our perception of lightness. We can make similar arguments about contour effects and spatial frequency channels, neither of which is obvious in our everyday experience but which

becomes visible to the perception researcher under controlled laboratory conditions.

Although laboratory research is often necessary to uncover perceptual mechanisms, we can sometimes hypothesize mechanisms based on everyday experience. Consider, for example, the following situation: You see a shadowy object in the dimly lit corner of a room and think it is a table. Upon closer inspection, however, it turns out to be a chair, or, perhaps, just a shadow. Situations such as this, in which our everyday perceptions are initially uncertain, have led Richard Gregory (1973a) to suggest that perception is governed by a mechanism he calls **hypothesis testing.**

Gregory's observation that sensory stimulation is sometimes uncertain led him to state that "we may think of sensory stimulation as providing *data for hypotheses* concerning the state of the external world" (p. 61). Your first hypothesis about the shadowy object in the corner ("That's a table.") was based on the rather indistinct sensory stimulation from the dimly lit corner. After you gained more information about the situation, your third hypothesis ("Oh, I see, that's actually a shadow.") turned out to be correct.

Some of the processes we have discussed in connection with lightness constancy can be considered in terms of hypothesis testing. Thus, we hypothesize that the light area on the wall in Figure 5.48 is due to the illumination streaming through the window rather than to an interesting paint job, since we can see the window on the left. There's a good chance that this hypothesis is correct, especially since there is a similar pattern of illumination on the far right. But it is *possible* (albeit unlikely) that the same artist who painted the key shadow in Figure 5.43 could have painted "sunlight" onto the walls of this restaurant.

Color Plate 5.1 is an example of a bush that fooled me into the wrong hypothesis. When I first looked at this bush, I thought that the ends of some of its branches looked brighter than the rest of the bush because they were sticking out and therefore appeared to be illuminated by the sunlight. This seemed reasonable until I looked at the branches more closely. As you can see in Color Plate 5.2, they were not, in fact, illuminated more brightly

F I G U R E   5. 48   *Sunlight in a Cafeteria* (1958), by Edward Hopper. (Yale University Art Gallery, New Haven, Conn.)

than the rest of the branches: They were actually a lighter green! Had I known that the new growth of these bushes is much lighter than the old growth, I probably wouldn't have been fooled. But my incorrect interpretation of the illumination, combined with my ignorance about how bushes grow, resulted in a faulty hypothesis, so I mistook a lightness change for a change in the illumination.

Looking back over this chapter, we can now appreciate that the range of explanations for our perceptions is as wide as the many methods and approaches we introduced in Chapter 1, with our explanations for brightness, contrast, and lightness ranging from lateral inhibition to spatial frequency channels to hypothesis testing. And we can also appreciate that these many explanations do not necessarily compete with one another. Perception is not a contest in which one mechanism must be the only correct one. Perception is the result of the coordinated workings of numerous mechanisms.

As we continue our exploration of perception in the chapters to follow, many of the basic principles of perception discussed in this chapter will reappear again both for the sense of vision and for the other senses as well.

Summary

1. Brightness is the perception of the intensity of light reflected from a surface. This intensity can be affected by the intensity of illumination or by the reflectance of a surface. Contrast is the perception of the difference in the light reflected from two areas.

2. The following principles of perception are introduced in this chapter.
   (a) Perception is multiply determined.
   (b) Presently, we can explain some perceptions physiologically, but can't explain others.

3. Mach bands are illusory light and dark bands that occur at borders between light and dark areas.

4. Lateral inhibition is the physiological mechanism underlying Mach bands and can partially explain the simultaneous contrast effect. Lateral inhibition cannot, however, totally explain simultaneous contrast, or the difference in the appearance of the two triangles in Figure 5.11.

5. It is important to distinguish between perceptual contrast—our *perception* of the difference in intensity reflected from two areas—and physical contrast, the difference in the intensity reflected from two areas.

6. Staring at a disc with a fuzzy contour can cause it to disappear. The reason this occurs is that, although the disc's image jiggles on the retina due to involuntary eye movements, only slight changes occur in the stimulation of receptors near the contour due to the fuzzy border. Since the visual system responds poorly to constant stimulation, the disc fades. Similar fading occurs when an image is stabilized on the retina, and stabilized image experiments show that the jiggling of contours maintains our perception of the area inside the contours.

7. Our perception of the contrast between two areas is affected by the spatial frequency of the stimulus. The contrast sensitivity function (CSF), a plot of contrast sensitivity versus spatial frequency, indicates that the visual system is most sensitive to sine-wave gratings with a spatial frequency of about 3 cycles per degree of visual angle.

8. Evidence from psychophysical selective adaptation experiments supports the idea that the CSF is generated by the activity of a number of spatial frequency channels. This idea is also supported by physiological evidence.

9. Contrast sensitivity provides more information about vision than does visual acuity because it provides information over a range of spatial frequencies and contrasts, whereas visual acuity provides information only about high-spatial-frequency, high-contrast vision.

10. The visual system must be able to work over a wide range of intensities while still maintaining good contrast sensitivity. It accomplishes this by working within a fairly narrow operating range that matches the average intensity of the scene. If a large change occurs in the average intensity of a scene, the operating range is shifted by the process of light or dark adaptation to match the new average intensity. This shift in operating curves with changes in illumination levels has been demonstrated physiologically.

11. Lightness is the property of objects that is related to an object's reflectance—the percentage of the light falling on the object that is reflected. Lightness constancy means that we perceive an object's lightness to be relatively constant, no matter what the illumination.

12. Lightness constancy is influenced by factors such as simultaneous contrast, the penumbra of shadows, and the observer's interpretation of how an object is illuminated.

13. The hypothesis testing mechanism of perception suggests that sensory stimulation provides data for hypotheses about the world. Perception, according to this idea, is a process of testing various hypotheses about what we are seeing. This process of hypothesis testing may be one of the mechanisms operating when we take the illumination conditions into account to determine our perception of lightness.

Boxes

1. A process called the spreading effect, or assimilation, can change our perception of the lightness of an area. Placing light lines inside a homogeneous field makes the field appear lighter.

2. Contour movement on the retina can be eliminated by having an observer look into a homogeneous field called a Ganzfeld. The effect of the Ganzfeld is similar to the effect of a stabilized image.

3. Like human vision, photographic papers have operating curves. These curves differ for high- and low-contrast paper.

Study Questions

1. Define brightness. Define contrast. Describe two different ways that we can change the brightness of a board. (145)
2. Define reflectance and lightness. (146)
3. What is a Mach band? Be sure you understand the difference between the *intensity distribution* of the stripes in Figure 5.3 and our *perception* of the brightness of the stripes. Where are the dark and light bands in the stripe pattern? (148)
4. What is lateral inhibition? How did Hartline et al. demonstrate lateral inhibition in the *Limulus*? (149)
5. Be sure you understand the calculation for the neural circuit in Figure 5.7. (151)
6. What is simultaneous contrast? How does lateral inhibition explain simultaneous contrast? What can't lateral inhibition explain about simultaneous contrast? About the brightnesses of the grey areas in Figure 5.11? (152)
7. What is the difference between perceptual contrast and physical contrast? (154)
8. If two areas reflect the same amount of light but one has a fuzzy contour and the other a sharp contour, which will appear to have more contrast? (155)
9. Explain why the fuzzy-contoured disc in Figure 5.13 fades while the sharp-contoured disc doesn't. What role do involuntary eye movements play in this process? (156) What basic principle of visual system operation can we propose, based on the way the visual system responds to the fuzzy and sharp discs? (156)
10. What is the stabilized image technique? What happens to vision when the image is stabilized? What does this result mean? (157)
11. Why might we expect that the center of the sharp disc should fade when it is viewed under normal (unstabilized) conditions? Why doesn't it? (157)
12. Describe Krauskopf's stabilized image experiment. What do the results prove? (158)
13. Describe a grating stimulus and define what we mean when we talk about a grating's waveform, physical contrast, and spatial frequency. (160)
14. What is the contrast sensitivity function (CSF)? How is it measured? What does the CSF tell us? (161)
15. What is a spatial frequency channel? How do the results of psychophysical selective adaptation experiments support the idea of spatial frequency channels? Is there any physiological evidence for these channels? (163)
16. How does the idea of spatial frequency channels explain the results of the size-adaptation demonstration of Figure 5.23? (165)
17. What is the advantage of contrast sensitivity measurements over visual acuity measures? What does contrast sensitivity tell us that visual acuity doesn't? As part of your answer describe Sekuler's experiment in which he compared the visual acuities and CSFs of old and young observers. (166)
18. What happens to an observer's ability to see contrast as he goes from high to low to high illumination? Relate this to what is happening to the dark adaptation curve. (168)
19. Draw operating curves (a) with a large operating range, and (b) with high-contrast sensitivity. (168)
20. Know how to determine how brightness changes as we increase the intensity from A to B in Figures 5.27 and 5.28. (168)
21. How does the visual system achieve good contrast sensitivity and a large operating range? (172)
22. What is the physiological evidence that operating curves change with adaptation? (172)
23. What is lightness? What do we mean when we say that lightness is a property of the surface? (173)
24. Describe Burzlaff's lightness constancy experiment. What does this experiment prove? (173)
25. How does the ratio principle explain lightness constancy? (176)
26. Describe Gelb's experiment. What does it show about the role of relationships in the perception of lightness? What does it show about the effect of the observer's knowledge on perception? (176)
27. What problem do shadows pose for lightness constancy? What is the difference between an illumination edge and a reflectance edge? What is the penumbra and what role does it play in lightness constancy? (177)
28. Describe the Mach card demonstration and explain how this demonstration shows that an observer's interpretation of how an object is illuminated affects her perception of the object's lightness. (179)
29. How does eliminating our perception of depth at a corner affect lightness constancy? (181)
30. Describe Gilchrist's experiment, in which he showed that our perception of an object's lightness is affected by our perception of how the object is illuminated. (181)
31. Explain the idea that perception is a process of hypothesis testing. Relate this to the perception of lightness constancy. (183)

Boxes

1. What is the spreading effect? Assimilation? Compare the spreading effect to simultaneous contrast. How does the spreading effect work in engravings? (153)
2. What is a Ganzfeld? What happens when you view one? What does this mean? (159)
3. Given two operating curves for photographic paper, be able to tell which paper would result in better reproduction of shades of grey. (171)

Glossary

Assimilation. See spreading effect.

Brightness. Perception of the intensity of light reflected from a surface. (145)

Contour. A narrow region that visually separates two areas. (155)

Contrast. Perception of differences in the light reflected from two areas. Also see *physical contrast*. (145)

Contrast sensitivity. Sensitivity to the difference in the light intensities in two adjacent areas. Contrast sensitivity is usually measured by taking the reciprocal of the minimum physical contrast that a grating must have so that the observer can see the bars of the grating. (163)

Contrast sensitivity function (CSF). A plot of contrast sensitivity versus the spatial frequency of a grating stimulus. (163)

Ganzfeld. A totally homogeneous field. (159)

Hypothesis testing. The idea that sensory stimulation provides data for hypotheses about the world. According to this idea, perceiving involves testing different hypotheses about what is causing stimulation. (183)

Illumination edge. An edge or contour in which the illumination on a surface changes. (177)

Involuntary eye movements. Involuntary jiggling of the eye. (156)

Lateral inhibition. Inhibition that is spread laterally across a nerve circuit. In the retina, lateral inhibition is spread by the horizontal and amacrine cells. (149)

Lateral plexus. A structure that transmits nerve impulses laterally in the Limulus eye. (149)

Lightness. Perception of reflectance. (147)

Lightness constancy. When our perception of an object's lightness remains constant under different intensities of illumination. (173)

Limulus. A primitive animal, also called the horseshoe crab, whose large visual receptors make it especially well suited for studying the electrophysiology of vision. (149)

Mach bands. A perceptual effect that causes a thin dark band on the dark side of a light-dark border and a thin light band on the light side of the border. (148)

Ommatidium. A structure in the eye of the *Limulus* that contains a small lens, located directly over a visual receptor. The *Limulus* eye is made up of hundreds of these ommatidia. (149)

Operating curve. A function relating to the psychological response of brightness to a light's physical intensity. (168)

Operating range. The range of intensities over which increases in light intensity cause increases in the brightness of the light. (168)

Penumbra. The fuzzy border on many shadows. The fuzziness of a shadow's border depends on how an object is illuminated. Objects illuminated by diffuse light cast fuzzy shadows (large penumbra), whereas objects illuminated by a point source of light cast sharp shadows (small penumbra). (178)

Perceptual contrast. Perception of difference in the light reflected from two areas. Perceptual contrast is referred to as contrast in this chapter. (154)

Physical contrast. Differences in light intensity in adjacent areas. (154)

Ratio principle. Two areas that reflect different amounts of light will look the same if the ratios of their intensities to the intensities of their surrounds are the same. (176)

Reflectance. The percentage of light reflected from a surface. (146)

Reflectance edge. An edge in which the reflectance of a surface changes. (177)

Selective adaptation. In this chapter selective adaptation refers to adaptation to a single spatial frequency or a narrow range of spatial frequencies. (163)

Sine-wave grating. A grating stimulus with a sine-wave intensity distribution. (161)

Spatial frequency channels. Hypothesized channels in the visual system that are sensitive to narrow ranges of spatial frequencies. (163)

Spreading effect (or Assimilation). Adding fine lines to a homogeneous field affects the lightness of the field. Light lines lighten the field and dark lines darken the field. (153)

Square-wave grating. A grating stimulus with a square-wave intensity distribution. (161)

Stabilized image. An image that is optically stabilized on the retina, so that when the eye moves, the image stays imaged at the same place on the retina. (157)

CHAPTER 6

Perceiving Objects and Forms

What's So Hard about Perceiving Objects?
Perceptual Organization: The Gestalt Approach
Modern Extensions of Gestalt Psychology
The Idea of Perceptual Processing
Preattentive and Focused Processing
Recognition-by-Components
The Computational Approach
Parts or Wholes?

Try asking someone what they see in a room. When you do this, you will probably hear responses like "a chair, some books on the desk, pictures on the wall." Perception, for most people, is first and foremost the perception of objects and their locations. This makes sense when we consider that, in dealing with the world, our main interactions are with objects located in particular places. We pick up the book to our left, or we are careful to walk around the chair in the middle of the room, and the fact that the book is red or the seat of the chair has a unique trapezoidal shape is of secondary importance to our perception of the book and chair as objects located in particular places.

WHAT'S SO HARD ABOUT PERCEIVING OBJECTS?

One characteristic of our ability to perceive objects is that it is usually effortless. We look at the chair and, with no particular effort, see a chair, unless it is extremely dark or it is hidden from view. And sometimes, even when most of the chair is not visible, as in Figure 6.1, we can still identify the partially hidden object as a chair.

Given the ease with which we perceive objects, we might assume that the process of object perception is simple. But we can appreciate that there is nothing simple about it by considering the difficulties involved in programming a computer to recognize even simple scenes. Although many of the early researchers in computer vision thought that it wouldn't be very difficult to design systems that could recognize objects or scenes, they soon found that although seeing is easy for humans, it is an extremely difficult task for computers. Even now, after decades of work on computer vision, most sophisticated computer programs can recognize simple shapes like those in Figure 6.2, but cannot correctly identify most of the varied objects that we see easily every day.

Why is the perception of objects so difficult for a computer? We can answer this question by considering the block scene in Figure 6.2. The computer's task is to use the two-dimensional information in images like the one in the figure to deter-

F I G U R E 6. 1 Mystery object behind wall.

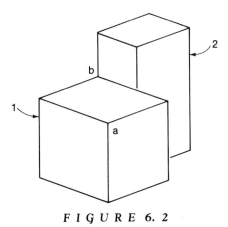

F I G U R E 6. 2

F I G U R E 6. 3 A given retinal image can be created by an infinite number of objects. Here we show three objects that, when viewed from the angle shown, cast the same image on the retina.

mine the actual three-dimensional reality of the scene. To do this, the computer must deal with the following problems:

1. Transforming a two-dimensional representation into three-dimensional objects. The problem arises when we realize that a given two-dimensional representation can be caused by many different three-dimensional objects. For example, the image of object 1, which we interpret as a cube, could be created by other geometrical objects, as shown in Figure 6.3.
2. Deciding whether three intersecting lines are part of the same object or are created by two different objects. For example, the intersection at (a) is the corner of object 1, but the intersection at (b) is created by objects 1 and 2 together.
3. Determining the shapes of objects that are partially hidden. Although we assume that object 2 is a rectangular solid, we do this by making an assumption about what is happening behind object 1 (just as we make an assumption that there is a rocking chair behind the wall in Figure 6.1).

These are only a few of the problems facing computer vision. Things become even more complex when we consider the many varied shapes we see in the real world (see Barrow & Tenenbaum, 1986; Beck, Hope, & Resenfeld, 1983; Brown, 1984; Hanson & Riseman, 1978; McArthur, 1982; Poggio, 1986; Winston, 1975 for more detailed discussions of the problems involved in computer vision).

BOX 6.1. / *Disorders of Object Perception*

Not everyone can easily identify common objects that they see every day. Objects like spoons, wristwatches, and pictures of common animals are either misidentified or looked at in puzzlement by people who suffer from **visual agnosia**—a condition caused by the brain damage resulting from strokes (an interruption of the blood supply serving the brain), tumors, or traumatic wounds. A person suffering from visual agnosia has no difficulty *seeing* objects but cannot name them, describe their use, and in some cases, cannot copy a picture of the object.

For example, a patient with agnosia might respond as follows to a picture of a telephone: "A dial . . . number . . . of course, it's a watch or some sort of machine." Patients like these can see isolated parts of each picture but can't synthesize these parts into an integrated whole. Thus, covering part of a picture has little effect on their performance. Whether they see the whole picture or only part of it, they can just identify isolated parts. This inability to synthesize an object into an integrated whole is also illustrated by the attempt, shown below, of a patient to copy a picture of an elephant or draw a picture of a man (Luria, 1966).

Some patients with visual agnosia are able to recognize objects when seen in a typical view such as the picture of the telephone on the left below, but are unable to recognize the object when seen in an "atypical" view, on the right (Warrington, 1982). Patients with a form of

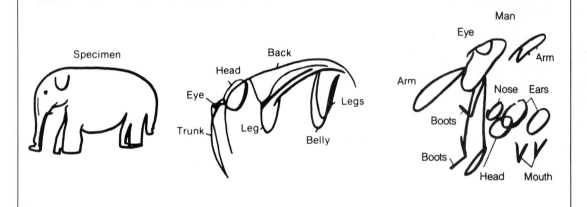

The point of this brief foray into computer vision is that although we are presented with the same information as the computer, in the form of a two-dimensional image of the scene on our retina, we are somehow able to translate this image into a correct perception of the scene. We are sometimes fooled (perhaps shape 2 is not really a rectangular solid), but most of the time we effortlessly arrive at a correct perception of the scene.

In this chapter we will describe some of the major attempts at explaining how we perceive objects. In doing this we will often be dealing not with three-dimensional objects but with simple two-dimensional shapes or forms, since understanding how we perceive simple forms is a good starting place for achieving our eventual goal of understanding how we perceive more complex objects and scenes.

Our approach in this chapter will be primarily psychophysical. That is, our explanations will be

agnosia called **prosopagnosia** cannot recognize faces, even those of close relatives, famous people, or people they have seen moments before.

What is the basis for these problems? Most forms of agnosia are associated with damage to cortical areas *outside of* the primary visual receiving area, with damage to the parietal and temporal lobes being most common. The initial analysis of the stimulus in the visual cortex may, therefore, be normal in these patients, but problems arise when this information is transmitted outside the visual cortex for further processing. We saw in Chapter 3 (p. 94) that there are neurons in the temporal lobe that respond best to complex stimuli like faces. These neurons often have extremely large receptive fields and respond equally well to both large and small stimuli, as well as to stimuli presented in different orientations (Gross & Mishkin, 1977; Sato, 1981; Rolls, 1981; Bruce et al., 1981). Perhaps, suggests A. Cowey (1982), these "higher-level" cells enable us to categorize objects irrespective of their exact shape, size, or angle of view (for example, "that's a telephone"). But when these cells are destroyed we lose our ability to categorize objects. Each different view is then seen as a unique object and cannot, therefore, be identified as anything familiar.

 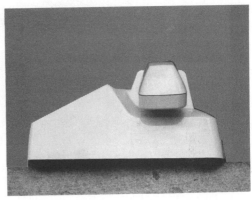

at the level of stimuli (see page 21). This is not to say that physiology is unimportant. In Chapter 3 (page 95) we considered the possible role of feature detectors in perceiving shapes. We concluded that although there is evidence supporting a role for feature detectors in form perception, at our present state of knowledge we are far from being able to explain the perception of even simple forms based on the firing of cortical feature detectors. Although it is certainly important to study how we perceive objects and forms at the level of physiology (see Boxes 6.1 and 6.2), our main priority in this chapter is to illustrate how an analysis of this problem at the level of stimuli can be rewarding.

We will begin by describing the early work of the Gestalt psychologists, which began in the 1920s, and will then describe more recent work that has evolved both from these early ideas and from recent work on computer vision and the information processing approach to perception.

B O X 6. 2. / *Two Visual Pathways: Object Vision and Spatial Vision*

Perceiving objects as integrated wholes that we can recognize from different points of view and in different positions in space depends, as we saw in Box 6.1, on cortical areas outside the primary visual receiving area. The idea that areas outside the visual cortex are important for vision was unthinkable based on what we knew about the brain in the 1950s, but we now know that as much as 40 percent of the cortex can be activated by visual stimuli (Mishkin, 1986).

Research by Mortimer Mishkin and coworkers (Mishkin, Ungerleider, & Macko, 1983) has shown that there are two separate visual pathways that extend from the primary visual receiving area in the occipital lobe to the parietal and temporal lobes. These pathways, shown in the figure below, serve two different functions. The one reaching the temporal area is crucial for *identifying objects,* whereas the one reaching the parietal area is crucial for *locating objects.*

We can understand the reasons for the conclusion that these two areas serve different functions by describing experiments involving two different kinds of problem-solving tasks. Let's first consider an *object discrimination* problem. A monkey is familiarized with one object, say a

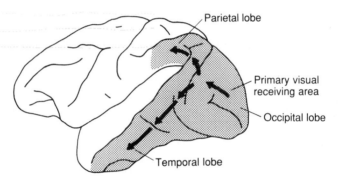

B O X 6.2 Cortex showing pathways from the primary visual receiving area in the occipital lobe to the parietal and temporal lobes. Sequences of arrows are shown to indicate that there are a number of synapses along these pathways.

PERCEPTUAL ORGANIZATION: THE GESTALT APPROACH

What Is Perceptual Organization?

When I was writing the first edition of this book, my son, Adam, was six years old. Often, as he was eating breakfast, he would tell me that he was about to eat an elephant, or some other animal, which had appeared in his scrambled eggs. Adam's perception of an elephant in his scrambled eggs means that the pieces of egg on his plate had become perceptually organized so that they looked like an elephant.

At 16 Adam still sees animals in his eggs, and my 10-year-old daughter Emily just reported seeing a gummy-bear in the clouds. But perceptual organization is not simply a curiosity that creates animals in food and in the clouds. **Perceptual orga-**

rectangular solid, and is then presented with a two-choice task like the one shown on the left below. To receive a reward the monkey must pick the "familiar" object, in this case the rectangular solid. Normal monkeys and monkeys with their parietal lobes removed can do this easily. However, removal of an area of the temporal lobes turns this into an extremely difficult task.

A different type of problem, called *landmark discrimination,* is shown on the right. Here, the monkey is rewarded for choosing the covered food well closer to the tall cylinder. This task can be done by a normal monkey or one with its temporal lobe removed, but it is difficult for monkeys lacking part of the parietal lobe.

Both of these problems are examples of higher-order visual functioning that goes far beyond the analysis carried out by <u>feature detectors in the primary visual receiving area</u>. The end result of processing in the temporal lobe is information about an object's physical properties that enables us to identify it when it is seen from different viewpoints and in different areas in space. The end result of processing in the parietal lobe is information about the object's location.

But this separation of the information needed for object identification and spatial location in two different areas of the brain creates a problem. How are these two types of information combined so we can both identify an object *and* know its location? Apparently, this takes place either in the limbic system, deep inside the brain, or in the frontal lobes, both areas which receive inputs from the parietal and temporal lobes.

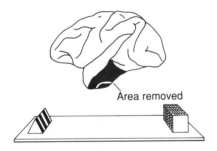

Object discrimination

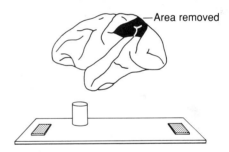

Landmark discrimination

nization, <u>the grouping of parts into larger units, is essential for making sense of the world.</u> When you look at a country scene and see a barnyard surrounded by trees, the process of organization enables you to separate the barnyard from the trees and to see each tree as a separate entity. Similarly, when you talk with a friend in a noisy room, the process of organization enables you to differentiate your friend's voice from all the other sounds that simultaneously reach your ears.

The Beginnings of Gestalt Psychology

Real progress in our understanding of perceptual organization began with a group called the Gestalt psychologists, which was formed about 1912 by Max Wertheimer (Figure 1.19). According to Edwin Boring (1950), the birth of **Gestalt psychology** can be traced to a train ride taken by Wertheimer in the summer of 1910. As the story goes, Wertheimer was on his way to a vacation in the Rhineland, in the west of Germany, when he suddenly experienced a flash of insight about movement perception. He got off the train at Frankfurt, checked into a hotel, and purchased a toy stroboscope (a device like a "flip book" in which still pictures appear to move when the pages are rapidly flipped). Wertheimer first began work in his hotel room but soon moved his makeshift setup to the psychology laboratory at the University of Frankfurt.

Wertheimer's experiments in movement perception at the Frankfurt lab, the results of which he published in 1912, focused on the apparent movement effect described in Chapter 1 (Figure 1.20), in which movement is perceived between two stationary stimuli that are flashed one after another. Wertheimer interpreted this result as an illustration of the principle that "the whole is different from the sum of its parts" (see p. 23).

Wertheimer also used this result to reject structuralism—the idea that perceptions are the result of addition of many elementary sensations (see page 22). He stated his objection to the analysis of scenes into elementary sensations as follows: "I stand at the window and see a house, trees, sky. Now on theoretical grounds I could try to count and say: 'Here there are . . . 327 brightnesses and hues.' Do I *have* '327'? No. I see sky, house, trees; and no one can really have these '327' as such." (Wertheimer, 1923; quoted in Treisman, 1986).

Wertheimer and his followers, who came to be known as the Gestalt psychologists, therefore rejected the idea that perceptions are constructed from sensations in favor of the idea that the stimulus must be considered as a whole. Much of the evidence for this view comes from examples which show that our perception of one part of a stimulus depends on the presence of other parts of the stimulus. Look, for example, at Figures 6.4 and 6.5. The horse in Figure 6.4 looks as if it is rearing back but the identical horse in Figure 6.5 appears to be moving forward. The presence of the rider in Figure 6.4 and the lead horse in Figure 6.5 make the same horse look different in the two pictures.

Figures 6.6, 6.7, 6.8, and 6.9 show other examples supporting the idea that our perception of parts of a stimulus depends on the overall stim-

F I G U R E 6. 4   A rearing horse. (From Arnheim, 1974.)

F I G U R E 6. 5   One horse following another horse. (From Arnheim, 1974.)

F I G U R E 6. 6   The white triangle with its base down in the above figure is constructed from subjective contours. When the black circles are covered the triangle vanishes, and when they are uncovered it reappears. (From Kanizsa, 1955.)

F I G U R E 6. 7 *Carapace No. 3* by Diane Sloan. (Collection of the Oakland Museum, gift of Mr. Joseph H. Chowning.)

ulus configuration. Figure 6.6 is an example of **subjective contour.** The contours of the triangle are not physically present; they are caused by the rest of the configuration. You can prove this to yourself by covering the three black objects with small pieces of paper. When you do this, the subjective contours vanish. No theory which proposes that perceptions are constructed from individual sensations can explain this result.

Figure 6.7 is a picture of a woman holding some flowers and a transparent veil. Though we can see some reflections on the right of the veil near the flowers, there are no reflections further to the left; and since the veil is transparent, it becomes almost invisible. How then do we know that the veil is there? The answer lies in the embroidery. The embroidery defines the veil and causes us to assume its presence even though we can't see it.

Look at the two vases in Figure 6.8. The one on the left has a glossy finish and the one on the right a dull finish. Or do they? Cover up the highlights on the left vase and observe what happens. It becomes the same as the right vase, because both vases are identical except that the highlights have been removed from the right vase. In this example, as in the previous ones, our perception of parts of

F I G U R E   6. 8   Two vases, showing how highlights on the surface on the left make the whole surface appear glossy. (From Beck, 1972.)

an object is determined by the other parts of the object.

Finally, consider the rolling wheel in Figure 6.9. A light placed on the rim of the wheel traces the path shown in (a). However, if we add a light to the center of the wheel, we perceive not the motion in (a) but, rather, the light on the rim as rotating around the central light (Duncker, 1929; Proffitt, Cutting, & Stier, 1979).

The Laws of Organization

The Gestalt psychologists were interested not only in demonstrating that the whole is different from the sum of its parts but also in determining the rules that specify how we organize small parts into wholes. Look at Figure 6.10. What do you see? If you see a dog, then you have succeeded in organizing a mass of black and white shapes into a dal-

(a)

(b)

F I G U R E   6. 9   The dots in (a) show the path traced by a light on the rim of a rotating wheel. We perceive this path when the light on the rim is the only one present. However, when another light is added to the center of the wheel, we perceive the light on the rim to be rotating around the center light, as in (b).

F I G U R E 6. 10 Some black and white shapes that become perceptually organized into a dalmation. (Photograph by R. C. James.)

mation! How does this particular arrangement of black and white shapes enable us to differentiate the spotted dog from the spotted background? A Gestalt psychologist would answer this question by referring to the **laws of organization.** These laws are a series of rules that describe what your per-

ception will be given certain stimulus conditions. Let's look at the five most important Gestalt laws.

Pragnanz. Pragnanz, roughly translated from the German, means "good figure." The **law of Pragnanz**—the central law of Gestalt psychology—which

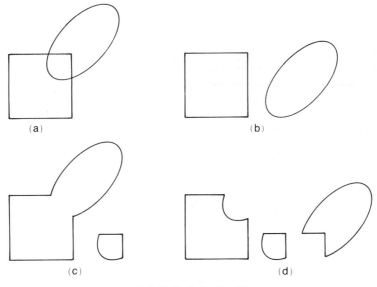

F I G U R E 6. 11

FIGURE 6. 12

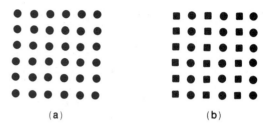

(a)   (b)

FIGURE 6. 13   (a) Perceived as horizontal rows or vertical columns or both. (b) Perceived as vertical columns.

is also called the **law of good figure,** or the **law of simplicity,** states: _Every stimulus pattern is seen in such a way that the resulting structure is as simple as possible._ According to the law of simplicity, you should perceive Figure 6.11(a) as a square and an elliptical object as in (b) because these two objects are simpler than some of the other possible per-

ceptions shown in (c) and (d). Similarly, Figure 6.12 is perceived as a triangle overlapping a rectangle and not as a complicated eleven-sided figure.

Similarity.   Most people perceive Figure 6.13(a) as either horizontal rows of circles, vertical columns of circles, or both. But when we change some

FIGURE 6. 14   Grouping due to similarity of lightness. The male and female dancers form separate groups due to similarity of lightness, with the males' dark suits causing them to be perceptually grouped and the females' light dresses causing them to be perceptually grouped. Similarity of orientation also contributes to the perceptual grouping of the dancers. (From "Cole." Photograph courtesy of the Pittsburgh Ballet Theater.)

FIGURE 6. 15 Grouping due to similarity of orientation. In this *pas de deux* from "The Nutcracker" the perceptual unity of the two dancers is greatly enhanced by the similarity of their arm and body orientations. (Top) The curve of the dancers' arms and bodies match closely. (Middle) The dancers' arms and legs become a series of parallel lines. (Bottom) The dancers' legs are parallel, and the mirror images of their arms further enhances the perceptual grouping. (Photographs courtesy of the Pittsburgh Ballet Theater.)

of the circles to squares, as in Figure 6.13(b), then most people perceive vertical columns of squares and circles. This perception illustrates the **law of similarity:** *similar things appear to be grouped together.* This law causes the circles to be grouped with other circles and the squares to be grouped with other squares. Grouping can also occur due to similarity of lightness (Figures 1.21 and 6.14), hue, orientation (Figure 6.15), or size.

Grouping also occurs for auditory stimuli. For example, notes that have similar pitches and that follow each other closely in time become perceptually grouped. We will consider this and other auditory grouping effects when we describe organizational processes in hearing in Chapter 11 (see page 403).

Good continuation. The series of points starting at A in Figure 6.16 flows smoothly to B. It does not go to C or D, because that path would involve making sharp turns and would violate the **law of good continuation,** which states: *points that, when connected, result in straight or smoothly curving lines are seen as belonging together, and lines tend to be seen in such a way as to follow the smoothest path.*

Good continuation is illustrated by the bridge and smokestack in Pissarro's painting *The Great Bridge at Rouen,* shown in Figure 6.17. Although the smoke cuts the bridge in two and cuts the smokestack into three pieces, we assume, due to good continuation, that the various parts belong together, and the bridge and smokestack, therefore, do not fall apart. Good continuation also comes into play in helping us to perceive a smoothly curving elliptical shape and a square in Figure 6.11(a).

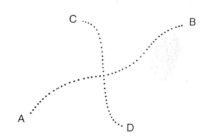

FIGURE 6. 16 Good continuation.

F I G U R E 6. 17   *The Great Bridge at Rouen* by Camille Pissarro (1896). (Museum of Art, Carnegie Institute, Pittsburgh, Pa.)

Proximity or nearness.   Figure 6.18(a) is perceived as horizontal rows of circles. This illustrates the **law of proximity:** *things that are near to each other appear to be grouped together.* And, although every other circle is changed to a square in Figure 6.18(b), we still perceive horizontal rows; in this case the law of proximity overpowers the law of similarity.

The fact that grouping can exist at different

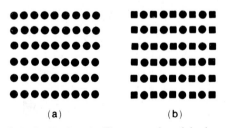

(a)   (b)

F I G U R E 6. 18   Two examples of the law of nearness: (a) perceived as horizontal rows of circles; (b) still perceived as horizontal rows, even though half of the circles have been changed to squares.

scales is illustrated by Figure 6.19. The small dots are grouped into triangular clusters because of their proximity. Further grouping then occurs as these clusters form larger triangles based on good figure (clusters 1, 2, and 3 group together to form a triangle, overpowering the potential grouping of clusters 3 and 4 on the basis of proximity). Finally, the large triangular units form two groups on the basis of proximity.

Common fate.   The two dancers in Figure 6.20 form a group by virtue of their nearness and similar orientation, but perhaps most important is their "common fate"—the fact that they are moving in the same direction. The **law of common fate** states that *things that are moving in the same direction appear to be grouped together.* This law often comes into play in ballet and modern dance. When one group of dancers moves together in one direction, they are perceived as a group separated from other danc-

F I G U R E 6. 19 Perceptual grouping existing at different scales. See text for details.

ers that are stationary or are moving in another direction.

Meaningfulness or familiarity. The **law of familiarity** states that *things are more likely to form groups if the groups appear familiar or meaningful* (Helson, 1933; Hochberg, 1971, p. 439).

DEMONSTRATION

Finding Faces in a Landscape

Consider the picture in Figure 6.21. At first glance this scene appears to contain mainly trees, rocks, and water. But upon closer inspection, you can see some faces in the trees in the background, and if you look more closely you can see that a number of faces are formed by various groups of rocks. There are, in fact, a total of 13 faces hidden in this pic-

ture. If you have trouble seeing all of them, try looking at the picture from a few feet away. This sometimes causes previously unseen faces to become visible.

The point of Figure 6.21 is that the perceptual organization of the rocks and trees changes when they change from "rocks in a stream" or "trees in a forest" into components of faces. Two rocks that initially are perceived separately in a stream become associated with each other when they become the left and right eyes of a face. In fact, once you perceive a particular grouping of rocks as a face, it is often difficult *not* to perceive them in this way—they have become permanently organized into a face.

Let's now apply some of these Gestalt laws to

F I G U R E 6. 20 Grouping due to common fate. The perceptual grouping of these dancers is enhanced both by their similarity of orientation and by common fate—the fact that they are both moving in the same direction at the same speed. (From "Mecuric Tidings." Photograph courtesy of the Pittsburgh Ballet Theater.)

FIGURE 6. 21 *The Forest Has Eyes* by Bev Doolittle (1985). Can you find 13 faces in this picture?

C O L O R P L A T E 7.1 The Blue Ridge Mountains of North Carolina. The blueness and fuzziness of the hills is caused by atmospheric perspective. See pages 231–233. Courtesy of North Carolina Department of Commerce.

C O L O R P L A T E 8.2 Gerard David (c. 1460–1523), *Rest on the Flight into Egypt*. See page 233.
Courtesy of the National Gallery of Art, Andrew W. Mellon Collection.

C O L O R   P L A T E   10.1   This mixed-media light box, titled *V-focus Tilting Room*, was created by Nancy Luomala to depict the double vision she has experienced since sustaining head injuries in an automobile accident. See Box 10.2, page 366.

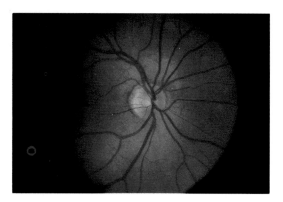

C O L O R   P L A T E   10.2 (a)   A normal retina as seen through an ophthalmoscope. The white area in the center is the optic disc. This picture shows only a small area of the retina around theoptic disc. The fovea (not visible) is located just past the far left edge of this picture.

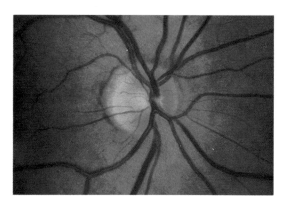

C O L O R   P L A T E   10.2 (b)   Close-up of the normal retina in Color Plate 10.2 (a).

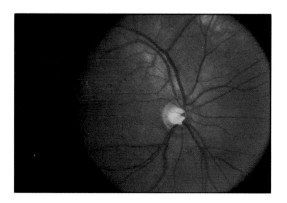

C O L O R   P L A T E   10.3 (a)   The retina in an eye with glaucoma. Cupping of the optic disc is indicated by the way the blood vessels vanish over a ridge in the cupped optic disc (see pages 370–371).

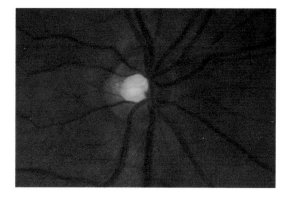

C O L O R   P L A T E   10.3 (b)   Close-up of a retina in an eye with glaucoma showing cupping of the optic disc. (Note that this is a different retina than the one in Plate 10.3 (a).)

F I G U R E 6. 22   Photograph by R. C. James.

the spotted dog in Figure 6.10. The initial difficulty we may experience in perceiving the dog occurs because of the similarity of the markings on the dog to the light and dark areas in the rest of the scene. But a closer look shows that there are differences between the dog's spots and the dark areas in the scene. Notice the orientation of the dark areas on the ground on which the dog is walking, indicated by the solid arrows in Figure 6.22. Then notice the different orientation formed by some of the small spots on the dog, indicated by the dashed arrows. Also notice that many of the spots on the dog are more rounded than the other spots in the picture. Grouping by similarity of shape is at work here.

But even more important than the law of similarity is how the area of the picture inside the circle influences our perception. This area, which, like the small spots, is differentiated from the shadows on the ground by its different orientation, also looks like a dog's head. The fact that this is a familiar shape helps us to separate it from its background. To show how the familiar dog's head influences our perception of the whole, cover this area with your finger. How does this affect your ability to separate the dog's body from its background? The

difficulty you experience in making this separation is yet another demonstration of the Gestalt idea that the whole is different from the sum of its parts.

Now that we've analyzed the dog picture, look at the picture in Figure 6.23. Although the patterns on the horses are similar to the patterns of the surroundings, we have no trouble perceiving the horses. How do the laws of organization operate in this picture? (Hint: Look for places where the laws of similarity, good continuation, and familiarity might be working.)

Figure-Ground Segregation

We perceive objects when they form figures against their backgrounds. This separation of figure and background, which is called **figure-ground segregation,** has been of great interest to the Gestalt psychologists, who studied patterns like the one in Figure 6.24, which was introduced by Danish psychologist Edgar Rubin in 1915. This is called a **reversible figure-ground** pattern, because it can be perceived either as two black faces looking at each other, in front of a white background, or as a white vase on a black background. Some of the properties of the figure and ground are:

FIGURE 6. 23   *Pintos* by Bev Doolittle (1979).

1. The figure is more "thinglike" and more memorable than the ground.
2. The figure is seen as being in front of the ground.
3. The ground is seen as unformed material and seems to extend behind the figure.
4. The contour separating the figure from the ground appears to belong to the figure.

You can demonstrate these properties to yourself by looking at Rubin's face-vase reversible figure-ground in Figure 6.24. Note that when the

FIGURE 6. 24   A version of Rubin's reversible face-vase figure.

vase is seen as figure, it appears to be in front of the black background, and when the faces are figure, they are sitting on top of the white background. Also notice that when you are perceiving the vase as figure it is difficult, if not impossible, to simultaneously perceive the faces. Remember that the ground is seen as "unformed material"; as soon as you perceive the white area as figure, the vase is seen in front and the black area becomes "unformed material" that extends behind the vase.

DEMONSTRATION

Determinants of Figure and Ground

Look at the following figures and decide, as quickly as possible, which areas are figure and which are ground:

Figure 6.25: On the left side which area is figure, white, or black? Which area is figure on the right side?

Figure 6.26: The white area or the black area?

Figure 6.27: The "cross-figure" or the "plus-figure"?

Figure 6.28: The vertical-horizontal cross or the tilted cross?

Figure 6.29a: The black areas or the white areas?

There are no "correct" answers to these questions, but experiments have shown that certain properties of the stimulus influence which areas are seen as figure and which are seen as ground. Some of these properties are:

FIGURE 6. 25 Symmetry and figure-ground. Look to the left and to the right and observe which colors become figure and which become ground. (Adapted from Hochberg, 1971.)

FIGURE 6. 26 The black columns are symmetrical and the white columns are convex. Which are seen as figure? (Kanizsa, 1979.)

1. *Symmetry.* Symmetrical areas tend to be seen as figure. In Figure 6.25 the symmetrical black areas on the left and the symmetrical white areas on the right are seen as figure.

2. *Convexity.* Convex (i.e., outwardly bulging)

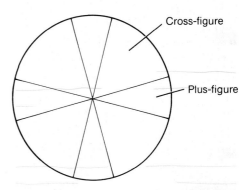

FIGURE 6. 27 Effect of area on figure-ground perception. Which is more likely to be seen as figure, the small plus-figure or the larger cross-figure?

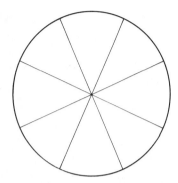

F I G U R E 6. 28 Effect of orientation on figure-ground perception. Which is easier to see as a figure, the vertical-horizontal cross or the tilted cross? What is your initial perception? Allow your perception to flip back and forth between the two alternatives. Which perception is present the longest?

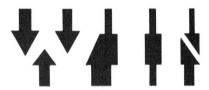

F I G U R E 6. 29 Which do you see as figure, the black area or the white area? After deciding, turn to the version of this figure on page 208.

shapes tend to be seen as figure, and convexity usually overpowers symmetry, as shown in Figure 6.26 in which the convex white areas tend to be perceived as figure over the symmetrical black areas.

3. *Area.* Stimuli with comparatively smaller areas are more likely to be seen as figure. This effect was demonstrated by an experiment in which subjects were shown stimuli such as the one in Figure 6.27. They were asked to report whether they saw the "plus-figure" or the "cross-figure" when the stimulus was first presented, and on each trial the area of the cross-figure was changed. The results of this experiment show that the smaller the area of the cross-figure, the more often it was seen as figure. A cross-figure angle of 70 degrees was seen as figure less than 10 percent of the time, but decreasing the size of the cross to 5 degrees caused it to be seen as figure 80 percent of the time (Kunnapas, 1957; see also Oyama, 1960).

4. *Orientation.* Vertical or horizontal orientations are more likely to be seen as figure than are other orientations. Thus, the vertical-horizontal cross in Figure 6.28 is easier to see as figure.

5. *Meaning.* As we saw in looking at Figures 6.22 and 6.23, meaningfulness is an important determinant of perceptual grouping, with meaningful objects more likely to be seen as figure. Thus, the black areas in Figure 6.29a, which includes three arrows, tend to be seen as figure. However, adding two more black areas on either side, as in Figure 6.29b, makes it easier to see that the white areas spell a word (WIN), making these areas more likely to be seen as figure.

In the examples above, the areas that become figure and ground are easy to distinguish from one another. For example, the black and white areas in Figures 6.24 and 6.29 are easily distinguishable. But what if these areas were more similar? We have already encountered this situation in the dog of Figure 6.10 and the horses of Figure 6.23. Although we are able to distinguish the dog and the horses as figures that stand out against the background, the similarity of their markings to the patterns in the background makes these figure-ground separations more difficult than if their markings were more different than the surroundings.

The dog and horses of Figures 6.10 and 6.23 are examples of *camouflage*—situations in which it is difficult to separate the figure from the ground, because of their similarity. An even better example of camouflage is shown in Figure 6.30. The close correspondence between the markings on the horses and on the trees helps to hide the horses from view. Thus, the *law of similarity* helps blur the distinction between figure and ground. Can you tell what other laws of organization are making it more difficult to segregate figure from ground in this picture?

What Does Gestalt Psychology Tell Us?

Gestalt psychology tells us that we should pay attention to the overall stimulus pattern. It also offers a number of laws of organization that help

F I G U R E 6. 30 *Woodland Encounter* by Bev Doolittle (1985).

govern the way we group parts of a stimulus together and the way we separate figure from ground; however, while the laws of organization seem to work well when applied to the examples picked to illustrate them, the operation of some of the laws is not always as straightforward as in the examples.

One problem lies in the application of the law of simplicity. How do we tell if one figure is simpler than another? This is not an easy question to answer. Although we can easily measure properties such as lightness or nearness, there is no easy way to measure simplicity.

D E M O N S T R A T I O N

Figures That Can Be
Seen in More Than One Way

Many figures can be seen in more than one way. Look at Figures 6.31 and 6.32 and decide (1) how you perceive them initially and (2) which other perceptions are possible.

Figure 6.31 can be seen as two overlapping rectangles, or as a rectangle and an upside-down L-shaped object in the same plane. Which of these two perceptions is "simpler?" Does the fact that the perception of two rectangles involves three rather than two dimensions make this perception more simple or more complex than the perception of a rectangle and an L-shaped object? Since the law of simplicity provides us with no rules for deter-

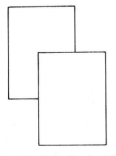

F I G U R E 6. 31

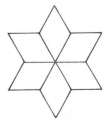

F I G U R E 6. 32

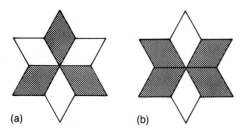

FIGURE 6. 33 Alternate perceptions of Figure 6.32.

mining which is simpler, it is hard to answer this question except to say that <u>most people tend to see this figure in three dimensions,</u> with one rectangle positioned in front of the other.

Figure 6.32 is often initially perceived as a flat six-pointed star; however, after it is viewed for a while, a number of alternative perceptions appear. For example, it can be perceived as two intersecting Vs, one right side up and one upside down, as in Figure 6.33(a) (the upside-down V is shaded). It can also be perceived as a three-finned propeller on top of a triangle. To see the figure in this way, try to perceive the shaded area of Figure 6.33(a) as the triangle and the light area as the three-finned propeller. (You can also reverse this perception by seeing the light area as the triangle and the shaded area as the fins of the propeller.) Finally, look at 6.33(b) and imagine that the shaded areas on the left and right represent the pages of opened books.

Obviously there are many possible perceptions of Figure 6.32 (in fact, my students have discovered others in addition to those described here: Can you find two chairs, each missing its legs on one side?). Although we might expect the law of simplicity to predict that the simplest perception would be the flat, symmetrical star, people often

FIGURE 6. 29 (Continued) In this version of Figure 6.29, which area is figure—white or black? Hint: Look for a three letter word.

see the seemingly more complex perceptions suggested by Figure 6.33. In fact, many people find that their perceptions change between two or even three different objects as they continue to view this figure. Can something be simple one minute and not simple the next? Unfortunately, the law of simplicity does not provide enough information about what simplicity is for us to know what it predicts about perception in situations such as this.

Another question we can ask about the Gestalt laws is: How applicable are they to real-life situations? Most examples of the Gestalt laws are illustrated by simple line drawings consisting of dots or lines. But what happens when we move from the flat pages of a book to the three-dimensional world where objects are separated in depth? In Chapter 7 we will see that <u>various kinds of depth information help us see that one object is in front of another, thereby making it unnecessary to use the laws of organization to explain why we see one thing as figure and another as ground.</u>

Another problem occurs when two Gestalt laws conflict with one another. Consider, for example, the two patterns in Figure 6.34(a). According to

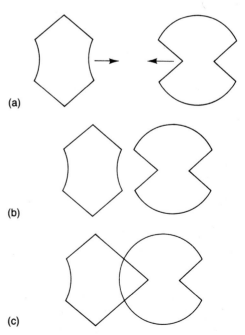

FIGURE 6. 34 Two symmetrical figures that turn into two overlapping asymmetrical figures when joined.

the law of simplicity, shouldn't we expect that if we were to move these patterns together we would continue to see two symmetrical patterns? Although this is a reasonable prediction, it does not occur, as indicated by Figure 6.34(c). As soon as the two patterns touch, another Gestalt law takes over and causes us to perceive them as two asymmetrical figures. (Can you figure out which law it is before reading further?)

Can the Gestalt laws explain why these two patterns lose their symmetry when they are joined? One way to explain the asymmetrical patterns that result is to say that the law of good continuation controls our perception when these two patterns are joined. (The intersection between the two patterns creates smooth continuations for the straight lines of the left pattern and for the curved line of the right pattern.)

But does this "explanation" really explain anything? It's really more a description of what's happening in this situation than an explanation that can help us predict what's going to happen in other situations. This tendency of the Gestalt approach to *describe* rather than to *explain* has led many present-day researchers to question the Gestalt approach. James Pomerantz (1981) has aptly described the Gestalt approach as the "look-at-the-figure-and-see-for-yourself" method: An observer looks at a figure and reports what he or she sees. Pomerantz and others have argued that we need a more quantitative approach to the Gestalt principles, and, in an attempt to do this, a number of people have begun to apply a more experimental approach to the study of the Gestalt laws. In the next section, we will describe some recent experiments resulting from this new approach to Gestalt psychology.

MODERN EXTENSIONS OF GESTALT PSYCHOLOGY

A number of modern researchers have taken the Gestalt principles beyond the descriptive level by asking a number of questions about the process of perceptual organization. We will consider three of these questions.

F I G U R E 6. 35   Which is more similar to the T, the *T* or the L?

What Stimulus Properties Are Responsible for Grouping?

Look at Figure 6.35. Which is more similar to the T, the tilted T or the L? Most subjects, when asked this question, respond that the tilted T is more similar to the T. With this result in hand and our knowledge of the Gestalt law of similarity, we would predict that Ts and tilted Ts should group together (since they are similar to one another), but that Ts and Ls should not (since they are not similar). However, by creating displays like the one in Figure 6.36, in which we create textures with groups of objects, we can see that the Ts and tilted Ts form two separate groups, whereas the Ts and Ls do not.

This result tells us that similarity, as judged by comparing one stimulus to another, is not a sure way to determine the stimulus properties responsible for perceptual grouping. In our example the relevant property is *orientation*, a property which, in other experiments, has also been shown to be important in determining perceptual grouping. For example, when Richard Olson and Fred Attneave (1970) measured the time it took for subjects to decide where the odd stimuli were in the displays in Figure 6.37, they found that subjects could do this rapidly (reaction time = 0.86 sec) if the stimuli differed in orientation, but took much longer (reaction time = 4.09 sec) if the stimuli contained lines with the same orientation.

How Does Grouping Affect Our Ability to Extract Information from a Display?

D E M O N S T R A T I O N

Detecting Targets in a Display

Your task is to determine whether a "T" or an "F" is present in the displays in Figure 6.38(a) and (b) at the bottom of the next page.

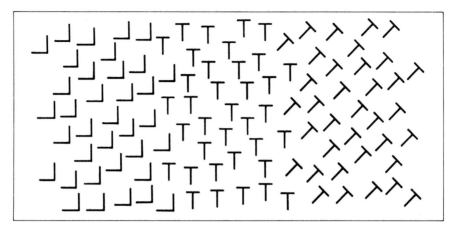

F I G U R E **6. 36**   The tilted Ts form a group in this display even though they are very similar in form to the upright Ts. Orientation is a powerful force responsible for perceptual grouping. (From Beck, 1966.)

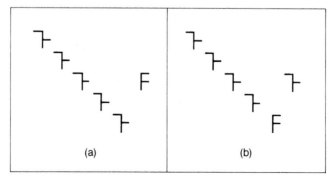

(a) RT = 0.86 sec   (b) RT = 4.09 sec

F I G U R E **6. 37**   Two of the stimuli used in Olson and Attneave's (1970) experiment.

(a)   (b)

F I G U R E **6. 38**   Two of the stimuli used in Prinzmetal and Banks' (1977) experiment, illustrating how grouping due to good continuation affects an observer's performance.

Which was easier? William Prinzmetal and William Banks (1977) found that observers identified the target letter faster in display (a) than in display (b). For the slower detection in (b) they concluded that the Gestalt principle of good continuation had caused the F in (b) to be grouped with the line of irrelevant stimuli, thereby making it hard to detect. In (a), however, the F is not grouped and, therefore, stands out more and is detected faster.

Now decide, as quickly as possible, whether there is a "T" or an "F" in displays (a) and (b) below.

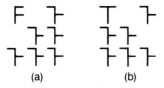

(a)   (b)

F I G U R E 6. 39 Two of the stimuli used in Banks and Prinzmetal's (1976) experiment, illustrating how grouping due to proximity affects an observer's performance.

Banks and Prinzmetal's (1976) observers detected the target letter faster in (a) than in (b), because in (b) the target is grouped, by proximity, with the irrelevant stimuli. In (a) this grouping does not occur, so the target is more easily detected. Both of these demonstrations show that Gestalt grouping affects an observer's ability to extract information from a display.

How Are Figure and Ground Analyzed by the Visual System?

The Gestalt psychologists specified some of the conditions that caused one region to be perceived as figure and another as ground, and, as we saw on page 204, they also observed that regions seen as figure have different properties than regions seen as ground. Bela Julesz (1978) has proposed that different kinds of perceptual analysis occur in areas perceived as figure and in areas perceived as ground. According to Julesz, analysis of the figure is con-

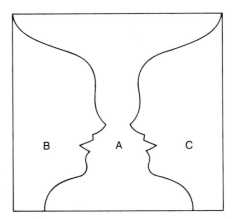

F I G U R E 6. 40 Rubin's faces-vase reversible figure used by Weisstein and Wong (1986). In their experiment, described in the text, vertical or tilted lines were flashed at locations A, B, or C. The lines' tilt, or lack of it, was more easily detected when the area on which the line was flashed was perceived as figure.

cerned with seeing fine details whereas analysis of the ground is concerned with seeing larger areas.

If "figure analysis" is concerned with details, then it should be easier to see sharply focused objects when they are superimposed on the figure than when they are superimposed on the ground. To test this idea, Naomi Weisstein and Eva Wong (1986) flashed vertical lines and slightly tilted lines onto a line drawing of Rubin's faces-vase reversible picture (Figure 6.40), and asked subjects to decide whether the line they saw was vertical or tilted. Since Rubin's figure is reversible, sometimes the faces (areas B and C) were seen as figure and sometimes the vase (area A) was seen as figure. On each trial, the subject indicated whether the vase or faces was the figure and the line was then flashed randomly on one of the areas. Subjects were three times more accurate at determining whether or not the line was tilted when it appeared on the figure. Thus, it does indeed appear that the process of figure analysis is concerned with processing information about detail.

The studies we have just described go beyond the early Gestalt psychologist's "look-at-the-figure-and-see-for-yourself" method and have begun to

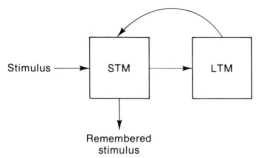

FIGURE 6.41 The kind of flow diagram used to break a cognitive process down into a sequence of steps. This diagram shows how memory is broken down into short-term memory (STM) and long-term memory (LTM). The important point for our purposes is not how memory operates but that these types of flow diagrams have been used to describe many different types of cognitive processes including, recently, some perceptual processes.

study **perceptual processing**—perception as the end product of a sequence of mental operations. This interest in perceptual processing can be traced to a number of influences. One of these is the growing popularity of **cognitive psychology** beginning in the 1960s, with its emphasis on the study of mental processes. Cognitive psychologists adopted the idea that the mind, like a computer, can be thought of as a system that processes information. This is similar to the idea that neurons process information; however, cognitive psychologists are concerned not with nerve impulses but with mental events. From this approach have come flow diagrams like the one in Figure 6.41, which breaks the process of memory down into a sequence of steps.

The idea that behaviors such as memory and problem solving can be analyzed into a sequence of mental events grew parallel with the growth in popularity of computers. This growing interest in computers influenced psychologists in a number of ways. Cognitive psychologists not only analyzed behaviors into flow diagrams like those used to write computer programs, but they also began writing computer programs to enable computers to solve problems, to play chess, and to perceive objects and simple scenes.

In the next section we will introduce the idea of perceptual processing as applied to form percep-

tion. In doing this, we will see that many researchers have concluded that to understand how we perceive forms and objects we must focus on how these forms and objects are constructed from smaller components.

THE IDEA OF PERCEPTUAL PROCESSING

The basic idea behind perceptual processing is that the observer carries out mental operations on the stimulus to arrive at a perception of the stimulus. Let's look at two examples of this approach.

Perception as Hypothesis Testing

In Chapter 5 we introduced Richard Gregory's idea that "we may think of sensory stimulation as providing data for hypotheses concerning the state of the external world" (1973, p. 61). Perception, according to this idea, is a process in which we may entertain a succession of hypotheses about what the pattern of light falling on our receptors really means. Gregory's idea that perception involves a process of hypothesis testing is similar to one proposed many years earlier by Hermann von Helmholtz (of the trichromatic theory of color vision). Helmholtz proposed the **likelihood principle:** we will perceive the object that is most likely to be caused by our sensory stimulation. According to this principle, if a number of possible objects could have caused a particular pattern of light and dark on the retina, we will perceive the object that is *most likely* to occur in that particular situation.

In the example in Chapter 5, in which you initially misperceive a shadow as a table, this process of selecting the hypothesis to pick the most likely object is conscious—you are aware of each of the hypotheses that leads, eventually, to your perception (see p. 183). But hypothesis testing does not always occur at a conscious level. We will see, as we discuss other ideas about perceptual processing, that we are usually not aware of the complex mental processes that occur as we perceive forms and objects.

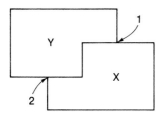

FIGURE 6. 42 Stimulus used by Peterson and Hochberg (1983), originally from Ratoosh (1949). See text for details.

Perception as a Process of Taking in Information by Eye Movements

In describing the constructivist approach to perception in Chapter 1, we introduced Julian Hochberg's idea that the observer takes an active role in perception by making a series of fixations on different parts of an object or a scene. Each fixation provides information about a small area, and our perception of the whole object or scene occurs when we combine the information from a number of fixations.

DEMONSTRATION

Where You Look Makes a Difference

Look at point 1 in Figure 6.42 and decide which shape appears in front, X or Y. Then shift your gaze to point 2 and again decide which is in front.

Mary Peterson and Julian Hochberg (1983) found that when subjects look at point 1 they tend to see X in front and when they look at point 2 they tend to see Y in front. The results of Peterson and Hochberg's experiments with this figure and a number of others show that our perception of an object depends on where on the object we look. For the stimulus in Figure 6.42 we base our perception on **local depth information**—information at one point on a figure that indicates depth. If local depth information is important in determining our perception, then, according to Peterson and Hochberg, we need to rethink the Gestalt idea that our perceptions are determined by the whole stimulus rather than by its parts.

Gregory's idea of hypothesis testing, Helmholtz' likelihood principle, and Hochberg's idea that our perceptions are affected by local depth information all see perception as involving an active observer who processes stimulus information. But what exactly is happening as an observer processes information from the stimulus? Hochberg says that what happens in local areas of the stimulus is important. But what is the nature of the processing that occurs as information is taken in at these local areas?

Recently, a number of researchers have begun to study the problem of information processing in perception in more detail. The basic conclusion of much of this research is that our perception of a whole object is constructed from information taken in from smaller parts. Specifically, this research says that in perceiving a stimulus, we analyze it into components or attributes.

In discussing this process of analysis, Anne Treisman points out that a horse "can be described as brown, fast-moving, rideable or as possessing any of hundreds of other properties." (1986, p. 35-14) The question, according to Treisman, is which of these properties are analyzed to enable us to perceive or recognize the horse? What are the basic units of analysis used by the visual system? We will consider this question by describing three approaches that postulate an analysis of forms or objects into components or attributes. We will begin by describing Treisman's idea of "preattentive and focused processing," we will then describe Irving Biederman's idea of "recognition-by-components," and finally David Marr's "computational approach."

PREATTENTIVE AND FOCUSED PROCESSING

Two Stages of Processing

Anne Treisman proposes that form perception takes place in two or more stages. In the **preattentive stage,** which is automatic and rapid, the stimulus is decomposed into a number of basic properties, which she calls **primitives**—the "basic words in

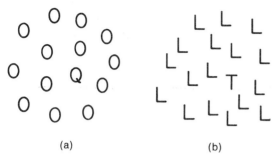

(a)   (b)

FIGURE 6.43 It's easy to find the Q in (a), but more difficult to find the T in (b). According to Treisman, the Q is found by an automatic preattentive process, whereas the T is found by a slower process involving focused attention.

the language of perception." (1986, p. 35-39.)*
One of the key properties of the preattentive stage is that it requires no conscious attention. That is, it occurs automatically without any effort on the part of the subject. An example of a task that requires no conscious attention is picking out the Q among the Os in Figure 6.43(a).

Once primitives are extracted they are combined in the **focused attention stage.** In contrast to the preattentive stage, this stage is not automatic and requires conscious attention. For example, in Figure 6.43(b) finding the T among the Ls requires a conscious search.

Determining the Primitives

We will now consider some of the ways that Treisman determined the identity of the primitives that are extracted in the preattentive stage.

DEMONSTRATION

Pop-Out Boundaries

What properties of objects in a field cause boundaries to become easily perceived? Look at Figure 6.36, Figure 6.44, and the one in Color Plate 6.1 and determine what property enables you to detect the boundary for each display.

_____

* The idea of preattentive processing was originally proposed by Ulrich Neisser (1967), who realized that some aspects of a stimulus are taken in automatically without conscious effort.

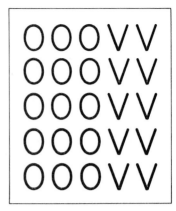

FIGURE 6.44 A pop-out boundary forms between the Os and Vs because of the difference between the curvature of the Os and the lines of the Vs.

Figure 6.36, Figure 6.44, and Color Plate 6.1 contain **pop-out boundaries,** boundaries that are seen almost immediately—they "pop out." These pop-out boundaries are associated with line tilt (Figure 6.36), curved shape (Figure 6.44), and color (Color Plate 6.1).

DEMONSTRATION

Visual Search

Find the target in each of the displays below. For each display, pay attention to how long it takes to find the target.

The target in this display is an "O."

FIGURE 6.45 Visual search stimulus. Finding the O among the Vs is almost instantaneous.

The target in this display is an "R."

F I G U R E 6. 46 Visual search stimulus. Finding the R among the Ps and Qs is not instantaneous unless, by chance, you happen to look at the R first.

In the first figure, identification of the O is almost instantaneous. It pops out because O's property of curvature differs from the V's property of straight lines. Notice that this is similar to the situation in Figure 6.43 in which we instantly perceive the Q among the Os because the Q contains a straight line not found in the Os.

In the second figure, finding the R probably took longer (unless by chance you happened to look at it right away). The longer search time for the R occurs because the target letter, R, contains a vertical line and a curved line, like the P, and a slanted line and a curved line, like the Q. When a target stimulus shares properties with other stimuli, we must focus our attention on each of the elements in the display until we find the target.

By measuring the time it takes for subjects to detect boundaries and to find target letters in search tasks, Treisman has identified the following primitives: curvature, tilt, color, line ends, and movement. In addition, closed areas, contrast, and brightness have been identified as primitives (Beck, 1982; Treisman, 1986).

Remember that these primitives are extracted from the stimulus during the first, preattentive, stage of processing. They are not combined until the second stage—the focused attention stage. Treisman has shown that these primitives exist independently of one another in the preattentive stage by using a procedure called the **illusory conjunction technique.**

We can understand this procedure by describing a typical experiment: A display consisting of a red X, a blue S, and a green T is flashed onto a screen for one fifth of a second, followed by a random dot pattern designed to eliminate any afterimage that might remain after the stimuli are turned off (see p. 20). When the subjects report what they have seen, **illusory conjunctions** like "red S" or "green X" occur on about a third of the trials. This result occurs even if the stimuli differ greatly in shape and size. For example, a small blue circle and a large green square could elicit the illusory conjunction, "blue square."

What does this result mean? According to Treisman, these reports of illusory conjunctions mean that each primitive exists independently of the others during the preattentive stage. That is, the primitives "redness," "curvature," or "tilted line" are not, at this early stage of processing, associated with a specific stimulus. They are, in Treisman's (1987) words, "free floating," and can, therefore, be incorrectly combined when stimuli are flashed briefly.

Now that we have described some of the properties of the primitives, we need to consider how these units are combined to form objects. Although our knowledge of how this combination takes place is still developing (Treisman, 1987), we can specify some of the things associated with the process.

Combining the Primitives

Focusing attention on locations. The process of combining units takes us from the preattentive stage, during which these units are analyzed automatically and unconsciously, to a stage that requires that the observer focus his or her attention at a particular location. Let's look at an experiment that supports the idea that attention *at a location* is important during this combination stage.

A display consisting of one orange X, many red Os, and many blue Xs is briefly flashed and is immediately followed by a random dot pattern designed to eliminate any afterimage that might

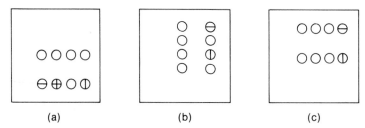

F I G U R E 6. 47 Stimuli used by Prinzmetal (1981). (a): A stimulus containing a +. (b) and (c): stimuli which, when briefly flashed, sometimes elicit the perception of a + due to the combination of a vertical and a horizontal line (an illusory conjunction). Illusory conjunctions are more easily formed in (b), when the lines are in the same perceptual group, than in (c), when they are in different perceptual groups.

remain after the stimulus is turned off. The subject's task is to indicate whether there is an orange X in the display and if there is to specify its location. Subjects find that even though they can often detect the presence of the orange X, they have difficulty specifying its location. The reason for this difficulty, according to Treisman, is that subjects can identify the presence of the orange X on the basis of just one primitive (color, in this case). Since only one primitive is involved, focused attention is not required, and the subject, therefore, does not pay attention to the object's location.

Consider, however, a task such as detecting a single blue O among many red Os and blue Xs. This task requires focused attention because to solve this problem the subject must locate an object that contains two properties: blueness *and* O-ness. To do this he or she must focus attention at a specific location. Thus, when subjects correctly identify the presence of the target in this task, they are also able to indicate its location.

The role of Gestalt grouping. Just because the perceptual process begins with small units does not mean that the Gestalt grouping principles do not play a role in perception. A number of experiments show that the process of combining units may be affected by the Gestalt principles of grouping. We have already seen from Banks and Prinzmetal's experiments (page 211) that grouping a target object with other objects by the law of nearness or good continuation makes it harder to single that object out for attention. William Prinzmetal (1981) has

also demonstrated the importance of Gestalt laws by using Treisman's illusory conjunction technique.

Prinzmetal flashed stimuli like those shown in Figure 6.47 and asked subjects to indicate whether they saw a + as in (a). Some of the stimuli, like those in (b) and (c), did not, however, contain + 's but + 's could be perceived as the result of illusory conjunctions of the vertical and horizontal lines. Prinzmetal found that subjects did, in fact, report illusory conjunctions on some trials. Thus, when (b) or (c) were presented, the vertical and horizontal lines would sometimes combine to form a +. The important result for our purposes, however, is that these illusory conjunctions occurred more often for stimulus (b) in which the lines were in the same perceptual group than for stimulus (c) in which the lines were in different perceptual groups. Since the lines are in the same physical positions in both (b) and (c), the greater rate of illusory conjunctions in (b) must be due to grouping according to the law of nearness.

Top-down and bottom-up processing. The analysis of objects into parts is called **bottom-up processing** because processing starts with basic units and our perception is then built on the foundation laid by these units. But it is clear that perception is influenced not only by the nature of the units that make up objects but also by the observer's knowledge of the world. We have already seen that this is so from the result of Palmer's experiment (Figure 1.29) and the rat–man demonstration (Figure 1.13) described in Chapter 1. These exper-

FIGURE 6.48 Stimulus used in Biederman's (1981) experiment. In this picture observers were asked to identify the fire hydrant.

iments showed that the meaning of a stimulus can affect our perception of the stimulus. This taking into account of meaning or familiarity is called **top-down processing,** because processing is based on "higher-level" information, such as the meaningful context in which a stimulus is seen, or other information that causes us to expect that another stimulus will be presented.

Another experiment that illustrates top-down processing was done by Irving Biederman (1981) using the stimulus in Figure 6.48. Biederman flashed this scene on a screen and asked observers to identify an object located at a particular place in the scene (they were told where to look immediately before seeing the picture). For the picture in Figure 6.48, observers were asked to identify the fire hydrant. Biederman found that observers made more errors when the hydrant was in a strange location, such as on top of the mailbox, than when it was located where it belonged, on the sidewalk. The observers' knowledge of where fire hydrants belong influenced their ability to recognize the hydrant.

This effect of meaning on perception comes into play during the focused attention stage, in which primitives are being combined. For example, our knowledge of the world allows us to rule out certain combinations of properties, making it

unlikely that we would see blue bananas or furry eggs. Also, our knowledge of the world must come into play when we respond to an object. Saying "That is a fire hydrant" is based on our prior knowledge of fire hydrants.

Thus, the overall process of form perception can, according to Treisman, be represented, in simplified form, by the diagram in Figure 6.49. This diagram conceives perception as being based both on bottom-up processing—preattentive isolation of individual properties and combination of these properties by focused attention—and on top-down processing—our knowledge of the way the world is put together and of the names and functions of various objects. In Treisman's words: "Normal perception falls somewhere between the extremes of prediction solely from prior knowledge and construction solely from sensory data" (1986, page 54).

RECOGNITION-BY-COMPONENTS

Treisman's work focuses on how different attributes, such as shape, color, texture, and size, are integrated into a single object. Irving Biederman

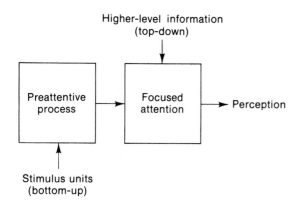

FIGURE 6. 49 Simplified flow diagram for Treisman's two-stage processing sequence. The preattentive stage acts on stimuli by breaking them down into primitives. This is a bottom-up process because it depends only on the physical properties of the stimuli. These primitives are then combined, in the focused attention stage, which is affected both by the stimulus input from the preattentive stage and by top-down processes such as the observer's knowledge of the way the world is put together and the observer's knowledge of the names and functions of various objects. The result of this processing is perception of a whole object.

(1987) has proposed a mechanism called **recognition-by-components** that is concerned not with how attributes like color and shape are combined but, rather, how we recognize three-dimensional objects based on our perception of the components that make up these objects.

The basic idea behind recognition-by-components is that we recognize an object by decomposing that object into basic components, or prim-

itives, called **geons** (for "geometric ions"). Biederman's primitives, unlike Treisman's, are *volumetric*. The cylinder, rectangular solid, and other volumes on the left of Figure 6.50 are some of the 36 different primitives in Biederman's system. These geons are, according to Biederman, the building blocks of perception, because it is possible to construct many thousands of objects by various arrangements of these components. Some examples of objects created from these components are shown on the right of Figure 6.50.

According to Biederman, these geons can be distinguished from one another even when observed from different viewpoints, because each geon has its own unique features that are visible from most viewpoints. For example, consider the "brick" and the "cylinder" geons in Figure 6.51. When seen from most viewpoints, the brick has three parallel edges, and the cylinder has only two. The cylinder has curved edges but the brick's edges are all straight, and the brick has three "arrow-vertices" whereas the cylinder has two "tangent Y vertices."

There are, however, some viewpoints from which we cannot see some of these properties. For example, if we look at the brick end-on, we see a square. But, according to Biederman, these situations, which give rise to what he calls **accidental properties,** occur only rarely. When they do occur, we find it difficult to recognize the object; however, in most cases, the properties shown in Figure 6.51, which Biederman calls **non-accidental properties,** are visible and allow us to distinguish between different geons from most viewpoints.

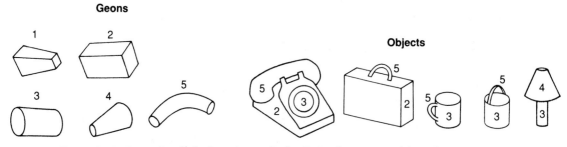

FIGURE 6. 50 Left: Some geons. Right: Some objects created from the geons on the left. The numbers on the objects indicate which geons are present. Note that recognizable objects can be formed by combining just two or three geons. Also note that the relations between the geons matter, as illustrated by the cup and the pail. (From Biederman, 1985.)

Brick geon   **Cylinder geon**

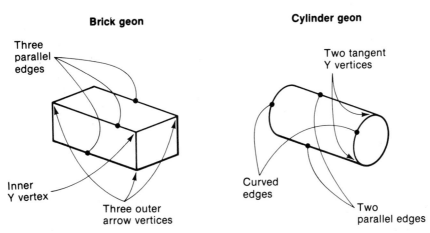

Three parallel edges

Inner Y vertex

Three outer arrow vertices

Two tangent Y vertices

Curved edges

Two parallel edges

F I G U R E 6. 51 Each geon has its own set of unique features that are visible from most viewpoints. Here two geons, a "brick" and a "cylinder," are labeled to indicate the features that enable us to distinguish them from each other. Note that these features are visible when we view the objects from most points of view. Only in special cases, such as end-on viewing, when the cylinder would be seen as a circle and the brick as a square, are we unable to see these features.

The basic principle governing recognition-by-components is the **principle of componential recovery,** which states that if an object's geons can be identified, then the object can be rapidly and correctly recognized. An important property of geons is that they can be identified even if partially obscured, as might occur if we saw an object behind foliage or in a snowstorm. This property is illustrated in Figure 6.52. We can identify this object (what is it?) even though over half of its contour

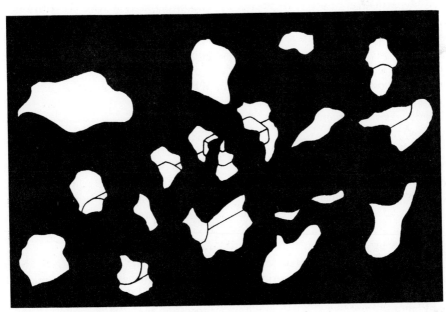

F I G U R E 6. 52 What is the object behind the mask? See the legend of Figure 6.53 for the answer (From Biederman, 1987).

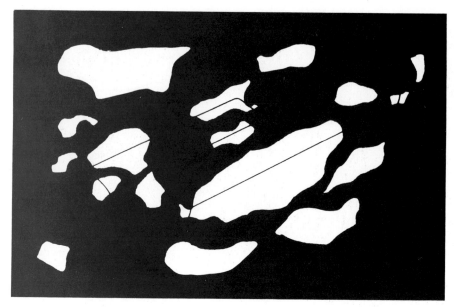

F I G U R E 6. 53   The same object as in Figure 6.52 (a flashlight) with geons obscured. See text for details. (From Biederman, 1987.)

is obscured. We can make this identification because the Gestalt principle of good continuation (page 199) completes the occluded contours so the geons that make up the object can be identified. If, however, we occlude the object so many of its intersections are obscured, as in Figure 6.53, we can no longer identify the geons, and it becomes impossible to recognize the object.

Another way to obscure an object's geons, and therefore make it difficult to recognize, is to view the object from an unusual viewpoint. For example, when we view the blender of Figure 6.54(a) from the unusual perspective in Figure 6.54(b) we can't see its basic geons and, therefore, have difficulty identifying it.

The basic message of Biederman's theory is that if enough information is available to enable us to identify an object's basic geons, we will be able to identify the object. Biederman has also shown that it is possible to identify objects if only a few of their geons are present. He demonstrated this by flashing line drawings like the ones in Figure 6.55 and asking subjects to name the object as rapidly as possible. The result of this experiment was that most objects could be named in less than a second based on only a few geons. For example,

although the airplane consists of nine geons when complete (Figure 6.55c), it was identified correctly 80 percent of the time when only three geons were present (Figure 6.55a) and 90 percent of the time when four geons were present (Figure 6.55b).

It is important to note that both Treisman's and Biederman's systems are recent proposals that are still being developed. Another recent proposal is David Marr's approach, which is called a **computational approach** because it postulates that perception is the end result of a mathematical analysis of the image on the retina.

THE COMPUTATIONAL APPROACH

We will describe Marr's system in general terms to give a flavor for it. Marr, who in 1977, at the age of 32, discovered that he had leukemia, spent the last two years of his life writing *Vision* (1982), a book that describes his work in more detail than we have space for here. This book, plus a number of papers (Marr, 1976; Marr & Hildreth, 1980; Marr & Nishihara, 1978), has influenced much of the research that has taken an information-processing approach to vision.

(a)   (b)

F I G U R E   6. 54   (a) A blender. (b) The same blender seen from a viewpoint that obscures most of its geons and therefore makes it difficult to recognize.

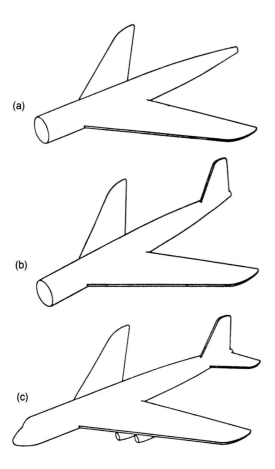

(a)

(b)

(c)

A basic step in analyzing an image, according to Marr, is the identification of an object's edges. We can appreciate the difficulty of doing this by looking at Figure 6.56. In this figure, intensity changes are caused both by the edges of the object *and* by shadows and highlights caused by the lighting conditions. To determine the shape of an object, the visual system must ignore these shadows and highlights and locate the object's true edges.

How does the visual system accomplish this? Marr proposes that the visual system does this (1) by analyzing the intensity changes in the image and (2) by taking into account properties of intensity changes that occur in the world. One of the properties of real-world intensity changes is that intensity usually changes gradually at the borders of shadows and highlights (remember from page 178 of Chapter 5 that shadows often have a fuzzy border called a penumbra). This property enables the visual system to ignore the borders created by shadows and highlights and to locate the object's real edges at places where sharp intensity changes occur. The actual procedure by which the visual system

F I G U R E   6. 55   An airplane, as represented (a) by three geons, (b) by four geons, and (c) by nine geons. (From Biederman, 1987.)

F I G U R E 6. 56 Intensity changes occur both at the edges of this object and at the borders created by the shadows and highlights on the surface of the object. To identify the object's shape, the visual system must identify the object's true edges.

are then processed further, by procedures we will not describe here (see Marr's *Vision* for details), to yield a representation of the object's surfaces and their layouts that Marr calls the **$2\frac{1}{2}$-D sketch.** The information in the $2\frac{1}{2}$-D sketch is then transformed into a **3-D representation** that we actually see.

One way to look at Marr's system is to think of it as a computer that is programmed to take into account certain physical properties of the world (for example, that shadows often have fuzzy borders). The data fed into this computer are the characteristics of the retinal image, particularly the pattern of light and dark areas in the image. The computer calculates the existence of objects in the environment based on this data. Our description of the way these calculations are carried out has been vague, both because these calculations are too complex to describe here and also because Marr did not have time to work out many of the specific details of his system.

The importance of Marr's system, even in its sketchy form, is that it proposes that we can perceive forms based solely on an analysis of the information in the retinal image. Marr's system does not rely on top-down processes that involve things like the observer's knowledge of what specific objects are used for (see Figure 1.29) or where certain objects are usually found (see Figure 6.48). It is, therefore, accurate to say that Marr's system relies on bottom-up processing. This feature makes Marr's approach compatible with computer vision, since computers are well suited to bottom-up processing, which depends only on manipulation of the data fed into the computer.

accomplishes this analysis involves computations that are too complicated to describe here. The important point for our purposes is not the specific details of Marr's procedure but the fact that his method is based on a *mathematical analysis* of the pattern of light and dark areas in the scene, combined with *rules based on the nature of the visible world.*

The mathematical analysis that locates an object's edges also yields a number of *primitives,* such as (1) blobs (closed loops), (2) segments of edges, (3) bars (open passages), and (4) terminations (the ends of edge segments). These primitives, plus the object's edges, make up the **raw primal sketch.**

The raw primal sketch is the result of the initial stage of computations, but we do not see it. Before conscious perception can occur, the visual system must process the information contained in the raw primal sketch. First, primitives that are similar in size and orientation are grouped, following Gestalt principles. These groups of primitives

PARTS OR WHOLES?

The research we have just described sees perception as a process that begins with the extraction of basic units called primitives. Though different units have been proposed by different researchers, all of these researchers are in agreement that perceptual processing begins at the level of basic units. This conclusion conflicts with the Gestalt idea that we perceive in terms of wholes. The reason for this conflict can be traced to the types of evidence used to support the Gestalt position and to support the "basic units" position.

The Gestalt emphasis on wholes is supported primarily by introspective evidence, like that cited by Wertheimer's statement that "I cannot see the '327' " (page 194). The Gestalt psychologists examined their perceptual experience and concluded that since we are much more aware of perception in terms of wholes, rather than in terms of parts, the basic mechanism of form perception must be *wholistic*. But the fact that we are not as *aware* of basic units does not mean that these units do not play a role in perception. Initial processing in terms of basic units, while not accessible to consciousness, may lead to the perceptions observed by the Gestalt psychologists in terms of wholes that are accessible to consciousness. The fact that we might not be conscious of these underlying mech-

anisms should not surprise us if we remember that at the physiological level, perception is caused by neural processing that is also hidden from consciousness.

Thus, although the Gestalt idea that wholes are important is true at the level of our experience in looking at pictures like the ones in Figures 6.5–6.9, it appears that the starting point for this wholistic perception is the units we have been calling primitives.

But just because there is evidence that perception begins at the level of primitives does not mean that we need to reject Gestalt psychology. You may have noticed that we mentioned Gestalt principles of grouping a number of times as we discussed primitives. Primitives may be the starting point for our perception of forms, but the Gestalt principles are part of the process that leads to our eventual perception of these forms.

Summary

1. Although perceiving objects appears to be simple, since we can usually do it with little effort, it is an extremely difficult task for computers.
2. Perceptual organization, the grouping of parts into larger units, is essential for making sense of the world. The Gestalt psychologists, who were especially interested in perceptual organization, rejected the structuralists' idea that perceptions are constructed from sensations and proposed, instead, the idea that "the whole is different from the sum of its parts."
3. The Gestalt laws of organization—Pragnanz, similarity, good continuation, common fate, nearness, and meaningfulness—provide us with rules for how parts of stimuli are grouped together.
4. A form is usually perceived as a figure in front of a background. A number of rules have been proposed to predict which part of a pattern will be perceived as the figure and which part will be perceived as the ground.
5. While the laws of organization can help to segregate figure and ground, these organizing principles can, if the figure and ground are similar, hinder the separation of figure and ground—a situation called camouflage.
6. The Gestalt laws of organization are sometimes difficult to apply. Some of the problems with them

include difficulty in telling when one object is simpler than another, conflicts between the laws, and the lack of applicability to the three-dimensional world.
7. The tendency of the Gestalt approach to describe rather than to explain has led many present-day researchers to propose that we need to apply a more quantitative approach to the Gestalt principles.
8. Recent research based on the Gestalt approach has concentrated on applying the experimental method to Gestalt psychology in an attempt to understand, in a more quantitative way, how these laws work. These experiments have focused on questions such as (a) what stimulus properties are responsible for grouping? (b) how does grouping affect our ability to extract information from a display? and (c) how are figure and ground analyzed by the visual system?
9. The idea behind perceptual processing is that the observer carries out mental operations on the stimulus to arrive at a perception of the stimulus. Examples of the application of this approach are Gregory's idea that perception involves a process of hypothesis testing and Hochberg's idea that perception is a process of taking in information with successive eye movements.
10. Treisman proposes that form perception takes place in two or more stages. In the preattentive stage the

stimulus is decomposed into a number of basic properties, or primitives. In the focused attention stage these primitives are combined. Treisman has used psychophysical techniques involving pop-out boundaries, visual search, and illusory conjunctions to determine the properties of the primitives.

11. The combination of primitives is influenced by Gestalt grouping principles and by top-down processing—processing that is based on higher-level information such as context and the observer's prior knowledge.

12. Biederman's recognition-by-components mechanism is concerned with how we recognize three-dimensional objects based on our perception of the components that make up these objects. According to this model we decompose objects into primitives called geons. According to the principle of componential recovery, if we can identify an object's geons, we can identify the object.

13. The computational approach to object perception, as described by Marr, is based on a mathematical analysis of the pattern of light and dark areas in the scene combined with rules based on the nature of the visible world.

14. Most recent research on form perception sees perception as a process that begins with the extraction of basic units called primitives. This idea can be reconciled with the more wholistic Gestalt approach if we realize that although primitives may be the starting point for our perception of forms, the Gestalt principles are part of the process that leads to the eventual perception of these forms.

Boxes

1. A person suffering from visual agnosia may have little trouble seeing an object but does have trouble naming the object, describing its use, or, in some cases, drawing a picture of the object. Most forms of visual agnosia are associated with damage to cortical areas outside the visual receiving area.

2. There are two separate visual pathways that extend from the primary visual receiving area. One, located in the temporal area, is responsible for identifying objects. The other, in the parietal area, is responsible for locating objects.

Study Questions

1. Describe three of the problems that make perception difficult for a computer. (188)
2. What school of psychology would try to explain the perception of an elephant in scrambled eggs in terms of rules of perceptual grouping? (192)
3. Describe Max Wertheimer's experiment which founded Gestalt psychology. What was Wertheimer's problem with structuralism? (193)
4. How does phi movement support the idea that the whole is more than the sum of its parts? (22, 194)
5. What is subjective contour and how is it relevant to Gestalt psychology? (195)
6. Describe each of the Gestalt laws of organization. (196)
7. What are the properties of figure and ground? (204)
8. Describe five factors that determine which of two areas will be seen as figure and which as ground. (205)
9. What is the connection between camouflage and the Gestalt laws of organization? (206)
10. What are some criticisms of the Gestalt laws? (207)
11. Describe the experiment of Figure 6.37. What do the results of this experiment have to do with Gestalt psychology? (209)
12. How can Gestalt laws like good continuation and proximity determine our ability to detect a target in a display? (209)
13. How does Julesz describe differences between the perceptual analysis that occurs for figure and ground? How do the results of Weisstein and Wong's experiment of Figure 6.40 relate to Julesz' idea? (211)
14. Describe Gregory's idea of hypothesis testing and Hochberg's idea that observers take in information by a sequence of fixations. How do these ideas relate to the idea that form perception can be thought of as a result of perceptual processing? (212)
15. Define: preattentive stage of processing; primitives; focused attention stage. (213)
16. Describe the "pop-out boundary" and visual search methods of determining the identity of the primitives that are extracted in the preattentive stage. (214)
17. Describe the illusory conjunction technique. What do the results of experiments done using this technique show? (215)
18. What process must occur for the primitives in Treisman's system to be combined? (215)
19. What is the role of Gestalt grouping in the process of combining primitives? (216)
20. What is bottom-up processing? Top-down process-

ing? Describe Biederman's experiment that demonstrates the effect of context on object identification. Relate these two processes to Treisman's model of form perception. (216)

21. What is a geon? How can geons be distinguished from one another? What are accidental properties? What is the principle of componential recovery? (218)

22. Why is Marr's system called a computational approach? (220)

23. Describe the first step in analyzing an image, according to Marr. (221)

24. What is the relationship between Marr's primitives and the raw primal sketch? Do we see the raw primal

sketch? What steps must happen before perception occurs? (222)

25. Why is Marr's system important? (222)

26. How is it possible to combine the Gestalt approach and the idea that form perception begins with basic units? (223)

Boxes

1. What is visual agnosia? (190)

2. Describe the two pathways for vision proposed by Mishkin. Where does each pathway go and what does it do? (192)

Glossary

Accidental properties. Properties of an object that occur when the object is viewed from an atypical viewpoint. For example, when we view a rectangular solid end-on we perceive a square. When this occurs we don't see the non-accidental properties that define our perception of the rectangular solid under most viewing conditions. (218)

Bottom-up processing. Processing in which a perception is constructed by first analyzing small units such as primitives. Treisman's preattentive stage of processing, in which a stimulus is analyzed into parts, is an example of bottom-up processing. (216)

Cognitive psychology. An approach to psychology that emphasizes the study of mental processes. (212)

Common fate, law of. Gestalt law: things that are moving in the same direction appear to be grouped together. (200)

Componential recovery, principle of. If an object's geons can be identified, then the object can be rapidly and correctly recognized. (219)

Computational approach. An approach to explaining object perception that treats perception as the end result of a mathematical analysis of the retinal image. (220)

Familiarity, law of. Gestalt law: Things are more likely to form groups if the groups appear familiar or meaningful. (201)

Figure-ground segregation. Segregation of a pattern into a figure and a background. The figure is seen as being in front of the ground, which extends behind the figure. (203)

Focused attention stage of processing. The stage of processing in which the primitives are combined. This stage requires conscious attention. (214)

Geon. "Geometric Ion": Volumetric primitives proposed by Biederman. (218)

Gestalt psychology. A school of psychologists that has focused on developing principles of perceptual organization. (193)

Good continuation, law of. Gestalt law: Points that, when connected, result in straight or smoothly curving lines are seen as belonging together, and lines tend to be seen in such a way as to follow the smoothest path. (199)

Good figure, law of. Gestalt law: Every stimulus pattern is seen so the resulting structure is as simple as possible. (198)

Illusory conjunctions. Illusory combinations of primitives that are perceived when stimuli containing a number of primitives are presented briefly. (215)

Illusory conjunction technique. A technique developed by Treisman, which shows that primitives exist independently from one another in the preattentive stage of processing. (215)

Laws of organization. Rules developed by the Gestalt psychologists, which describe how small elements are grouped into larger configurations. (197)

Likelihood principle. We will perceive the object that is most likely to be caused by our sensory stimulation. This principle was proposed by Helmholtz. (212)

Local depth information. Information at a localized place on a figure that indicates depth. (213)

Non-accidental properties. Unique features that enable us to distinguish between different geons from most viewpoints. See accidental properties. (218)

Perceptual organization. The perceptual grouping of small units into larger forms. (192)

Perceptual processing. The mental processing that occurs during the process of perception. (212)

Pop-out boundaries. Boundaries between areas in a display that are seen almost immediately—they "pop out." (214)

Pragnanz, law of. Also called the law of good figure or the law of simplicity. States that every stimulus pattern is seen in such a way that the resulting structure is as simple as possible. (197)

Preattentive stage of processing. An automatic and rapid stage of processing, during which a stimulus is decomposed into primitives. (213)

Primitives. Basic properties of a stimulus. For example, Treisman has proposed primitives such as color, line tilt, and curvature. Biederman's primitives are volumetric shapes. (213)

Prosopagnosia. A form of visual agnosia in which the person can't recognize faces. (191)

Proximity, law of. Gestalt law. Also called the law of nearness. Things that are near to each other appear to be grouped together. (200)

Raw primal sketch. In Marr's computational approach to object perception, the raw primal sketch consists of an object's primitives and edges. (222)

Recognition-by-components. A mechanism of object perception proposed by Biederman, in which we recognize objects by decomposing them into primitives called geons. (218)

Reversible figure-ground. A figure-ground pattern that reverses as it is viewed so the figure becomes the ground and the ground becomes the figure. (203)

Similarity, law of. Gestalt law: Similar things appear to be grouped together. (199)

Simplicity, law of. See Good figure, law of.

Subjective contour. Perception of a contour when no contour is physically present. (195)

3-D representation. The end result of Marr's computational process—the perception of the three-dimensional stimulus. (222)

Top-down processing. Processing that starts with the analysis of high-level information, such as the context in which a stimulus is seen. (217)

$2\frac{1}{2}$-D sketch. The second stage of Marr's computational process. This stage is the result of processing the primitives. The resulting $2\frac{1}{2}$-D sketch is then transformed into the *three-dimensional representation*. (222)

Visual agnosia. A condition in which a person can see clearly but has difficulty recognizing what he sees. This condition, which is often caused by brain injuries, makes it difficult for people to synthesize parts of an object into an integrated whole. (190)

CHAPTER 7

Perceiving Depth and Size

Imagine that you are standing on a hill looking out over the neighborhood of Figure 7.1. Imagine that you are actually *there, observing the three-dimensional scene.* You can see from the car in the foreground down to the cross street at the bottom of the hill, and then up the next hill to the houses that line the ridge in the distance. And it takes no particular skill on your part to know that the car is nearby and the ridge is far away.

How is it possible that we can perceive the depth in this scene when the light reflected from this scene is imaged on the two-dimensional surface of our retinas? In this chapter, we will see that there are many answers to this question, both because depth is determined by a number of different factors and because of different theoretical approaches to answering the question.

One theoretical approach, called **cue theory,** focuses on identifying information in the retinal image that is correlated with depth in the world. We begin this chapter by considering this approach to depth perception and will also consider how this approach explains the perception of size and the perception of visual illusions—two things that are closely related to our perception of depth.

After discussing the cue approach we will consider a second theoretical approach, the **ecological approach** proposed by J. J. Gibson (see page 25). Rather than focusing on information for depth on the retina, this approach focuses on identifying information "out there" in the environment that is used by observers moving through that environment.

THE CUE APPROACH

The cue approach to depth perception postulates connections between stimuli in the environment, the images these stimuli present to the retina, and perceived depth. For example, if one object partially covers another object, as the houses in the foreground of Figure 7.1 cover the houses in the background, the object that is partially covered must be at a greater distance than the object that

227

F I G U R E 7. 1   A neighborhood in Pittsburgh that contains many depth cues.

is covering it. This situation, which is called over-lap, is a signal, or cue, that one object is in front of another. According to cue theory, the connection between this cue and depth is learned through a person's previous experience with the environment. After this learning has occurred, the association between particular cues and depth becomes automatic, and when **depth cues** are present we experience the world in three dimensions.

Another way of stating the cue approach is to say that our perception of depth cues enables us to make *inferences* about the depth in a scene. For example, we infer that A is in front of B by reasoning that "if A covers B, then A is in front of B." This way of describing the cue approach emphasizes its constructivist nature. Remember from Chapter 1 (p. 23) that the constructivist approach assigns an active role to the observer, postulating that perception occurs as the result of physiological or mental processing. We emphasize the constructivist nature of the cue approach, because at the end of the chapter we will consider the ecological analysis of depth perception, an approach that differs greatly from constructivism. Thus, one purpose of this chapter is to describe both the cue and ecological approaches to depth and size perception

so we can draw contrasts between the two.

Rather than simply presenting a list of all of the depth cues, we will divide them into the following four groups, based on their properties:

1. **Oculomotor cues:** cues that depend on our ability to sense the position of our eyes and tension in our eye muscles.
2. **Pictorial cues:** cues that can be depicted in a still picture.
3. **Motion-produced cues:** cues that depend on movement of the observer, or movement of objects in the environment.
4. **Binocular disparity:** a cue that depends on the fact that slightly different images of a scene are formed on each eye.

We will now describe each of these types of depth cues.

OCULOMOTOR CUES

Convergence and Accommodation

Convergence and accommodation provide information from the muscles of the eye.

Feelings in Your Eyes

Look at your finger as you hold it at arm's length. Then slowly move your finger toward your nose and become aware of how, as your finger moves closer, you feel your eyes looking inward and you feel increasing tension inside your eyes.

The feelings you experience as you move your finger closer are caused by (1) **convergence** as your eye muscles cause your eyes to look inward, as in Figure 7.2(a), and (2) **accommodation** as the lens bulges to focus on a near object (see Figure 3.10 and page 72). If you move your finger farther away, the eyes diverge, as in Figure 7.2(b), and the lens flattens.

Convergence and accommodation can serve as cues to depth because the shape of the lens and the position of the eyes are correlated with the distance of the object we are observing. These cues are, however, effective only at distances closer than about 5–10 feet from the observer (see Liebowitz, Shina, & Hennessy, 1972).

PICTORIAL CUES

Pictorial cues can be represented in a picture—either the picture formed on the retina or pictures like the illustrations in this book.

Overlap

We have already described the depth cue of **overlap.** If object A covers part of object B, then object A is seen as being in front of object B. Note that overlap does not provide information about an

(a)   (b)

F I G U R E 7. 2 (a) Convergence of the eyes occurs when a person looks at something very close. (b) Divergence occurs (right) when he looks at something far away.

—B

—A

F I G U R E   7. 3   *Place des Lices, St. Tropez* by Paul Signac (1893). (Museum of Art, Carnegie Institute, Pittsburgh, Pa.)

object's distance from us; instead, it indicates *relative depth*—that one object is closer than another object.

Paul Signac's painting *Place des Lices, St. Tropez* (1893), shown in Figure 7.3, makes extensive use of overlap. Place a piece of paper so that it covers everything below mark A and notice how overlap helps you determine the relative positions in depth of the tree branches in the top part of the picture. Then move your paper up that so it covers everything below mark B. Since there is little overlap in the upper left of the picture, it is difficult to tell which branches are in front and which are in back.

We usually find it easy to judge when one object is overlapping another. But what is it about two stimuli that makes one appear to cover the other? Hermann von Helmholtz (see Hochberg, 1971, p. 498) pointed out that the contour of the

object seen as being in front usually does not change its direction where it intersects the object seen as being in back. Helmholtz' rule usually works, as in Figure 7.4(a), but there are exceptions, as in Figure 7.4(b), in which the star appears to be in front even though its contour changes direction where it intersects with the cross.

Size in the Field of View

In addition to noticing that the houses in the background in Figure 7.1 are overlapped by those in the foreground, you can also see that the houses in the background take up less of your field of view than those in the foreground. The cue of **size in the field of view,** which apparently has fooled the large person in Figure 7.5 into thinking that a small person is far away, was demonstrated by Adelbert Ames, who had observers view illuminated bal-

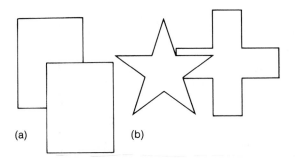

(a)   (b)

F I G U R E 7. 4 (a) The contour of the rectangle that appears in front does not change direction where it intersects the rectangle that appears in back. This example therefore conforms to Helmholtz' rule. (b) An exception to Helmholtz' "rule". Here, the star appears to be in front even though its contour changes its direction in the two places where it intersects the cross.

loons in a darkened room. When he increased the size of one balloon by pumping more air into it,

the observers reported that the expanding balloon appeared to be moving closer. Larger size causes an object to appear closer.

Height in the Field of View

The houses in the background of Figure 7.1 not only take up less of your field of view than those in front but they are also higher in the scene. This is the cue of **height in the field of view.** Objects that are *higher* in your field of view, like the men in Figure 7.6, are usually seen as being more distant. This rule holds for objects like the men that are below the horizon line, but objects like the clouds, that are above the horizon line, appear more distant when they are *lower* in your field of view.

Not only are the more distant houses of Figure 7.1 the highest in the scene, but they are also slightly less sharp than those in the foreground. This brings us to our next pictorial cue, atmospheric perspective.

"Excuse me for shouting—I thought you were farther away."

F I G U R E 7. 5 (Reproduced by special permission of *Playboy* Magazine. Copyright 1971 by Playboy.)

F I G U R E 7. 6   Relative height. Other things being equal, objects below the horizon that appear higher in the field of view are seen as being farther away. Objects above the horizon that appear lower in the field of view are seen as being farther away.

Atmospheric Perspective

Atmospheric (or ariel) perspective causes us to see distant objects as less sharp because we must look through the air and the particles suspended in the air between us and the object. The farther away an object is, the more air and particles we have to look through, and this makes far objects look less sharp than close objects. Figure 7.7, which shows some of the buildings of downtown Pittsburgh from a nearby neighborhood, illustrates atmospheric perspective. Compare the sharpness of the church in the foreground to the less sharp buildings in the background.

If instead of viewing buildings in Pittsburgh you were to view craters on the moon, where there is no atmosphere, and hence no atmospheric perspective, the far craters would look just as sharp as near ones. But on earth there is atmospheric perspective, with the exact amount being dependent on the nature of the atmosphere.

An example of how atmospheric perspective depends on the nature of the atmosphere occurred when one of my friends took a trip from Pittsburgh to Montana. He started walking toward a moun-

tain that appeared to be perhaps a two- or three-hour hike away but found after three hours of hiking that he was still far from the mountain. Since my friend's perceptions were "calibrated" for Pittsburgh, he found it difficult to accurately estimate distances in the clearer air of Montana, so a mountain that would have looked three hours away in Pittsburgh was over six hours away in Montana!

In addition to making far objects look fuzzy, the atmosphere also makes them look blue. In Color Plate 7.1 you can see that the hills in the background look much bluer than the trees and grass in the foreground. (Review Box 4.1 for an explanation of this blueness.)

Atmospheric perspective was widely used by painters in the 15th and 16th centuries, and many of the art academies of the day hung a series of blue-tinted curtains between the art students and the objects they were painting in order to make these students paint far-away objects blue. This training often resulted in an exaggeration of atmospheric perspective, so that mountains often appeared much bluer in the painting than in the original scene. For example, look at the distant blue hills in Gerard David's painting *Rest on the Flight into Egypt*, shown in Color Plate 7.2 (Also note how Joseph's small size in the field of view enhances the impression of distance between him and Mary.)

Familiar Size

Look at the coins in Figure 7.8. If they were real coins, which would you say is closer? If you are influenced by your knowledge of the actual size of dimes, quarters, and half-dollars, you would probably say that the dime is closer. If you did, the cue of **familiar size** is influencing your judgment of depth. An experiment by William Epstein (1965) shows that under certain conditions, our knowledge of an object's size can influence our perception of that object's depth. The stimuli in Epstein's experiment were photographs of a dime (enlarged to the size of a quarter), a quarter (actual size), and a half-dollar (reduced to the size of a quarter). By placing

F I G U R E 7. 7 Atmospheric perspective causes details of the buildings in the background to be less sharp than details of the church in the foreground. This is a subtle example of atmospheric perspective. Increased pollution, fog, or mist can increase atmospheric perspective, so that far-away details become difficult or impossible to see.

these photographs in a darkened room, illuminating them with a spot of light, and having subjects view them with one eye, Epstein created the illusion that these pictures were real coins.

The observer's task was to estimate the distance of each of the coin photographs. Although each photograph was positioned at the same distance, the dime was estimated to be closer than the quarter, which was estimated as closer than the half-dollar (Figure 7.9). This result is exactly what we would expect if familiar size were influencing the observer's judgment of distance. Consider the oversized dime. For a dime to appear as large as it did to the observers (who did not know that the dime was actually over twice its normal size), it

would have to be close. Similarly, for a half-dollar to appear as small as it did, it would have to be far away. But the quarter, which was its actual size,

F I G U R E 7. 8 Line drawings of the stimuli used in Epstein's (1965) familiar size experiment (the actual stimuli were photographs).

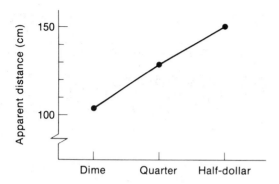

F I G U R E 7. 9 Results of Epstein's (1965) familiar size experiment. Although the oversized dime, the actual-sized quarter, and the undersized half-dollar were actually at the same distance, they were perceived to be at different distances when viewed monocularly.

was estimated to be at just about the right distance. Clearly, the observers' judgments were influenced by their knowledge of the sizes of real dimes, quarters, and half-dollars.

The result shown in Figure 7.9 did not, however, occur when the observers opened both eyes. When they did this they were able to tell that all of the coins were at the same distance. As we will see below, the use of two eyes provides important information for the perception of depth; so, when the observers in Epstein's experiment used two eyes, this extra information enabled them to disregard the effect of familiar size and correctly judge the distances of the oversized dime and undersized half-dollar. The cue of familiar size is, therefore, most effective when other information about depth is absent (see also Schiffman, 1967; Coltheart, 1970).

Linear Perspective

How can we create a three-dimensional impression of depth on the two-dimensional surface of a canvas? This question has concerned artists since before the ancient Greeks, but it wasn't until 1435 that

Leon Battista Alberti wrote *De Pictura*, the first book describing the principles of a drawing system called **linear perspective,** which made it possible to convincingly depict depth on a two-dimensional surface (see White, 1968; Hagen, 1979, 1986; Kubovy, 1986). Alberti's book describes a geometrical procedure for drawing a picture in linear perspective.

Another way of creating a perspective picture is based on the idea stated by Leonardo da Vinci that "perspective is nothing else than seeing a place behind a plane of glass, quite transparent, on the surface of which the objects behind the glass are to be drawn" (Gombrich, 1960). By using this technique, which has been called **Alberti's window,** anyone can draw in perspective. You need only obtain a transparent surface such as a piece of glass or a rigid piece of transparent plastic; then, keeping your eye fixed in one place, look at a scene through the transparent surface and trace the contours of the scene onto the surface. This procedure is being used by the artist in Figure 7.10; instead of drawing the picture on the window, however, he is using a grid to transfer it to a canvas. This procedure results in a picture drawn in linear perspective that creates an impression of depth on the canvas. Another way to create a perspective picture is to take a photograph. The optical system of a camera accomplishes essentially the same thing as Alberti's window and records the result on film.

When a picture is drawn in linear perspective, an interesting result occurs: Lines that are parallel in the scene (such as the sides of the street in Figure 7.1) converge as they get farther away. The greater the distance, the greater the convergence, until, at a distance of infinity (far away!), these lines meet at a vanishing point. What is important for our purposes is that this convergence occurs not only in perspective pictures, such as Figure 7.11, but also occurs in the world. This convergence of parallel lines, to which most people have been introduced by viewing railroad tracks that meet far in the distance, is usually referred to as the depth cue of **linear perspective.**

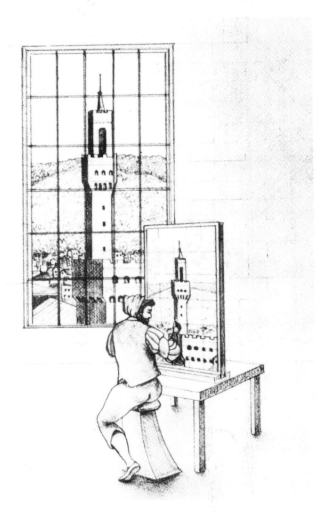

F I G U R E 7. 10 An artist drawing a picture in perspective using the method of Alberti's window.

F I G U R E 7. 11 (below) *A Street with Various Buildings, Colonnades, and an Arch,* c. 1500, artist unknown (School of Donate Brumante). This is an example of a picture drawn in perspective so that lines that are parallel in the scene converge to a vanishing point if extended into the distance. Something interesting happens in this picture near the last building on the left. The squares in this part of the street are not lined up exactly parallel with the squares in the foreground, and this creates the impression of a slight rise in the street. We can't tell, however, whether the artist meant to show a slight rise in the street, or whether this rise is the result of faulty perspective. (Museum of Art, Carnegie Institute, Pittsburgh, Pa.)

MOVEMENT-PRODUCED CUES

All of the cues we have described so far provide information about depth to a stationary observer. As we stand on the hill observing the scene in Figure 7.1, these cues contribute to our perception of depth in the scene. If, however, we decide to take a walk, new cues emerge that further enhance our perception of depth. Hermann von Helmholtz (1866/1911) describes the following situation in which movement enhances depth perception:

Suppose, for instance, that a person is standing still in a thick woods, where it is impossible for him to distinguish, except vaguely and roughly, in the mass of foliage and branches all around him what belongs to one tree and what to another. . . . But the moment he begins to move forward, everything disentangles itself, and immediately he gets an apperception of the material contents of the woods and their relations to each other in space . . . . (p. 296).

We will describe two different movement-produced cues: (1) motion parallax and (2) deletion and accretion.

Motion Parallax

Elaborating further on the effect of movement on depth perception, Helmholtz (1866, p. 295) states:

In walking along, the objects that are at rest by the wayside . . . appear to glide past us in our field of view . . . . More distant objects do the same only more slowly . . . . Evidently, under these circumstances, the apparent angular velocities of objects in the field of view will be inversely proportional to their real distances; and, consequently, safe conclusions can be drawn as to the real distance of the body from its apparent angular velocity.

This effect is particularly obvious when you look out the side window of a moving car or train. Nearby objects appear to speed by in a blur, while objects on the horizon move very slowly. This difference in the speed of movement for near and far objects is called **motion parallax,** and we can use this cue to perceive the depths of objects based on how fast they move as we move: Far objects move slowly; near objects move rapidly.

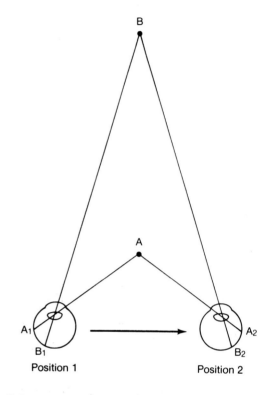

F I G U R E 7. 12   One eye, moving from left to right, showing how the images of two objects (A and B) change their position on the retina due to this movement. Notice that the image of the near object, A, moves farther on the retina than the image of the far object, B.

We can understand why this motion parallax effect occurs by looking at the eye in Figure 7.12. This figure shows what happens to the images of two objects, a near object at A and a far object at B, when a single eye moves from position 1 to position 2. First consider how the image of the near object moves across the retina as the eye moves from 1 to 2. When the eye is at 1, the image of object A is at A1 on the retina; and when the eye has moved to 2, the image of object A has moved all the way across the retina to A2. This means that when the eye moves from position 1 to position 2, the image of object A moves from one side

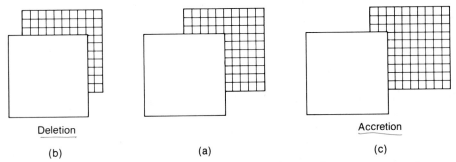

Deletion   Accretion

(b)   (a)   (c)

F I G U R E 7. 13   Deletion and accretion occur when an observer moves in a direction *not* perpendicular to two surfaces that are at different depths. If an observer perceives the two surfaces as in (a) and then moves to the *left*, deletion occurs so the front object covers more of the back one, as in (b). If the observer starts at (a) and moves to the *right*, accretion occurs so the front object covers less of the back one, as in (c). Try this with two objects.

of the observer's field of view to the other. The image of object B, on the other hand, moves only from B1 to B2 on the retina and, therefore, moves only a short distance across the observer's field of view. Thus, as the observer moves from left to right, the near object travels a large distance across the retina and therefore travels rapidly across the observer's field of view, but the far object travels a much smaller distance across the retina and therefore travels much more slowly across the observer's field of view.

Deletion and Accretion

When two surfaces are located at different distances, as in Figure 7.13(a), any movement that is not perpendicular to these surfaces causes them to appear to move relative to one another, with the back surface covered up, or **deleted,** by the one in front when the observer moves in one direction [Figure 7.13(b)], or with the back surface uncovered, or **accreted,** when the observer moves in the other direction [Figure 7.13(c)]. This cue, which is related both to motion parallax, since surfaces appear to move relative to one another, and to overlap, since one surface partially covers the other, is especially effective for detecting depth at an edge (Kaplan, 1969).

BINOCULAR DISPARITY

This cue has been saved for last because it is the most important cue for depth. All the other cues we have discussed, with the exception of convergence, are **monocular depth cues** because they still work if we look through only one eye, but binocular disparity is a **binocular depth cue** because it depends on both eyes. This cue is based on the fact that our eyes see the world from the slightly different positions determined by the distance between them. Because of this we see two different views of the world.

Two Eyes: Two Viewpoints

D E M O N S T R A T I O N

Looking Around Your Finger

With only your right eye open hold one finger upright about 6 inches in front of you. Then position a finger from your other hand about 6 inches farther back, so that it is completely hidden by the front finger. Now close your right eye and open your left eye, and the rear finger becomes visible. Since the left eye sees from a different point of view, it has looked around your front finger.

F I G U R E 7. 14   A stereoscopic photograph from the Super Bowl Pittsburgh Steelers of the 1970s. This photograph shows Terry Bradshaw (right) of the Steelers talking to Joe Ferguson of the Buffalo Bills after a game at Three Rivers Stadium in Pittsburgh. The picture on the left is the view seen by the left eye, and the picture on the right is the view seen by the right eye. Although the two pictures may at first glance look the same, a closer look shows that the relationship between the foreground and background is different in the two views. For example, compare the distance between Bradshaw's head and the lighted upper stands in the background, or compare the people in the stands in the space between Bradshaw and Ferguson. This slight displacement results in binocular disparity when these two views are presented to each eye separately in a stereoscope and we see the scene in depth. (Stereogram by Mike Chikiris, Pittsburgh Stereogram Company, Pittsburgh, Pa., 1977.)

The fact that the two eyes see different views of the world was used by the physicist Charles Wheatstone (1802–1875) to create the **stereoscope,** a device which produces a convincing illusion of depth using two slightly different pictures. This device, extremely popular among adults in the 1800s and now familiar to most children as the View Master, presents two photographs that are made with a camera with two lenses separated by the same distance as the eyes. This results in two slightly different views, like those shown in Figure 7.14. The stereoscope presents the left picture to the left eye and the right picture to the right eye so that they combine to result in a convincing three-dimensional perception of the scene.

D E M O N S T R A T I O N

Binocular Depth from a Picture, without a Stereoscope

Place a 4 × 6 card vertically, long side up, between the two pictures below and place your nose against the card so you are seeing the left-hand drawing with just your left eye and the right-hand drawing with just your right eye. (Blink back and forth to

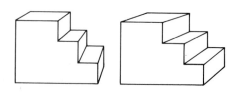

F I G U R E 7. 15

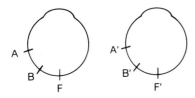

F I G U R E 7. 16 Corresponding points on the two retinas. To determine corresponding points, slide one eye on top of the other one.

The principle behind the stereoscope—presenting one image to the left eye and the other to the right eye—has also been used in 3-D movies. These movies became quite popular when introduced commercially in the 1950s, and I still vividly remember a scene from a film called *The Maze,* in which a terrible frog-like creature plummeted from a castle window directly toward me! Luckily, I survived to write this book.

Looking into a stereoscope shows that when our two eyes receive slightly different images of the same scene, we experience an impression of depth. But why does this impression occur? To understand this, we must introduce the concept of **corresponding retinal points.**

Corresponding Retinal Points

confirm this.) Then *relax* and wait for the two drawings to merge. When the drawings form a single image, you should see the stairs in depth, just as you would if you looked at them through a stereoscope.

For every point on one retina, there is a corresponding point on the other. Corresponding points are the places on each retina that would overlap if one retina could be slid on top of the other. So, the two foveas, F and F′, fall on corresponding points, as shown in Figure 7.16, and A and A′ and

F I G U R E 7. 17 When the lifeguard looks at Ralph, this causes the images of Ralph, Susan, and Harry to fall on the horoptor indicated by the dashed line. This means that Ralph's, Susan's, and Harry's images fall on corresponding points on the lifeguard's retina, and the images of all of the other swimmers fall on noncorresponding points.

B O X 7. 1 / *Flatness Cues in Pictures*

Is it possible to create a picture of a three-dimensional scene that is so realistic that an observer will mistake it for the actual scene? The answer to this question is "yes," but only if special precautions are taken to eliminate the picture's **flatness cues.** Flatness cues are aspects of the picture that signal the flatness of the picture. Some of them are:

1. Motion parallax does not occur when a viewer moves relative to a pictured scene. When we walk past a real scene, we experience motion parallax, which causes objects to change their positions in relation to one another. Demonstrate this to yourself by holding up one finger on each hand, about 6 inches apart and one in front of the other. While observing the fingers with one eye, move your head back and forth and notice how the front finger moves back and forth so it is sometimes seen to the left of the rear finger and sometimes to the right. But if you try this procedure on a *picture* of your fingers, the pictured fingers do not move relative to one another. This lack of motion parallax is a cue that the picture is flat.

2. Binocular disparity does not occur when viewing pictures. Remember the demonstration on page 237, in which you looked at your two fingers first with one eye and then with the other? By blinking back and forth, you saw two different views of your fingers. But what happens if you try this on a *picture* of two objects? Blinking back and forth has no effect on your perception of the object's position. We do not experience binocular disparity when looking at a picture, and this lack of disparity serves as a cue that we are looking at a flat picture.

3. We can see brushstrokes, glare, and the edges of the picture. All of these things tell us that we are looking at a flat picture.

How can we eliminate these flatness cues? We can do this by viewing the picture through a peephole that is close enough to the picture so we don't see the edges of the picture but is far enough away so we can't see the picture's brushstrokes (if it's a painting). But most important of all, viewing through a peephole makes movement impossible and without movement we can't tell that there is no motion parallax. Also, when we are viewing with one eye our brain can't tell that there is no binocular disparity, since it can't compare the images from the two eyes.

Though looking through a peephole may be a strange way to view a picture, this viewing method can so increase the illusion of depth that an unsuspecting viewer will be fooled into thinking she is looking at an actual scene instead of a picture. Patricia and Olin Smith (1961) achieved

---

B and B′ also fall on corresponding points.

To apply our knowledge of corresponding points to depth perception, let's assume that you are sitting in the lifeguard chair of Figure 7.17. If you look directly at your friend Ralph, his image will fall on your foveas (F and F′), which are corresponding points. However, Ralph is not the only person whose image falls on corresponding points.

The images of everyone who is located on the dashed line also fall on corresponding points. This dashed line, which is called the **horoptor,** is part of an imaginary surface that passes through the point of fixation (Ralph's head) and, in our example, also through the heads of Harry and Susan. This means that Harry's and Susan's images fall on corresponding points on the retina, as shown in Figure 7.18.

this illusion by having observers view a large photograph of a room through a peephole and found that the observers, unaware that they were looking at a photograph, thought they were viewing a real room.

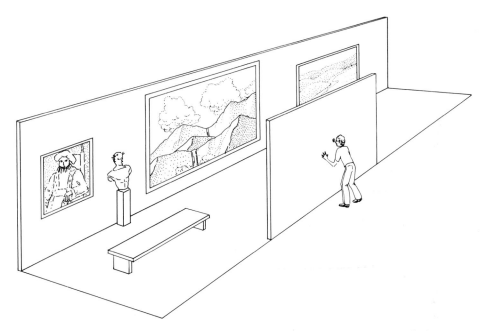

Peephole viewing can increase the impression of depth in a picture by eliminating flatness cues.

(It is important to remember that the situation we are describing here holds only as long as you are looking at Ralph. If you change your point of fixation, then a new horoptor is created that passes through the new point of fixation.)

What does this have to do with depth perception? To answer this question, let's continue looking at Ralph, and consider where Carol's and Charlie's images fall on the retina. Since their heads are not located on the horoptor, their images fall on **noncorresponding,** (or **disparate**) **points,** as indicated in Figure 7.19. For example, Carol's image falls on noncorresponding points B and G'. (Note that if you slid the retinas on top of each other, points B and G' would not overlap and are therefore noncorresponding.) The corresponding point

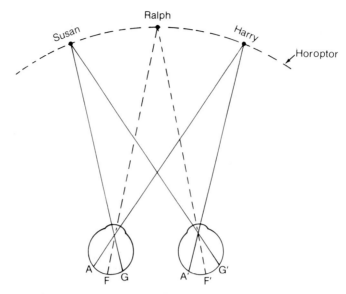

F I G U R E 7. 18 What's happening to the images of Susan, Ralph, and Harry inside the lifeguard's eye? Susan's image falls on corresponding points G and G′, Ralph's falls on the foveas F and F′ (which are corresponding points), and Harry's falls on corresponding points A and A′.

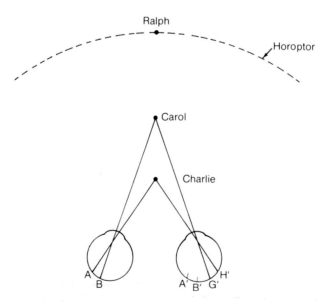

F I G U R E 7. 19 What's happening to the images of Carol and Charlie in the lifeguard's eye? Since Carol and Charlie are not located on the horoptor, their images fall on noncorresponding points.

FIGURE 7.20 The response of a binocular depth cell in the visual cortex of the monkey. The positions of the cross-hairs indicate the position of the bar for the right eye (RE) and the left eye (LE). This cell responds to movement of the bar in either direction (indicated by the arrows) and responds best when the two bars are presented simultaneously but are displaced 30 minutes in position as shown in record (c). In records (f) and (g), bars are presented to the same positions as in record (c), but each bar is presented to the left and right eye separately. The cell does not respond in (f) and (g) because both eyes must be stimulated to cause a binocular depth cell to fire. (From Hubel & Wiesel, 1970b.)

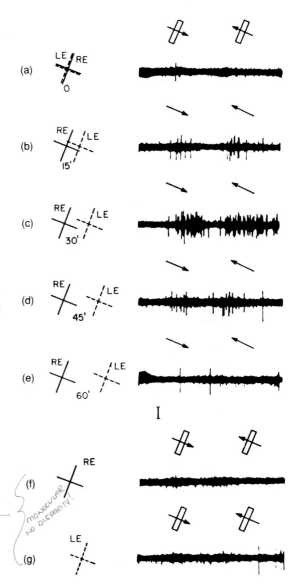

to B is, in fact, located at B′, far from G′. The distance between G′ and B′ is called the **degree of disparity,** and the key to binocular depth perception is that *the farther the object is from the horoptor, the greater is the degree of disparity.* You can see this by comparing the disparity of Carol's and Charlie's images in Figure 7.19. Carol's disparity is, as we saw above, the distance between G′ and B′, whereas Charlie's is the distance between H′ and A′. Charlie's images are more disparate because he is located farther from the horoptor. Thus, knowing the amount of disparity tells us how far Charlie and Carol are from where we are looking. Since Charlie's disparity is greater than Carol's, he must be located farther from the horoptor and, therefore, closer to us.

Disparity Information and the Brain

Though we can now see that disparity provides information about the relative distances of objects in a scene (or swimmers in a pool), one problem remains. How is this information used by the brain? This question was answered by Horace Barlow, Colin Blakemore, and John Pettigrew (1967), who found cells in the cortex of the cat that respond best to stimuli that fall on points separated by a specific degree of disparity on the two retinas. Records from such a cell in the visual cortex of the monkey, which David Hubel and Torsten Wiesel (1970b)

call a **binocular depth cell,** are shown in Figure 7.20. Record (a) shows that this cell does not respond when corresponding points (indicated by the overlap of the cross-hairs) on the two eyes are simultaneously stimulated by a bar moving either from left to right or from right to left. Records (b), (c), (d), and (e) show that this cell does respond,

BOX 7. 2 / Depth in Random Dot Patterns

The depth cue of *retinal disparity* is used to create an illusion of depth from two-dimensional pictures in stereoscopes, which present the left eye's view to the left eye and the right eye's view to the right eye. Although the disparity created by presenting a different view to each eye creates depth in these stereoscopic pictures, most stereoscopic pictures contain depth information in addition to disparity. *Relative size, overlap, relative height,* and other *monocular depth cues* may contribute to the depth seen in stereoscopic pictures. Bela Julesz (1971), however, has created the illusion of depth by using a stereoscope with random dot patterns, which contain no depth information other than disparity. Two such

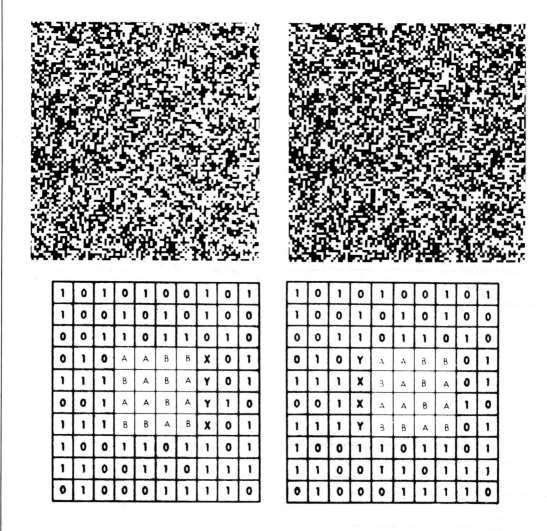

random dot patterns, which constitute a **random dot stereogram,** are shown here.

These patterns were constructed by first generating two identical random dot patterns with a computer and then shifting a square-shaped section of the dots to the right, in the pattern on the right. This shift is too subtle to see in these dot patterns, but we can understand how it is accomplished, by looking at the diagrams below the dot patterns. In these diagrams, the black dots and white dots in the patterns are indicated by 0s and 1s and by As and Bs. The As and Bs indicate the square-shaped section where the shift takes place. Notice that the As

and Bs are shifted one unit to the right in the right pattern. The Xs and Ys indicate areas uncovered by the shift that must be filled in with new black dots and white dots to complete the pattern.

The effect of shifting one section of the pattern in this way is to create disparity, which causes the perception of depth when the patterns are viewed in stereoscope. When these patterns are viewed stereoscopically, we perceive a small square floating above the background. This demonstration shows that even when no other depth information is present, retinal disparity can cause the perception of depth.

however, when the disparity of the moving bar is increased, with the maximum response occurring in record (c) at 30 minutes (half a degree) of disparity. Records (f) and (g) indicate that when each eye is *individually* stimulated by bars separated by 30 minutes of arc no response occurs, even though a large response results when these same bars are presented simultaneously, as in (c).

The existence of binocular depth cells in the cat and monkey means that if the animal's convergence is fixed (that is, if its eyes are positioned to look at a particular point in space and don't move), cells that fire best to different disparities will be excited by stimuli lying at different distances from the animal. Thus, in Figure 7.17, each swimmer causes a different group of the lifeguard's binocular depth cells to fire, which signals information about the distance between the lifeguard and each swimmer.

This description of binocular disparity completes our list of depth cues. Although no single cue is crucial for our perception of depth (we can eliminate any monocular depth cue or close one eye to eliminate binocular disparity and still see in depth), the more cues we have, the better our

chances of accurately deducing the three dimensions of the world from the two-dimensional information on our retinas.

At the end of this chapter we will discuss some of the strengths and weaknesses of the cue approach to depth perception, but first we will consider the perception of size.

PERCEIVING SIZE

Why are we discussing size perception in the same chapter as depth perception? We do this because our perception of size is greatly influenced by our perception of depth. To understand why this is so, we need to consider how an object's visual angle and retinal size are influenced by the object's distance and by the object's size.

Visual Angle, Retinal Size, and Distance

Visual angle, which we introduced in Chapter 3 (p. 65), is the angle between lines extended from the observer's eye to the top and bottom (or left and right sides) of an object (Figure 3.2). Figure 7.21 shows how the visual angle is affected by the object's distance: The closer the object, the larger the visual angle. Figure 7.22 shows how the visual angle is affected by the object's size. The larger the object's size, the larger the visual angle.

Since the visual angle is determined by both the object's size *and* its distance from the observer, we cannot determine the visual angle if we know only one or the other. A huge, far-away object can have a small visual angle, and, as illustrated in Figure 7.23, a small object that is close can have a visual angle equal to a large object that is farther away (see Box 7.3 and page 67).

Visual angle is important in discussing size perception because an object's visual angle is directly related to the size of that object's image on the retina. You can see this by looking at Figures 7.21,

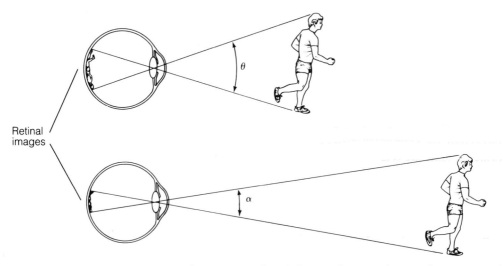

Retinal images

F I G U R E 7. 21   Increasing an object's distance decreases the size of its image on the retina and decreases its visual angle. In the bottom picture the man is twice as far from the eye as in the top picture, so the size of his image on the retina is half as large as it is in the top picture.

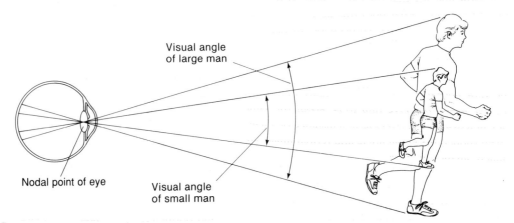

Visual angle of large man

Nodal point of eye

Visual angle of small man

F I G U R E 7. 22   If two objects are at the same distance, the one that is larger will have a larger visual angle.

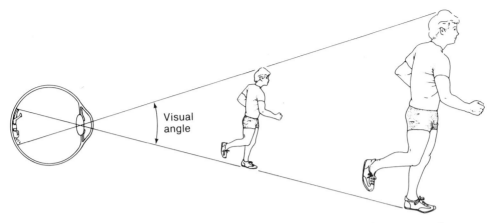

F I G U R E 7. 23 Two objects with the same visual angle have the same retinal size.

7.22, and 7.23. When the visual angle is large, the retinal image is large (Figures 7.21 and 7.22), and when two objects have the same visual angle, their retinal images are the same size (Figure 7.23). Since visual angle and retinal size are so closely related, we will use these terms interchangeably in the remainder of our discussion.

Perceiving Size as Visual Angle Changes

How do we perceive an object's size as its visual angle (or retinal size) changes? To answer this question, imagine that, when looking at a person who is 4 feet away, you perceive the person to be 6 feet tall. Now imagine that the person doubles his distance to 8 feet. What does this do to the size of his image on your retina? (It decreases by half. To convince yourself that this is so, look at Figure 7.21.) Does this halving of the size of the retinal image cause the person to appear half as large, so he now appears 3 feet tall? Probably not. Most people would perceive him to be about the same size at a distance of 8 feet as at a distance of 4 feet, even though his visual angle and retinal image are much smaller at 8 feet. In fact, the same result occurs if we replace the person with an unfamiliar stimulus, such as a board. Moving the board away decreases its visual angle but causes little or no change in our perception of its size. Thus, our perception of an object's size remains constant as the size of the object's image on the retina changes.

The fact that we perceive an object's size as remaining constant at different distances is called **size constancy.** According to the **law of size constancy** we correctly perceive an object's *physical size* no matter what its distance from us or the size of its image on our retina. The phenomenon of size constancy means that our perception of size must depend on information in addition to the size of the retinal image. In a classic experiment, A. H. Holway and Edwin Boring (1941) showed that size constancy depends on our perception of depth.

Size Constancy and Depth Perception

The setup for Holway and Boring's experiment is shown in Figure 7.24. The observer sits at the intersection of two hallways so that he sees a luminous test circle when looking down the right hallway and a luminous comparison circle when looking down the left hallway. The comparison circle is always 10 feet from the observer, but test circles are presented at distances ranging from 10 feet to 120 feet. On each trial, the observer's task is to adjust the size of the comparison circle to match that of the test circle. The key to this experiment is that each test circle has a visual angle of one degree. Thus, as shown in the top view of Holway and Boring's setup in Figure 7.25, larger and larger test circles must be used as distance increases in order to keep the visual angle constant at one degree.

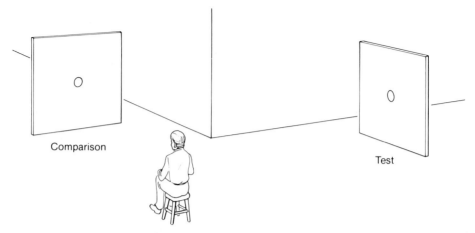

F I G U R E 7. 24   Setup of Holway and Boring's (1941) experiment. The observer adjusts the size of the comparison stimulus to match the size of the test stimulus.

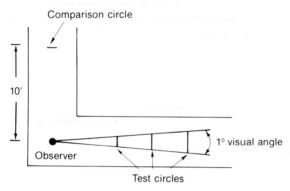

F I G U R E 7. 25   Top view of Holway and Boring's experiment. The key feature of this experiment is that the test circles all have the same visual angle and therefore cast the same image on the observer's retina. (Adapted from Holway & Boring, 1941.)

Note that in this phase of the experiment, many depth cues are available to the observer.

The results of this experiment are indicated by line 1 in Figure 7.26. It is clear that the observers based their judgments on the physical sizes of the circles, since large test circles that were far from the observer were matched by large comparison circles, and small test circles that were closer to the observer were matched by small comparison circles. The fact that the comparison circles were always adjusted to match the actual size of the test circles, even though all test circles had the same visual angle and therefore cast identical images on the retina, supports the law of size constancy.

Holway and Boring then asked how the presence of depth information affected the observer's perception of size. To determine the role of depth in size perception, Holway and Boring systematically eliminated depth cues from the hallway by having the observer view the test circles with one eye (line 2), by having the observer view the test circles through a peephole (line 3), and by adding drapes to the hallway to eliminate reflections (line 4). The results of these experiments indicate that as it becomes harder to determine the distance of the test circles our observer's judgments cease to follow the law of size constancy. When the observer looks down the draped hallway through a peephole, he judges all of the test circles to have about the same size (lower dashed line)—the result that would be predicted by the **law of visual angle.** The law of visual angle states that our perception of an object's size is determined solely by its visual angle. In a later experiment similar to Holway and Boring's, all depth cues were eliminated by using screens that permitted the observer to see only the test circles. Under these conditions, size constancy was completely eliminated, and the observer's perceptions followed the law of visual angle (Lichten & Lurie, 1950).

B O X   7. 3   /   *The Sun, the Moon, and the Law of Visual Angle*

Astronomy was full of such intriguing but meaningless coincidences. The most famous was the fact that, from the earth, both Sun and Moon have the same apparent diameter.
—Arthur C. Clarke, *2010:Odyssey Two*

Do the sun and moon appear to be about the same size to you? This is not a particularly easy question to answer, because we usually don't see the sun and moon together, and on the occasions when the moon is visible during the day, it is located far away from the sun in the sky. But there is one time when we see both the sun and moon together—during an eclipse of the sun. Although we can see the flaming corona of the sun surrounding the moon, as shown in the figure below, the moon's disc almost exactly covers the disc of the sun. We perceive the sizes of the sun and moon to be the same, simply because two objects with the same visual angle cast equal images on the retina. If we calculate the visual angles of the sun and moon, the result is 0.5 degrees for both. As you can see in the figure on the right, the moon is small (diameter = 2,200 miles) but close (245,000 miles from earth), while the sun is large (diameter = 865,400 miles) but far away (93 million miles from earth). The situation, therefore, is similar to the one depicted in Figure 7.23, in which a small object that is close casts the same-sized image on the retina as a large object that is far away.

In addition to being an interesting astronomical curiosity, the fact that the sun and moon have both the same visual angle *and* the same perceived size indicates that we perceive the sizes of these objects according to the law of visual angle. (If the sizes of the sun and moon were perceived according to the law of size constancy, the sun would appear to be almost 400 times the diameter of the moon.) Our perception according to the law of visual angle is not surprising, since we have no way of judging the relative distances of the sun and the moon; as we saw from the results of Holway and Boring's experiment, when we can't judge an object's distance, our perception of size is determined by the object's visual angle.

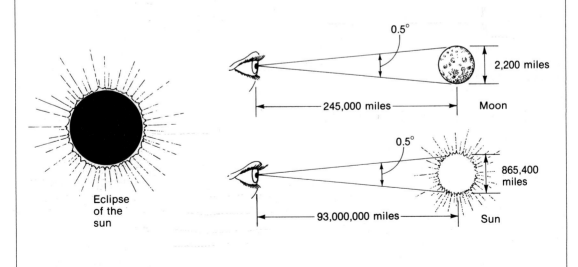

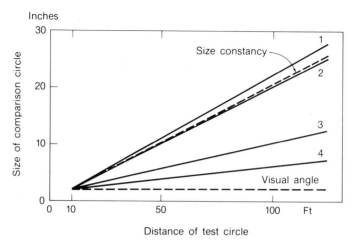

FIGURE 7.26 Results of Holway and Boring's experiment. The dashed line marked "size constancy" is the result that would be expected if the observers adjust the size of the comparison circle to match the physical size of the test circle. The line marked "visual angle" is the result that would be expected if the observers adjust the size of the comparison circle to match the visual angle of the test circle. (Adapted from Holway & Boring, 1941.)

The results of Holway and Boring's experiment indicate the importance of depth information in perceiving size. This linkage between depth and size perception has led to the proposal that a *constancy scaling mechanism* supplements the information available on the retina by taking an object's distance into account (Gregory, 1966). We will call this constancy scaling mechanism **size-distance scaling.** Thus, when a 6-foot-tall person is far away and casts a small image on your retina, the size-distance scaling mechanism takes his distance into account and you still perceive him to be 6 feet tall.

DEMONSTRATION

Size-Distance Scaling and Emmert's Law

You can demonstrate size-distance scaling to yourself. Look at the center of the circle in Figure 7.27 for about 60 seconds. Then look at the white space to the side of the circle and blink to see the circle's afterimage. Now repeat this procedure, but look at a wall far across the room. Blink to bring back the afterimage if it fades. You should see that the size of the afterimage depends on where you look. If you look at a distant surface such as the far wall of

FIGURE 7.27

the room, you see a large afterimage that appears to be far away. If you look at a near surface such as the page of this book, you see a small afterimage that appears to be close.

Figure 7.28 illustrates the principle underlying the effect you just experienced, which was first described by Emmert in 1881. Staring at the circle in Figure 7.27 bleaches a small circular area of visual pigment on your retina. This bleached area of the retina determines the *retinal size* of the afterimage and stays constant. The *perceived size* of the afterimage, as shown in Figure 7.28, is determined by the distance of the surface against which the afterimage is viewed. This relationship between the apparent distance of an afterimage and its perceived size is known as **Emmert's law:** the farther away an afterimage appears, the larger it will appear. Stated mathematically, this law is: Sp = K(Sr ×

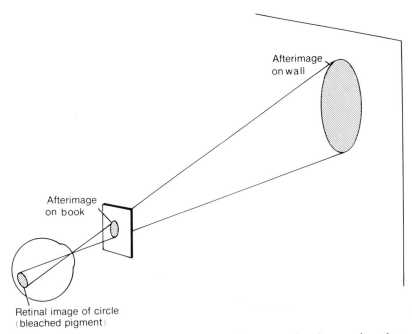

F I G U R E 7. 28 The principle behind the observation that the size of an afterimage increases as the afterimage is viewed against more distant surfaces.

Dp), where Sp is the perceived size of the after-image, K is a constant, Sr is the size of the retinal image, and Dp is the perceived distance of the afterimage. Thus, the size of the afterimage gets larger when you view it against a far wall because viewing it against the wall increases the perceived distance (Dp), but the size of the retinal image (Sr) stays constant.

This same equation can be applied to size constancy—the fact that your perception of a person's size remains constant as the person walks away. As the person walks away, the size of her image on your retina (Sr) gets smaller, but your perception of the person's distance (Dp) gets larger. These two changes cancel each other and the net result is that your perception of the person's size (Sp) remains constant.

DEMONSTRATION

Size-distance Scaling in the Mirror

Think about the last time you looked in the mirror. How big did you appear? Normal sized? Smaller or

larger than normal? Now actually look in the mirror and ask yourself those questions. Then increase your distance from the mirror. When you do this do you appear smaller or do you appear to stay the same size? Ordinarily, people appear normal sized in the mirror and appear to remain the same size, no matter what their distance from the mirror.

Look in the mirror and draw an outline around your head with a piece of soap. What you will see, as indicated in Figure 7.29, is that the image of your head *on the surface of the mirror* is exactly half the size of your head. Now try moving back while keeping your head centered in the outline you have drawn. What happens to the size of the image inside the outline?

What's going on in the mirror? Let's first consider the image you see when you look into the mirror. As you can see from Figure 7.29, moving back from the mirror causes two effects: (1) a decrease in the image's visual angle and (2) an increase in your perception of the image's distance.

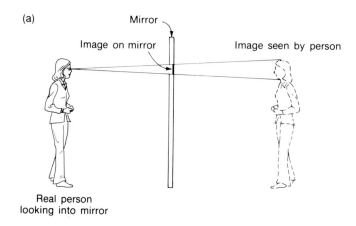

(a)

Mirror

Image on mirror

Image seen by person

Real person
looking into mirror

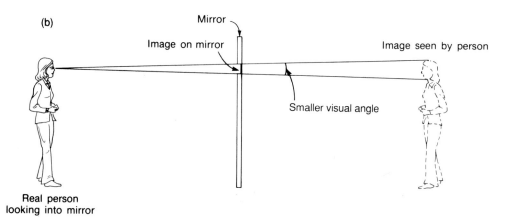

(b)

Mirror

Image on mirror

Image seen by person

Smaller visual angle

Real person
looking into mirror

F I G U R E 7. 29

If visual angle were controlling your perception of size, your image in the mirror would appear to shrink as you moved back. This is not, however, what happens. Instead, your size-distance scaling mechanism takes your increased distance into account and causes you to perceive your head in terms of its real size at all viewing distances.

But what about the image *on the surface of the mirror?* This image is always half the size of your head because the mirror is always half way between you and your image, as shown in Figure 7.29. You are usually not aware of the small size of the image on the surface of the mirror because your attention is usually focused not on the surface of the mirror but on the image in back of the mirror.

Can We Perceive an Object's Visual Angle?

You might now be thinking that while you can indeed see a 6-foot-tall person as staying 6 feet tall when he is far away, he does look different than when he is close. You're right. The person's visual angle *is* smaller when he is far away, and even though the size-distance scaling mechanism causes us to see him at his correct 6-foot size, there is still information available that tells us that his visual angle is small. Perhaps the most obvious information that tells us this is that when the person is far away, he takes up a much smaller fraction of your field of view than when he is close. When a person stands

2 feet from you, he may cover almost your entire field of view, but when he is the length of a football field away, he is just one small object in a large field of view. In fact, experiments have shown that when observers are asked to judge an object's visual angle, they can do so, though they tend to somewhat overestimate the visual angle, probably because they can't completely overcome the tendency to perceive in terms of size constancy when good depth information is available (Gilinsky, 1965).

Though it is possible to estimate the visual angle of an object, our everyday experience is dominated by size constancy. A faraway mountain looks huge, even though its visual angle may be smaller than many nearby objects, and our 6-foot-tall person appears 6 feet tall, no matter where he is. This dominance of size constancy occurs because our everyday experience usually includes abundant depth information. In some situations, however, erroneous depth information may lead us to perceive illusions of size.

ILLUSIONS OF SIZE

Size illusions due to erroneous depth information sometimes occur in our everyday experience. I remember once looking into a room through a window that had a small decal on it. I misperceived the depth of the decal because instead of seeing it as being attached to the window, I thought it was attached to the far wall of the room. This incorrect perception of the decal's distance made it look huge. But as I realized that it was actually attached to the nearby window, my perception changed, and it became the small decal that it actually was.

Another example of a situation in which poor depth information leads to inaccurate size perception is this description of the effect of inclement weather at an Antarctic research base (*The New Yorker*, March, 1981).

The most treacherous weather phenomenon is something known as a whiteout, in which light is reflected from a thick cloud cover and back up from the snow, obscuring the horizon and surface definition, and surrounding one with a dazzling whiteness. Someone flying a helicopter during a whiteout can't tell up from down;

pilots have been known to drop smoke grenades to determine their altitude only to find that they were a few feet above the ground. Others have flown at full power directly into the ice. What one can see is distorted—a discarded matchbox may look like a tent or a vehicle.

Illusions of size have also been produced in a number of different ways by psychologists. The most famous of these illusions is called the Ames room.

The Ames Room

The **Ames room**, which was first constructed by Adelbert Ames, causes two people of equal size to appear very different (Ittleson, 1952). In the photograph of the observer's view of an Ames room in Figure 7.30, you can see that the man on the right looks much bigger than the one on the left. This perception occurs even though the two men are actually the same size. The reason for this erroneous perception of size lies in the construction of the room. Because of the shapes of the wall and windows at the rear of the room, it looks like a normal rectangular room when viewed from a particular observation point; however, as shown in the diagram in Figure 7.31, the Ames room is, in fact, shaped so that the left corner of the room is almost twice as far away from us as the right corner.

What's happening in the Ames room? Due to the construction of the room, the man on the left has a much smaller visual angle than the man on the right. We think, however, that we are looking into a normal rectangular room, and our perception that both men are at the same distance prevents our size-distance scaling mechanism from correcting for the left man's greater depth. We therefore use the only other available information—the visual angles of the two men. Since the man on the right has a larger visual angle than the one on the left, he looks taller. You can think about this in another way: If you perceive two people to be the same distance from you, the one who has the larger visual angle will appear larger. This is really a statement of the obvious: If a tall and short person stand next to each other, you perceive the tall person as being taller. The Ames room causes you to think that you are seeing two men at the same distance, which makes the closer one, with the larger visual angle, appear to be taller.

Look at Figure 7.32. When I saw this photograph in my local newspaper, I thought something strange was going on. Why did the man on the right appear huge compared to the one on the left? When I showed this picture to other people, they also were confused. This confusion was resolved only after I obtained the more complete version of the photograph in Figure 7.33 from the paper. Once the rest of the photograph was revealed, the depth relations between the two men became clear and the relative sizes made sense. Both the cropped version of the photograph in Figure 7.32 and the Ames room contain inaccurate depth information, and this makes it difficult for us to perceive the correct sizes of objects in the photograph or in the room.

The Moon Illusion

The **moon illusion** is another perceptual effect that depends on the perception of depth. You may have noticed that when the moon is on the horizon it appears much larger than when it is directly overhead, at its **zenith**. This difference in the perceived sizes of the horizon and zenith moons, shown in Figure 7.34, is called the moon illusion. People have been aware of this illusion for centuries, and many explanations have been proposed for it. Early explanations of the moon illusion invoked the **apparent distance theory,** which is based on the idea that an object on the horizon, which is viewed across the filled space of the terrain, should appear to be farther away than an object at the zenith, which is viewed through the empty space of the sky. If a far object has the same visual angle as a near object, the far object will appear larger (as we have seen from the results of Holway and Boring's experiment). The apparent distance theory, therefore, states that since the horizon and zenith moons have the same visual angle, the farther-appearing horizon moon should appear larger.

F I G U R E 7. 30   The Ames room. All three men are actually the same height. (Wittreich, 1959; photograph courtesy of William Vandivert.)

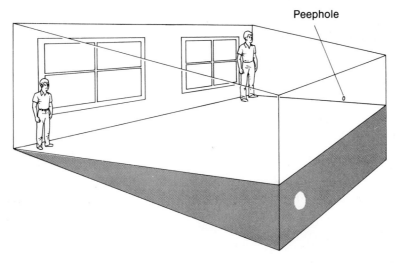

F I G U R E 7. 31 The Ames room, showing its true shape. The man on the left is actually almost twice as far away as the man on the right; however, when the room is viewed through the peephole this difference in distance is not seen. In order for the room to look normal when viewed through the peephole, it is necessary to enlarge the left side of the room.

F I G U R E 7. 32 Picture of two men from a newspaper story. The way the picture is cropped, plus the low contrast due to the nature of newspaper pictures, reduces depth information in the picture. (Photograph by Tony Tye, Pittsburgh Post-Gazette.)

F I G U R E 7. 33   The picture from Figure 7.32 with added depth information.

D E M O N S T R A T I O N

The Visual Angle of the Moon

Do the horizon and zenith moons really have the same visual angle? Since the moon's physical size (2,160 miles in diameter) and distance from the earth (239,000 miles) are constant throughout the night, the moon's visual angle must be constant. You can verify this in two ways: (1) Photograph the horizon and zenith moons and measure the resulting photograph. You will find that the diameters of the resulting pictures of the horizon and

F I G U R E 7. 34 An artist's conception of the moon illusion showing the moon on the horizon and high in the sky simultaneously.

zenith moons are identical. (2) View the moon through a 1/4-inch-diameter hole (the size produced by most standard hole punches) held at arm's length. For most people, the moon will just fit inside this hole, and the fit will appear exactly the same whether the moon is at the horizon or at its zenith.

Several hundred years after the proposal of the apparent distance theory, Edwin Boring and Alfred Holway questioned the basis of this theory by asking people to tell them whether the horizon or the zenith moon looked closer. When asked to make this judgment, most people said that the horizon moon looked closer, and when asked why, they said that the horizon moon looked closer because it appeared larger. Since Boring's observers contradicted the idea from apparent distance theory that the horizon moon looks farther away, Boring and Holway (1940a, 1940b; Boring, 1943) rejected this explanation of the moon illusion and did a series of experiments that led them to propose another explanation.

In their experiments, Boring and Holway projected a small artificial moon onto a screen, 3.5 meters from the observer, then had the observer adjust the size of this artificial moon to match the perceived size of the real moon. However, rather than letting observers tilt their heads up to look at the zenith moon, Boring and Holway had them face forward and elevate their eyes. When observers elevated their eyes to view the zenith moon (Figure 7.35a), they equated the zenith moon with a smaller artificial moon on the nearby screen. Furthermore, when observers lay on their backs so they could view the zenith moon without elevating their eyes (Figure 7.35b), they equated the zenith moon with a large artificial moon. Thus, Boring and Holway proposed the **eye elevation hypothesis**—that the moon illusion was due to the position of the observer's eyes in his or her head, with elevated eyes causing the zenith moon to appear smaller.

Boring's eye elevation hypothesis became the accepted explanation of the moon illusion, despite the fact that Boring could think of no reason why elevating the eyes should cause the moon to appear smaller. In 1962, however, Lloyd Kaufman and Irvin Rock (1962a, 1962b; Rock & Kaufman, 1962) questioned the eye elevation hypothesis for two reasons. First, they saw no significant difference in the size of the moon when they viewed it with their eyes elevated or straight ahead. Second, they questioned Boring's method for determining the perceived size of the moon. Kaufman and Rock felt that it was asking too much of the observers to have them match the size of a faraway object such as the moon with a nearby object, such as an artificial moon only 3.5 meters away. In fact, in the description of his experiment, Boring states that observers found it difficult to match the sizes of the real and artificial moons because of the great distance between them.

Instead of asking observers to match the distant real moon with a nearby artificial moon, Kaufman and Rock built a projection system that enabled observers to match the size of one artificial moon, seen against the zenith sky, by adjusting the size of another artificial moon, seen against the horizon sky. These similar moons greatly simplified the observer's task, and with this new method of measuring the illusion, Kaufman and Rock retested the eye elevation hypothesis. They found that eye elevation had no essential effect on the perceived size of the moon, and therefore they concluded that

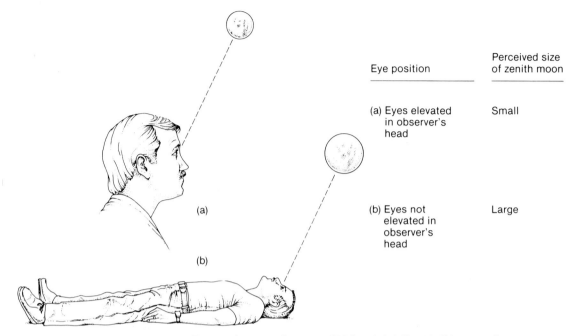

Eye position	Perceived size of zenith moon
(a) Eyes elevated in observer's head	Small
(b) Eyes not elevated in observer's head	Large

F I G U R E   7. 35   Two conditions in Boring and Holway's (1940a, 1940b) moon illusion experiment. Boring and Holway concluded that elevation of the observer's eyes was responsible for the illusion, since their observers perceived the zenith moon to be small when they elevated their eyes (top) but perceived it to be large when they lay on their backs and viewed the zenith moon without elevating their eyes (bottom).

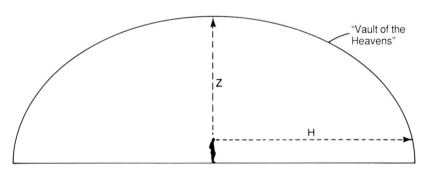

F I G U R E   7. 36   If observers are asked to consider that the sky is a surface and are asked to compare the distance to the horizon (H) and the distance to the top of the sky (Z) on a clear moonless night, they usually say that the horizon appears farther away. The result is a flattened *vault of the heavens* as shown above.

the results on which Boring and Holway based their eye elevation hypothesis were in error.

Having rejected the eye elevation hypothesis, Kaufman and Rock returned to the apparent distance theory, which Boring had rejected because his observers said that the horizon moon looked closer than the zenith moon. Instead of asking observers to judge the distance of the horizon and zenith moons, Kaufman and Rock asked observers to imagine that the moonless sky was a surface and to decide whether the surface seemed farther away at the horizon or at the zenith. When they did this, observers said that the horizon appeared farther away. This result is consistent with observations by other investigators that the surface of the sky appears flattened, as shown in Figure 7.36, and if we assume that the moon is actually perceived to be on the surface of the sky, this result confirms the idea, proposed in apparent distance theory, that the horizon moon appears farther away than the zenith moon.

After resurrecting the apparent distance theory, Kaufman and Rock still had to show that the enlarged perceived size of the horizon moon was, in fact, the result of viewing the moon over the terrain, which caused it to appear farther away. They demonstrated this in a number of ways. They found that when the horizon moon was viewed over the terrain, it appeared over 1.3 times larger than the zenith moon; however, when the terrain was masked off so that the horizon moon was viewed through a hole in a sheet of cardboard, the illusion vanished. When Kaufman and Rock took their apparatus to a place where the visible horizon was about 2 miles away in one direction and only about 2,000 feet away in another direction, they found that the horizon moon appeared much larger when viewed over the far horizon than when viewed over the near horizon. A number of other experiments in which Kaufman and Rock varied the apparent distance to the horizon resulted in the same conclusion: The apparent distance theory was correct—the horizon moon looks larger because it appears farther away.*

The principle involved in Kaufman and Rock's explanation of the moon illusion is the same one that causes an afterimage to appear larger if it is viewed against a faraway surface. Just as the near and far afterimages of Figure 7.28 have the same visual angles, so do the zenith and horizon moons. The afterimage that appears to be on the wall across the room simulates the horizon moon; the circle appears farther away, so your size-distance scaling mechanism makes it appear larger. The afterimage

*Not everyone agrees with Kaufman and Rock's apparent distance explanation of the moon illusion. See Baird (1982), Baird and Wagner (1982), and Restle (1970) for explanations for this illusion based on the idea that we compare the size of the moon to the sizes of other objects in the environment.

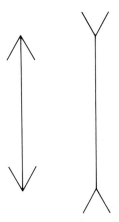

FIGURE 7. 37 The Muller-Lyer illusion. Both lines are actually the same length.

that appears to be on the page of the book simulates the zenith moon; the circle appears closer, so your scaling mechanism makes it appear smaller.

The Muller-Lyer and Ponzo Illusions

The **Muller-Lyer illusion**, shown in Figure 7.37, is analogous to the moon illusion in that the two central lines are actually equal in length and therefore have the same visual angle, but the line on the right looks longer. Why does this occur? Richard Gregory (1966) has explained this illusion on the basis of what he called **misapplied size constancy**. He points out that size constancy normally helps us maintain a stable perception of objects by taking distance into account. Thus, size constancy causes a 6-foot-tall person to appear 6 feet tall, no matter what his distance. Gregory, however, proposes that this mechanism, which helps us maintain stable perceptions in the three-dimensional world, sometimes creates illusions when applied to objects drawn on a two-dimensional surface. We can see how this works by comparing the left and right lines of Figure 7.37 to the left and right pictures of Figure 7.38. Gregory suggests that the fins on the right line make this line look like part of the inside corner of a room and the fins on the left line make this line look like part of the outside corner of a building. Since the inside corner of a room tends to look farther away than the outside corner of a building, we see the right line as being

F I G U R E 7. 38 According to Gregory (1973), the Muller-Lyer line on the left in Figure 7.37 corresponds to the outside corner of a building and the line on the right corresponds to the inside corner of a room.

farther away, and our size-distance scaling mechanism causes this line to appear longer.

At this point you may say that while the Muller-Lyer figures may remind Gregory of the inside corner of a room or the outside corner of a building, they don't look that way to you (or at least they didn't until Gregory told you to see them that way). But, according to Gregory, it is not necessary that you be consciously aware that the Muller-Lyer lines can represent three-dimensional structures; your perceptual system unconsciously takes the depth information contained in the Muller-Lyer figures into account, and your size-distance scaling mechanism causes the left line to shrink and the right line to expand. This theory of visual illusions can also be applied to other illusions that contain depth information, such as the **Ponzo (or railroad track) illusion,** shown in Figure 7.39. Here, both horizontal lines have the same visual angle, but the one on top appears farther away and is therefore perceived as larger.

Gregory's theory of visual illusions has not,

however, gone unchallenged. For example, P. DeLucia and Julian Hochberg (1985, 1986; Hochberg, 1987) have shown that the Muller-Lyer illusion occurs for a three-dimensional display like the one in Figure 7.40 in which it is obvious that the spaces between the two sets of fins are not at different depths. And figures like the "dumbbell figure" in Figure 7.41, which contain no obvious perspective or depth, still result in an illusion. The illusions created by the stimuli in Figures 7.40 and 7.41 are difficult for Gregory's theory to explain.

Unfortunately, a satisfactory alternative to Gregory's theory has yet to be proposed. J. O. Robinson (1972) surveys all the current theories of visual illusions in his book *The Psychology of Visual Illusion* and concludes that "no theory has been able to survive rigorous test." He suggests that there are so many different visual illusions that it is probably unlikely that any one theory can explain them all.

All of our demonstrations of how size depends on depth have been explained within the construc-

F I G U R E 7. 39 The Ponzo or railroad track illusion. The two horizontal rectangles are the same length on the page (measure them), but the far one appears larger.

tivist tradition. Our perception of size, according to this idea, is the outcome of processing in which both retinal size and perceived distance are taken into account. But this is not the only way to explain size perception. The ecological approach, which is most closely identified with J. J. Gibson (page 25), proposes, among other things, that this kind of calculation is not necessary for the perception of either depth or size. We will first consider the basic principles of the ecological approach and will then apply these principles to depth and size perception.

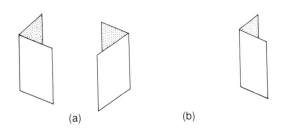

(a)   (b)

F I G U R E 7. 40 A three-dimensional Muller-Lyer illusion. The 2-foot high wooden "fins" stand on the floor. Although the distances between the corners of the fins at *a* and *b* are the same, distance *b* appears larger, just as in the two-dimensional Muller-Lyer illusion. Gregory's explanation of the illusion in terms of misapplied size constancy does not work in this case, since it is obvious that the spaces between the sets of fins are not at different depths.

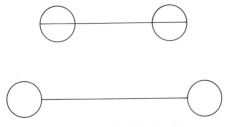

F I G U R E 7. 41 The "dumbbell" version of the Muller-Lyer illusion. As in the Muller-Lyer illusion, the two lines are actually the same length.

B O X 7. 4 / *Shape Constancy*

D E M O N S T R A T I O N

Viewing a Penny at an Angle

Place a penny on your desk, then view it from a height of 5 inches and a distance of 20 inches, as shown in the figure below. While viewing the penny, decide which shape on the far right of the facing page [viewed straight-on as shown in (a)] most clearly matches your perception of the penny's shape at an angle. Note which shape you picked and read on.

To understand the rationale behind this demonstration, we need to realize that when we look directly down onto the penny, it casts a circular image on our retina, but when we look at the penny at an angle, as we did in the demonstration, it casts an elliptical image on our retina. If you picked stimulus number 1, then your perception matches the elliptical she ̣e of the coin's image on your retina. If you p ̣ked number 6, then your perception matches the circular physical shape of the coin. Most people pick number

3, 4, or 5, because they perceive the coin to be elliptical, though not as elliptical as the coin's shape on their retina.

In 1931 Robert Thouless conducted an experiment similar to the one you just did. His observers viewed a circle at a slant and picked the shape that most closely matched their perception. Figure (b) shows the results of one of Thouless' experiments. The circle represents the physical shape of the circle, and the shaded ellipse represents the shape of the retinal image when the circle is viewed at an angle. The dashed line shows the shape that Thouless' observers said matched their perception of the circle viewed at an angle. Thouless' observers saw the circle at a slant as elliptical, though not as elliptical as the circle's shape on the retina. Thouless' result is an example of **shape constancy**—the tendency to see the true shapes of objects, even when they are seen in different orientations. Note, however, that Thouless' observers demonstrated only *partial shape constancy*. Full shape constancy would require that the perceived shape of the circle exactly match the physical shape of the circle.

THE ECOLOGICAL APPROACH

Basic Principles

The basic principles of the ecological approach, as proposed by Gibson, are as follows:

1. Perception is best studied in terms of the moving observer. This emphasis on movement reflects the fact that since people are rarely totally stationary, most of our perception occurs as we move through the environment. Many traditional perception experiments restrain subjects by placing their heads in a chin rest, a situation foreign to real life.

2. Perception is best studied not in terms of the static image on the retina but, rather, in terms of the information contained in the optic array (*see p. 69*). The optic array, illustrated in Figure 7.42, is the structured pattern of light converging on the observer's eye from the environment. Perception is determined by the way the optic array changes as the observer moves through the environment, because these changes in the optic array contain information that enables us to perceive various qualities of the environment.

What determines shape constancy? Thouless found that eliminating a person's ability to see the object's orientation causes shape constancy to vanish and concluded that shape constancy involves a taking into account of the object's orientation in space. Under normal conditions, when orientation is easily perceived, shape constancy works and our perception is close to the object's physical shape. Thus, as you sit down to eat, your circular dinner plate doesn't deform to match the elliptical shape it is casting on your retina. Just as your visual system takes distance into account to maintain a constant perception of size, it also takes orientation into account to maintain a constant perception of shape.

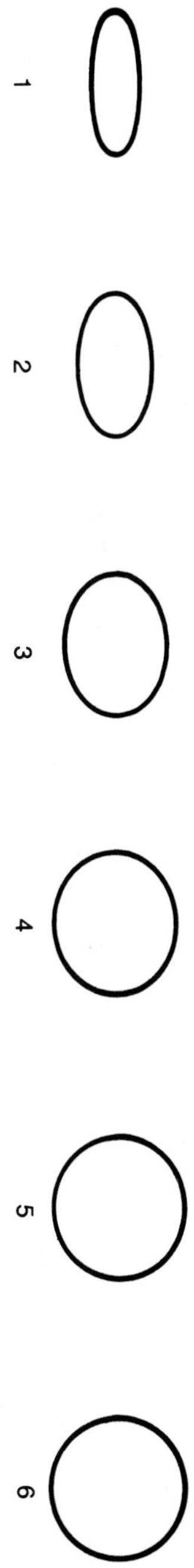

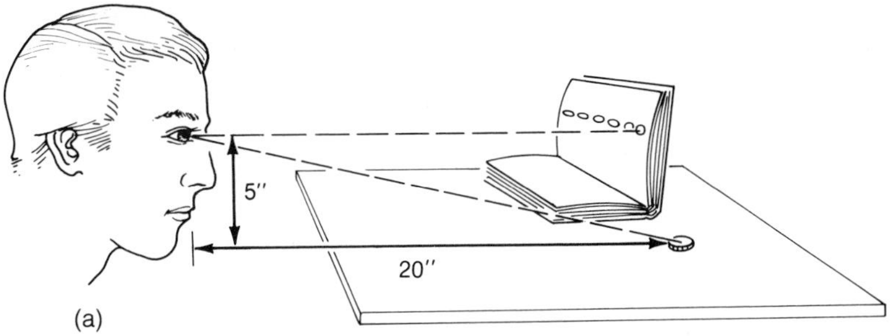

(a)

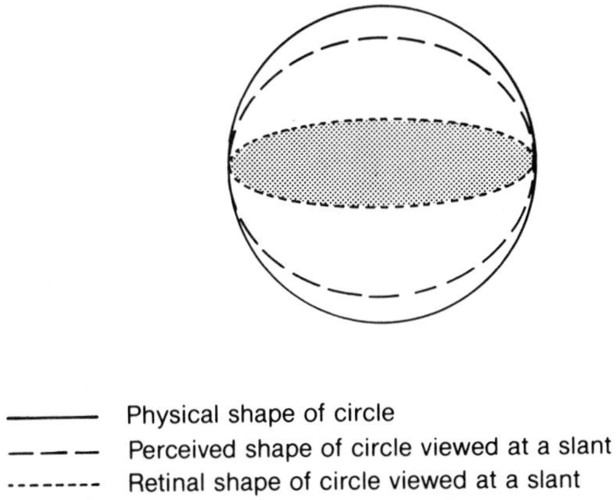

5"

20"

(b)

——— Physical shape of circle

— — — Perceived shape of circle viewed at a slant

- - - - - - Retinal shape of circle viewed at a slant

1

2

3

4

5

6

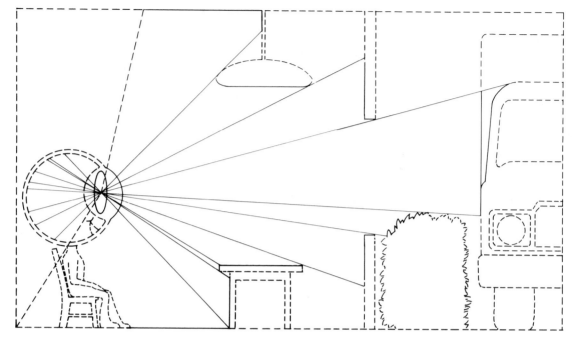

F I G U R E 7. 42   The optic array is the structured pattern of light reaching our observer's eye from the environment. Environmental surfaces visible to our observer are indicated by solid lines, invisible surfaces by dashed lines. Each of the visible surfaces structures the pattern of light entering the observer's eye.

3. There is enough information in the optic array to make "calculations" or processing unnecessary. This point refers back to the constructivists' idea that perception depends on calculations or processing. Why do the constructivists feel calculations are necessary? One reason we need to make calculations, according to the constructivists, is because the information we receive from the environment is ambiguous. For example, a retinal image of a particular size could be caused by a small object that is close or by a large object that is far away. Therefore, to determine the size of the object we must also take its distance into account, and this requires a calculation by the size-distance scaling mechanism.

Gibson feels that the constructivists' reasoning becomes irrelevant if we realize that there is enough information in the optic array to specify perceptions like size and depth without the need

for calculations. To understand what he means by this, let's look at the information provided by the optic array.

The Information in the Optic Array

Gibson's approach to perception grew out of some perception experiments he did during World War II, in which he tried to determine how to improve a pilot's ability to land an airplane. From these experiments, Gibson concluded that the traditional depth cues such as overlap, size in the field of view, and height in the field of view, which all depend on objects or groups of objects that protrude into the air, could not sufficiently explain how an airplane pilot judges the distance to a runway as he comes in for a landing. Gibson proposed instead that the crucial information for depth per-

F I G U R E 7. 43 A texture gradient made up of ridges in the sand. If viewed from directly above we would see that the distance between each sand ridge is approximately equal; however, when viewed from the ground the ridges are spaced closer and closer together as distance increases. (Photograph courtesy of Philip Brodatz, 1976.)

ception is defined by surfaces in the environment. Let's consider some examples of this information:

Texture gradients. One way information is contained on surfaces in the environment is in **texture gradients** such as the one created by the ridges in the sand of Figure 7.43. This figure shows how the elements that make up a textured surface appear to be packed closer and closer together as the surface stretches into the distance. This gradient results in an impression of depth, and the spacing of the gradient's elements provides information about the distance at any point on the gradient. Other examples of texture gradients are the modern painting in Figure 7.44, the squares on the Renaissance street of Figure 7.11, and the checkerboard of Figure 7.45(b).

These texture gradients share with depth cues such features as linear perspective (the way parallel lines in the gradients of Figures 7.11 and 7.45 converge toward a vanishing point) and size in the field of view (the way the more distant elements of the gradients get smaller). However, an important difference between texture gradients and depth cues is that gradients contain **invariant information** that the depth cues lack.

By invariant information we mean that the information for depth provided by the texture gradient remains invariant—or constant—even if the observer changes her position on the gradient. Though an observer's movement may cause the contours of the gradient to sweep across the retina, the elements of the gradient always appear more closely spaced as distance increases, and there is always information on the gradient that enables you to determine the distance between where you are and another point on the gradient. For example, consider the checkerboard of Figure 7.45. All you need to do is count the number of elements between two points on the gradient to determine the distance to 3 when you are at 1 (7.45b), when you are at 2 (7.45c), or when you are anywhere else on the gradient. According to Gibson, this kind of invariant information determines our perception as we move through the environment.

Texture gradients also supply information about

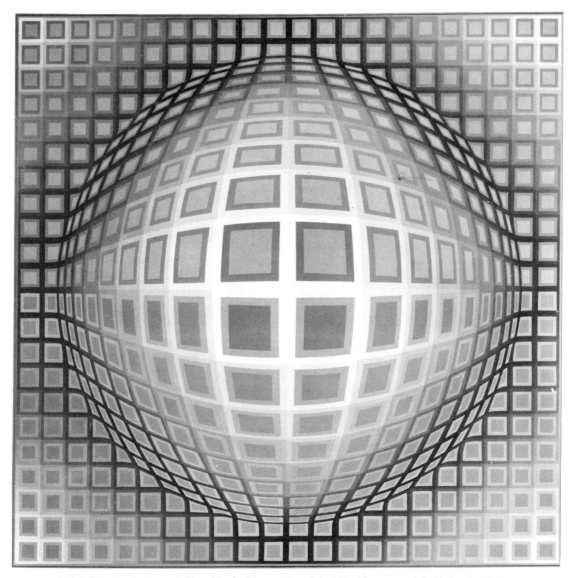

F I G U R E 7. 44 *Vega-Nor* by Victor Vasarely, 1969. (Courtesy of the Albright-Knox
Art Gallery, Buffalo, New York. Gift of Seymour H. Knox, 1969.)

the orientations of surfaces. For example, the orientations of the sides of the solid in Figure 7.46 are indicated by how the density of the texture changes on each face, with large changes in texture, as for face A, indicating that the surface is seen at an angle, and small changes, as for face B, indicating that the surface is seen almost straight on.

Texture gradients also provide a basis for size constancy, and it is here that the contrast between the ecological and cue approaches is most obvious. Remember that the cue approach, in the constructivist tradition, postulates that size constancy is the result of a calculation which takes both the size of the retinal image and distance into account. Such a calculation is not necessary, according to the eco-

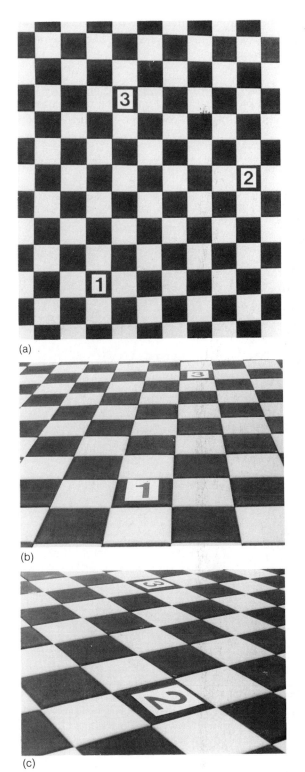

(a)

(b)

(c)

F I G U R E 7. 45 (a) Top view of a checkerboard pattern showing the location of 1, 2, and 3. (b) Looking at 3 from 1. (c) Looking at 3 from 2. No matter where you are on a texture gradient, information is present that indicates distance. When we are standing at 1 the number of gradient units indicates the distance of 3. If we move to 2, we can still use the information provided by the number of texture units to determine the distance to 3.

logical approach, because an object's size is indicated by the number of units its base covers on a texture gradient. This principle is illustrated in Figure 7.47, which shows two cylinders on the texture gradient formed by a cobblestone street. That the bases of the front and near cylinders both cover about half a unit on the gradient indicates *directly* that the bases are the same size. A calculation in which retinal size and perceived distance are taken into account is simply not necessary. Perception, according to Gibson, is therefore not a construction but happens *directly* from the information in the optic array. Gibson calls this perception without calculation **direct perception.**

Flow patterns. Another example of invariant information is the way elements in the environment flow past a moving observer. An observer looking to the side while moving forward, like a person looking out the side window of a moving car, sees a gradient of flow, with the speed of move-

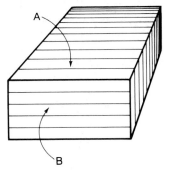

F I G U R E 7. 46 The texture gradients on this rectangular solid provide information regarding the orientation of the solid's surfaces.

F I G U R E 7. 47 A texture gradient with two cylinders. According to Gibson, the fact that the base of both cylinders cover the same number of units on the gradient provides direct information that the bases of the two cylinders are the same size.

ment rapid in the foreground and becoming slower as distance is increased. This is similar to the depth cue of movement parallax, although in Gibson's system the emphasis is on the flow of the whole field rather than on the movement of individual objects.

The deletion and accretion at edges that are at different depths (Figure 7.13) are also mentioned by Gibson as information that signals depth to the moving observer.

Gibson also considers the flow that occurs as a person moves forward. In this case, the environment flows past the observer on all sides and, according to Gibson, this flow provides information that helps the person negotiate her way through the environment. Since this information is concerned more with how an observer moves through

the environment than with depth perception, we will wait until the next chapter to discuss this aspect of flow.

The horizon ratio. We have seen that our perception of size can be determined by the number of units an object occludes on a texture gradient.

F I G U R E 7. 48 According to the horizon ratio principle, the horizon line intersects the telephone poles and tree at a height equal to the viewer's eye level. Objects that are the same size, such as the three telephone poles, have the same horizon ratio. Since a larger proportion of the tree is above the horizon, we perceive it as larger than the telephone poles.

Another source of information for size is the **horizon ratio** (Gibson, 1950; Sedgwick, 1973, 1983). The **horizon ratio principle** states that if a person is standing on flat terrain, a point on an object that intersects the horizon will be one eye-height above the ground. In addition, if two objects that are in contact with the ground are the same size, the proportions of the objects above and below the horizon will be the same. For example, since all of the telephone poles in Figure 7.48 have the same horizon ratio, we know they are the same size. We also know that the tree is larger than the telephone poles because the ratio, portion above the horizon/portion below the horizon, is greater for the tree than for the telephone poles.

The horizon ratio has both properties considered important by Gibson. The ratio is invariant with the observer's position in the scene, so although the size of a telephone pole may become larger in the field of view as an observer approaches it, the proportion of the pole that is above and below the horizon line remains constant. And since the horizon ratio supplies all of the information we need to know that the telephone poles are all the same size, calculation or processing is not necessary. We *directly* perceive the pole's height.

In this chapter we have presented the basic principles of two major approaches to depth and size perception, the constructivist approach and the ecological approach. Which approach is "correct"? The answer to this question depends on whom you ask.

Most researchers subscribe to the idea that we construct our perceptions from multiple sources of information; for example, to perceive size we take into account both retinal size and perceived distance. However, the ecological approach also has its supporters, and there have been lively debates in the perception literature in which the different sides have argued their points of view (Cutting, 1986; Epstein, 1977; Fodor & Pylyshyn, 1981; Gibson, 1979; Runeson, 1977; Ullman, 1980). As with many opposing views, both contribute to our understanding. Both depth cues and invariant information probably contribute to our perception of depth and size, and most researchers acknowledge the importance of studying perception in natural settings and considering the information generated by the moving observer. The major disagreement between "ecologists" and "constructivists" is about whether or not perceptual experience can be fully explained in terms of information obtained directly from the optic array.

One of the most important contributions of the ecological approach is its emphasis on studying perception in natural environments, and especially its emphasis on considering the role of movement in perception. As we discuss movement and events in the next chapter, we will see that a number of ecologically oriented researchers have made important contributions to our understanding of how people perceive as they move through the environment.

Summary

1. Our perception of the three-dimensional environment depends on information imaged on the two-dimensional surface of the retina. The cue approach to depth perception postulates that our perception of depth cues in the retinal image enables us to make inferences about the depth in a scene. The cue approach is a constructivist approach to depth perception.
2. The following cues convey information about depth in the environment: (a) Oculomotor cues: accommodation and convergence. (b) Pictorial cues: overlap, size and height in the field of view, atmospheric perspective, familiar size, and linear perspective. (c) Movement-produced cues: motion parallax, deletion and accretion. (d) Binocular disparity.
3. The cue of binocular disparity depends on the fact that each eye receives a slightly different view of the world. The horoptor is an imaginary line that passes through the point of fixation. The images of objects that fall on the horoptor fall on corresponding points on the two retinas. The images of objects that fall in front of or in back of the horoptor fall on noncorresponding, or disparate, points on the

retinas. An object's degree of disparity indicates its distance from the horoptor.

4. Binocular depth cells respond when the retina is stimulated by images with a specific degree of disparity.

5. An object's visual angle is directly related to the size of that object's image on the retina. Thus, when visual angle decreases so does the size of the retinal image.

6. The law of size constancy states that we perceive an object's size as staying constant, no matter what its distance.

7. Holway and Boring's experiment showed that when depth information is available, the law of size constancy holds, but when depth information is unavailable, the law of visual angle holds.

8. The link between depth and size demonstrated by Holway and Boring and others has led to the proposal that a size-distance scaling mechanism supplements the information available on the retina by taking an object's distance into account.

9. Emmert's law states that the size of an afterimage depends on the distance of the surface against which it is viewed—the more distant the surface, the larger the afterimage. This effect illustrates size-distance scaling.

10. Although it is possible to judge an object's visual angle, our everyday experience is dominated by size constancy.

11. Illusions of size such as the Ames room, the moon illusion, the Muller-Lyer illusion, and the Ponzo illusion have been explained by the operation of the size-distance scaling mechanism in the presence of erroneous depth information. Recent experiments indicate, however, that size-distance scaling may not completely explain these illusions.

12. Three of the basic principles of the ecological approach to perception are: (a) perception is best studied in terms of the moving observer; (b) perception is best studied not in terms of the static image on the retina but in terms of information contained in the way the optic array changes as the observer moves through the environment; (c) there is enough information in the optic array to make calculations or processing unnecessary.

13. Among the sources of information in the optic array are (a) texture gradients, (b) flow patterns, and (c) the horizon ratio. According to Gibson, certain information remains constant, or invariant, as the observer moves through the environment. Gibson feels that we perceive these invariants directly, without any mental processing.

Boxes

1. Flatness information is provided by a picture's lack of movement parallax and binocular disparity and by the perception of brush strokes, glare, and the frame of the picture. A convincing illusion of depth can be achieved if a picture which is drawn in linear perspective and uses sufficient depth cues is viewed through a peephole with one eye.

2. Random dot stereograms show that the cue of binocular disparity alone is sufficient to create an impression of depth.

3. The sun and the moon have the same visual angle and appear the same size in the sky. Since we can't perceive their distances, we perceive their size based on their visual angles.

4. Shape constancy occurs when you view an object at an angle and your perception of the object's shape corresponds to its physical shape rather than to the shape of its retinal image.

Study Questions

1. What is the major idea behind the cue approach to depth perception? (227)

2. What are the four groups of depth cues? (228)

3. Describe the depth cues of accommodation, convergence, overlap, relative size, relative height, atmospheric perspective, and familiar size. Describe Epstein's familiar size experiment. (229)

4. What is linear perspective? How can Alberti's window be used to draw a picture in linear perspective? What happens to lines that are parallel in a scene when the scene is depicted in linear perspective? (234)

5. What is motion parallax? Deletion and accretion? Be sure to understand the principle behind Figure 7.15. (238)

6. What are the monocular depth cues? (237)

7. What are corresponding retinal points? Given one point on a retina, be able to locate the corresponding point on the other retina. (239)

8. When you fixate on one point, which objects in space fall on corresponding points on the retina? (239)

9. What is the horoptor? What happens to the horoptor when you change your point of fixation? (239)

10. If an object is located in front of the horoptor or in back of the horoptor, where do the images of the object fall on the retina? (243)
11. What is disparity? How do we determine the degree of disparity? How does disparity result in depth perception? (243)
12. Describe the properties of binocular depth cells. When do they fire? When don't they fire? (243)
13. How is an object's visual angle affected by the object's distance? By its size? What is the relation between visual angle and the size of an object's image on the retina? (246)
14. Define size constancy. (247)
15. Describe Holway and Boring's experiment. Be sure you understand the results of this experiment as plotted in Figure 7.26. (247)
16. What do the results of Holway and Boring's experiments tell us about the conditions under which size constancy occurs? What is size-distance scaling? What is the law of visual angle? Under what conditions does the law of visual angle hold? (248)
17. What is Emmert's law? How is it related to the idea of size-distance scaling? (250)
18. How big is the tracing of the image of your head in a mirror compared to the size of your real head? Why does your head appear to be its correct size in the mirror? (252)
19. How well can we estimate an object's visual angle? (253)
20. What is the Ames room? How does it work? How do the visual angles of the two people in the opposite corners of the room compare? What does the Ames room show? (253)
21. What is the moon illusion? Describe the apparent distance theory of the moon illusion. (254)
22. How do the visual angles of the horizon and zenith moons compare? (256)
23. Describe the eye elevation hypothesis. What are Kaufman and Rock's criticisms of the eye elevation hypothesis? (257)
24. Describe Kaufman and Rock's experiment and their explanation of the moon illusion. What is the evidence that the moon appears closer when it is at the horizon? (258)
25. What are the Muller-Lyer and Ponzo illusions? How does Gregory explain these illusions? (259)
26. Is Gregory's explanation of the illusions correct? (260)
27. What are the three basic principles of the ecological approach to perception? (262)
28. What is a texture gradient? What property does it have that the depth cues lack? How do texture gradients provide information about an object's distance, an object's size, or the orientation of surfaces? (265)
29. What is direct perception? (267)
30. What is the horizon ratio? How does it provide information about an object's size? (269)

Boxes

1. What are flatness cues? Under what conditions can these cues be eliminated or minimized? What is the result of eliminating the flatness cues? (240)
2. What is a random dot stereogram? How is it viewed? What do we see when we view it correctly? What does this show? (244)
3. Compare the visual angles of the sun and the moon. Does our perception of the sizes of the sun and the moon follow the law of size constancy or the law of visual angle? Explain your answer. (249)
4. What is shape constancy? How does your perception of the shape of a circle viewed at an angle compare to the shape of the circle's image on your retina? What determines shape constancy? (262)

Glossary

Accommodation. A possible depth cue. Muscular sensations that occur when the eye accommodates to bring objects at different distances into focus may provide information regarding the distance of that object. (229)

Accretion. The uncovering of the farther of two surfaces due to observer movement. (237)

Aerial perspective. See atmospheric perspective.

Alberti's window. Used to draw a picture in perspective, Alberti's window is a transparent surface on which an artist traces the scene viewed through the surface. (234)

Ames room. A distorted room first built by Adelbert Ames that creates an erroneous perception of the sizes of people in the room. The room is constructed so it appears that two people at the far wall of the room appear to stand at the same distance from an observer. In actuality, one of the people is much farther away than the other. (253)

Apparent distance theory. An explanation of the moon illusion that is based on the idea that the horizon moon, which is viewed across the filled space of the terrain, should appear farther away than the zenith moon, which is viewed through the empty space of the sky. This theory states that since the horizon and zenith moons have the same visual angle, the farther-appearing horizon moon should appear larger. (254)

Atmospheric perspective. A depth cue. Objects that are farther away look more blurred and bluer than objects that are closer, because we must look through more air and particles to see them. (231)

Binocular depth cell. A neuron in the visual cortex that responds best to stimuli that fall on points separated by a specific degree of disparity on the two retinas. (243)

Binocular depth cue. A depth cue that requires the participation of both eyes. Binocular disparity is the major binocular depth cue. (237)

Binocular disparity. When the retinal images of an object fall on disparate points on the two retinas. (237)

Convergence. A possible depth cue. Muscular sensations that occur when the eyes move inward (convergence) or outward (divergence) to view objects at different distances may provide information regarding the depth of that object. (229)

Corresponding retinal points. The points on each retina that would overlap if one retina were slid on top of the other. (239)

Cue theory. The approach to depth perception that focuses on identifying information in the retinal image that is correlated with depth in the world. (227)

Degree of disparity. If the two retinas are stimulated by images which fall on disparate (noncorresponding) points, the degree of disparity is the distance one of the images must be moved so that both images will fall on corresponding points. (243)

Deletion. The covering of the farther of two surfaces due to observer movement. (237)

Depth cues. Two-dimensional information on the retina that is correlated with depth in the scene. (228)

Direct perception. J. J. Gibson's idea that we pick up the information provided by invariants directly and that perceptions result from this information without the need for any further processing. (267)

Disparate points. See noncorresponding points.

Ecological approach. An approach to perception that focuses on identifying information in the environment that is used for perception by a moving observer. (227)

Emmert's law. States that the size of an afterimage depends on the distance of the surface against which the afterimage is viewed. The farther away the surface against which an afterimage is viewed, the larger the afterimage appears. (250)

Eye elevation hypothesis. An explanation of the moon illusion; it hypothesizes that the zenith moon looks smaller than the horizon moon because we move our eyes upward to observe the zenith moon. (257)

Familiar size. A depth cue. Our knowledge of an object's actual size sometimes influences our perception of an object's distance. (233)

Flatness cues. Information that indicates a picture is flat. For example, one flatness cue is that movement parallax does not occur in a picture as an observer moves relative to the picture. (240)

Height in the field of view. A depth cue. Objects that rest on a surface below the horizon and are higher in the field of view are usually seen as being more distant. (231)

Horizon ratio. The proportion of an object that is above the horizon divided by the proportion that is below the horizon. (269)

Horizon ratio principle. If a person is standing on flat terrain, a point on an object that intersects the horizon will be one eye-height above the ground. Thus, if two objects that are in contact with the ground are the same size, the proportions of the objects above and below the horizon will be the same. (269)

Horoptor. An imaginary surface that passes through the point of fixation. Objects falling on this surface result in retinal images that fall on corresponding points on the two retinas. (239)

Invariant information. Environmental properties that do not change as the observer moves. For example, the spacing, or texture, of the elements in a texture gradient does not change as the observer moves on the gradient. The texture of the gradient, therefore, supplies invariant information for depth perception. (265)

Linear perspective (depth cue). Parallel lines (like railroad tracks) converge toward each other as they get farther away. This convergence of parallel lines is a depth cue, with greater convergence indicating greater distance. (237)

Linear perspective (drawing system). A method of representing three-dimensional space on a two-dimensional surface. (235)

Misapplied size constancy. The idea that when mechanisms that help maintain size constancy in the three-dimensional world are applied to two-dimensional pictures, an illusion of size sometimes results. (259)

Monocular depth cues. Depth cues such as overlap, relative size, relative height, familiar size, linear perspective, movement parallax, and accommodation which work if we use only one eye. (237)

Moon illusion. The moon appears to be larger when it is on or near the horizon than when it is high in the sky. (254)

Motion-produced cues. Cues that depend on movement of the observer, or movement of objects in the environment. (229)

Motion parallax. A depth cue. As an observer moves, nearby objects appear to move rapidly whereas far objects appear to move slowly. (236)

Muller-Lyer illusion. An illusion which causes two lines of equal length to appear different lengths because of the addition of outward-facing "arrows" on one line and inward-facing on the other line. (259)

Noncorresponding (disparate) points. Two points, one on each retina, that would not overlap if the retinas were slid onto each other. (241)

Oculomotor cues. Cues that depend on our ability to sense the position of our eyes and tension in our eye muscles. (229)

Overlap. A depth cue. If object A covers object B, then object A is seen as being in front of object B. (229)

Pictorial depth cues. Depth cues such as overlap, relative height, and relative size that can be depicted in pictures. (229)

Ponzo illusion. Also called the railroad track illusion. A size illusion in which two rectangles of equal length that are drawn between two converging lines appear to be different in length. (260)

Railroad track illusion. See Ponzo illusion.

Random dot stereogram. A stereogram in which the stimuli are pictures of random dots. If one section of this pattern is shifted slightly in one direction, the resulting disparity causes the perception of depth when the patterns are viewed in a stereoscope. (245)

Shape constancy. When our perception of an object's shape remains constant even when we view the object from different angles. (262)

Size constancy. When the perceived size of a stimulus remains constant even when we view the object from different distances. (247)

Size constancy, law of. States that our perception of an object's size remains constant, no matter what its distance from us. (247)

Size-distance scaling. A hypothesized mechanism that helps maintain our perception of size constancy by taking an object's distance into account. (250)

Size in the field of view. A depth cue. Objects that take up a small part of the field of view are, everything else being equal, perceived as farther away than objects that take up a large part of the field of view. (230)

Stereoscope. A device that presents pictures to the left and right eyes so that the binocular disparity a person would experience when viewing an actual scene is duplicated. The result is a convincing illusion of depth. (237)

Texture gradient. The pattern formed by a regularly textured surface that extends away from the observer. The elements in a texture gradient appear smaller as distance from the observer increases. (265)

Visual angle, law of. States that our perception of an object's size is determined solely by its visual angle. (248)

Zenith. The sky directly overhead. (254)

Perceiving Movement and Events

If asked what aspect of vision means the most to them, a watchmaker may answer 'acuity,' a night flier 'sensitivity,' and an artist 'color.' But to animals which invented the vertebrate eye, and hold the patents on most of the features of the human model, the visual registration of movement was of the greatest importance.

Gordon Walls (1942), p. 342

Motion perception evolved early, according to the comparative physiologist Gordon Walls, because, as the act of movement is intimately associated with life, the perception of this movement is intimately associated with survival. Predators who can detect the movement of potential prey will be more likely to catch that prey, and prey who can detect the movement of potential predators are more likely to survive.

While modern-day humans may not need movement perception to avoid predators, we not only need it to avoid cars and other moving objects in our environment, but it serves a number of other functions as well.

(1) Movement attracts our attention. If you are in a crowd and want to attract someone's attention, one of the best things you can do is wave your arms. Movement in the periphery usually triggers an eye movement to bring the moving object's image onto our foveas so we can see it clearly.

(2) Movement of an object relative to an observer provides information about the object's three-dimensional shape. We may not be sure of an unfamiliar object's shape if we see it from just one viewpoint, but if it moves relative to us or if we walk around it, its shape becomes obvious.

(3) Movement provides information that helps us segregate figure from ground. A good example of this is provided by a camouflaged animal who remains invisible as long as it is still, but who becomes instantly visible as soon as it moves. Movement segregates figure (the animal) from ground (the rest of the environment).

(4) Movement provides information that enables us to actively interact with the environment. As we walk down the sidewalk or drive down the street, movement of elements of the environment provides information that keeps us on course

F I G U R E 8. 1 Our environment is dominated by movement. This movement can be caused by the movement of objects in the environment, as shown in this picture, or by movement of the observer. (Photograph: *A Passing Umbrella* by Kenneth Antol, 1983.)

and helps us avoid bumping into things. Our perception of movement is also crucial for doing things like hitting or catching a baseball, playing tennis, or playing a video game. In these situations we both perceive an object's movement and coordinate our own movement with that of the moving object. A dramatic illustration of this coordination occurs every time a fly ball is hit toward the outfield in a baseball game. Even though the ball is traveling at over 100 miles per hour, the outfielder can determine nearly instantly, based on watching just the initial flight of the ball, where the ball will land and whether there is sufficient time to reach it before it hits the ground (Todd, 1981).

But perhaps the most dramatic illustration of

the importance of movement perception comes from those rare cases in which cortical damage eliminates a person's ability to perceive movement. Such a case, described in Box 8.1, emphasizes the crucial role that movement perception plays in our day-to-day lives.

In this chapter we will consider how movement is perceived by a person who passively watches movement and by a person who actively moves through the environment, thereby creating movement and perceiving it at the same time. In looking at research on movement as observed by a passive observer, we will be describing the traditional approach to the study of movement perception, which dates back over 100 years and still flourishes

Movement	Stimulus	Conditions
(a) Real	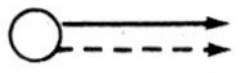	Light physically moves.
(b) Apparent	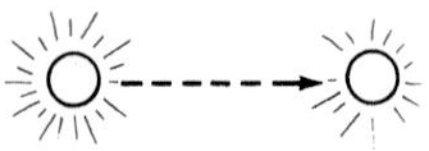	Lights flashed one after another with about 40–200 msec. in between. Movement is perceived from one light to the other.
(c) Induced	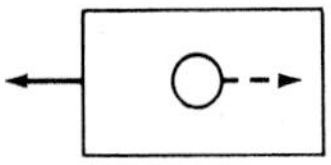	Light surrounded by a larger object which is moved. Light appears to move in opposite direction.
(d) Autokinetic		Light viewed in a completely dark room. Movement can be perceived in any direction.
(e) Movement aftereffect	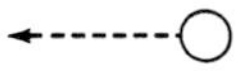	Moving stripes (see Figure 8.4) are viewed prior to viewing light. Light appears to move in opposite direction to stripe movement.

F I G U R E 8. 2 Five ways to make a spot of light appear to move. Solid arrows indicate actual physical movement and dashed arrows indicate perceived movement of the light. Note that the light physically moves only in (a). In all other cases perceived movement occurs in the absence of physical movement of the spot.

today. Most of this work has been done in laboratory settings and has focused on determining (1) how properties of the stimulus like speed, size, and location affect our perception of movement, and (2) the physiological mechanisms that underly our perception of movement. As we discuss this approach we will encounter mechanisms such as movement detectors and neural circuits that we are familiar with from previous chapters.

Research on movement perception by the active observer is more recent. Much of this research has been inspired by the work of J. J. Gibson, who, as we saw in the last chapter, favored an ecological approach to perception. This approach to movement perception usually uses more naturalistic stimuli than are used in the more traditional studies, and often considers movement perception as the perception of *events*. When we discuss this approach in the second part of this chapter, one of our tasks will be to pose the question: "What is an event?"

To begin our discussion of motion perception, we will start with a very simple stimulus—a spot of light. And we will answer the following question about this spot: "What are five ways to make the spot of light appear to move?"

FIVE WAYS TO MAKE A SPOT OF LIGHT APPEAR TO MOVE

In the list that follows we present five different ways to make a spot of light appear to move. We say *appear* to move because in only one case does the light actually move. In the other four cases the light remains stationary and we experience the *illusion* that it is moving.

1. **Real movement.** Real movement means that an object is continuously displaced from one point to another, as shown in Figure 8.2(a).

2. **Apparent movement** or **stroboscopic movement.** We can create an illusion of movement between two lights by flashing one light on and off, waiting about 60 msec (1 msec = 1/1,000 sec) and then flashing the other light on and off (Figures 1.19; 8.2b). The study of apparent movement led Gestalt psychologist Max Wertheimer to the proposal that "the whole is different from the sum of its parts" (see Chapter 6). The movement you perceive in a film, which is actually a series of still pictures, is apparent movement (Figure 8.3).

3. **Induced movement.** Another way to make the spot appear to move is to surround it with another object and then move this other object. Figure 8.2(c) indicates that moving the rectangle to the left causes the dot inside the rectangle to appear to move to the right. You've experienced induced movement if you've seen the moon racing through the clouds on a windy night. The moving clouds induce movement in the stationary moon.

4. **Autokinetic movement.** Perhaps the simplest way to make the light appear to move is to turn out all the room lights, as indicated in Figure 8.2(d). When the surrounding framework of the room is not visible, the small stationary light appears to move, usually in a rather erratic path.

5. **Aftereffects of movement.** If an observer first views a pattern that is moving in one direction, such as the moving belt of stripes in Figure 8.4, and then views the spot of light,

F I G U R E   8. 3   Seven frames from Edwin S. Porter's 1903 film, *The Great Train Robbery*. This sequence lasts about four-tenths of a second when projected.

the spot (and its surroundings) will appear to move in a direction opposite to the movement of the stripes (Figure 8.2e).

We will now describe each of these ways of making the spot appear to move in more detail.

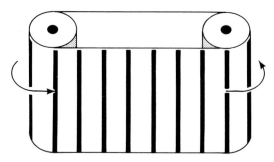

FIGURE 8. 4 Stimulus for the movement aftereffect of Figure 8.2(e).

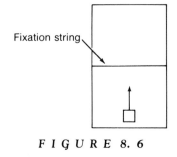

FIGURE 8. 6

REAL MOVEMENT

Factors That Influence Our Perception of Real Movement

Much of the research on real movement has focused on determining which factors influence (1) our *threshold* for perceiving movement and (2) our perception of the *velocity* of movement.

The threshold for perceiving movement in a homogeneous field is a velocity of about one-sixth to one-third of a degree of visual angle per second (Aubert, 1886). This means that you would just barely perceive the movement of the spot in Figure 8.5 if, when viewed from a distance of 1 foot, it takes about 14 seconds to travel from A to B. If, however, we add vertical lines to the space between A and B, the spot's movement can be perceived even at velocities as low as one-sixtieth of a degree of visual angle per second (which translates into a travel time of 280 seconds from A to B). Thus, our perception of movement does not depend only on the dot. We must also take the surroundings into account.

The surroundings affect not only the threshold for movement but also our perception of *velocity*. When an observer fixates on a string, in a dis-

play like the one in Figure 8.6, and then watches a small object move from the bottom to the top of the rectangle at a constant speed, the object appears to accelerate when near the bottom or top of the rectangle or when near the fixation string at the center of the rectangle (Brown, 1931a).

Our perception of velocity is also affected by the size of both the moving object and the framework through which it moves. J. F. Brown (1931b) asked an observer sitting in a dimly lit room to adjust the speed of a large dot moving across a large rectangle so it was equal to the speed of a small dot moving across a small rectangle (Figure 8.7). If the large rectangle was ten times larger than the small one, the large dot had to move seven times faster than the small one for them to appear to move at the same speed. In other words, a cat in a large cage must move much faster than a mouse in a small cage if they are to appear to move at the same speed. This effect, which is called **velocity trans-**

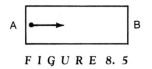

FIGURE 8. 5

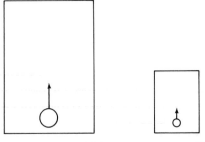

FIGURE 8. 7 Velocity transposition. The large circle must move faster than the small circle to appear to be moving at the same speed.

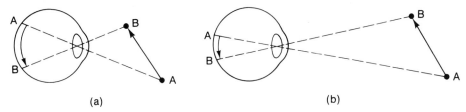

F I G U R E 8. 8 Movement occurs between A and B. When the movement is far, as in (b), the visual angle and distance moved across the retina is less than when the movement is closer as in (a). Since it takes the same time to move from A to B in both cases, the speed of movement across the retina in (b) is slower than in (a).

position, shows that two images moving across the visual field at different speeds can be perceived to be moving at the same speed.

Velocity transposition plays a role in our perception of film. Imagine that you are viewing a film in which a car drives from the left to the right side of the screen in 3 seconds. If you then move the projector back so that the size of the image on the screen increases, the car now moves across a greater distance, but it still takes 3 seconds. (If this weren't so, films with larger images would take longer!) According to the principle of velocity transposition, we should perceive the car to be moving at about the same speed in both cases. Thus, a car that appears to be traveling 50 miles per hour on a small screen will not appear to be traveling 100 miles per hour on a screen that is twice as large.

The above examples show that there is a lack of correspondence between (1) how rapidly the image of an object moves across the retina, and (2) the perceived speed of that object. Another way to demonstrate this lack of correspondence is to increase the distance between the moving object and the observer, as in Figure 8.8. Increasing distance decreases the visual angle through which the moving object travels and therefore decreases the speed with which it moves across the retina. But Brown (1931b) showed that increasing the distance by a factor of 20 only decreases the perceived velocity by about half. A large change in retinal velocity is accompanied by only a small change in perceived velocity. This effect is called **speed constancy.**

The lack of correlation between retinal and

perceived velocity also occurs when an observer follows a moving object with his eyes. When a person fixates on a moving object, the object's image remains stationary on the retina. Even so, the object still appears to be moving and, in fact, this movement appears about one and a half to two times *faster* than when the eyes are stationary and the object's image moves across the retina!

We have seen that we perceive movement both (1) when the eyes are stationary, so the image of the stimulus moves across the retina, and (2) when the eyes are tracking a moving stimulus, so its image stays stationary on the retina. We will now consider a number of mechanisms that have been proposed to explain movement perception, beginning with the situation in which a stimulus moves across the retina.

Mechanisms for the Perception of Real Movement

Movement detectors. When an image moves across the retina, it stimulates a series of receptors, one after another. We saw in Chapter 3 that there are neurons in the visual system, like complex cortical cells, that respond best when a stimulus moves across the retina in a particular direction. These *movement detectors* are created by circuits like the one in Figure 8.9. In this simplified circuit, excitation and inhibition interact to create a cell that responds only to movement from right to left.

To understand how this circuit works, let's look at what happens as we stimulate each receptor in turn, beginning with receptor A and moving toward

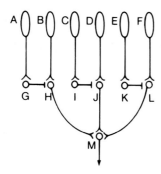

FIGURE 8.9 A neural circuit that creates a neuron (M) that responds to movement of a stimulus across the receptors from right to left but does not respond to movement from left to right.

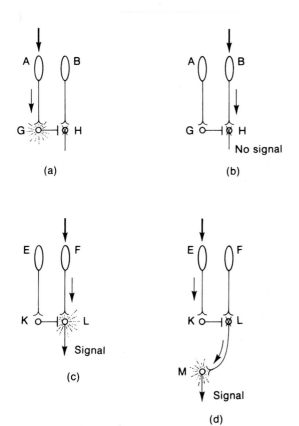

FIGURE 8.10 What happens as a light moves across the receptors of Figure 8.9. See text for details.

the right. Receptor A synapses with G, so stimulation of A excites G, which then sends an inhibitory signal to H. (The "X" across H in Figure 8.10(a) indicates that H is being inhibited). While this is occurring, the stimulus moves to receptor B and causes it to fire and to send an excitatory signal to H (Figure 8.10b). But since H has been inhibited by G, it does not fire. Thus, the signals from receptors A and B do not get past H, and therefore never reach M, the neuron at the end of the circuit. This process is repeated as the stimulus moves across the remaining receptors, with the net result being no response in M.

The outcome is different, however, if we begin at receptor F and move the light to the left. Receptor F sends a signal to L, which causes it to fire, as shown in Figure 8.10(c). The light then moves to receptor E, which causes K to send inhibition to L. This inhibition, however, arrives too late. L has already fired and has stimulated M (Figure 8.10d). This process is repeated as the spot moves across the remaining receptors, with the net result being that M fires. Thus, neuron M fires to movement from right to left but does not fire to movement from left to right.

Figure 8.11 shows how a complex cell in the cat's cortex responds to different directions of movement. The cell is tuned to respond best to a moving bar oriented at about +20 degrees and responds less well on either side of this orientation, eventually dropping to the cell's spontaneous firing level.

Based on this tuning curve, we might be tempted to propose that the firing of the neuron provides the information we need to perceive movement at +20 degrees. But if we remember our discussion of sensory coding on page 53, we know that we can't determine the direction a stimulus is moving by simply monitoring the firing rate of one cell. This is so because a cell's firing rate is affected not only by the direction of movement but also by the velocity and the intensity of the stimulus. For example, our cell in Figure 8.11 might fire equally well in response to a low-intensity bar oriented at +20 degrees and to a high-intensity bar oriented at +30 degrees. Thus, a particular

B O X 8. 1 / *A Frozen World: A Loss of Movement Perception in a Woman with Cortical Damage*

Is there an area of the cortex that is particularly important for movement perception? Some researchers who have recorded from cortical neurons have suggested that the answer to this question is "yes" (Zeki, 1978), and a recent report by J. Zihl, D. von Cramon, and N. Mai (1983) of a woman who lost much of her ability to perceive movement because of damage to her cortex supports the idea that movement perception depends on an area outside the primary visual receiving area.

The patient was admitted to the hospital after complaining of severe headaches, vertigo, and nausea. A brain scan and other testing indicated that an area of cerebral cortex around the border of the occipital and temporal lobes was damaged. The result of this damage, an inability to see movement in many situations, is described as follows in the report of her case:

> The visual disorder complained of by the patient was a loss of movement vision in all three dimensions. She had difficulty, for example, in pouring tea or coffee into a cup because the fluid appeared to be frozen, like a glacier. In addition, she could not stop pouring at the right time since she was unable to perceive the movement in the cup (or a pot) when the fluid rose. Furthermore the patient complained of difficulties in following a dialogue because she could not see the movements of the face, and, especially, the mouth of the speaker. In a room where more than two other people were walking she felt very insecure and unwell, and usually left the room immediately, because 'people were suddenly here or there but I have not seen them moving.' The patient experienced the same problem but to an even more marked extent in crowded streets or places, which she therefore avoided as much as possible. She could not

cross the street because of her inability to judge the speed of a car, but she could identify the car itself without difficulty. 'When I'm looking at the car first, it seems far away. But then, when I want to cross the road, suddenly the car is very near.' She gradually learned to 'estimate' the distance of moving vehicles by means of the sound becoming louder. (p. 315)

Psychophysical testing indicated that the patient could perceive only slow horizontal or vertical movement and that movement vision in depth was completely abolished. Although it is difficult to exactly locate the area of cortical damage in cases such as this, it appears that damage occurred in an area that, in the monkey, is rich in movement-sensitive cells, many of which prefer movement in depth. One thing that is clear is that the damaged area is outside the primary visual receiving area. This may sound familiar, since in Boxes 6.1 and 6.2 we described research which shows that our ability to identify and locate objects depends on processing that takes place outside the primary visual receiving area.

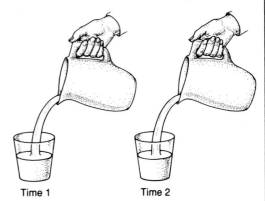

Time 1   Time 2

Zihl's patient perceived no change in the level of the water being poured into a cup.

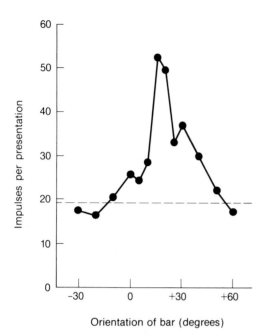

firing rate does not tell us the direction of the bar's movement.

The brain deals with this problem by analyzing the overall *pattern* of responses from many cells. Thus, as our +20 degree bar moves across the retina, it causes large bursts of firing in cells that prefer this orientation and smaller bursts in cells that prefer other orientations. The resulting *pattern* of response, which holds over a wide range of intensities, signals the bar's direction of movement. You may recognize this idea from Chapter 2 (page 53), as the *across-fiber-pattern theory of sensory coding.*

The velocity of a bar's movement may be signaled in a similar fashion. Just as there are movement detectors tuned to respond best to different directions of movement, so there are cells in the visual system tuned to respond best to different velocities. Figure 8.12 shows **velocity tuning curves** for two cells in the cat's LGN, one (A) that responds best at low velocities, and another (B) that responds best at high velocities.

So far, the brain's detection of movement seems fairly straightforward: Movement detectors sensitive to different directions and velocities of movement fire as the stimulus moves across the retina.

FIGURE 8.11 "Directional tuning curve" showing the relationship between the orientation of a moving bar and the response of a complex cell in the cat's cortex. The cell responds best when the bar is oriented at about 15–20 degrees. The dashed line indicates the rate of spontaneous firing. (Blakemore & Tobin, 1972.)

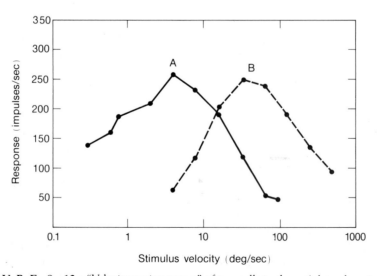

FIGURE 8.12 "Velocity tuning curves" of two cells in the cat's lateral geniculate nucleus. Cell A responds best to slow movement of a bar across the retina, and cell B responds best to rapid movement of the bar across the retina. (Frishman, 1979.)

However, movement detectors cannot explain movement perception in cases (1) when you perceive movement when there is *no* movement on the retina, as when you follow a moving object with your eyes so your eye movements keep the object's image stationary on your fovea, and (2) when you perceive no movement when there *is* movement on the retina, as when you move your eyes to look at different parts of a scene or as you walk through a scene. Though the image of the scene moves across your retina, you do not perceive the scene as moving.

In order to deal with these two situations, we need a mechanism that can tell whether retinal stimulation results from movement of the stimulus, movement of the observer, or both. We will now consider two possible mechanisms: (1) corollary discharge theory and (2) information from the optic array.

The corollary discharge. The idea underlying **corollary discharge theory** is that information about the observer's eye movements is provided by signals generated when the observer moves, or tries to move, her eyes (von Holst, 1954; Teuber, 1960; Gyr, 1972). Let's consider how this theory works, by following what happens in the circuit shown in Figure 8.13 when an observer decides to move her eyes to the left.

When the observer decides to move her eyes to the left, a motor signal (M) travels from the motor area of the brain to the eye muscles and causes the eyes to move to the left. This eye movement causes the image of whatever is in the observer's view to move across the retina, and this movement results in a **sensory movement signal** (S) in the optic nerve. We call this a sensory *movement* signal to differentiate it from the sensory signal present when the eye is stationary.

If the sensory movement signal, which indicates that an image has moved across the retina, reaches the cortex, it will cause the observer to perceive the scene as moving. But the scene isn't moving. Only the eyes have moved. It is here that the corollary discharge (C) comes into play. The **corollary discharge,** which is transmitted to the **comparator,** is a copy of the motor signal that is

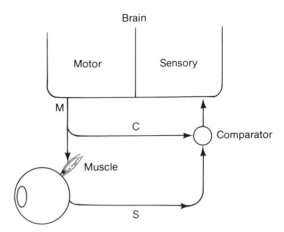

FIGURE 8.13 Diagram of the corollary discharge model. The brain is divided into two areas: the motor area which sends motor signals to muscles, and the sensory area which receives sensory signals from the sense organs. The exact location of the comparator is not specified. (From Teuber, 1960.)

sent from the brain to the eye muscles. The corollary discharge informs the comparator that a signal to move left has been sent to the eye. This information cancels the sensory movement signal and thereby causes the scene to be perceived as stationary.

According to this model, we will see movement when just the sensory movement signal is sent to the comparator, or when just the corollary discharge is sent to the comparator, but will not see movement if both the sensory movement signal and the corollary discharge reach the comparator together. The model has been tested by creating situations in which just the corollary discharge reaches the comparator. In this situation we should, according to the model, perceive movement. We can produce a corollary discharge that is not accompanied by a sensory movement signal in four ways:

1. By paralyzing the eye muscles.

In this situation, when the observer tries to move his eyes, the motor signal sent to the eye muscles results in a corollary discharge but, since the paralyzed eye remains stationary, there is no sensory movement signal (Figure 8.14a). In such

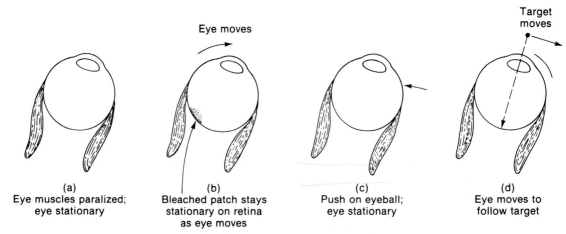

Eye moves

Target moves

(a)
Eye muscles paralized;
eye stationary

(b)
Bleached patch stays
stationary on retina
as eye moves

(c)
Push on eyeball;
eye stationary

(d)
Eye moves to
follow target

F I G U R E 8. 14 Voluntary movement of our eyes usually generates both a corollary discharge (because we send a signal to our eye muscles) and a sensory movement signal (because movement of the eyes usually causes movement of an image across the retina). There are, however, ways to create a corollary discharge without generating a sensory movement signal. In all four examples shown above, a signal is sent to the eye muscles and a corollary discharge is generated. No sensory movement signal is generated, because (a) the eye is paralyzed so that the signal sent to the muscle cannot cause the eye to move; (b) staring at a spot for about 30 seconds bleaches a patch of retina and generates an afterimage—the bleached spot stays on the same place on the retina as the eye moves; (c) when we push on the eyeball we can send signals to the muscles to hold the eye steady, and (d) the eye moves to track a moving object, so the object's image remains stationary on the retina.

an experiment, John Stevens (Stevens, et al., 1976) was temporarily immobilized by a paralytic drug injected into his circulation. When Stevens tried to move his eyes, the scene in front of him appeared to jump to a new position, just as predicted by the corollary discharge model. (Also see Matin, Picoult, Stevens, Edwards, & MacArthur, 1982 for another paralysis experiment.)

2. By observing an afterimage as you move your eyes in a dark room.

D E M O N S T R A T I O N

Using an Afterimage to Eliminate the Sensory Movement Signal

Illuminate page 250 with your desk lamp and look steadily at the circle in Figure 7.27 for about 60 seconds. Then go into your closet (or a completely

dark room) and observe what happens to the circle's afterimage (blink to make it come back if it fades) as you look around. Notice that the afterimage moves in synchrony with your eye movements.

The movement of the afterimage in the dark cannot be due to movement of an image on the retina since the circle's image always remains on the same place on the retina. There is, therefore, no sensory movement signal. A corollary discharge is, however, generated by the signals that caused your eye muscles to move your eyes. Since the corollary discharge is not canceled by a sensory movement signal, you see the afterimage move as your eyes move (Figure 8.14b).

3. By pushing on your eyeball while keeping your eye steady.

F I G U R E 8. 15 Why is this man smiling? Because every time he pushes on his eyeball he sees the world jiggle.

DEMONSTRATION

Pushing on Your Eyeball

While looking steadily at one point, *gently* push back and forth on the side of your eyelid, as shown in Figure 8.15. As you do this you will see the scene move.

Why do you see movement when you push on your eyeball? The traditional explanation for this result was that pushing on your eyeball causes your eye to move and this causes the image of the scene to move on your retina. Since there is, however, no corollary discharge (you moved your eye with your finger rather than by sending a signal from your brain to your eye muscles), the sensory movement signal is not canceled, and you perceive movement.

Recently, however, Lawrence Stark and Bruce Bridgeman (1983) have provided an explanation

to replace the "traditional" one above. The problem with the traditional explanation, according to Stark and Bridgeman, is that pushing on the eyeball does not necessarily cause it to move. They showed that when subjects push on their eyeball while keeping their eye fixated on a particular point, their eyes either do not move or move very little. Why don't the eyes move? Because to maintain steady fixation, the eye muscles are pushing against the force of the finger. Thus, by pushing on the eyeball we have created a corollary discharge (the signal sent to the eye muscles to hold the eye in place), and since there is no sensory movement signal to cancel it, we see movement (Figure 8.14c).

4. By following a moving object with your eyes.

Let's now consider how corollary discharge theory explains our perception of movement in the more normal situation in which an observer follows a moving car with her eyes as it drives past. Since the eyes move to follow the car, the car's

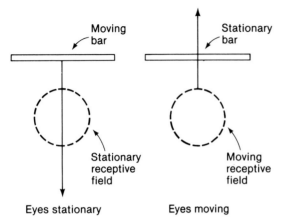

F I G U R E 8. 16 The two conditions in the experiment in which Robinson and Wurtz (1976) recorded from single cells in the monkey's superior colliculus. In the first condition (left), the monkey's eyes remained stationary and a bar was moved across the cell's receptive field. In the second condition (right), the bar remained stationary and the monkey moved its eyes so that the cell's receptive field moved across the bar.

F I G U R E 8. 17 A person moving from left to right past a stationary observer. In this situation the person moves across the observer's field of view as indicated by the arrows, but the background remains stationary.

image remains stationary on the observer's retinas and no sensory movement signal occurs. But since the eye is moving, a corollary discharge reaches the comparator. This signal is not canceled by a sensory movement signal, and our observer perceives the car to be moving. But what about the rest of the scene? As the observer follows the car with her eyes, the image of the rest of the scene sweeps across her retina, which generates a sensory movement signal. However, this sensory movement signal is canceled by the corollary discharge due to the eye movement, and she therefore perceives the rest of the scene as stationary.

Corollary discharge theory explains many of the facts of movement perception and has been supported by some recent single-cell recordings. Cells have been found in the monkey's superior colliculus that increase their firing rate when the eye is stationary and a bar moves across the cell's receptive field (Figure 8.16 left), but decrease their firing rate when the eye moves so that the receptive field moves across a stationary bar (Figure 8.16 right) Robinson & Wurtz, 1976). (See Figure 3.13 for the location of the superior colliculus, which

plays an important role in controlling eye movements.) Note that in both cases, the bar traverses the receptive field; but when the eye is stationary, the cell fires, and when the eye is moving, the cell does not fire.

This result is exactly what corollary discharge theory predicts. When the eye is stationary, the bar moves across the cell's receptive field, and since the resulting movement signal is not canceled by a corollary discharge, the cell fires. However, when the eye moves, the sensory movement signal generated when the bar sweeps across the receptive field is canceled by the corollary discharge generated by the eye movement, and the cell doesn't fire. The behavior of these superior colliculus cells, therefore, supports the idea that a corollary discharge inhibits firing when the eye moves. This enables the visual system to differentiate between movement on the retina that results from movement of a stimulus and movement on the retina that results from movement of the eyes.

Information in the optic array. We saw in the last chapter that J. J. Gibson believed in an ecological

F I G U R E 8. 18 A person moving from left to right as in Figure 8.17, but the observer follows the person with her eyes. This causes the image of the moving person to remain stationary, while the background flows from right to left, as indicated by the arrows.

F I G U R E 8. 19 The observer moves from left to right past a stationary person causing the image of the person *and* the background to move from right to left across the observer's field of view, as indicated by the arrows.

approach that saw perception as a process of extracting information from the optic array. Gibson is concerned not with physiological mechanisms, like movement detectors or the corollary discharge, but, rather, with how information in the stimulus leads to our perception of movement. To understand Gibson's thinking, let's look at how he would explain three different situations.

1. A person walks past a stationary observer. This is the case most easily handled by movement detectors, since an object (our walking person) is sweeping across the retina, as shown in Figure 8.17. Gibson, however, would say that our perception of movement is determined by the fact that our walking person is moving relative to the background—he covers and then uncovers part of the background as he walks by.

2. A person walks past the observer, who moves his eyes to follow the person. In this situation, (Figure 8.18), the image of the moving person remains stationary on the observer's retina, but the image of the background moves across

the retina in a direction opposite to the person's movement. We perceive movement even though the walking person does not move on our retina, because the walking person moves relative to the background. According to Gibson, in both this situation and the one above, the walking person's movement relative to the background is the crucial information we need to perceive the person as moving.

3. The *observer* walks past a stationary person. This creates the situation shown in Figure 8.19: Both the person and the background sweep across the observer's retina. That the person and background do not move relative to one another provides information that it is the observer that is moving, and not the person or the background. In this situation we perceive no movement, despite much movement on our retina, because there is no movement relative to the background.

Gibson's explanations work in an environment in which the background is visible, but they can't explain how we perceive movement when the

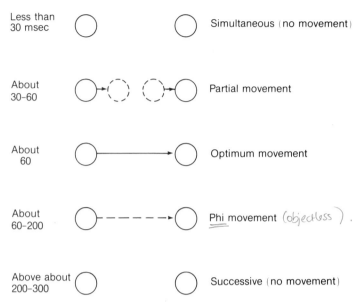

Less than 30 msec — Simultaneous (no movement)

About 30–60 — Partial movement

About 60 — Optimum movement

About 60–200 — Phi movement (objectless).

Above about 200–300 — Successive (no movement)

F I G U R E 8. 20 The perception of apparent movement depends on the time interval between two flashing lights. As the time interval is increased, the observer's perception goes through the stages shown above.

background is not visible, as in the case of a spot of light seen in a dark room or if an object is seen against a completely textureless background. To Gibson these are artificial situations that might occur in perception laboratories but are rare in real life, and his theory is purposely not designed to explain these "special cases."

APPARENT MOVEMENT

Movement Between Two Lights

Apparent movement was first demonstrated in 1875 by Exner, who showed that when two electrical sparks are discharged next to each other briefly separated in time, movement appears to occur across the space between them. However, it wasn't until Max Wertheimer's paper of 1912 (see page 194) that research on apparent movement began in earnest. Wertheimer and later workers found that the nature of the movement that occurs between two flashing lights depends on both the timing between the flashes and the distance between the lights.

Figure 8.20 shows how our perception of two flashes of light changes as the time interval between the two flashes, the **interstimulus interval (ISI),** is increased (Graham, 1965). When the ISI is less than about 30 msec, the lights appear to flash on and off simultaneously. As the interval is increased above 30 msec, **partial movement** is perceived between the two lights; and at a separation of about 60 msec, the lights appear to move continuously from one to the other. This continuous movement is called **optimal movement,** because it looks just like real movement. At intervals between about 60 and 200 msec, a type of movement called **phi movement,** or **objectless movement,** is perceived between the two lights. It is called objectless movement because, while movement appears to occur between the two lights, it is difficult to actually perceive an object moving across the space between them. Finally, at time intervals above about 200–400 msec, *no* movement is perceived between the two lights; they appear successively, with first one flashing on and off, and then the other.

The distance between the two lights also affects the perception of apparent movement. As the dis-

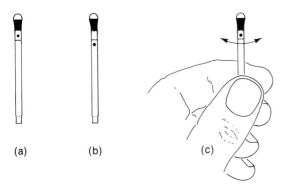

F I G U R E 8. 21 We can create apparent movement by drawing a dot on each side of a match as shown in (a) and (b), and by flipping the match back and forth, as shown in (c).

tance increases, either the time interval between the two flashes or the intensity of the flashes must be increased to maintain the same perception of movement.

DEMONSTRATION

A Demonstration of Apparent Movement

You can demonstrate some of the effects in Figure 8.21 to yourself, as follows: Place a dot on one side of a match as shown in Figure 8.21(a) and, slightly farther down, place a dot on the other side, as in (b). Then, with the match between your thumb and forefinger, as shown in (c), slowly begin to roll the match back and forth. Notice how at slow speeds (long ISIs) you just see the dots one after another. Then, as you increase the speed, notice when movement occurs. Would you classify this movement as "optimal" or "objectless"? At very high speeds (short ISIs) you will see both dots simultaneously, with no movement between them.

Movement in Complex Displays

The above approach to movement perception, using a simple display in which two lights are flashed one after the other, is a logical starting point for the study of apparent movement. In this simple case, movement must occur from one light to the other

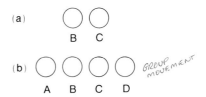

F I G U R E 8. 22 The stimuli used in Ternus' (1926) apparent movement experiment which demonstrated *phenomenal identity.*

since there are only two elements in the display. However, when more complex displays are used, the resulting movement is often not so straightforward. For example, in 1926 J. Ternus did an experiment in which he showed that the nature of apparent movement depends on the overall configuration of the stimulus.

To understand Ternus' experiment, let's first consider what happens when we flash the two lights in Figure 8.22(a) on and off simultaneously and then, after a brief time interval, flash them both on and off again. When we do this, we simply see lights B and C flashing on and off twice, with no movement between them. For his experiment, Ternus added lights at positions A and D, as shown in Figure 8.22(b). He first flashed the group A-B-C, then, after a brief time interval, flashed the group B-C-D. Flashing the lights in this way creates a perception of **group movement**—that is, each dot in the group A-B-C appears to move one position to the right, so A moves to B, B to C, and C to D. Notice that in this situation, lights B and C are flashing on and off just as they did in (a), but adding lights at A and D and flashing the lights in groups of three causes B and C to appear to move to the right. This movement demonstrates what Ternus called **phenomenal identity,** because the group A-B-C retains its identity; the three lights are seen to move together as a whole, even though lights B and C are simply flashing on and off in the same position.

Ternus, who was one of the early Gestalt psychologists (see Chapter 6), used this result to support the Gestalt idea that the whole is different from the sum of its parts. His demonstration of phenomenal identity did support this idea but didn't

---

B O X   8. 2   /   *Apparent Motion: Some Interesting Effects*

Apparent motion is usually illustrated by examples like the one in Figure 8.2(b): two round lights flashing one after the other that create an illusion of movement in a straight line between the two lights. But apparent motion occurs in other situations, as well. Let's look at a few of them.

Apparent movement can be influenced by an object's shape. Look at the apparent movement stimuli in the figure at right. Paul Kolers (1972) asked the following questions about these stimuli: What will happen in (a) if rectangle A flashes on and off followed by B and C flashing together? Answer: A appears to split and move simultaneously to B and C. What if we do the same thing, but turn rectangles B and C on their side, as in (b)? Answer: The center rectangle splits and its parts rotate in opposite directions to move to new orientations at positions B and C (also see Proffitt, Gilden, Kaiser, & Whelan, 1988). What if one of the side rectangles is horizontal and the other vertical, as in (c)? Answer: Movement occurs only to the more similar rectangle C, even though it is more distant; the closer horizontal rectangle B blinks on and off. Kolers calls this last effect **figural selection.**

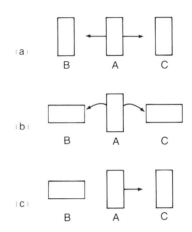

Apparent movement can be influenced by the observer's past experience. Max Wertheimer (1912) demonstrated the effect of past experience on apparent movement by flashing two lines, *a* and *b*, one after another, so that line *a* appeared to move downward through the 60-degree angle to *b*, as shown in figure (a) on the next page. This is the usual result observed when two lines at an angle are presented; movement occurs through the smaller 60-degree angle rather than through the larger 120-degree angle.

---

add much to our knowledge of the mechanisms underlying apparent movement. However, 50 years later, modern researchers used Ternus' effect to show that there are two different mechanisms for apparent movement, one that is responsible for the perception of movement that occurs when there is a brief interval between flashes, and another that is responsible for the perception of movement that occurs when there is a longer interval between flashes.

We are now going to describe the experiments that demonstrated this. First we will show how the Ternus effect was used to demonstrate the existence of these two mechanisms. Then we will look

at some additional experiments that showed that these two mechanisms have different properties.

The purpose of the discussion on the next few pages is not just to present some "facts" about movement perception but to illustrate how a specific idea has been developed by researchers. You will see how experiments which supported the initial idea—"that there are two mechanisms responsible for apparent movement"—were followed by additional experiments that not only supported the idea of two mechanisms but also discovered a number of additional differences between them. We will begin by describing the experiment that used the Ternus stimulus.

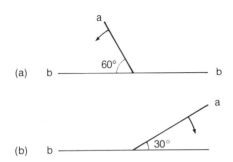

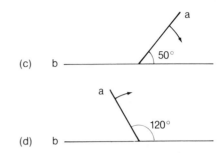

However, when Wertheimer first flashed the lines so they moved through 30-degree and 50-degree angles, as shown in (b) and (c), and then presented the arrangement in (a), line *a* was perceived to move through the larger 120-degree angle, as shown in (d). Thus, apparent movement can be affected by the observer's previous experience.

Apparent movement can occur along a curved path. Although the apparent movement between two flashing stimuli usually follows the shortest straight line between the stimuli, Roger Shepard and Susan Zare (1983) have shown that apparent movement can occur along a curved path if a dim curved band of light is flashed during the time interval between the flashing of the two

stimuli. This effect, which they call **path-guided apparent motion,** can cause apparent movement over an extremely curved path, as shown in the diagram below.

These three examples, plus the examples of apparent movement in complex displays described in the text, show that there is much more to be explained about apparent movement than simply why movement occurs in a straight-line path from one flashing dot to another.

Two Systems for Apparent Movement

The existence of two different movement systems, an idea originally proposed by Oliver Braddick (1974), was demonstrated in an experiment by Alan Pantle and Lucinda Picciano (1976) using the Ternus stimulus. They presented Ternus' display repeatedly, ABC-BCD-ABC-BCD, and so on. When the ISI between each group was above about 50 msec, observers saw the groups of three lights move back and forth together, as shown in Figure 8.23(a). This is the movement Ternus' observers reported 50 years earlier. However, when the ISI was below 50 msec, observers saw the two over-

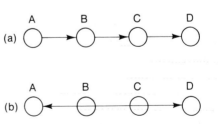

F I G U R E 8. 23 Two ways of seeing apparent movement in the Ternus display. (a) At longer ISIs subjects see all three dots moving together; (b) at shorter ISIs they see B and C as stationary and A and D as moving back and forth.

lapping dots, B and C, as stationary and saw a third dot moving back and forth from one end of the display to the other, as shown in Figure 8.23(b).

But just showing that different perceptual effects occur at different ISIs does not prove that there are two different mechanisms of apparent movement. To establish the existence of different mechanisms, we need to uncover further differences between the two types of movement. Pantle and Picciano did this by using a technique called **dichoptic presentation.** In a dichoptic presentation, one stimulus (lights A, B, and C of the Ternus display) is presented to the left eye and the other stimulus (B, C, and D) is presented to the right eye. When Pantle and Picciano presented the stimuli in this way, their observers saw only movement of the three lights together as in Figure 8.23(a).

Consider what this result means. Since signals from the left and right eyes do not meet until they reach binocular cells in the cortex (remember that in the lateral geniculate nucleus signals from each eye remain separated), the mechanism responsible for the movement observed by Pantle and Picciano's observers must reside in cortical cells that receive inputs from both eyes. In contrast, movement like that in Figure 8.23(b) only occurs when the two stimuli are presented to the same eye and therefore probably involves neurons that receive signals from only one eye.

These results enable us to say with more confidence that these two kinds of movement are served by different mechanisms. We will call the mechanism that causes the type of movement shown in Figure 8.23(a) the **high-level system.** This system is slow (remember that it only occurs at ISIs greater than 50 msec) and resides in binocular neurons. We will call the mechanism that causes the type of movement shown in Figure 8.23(b) the **low-level system.** This system is fast and resides in monocular neurons.

In addition to differing in speed and location, the high- and low-level systems also differ in another important way: In the rapid, low-level system, movement occurs *before* the visual system processes information about the form of the stimulus. In the slower high-level system, movement occurs *after*

the visual system processes information about the form of the stimulus. To understand what we mean by this, let's look at the experiments that support both of these statements.

The Low-Level System: Movement Before Form

When you say "I saw the square move" you are linking your perception of movement to your perception of a specific form. Although form and movement are linked in our consciousness, it appears that these two qualities may be processed separately by the visual system. This separation of form and movement processing for the low-level system is illustrated by a demonstration that uses a stimulus display called a **random dot kinematogram.** To understand this demonstration we need to first describe the random dot kinematogram stimulus.

The random dot kinematogram is based on the random dot stereogram, a stimulus we described in Chapter 7 (Box 7.2, page 244). The random dot stereogram in Box 7.2 was constructed by starting with two identical displays of random dots, and then by shifting a square area in the middle of the right display slightly to the right. When one display is presented to the left eye and one to the right, the shifted area in the center creates binocular disparity and the viewer sees a small square in depth.

When the left side of a stereogram is presented briefly to one eye and, after a short ISI, the right side is presented briefly to the same eye, the stereogram becomes a random dot kinematogram. When the ISI between presentations is short, observers see a small square in the middle of the display that appears to move from left to right (Figure 8.24).

Why do we perceive this moving square? After all, when we look at the left and right halves of the kinematogram all we see are random dots. (Look at the stereograms in Box 7.2 to convince yourself that this is true.) Neither random dot pattern, when considered alone, contains a small square. The small moving square exists only when the two patterns are presented one after the other. Thus, we are not flashing a square in two different positions. We are

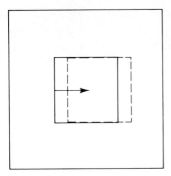

F I G U R E 8. 24 Movement of a square is perceived when the two stimuli of the random dot kinematogram are flashed one after the other.

flashing two arrays of random dots in which some of the dots are in the same positions in the two arrays, and the dots in an area in the center of one array are shifted slightly to the right. The visual system creates movement by somehow matching the shifted dots in the two patterns. When apparent motion occurs for all of the corresponding pairs of dots simultaneously, we see a moving square.

Now that we realize that kinematogram movement is the result of the simultaneous movement of individual elements, we can appreciate that the movement we observe when flashing the kinematogram takes place *before* the stimulus has any *form*. Form perception ("I see a square") occurs only *after* the individual elements have all moved. Thus, the kinematogram movement determined by the low-level system occurs *before* form processing has taken place (Figure 8.25). This is different from movement determined by the high-level system, for which, as we will now see, the situation is reversed.

The High-Level System: Form Before Movement

We can show that form processing comes before movement perception for the high-level system by flashing the two stimuli in Figure 8.26 (Ramachandran, Rao, & Vidyasagar, 1973). Although there are no points in frame 1 that correspond to points in frame 2, when we flash these stimuli one after another, we see a moving square. Our perception of movement in this case cannot, therefore, depend on the formless point-by-point matching that occurs for the kinematograms. Instead, our perception of movement depends on a matching of the square on the left with the square on the right. For the high-level system, form is processed first and then movement occurs (Figure 8.27).

Finally, let's consider how cognitive factors affect the two movement systems.

Cognitive Factors and the Two Movement Systems

The high-level system differs from the low-level system in its susceptibility to cognitive factors. For example, let's consider what happens when, under conditions that favor operation of the high-level system, the triangle and circle on the left of Figure 8.28 are presented together and are then followed by the triangle on the right. When we do this, both the triangle and circle appear to move to the right, but when the circle reaches the triangle, it disappears *behind* the triangle. Vilayanur Ramachandran (1981) suggests that the circle's disappearance reflects the perceptual system's application of the following rule, based on its knowledge of the world: *It is more*

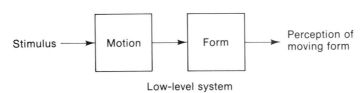

Low-level system

F I G U R E 8. 25 In the low-level apparent movement system, motion is processed before form.

F I G U R E   8. 26   Stimulus for Ramachandarian et al. (1973) experiment. See text for details.

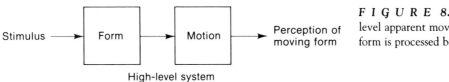

High-level system

F I G U R E   8. 27   In the high-level apparent movement system, (left) form is processed before motion.

likely for an object to disappear behind another object than for an object to fuse into another object. This demonstration and others show that the movement determined by the high-level system can be affected by our knowledge of the world. Other experiments, in which the low-level system is tested, show that this system responds automatically to patterns of light and dark on the retina and is therefore not affected by our knowledge of the world.

Summary of the Differences Between Low-level and High-level Movement Systems

What emerges from all of the experiments we have described, plus many others, is that there are a number of differences between the low-level and high-level systems. These differences are summarized in Table 8.1 on the facing page.

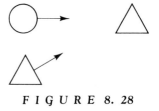

F I G U R E   8. 28

The information in this table represents a large step from the original observation that two lights flashed one after another cause an illusion of movement between them. We now know that there are two very different mechanisms responsible for apparent movement. Other research, which we haven't described here, has discovered even more differences between these two mechanisms (see Anstis, 1980; Braddick, 1980).

T A B L E 8. 1 / *Differences between the High- and Low-level Systems*

	Low-level System	High-level System
Speed	Fast (short ISIs)	Slow (longer ISIs)
Movement perception occurs before form processing?	Yes	No
Influenced by cognitive factors?	No	Yes
Anatomical location	Monocular cells	Binocular cortical cells

INDUCED MOVEMENT

One example of induced movement, mentioned earlier, is the perception that the moon is racing through the clouds when the clouds are moving and not the moon. You also may have experienced an induced movement effect while sitting in your car at a stoplight. As you feel your car moving backward, you jam on the brakes, only to realize that your car is standing still and the one next to you is moving forward. Another example of induced movement is the way a pigeon's head appears to move when the pigeon walks. When asked to describe how a pigeon's head moves, most people say that the head moves forward and then backward every time the pigeon takes a step. But films of pigeons walking show that this isn't so; the pigeon's head does move forward, but then the pigeon's body moves forward under the head, making the pigeon's head appear to move backward, as shown in Figure 8.29.

In two of the above examples, a small object (the distant moon, the pigeon's head) appears to move because of the movement of a large object (the clouds, the pigeon's body). This general characteristic of induced movement was described by Karl Duncker in 1929. Duncker had observers sit in a darkened room and observe a small luminous circle inside a luminous rectangle, as shown in Figure 8.30. When Duncker moved the rectangle to the right, his observers reported that the circle appeared to move to the left.

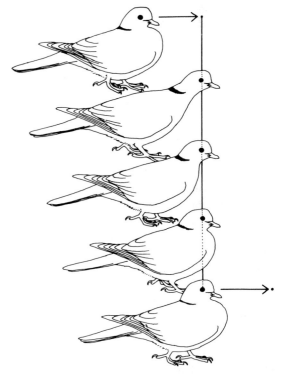

F I G U R E 8. 29 How a pigeon walks. These pictures, which were taken from a film of a pigeon walking, show that a pigeon moves its head forward and then moves its body forward while keeping its head stationary. The pigeon's head never moves backward. (Figure courtesy of Mark Friedman; see Friedman, 1975.)

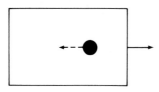

F I G U R E 8. 30 Duncker's (1929) induced movement demonstration as demonstrated by Wallach (1959). When the rectangle is moved to the right as indicated by the solid arrow, the disc inside the rectangle appears to move to the left as indicated by the dashed arrow.

D E M O N S T R A T I O N

Inducing Movement in a Dot

You can demonstrate induced movement to yourself by sticking a small dot of paper to the screen of your television set, as shown in Figure 8.31, and watching a program in which the television camera moves back and forth across a scene or follows a moving person or car (football, basketball, or hockey games are particularly good). These camera move- ments cause the entire TV image to move across the screen, which will induce movement in your dot. The movement you see, however, will not be as impressive as that observed by Duncker's observers, because the stationary border of the TV screen exerts a stabilizing influence on the dot.

An experiment by Sakata and coworkers (1977) shows that there are neurons in the monkey's cortex that fire under the same conditions that cause humans to perceive induced movement. These neurons, located in the posterior parietal association cortex—an area between the occipital and parietal lobes (see Figure 2.9)—increase their firing rate when a spot of light moves downward and decrease their firing rate when the spot moves upward (Figure 8.32a). The interesting thing about these neurons is the way they fire when we keep the dot stationary and move a surrounding frame, as shown in Figure 8.32(b). These neurons increase their firing when the frame moves up and decrease their firing when the frame moves down. The

F I G U R E 8. 31 As these basketball players race down the court, the dot stuck to the center of the TV screen races with them!

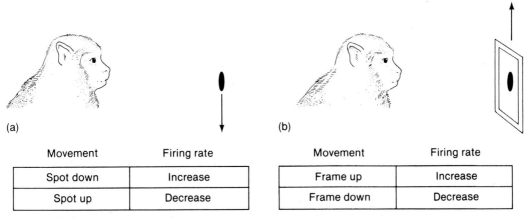

Movement	Firing rate
Spot down	Increase
Spot up	Decrease

Movement	Firing rate
Frame up	Increase
Frame down	Decrease

F I G U R E 8. 32 The response of a neuron that might be involved in the perception of induced movement. This neuron increases its firing rate when the spot moves down (left) or when the frame moves up (right). According to Duncker's result (Figure 8.30), upward movement of the frame should make the spot appear to move down.

important point here is that when a person perceives induced movement, movement of a frame in one direction makes a spot appear to move in the opposite direction, and this is exactly how these cells respond: They increase their firing when the spot moves down *or* the frame moves up, and decrease their firing when the spot moves up *or* the frame moves down.

AUTOKINETIC MOVEMENT

I first became aware of autokinetic movement while I was looking up at the stars on a dark night. I noticed that a star which was separated somewhat from the others appeared to be moving. "That must be an airplane," I thought. Although it continued to move as I watched, it stayed in about the same area of sky. I then realized that the "airplane" was a star and I was experiencing an illusion, which I later learned was called autokinetic movement, or the autokinetic effect.

D E M O N S T R A T I O N

Observing Autokinetic Movement

The most pleasurable way to observe autokinetic movement is to repeat my outdoor observation above by observing an isolated star. If that isn't possible, you can observe autokinetic movement indoors. Obtain a light that is dim enough so you can't see any of the other objects in a completely darkened room (the tip of a lighted cigarette works). What happens as you watch the light? If it moves, can you influence the movement by "willing" the light to move in a particular direction? (See below.)

An interesting feature of the autokinetic effect is that it can be influenced by suggestion. In 1935 Muzafer Sherif, a social psychologist, did an experiment in which he instructed observers as follows: "When the room is completely dark I shall give you the signal 'ready' and then show you a point of light. After a short time the light will start to move. As soon as you see it move, press the key. A few seconds later the light will disappear. Then tell me the distance it moved."

Sherif's experiment was run both for individual observers and for groups of two or three at a time, and the results depended on whether the observers were run individually or in groups. When run individually, observers reported that the dot moved anywhere from 0.8 to 7.4 inches, but when run in groups of three, all observers reported after a few trials that the dot moved about 4 inches.

When run together, the observers apparently influenced each other, and their perceptions became the same.

Because the autokinetic effect is so open to suggestion, Allan Rechtschaffen and Sarnoff Mednick (1955), two clinical psychologists, proposed that the effect be used as a personality test. To administer this test, which they called the **autokinetic word technique,** they had observers view a spot of light in a dark room. The observers were told that they were being tested on their ability to see words written by a point of light and should report any words or letters they saw. All observers reported seeing words, showing that the experi-

F I G U R E 8. 33   To see the waterfall illusion, stare at one spot on a real waterfall and then look off to the side. The effect only works with waterfalls that fill only a small part of your field of view. (Niagara Falls *won't* work!)

menters' suggestion was effective, since most observers do not spontaneously report seeing words. Though many of the words were simple ones, such as "and," "on," and "the," a number of subjects gave long, rather revealing responses. One subject, after giving a number of responses of a highly personal nature, indignantly asked the experimenter, "Where did you get all of that information about me?"

AFTEREFFECTS OF MOVEMENT

The Waterfall Illusion

Figure 8.33 shows a picture of the stimulus for an illusion of movement unsurprisingly called the **waterfall illusion.** If you stare for about 30–60 seconds at a waterfall or a rapidly flowing stream that fills only part of your field of view and then look away at some other part of the scene, the scene will appear to move in a direction opposite to the original direction of flow. This is called an aftereffect of movement, because the observer must first view an **inducing stimulus,** such as the waterfall, to get the effect.

Stuart Anstis and Richard Gregory (1964) showed that the waterfall illusion depends on the movement of the inducing stimulus across the retina. Instead of having observers view a waterfall, they had them view a belt of horizontally moving, vertical black and white stripes, similar to that in Figure 8.4. The observers viewed these moving stripes either with their eyes stationary, so the pattern moved across the retina, or with their eyes tracking the moving stripes, so the pattern remained stationary on the retina. In both the "eyes stationary" and "eyes tracking" conditions, the observers perceived the movement of the stripes, but an aftereffect of movement occurred only after the "eyes stationary" condition. Thus, the important factor in determining this aftereffect is not the perception of the stripes' movement but the movement of the stripes across the retina.

That the waterfall illusion occurs only if the inducing stimulus moves across the retina supports the idea that movement detectors, which respond only to movement across the retina, may help create this illusion. In fact, by recording from directionally selective cells in the rabbit's retina, Horace Barlow and Robert Hill (1963) have found electrophysiological evidence that movement detectors are involved in the waterfall illusion. Figure 8.34 shows their results. When the stimulus is moved across the cell's receptive field, the firing rate increases to above the cell's spontaneous level, and when the stimulus is turned off, the firing rate falls to below the cell's spontaneous level.

Barlow and Hill hypothesize that this cell (which we will call A) is paired with another cell (B), which is directionally selective in the opposite direction. After stimulation of A is stopped, its firing rate drops to below its spontaneous level; therefore A is firing at a lower rate than B, which is still firing at its spontaneous level. We perceive movement in the preferred direction of B, because it is firing at a greater rate than A. Thus, according to Barlow and Hill, aftereffects of movement result from temporary imbalances of the discharges of cells that respond in opposite directions.

Although Barlow and Hill's proposed mechanism may be correct, we should not fall into the trap of assuming, based on their observations of neurons in the rabbit's retina, that our perception of the waterfall illusion results solely from activity in the retina. While the rabbit retina contains directionally selective neurons, the monkey retina does not (see page 94). In addition, psychophysical experiments show that the illusion can be transferred between the two eyes. That is, if the inducing stimulus is presented to one eye, the illusion of movement can be observed with the other eye. Thus, the neural processes that cause this illusion in humans are probably located in the cortex (see Barlow & Brindley, 1963; Mitchell & Ware, 1974).

DEMONSTRATION

The Spiral Aftereffect

The **spiral aftereffect** is an illusion of movement similar to the waterfall illusion. You can observe this effect by xeroxing the spiral in Figure 8.35 and placing it on a turntable. Set the turntable for a

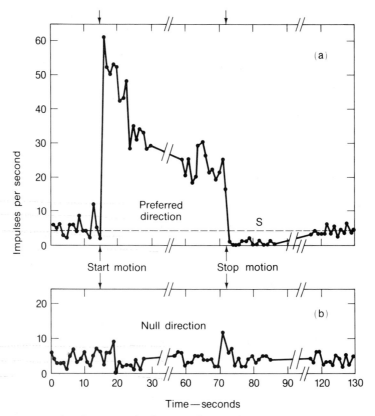

FIGURE 8.34 Response of a directionally selective cell in the rabbit's retina to a stimulus moving in its preferred direction. In (a) we see that during 60 seconds of continuous stimulation the rate of nerve firing stays above the spontaneous level, S. After the stimulation is stopped, firing decreases to below the spontaneous level for about 30 seconds. (b) shows the same stimulus conditions as in (a), but in the cell's "null direction" (opposite to the preferred direction), showing that stimulation in the null direction has no effect on the response of this cell. (Barlow & Hill, 1963.)

speed of 33⅓ and look at the center of the rotating spiral for 30–60 seconds. Then look at a nearby object and observe what happens.

EVENT PERCEPTION

Our discussion of movement perception up to now has been concerned with our ability to detect real movement and with the conditions that lead to our perception of different illusions of movement. But movement is far more than simply an aspect of the environment that we detect. As we stated at the beginning of this chapter, movement perception provides information about three-dimensional shape, it provides information that helps us to segregate figure from ground, and it enables us to interact with the environment. In the remainder of this chapter we are going to focus on the connection between movement perception and these other aspects of our environment. To do this we will describe research that many researchers classify as being concerned with "event perception."

What is an **event**? Most people agree that when an event occurs "something happens," and in most

FIGURE 8. 35

cases that "something" is associated with movement. Although psychologists have had difficulty in agreeing on a single definition of an event, most definitions include the idea of movement or change. For example, Dennis Proffitt and James Cutting (1980) define an event as "an object undergoing change, such as movement."

The important thing about the study of event perception for our purposes is the philosophical position that motivates it. This position, which has its roots in work by the Swedish psychologist Gunnar Johansson (1950) and in J. J. Gibson's ecological approach, is stated by William Warren and Robert Shaw (1985) as follows:

The common insight behind an "event" approach is that, unlike most perceptual psychologists' stimulus displays, the natural world doesn't usually sit still for a perceiver, nor does a perceiver typically sit still when exploring his or her surroundings. Our perceptual encounters with the world are dominated by *events,* or changes in structure over time. But far from complicating the act of perceiving, such transformations appear to yield more efficient, stable, and veridical perception, by providing more information about the object or event observed." (p. xiii)

The key part of this statement is the last sentence. What is important is not the movement itself but that it provides information that "yields more efficient, stable and veridical perception."* In our description of the research inspired by this philosophy, we will focus on research that investigates:

1. How movement of a stimulus provides information that
   a. reveals structure in the stimulus.
   b. causes the perception of cause and effect relationships between moving stimuli.
   c. causes people to assign motivation and personalities to certain types of moving stimuli.
2. The role of visual information in determining our ability to keep our balance and to interact with our environment as we move through it.

Creating Structure Through Motion

We can understand why movement is important in determining our perception of an object's structure by returning to a point we made at the beginning of Chapter 6—that a given two-dimensional representation can be caused by many different three-dimensional objects. Thus, both the cubes and the other shape in Figure 6.2 can, when viewed from a particular angle, result in the same two-dimensional image on the surface of the retina. Another example of this situation is shown in Figure 8.36. In view (a) we see what looks like two rectangles, one in front of the other. But moving to another position reveals the view in (b), and we see that the rectangle we thought was in front is actually in back and the rectangle we thought was in back isn't even a rectangle at all. Thus, although the two-dimensional representation in (a) looks reasonable, it is actually an ambiguous image that misleads us into the wrong conclusion about the shapes of the objects in the display. By moving we eliminate this ambiguity—an example of how movement can reveal the correct structure of a stimulus.

---

*Veridical perception occurs when the perception of a stimulus's properties matches the physical properties of the stimulus (from Chapter 4, p. 140).

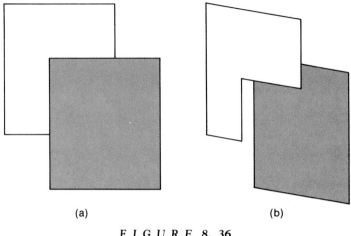

(a)   (b)

F I G U R E 8. 36

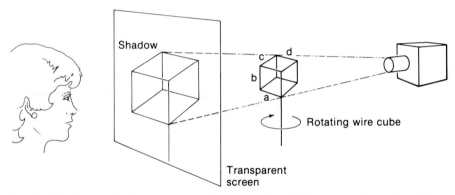

F I G U R E 8. 37 Setup similar to the one used by Wallach and O'Connell (1953) to demonstrate the kinetic depth effect.

Let's now look at some other examples of how movement reveals three-dimensional structure.

The kinetic depth effect. The most well-known demonstration of how movement can cause us to perceive structure is the **kinetic depth effect,** in which the three-dimensional structure of a stimulus can be perceived from a moving two-dimensional image. This effect was demonstrated by Hans Wallach and D. N. O'Connell (1953) by casting a shadow of a cube on a transparent screen, as shown in Figure 8.37. When the shadow is stationary it looks flat, but when the cube is rotated, as indicated by the arrow, the shadow takes on a three-

dimensional appearance, even though it is seen on a two-dimensional surface. Movement, therefore, can create the perception of three-dimensional structure on a two-dimensional surface.

D E M O N S T R A T I O N

The Kinetic Depth Effect with Pipe Cleaners

You can demonstrate the kinetic depth effect to yourself by bending a pipe cleaner so it reproduces sides a, b, c, and d of the shape in Figure 8.37. Then cast a shadow of the pipe cleaner on a piece of paper, as shown in Figure 8.38, and, while viewing the shadow from the other side of the paper,

F I G U R E 8. 38 Shadow-casting by a bent pipe cleaner. To achieve a sharp shadow, position the pipe cleaner about 2 feet from your desk lamp. (If it is too close to the lamp the shadow will be fuzzy.) To perceive the kinetic depth effect, rotate the pipe cleaner between your fingers while observing the shadow from the other side of the paper.

rotate the pipe cleaner. The result should be a more three-dimensional perception than when the shadow was stationary.

Perceiving common and relative movements. In our encounters with movement in the environment, we often see objects that are moving relative to other objects. Objects moving relative to one another sometimes create a structure that doesn't exist for either object alone. To illustrate this to yourself, do the following demonstration.

D E M O N S T R A T I O N

Perceiving Moving Dots

Between pages 303 and 341 there is a dot in the middle right edge of your book. By flipping the pages of your book from the back toward the front

you will perceive this dot to move back and forth along a diagonal path. The same dot also appears between pages 345 and 381, with two other dots above and below. When you flip these pages, the two outer dots will appear to move back and forth along a horizontal path. The important thing to notice when you observe the movement of this three-dot display is how the central dot appears to move. Although the central dot is moving in exactly the same way as it was when alone, it is *perceived* differently, with its diagonal movement replaced by an up and down movement between the two horizontally moving dots (Figure 8.39).

The moving dots are just one of many demonstrations provided by the Swedish psychologist Gunnar Johansson (1975, 1982, 1985) to show how movement of one element can be influenced by its

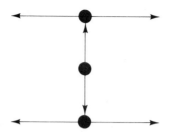

F I G U R E 8. 39 The central dot moves in a diagonal path. When accompanied by two other sideways moving dots, the central dot is perceived to move up and down between the other two dots.

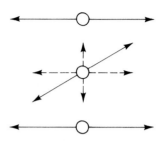

F I G U R E 8. 40 Vector analysis of the dots' movement. The diagonal movement of the center dot can be broken down into horizontal and vertical vectors (dashed lines).

relationship to other elements. The demonstration you have just seen illustrates the Gestalt principle that "the whole is different from the sum of its parts," since our perception of the motion of the central dot changes when we add the other two dots. But Johansson has extended the analysis of

this phenomenon beyond this simple Gestalt maxim, by explaining it in terms of what he calls **perceptual vector analysis.**

We can understand why our perception of the center dot's movement changes when we add the other two dots by breaking its movement into vec-

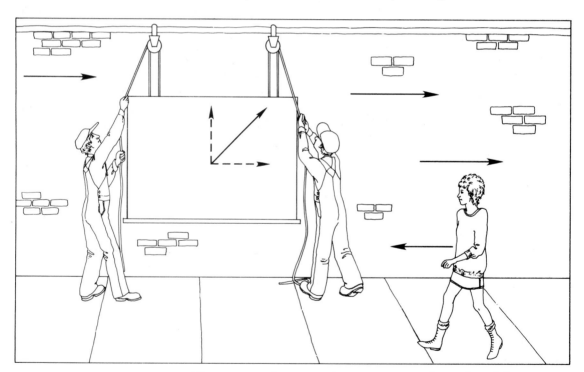

F I G U R E 8. 41 The movement that occurs when a person moves from right to left in front of a wall where a billboard is being raised. The wall's image moves from left to right, as indicated by the solid horizontal arrows. The billboard's image moves diagonally, as indicated by the diagonal arrow. This diagonal movement of the billboard relative to the person can be broken into horizontal and vertical vectors (dashed lines).

tors. Vectors are arrows that separate angular movement into horizontal and vertical components. The vectors present in our three-dot display are shown in Figure 8.40.

In Figure 8.40 we can see that all of the dots have horizontal vectors in common. These common vectors define the *common movement* of the dots—all of the dots have a horizontal component of movement. The vector that remains, for our central dot, defines the *relative movement* of the dot—its movement relative to the other dots. According to Johansson, our visual system "partials out," or subtracts, the common vectors shared by all three dots. Doing this leaves the central dot's vertical vector, which causes us to perceive the dot as moving up and down relative to the other dots, as it simultaneously moves sideways to follow them.

Our perception of the central dot's movement is not simply a laboratory curiosity. Suppose, for example, as you are walking past a wall, you see a billboard being raised in front of the wall as shown in Figure 8.41. Your movement causes the wall's image to move across your retina horizontally, and the combination of your horizontal movement and the billboard's upward movement causes the billboard's image to move across your retina at an angle, as shown by the solid arrow on the billboard. However, your perceptual system breaks the diagonal movement of the billboard into horizontal and vertical vectors (dashed arrows). When we subtract the common movement of the billboard and the wall, indicated by the horizontal vectors, the billboard's remaining vertical vector determines your perception of the billboard's movement relative to the wall: It appears to be rising vertically in front of the wall (Johansson, 1985).

Johansson's early work was done using simple computer-generated dot stimuli like the ones in Figure 8.40. To extend his research to more complex stimuli that we might encounter in everyday life, he began a series of experiments on **biological motion** in which dots of light were moved not by a computer but by a walking person.

The perception of biological motion. The stimulus for Johansson's biological motion experiments was a human outfitted with 12 small lights, as shown

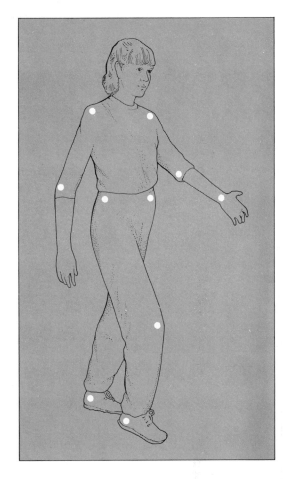

F I G U R E   8. 42   A person wearing lights for a biological movement experiment. In the actual experiment the room is totally dark, so only the lights can be seen.

in Figure 8.42. This person was filmed in a dark room so only the lights could be seen, with the result being a film that begins with the person still and then shows her walking and engaging in various other movements. When the configuration of lights attached to the person was stationary, subjects reported seeing a meaningless pattern of lights. However, as soon as the person got up and started walking, subjects were able to instantly identify the movement as being produced by a walking person. Thus, movement creates a structure (a person walking) out of what was initially perceived as a random arrangement of dots. This is particularly

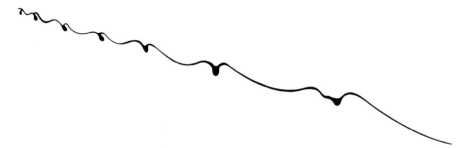

F I G U R E 8. 43 The path traced by one of the lights attached to the walking person's ankle. When viewing all of the lights moving together, the observer is unaware of these individual movements but, instead, perceives the entire configuration as a walking person.

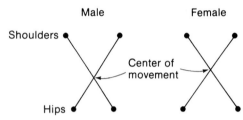

F I G U R E 8. 44 Center of movement for males and females. According to Cutting and Proffitt (1981) we are able to use information about the center of movement to tell whether a "light walker" is a male or a female.

impressive when we consider the paths of an individual light, shown in Figure 8.43. Observers do not perceive the individual bouncing movements of each light but, instead, perceive the entire configuration as a walking person.

Following Johansson's lead, Lynn Kozlowski and James Cutting (1977) found that observers can go beyond simply identifying the moving lights as walking people. Observers can label the moving lights as belonging to male or female walkers with 60–70 percent accuracy. And Sverker Runeson and Gunilla Frykholm (1981) found that observers can accurately estimate the amount of weight being lifted by a person on the basis of the information provided by lights attached to the person.

The conclusion to be drawn from these experiments is that the visual system sees more than moving "lights." The visual system extracts information from patterns of movement that enable observers to perceive *events*. Thus, moving lights provide information that is translated into perceptions such as "I see a man walking" or "I see a person lifting a heavy weight."

But exactly what *is* this information? Cutting and Proffitt (1981) suggest that the crucial information for determining whether a person is male or female is the person's **center of movement.** This center, the point around which all other movements have regular patterns, is higher for females than for males (Figure 8.44).

Movement and the Perception of Causality

When we see a hammer driving a nail into a board or a knife cutting bread, we are perceiving causality: The hammer causes the nail to go into the board, and the knife causes the bread to be cut. The perception of movement is one important component of these and many other situations in which we perceive causality. Although in some situations, such as a match causing a piece of paper to burn, we may conclude that one event causes another in the absence of movement, the majority of examples of the percept of causality involve movement. One researcher in particular, Albert Michotte (1963), in his book *The Perception of Causality*, concentrates his attention on situations in which our perception of causality is linked to our perception of movement.

According to Michotte, the most important factor in determining whether we perceive event A as causing event B is the timing between them.

F I G U R E 8. 45 Stimuli like those used by Michotte (1963).

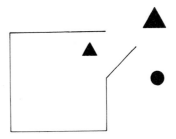

F I G U R E 8. 46 A scene from Heider and Simmel's (1944) film.

Michotte illustrates this by pointing out that if a gust of wind blows a door shut and a light immediately goes on at the other end of the corridor, the impression of a causal relationship between the door closing and the light going on is forced upon us. Even though we may think it unlikely that shutting a door would turn on a light (although this is certainly not impossible, since shutting a refrigerator door turns *off* a light), the timing between the door and light may, as Michotte says, *force* an impression of a causal relationship upon us.

In order to experimentally study the effect of timing on the perception of causality, Michotte used stimuli such as squares A and B in Figure 8.45. Square A moves toward square B; then, after A reaches B, B moves away from A. By varying the timing between the movement of A and B, Michotte has identified the conditions that result in what he calls the **launching effect**—the perception that object A appears to "launch" object B. Michotte reported that this perception occurs when the interval between A arriving and B leaving is 200 msec or less. Recent research sets this minimum interval at less than 50 msec. (Kaiser & Proffitt, 1987). Thus, the time interval between two events must be very short if we are to perceive a causal relationship between them.

Movement and the Perception of Motives and Personality

Another effect of movement is to give "life" to inanimate objects, because a major property of living things is mobility. While this hardly means that we conclude that all moving things are alive, Fritz Heider and Marianne Simmel (1944) have shown that movement can give personalities, feelings, and motives to geometrical figures. They showed a 2½-minute film, the cast of which appears in Figure 8.46: a "house" inhabited by a large triangle, a small triangle, and a disc. In the film these geometrical figures move and interact with each other in various ways. For example, the large triangle might bump into the smaller one, or the disc might move inside the house and then outside again.

The observer's task was to watch the film and write down what happened. Thirty-three of the 34 observers interpreted the film in terms of animate beings. That is, they gave human or animal properties to each geometrical figure on the basis of the figure's movements and size. When asked specifically about the figures, observers showed no hesitation in assigning personality characteristics to them. Many people felt the big triangle was a "male" since it was bigger, and everyone disliked it since it picked on the smaller triangle. The small triangle, on the other hand, was perceived as being "heroic, brave, timid, cagey, and sly." Thus, movement can give geometrical figures qualities usually associated with living things.

Vision and Balance

One of the most important functions of movement perception is its role in helping us to interact with our environment. David Lee and coworkers (1983) have this function in mind when they say that "the visual and motor systems evolved together to support life's activities." Only recently, however, have researchers looked closely at the link between vision and our active interaction with the environment. We will begin our description of this research by considering the role of vision in a basic function—keeping our balance.

J. J. Gibson (1966) suggested that vision is

one of the **proprioceptive senses**—that is, one of the senses responsible for sensing the location, orientation, and movement of the body. This was seen as an unconventional suggestion when it was made, because the senses usually identified as proprioceptive are the vestibular system of the inner ear, which is generally considered to be the major mechanism for balance, and the receptors in our muscles and joints, which help us sense the positions of our limbs. Gibson's assertion is, however, correct, as we can illustrate by a simple demonstration.

DEMONSTRATION

Keeping Your Balance

Keeping your balance is something you take for granted. Even when standing on one foot most people can keep their balance with little effort. Try it. Then after demonstrating your ability to balance on one foot, repeat this demonstration, but with your eyes closed. You may be surprised at how difficult balance becomes when you can't see. Vision provides a frame of reference that helps our muscles constantly make adjustments to help us maintain our balance.

The importance of vision for keeping our balance has been demonstrated in another way in an experiment by David Lee and Eric Aronson (1974). Lee and Aronson placed 13–16-month-old toddlers in the "swinging room" in Figure 8.47. In this room the floor is stationary but the walls and ceiling of the room can swing forward and backward.

The idea behind the swinging room was to duplicate the visual stimulation that normally occurs as our bodies sway forward and backward. When we sway forward we create an expanding **optic flow pattern**[*] like the one in Figure 8.48(a), and when we sway backward we create a contracting pattern like the one in Figure 8.48(b). These flow patterns provide information about or body sway and, without realizing it, we are constantly using this infor-

---

[*]The "optic flow pattern" is sometimes called the "optic flow field." Both terms mean essentially the same thing.

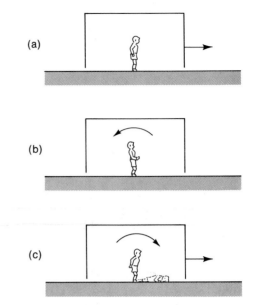

FIGURE 8. 47 Lee's swinging room. (a) Moving the room forward creates an optic flow pattern as in Figure 8.48b that occurs when a person sways backward, as in (b). In compensating for this apparent sway, subjects sway forward, as in (c), and often lose their balance and fall down.

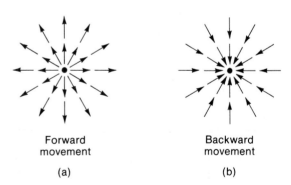

FIGURE 8. 48 Flow patterns that occur (a) when we move forward and (b) when we move backward.

mation to make corrections for this sway so we can stand upright. Lee and Aronson reasoned that if they created a flow pattern that makes a person think he is leaning forward or backward, they could cause him to lean in the opposite direction to compensate.

F I G U R E 8. 49 The flow of the environment as seen from a car speeding across a bridge toward point A. The flow, shown by the arrows, is more rapid closer to the car (as indicated by the increased blur) but occurs everywhere except A, the focus of expansion, toward which the car is moving. (Also see Figure 8.48a)

They accomplished this by moving the room either toward or away from the standing children, and the children responded as predicted. When the room moved toward them (creating the flow pattern for swaying forward), they leaned back, and when it moved away (creating the flow pattern for swaying backward), they leaned forward. In fact, many of the children did more than just lean: 26 percent swayed, 23 percent staggered, and 33 percent fell down! Adults were also affected by the swinging room. If they braced themselves, "oscillating the experimental room through as little as 6 mm caused adult subjects to sway approximately in phase with this movement. The subjects were like puppets visually hooked to their surroundings and were unaware of the real cause of their disturbance" (Lee, 1980, p. 173). Adults who didn't brace themselves could, like the infants, be knocked over by the moving room. Thus, vision is such a powerful determinant of balance that it can override the traditional sources of balance information provided by the inner ear and the receptors in the muscles and joints.

Moving Through the Environment

In moving through the environment, we encounter a number of problems, the most important of which are how to stay on course and how to avoid bumping into things. For example, when driving a car we want to be able to stay on the road and avoid hitting the car in front of us. Much research on event perception has focused on how we go about solving these two problems, with the major goal being to specify how the optic array provides information that enables us to stay on course and avoid hitting other objects. Let's consider some of the proposed sources of information.

Focus of expansion of the optic flow pattern. J. J. Gibson proposed that a major source of information for the moving observer is the optic flow pattern. Optic flow is created by the movement of elements in the optic array that occurs as an observer moves through the environment. For example, when looking out the front window of a moving car, or when walking down the street, elements flow past you on all sides, as illustrated in Figure 8.49.

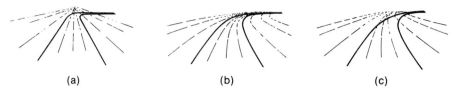

(a)   (b)   (c)

FIGURE 8. 50 Optic flow lines for (a) movement along a straight stretch of road;
(b) correct negotiation of a curved stretch of road; and (c) incorrect negotiation of a curved
stretch of road. In (c) the car will go off the road unless a steering correction is made.

The size of the arrows in this figure indicates the rate of flow. We can see that at greater distances the rate becomes less, until it reaches the **focus of expansion (f.o.e.),** the point of zero expansion in the distance. Gibson proposed that the f.o.e. always remains centered on the observer's destination and, therefore, provides *invariant* information indicating where the observer is heading. Thus, to reach a particular place, it is simply necessary, according to Gibson, to keep that place centered on the f.o.e. of the optic flow pattern.

One problem, however, with the f.o.e. as a source of information for the observer's destination is that moving observers rarely look directly at where they are going. Automobile drivers tend to look at the center lines and at the road's edge, so even if the f.o.e. does provide information about where the driver is headed, there is no guarantee that this information is used (Schiff, 1980).

Optic flow lines. The fact that drivers look at the center line and at the road's edge supports David Lee's (1974, 1980) idea that a feature of the optic flow pattern other than its f.o.e. may be used by drivers to help them stay on course. Consider Figure 8.50(a), which shows a straight stretch of road and a bend. If the driver is on course on the straight stretch, the optic flow line that passes from view directly below the driver, which Lee calls the **loco-motor flow line,** is centered on the road. This line indicates the course the car will follow if no changes are made in steering. In addition, when the driver is on course, the optic flow lines and the edges of the road coincide, as in Figure 8.50(a) for the straight stretch of road and Figure 8.50(b) for the curved stretch. In Figure 8.50(c) the optic flow lines and

the road do not match, a situation to be avoided if you want to stay on the road.

Not only do optic flow lines provide information that drivers are likely to pay attention to, but they offer the advantage of being useful when negotiating curved roads, where the f.o.e. would be useless since the "destination point" is constantly changing throughout a curve.

Motion parallax. We saw in Chapter 7 that motion parallax can serve as a cue for depth perception. James Cutting (1986) has suggested that it can also help indicate where we are going. Motion parallax achieves this by a very simple mechanism: When we look in a direction that is *not* the direction in which we are moving, we see motion parallax—objects farther from the object we are looking at appear to move in the direction we are moving, and objects closer than the object we are looking at appear to move in the opposite direction (Figure 8.51). If, however, we are looking in the same direction we are moving, there is no motion parallax—objects along our line of sight do not move relative to one another. Thus, to maintain a course along the direction you are looking, all you need to do is to move so there is no motion parallax along your line of sight.

DEMONSTRATION

Motion Parallax and the Line of Sight

To illustrate the principle described above, line up three objects on your desk, one near you, another about 1 foot away, and a third 2 feet away, as shown in Figure 8.52. Now move your head at an angle to these objects (path A) while looking at the cen-

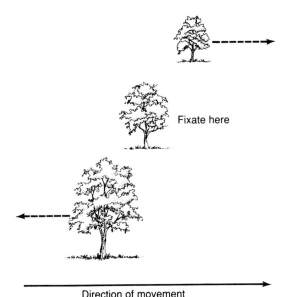

Fixate here

Direction of movement

F I G U R E 8. 51 Motion parallax. If we are moving from left to right past three trees that are at different distances, while fixating on the center one, the near tree appears to move in the direction opposite to our direction of movement, and the far tree appears to move in the same direction we are moving (dashed lines).

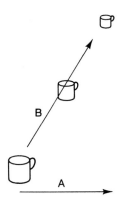

F I G U R E 8. 52 Movement along path A while looking at the center cup will duplicate the situation in Figure 8.51 and you will observe sideways movement of the near and far cups caused by motion parallax. If, however, you move along path B, which is in line with the cups, you will perceive no motion parallax. Thus, you can maintain a course along a direction you are looking by moving so that there is no motion parallax along your line of sight.

ter object. When you do this you should notice the effects of motion parallax: The far object appears to move in the direction you are moving and the near object appears to move in the opposite direction. If, however, you move along a path that is directly in line with the objects (path B), motion parallax is eliminated and the objects do not move sideways relative to one another. In this condition, your direction of movement matches your line of sight.

Angular expansion. Information about flow in the optic array not only helps a driver stay on course but also informs him as to the possibility of colliding with another vehicle. Consider the situation that occurs if you are following another car. If you stay at the same distance from this car, its angle in your field of view remains constant. If, however, you are gaining on the other car, its angle expands until eventually (if you don't brake or change lanes to pass) you will collide with the other car. David Lee (1976) has shown that the **rate of angular expansion** provides information that enables drivers to estimate when they will collide if they maintain their same speed and course.

The idea that the rate of angular expansion does provide this information is supported by experiments in which an observer views a film of an object that is expanding as if it were on a collision course with the observer (Figure 8.53). The film is stopped before the "collision" and the

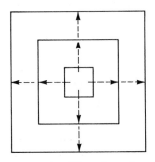

F I G U R E 8. 53 Three "snapshots" of a square as it moves directly toward an observer. The dashed arrows indicate that the square appears to be expanding outward as it moves closer.

observers are asked to estimate how long it will be before a collision would have occurred. The observers estimated longer collision times for longer actual collision times, although they tended to underestimate the actual time to collision (Schiff & Detwiller, 1979; McLeod & Ross, 1983). It appears, therefore, that the rate of angular expansion provides information which can be used to avoid colliding with other objects in the environment.

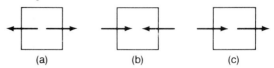

F I G U R E 8. 54 Stimuli used by Regan and Cynader (1979) to stimulate a neuron in the visual cortex of the cat that fires when the sides of a rectangle move away from each other (a) or toward each other (b) but does not fire when the two sides move in the same direction (c).

MOVEMENT PERCEPTION AND MULTIPLE APPROACHES TO PERCEPTION

This chapter has contained a little of everything: movement that is real and movement that is illusory; movement perception explained by neural firing and movement perception explained by optic flow; movement that is observed by a passive observer and movement that is created by an observer's movement through the environment.

There are a number of messages in this diversity which are important to acknowledge, because these messages are valid not only for movement perception but for perception in general.

(1) Since "movement perception" is not just one phenomenon, it cannot be explained by a single mechanism. As we have seen, there are at least five different ways to make a spot of light appear to move, and we have also seen that there are at least two different mechanisms responsible for apparent movement. Julian Hochberg (1986) captures this idea of multiple mechanisms with his statement that ". . . one can suggest that there are multiple mechanisms and multiple modes of experience, elicited by different aspects of relative motion in the world, and that each mechanism may have quite different characteristics" (p. 22-35).

(2) Movement perception can be understood at a number of different levels of analysis. We have, throughout this book, emphasized the idea that we can look for mechanisms at the level of stimuli and at the level of physiology. These two levels are well represented in our discussion of movement perception. For example, we can try to explain movement perception by looking for information in the optic array or by looking for information in neural discharges.

Often, researchers who are committed to a particular approach take the view that their approach is the only "correct" way to truly understand perception. This is not, however, the case. A full understanding of perception can be achieved only by combining the knowledge provided by a number of different approaches.

(3) Although movement perception presents a number of different phenomena, each of which can be analyzed at a number of different levels, these different phenomena and levels are not necessarily independent of one another. An example of "cross-talk" between two approaches is provided by D. Regan and Max Cynader's (1979) demonstration that there are neurons in the cat's cortex that respond to stimuli that have properties in common with the optic flow pattern. These neurons respond strongly to a rectangle when the sides are moved either out, as in Figure 8.54(a) or in, as in (b), but do not respond when the sides move in the same direction, as in (c). Since the type of movement this neuron responds to is similar to the movement created by optic flow (see Figures 8.48 and 8.49), these neurons may help signal optic flow information. Here we have an example of the combination of two very different approaches—physiological and ecological—that provides a more complete picture of how optic flow patterns operate than is provided by either approach alone.

The three "messages" described above do not apply only to movement perception. If you were to look back at the previous four chapters, you would see that the qualities of contrast, color, form, and depth all provide examples of multiple mechanisms that have been studied by a number of different approaches. In the next chapter, on the development of perception, we will provide further examples of this by first focusing on psychophysical studies of the perception of human infants and then looking at the results of physiological studies on the development of the visual systems of cats and monkeys.

Summary

1. Our perception of movement serves a number of functions. Movement (a) attracts attention, (b) provides information about an objects' three-dimensional shape, (c) provides information that helps segregate figure from ground, and (d) provides information that enables us to interact actively with the environment.

2. There are five ways to make a spot of light appear to move: (1) make the spot physically move (real movement); (2) flash two lights in different positions on and off one after the other (stroboscopic movement); (3) move a large object that surrounds the spot (induced movement); (4) view the spot in a completely dark room (autokinetic movement); and (5) view the spot after viewing a moving pattern such as a belt of vertical stripes (movement aftereffect).

3. The threshold for real movement depends on the background. Movement is more easily seen if the object moves across a structured background.

4. Perception of velocity depends on the surroundings. The phenomena of velocity transposition and speed constancy indicate that perceived velocity does not depend on retinal velocity.

5. Motion detectors, tuned to respond to movement in a specific direction, provide a mechanism to explain how we perceive the movement of a stimulus across the retina but cannot deal with situations such as tracking a stimulus, in which movement is perceived in the absence of movement across the retina, or situations such as walking through a scene, in which movement is not perceived even though stimuli move across the retina.

6. The corollary discharge provides a mechanism to differentiate between stimulation due to observer movement and stimulus movement, and although the corollary discharge is hypothetical, there is neurophysiological evidence for its existence.

7. Gibson has suggested that we can determine when stimulation is due to movement of the stimulus, movement of the observer, or both by observing whether an object is displaced relative to the background. This idea, however, cannot explain our perception of movement when no structured background is present.

8. Apparent movement is affected by the time interval between two flashes. As time between the flashes is increased, observers first see the lights flash on and off simultaneously (no movement), then see partial movement, optimal movement, and phi movement between the lights, and at long time intervals see the lights flash on and off successively. Apparent movement is also affected by the space between the stimuli and the intensity of the stimuli.

9. The principle of phenomenal identity, first demonstrated by Ternus, shows that complex displays often move together as a whole in apparent movement.

10. Recent research has shown that there are two systems for apparent movement: (1) a high-level system that is slow, is influenced by cognitive factors, involves binocular neurons, and in which form is processed before movement, and (2) a low-level system that is fast, is not influenced by cognitive factors, involves monocular cells, and in which movement is processed before form.

11. Movement is induced in a small object when this object is surrounded by a larger object that is moving. Recently, a neuron has been discovered that may be involved in the perception of induced movement.

12. Autokinetic movement is the illusory movement of a stationary spot of light in dark surroundings. This illusion can be modified by suggestion.

13. The waterfall illusion and the spiral aftereffect are aftereffects of motion. They occur only if the inducing pattern moves on the retina.

14. There is no good explanation for the autokinetic effect, but the action of directionally selective movement detectors can explain the waterfall illusion.

15. Event perception is concerned with the movement

of objects and with how this movement provides information that enhances our ability to perceive these objects.

16. Examples of situations in which movement creates a perception of structure are:

(a) the kinetic depth effect—the three-dimensional structure of a stimulus is perceived from a moving two-dimensional image.

(b) perceiving movement of objects relative to one another—in which our perception of one object's movement is influenced by its proximity to other moving objects. Johansson has explained these effects in terms of perceptual vector analysis.

(c) the perception of biological motion—the movement of lights attached to a person creates structure (a person walking) out of what was initially perceived as a random arrangement of dots.

17. Michotte's demonstration of the launching effect shows that with the correct timing the movement of object A can be perceived to cause the movement of object B.

18. Movement can give human qualities to geometrical objects.

19. One of the most important functions of movement perception is its role in helping us interact with the environment. Lee's "swinging room" experiment shows that vision is important for keeping our balance.

20. The following sources of information have been proposed to help us stay on course and avoid bumping into things:

(a) focus of expansion of the optic flow pattern

(b) optic flow lines

(c) motion parallax

(d) angular expansion

Boxes

1. Damage to an area outside the visual receiving area can cause the loss of ability to perceive movement in depth.

2. Apparent movement can be influenced by an object's shape and by the observer's past experience. Path-guided apparent motion, apparent movement along a curved path, occurs when a dim curved band is flashed during the interval between two apparent movement stimuli.

Study Questions

1. Name four functions of movement perception. (274)
2. Describe five ways to make a spot of light appear to move. Which of these ways involve real movement? (277)
3. What is the evidence that our perception of an object's velocity is influenced by its surroundings? What is velocity transposition? (278)
4. What is the evidence that there is a lack of correspondence between the velocity of the image moving across the retina and perceived velocity? What is speed constancy? (279)
5. Understand the principle behind the movement-detecting circuit in Figure 8.9. (280)
6. Can the direction an object is moving be signaled by the response of a single complex cortical cell that is tuned to respond best to a specific orientation of movement? (280)
7. How might the velocity of movement be signaled by a movement detector? What is a velocity tuning curve? (282)
8. Describe corollary discharge theory. Know how the sensory movement signal and the corollary discharge determine movement perception by interacting at the comparator. (283)
9. Describe four ways to produce a corollary discharge without generating a sensory movement signal. For each way, indicate what is perceived. (283)
10. What are the two explanations that have been proposed to explain why you see movement when you push on your eyeball? Which one is correct? (285)
11. Describe the relationship between Robinson and Wurtz' cell in the monkey superior colliculus and corollary discharge theory. (286)
12. What kind of information in a scene enables us to correctly detect which parts of the scene are moving and which are stationary when (a) an object moves past a stationary observer, (b) an object moves past a stationary observer who is following the object with her eyes, and (c) an observer moves past a stationary object. (287)
13. Describe the stages of stroboscopic movement that occur as we increase the time interval between two flashing lights. (288)
14. Describe Ternus' experiment that illustrates phenomenal identity. (289)
15. What are the two systems for apparent movement? Describe Pantle and Picciano's experiments that illustrate some of the properties of these systems. (291)
16. In what order do the high- and low-level systems

process information about form and movement? How is the random dot kinematogram used to answer this question for the low-level system? (292)

17. Describe the experiment that shows that form processing comes before movement perception for the high-level system. (293)

18. How do cognitive factors influence movement produced by the high- and low-level systems? (293)

19. Cite two examples of induced movement. Describe Duncker's demonstration of induced movement. (295)

20. Describe the neuron which may be involved in the perception of induced movement. (296)

21. What is autokinetic movement? What evidence indicates that our perception of autokinetic movement can be influenced by suggestion? (297)

22. What is the waterfall illusion? How did Anstis and Gregory show that the waterfall illusion depends on the movement of the inducing stimulus across the retina? (299)

23. What electrophysiological evidence indicates that movement detectors may be involved in the waterfall illusion? (299)

24. What is an event? What is the philosophical position that motivates the study of event perception? (300)

25. Describe the following ways that structure can be created by motion: (a) the kinetic depth effect, (b) perceiving objects moving relative to one another,

and (c) biological motion. (301)

26. How does Johansson use perceptual vector analysis to explain how we perceive objects moving relative to one another? (304)

27. How did Michotte illustrate the perceptual of causality? What is the role of timing in the perception of causality? (306)

28. How was it shown that movement can give "life" to inanimate objects? (307)

29. J. J. Gibson suggested that vision is one of the proprioceptive senses. What did he mean by this? (308)

30. Describe Lee's swinging room experiments. What is the relation between the optic flow pattern and our perception of body sway? (308)

31. Describe the following sources of information that help us to stay on course and avoid bumping into objects: (a) focus of expansion of the optic flow pattern, (b) optic flow lines, (c) motion parallax, and (d) angular expansion. (309)

32. Describe how neurons studied by Max Cynader may signal the presence of optic flow. (312)

Boxes

1. Describe the case of the woman who saw the world as "frozen." What does this case demonstrate? (281)

2. Describe how shape, expectation, and guided paths influence our perception of apparent motion. (290)

Glossary

Aftereffect of movement. Illusory movement of a stationary object that occurs after viewing a moving inducing stimulus for 30–60 seconds. The spiral aftereffect and the waterfall illusion are examples of aftereffects of movement. (277)

Angular expansion, rate of. The rate that an object's visual angle expands as it gets closer to an observer. (311)

Apparent movement. An illusion of movement that occurs between two objects that are separated in space, when the objects are flashed on and off one after another, separated by a time interval of about 50–100 msec. (277)

Autokinetic movement. Illusory movement of a stationary spot of light that occurs when the light is viewed in the dark so that the surroundings are not visible. (277)

Autokinetic word technique. A test in which observers are told that a spot of light viewed in a dark room will move to spell letters or words. In actuality, the

light is stationary, but the autokinetic effect combined with the suggestion that letters or words will be perceived causes many observers to perceive a moving spot that spells letters or words. (298)

Biological motion. Motion produced by biological organisms. Most of the experiments on biological motion have used walking humans as stimuli. (305)

Center of movement. The point on a person's body around which all other movements have regular patterns. (306)

Comparator. A structure hypothesized by the corollary discharge theory of movement perception. The corollary discharge signal and the sensory movement signal meet at the comparator. (283)

Corollary discharge. A copy of the signal sent from the motor area of the brain to the eye muscles. The corollary discharge is sent, not to the eye muscles, but to the hypothetical comparator of corollary discharge theory. (283)

Corollary discharge theory. According to the corollary

discharge theory of motion perception, the corollary discharge signal is sent to a structure called the "comparator" where the information in the corollary discharge is compared to the sensory movement signal. If the corollary discharge and the sensory movement signal do not cancel each other, movement is perceived. (283)

Dichoptic presentation. Presenting one stimulus to the left eye and another stimulus to the right eye. (292)

Event. An object undergoing change, such as movement. (300)

Figural selection. When one object is flashed on and off, followed by two or more other objects located at approximately the same distance from the first object, stroboscopic movement will occur to the object most similar in shape to the first object. (290)

Focus of expansion (f.o.e.) The point in the flow pattern caused by observer movement in which there is no expansion. According to Gibson, the focus of expansion always remains centered on the observer's destination. (310)

Group movement. When using Ternus' three-component stimulus, group movement is perceived when dots in positions A, B, and C appear to move as a group to positions B, C, and D. (289)

High-level system. The apparent movement system that causes group movement of dots in the Ternus display. See Table 8.1 for the properties of this system. (292)

Induced movement. Illusory movement of one object that is caused by the movement of another object that is nearby. (277)

Inducing stimulus. A moving stimulus, such as a waterfall or the moving belt of Figure 8.4, that, after being viewed, causes an aftereffect of movement. (299)

Interstimulus interval (ISI). The time interval between two flashes of light in an apparent movement display. (288)

Kinematogram, random dot. See Random dot kinematogram.

Kinetic depth effect. When a stimulus's three-dimensional structure becomes apparent from viewing a two-dimensional image of the stimulus as it rotates. (302)

Launching effect. When one shape moves toward another shape, stops, and then the other shape begins moving immediately or after a brief time interval, it appears that the first shape has "launched" the second shape into motion. (307)

Locomotor flow line. The flow line that passes directly under a moving observer. (310)

Low-level system. A rapid apparent movement system. See Table 8.1 for the properties of this system. (292)

Objectless movement. Apparent movement between two stimuli in which it is difficult to actually perceive an object moving across the space between them. Also called phi movement. (288)

Optic flow pattern. The flow pattern that occurs when an observer moves relative to the environment. Forward movement causes an expanding optic flow pattern, whereas backward movement causes a contracting optic flow pattern. The term *optic flow field* is used by some researchers to refer to this flow pattern. (308)

Optimal movement. Stroboscopic movement that looks identical to real movement. (288)

Partial movement. Stroboscopic movement in which the illusion of movement between two objects is not complete; one object, therefore, appears to move only part way across the space separating the two objects. (288)

Path-guided apparent movement. Apparent movement that occurs along a dim path that is flashed between two apparent movement stimuli. (291)

Perceptual vector analysis. A procedure suggested by Johansson in which the movement of each object in a group is broken down into horizontal and vertical vectors. Identical vectors cancel each other, leaving vectors that indicate how objects appear to move relative to one another. (304)

Phenomenal identity. A stroboscopic movement effect that occurs when a group of lights appears to move as a whole to a new position. (289)

Phi movement. See Objectless movement.

Proprioceptive senses. The senses responsible for sensing the location, orientation, and movement of the body. (308)

Random dot kinematogram. Stimulus that occurs when the left and right parts of a random dot sereogram are flashed, one after the other, to the same eye. (292)

Rate of angular expansion. See Angular expansion, rate of.

Real movement. Physical movement of a stimulus. (277)

Sensory movement signal. The electrical signal generated by movement of an image across the retina. This is one of the signals which plays a role in the corollary discharge theory of movement perception. (283)

Speed constancy. Our perception of an object's speed stays fairly constant even when the object is viewed from different distances which change the speed at which the object's image moves across the retina. (279)

Spiral aftereffect. An aftereffect of movement. Objects that are viewed immediately after viewing a rotating spiral for 30–60 seconds appear to shrink or expand. (299)

Stroboscopic movement. See Apparent movement.

Vectors. Arrows that indicate the separation of angular movement into horizontal and vertical components. (304)

Velocity transposition. When a large object moving across a large space must move faster than a small object moving across a small space in order for the two objects to be perceived to be moving at the same speed. (278)

Velocity tuning curve. A plot of firing rate versus velocity for an individual neuron. The velocity tuning curve indicates the range of stimulus velocities that cause a neuron to fire. (282)

Waterfall illusion. An aftereffect of movement. Objects that are viewed immediately after viewing the downward flow of a waterfall for 30–60 seconds appear to move up. (299)

Perceptual Development

We have seen that the complex network of neurons called the visual system endows us with truly amazing capacities. We can see fine details and keep them in focus when an object moves from close to far away. We see something move and can follow the moving object with our eyes, keeping its image on our foveas so we can see the object clearly. We perceive the depths and sizes of things in the world and are fortunate enough to have a visual system that colors these objects with thousands of different hues. And these objects are not simply meaningless shapes; they are recognizable things to which we attach meanings.

Our visual system does all these things and more, and, as we mentioned at the beginning of this book, it accomplishes these things with such apparent ease that we take perception for granted. But were we born with the abilities to see fine details, follow moving objects, and perceive depths,

forms, and colors? Most 19th-century psychologists would answer this question by saying that infants experience a totally confusing perceptual world, in which they either perceive nothing or make little sense of what they do perceive.

We will see that this view of infant perception underestimates the infant's capacities. The newborn can see much more than the 19th-century psychologists gave them credit for, and their abilities develop rapidly over the first months of life.

In the first part of this chapter we will describe (1) the perceptual capacities of the newborn and (2) how these capacities develop as the infant gets older. In addition to describing when various capacities emerge, we will also consider how both *genetics* and *experience* determine perceptual development. We will consider this issue both in the context of the results of psychophysical studies on infants that are described in the first part of the chapter, and in the context of the results of physiological studies of cats and monkeys that we will describe in the second part of the chapter.

We begin this chapter by describing some of the methods that are used to measure infant perception.

MEASURING INFANT PERCEPTION

Problems in Measuring Infant Perception

Why is it that the early psychologists thought that the infant's perceptual world was either non-existent or very confusing, whereas present-day psychologists think that infants have some perceptual abilities? Did infants learn to see better between 1890 and 1980? Obviously not. What did happen is that psychologists learned how to measure the infants' perceptual abilities that were there all along. Measuring infant perception is a difficult problem that has only recently been solved.

To appreciate the difficulties in measuring infant perception, let's consider the problem of measuring visual acuity, the ability to see details. To do this in an adult, all we have to do is ask the person to read the letters on an eye chart. But what do we do for an infant, who can't understand or respond to instructions?

The first step is to pose the correct question. To understand what we mean by this, let's consider another way of measuring acuity in adults. Instead of an eye chart we could present two fields like the ones in Figure 9.1. One is a black and white grating and the other is a homogeneous grey field that reflects the same amount of light that the grating would reflect if its bars were smeared out evenly over the whole area. To measure acuity, we simply ask our subject to tell us which display has the bars. This is easy when the bars are large, as in the figure, but becomes more difficult as we decrease the size of the bars, until the bars become so fine that they cannot be seen and the grating becomes indiscriminable from the grey card. At this point, our subject would be able to pick the grating with only chance (50 percent) accuracy.

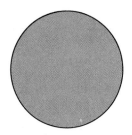

F I G U R E 9. 1 Grating stimulus and grey field of the same average intensity.

The key to our new procedure is that we have changed the question from "What do you see?" to "Can you tell the difference between A and B?" And posing this question to infants enables us to measure their acuity. The trick is to find a way for them to answer the question, and since they can't do this by talking to us, they do it with the behaviors they have available. Two of these behaviors are *looking* and *reaching*.

Looking

Preferential looking. The fact that an infant looks in different directions in response to stimuli in its environment (Figure 9.2) provides a response we can use to determine whether he or she can tell the difference between two stimuli. This response has been used in a technique called **preferential looking (PL),** in which two stimuli are presented to the infant and the experimenter watches the infant's eyes to see whether the infant looks at one of the stimuli more than the other. If the infant does look at one stimulus more than the other, we conclude that he or she can tell the difference between them.

The reason PL works is that infants have **spontaneous looking preferences.** That is, they prefer to look at certain types of stimuli. For measuring acuity we can make use of the fact that infants choose to look at objects with contours, such as the one in Figure 9.3(a) or our grating in Figure 9.1(a), over one that is homogeneous, such as the one in Figure 9.3(b) (Fantz, Ordy, & Udelf, 1962). To measure acuity, we can use the procedure we described for the adult, but instead of verbally

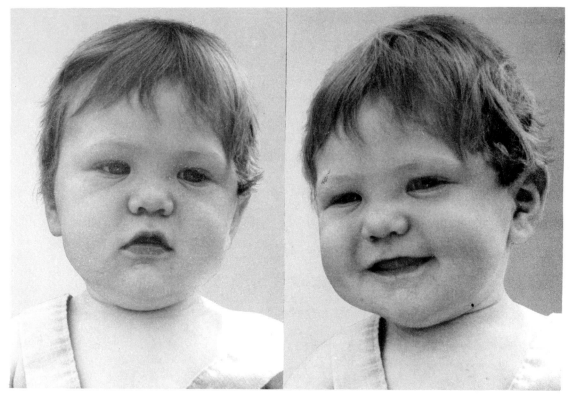

F I G U R E 9. 2 An infant looking in different directions in response to stimuli at different positions in space.

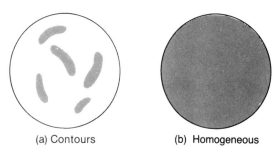

(a) Contours   (b) Homogeneous

F I G U R E 9. 3 Infants will look longer at contours than at a homogeneous field if given a choice.

reporting which stimulus has the bars, the infant responds by moving his or her eyes to the contoured side. As we decrease the size of the bars, it becomes more difficult for the infant to tell the difference between the grating and grey stimuli,

until, when they become indiscriminable, the infant looks at each display equally. We can, therefore, determine the infant's acuity by determining the narrowest stripe width that results in preferential looking. (Figure 9.4)

Habituation. In the example above, we used the infant's spontaneous looking preference for contours to help us measure acuity. But what if the infant shows no spontaneous preference between two stimuli? How, in this case, can we get the infant to tell us whether he or she can tell the difference between these two stimuli?

The solution to this problem makes use of the fact that if infants are given a choice between a familiar stimulus and a novel one, the infant is more likely to look at the novel one (Fagan, 1976; Slater, Morison, & Rose, 1984). With this fact in

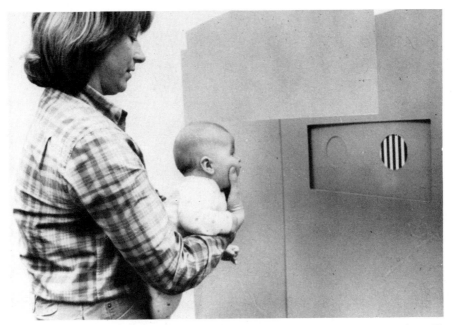

F I G U R E 9. 4 An infant being tested using the preferential looking procedure. The mother holds the infant in front of the display—a grating on the right and a homogeneous grey field with the same average intensity as the grating on the left. An experimenter, who does not know which side the grating is on, on any given trial, looks through a peephole (barely visible between the grating and the grey field) and judges whether the infant is looking to the left or to the right. (Photograph courtesy of Velma Dobson.)

hand, we can now *create* a preference for one of the two stimuli by familiarizing the infant with one stimulus but not with the other. In this technique, which is called **habituation,** one stimulus (A) is presented to the infant repeatedly, and the infant's looking time is measured for each presentation. As the infant becomes more familiar with A, he or she habituates to it, looking less and less on each trial, as shown in Figure 9.5.

F I G U R E 9. 5 In the habituation procedure, the amount of time that the infant looks at a stimulus decreases during habituation. When the stimulus is changed (at the dashed vertical line), the infant either continues to habituate (indicating that the new stimulus appears similar to the old one) or dishabituates (indicating that the new stimulus appears different from the old one).

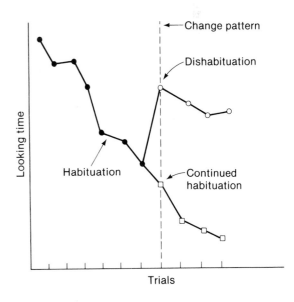

We can see from Figure 9.5 that by the seventh habituation trial the infant is looking much less at A than on the first trial. We now determine whether the infant can tell the difference between A and another stimulus, B, by presenting B on the eighth trial. If the infant can tell the difference between A and B, it will increase its looking time to the presentation of B on trial 8 (open circles), since B is a novel stimulus. If, however, the infant cannot tell the difference between A and B, he will continue to habituate to B (since it will not be perceived as novel), as shown by the open squares in Figure 9.5. This habituation has been observed in newborn infants (Slater, Morison, & Rose, 1984; Granrud, 1987).

Reaching

The response of reaching has been useful in studying depth perception, because infants older than 4 months have a **spontaneous reaching preference** to reach for the nearer of two objects (Granrud, Yonas, & Petterson, 1984; Granrud, 1986).

Visual Scanning

In using the looking response to measure acuity, we measure whether the infant looks at A or at B. We measure **visual scanning** to specify more precisely where an infant is looking or to specify the exact order in which the infant looks at various parts of an object. By photographing the infant's eyes as he looks at an object, we can answer questions such as, "What part of a stimulus does the infant look at?" or "Where does the infant look first?"

Visual Evoked Potential

Our final technique for measuring infant perception is a physiological technique in which electrical signals are recorded by 1/4-inch-diameter disc electrodes placed on the back of the infant's head, over the visual cortex. The infant looks at a grey field, which is briefly replaced by either a field of alternating black-and-white stripes or a checker-

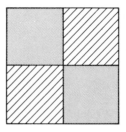

F I G U R E   9. 6   Stimuli used by Adams et al. (1986) to assess the color vision of 5-day-old infants. The stimulus on the left is a checkerboard with two grey squares and two hued squares. The stimulus on the right is a solid grey square with the same size and average intensity as the checkerboard.

board pattern. If the stripes or checks are large enough to be resolved by the visual system, a **visual evoked potential (VEP)** is generated in the visual cortex; however, if the pattern cannot be resolved, no response is generated. Thus, the VEP provides an objective measure of the resolving power of the visual system and is, therefore, well suited for studying the development of visual acuity.

We will now look at research which has used the four methods above to determine an infant's perceptual capacities at birth and to trace the development of these capacities during the first months of life.

COLOR VISION

We describe color vision first, because it is one of the first capacities to appear. Let's look at an experiment by Russell Adams, Daphne Maurer, and Margaret Davis (1986) that shows that newborns have some color vision. They showed 1- to 5-day-old infants either (1) a checkerboard pattern like the one in Figure 9.6, with two grey checks and two hued checks (either red, green, yellow, or blue), or (2) a solid grey square with the same average intensity as the checkerboard. Since infants prefer patterned over unpatterned stimuli, Adams reasoned that if the infants could tell the difference between the colored and grey checks, they would look longer at the checkerboard stimulus than at the grey stimulus. However, infants lacking color vision wouldn't be able to tell the difference between the colored and grey checks, making the checkerboard look solid. These infants would, therefore, look at the checkerboard and solid stimuli equally.

Adams took precautions to be sure that the grey and colored checks appeared equally bright to the infants, so they could perceive a checkerboard *only* if they could perceive the difference in hue between the grey and colored checks (see "Color vision in animals," page 135, for a discussion of this problem).

Adams found that infants looked at the checkerboard stimulus longer than the solid grey stimulus if the colored checks were red, yellow, or green, but showed no looking preference if the colored checks were blue. They concluded, therefore, that 1–5-day-old infants can perceive reds, greens, and yellows, but that the system for the perception of blue is not yet developed (see "What's special about blue?", Box 4.3). Newborns, therefore, can see some colors but are partially color-blind compared to adult, trichromatic observers (see p. 133). Other researchers have found that by 2–3 months of age infants may have color vision that is close to that of a normal adult, although there is still some uncertainty as to when the infant's color vision exactly matches adult color vision (Bornstein, 1976; Werner & Wooten, 1979).

Whether or not infants have "adult" color vision by 3 months of age, the infant's ability to see color at an early age supports the idea that the development of color vision does not depend on experience with the environment but, rather, is genetically programmed. The question of whether a particular perceptual capacity is genetically programmed or is environmentally determined is one that we will be concerned with throughout this chapter. Let's, therefore, discuss this question before proceeding further.

One way to answer this question is to consider the age at which a particular capacity appears. If a capacity is present at birth, as is color vision, we can conclude that it is the result of genetic pro-

gramming. But if a capacity is not present at birth, but takes some time to develop, then the relative roles of genetic programming and environmental experience become less certain. If, for example, a particular capacity doesn't appear until 4 months of age, it is possible that 4 months of environmental experience are required for development *or* that the capacity is genetically programmed to mature at 4 months.

To illustrate this latter possibility let's consider the nonperceptual example of a genetically programmed characteristic that appears late: the appearance of facial hair on teenaged boys. Even though this secondary sex characteristic doesn't appear until many years after birth, no one seriously suggests that the growth of facial hair depends on experience with the environment. Similarly, the appearance of many perceptual abilities may be genetically programmed to appear at various times during the first year of life. For example, in the next section we will see that visual acuity is poor at birth but increases to nearly adult levels during the first 6 months of life. But this developmental course appears to depend more on the maturation of the cone receptors and connections between neurons in the visual cortex than on experience with the environment.

It would, however, be incorrect to conclude that genetic programming is the only thing responsible for the development of perception. There is good evidence, which we will describe in the second half of this chapter, that cats, monkeys, and humans must grow up experiencing a normal visual environment if their visual systems are to develop normally. Normal experience, therefore, is often a prerequisite for normal development, even for capacities that are genetically programmed to mature at a particular time. And we should not overlook the fact that experience with the environment may be essential for the development of some perceptual abilities, especially those that are complex and appear later in life.

Keeping the above considerations in mind, let's now continue our survey of perceptual development by looking at the results of research on the development of visual acuity.

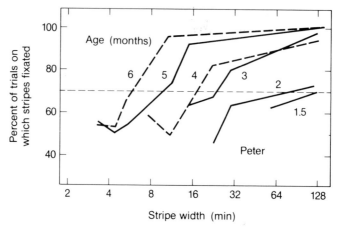

F I G U R E 9. 7 A series of psychophysical functions obtained using the preferential looking technique for a single subject at ages 1.5–6 months. Each of these functions represents the results of many trials in which the infant is presented with a choice between a striped stimulus and a homogeneous grey stimulus. The subject's threshold is defined as the stripe width at which he looks at the striped pattern on 70 percent of the trials. The fact that the functions move to the left as the infant gets older indicates that he can perceive finer and finer stripes. (See Appendix A for a discussion of this type of psychophysical function.) (Teller, Morse, Borton, & Regal, 1974.)

SEEING DETAILS

Visual Acuity

Visual acuity has been measured using the preferential looking technique, as described above, and also by measuring the smallest stripe width that results in a visual evoked potential. Although acuity tends to be slightly higher when measured with the VEP (for reasons we won't go into here), the general result is the same for both methods: Acuity is poor at first (about 20/400–20/600 at 1 month),[*] and then rapidly increases over the first 6 months to just below the adult level of 20/20 (Harris et al., 1976; Salapatek, Bechtold, & Bushness, 1976; Banks & Salapatek, 1978; Dobson & Teller, 1978). This improvement in acuity with age is shown in Figure 9.7, which shows a series of psychophysical functions from one subject derived using the PL technique, and Figure 9.8, which shows acuities for a number of subjects measured with the VEP.

[*] "20/400" means that the infant must view a stimulus from 20 feet to see the same thing a normal adult observer can see from a distance of 400 feet. See Chapter 10, page 372.

The rapid improvement of acuity until the sixth month is followed by a leveling-off period, and full adult acuity is not reached until sometime after 1 year of age.

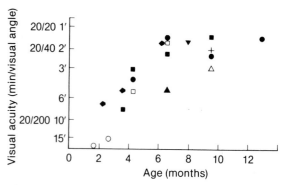

F I G U R E 9. 8 The improvement of acuity over the first year of life, as measured by the visual evoked potential. The numbers on the vertical axis indicate the smallest stripe width in minutes of visual angle that results in a detectable evoked response. Snellen acuity values (see Chapter 10) are also indicated on this axis. The different symbols represent measurements on different subjects. (Pirchio, Spinelli, Fiorentini, & Maffei, 1978.)

Why is acuity so low at birth? One of the major reasons is the undeveloped state of the newborn's retina and visual cortex. Although the peripheral retina, which contains mostly rods, appears adult-like in the newborn, the fovea, which with its closely packed cones is responsible for the adult's high acuity, contains widely spaced and very poorly developed cone receptors (Abramov et al. 1982). The cone density at birth is less than a third the density in the adult, and the cones' outer segments, which contain the light-sensitive visual pigment, are less than one-tenth the length of those in the adult (Yuodelis & Hendrickson, 1986; Hendrickson & Yuodelis, 1984).

On the basis of this alone, we would expect the infant's acuity to be less than an adult's, but, in addition, the visual cortex is also undeveloped at birth. Figure 9.9 shows the state of cortical

development at birth, 3 months, and 6 months (Conel, 1939, 1947, 1951). These pictures indicate that the visual cortex is only partially developed at birth and becomes more developed at 3 and at 6 months. Most significant about these pictures is the large jump in development between birth and about 3 months, just the time when there is a steep rise in acuity.

Contrast Sensitivity

Visual acuity, which is typically measured with high-contrast stimuli, indicates the visual system's capacity to resolve fine details under optimum conditions. Acuity tells us little, however, about how well we can see under lower contrasts and how well we can see forms larger than fine details. As we saw in Chapter 5, we can determine the visual system's

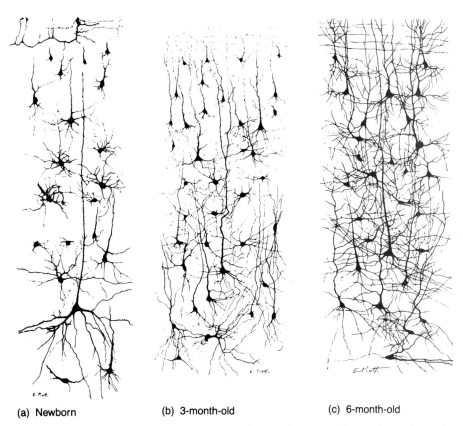

(a) Newborn   **(b) 3-month-old**   **(c) 6-month-old**

F I G U R E 9. 9   Drawings of neurons in the visual cortex of the newborn, 3-month-old, and 6-month-old human infant. (Conel, 1939, 1947, 1951.)

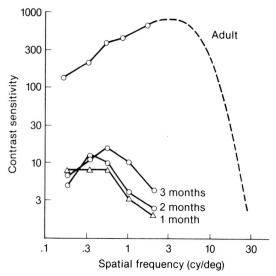

F I G U R E 9. 10 Contrast sensitivity functions for an adult and for infants tested at 1, 2, and 3 months of age.

ability to see forms of different sizes at a wide range of contrasts, by measuring the contrast sensitivity function (CSF). We measure this function in infants using the same PL technique that we use to measure acuity, but we present sine-wave gratings of different contrasts to the infant instead of the high-contrast black-and-white gratings used to measure acuity. (See pp. 161–168 in Chapter 5, for a detailed description of the CSF.)

Contrast sensitivity functions for 1-, 2-, and 3-month-old infants and for adults, all determined with the preferential looking technique, are shown in Figure 9.10 (Salapatek & Banks, 1978; Banks & Salapatek, 1978, 1981; Banks, 1982). Similar results have been obtained by using the visual evoked potential, which also indicates that the contrast sensitivity of 6-month-olds is much better than that of 3-month-olds but is still slightly below adult sensitivity (Pirchio et al., 1978). Other studies show that full adult contrast sensitivity is not achieved until 5–8 years of age (Bradley & Freeman, 1982).

Comparing the infant CSF curves with the adult curve indicates that (1) the infant's contrast sensitivity is lower than the adult's by a factor of 50–100 at all frequencies; (2) the infant's sensitivity is restricted to lower frequencies; and (3) the infant can see little or nothing at frequencies above about 2–3 cycles per degree, the frequencies to which the adult is most sensitive.

What does the young infant's depressed CSF tell us about its visual world? Clearly, the infant is sensitive to only a small fraction of the pattern information available to the adult. At 1 month, the infant can see no fine details and can see only relatively large objects with high contrast. The vision of infants at this age is slightly worse than adult night vision (Pirchio et al., 1978; Fiorentini & Maffei, 1973), a finding consistent with the fact that the undeveloped state of the infants' fovea forces them to see primarily with their rod-dominated peripheral retina.

We should not conclude from the young infant's poor vision, however, that it can see nothing at

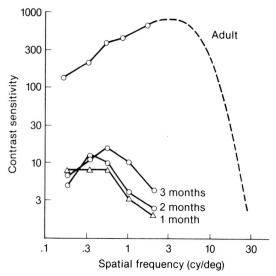
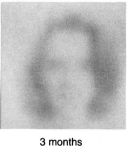

| 1 month | 2 months | 3 months | Adult |

F I G U R E 9. 11 Simulations of what 1-, 2-, and 3-month-old infants see when they look at the woman's face from a distance of about 50 cm. These pictures were obtained by using a mathematical procedure that applies infant contrast sensitivity functions to the photograph on the right, which depicts what an adult perceives. (From Ginsburg, 1983.)

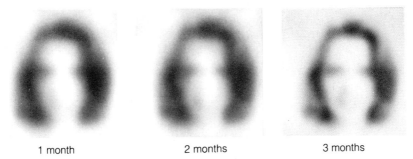

1 month   2 months   3 months

F I G U R E 9. 12   The infant perceptions from Figure 9.10, with the contrast enhanced to make it easier to see the improvement in vision that occurs between 1 and 3 months. (From Ginsburg, 1983.)

all. At very close distances, a young infant can make out some gross features, as indicated in Figure 9.11, which simulates how 1-, 2-, and 3-month-old infants perceive a woman's face from a distance of about 50 cm. At 1 month the contrast is so low that it is difficult to make out facial expressions, but it is possible to see very high-contrast areas, such as the contour between the woman's hairline and forehead. By 3 months, however, the infant's contrast perception has improved so that the perception of facial expressions is possible, and behavioral tests indicate that by 3–4 months, infants can tell the difference between a face that looks happy and faces surprised, angry, or neutral (LaBarbera, Izard, Vietze, & Parisi, 1976; Young-Browne et al., 1977). In Figure 9.12 the contrast is enhanced to show the improvement between 1 and 3 months.

The improvement in the perception of details and contrast, which begins almost as soon as the infant is born and brings the infant to nearly adult levels by 6 months of age, makes possible the development of accommodation, the mechanism that enables the infant to adjust its focus to see near and far objects.

Accommodation

We saw in Chapter 3 that adults have the ability to accommodate—to change the shape of their lens—so they can see both near and far objects clearly. This capacity, however, is poorly developed at birth, and for good reason: The purpose of accommodation is to bring out-of-focus vision into focus, but if everything is out of focus, accommodation clearly can't work. But as the infant's world becomes more and more detailed, the need for accommodation, and the possibility that it might work, increases. In fact, Martin Banks (1980) has shown that infants as young as 1 month old have the ability to accommodate slightly and that by 3 months they can accommodate nearly as well as adults (also see Howland, Boothe, & Kiorpes, 1981).

Banks measured infants' ability to accommodate by using an instrument called a retinoscope (see Chapter 10, p. 373). This device, which enables an examiner to determine how well a person's eye focuses light, was used to determine the infant's ability to focus on a high-contrast checkerboard pattern placed at different distances from its eye. Banks found that by 3 months of age, infants will change their focus as the checkerboard is moved to different distances, in much the same way as adults. Thus, infants as young as 3 months of age have the capacity to accommodate to very high-contrast targets. Infants may not be able to use this capacity to accommodate to low-contrast targets they cannot see; however, as their vision becomes clearer, their capacity to accommodate enables them to bring more and more of their visual world into focus at different distances.

DEPTH PERCEPTION

What enables us to see in depth? In Chapter 7 we saw that depth is determined by a number of different sources of information or "cues." Research

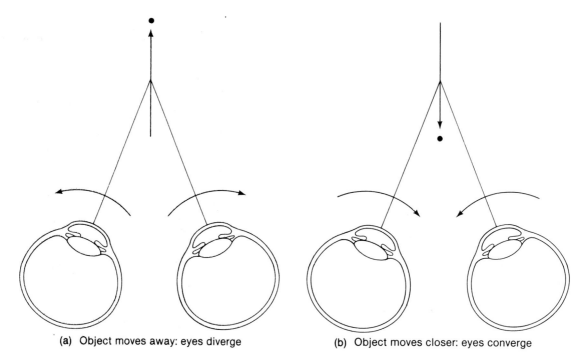

(a) Object moves away: eyes diverge   (b) Object moves closer: eyes converge

F I G U R E 9. 13   If an infant is fixating on an object that is moving, its eyes (a) diverge (rotate outward) as it follows an object that is moving away and (b) converge (rotate inward) as it follows an object that is moving closer.

on the development of depth perception has studied each of these cues in isolation and has found that different cues become operative at different times. We will begin by considering binocular disparity, one of the first sources of depth information to develop.

Binocular Disparity

We saw in Chapter 7 that we see the world with two eyes that have different points of view, about 8 cm apart. This double view of the world provides binocular disparity information that enables us to see the world in depth (review binocular disparity on pp. 239–245). Before binocular disparity can work, however, both eyes must be able to binocularly fixate—to direct their foveas to exactly the same place. At birth the capacity to binocularly fixate is present in only a crude form (Slater & Findlay, 1975), so binocular fixation is imprecise, especially for objects that are changing in depth.

To determine when precise **binocular fixation**

develops, Richard Aslin (1977) did a simple experiment. He filmed infants' eyes while moving a target between a near point, 12 cm away, and a far point, 57 cm away. If the infant directs both eyes at the target, then the eyes should diverge (rotate outward) as the target moves away, as shown in Figure 9.13(a) and should converge (rotate inward) as the target moves closer, as shown in Figure 9.13(b). Aslin's films indicate that while some divergence and convergence does occur in 1- and 2-month-old infants, these eye movements do not reliably point both eyes at the target until about 3 months of age.

Although binocular fixation may be present by 3 months of age, this does not guarantee that the infant can use the resulting disparity information to perceive depth. To determine when infants can use this information to perceive depth, Robert Fox and coworkers (Fox, Aslin, Shea, & Dumais, 1980; Shea, Fox, Aslin, & Dumais, 1980) presented random dot stereograms to infants ranging in age from $2\frac{1}{2}$ to 6 months. Before describing Fox's experiment, let's briefly review the idea behind stereograms (for a more detailed description of stereograms, see p. 240–241 in Chapter 7).

A stereogram consists of two pictures like those in Figure 7.14, one made from the point of view of each eye. When we use a special viewer to present the left picture to the left eye and the right picture to the right eye, the disparity information provided by the different views results in a striking perception of depth. As we saw in Chapter 7, however, the depth we see in stereograms as in Figure 7.14 may be due not only to the disparity between the two pictures but also to monocular depth cues such as overlap, perspective convergence, and relative height. One way to eliminate these monocular cues is to use random dot stereograms, like the ones in Box 7.2 (see p. 244 for a description of how random dot stereograms work).

The beauty of a random dot stereogram is that the disparity information in the stereogram results

in a perception of depth only if (1) the stereogram is observed with a viewer that presents one picture to the left eye and the other picture to the right eye and (2) the observer's visual system can convert this disparity information into an impression of depth. Thus, if we present a random dot stereogram to an infant whose visual system is not yet able to use disparity information, all he or she will see is a random collection of dots.

In Fox's experiment, a child wearing special viewing glasses was seated in its mother's lap in front of a television screen as shown in Figure 9.14. The child viewed a random dot stereogram that looked, to an observer sensitive to disparity information, like a rectangle-in-depth, moving either to the left or to the right. Fox's premise was that an infant sensitive to disparity will move his or her eyes to follow the moving rectangle. He found that infants younger than about 3 months of age would not follow the rectangle, but infants between $3\frac{1}{2}$

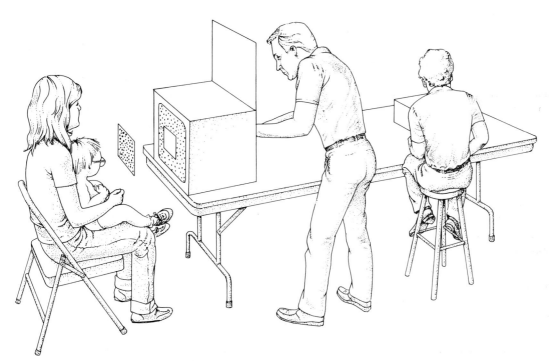

F I G U R E 9. 14 The setup used by Fox, Aslin, Shea, & Dumais (1980) to test infants' ability to use binocular disparity information. If the infant can use disparity information to see depth, he or she sees a rectangle moving back and forth in front of the screen.

B O X   9. 1   /   *Sensory-Motor Coordination*

Although you may often sit in one place to watch a film, a television program, or even a lecture on perception, much of your visual experience occurs as you interact more actively with your environment. This active interaction with the environment—which ranges from simple actions, such as turning the pages in this book, to more complex actions, such as figure skating or gymnastics—involves **sensory-motor coordination.** Although many of your day-to-day tasks may seem easy to you now, you originally had to learn to coordinate your movements with your perceptions to do even the simplest things. How did you develop this ability?

Richard Held (1965) has suggested that a person must actively interact with the environment to develop sensory-motor coordination. To support this idea, Held did an experiment in which he disrupted sensory-motor coordination by having a person wear prism goggles that shift perception to the left or right. A person wearing the goggles often has trouble picking up things and often bumps into things, because they are not where they appear to be. Eventually, however, the person adapts to the displaced vision and can function while wearing the goggles.

That a person can adapt to displaced vision is nothing new—psychologists have been putting prism goggles on people (and on themselves) since before the turn of the century—but Held added something new. He had one person wear the goggles while walking along an outdoor path and another person wear them while being pushed in a wheelchair along the same path. Thus, both people were exposed to similar visual stimulation, but the walking person was active whereas the other was passive. After this trip along the path, Held tested the extent of adaptation to the goggles and found that the active person adapted to the goggles but the passive person did not. This result supports the idea that active or **self-produced movement** is necessary to adapt to the displaced vision caused by prism goggles.

To show that self-produced movement is important not only for the sensory-motor coordination involved in an adult's adaptation to prism goggles but also for a newborn's development of sensory-motor coordination, Held and Alan Hein (1963) did an experiment in which two dark-reared kittens were given their first visual experience in the "kitten carousel" shown in the figure. As the active kitten walked, it transported the passive kitten riding in the gondola. Just as in the goggle experiment described above, both kittens received the same visual stimulation, but this stimulation was caused by self-produced movement only for the active kitten. As predicted, the active kitten developed good sensory-motor coordination, as indicated by its ability to blink at an approaching object, and to put out its paws to ward off collision when carried downward toward a surface; the passive kitten, however, had poor sensory-motor coordination, as indicated by its inability to do these things.

---

and 6 months of age would follow it. He therefore concluded that the ability to use disparity information to perceive depth emerges sometime between $3\frac{1}{2}$ and 6 months of age.

Richard Held and his group (Held, Birch, & Gwiazala, 1980) have also shown that infants develop the ability to use disparity information by about $3\frac{1}{2}$ months of age. He did this by measuring infants' **stereoacuity,** the ability to resolve differences in disparity. The question Held asked was, "What is the smallest disparity that results in an infant's perception of depth?" (Remember, from Chapter 7, that when images fall on corresponding points on the two eyes the disparity is zero, and

Thus, to develop sensory-motor coordination, it is necessary not only to be exposed to changing visual stimulation but also to cause the scene to change by means of self-produced movement.

It is this interaction between changes in visual stimulation and the movement which produces these changes that helps you to coordinate what you do with what you see.

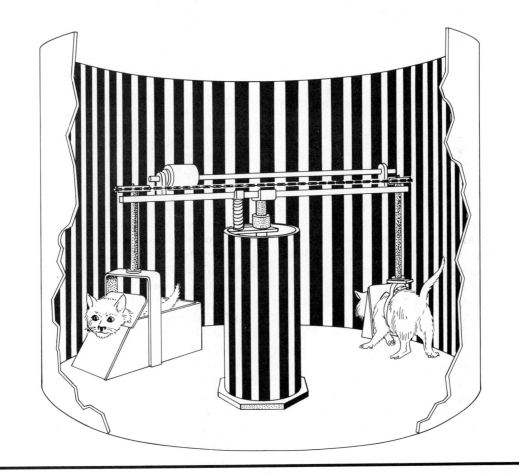

the more one of the images deviates from being on corresponding points, the greater the disparity.)

Held measured the infants' stereoacuity by having them view the display shown in Figure 9.15. One stimulus in this display is a flat picture of three black bars and the other is a stereogram, which when viewed through special glasses, appears three-

dimensional to adults. This type of stereogram can create smaller differences in disparity than the random dot stereogram and therefore provides a more sensitive measure of the infants' abilities.

Held used the preferential looking technique. The infants, who sat on their mother's laps and wore special viewing glasses, saw the bar stereo-

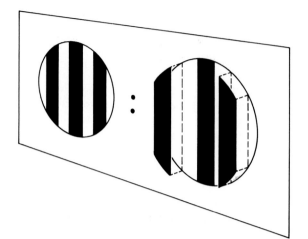

F I G U R E 9. 15 Stimuli used by Held, Birch, & Gwiazda (1980) to test stereoacuity. The pattern on the left is a two-dimensional grating. The one on the right is a stereogram which looks three-dimensional when viewed through special glasses. This three-dimensional perception occurs, however, only if the subject can perceive depth based on disparity.

gram on one side of the display and the flat bar pattern on the other side. Infants, if given a choice, prefer a three-dimensional stimulus to a two-dimensional one (Fantz, 1965), so if they perceive depth based on disparity, they look preferentially at the stereogram.

Held's results agreed with Fox's—by about $3\frac{1}{2}$ months of age infants are able to use disparity to perceive depth. By showing the infants stereograms with a number of different disparities, Held was able to trace the development of the ability to use disparity. At $3\frac{1}{2}$ months infants are able to detect disparities of about 1 degree of visual angle, and their stereoacuity increases rapidly to less than 1 minute of visual angle over the next month. (1 minute of visual angle = 1/60 degree). Thus, Held showed that once the ability to detect disparity appears, infants show a rapid increase in stereoacuity to fairly good levels by between 4 and 5 months of age. (Full development to adult levels, which can be as high as a few *seconds* of visual angle [1 second = 1/60 minute], does not occur until later.)

Pictorial Cues

In addition to the binocular cue of disparity, there are a number of cues such as shading, interposition, texture gradients, linear perspective, familiar size, relative size and height in the field of view. These cues, which we called pictorial cues in Chapter 7 because they can be depicted in pictures, develop after binocular disparity. The evidence for this is provided by experiments done by Albert Yonas, Carl Granrud, and their colleagues, who have shown that infants begin to use interposition, familiar size, relative size, shading, linear perspective, and texture gradients sometime between 5 and 7 months of age (Yonas, Petterson, & Granrud, 1982; Granrud & Yonas, 1984; Granrud, Yonas, & Opland, 1985; Granrud, Haake, & Yonas, 1985; Yonas, Granrud, Arterbery & Hanson, 1986). Let's look at two of their experiments, one for interposition (Granrud & Yonas, 1984) and one for familiar size (Granrud, Haake, & Yonas, 1985).

Infants' ability to perceive depth from interposition was tested by showing them two-dimensional cardboard cutouts of the displays shown in Figure 9.16. Viewing was monocular, because binocular viewing would indicate that the displays were flat, thereby lowering the chances that the infant would respond to the pictorially induced depth. The display in (a) contains the depth cue of interposition, whereas the ones in (b) and (c) do not, so if infants are sensitive to interposition they should reach for (a) more than for (b) or (c). This was the result for 7-month-olds but not for 5-month-olds. Thus, the ability to perceive depth based on interposition appears sometime between 5 and 7 months.

A two-part experiment tested for familiar size. In the *familiarization phase*, 7-month-old infants played with a pair of wooden objects for 10 minutes. One of these objects was large and one was small, as shown in Figure 9.17(a) and (b). In the *test phase*, the two objects were presented at the same distance from the infant (Figure 9.17c). The prediction in this experiment is that infants sensitive to familiar size would perceive the right object in 9.17(c) to be closer after playing with pair (a)

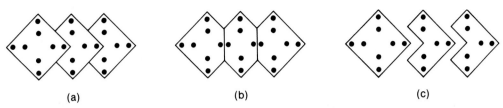

F I G U R E 9. 16 Stimuli for Granrud and Yonas's (1984) interposition experiment. See text for details.

or perceive the left object in Figure 9.17(c) as closer after playing with pair (b).

The 7-month-olds reached for the "apparently nearer" stimulus predicted by familiar size when they viewed the test stimuli monocularly, but didn't reach for this stimulus when viewing the stimuli binocularly. This lack of familiar size response in the binocular condition is exactly what we would expect, since binocular disparity indicates that the two objects are, in fact, at the same distance. But when this depth information is eliminated by monocular viewing, familiar size creates an impression of depth, just as it does for adults (see page 233). The 5-month-olds, who were only tested in the monocular condition, did not reach more for the "apparently nearer" object in the test phase, indicating that the infants were not responsive to familiar size. Thus, just as for interposition, the ability to use familiar size to perceive depth develops sometime between 5 and 7 months.

This experiment is interesting not only because it indicates when the ability to use familiar size develops, but also because the infant's response in

the test phase does not depend on information present in the optic array (since there is no information to indicate depth). Rather, it depends on his ability to remember the sizes of the objects he played with in the familiarization phase. The 7-month-old infants' depth response is, therefore, a "construction" based on both the information in the optic array *and* the infants' memory for the sizes of the objects.

FORM PERCEPTION

We have seen that during the first 6 months of life, infants develop good detail vision. But does this mean that they can perceive forms? Many experiments have shown that newborns and older infants look at some forms more than others. For example, when given a choice between curved and straight contours, newborns look more at the curved contours (Fantz, Fagan, & Miranda, 1975). While this result tells us that newborns can tell the difference between two different forms, it doesn't tell us what

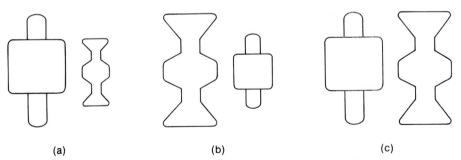

F I G U R E 9. 17 Stimuli for Granrud, Haake, and Yonas's (1985) familiar size experiment. See text for details.

Subject number   6   25   17   20   15

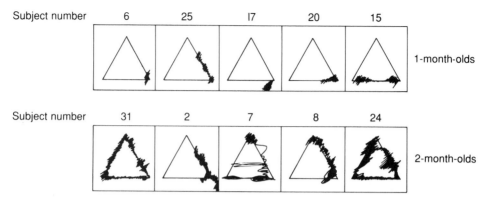

1-month-olds

Subject number   31   2   7   8   24

2-month-olds

F I G U R E 9. 18   How 1- and 2-month-olds look at triangles. (Salapatek, 1975.)

they are perceiving. Are the infants perceiving in terms of a form's individual parts or in terms of the whole form? The available evidence indicates that early perception is in terms of parts, and only later are whole forms perceived.

One way to investigate the problem of the perception of parts versus wholes is to measure the visual scanning of infants as they view patterns. Philip Salapatek (1975) measured the visual scanning of 1- and 2-month-old infants by filming the infants' eyes as they looked at triangles and other geometrical objects. His results, shown in Figure 9.18, indicate that 1-month-old infants tend to look at a single vertex of a triangle, whereas 2-month-old infants are more likely to scan more of the triangle. A similar situation occurs when infants look at a face or a picture of a face. The 1-month-old infants either don't look at the face at all or look at only a limited portion of it, usually near the perimeter; 2-month-olds, however, look at the face more often, and when they do they scan more broadly and often look at the details inside the face (Maurer & Salapatek, 1976). This finding fits the observations made by many parents that babies don't look into their eyes until about 2 months of age. Thus, at 2 months, infants begin to scan patterns more as a whole and begin to pay attention to things inside the pattern.

This more extensive scanning at about 2 months, however, does not tell us whether the infant *perceives* the form as a whole. The infant may be

fixating the individual parts of a form, without combining or integrating them into the perception of a whole form. One approach to investigating this problem is to present two forms that have the same parts but are arranged differently. Such experiments show that newborns look equally often at two pictures of faces, one of which has normally arranged features and the other of which has its features reorganized so that the eyes, nose, mouth, and other parts of the face are not in their usual positions (Figure 9.19). Four-month-old infants, however, prefer to look at the normal faces (Fantz et al., 1975; Kagan, Henker, Hen-Tov, Levine, & Lewis, 1966). This result suggests that the older

F I G U R E 9. 19   Stimuli from Fantz's experiments, in which he showed that newborns spend about the same amount of time looking at the normally arranged face and the scrambled face, but that 4-month-olds prefer to look at the normally arranged face. (Also see Maurer, 1985.)

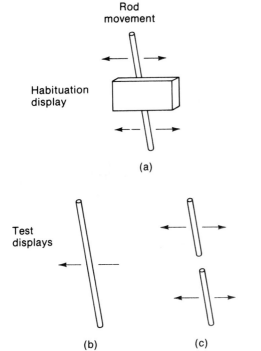

Rod movement

Habituation display

(a)

Test displays

(b)   (c)

F I G U R E   9. 20   Stimuli for the Kellman and Spelke (1983) experiment.

infants may be perceiving the faces as wholes rather than as individual features (also see Maurer, 1985).

Increasing age brings more advanced capacities for form perception. For example, Philip Kellman and Elizabeth Spelke (1983) used a habituation procedure to show that infants perceive objects as continuing behind an occluding object. To do this, they habituated 4-month-old infants to a rod moving back and forth behind a block (Figure 9.20a). After presenting the display until the infants' looking time had decreased to a low level, the test stimuli shown in Figure 9.20(b) and (c) were presented.

If the infant had perceived the display in (a) as a long rod moving behind the block, then we would expect that in the habituation trials he would look longer at the two rods in (c). (Remember that in the habituation procedure, it is assumed that the infant will look longer at a *novel* stimulus than at a familiar one. Thus, if the infant saw the rod

as continuing behind the block, the two short rods would be the novel stimulus.) This is, in fact, what happened, leading Kellman and Spelke to conclude that 4-month-old infants perceive the partly occluded stick as continuing behind the block. This result does not occur however, if the rod is stationary. At 4 months, therefore, an infant can perceive one object as extending behind another, but only if the two parts of the object are moving together.

Four-month-old infants can also perceive the biological motion created by a walking person. In Chapter 8 we saw that people can easily identify as a person the patterns of movement created by 12 lights attached to a person walking in a dark room. Robert Fox and Cynthia McDaniel (1982) used the PL technique to determine whether infants are also capable of recognizing this biological motion. One videotape of the lights attached to a running person was shown on one screen and another videotape of randomly moving lights was shown on the other screen. When placed in front of the two screens, 2-month-old infants showed no preference, looking at both screens equally. But 4- and 6-month-old infants looked at the biological motion tape about 70 percent of the time. Thus, by 4 months infants can tell the difference between these two types of motion and prefer the biological motion. Since the ability to perceive biological motion occurs at a very young age, Fox and McDaniel hypothesize that this ability is determined genetically rather than being slowly acquired due to experience (also see Berthenal, Proffitt, Spetner, & Thomas, 1985).

CONSTANCY: INVARIANCE ACROSS TRANSFORMATIONS

As we saw when we discussed size and shape constancy in Chapter 7, our perception of an object's size and shape remains fairly constant in the face of large changes in the retinal image. Thus, we perceive an objects' size as constant as we view it from different distances and we perceive its shape as constant as we view it from different angles.

Size constancy has been reported in infants by 3 months of age (Granrud, Artenbery, & Yonas,

(a)   (b)

F I G U R E 9. 21 Some of the stimuli used in Fagan's (1976) experiment in which he showed that after seeing one pose of a face, 7-month-old infants can recognize this face when it is seen in a different pose.

1985) and 3-month-old infants perceive the shape of a square as remaining constant even when viewed from different angles (Caron, Caron, & Carlson, 1979; Cook & Birch, 1984). By the age of 5–6 months, infants can generalize from one pose of a

face to another. Joseph Fagan (1976) habituated 7-month-old infants to the training face in Figure 9.21(a), by presenting it for 40 seconds. When he then presented the test face in a different pose and paired it with a new face, as shown in Figure 9.21(b), the infants indicated that they recognized the test face, by looking more at the new face.

That infants can recognize different views of the same face indicates that they can perceive *invariance across transformations.* That is, even though the face is transformed by changing its position, things such as the relationships between features, the eyes, nose, and mouth, remain constant, or invariant, and the infant apparently can recognize these invariant relationships.

The above descriptions of the infant's ability to perceive forms indicates that the infant's perception comes a long way during the first 6 months of life. In fact, 6–8-month-old infants not only can recognize the invariant features of faces but can recognize the similarities between a sequence of light flashes and a similarly timed sequence of tones (Allen, Walker, Symonds, & Marcell, 1977), and can identify the shape of a visually presented object they had previously felt (Bryant, Jones, Claxton, & Perkins, 1972).

As psychologists continue to study infant perception, they are uncovering more and more capacities at earlier ages. Looking at the results we have presented, which are summarized in Figure 9.22, we can see that by the time an infant is 7 months old it has acquired most of its basic perceptual abilities. This does not mean, however, that perceptual development is over. As the child

Age in months	
7	
6	Pictorial depth cues
5	
4	Biological motion / Binocular disparity
3	Color vision: trichromatic (?) / Accommodation / Reliable binocular fixation
2	Scanning whole figures
1	
0	Color vision (dichromatic)

Acuity: 20/40

Moving object extends behind occluding object

Size and shape constancy

Acuity: 20/500

F I G U R E 9. 22 Approximate ages at which various perceptual capacities appear.

gets older, important cognitive abilities emerge that enrich the basic perceptual abilities that appear during the first year. For example, even though a 3–6-month-old infant may be able to tell the difference between lights in biological motion and lights in nonbiological motion, a true understanding of the meaning of these moving lights may take years to develop.

GENETIC PROGRAMMING OR ENVIRONMENTAL INFLUENCE?

Now that we have described the course of perceptual development in human infants, we are ready to take a more physiological approach to our question, "What are the roles of *genetics* and *experience* in determining perceptual development?" The two extreme answers to this question are:

1. The entire process of perceptual development is genetically programmed, so that whatever the environmental conditions, development will run its course.
2. The entire process of perceptual development depends on experience, so that development depends on the environmental conditions.

These two possibilities represent the extremes of what has been called the nature versus nurture debate, and, as is usually the case when dealing with extremes, the correct answer lies somewhere between these two. As Richard Aslin (1981) states in a paper reviewing research on perceptual development, "There can be little doubt that development is determined by a combination of genetic and environmental factors operating in a complex manner." Much of the evidence that led Aslin to this conclusion has come (1) from experiments which look at the way single neurons in the cortex of newborn cats and monkeys respond, (2) from **deprivation experiments** in which the effect of the environment is determined by depriving animals of contact with the environment, and (3) from **selective rearing** experiments in which animals are reared in environments that differ from their normal environment. We will now consider each of these lines of evidence, in turn.

CORTICAL CELLS IN NEWBORN CATS AND MONKEYS

We know that the human infant's visual system is not totally developed at birth. However, newborn cats and monkeys (who have been the main subjects of deprivation experiments) have more highly developed visual systems than the newborn human. To determine the state of the visual systems of newborn cats and monkeys, responses of neurons in the cortex are measured. The first study of this kind was done by Hubel and Wiesel, on kittens in 1963. (Remember from Chapters 2 and 3 that Hubel and Wiesel were also the first investigators to determine the characteristics of simple, complex, and hypercomplex cells in the cat's cortex.) To be sure that their kittens had no visual experience before they were tested, Hubel and Wiesel either tested them before they opened their eyes or put occluders (which eliminated all patterned stimuli) on the kittens' eyes as soon as they opened, at 8–10 days, and tested the kittens shortly afterward.

Hubel and Wiesel found that 8–16-day-old kittens, who have never seen patterned light, have receptive fields very similar to those of adult cats. That is, they found cells in the cortex of these visually inexperienced kittens that correspond to the simple, complex, and hypercomplex cells seen in the adult. Furthermore, they found that most cells, as in the adult, respond to stimulation of both eyes, and they also found evidence for columns of cells with identical receptive field orientations. The major difference between the cells of a kitten and an adult cat is that the response of the kitten's cells is more sluggish.

Hubel and Wiesel's report of adult-like *orientation preferences* in the newborn proved to be controversial; although some later experiments supported their results (Sherk & Stryker, 1976; Wiesel and Hubel, 1974), others questioned the idea that development is so adult-like at such an early age (Blakemore & Van Sluyters, 1975; Pettigrew, 1974; Buissert & Imbert, 1976; Imbert & Bonds, 1979). The general consensus of many experts at this point is that the cat's neurons have adult-like orientation preferences by 6 weeks of age (Mitchell & Timney, 1984).

The results regarding the **binocularity** of cells in the newborn kitten are more clear. There is general agreement with Hubel and Wiesel's finding that most cells in the newborn respond to stimulation of both eyes. But just because binocular cells are present does not mean that the newborn kitten can use binocular disparity to perceive depth. For the visual system to make use of binocular disparity to perceive depth, the eyes must be precisely aligned so that small disparities between images that fall on the two retinas can be detected. Pettigrew (1974) finds that although most cells in the newborn kitten can respond to stimulation of both eyes, the eyes are poorly aligned. Not until about 5 weeks of age are the eyes aligned so that the kitten can make use of binocular disparity information.

While the early development of the cat's visual system argues for a genetic component of perceptual development, we can also show that changing the environment has a large effect on both the response of neurons in the visual cortex and on the perception controlled by these neurons. We will first describe how depriving cats and monkeys of light affects acuity and binocularity.

THE EFFECTS OF DEPRIVATION

In describing these deprivation experiments, we will see not only that changing the environment affects the visual system but that the effects that do occur depend on *when* the environment is changed. We will begin by describing how rearing an animal in the dark or in diffuse light affects its acuity.

Deprivation and Acuity

If a kitten or monkey is deprived of all vision by being reared in the dark, or is deprived of pattern vision by occluding both eyes, acuity decreases. The longer the deprivation, the greater the decrease

in acuity, and the less the chance of recovery once the animal is exposed to the light.

More drastic effects occur if the animal is deprived of vision by occluding only one eye, a procedure called **monocular deprivation.** Cats and monkeys that have been monocularly deprived become blind in the deprived eye and recover much less than if deprived of light in both eyes. For example, monkeys reared in the dark for the first 3–6 months of life can recover substantial acuity within a month (Regal et al.,1976), but if deprived of vision in one eye for a similar period, may never recover vision in the deprived eye (von Noorden, 1973).

These large reductions in acuity can be linked to the fact that deprivation causes visual neurons to become unresponsive. For example, monocular deprivation of a kitten from birth until 8–14 weeks causes most of its cortical neurons to become unresponsive to stimulation of the deprived eye. An important consequence of this decrease in responsiveness is a decrease in the animal's capacity for binocular vision. Although about 80 percent of cells in the visual cortex of the adult cat respond to stimulation of both eyes, none of the cells of monocularly reared kittens respond to stimulation of both eyes. This finding has led to much research on how deprivation affects binocularity.

Deprivation and Binocularity

Development of normal binocularity depends on the presence of coordinated inputs to the left and right eyes. Researchers have used two techniques—(1) monocular deprivation and (2) creating misalignment of the images in the two eyes—to determine the effects of disrupting this input. We will consider each of these techniques in turn.

Monocular rearing. The effect of monocular rearing on binocularity is illustrated most clearly by **ocular dominance histograms** such as those in Figure 9.23. These histograms are determined by recording from a large number of cells and then rating each cell's ability to respond to stimulation of both the **contralateral eye** (the eye on the oppo-

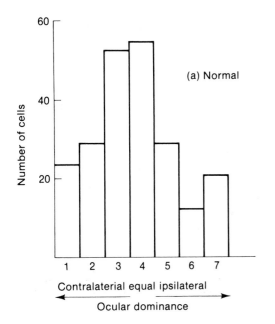

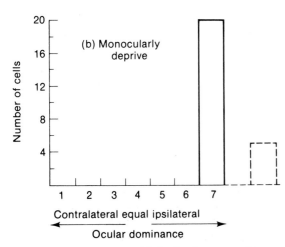

site side of the head from the cell) and the **ipsilateral eye** (the eye on the same side as the cell). Each cell is placed in one of the following categories according to the degree of **ocular dominance:**

Category	Description
1	Cell responds only to stimulation of the contralateral eye. Thus, if the cell is in the right hemisphere, it responds only to stimulation of the left eye.
2	Cell responds much more to stimulation of the contralateral eye than to stimulation of the ipsilateral eye.
3	Cell responds slightly more to stimulation of the contralateral eye.
4	Cell responds equally to stimulation of each eye.
5	Cell responds slightly more to stimulation of the ipsilateral eye.
6	Cell responds much more to stimulation of the ipsilateral eye.
7	Cell responds only to stimulation of the ipsilateral eye.

F I G U R E 9. 23 (a) Ocular dominance histogram for 223 cells recorded from the visual cortex of adult cats. Note that there are a large number of cells that respond to stimulation of both eyes. (b) Ocular dominance histogram of 25 cells recorded from the visual cortex of a 2½ -month-old kitten that was reared with its right eye occluded until the time of the experiment. The dashed bar on the right indicates that five cells did not respond to stimulation of either eye. The solid bar indicates that all 20 cells that did respond to stimulation responded only to the eye which was opened during rearing. (Wiesel & Hubel, 1963.)

The histograms in Figure 9.23 show the striking effect of monocular deprivation on the way the kitten's cells respond to stimulation of each eye. Whereas most of the cells in the normal cat respond to both eyes, and therefore fall in categories 2–6 of the histogram, all the cells in the deprived kitten respond only to the undeprived eye and are placed in category 7.

Hubel and Wiesel found that the longer kittens are monocularly deprived from birth, the greater the abnormalities in their ocular dominance histograms; however, if we postpone the deprivation until the kittens become adult cats, even long periods of monocular deprivation have no effect on their ocular dominance histograms. This finding led Hubel

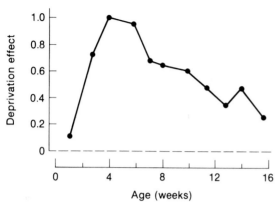

FIGURE 9. 24 Profile of the sensitive period for monocular deprivation in kittens. "Deprivation effect" (vertical axis) indicates how severely 10–12 days of monocular deprivation imposed at the ages on the horizontal axis disrupted binocularity. This curve indicates that monocular deprivation causes substantial effects as long as 4 months after birth. Other measurements indicate that deprivation effects continue to occur up until about 6 months of age. (From Olson & Freeman, 1980.)

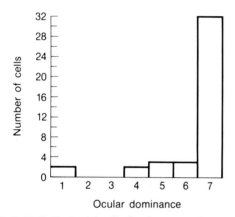

FIGURE 9. 25 Ocular dominance histogram of a kitten that had one eye occluded for 24 hours following four weeks of normal vision. (Olson & Freeman, 1975.)

and Wiesel to propose a **sensitive period,** early in the kitten's life, during which monocular deprivation has a large effect; once this period is past, however, deprivation has little effect.

To investigate this idea, Hubel and Wiesel (1970a) monocularly deprived kittens at various times after birth. They found that deprivation for

only 3 days between the fourth and fifth week causes a large change in the ocular dominance histograms. But when deprivation was started past about the eighth week, smaller effects were observed, until even long periods of deprivation at 4 months caused no effect. Hubel and Wiesel concluded that the sensitive period for susceptibility to monocular deprivation begins in the fourth week and extends to about 4 months of age. Later research, using long periods of deprivation and more sensitive tests of brain function, has shown that monocular deprivation can cause effects as late as the sixth month in cats (Figure 9.24) (Olson & Freeman, 1980; Cynader, Timney, & Mitchell, 1980; Jones, Spear, & Tong, 1984).

Deprivation does not have to be long to cause large effects. If carried out during the sensitive period, extremely brief deprivations can cause large effects on the ocular dominance of cells in the kitten's cortex. For example, C. R. Olson and Ralph Freeman (1975) found that occluding one eye of a 4-week-old kitten, for only *one day,* causes the large effect on the ocular dominance histogram shown in Figure 9.25.

The large effects of monocular deprivation on the kitten's visual system led researchers to also investigate how binocularity is influenced by misalignment of the images in the two eyes.

Image misalignment and binocularity. Misalignment of the images in the two eyes can be accomplished by either cutting the eye muscles or by fitting the animal with a helmet that contains small optical prisms. Cutting the eye muscles causes the eyes to become misaligned, as shown in Figure 9.26, and optical prisms, shown in Figure 9.27, change the direction of the light entering the eyes. Both procedures cause effects similar to those observed after monocular deprivation. Whereas 80 percent of cortical cells in normal cats respond to stimulation of both eyes, only 20 percent of the cells in cats with cut eye muscles respond to stimulation of both eyes (Hubel and Wiesel, 1965b). Similarly, M. L. J. Crawford and G. K. von Noorden (1980) found that 70 percent of cortical cells in normal monkeys respond to stimulation of both eyes, but less than 10 percent of the cells in monkeys that

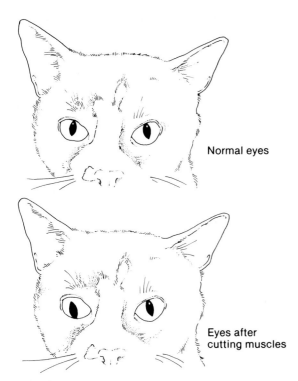

FIGURE 9.26 The appearance of a normal cat's eyes and the eyes of a cat whose eyes are misaligned due to cutting of its eye muscles.

FIGURE 9.27 A monkey wearing an optical prism-helmet, which causes a misalignment of the images in the two eyes. (Crawford & von Noorden, 1980.)

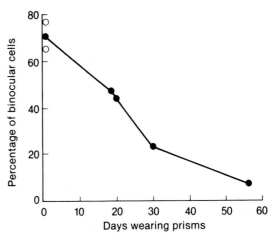

FIGURE 9.28 The percentage of cells that respond to stimulation of both eyes starts out at about 70 percent in normal monkeys, but then decreases to less than 10 percent after wearing a prism-helmet for 60 days. (Crawford & von Noorden, 1980.)

have worn the prism-helmets for 60 days respond to stimulation of both eyes. Figure 9.28 shows that the number of cells responding to both eyes decreases as the prisms are worn for longer periods of time (see also Smith, 1979).

This loss of binocular cells has a large behavioral effect. Monkeys with few remaining binocular cells due to prism-rearing are unable to detect depth in random dot stereograms, indicating that they have lost the ability to use binocular disparity to perceive depth (Crawford, et al., 1984).

All of the experiments we have discussed so far show that the visual systems of young cats and monkeys are very sensitive to changes in the visual environment. This sensitivity to the environment has been called **cortical malleability,** because the cortex is malleable—changeable—for a long period after birth.

A possible reason for cortical malleability. It has been suggested that cortical malleability serves a very important purpose—it enables binocular neurons to adjust to the increased spacing between the eyes that occurs as we grow from infants to adults. To understand what we mean by this we need to remember, from Chapter 7, that for a neuron to be able to signal binocular disparity, its receptive field

F I G U R E 9. 29 Frontal eyes (left) and lateral eyes (right). There is a large degree of overlap between the view seen by each eye of frontal-eyed animals, but there is little overlap of the views seen by each eye of lateral-eyed animals.

in the left eye must be in exactly the right relation to its receptive field in the right eye. But as we grow, the spacing between our eyes changes, so two receptive fields that would be lined up for closely spaced eyes would be thrown out of alignment for widely spaced eyes. Cortical malleability enables neurons to compensate for this slow, but substantial, change in eye spacing, thereby enabling the receptive fields to maintain their appropriate relationship to one another.

The idea that cortical malleability is necessary for binocular depth perception is supported by comparisons of animals with frontal eyes, in which there is a large overlap of the views of the two eyes, with animals with lateral eyes, in which there is little overlap of the views of the two eyes (Figure 9.29). While the neurons of animals with frontal eyes like cats and monkeys are greatly affected by deprivation, the neurons of animals with lateral eyes like rabbits and rats are only slightly affected by deprivation. Apparently, the visual cortex of a lateral-eyed animal lacks malleability because its neurons don't need to be constantly "recalibrated" as the spacing between the eyes changes (Mitchell & Timney, 1984).

The research on visual acuity and binocularity supports the idea that experience doesn't simply *maintain* the visual system, but, rather, that it plays an active role in its development. Further evidence for this idea is provided by selective rearing experiments.

THE EFFECTS OF SELECTIVE REARING

If visual experience plays an active role in shaping the development of visual neurons, then raising animals in environments different than their normal environments might cause their neurons to develop different-than-normal response characteristics. This is the idea behind selective rearing experiments, which expose animals to specific types of environments.

In the first selective rearing experiments, kittens were exposed to either vertical or horizontal stripes, in two ways, by two different groups of researchers. Colin Blakemore and Grahame Cooper (1970) placed kittens in striped tubes like the one in Figure 9.30, while Helmut Hirsch and D. N.

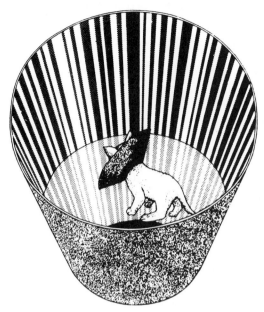

FIGURE 9. 30 Blakemore and Cooper's (1970) striped tube. The kitten wore a black ruff to mask its body from its eyes and stood on a glass platform in the middle of the cylinder. A spotlight (not shown) illuminated the walls from above.

Spinelli (1970, 1971) fitted kittens with goggles that presented vertical stripes to one eye and horizontal stripes to the other, as shown in Figure 9.31.

Blakemore and Cooper's kittens were kept in the dark from birth to 2 weeks of age, at which time they were placed in the tube for 5 hours a day; the rest of the time they remained in the dark. Since the kittens sat on a Plexiglas platform and the tube extended both above and below them, there were no visible corners or edges in their environment other than the vertical or horizontal stripes on the sides of the tube. The kittens wore neck ruffs to prevent them from turning vertical stripes into oblique or horizontal stripes by turning their heads; however, according to Blakemore and Cooper, "The kittens did not seem upset by the monotony of their surroundings and they sat for long periods inspecting the walls of the tube" (p. 477).

After 5 months, the selective rearing was stopped and the kittens were placed in the dark except for brief sessions in which their vision was

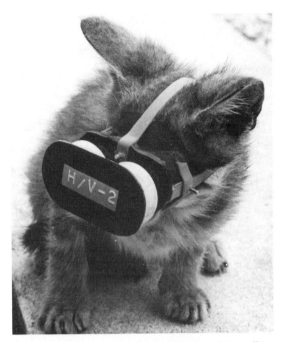

FIGURE 9. 31 One of Hirsch and Spinelli's (1971) cats wearing goggles. The vertically and horizontally striped stimulus patterns are mounted on the inside surface of the black rectangular sheet on the front of the goggles. The neck ruff, which the cats normally wore, is not shown.

tested. This testing uncovered a number of defects in their visual behavior. Their head movements were jerky when following moving objects; they tried to touch moving objects that were across the room, far from their reach; and they often bumped into things. Most important, however, these kittens seemed blind to stripes orthogonal (at 90 degrees) to the orientation of the stripes in the environment in which they were reared.

In one test, Blakemore and Cooper held a rod in front of two kittens, one of which had been raised in a vertical environment and the other in a horizontal environment. When the rod was held in a vertical position and shaken, the vertically reared kitten played with it while the horizontally reared kitten ignored it. When the rod was changed to a horizontal position, the kittens traded roles: The horizontally reared kitten played with the rod, while the vertically reared kitten ignored it.

Following these behavioral tests, Blakemore

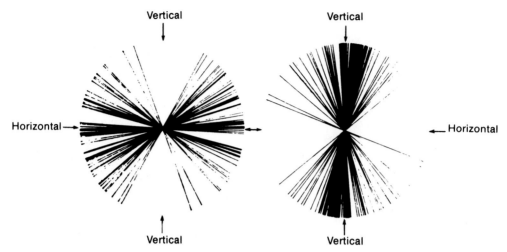

F I G U R E 9. 32   Distribution of optimal orientations for 52 cells from a horizontally experienced cat, on the left, and for 72 cells from a vertically experienced cat, on the right. (Blakemore & Cooper, 1970.)

and Cooper recorded from cells in the visual cortex and determined the stimulus orientation that caused the largest response from each cell. Their results are shown in Figure 9.32. These plots, in which each line represents the optimum orientation for a single cell, show that many of the cells of the horizontally reared cat respond best to horizontal stimuli, but none respond to vertical stimuli. The cells of the vertically reared cat, on the other hand, respond best to vertical stimuli, but none respond to horizontal stimuli. These results, combined with the behavioral results described above, indicate a correspondence between the directional selectivity of cortical neurons and the cat's ability to perceive stimuli in different orientations. Other investigators have found similar connections between behavior and cortical physiology (Hirsch, 1972; Muir & Mitchell, 1975; Blasdel, Mitchell, Muir, & Pettigrew, 1977).

The results of Hirsch and Spinelli's experiments, in which kittens wore goggles instead of being reared in a tube, were even more striking: They found few cells that deviated from the horizontal (for cells connected to the eye exposed to horizontal stripes) or vertical (for cells connected to the eye exposed to vertical stripes) by more than 5–10 degrees. Thus, Hirsch and Spinelli's goggle-

rearing results show that cells respond to orientations very close to the orientations seen during rearing.

In one of the most amazing results of all of the selective experiments, Colin Blakemore and Donald Mitchell (1973) demonstrated that *one hour* of exposure to the striped tube could drastically change the cells in the kitten's cortex. They kept a kitten in the dark until 28 days of age, placed the kitten in a tube with vertical stripes for 1 hour, and then put the kitten back into the dark until recording was carried out, at about 42 days of age. The results of this 1-hour exposure to an environment of vertical stripes is a transformed cortex! (Figure 9.33) As in the kittens exposed to vertical stripes for much longer periods of time, most cells respond best to vertical or near-vertical orientations.

These large effects on the properties of cortical cells caused by vertical or horizontal rearing stimulated a large number of experiments in which animals were exposed to many different environments. In general, their results paralleled those of vertical and horizontal rearing experiments, in that the properties of the kitten's receptive fields tended to resemble the environment to which the kitten was exposed. The results of some of these experiments are described in Table 9.1.

TABLE 9.1 / *Effects of Selective Rearing Experiments*

Rearing Stimulus	Cortical Cells
1. Moving white spots (Van Sluyters & Blakemore, 1973)	Most cells respond as well to spots as to lines (normally, lines are preferred). Many cells respond best to moving spots of about the same size as those seen during rearing.
2. Random array of point sources of light, bright stars on a dark sky (Pettigrew & Freeman, 1973).	Many cells are "spot detectors," which respond best to very small moving targets and respond poorly to linear contours.
3. Strobe light flashing at 2 flashes per second (Olson & Pettigrew, 1974).	Cells show little preference for line over spot stimulus. Only 45 percent of cells are orientation specific, compared with 86 percent in the normal cat.
4. Stripes moving in one direction (Tretter, Cynader, & Singer, 1975; Cynader, Berman, & Hein, 1975).	More cells respond to lines moving in the direction of movement experienced during rearing.

FIGURE 9.33 The effect of spending 1 hour in an environment of vertical stripes at 28 days of age on the optimal orientation of cortical cells. (Blakemore & Mitchell, 1973.)

that respond best to verticals. In support of this idea, it has been found that if an electrode obliquely penetrates the cortex of a kitten that has been reared viewing only vertical contours, it encounters long sequences of vertically selective neurons, as shown in Figure 9.34a (Rauschecher & Singer, 1981). Remember from Chapter 3 (Figure 3.10) that in a normal cat this type of oblique penetration encounters neurons that respond to many orientations (Figure 9.34b), as the electrode passes through many different orientation columns.

Also supporting the instructive acquisition hypothesis is the finding that a much larger-than-

What causes these large environmental effects? One proposed explanation is the **instructive acquisition hypothesis.** This proposes that the environment *instructs* a neuron's development so it *acquires* the ability to respond in a certain way. Thus, when a cat is raised in a vertical environment, cells that originally responded best to other-than-vertical orientations are "instructed" to change into cells

FIGURE 9.34 (a) When an electrode obliquely penetrates the visual cortex of a kitten that has been reared in a vertical environment, the electrode encounters long sequences of neurons maximally responsive to vertical orientations. (b) In a normally reared kitten an oblique electrode penetration encounters neurons with different orientation preferences as the electrode passes through different orientation columns.

normal volume of the cortex of monocularly reared monkeys is taken over by neurons that respond to the stimulated (nondeprived) eye (LeVay, Wiesel, & Hubel, 1980; also see Blakemore, 1974, 1976, 1977).

But not all researchers agree with the instructive acquisition hypothesis. Some argue that even if "instruction" does take place, it has its limits. Josef Rauschecker and Wolf Singer (1981) argue, for example, that while experience *can* change the orientation to which a neuron responds, a neuron can't adopt a preference for an orientation to which it has never responded. Thus, we may be able to create a vertically preferring neuron from one that had some vertical response, but we cannot create such a neuron from one that has never responded to this orientation.

A stronger argument against the instructive acquisition hypothesis is provided by evidence that selective rearing may cause some neurons to degenerate. According to the **selective degeneration hypothesis,** neurons that are not stimulated by a particular environment lose their ability to respond, leaving only those neurons that are stimulated by the rearing environment. This explanation is supported by studies that show that when cats are reared with horizontal/vertical goggles, many cells respond abnormally, or become completely unresponsive (Stryker, Sherk, Leventhal, & Hirsch, 1978). Presumably, these unresponsive cells are the ones that were not stimulated by the kitten's selective environment.

When asked to choose between these two hypotheses, all researchers do not agree. Some favor one hypothesis, some the other, and some say that both may be operating. While it is certainly clear that early environmental experience can modify the visual system, the exact mechanisms responsible for this modification are still controversial.

The demonstration that large physiological and behavioral changes occur in monocularly and selectively reared cats and monkeys has caused numerous investigators to look at analogous cases in humans. Scientists, of course, are not rearing human babies with one eye occluded or in vertically or horizontally striped tubes. However, early

medical problems often result in a duplication of some of the deprivations that have been carried out on cats and monkeys, and there is evidence that these human "deprivations" cause physiological and perceptual effects analogous to the changes observed in cats and monkeys.

THE EFFECTS OF VISUAL DEPRIVATION ON HUMANS

Monocular Rearing Due to Eye Patching

In Hubel and Wiesel's monocular rearing experiments, cats that had one eye occluded between 4 and 8 weeks of age essentially lost the use of that eye, as indicated behaviorally and by the fact that no cortical cells would fire to stimulation of the previously occluded eye. There is increasing evidence that **amblyopia**—a large reduction in the visual acuity in one eye—may sometimes occur in humans who, as young children, had reduced use of one eye due to patching following an eye operation.

This evidence has been provided by Shinobu Awaya and coworkers (1973), who investigated the histories of 19 patients with amblyopia and found that all had had their amblyopic (low visual acuity) eye closed early in life, following an eye operation, with most of the closures occurring during the first year. This type of amblyopia has therefore been called **stimulus deprivation amblyopia** to distinguish it from amblyopia due to other causes (von Noorden & Maumanee, 1968). It seems likely that the same mechanisms are responsible for stimulus deprivation amblyopia and the loss of vision in Hubel and Wiesel's monocularly reared kittens.

Early Strabismus

Another cause of reduced vision in one eye is **strabismus,** an imbalance in the eye muscles that upsets the coordination between the two eyes. We saw that cutting the eye muscles in animals causes a loss of cortical cells that respond to stimulation of

---

B O X   9. 2   /   *The Case of S.B.: Recovery from Lifelong Blindness*

Richard Gregory and Jean Wallace (1963) tell the story of S.B., a 53-year-old man blind since the age of 10 months, who had a corneal transplant operation (see Chapter 10, p. 361) in an attempt to restore his sight. Before the operation, S.B. could see light and dark and had very rudimentary pattern vision, being able to see fingers at a distance of about 9 inches. S.B.'s first visual experience, immediately after the operation, was a blurred perception of the surgeon's face, which S.B. knew was a face only because he heard the surgeon's voice and knew that voices come from faces.

When Gregory and Wallace examined S.B., 48 days after the operation, they found that he did not look at the objects around him as normally sighted people do. He could name objects only when they were called to his attention, and even though he could recognize large letters, he had difficulty recognizing faces and appeared unaware of facial expressions. He also experienced distortions of depth; for example, when looking down from a window 30–40 feet above the ground, he thought he could safely lower himself down with his hands. Only after seeing the same window from the outside did he realize that this would be impossible.

When Gregory and Wallace visited S.B. at his home, about 6 months after the operation, they found that his vision had improved considerably. He could recognize the faces of friends from about 15 feet away, cross streets confidently, and draw fairly detailed pictures of objects in his environment.

This case is one of the more successful reports of recovery from blindness. S.B.'s ability to perceive details indicates that his long deprivation of form vision did not cause the extensive permanent damage to his visual system experienced by dark-reared cats and monkeys. Apparently,

enough patterns were imaged on S.B.'s retinas to keep his cortical cells from becoming completely inactive, and this enabled him to regain some form perception.

Most people would regard the regaining of sight experienced by S.B. to be a happy event. Strangely enough, however, a common reaction to the regaining of sight is depression and unhappiness. Though S.B.'s sight had improved enormously when Gregory and Wallace visited him 6 months after he left the hospital, they noticed that he appeared dispirited. Before the operation, S.B. was a cheerful and outgoing person, but as time progressed after the operation, he became more and more depressed.

What causes this depression? One theory, proposed by Alberto Valvo (1968), is that it is difficult to deal with the dramatic change from the world of touch to the world of vision, where everything is done differently. Consider this entry in the diary of a 35-year-old man who had an operation similar to S.B.'s: "Paradoxically, when my sight started improving I began to feel depressed. I often experienced periods of crying. . . . In the evening I preferred to rest in a dark room. Some days I felt confused: I did not know whether to touch or to look. . . . Recovery of vision has been a long and hard road for me, like entering a strange world. In these moments of depression I sometimes wondered if I was happier before. . . ."

Despite his depression, this man expresses hope for the future, stating that, "i know that there is still room for improvement and I am determined to do my best to accomplish it." S.B., however, never regained the cheerfulness he once possessed. His increasing depression led him to withdraw from active life, and he died 3 years after the operation.

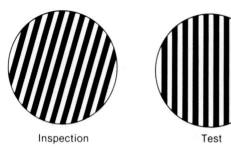

F I G U R E 9. 35 Stimuli for measuring the tilt aftereffect. Stare at the inspection pattern on the left for about 60 seconds and then transfer your gaze to the test lines on the right. If you see the test lines as tilted, you are experiencing the tilt aftereffect.

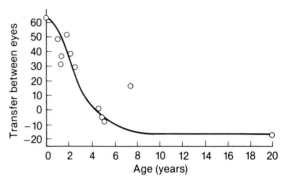

F I G U R E 9. 36 The degree of interocular transfer of the tilt aftereffect as a function of the age at which surgery was performed to correct strabismus. (From Banks, Aslin, & Letson, 1975.)

both eyes. Numerous investigators have recently found evidence of a similar lack of binocularly driven cells in people who had strabismus as young children. Strabismus can be corrected by a muscle operation that restores the balance between the two eyes. However, if this operation is not performed until the child is 4–5 years of age, a loss of binocularly driven cells can occur similar to that observed in monocularly deprived cats or cats with artificially produced strabismus.

How do we know that people who had early strabismus lack binocularly driven cells? Obviously, we can't record from single neurons in the human cortex. We can, however, use a perceptual effect called the **tilt aftereffect** that enables us to estimate the binocularity of a person's cortical neurons.

D E M O N S T R A T I O N

The Tilt Aftereffect

You can illustrate the tilt aftereffect to yourself, by staring for about 60 seconds at the adaptation lines on the left of Figure 9.35 and then transferring your gaze to the test lines on the right. If the aftereffect is successful, the lines on the right will appear to be slightly tilted even though, in reality, they are vertical.

The tilt aftereffect can be used to measure binocularity because of the phenomenon of **interocular transfer.** If an observer looks at the adap-

tation lines with one eye and then looks at the test lines with the other eye, the aftereffect will transfer between the eyes (try this). This transfer, which causes an effect about 60–70 percent as strong as the effect that occurs if the adaptation and test lines are viewed with the same eye, indicates that information from one eye must be being shared with the other. Since the first place that neurons from the left and right eyes meet is the visual cortex (remember that little or no interaction between the eyes occurs in the later geniculate nucleus), this information sharing between the two eyes must take place at the level of the visual cortex, or higher. The degree of transfer of the tilt aftereffect, therefore, can be used to assess the state of binocularly driven cells in the cortex (Aslin & Banks, 1978; Mitchell & Ware, 1974; Ware & Mitchell, 1974; Mitchell, Reardon, & Muir, 1975).

Armed with the tilt aftereffect, Martin Banks, Richard Aslin, and Robert Letson (1975) measured the degree of interocular transfer in people who had strabismus early in life. Figure 9.36 plots the magnitude of interocular transfer as a function of the age at which 12 people born with strabismus had corrective surgery. When the surgery was carried out early in the person's life, interocular transfer is high, indicating good binocular function, but if surgery was delayed, interocular transfer is poor, indicating poor binocular function. Based on the results in Figure 9.36, other data from their exper-

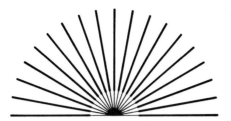 

F I G U R E   9. 37   Left: astigmatic fan chart used to test for astigmatism. Right: an astigmatic patient will perceive the lines in one orientation (in this case vertical) as sharp and the lines in the other orientation as blurred. (From Trevor-Roper, 1970.)

iments, and data from similar experiments by A. Hohmann and Otto Creutzfeldt (1975), Aslin and Banks (1978) concluded that a sensitive period for binocular development in humans begins during the first year of life, reaches a peak during the second year, and decreases by 4–8 years of age.

Early Astigmatism

Another human analogue of the animal deprivation experiments is provided by people who have **astigmatism** early in life. Astigmatism, which is caused by a distortion in the cornea, results in an image that is out of focus either in the horizontal or vertical, as shown in Figure 9.37. Thus, a person who has an astigmatism at an early age is exposed to an environment in which lines in one orientation are imaged sharply on the retina but lines 90 degrees from this orientation are out of focus.

Ralph Freeman and John Pettigrew (1973) showed that cats reared with an artificial astigmatism, created by wearing a mask containing astigmatic lenses, develop cortical cells that favor whichever orientation is in sharp focus during rearing. This result in cats resembles a condition known as **meridional amblyopia** in humans. People with this condition have astigmatisms that cannot be optically corrected. That is, even if these people wear glasses that compensate for their distorted corneas so that all orientations are sharply imaged on the retina, they still have impaired acuity for objects in the orientation originally blurred by their astigmatism.

To show that a person with meridional amblyopia has decreased visual acuity in one orientation,

even when his or her vision is optically corrected so that the retinal image is sharp, Donald Mitchell and Frances Wilkinson (1974) carefully measured the optically corrected vision of a person with meridional amblyopia and obtained the top curve in Figure 9.38. This observer has an astigmatism that blurs horizontal images (orientations = 0 and 180 degrees), and the curve indicates that this observer's acuity is lowest at these orientations and is best at the vertical orientation of 90 degrees.

Anticipating arguments that the results in the upper curve of Figure 9.38 could be due to an imperfect optical correction, Mitchell and Wilkinson used a laser to present a sharp image to the observer's retina. This laser bypasses the observer's distorted cornea and therefore ensures that the image is focused sharply on the retina. The results of this method of stimulus presentation, shown by the lower curve in Figure 9.38, indicate that the differences in acuity for horizontal and vertical orientations (observed in the upper curve) remain.

The results of Figure 9.38 indicate that the decreased acuity for horizontal orientations must result not from the way the image is focused on the retina but, probably, from changes that have taken place in the observer's brain. Just as the neurons of Freeman and Pettigrew's astigmatic cats respond less well to orientations blurred by the astigmatism, so the neurons of the observer in Figure 9.38 may respond less well to lines oriented at 0 and 180 degrees. This idea is further supported by other findings: In astigmatic observers with optically corrected vision, the visually evoked potential is lowest in response to stimuli oriented in the direction originally blurred by the astigmatism (Freeman &

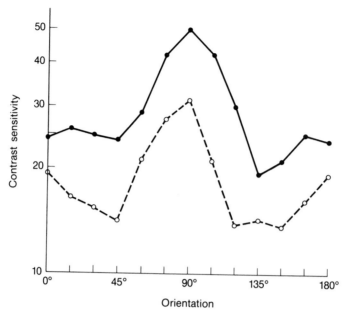

F I G U R E 9. 38   A plot of contrast sensitivity for different orientations (see text for details). (From Mitchell & Wilkinson, 1974.)

Thibos, 1973). Apparently, the selective rearing effects observed in cats can also affect the vision of humans.

In this chapter we have seen that the basic visual capacities of color vision, visual acuity, depth perception, form perception, and perceptual constancy develop to nearly adult levels during the first year of life. We have also seen that the development of some of these capacities depends on the presence of normal visual input early in life.

It may be surprising to think that the infant's visual capacities are well developed before most infants can walk or talk. But perhaps this rapid development is not so surprising when we consider the development that follows: An infant that seemed helpless just months earlier suddenly learns to walk and turns into a toddler-in-motion. And this same toddler also begins learning to talk.

The rapid perceptual development that precedes these newly emerging motor and cognitive capacities provides the child with the perceptual tools it needs to develop in these other areas. Additional perceptual development does occur after the first year, much of it linked to the child's constantly expanding cognitive capacities. But the perceptual development of the first year provides the foundation for the cognitive development that follows.

Summary

1. We can measure infant perception by asking infants the question: "Can you tell the difference between A and B?"and by using their looking or reaching behaviors to determine their answers to this question.
2. Specific techniques to measure infant perception include (a) the preferential looking technique, (b) the habituation procedure, (c) measuring reaching behavior, (d) measuring visual scanning, and (e) the visual evoked potential.
3. Infants 1–5 days old can perceive reds, greens, and yellows but their system for the perception of blue is not yet developed. By 2–3 months infants have

color vision that is close to adult color vision.

4. The visual acuity of human infants can be measured by the preferential looking technique and the evoked potential technique. Both techniques indicate that 1–2-month-old infants have poor visual acuity. This poor visual acuity is due to the fact that the infants' foveal cone receptors and cortical connections are poorly developed. Acuity improves rapidly, however, over the first 6 months of life. Acuity approaches adult levels by 1 year, but adult levels are not achieved until sometime after 1 year of age.

5. The infant's contrast sensitivity is much lower than the adult's at all frequencies. What sensitivity the infant does have is restricted to lower frequencies. By 6 months of age the infant's contrast sensitivity has considerably improved but is still below adult levels.

6. Infants as young as 1 month old have the ability to accommodate slightly, and by 3 months they can accommodate nearly as well as adults.

7. Reliable binocular fixation does not occur until about 3 months of age. The ability to use disparity information to perceive depth emerges sometime between $3\frac{1}{2}$ and 6 months of age.

8. Measurements of stereoacuity indicate that by about $3\frac{1}{2}$ months of age infants are able to use disparity to perceive depth. Once this ability emerges, stereoacuity develops rapidly over the next month.

9. The ability to use pictorial depth cues like interposition, familiar size, relative size, shading, linear perspective, and texture gradients does not develop until between 5–7 months of age.

10. Very young infants tend to see forms in parts, but as they get older they perceive more in terms of wholes. Increasing age brings more advanced capacities for form perception.

11. By 4 months of age infants can perceive a partially occluded moving stick as continuing behind another object and can tell the difference between biological motion and random motion.

12. Size constancy has been reported in infants by 3 months of age and by 5–6 months infants can generalize from one pose of a face to another. These infants can, therefore, perceive invariance across transformations.

13. A large number (but not all) of the cells in the cortex of the newborn kitten are selective for orientation, but it is not until 4–6 weeks that the majority of these cells reach adult standards of orientation selectivity.

14. Most cells in the newborn kitten respond to stimulation of both eyes. It is not until about 5 weeks of age, however, that the kitten's eyes are aligned so it can make use of binocular disparity information.

15. Depriving a kitten or monkey of all vision by rearing in the dark causes a decrease in acuity, with longer deprivation decreasing the chances of recovery. More drastic and long-lasting effects occur when vision is monocularly deprived. Monocular deprivation also causes large decreases in binocularity.

16. The sensitive period for susceptibility to monocular deprivation extends from about the fourth week to 6 months in cats. Deprivation for even one day during the sensitive period can have a large effect.

17. Rearing under conditions of image misalignment caused by cutting the eye muscles or wearing prisms causes a large decrease in binocularity as measured both electrophysiologically and behaviorally.

18. Cortical malleability refers to the fact that the cortex is sensitive to environmental manipulations. This malleability may serve the purpose of enabling binocular neurons to adjust to the increased spacing between the eyes that occurs as we grow from infants to adults.

19. Kittens reared in all horizontal—or all vertical—environments have neurons in the cortex that respond primarily to the orientation present during rearing. Exposure for as little as 1 hour during the sensitive period has a large effect. These physiological changes are accompanied by behavioral indications of severely reduced vision for orientations orthogonal to the rearing orientation.

20. Rearing in environments consisting of moving white spots, point sources of light, strobe lights, and stripes moving in one direction results in cortical cells that respond preferentially to stimuli resembling the stimuli present during rearing.

21. Two mechanisms, instructive acquisition and selective degeneration, have been proposed to explain the effects of selective rearing on the visual system. There is evidence supporting both hypotheses, so it is possible that both may be operating during selective rearing.

22. Children who have one eye patched early in life, due to an eye operation, often develop stimulus deprivation amblyopia, a loss of acuity in the deprived eye. This amblyopia may be caused by the same mechanism that impairs vision in monocularly deprived kittens.

23. Children who develop a squint due to early strabismus often develop an inability to use disparity information from the two eyes to see depth. There appears to be a critical period for binocular development that begins during the first year of life, reaches a peak during the second year, and decreases by 4–8 years of age.

24. Meridional amblyopia, a loss of acuity for stimuli of a particular orientation, may result from an early astigmatism that causes loss of cortical cells responsive to that orientation.

Boxes

1. To develop sensory-motor coordination it is necessary not only to be exposed to changing visual stimulation but also to cause the scene to change by means of self-produced movement.
2. In some cases of prolonged deprivation of patterned stimulation due to an opaque cornea, vision has been restored by transplanting a new cornea. This restoration of vision occurs only gradually and is sometimes accompanied by an emotional reaction, perhaps caused by the difficulty in moving from the world of the blind to the world of the sighted.

Study Questions

1. What questions do psychologists ask infants in order to determine what they can see? What behaviors do the infants use to answer the psychologists' questions? (319)
2. Describe the preferential looking procedure. Why does it work? (319)
3. Describe the habituation procedure. Why does it work? (321)
4. What are three other procedures for measuring infant perception? (322)
5. Describe the Adams et al. study that measured the newborn's color vision capacities. What did this experiment show about the newborn's capacity for color vision? By what age do infants have color vision close to that of an adult? (322)
6. Under what conditions can we be certain that a particular capacity is due to genetic programming? (323)
7. What methods have been used to measure visual acuity in infants? Describe the time course of the development of visual acuity. (324)
8. What is the state of development of the human fovea and visual cortex at birth? (325)
9. Describe the infant contrast sensitivity function. What kinds of features can 1-month- and 3-month-old infants perceive? (326)
10. How did Banks measure infant accommodation? At what age is infant accommodation similar to that of adults? (327)
11. How did Aslin measure binocular fixation in infants? At what age does reliable binocular fixation appear in infants? Why must the development of binocular fixation precede the development of binocular disparity? (328)
12. How did Fox measure infants' ability to use binocular disparity information to see depth? What is stereoacuity and what does it tell us about the ability to perceive depth? How did Held measure it in infants? At what age does the ability to use disparity information emerge? (329)
13. Describe experiments that tested infants' ability to use the cues of interposition and familiar size to perceive depth. At what age do infants become responsive to most of the pictorial depth cues? (332)

14. Do newborns demonstrate any capacity for form perception? (333)
15. How does an infant's pattern of eye fixations change between 1 and 2 months of age? (334)
16. At what age may infants begin perceiving faces as wholes rather than as individual parts? (335)
17. Describe the procedure that showed that infants perceive objects as continuing behind an occluding object. (335)
18. How was it shown that infants can tell the difference between biological and nonbiological motion? (335)
19. Describe Fagan's experiment which shows that a 5–6-month-old infant can generalize from one facial pose to another. (336)
20. Know the order and approximate age at which each of the infants' perceptual capacities emerge. (336)
21. How well do neurons in the newborn kitten's cortex respond to orientation? Taking a number of studies into account, at what age can we conclude that most cells in the kitten's cortex reach adult standards for orientation selectivity? (337)
22. How well do neurons in the newborn kitten's cortex respond to stimulation of both eyes? How well are the kitten's eyes lined up at birth? (338)
23. How do binocular deprivation and monocular deprivation affect visual acuity in kittens and monkeys? (338)
24. What is ocular dominance? Understand how to read ocular dominance histograms like the one in Figure 9.22. How does monocular rearing affect binocularity? (339)
25. What is the sensitive period for monocular deprivation in the cat? How long does deprivation have to be to cause large effects? (340)
26. What percentage of cortical cells in the normal cat respond to stimulation of both eyes? (340)
27. How does the wearing of prisms affect binocularity, as determined both electrophysiologically and behaviorally in the monkey? (340)
28. What is cortical malleability and what is its possible function? What evidence supports this hypothesis about its function? (341)
29. What is a selective rearing experiment? Describe

two ways of rearing a cat in a selective environment. (342)

30. Describe the results of selective rearing experiments. How does selective rearing affect (a) the orientation selectivity of the kitten's cells? (b) the kitten's behavior? (344)

31. Are long exposures to selective rearing conditions necessary to get selective rearing effects? What is the general finding of selective rearing experiments? (344)

32. What two ideas have been proposed regarding the reasons for the changes in cortical neurons caused by selective rearing? What evidence supports each of these ideas? (345)

33. What is amblyopia? Stimulus deprivation amblyopia? What evidence suggests that stimulus deprivation amblyopia is due to early eye closure? Is there any parallel between stimulus deprivation amblyopia observed in humans and the effects of monocular deprivation on kittens? (346)

34. What is strabismus? Describe how the tilt aftereffect was used to show that people with early strabismus lack binocularly driven cells. What is the sensitive period for the development of binocular function in humans? (346)

35. What happens to the cortical cells of a cat that is reared wearing an astigmatic lens? (349)

36. What is meridional amblyopia? What causes the decreased acuity of meridional amblyopia? Why can't it be corrected with glasses? (349)

Boxes

1. What happens to a person's perception when he or she wears prism goggles? What is the difference between wearing prism goggles while walking and wearing prism goggles while being pushed in a wheelchair? Describe the kitten carousel experiment. How do the results of this experiment relate to the prism goggle experiments? (330)

2. Was S.B. able to see clearly immediately after his operation? What could he see 48 days after the operation? 6 months after the operation? What often happens to the emotional state of people whose sight has been restored after long blindness? What reason has been proposed for these emotional effects? (347)

Glossary

Amblyopia. A large reduction in the acuity in one eye. (346)

Astigmatism. A condition in which vision is blurred in some orientations due to a misshapen cornea. (349)

Binocular fixation. Fixating on an object with both eyes simultaneously. (328)

Binocularity. A neuron is binocular if it responds to stimulation of both the left and right eyes. (338)

Contralateral eye. The eye on the opposite side of the head from a cortical recording electrode. (338)

Cortical malleability. The ability of neurons in the visual cortex to change their properties in response to environmental changes. (341)

Deprivation experiments. Experiments in which an animal is deprived of some aspect of visual experience during rearing, followed by an assessment of the effect of the deprivation on the animal's behavior and/or physiology. (337)

Habituation. When the same stimulus is presented repeatedly, infants look at the stimulus less and less on each succeeding trial. (321)

Interocular transfer. When presenting an adaptation stimulus to one eye results in an aftereffect in the other eye. (348)

Instructive acquisition hypothesis. The hypothesis that the environment instructs a neuron's development so it acquires the ability to respond in a certain way. This hypothesis has been proposed to explain the effects of selective rearing experiments. (345)

Ipsilateral eye. The eye on the same side of the head as a cortical recording electrode. (339)

Meridional amblyopia. An astigmatism that cannot be completely corrected with corrective lenses. (349)

Monocular deprivation. Rearing an animal with one eye occluded so that the animal receives visual input through only the unoccluded eye. (338)

Ocular dominance. The degree to which a neuron is influenced by stimulation of each eye. A neuron has a large amount of ocular dominance if it responds only to stimulation of one eye. There is no ocular dominance if the neuron responds equally to stimulation of both eyes. (339)

Ocular dominance histogram. A histogram that indicates the degree of ocular dominance of a large population of neurons. (338)

Preferential looking (PL). A technique used to measure perception in infants. Two stimuli are presented and the infant's looking behavior is monitored to determine the amount of time the infant spends viewing each stimulus. (319)

Selective degeneration hypothesis. The idea that selective rearing causes degeneration of cells that are sensitive to patterns not present during rearing. For example, according to this hypothesis, cells that are sensitive to vertical lines will degenerate if an animal is exposed to an environment that consists only of horizontal lines. (346)

Selective rearing. Rearing an animal in an environment which contains only one kind of pattern. For example, vertical stripes or horizontal stripes. (337)

Self-produced movement. Movement produced by an organism. For example, walking through the environment, as opposed to being pushed through the environment in a wheelchair. (330)

Sensitive period. A period of time, usually early in an organism's life, during which changes in the environment have a large effect on the organism's physiology or behavior. (340)

Sensory-motor coordination. Coordination between perception and movement. For example, picking up an object involves coordination between seeing the object and the movement necessary to reach for it. (330).

Spontaneous looking preference. Infants prefer to look at certain types of stimuli. This property of infant behavior is the basis of the preferential looking technique. (319)

Spontaneous reaching preference. Infants tend to reach for the nearer of two objects. This property of infant behavior enables us to use reaching behavior to measure an infant's depth perception. (322)

Stereoacuity. The ability to resolve small differences in disparity. (330)

Stimulus deprivation amblyopia. Amblyopia due to early closure of one eye. (346)

Strabismus. A condition in which there is an imbalance in the eye muscles that upsets the coordination between the two eyes. (346)

Tilt aftereffect. Staring at an adapting field of tilted lines and then looking at vertical lines causes the vertical lines to appear to be tilted in a direction opposite to the tilt of the adapting field. (348)

Visual evoked potential (VEP). An electrical response to visual stimulation recorded by placing disc electrodes on the back of the head. This potential reflects the activity of a large population of neurons in the visual cortex. (322)

Visual scanning. The eye movements made when looking at different parts of an object. (322)

CHAPTER **10**

What Can Go Wrong?

Focusing Problems

Decreased Transmission of Light

Damage to the Retina

Optic Nerve Damage

The Eye Examination

Clinical Aspects of Vision

Although it is obvious that the man in Figure 10.1 is examining the woman's eye, most people do not understand exactly what he is seeing or what he is looking for. Even though over 100 million Americans have had their eyes examined by an eye specialist in the process of being fitted for glasses or contact lenses, few of them understand, except in the most general sense, what is going on during these examinations. One of the purposes of this chapter is to demystify what goes on during an eye exam.

Before we can understand what the eye specialist looks for during an eye examination, we must understand the major problems that can cause poor vision. We will, therefore, start this chapter by describing these problems and how they are treated to improve or restore vision. After we understand the nature of the most common causes of visual problems, we will describe how a routine eye examination can detect these problems.

WHAT CAN GO WRONG?

There are four major types of problems that can cause poor vision:

1. Light is not focused clearly on the retina. Problems in focusing light can occur because the eyeball is too short or too long or because the lens does not function properly. We will describe the following specific problems: myopia (nearsightedness), hyperopia (farsightedness), and astigmatism.

2. Light is blurred as it enters the eye. Scarring of the cornea or clouding of the lens blurs light as it enters the eye. Specific problems: corneal injury or disease, cataract.

3. There is damage to the retina. The retina can be damaged by disruption of the vessels that supply it with blood, by its separation from the blood supply, and by diseases that attack its receptors. Specific problems: macular degeneration, diabetic retinopathy, detached retina, hereditary retinal degeneration.

4. There is damage to the optic nerve. The optic nerve can degenerate. When this degeneration is due to a pressure buildup inside the eyeball the cause is glaucoma. In addition, degeneration can be caused by poor retinal circulation, toxic substances, or presence of a tumor. We will focus on glaucoma in our discussion.

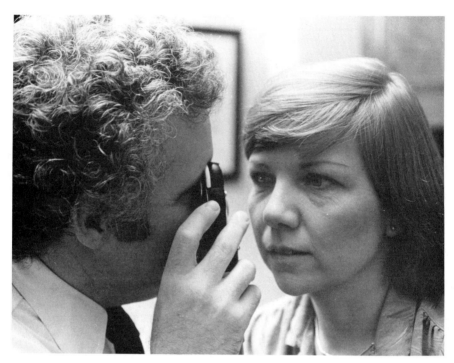

F I G U R E 10. 1   Ophthalmologist examining patient.

We begin by considering a problem that affects more people than all the others combined: an inability to focus incoming light onto the retina.

FOCUSING PROBLEMS

In Chapter 3 (pp. 70–73) we described the optical system of the eye—the cornea and the lens—which, if everything is working properly, bring light entering the eye to a sharp focus on the retina. We also described the process of accommodation, which adjusts the focusing power of the eye to bring both near and far objects into focus.

We will now consider myopia, hyperopia, and astigmatism, three problems which affect the person's ability to focus an image on the retina.

Myopia

Myopia, or nearsightedness, is an inability to see distant objects clearly. The reason for this difficulty, which affects over 70 million Americans,

can be understood by looking at Figure 10.2a: In the myopic eye, parallel rays of light are brought to a focus in front of the retina so the image reaching the retina is blurred. This problem can be caused by either of two factors: (1) **refractive myopia:** The cornea and/or lens bend the light too much, or (2) **axial myopia:** The eyeball is too long. Either way, light comes to a focus in front of the retina, so the image on the retina is out of focus, and faraway objects look blurred.

How can we deal with this problem? Accommodation (see p. 72) can't help us because increasing the power of the lens moves the focus point forward, as we saw in Figure 3.10, and this only makes matters worse. We can, however, cause the image to fall on the retina by moving our stimulus closer. To understand why this is so, consider what happens when we move our spot of light closer to a normal eye. When the spot of light is far from the eye, the resulting parallel rays are focused on the retina (Figure 3.10a), but when we move the spot closer, the focus point moves back (Figure 3.10b). The same thing happens in a myopic eye:

B O X   10. 1   /   *Vision Problems in the United States*

Blindness and visual disability exact an enormous toll on both the people who are affected and on society. Consider these facts:

- 100 million people wear glasses or contact lenses.
- 10 million people over 25 have some noncorrectable loss of sight.
- 1.4 million people can't see ordinary newsprint, even with glasses.

- 500,000 people are legally blind.
- 47,000 new cases of blindness are reported every year.
- 34 million office visits are made each year for eye care.
- 770,000 eye operations are performed each year.
- Over $5 billion are spent each year on doctors' bills and benefits related to eye care.

Source: *Vision Problems in the United States,* National Society to Prevent Blindness, New York, 1978.

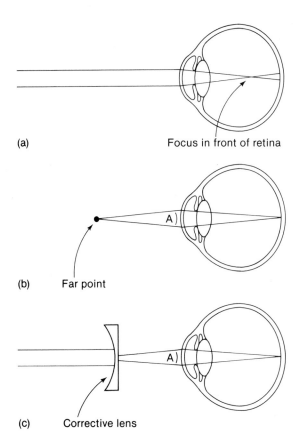

(a)   Focus in front of retina

(b)   Far point

(c)   Corrective lens

When the spot of light is far from the eye, rays are focused in front of the retina (Figure 10.2a), but when we move the spot closer, the focus point moves back, and if we move the spot close enough, we can push the focus point onto the retina (Figure 10.2b). The distance at which the spot of light becomes focused on the retina is called the **far point** and when our spot of light is at the far point, a myope can see it clearly.

What happens if we move our spot of light closer than the far point? Moving the spot closer pushes the focus point back behind the retina (see Figure 3.10b) but, fortunately, we can now use accommodation to push the focus point forward, back onto the retina. A myope, therefore, can see objects clearly if they are at the far point or closer.

Moving objects closer to the eye enables the

F I G U R E   10. 2   Focusing of light by the myopic (nearsighted) eye. (a) Parallel rays from a distant spot of light are brought to a focus in front of the retina, so distant objects appear blurred. (b) As the spot of light is moved closer to the eye, the focus point is pushed back until, at the far point, rays are focused on the retina and vision becomes clear. Vision is blurred beyond the far point. (c) A corrective lens, which bends light so it enters the eye at the same angle as light coming from the far point, brings light to a focus on the retina. Angle A is the same in (b) and (c).

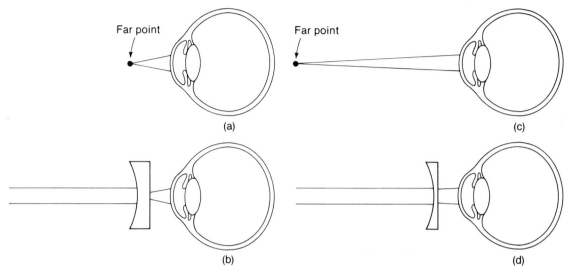

F I G U R E 10. 3 The strength of a lens required to correct myopic vision depends on the location of the far point. (a) Close far point requiring (b) strong corrective lens. (c) Distant far point requiring (d) weak corrective lens.

myope to see nearby objects clearly (which is why a myopic person is called "nearsighted"), but it still leaves the myope with fuzzy vision for objects beyond the far point. The solution to this problem is well known to anyone with myopia: corrective glasses or contact lenses. These corrective lenses bend incoming light so that it is focused as if it is at the far point, as illustrated in Figure 10.2(c). Notice that the lens placed in front of the eye causes the light to enter the eye at exactly the same angle as light coming from the far point in Figure 10.2(b).

Before leaving our discussion of myopia, let's consider one more problem: How strong must a corrective lens be to give the myope clear far vision? To answer this question, we have to keep in mind what is required of a corrective lens: It must bend parallel rays so that light enters the eye at the same angle as a spot of light positioned at the far point. Figure 10.3 shows what this means for two different locations of the far point. When the far point is close, as in Figure 10.3(a), we need a powerful corrective lens to bend the light in the large angle shown in Figure 10.3(b). However, when the far point is distant, as in Figure 10.3(c), we need only a weak corrective lens to bend the light in the small angle shown in Figure 10.3(d). Thus, the strength

of the corrective lens depends on the location of the far point: A powerful lens is needed to correct vision when the far point is close, and a weak lens is needed to correct vision when the far point is distant.

When ophthalmologists or optometrists write a prescription for corrective lenses, they specify the strength of the lens in **diopters,** using the following relationship: number of diopters = 1/far point in meters. Thus, a slightly myopic person with a far point at 1 meter (100 cm) requires a 1 diopter correction (diopters = 1/1 = 1.0). However, a very myopic person with a far point at 2/10 of a meter (20 cm) requires a 5 diopter correction (diopters = 1/0.2 = 5.0). This relationship between the distance of the far point and the required number of diopters of correction is shown in Figure 10.4.

Hyperopia

A person with **hyperopia,** or **farsightedness,** can see distant objects clearly but has trouble seeing nearby objects. We can understand hyperopia by looking at Figure 10.5. In the hyperopic eye, the

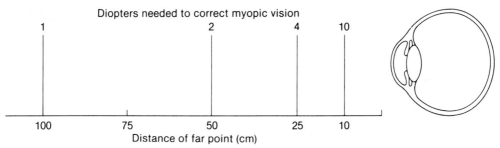

F I G U R E 10. 4 The number of diopters of lens power needed to correct myopic vision for different far points. Without a corrective lens, vision is blurred at distances greater than the far point. A far point of 10 cm represents severe myopia, and a far point of 100 cm represents mild myopia.

focus point for parallel rays of light is located behind the retina, usually because the eyeball is too short. By accommodating to bring the focus point back to the retina, hyperopes are able to see distant objects clearly.

Nearby objects, however, are more difficult

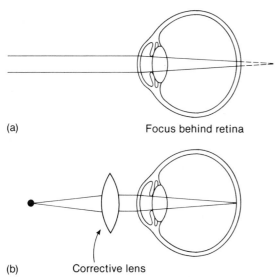

(a)   Focus behind retina

(b)   Corrective lens

F I G U R E 10. 5 Focusing of light by the hyperopic (farsighted) eye. (a) Parallel rays from a distant spot of light are brought to a focus behind the retina, so, without accommodation, far objects are blurred. Hyperopes can, however, achieve clear vision for distant objects by accommodating. (b) If hyperopia is severe, the constant accommodation needed for clear vision may cause eyestrain, and a corrective lens is required.

for the hyperope to deal with because, as we saw in Figures 3.10 and 10.2, moving an object closer pushes the focus point farther back. The hyperope's focus point, behind the retina for far objects, is pushed even farther back for nearby objects, so the hyperope must exert a great deal of accommodation to return the focus point to the retina. The hyperope's constant accommodation when looking at nearby objects (as in reading or doing close-up work) results in eyestrain and, in older people, headaches. Headaches do not usually occur in young people since they can accommodate easily, but older people, who have more difficulty accommodating due to presbyopia (see page 73), are more likely to experience headaches, and may therefore require a corrective lens which brings the focus point forward onto the retina, as shown in Figure 10.5.

Astigmatism

Imagine what it would be like to see everything through a pane of old-fashioned wavy glass, which causes some things to be in focus and others to be blurred. This describes the experience of a person with a severe **astigmatism,** because an astigmatic person sees through a misshapen cornea, which correctly focuses some of the light reaching the retina but distorts other light. The normal cornea is spherical, curved like a round kitchen bowl, but an astigmatic cornea is somewhat elliptical, curved like the inside of a teaspoon. Because of this elliptical curvature, a person with astigmatism will see the "astigmatic fan" in Figure 9.37 partially in focus and partially out of focus. As in hyperopia, eyestrain is a symptom of astigmatism, because no matter how much the person accommodates to try to achieve clear vision, something is always out of focus. Fortunately, astigmatism can be corrected by glasses or contact lenses.

DECREASED TRANSMISSION OF LIGHT

The focusing problems described above are the most prevalent visual problems, as evidenced by the large number of people who wear glasses. Because these problems usually can be corrected with glasses or contact lenses, most people with focusing problems see normally or suffer only mild losses of vision. We will now consider situations in which disease or physical damage can cause severe visual losses or, in some cases, blindness. But before we begin to discuss these problems, we should define what we mean by **blindness.**

What Is Blindness?

It is a common conception that a person who is blind lives in a world of total darkness or formless diffuse light. While this description is true for some blind people, many people who are classified as legally blind do have some vision and many can read with the aid of a strong magnifying glass. According to the definition accepted in most states, a person is considered legally blind if, after correction with glasses or contact lenses, he or she has visual acuity of 20/200 or less in the better eye. To understand this definition, consider that 20/20 acuity means that a person can see at 20 feet what a person with normal vision can see at 20 feet. However, a person with an acuity of 20/200 needs to be at a distance of 20 feet to see what a person with normal vision can see from a distance of 200 feet.

When we define blindness in terms of visual acuity, we are evaluating a person's ability to see with his or her fovea (which, as we saw in Chapter

3, is the cone-rich area of the retina that is responsible for detail vision). While poor foveal vision is the most common definition of blindness, a person with good foveal vision but little peripheral vision can also be considered legally blind. Thus, a person with normal (20/20) foveal vision but little or no vision in the periphery can be legally blind. This situation, which is called **tunnel vision,** results from diseases we will discuss below, such as advanced glaucoma or retinitis pigmentosa (a form of retinal degeneration), which affect peripheral vision but leave the foveal cones unharmed.

Corneal Disease and Injury

The **cornea,** which is responsible for about 70 percent of the eye's focusing power (Lerman, 1966), is the window to vision, because light first passes through this structure on its way to the retina. In order for a sharp image to be formed on the retina the cornea must be transparent, but this transparency is occasionally lost when injury, infection, or allergic reactions cause the formation of scar tissue on the cornea. This scar tissue causes decreased

- 2 million cases of corneal disease are diagnosed each year.
- 1.3 million injuries occur each year.
- The most common causes of eye injuries are (in order of incidence) metal pieces, contact lenses, motor vehicles, chemicals, baseballs, and glass.
- More than 35,000 Americans suffer eye injuries from sports each year. Baseball, racquet sports, and basketball account for the largest number of sports-related injuries.
- Corneal problems are the leading cause of monocular (one-eyed) blindness.
- Over 10,000 corneal transplant operations are performed each year.

Note: All data in this chapter regarding the incidence of vision problems are from *Vision Problems in the United States,* National Society to Prevent Blindness, New York, 1978. Note that these numbers refer only to vision problems in the United States.

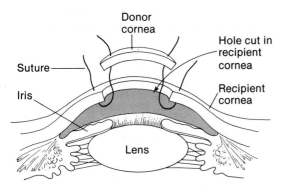

F I G U R E 10. 6 Corneal transplant operation. The scarred part of the cornea has been removed, and the donor cornea is about to be sutured in place.

visual acuity and sometimes makes lights appear to be surrounded by a halo, which looks like a shimmering rainbow. In addition, **corneal disease and injury** can also cause pain. Drugs, which can often bring the cornea back to its transparent state, are the first treatment for corneal problems. If drugs fail, however, clear vision can often be restored by a **corneal transplant** operation. The basic principle underlying this operation is shown in Figure 10.6. The scarred area of the cornea, usually a disc about 6–8 mm in diameter, is removed and replaced by a piece of cornea taken from a donor. For best results, this donor should be a young adult who died from an acute disease or from an injury that left the corneal tissue in good condition. In the past, a major problem with this operation was the necessity of transplanting the donor cornea within a few hours after the donor's death. Recently, however, two procedures have been developed that make it possible to store corneal material for long periods of time. A donor cornea stored at 4 °C in a special solution called M-K will keep for up to a week, and a cornea that is slowly brought down to a temperature of −120 °C (a technique called **cryopreservation**) will keep indefinitely.

One of the major problems which must be dealt with in operations such as heart and liver transplants is rejection of the organ, which can occur because of antibodies carried in the blood. Rejection is not, however, a problem for corneal transplants because the cornea is not in contact with the blood supply. Thus, of the over 10,000 corneal transplants performed every year, 85 percent are successful. Remember, however, that a corneal transplant operation involves only a small piece of the eye—there is no such thing as an eye transplant. Indeed, the problems involved in transplanting a whole eye are overwhelming. For one thing, the optic nerve and retina are sensitive to lack of oxygen, so once the circulation is cut off, irreversible damage occurs within minutes, just as is the case for the brain. Thus, keeping the donor's eye alive presents a serious problem. And even if it were possible to keep an eye alive, there is the problem of connecting the one million optic nerve fibers of the donor's eye to the corresponding nerve fibers of the patient's optic nerve. At this point, whole eye transplants are purely science fiction.

Clouding of the Lens (Cataract)

Like the cornea, the **lens** is transparent and is important for focusing a sharp image of the incoming light on the retina. Clouding of the lens, which is called a **cataract,** is sometimes present at birth (**congenital cataract**), can be caused by another eye disease (**secondary cataract**), or can be caused by injury (**traumatic cataract**), but the most common cause of cataract is old age (**senile cataract**). Cataracts develop, for reasons as yet unknown, in 75 percent of people over 65 and in 95 percent of people over 85.

Although millions of people have cataracts, in only about 15 percent of the cases does the cat-

---

- Cataracts are the third leading cause of blindness, accounting for 42,000 cases.
- 41.2 million people over 40 have cataracts.
- Three out of 4 people over 65 (25 million people) have cataracts.
- 5–10 million people become visually disabled every year due to cataracts.
- 300,000 to 400,000 cataract operations are performed every year.

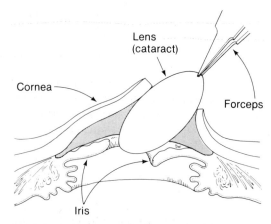

Last stage of a cataract operation. The figure shows the lens being removed from the eye with forceps.

aract interfere with a person's normal activities, and only 5 percent are serious enough to require surgery—the only treatment.

The basic principle underlying a cataract operation is illustrated in Figure 10.7. A small opening is made in the eye, through which the lens is removed, either by pushing on the eyeball to force the lens out and then removing it with forceps or by a method called **phacoemulsification,** which uses ultrasound to remove the lens. A hollow needle-like instrument, vibrating 40,000 times per second, is inserted into the lens, the high-frequency vibrations break up the lens, and the resulting pieces are sucked out of the eye through the hollow needle.

Removal of the clouded lens clears a path so that light can reach the retina unobstructed, but in removing the lens we have also removed some of the eye's focusing power. (Remember that the cornea accounts for 70 percent of the eye's focusing power; the lens is responsible for the remaining 30 percent.) Although we can fit the patient with glasses, this creates problems of its own, because glasses can enlarge the image falling on the retina by as much as 20–35 percent. If one eye receives this enlarged image and the other receives a normal image, the brain cannot combine the two images to form a single, clear perception. A better solution is to fit the patient with contact lenses, which

only enlarge the image by about 6 percent, but many older people have difficulty inserting and removing these lenses every day. They need a lens that neither changes image size nor requires daily insertion and removal. This need appears to be met by a relatively new development in the treatment of cataract—the **intraocular lens.**

The idea of implanting a lens inside the eye where the old lens used to be goes back 200 years, but the first workable design for an intraocular lens was not proposed until 1949. The lenses introduced in the 1950s were not, however, very successful because they were too heavy, but recent developments in lightweight plastics have resulted in ultra lightweight lenses, like the one shown in Figure 10.8. Although the intraocular lens was still considered experimental in the early 1970s, today the intraocular lens is a routine part of the cataract operation.

DAMAGE TO THE RETINA

The retina's source of life is the nourishment it receives from the retinal circulation and from the **pigment epithelium** upon which it rests. All four conditions described below affect the retinal circulation or the relationship between the retina and the pigment epithelium in some way, resulting in a loss of vision.

Diabetic Retinopathy

Before the isolation of insulin in 1922, most people with severe **diabetes,** a condition in which the body doesn't produce enough insulin, had a life expectancy of less than 20 years. The synthesis of insulin (which won the 1923 Nobel prize for its discoverers) greatly increased the life expectancy of diabetics, but one result of this greater life expectancy has been a great increase in an eye problem called **diabetic retinopathy.** Of the 10 million diabetics in the United States, about 4 million show some signs of this problem.

Figure 10.9 shows what happens as the disease progresses. At first the capillaries swell, as shown

(a)

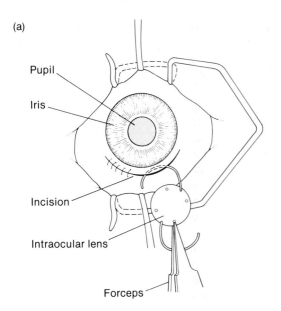

Pupil

Iris

Incision

Intraocular lens

Forceps

(b)

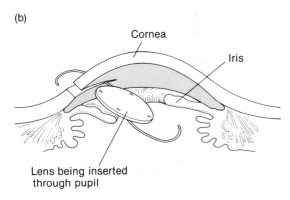

Cornea

Iris

Lens being inserted
through pupil

(c)

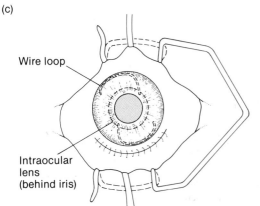

Wire loop

Intraocular
lens
(behind iris)

F I G U R E 10. 8 Installing an intraocular lens in the eye after the cataract (the person's clouded lens) has been removed. (a) Top view of the eye, showing lens being inserted into the eye through an incision. (b) Side view, showing the lens partially inserted. (c) Top view, showing the lens in place behind the iris. The small wire loops hold the lens in place.

- 4 million people suffer from diabetic retinopathy.
- Diabetic retinopathy accounts for 37,000 cases of blindness.
- 300,000 diabetics suffer severe decreases in vision due to diabetic retinopathy.

in Figure 10.9(a). Most cases of diabetic retinopathy stop here; even so, a large number of diabetics suffer vision losses even when the disease stops at this point. Further progression of the disease, which occurs in a small percentage of patients, involves a process called **neovascularization.** Abnormal new blood vessels are formed, as shown in Figure 10.9(b), which do not supply the retina with adequate oxygen and which may rupture and bleed into the **vitreous humor** (the jelly-like substance that fills the eyeball), interfering with the passage of light to the retina and causing, in some cases, scarring and retinal detachment (see below).

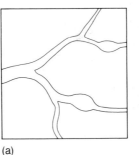
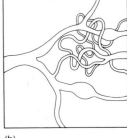

(a)   (b)

F I G U R E 10. 9 Blood vessels in diabetic retinopathy. (a) In early stages of the disease, blood vessels swell and leak slightly. (b) In later stages, abnormal new blood vessels (neovascularization) grow on the surface of the retina.

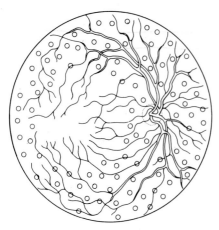

F I G U R E 10. 10 Laser photocoagulation for the treatment of diabetic retinopathy. The picture shown here illustrates the technique of panretinal photocoagulation. Each dot represents a small laser burn.

One technique for stopping neovascularization is called **laser photocoagulation,** in which a laser beam of high-energy light is aimed at leaking blood vessels. The laser "photocoagulates," or seals off, these vessels, thereby stopping the bleeding. Recently, a new procedure called **panretinal photocoagulation** has been used with some success. In this technique, the laser scatters 2,000 or more tiny burns on the retina, as shown in Figure 10.10. The burns do not directly hit the leaking blood vessels, but by destroying part of the retina they decrease the retina's need for oxygen, which causes the leaking blood vessels to dry up and go away. If laser photocoagulation is not successful in stopping neovascularization, a procedure called a **vitrectomy,** shown in Figure 10.11, is used to eliminate the blood inside the eye. In this operation, which is done only as a last resort, a hollow needle placed inside the eye sucks out the vitreous humor and the blood which is blocking vision, then replaces the vitreous humor with a salt solution. While this procedure removes the blood inside the eye, it does not stop neovascularization, which caused the bleeding in the first place.

Although a complete cure for diabetic retinopathy has not yet been discovered, a recent series of tests carried out by the National Eye Institute

F I G U R E 10. 11 Vitrectomy. The hollow needle inserted into the eyeball first sucks out the liquid inside the eye and then fills the eyeball with a salt solution.

indicates that laser photocoagulation reduces by 60 percent the chance that someone with diabetic retinopathy will suffer severe visual loss.

Macular Degeneration

Imagine your frustration if you could see everywhere *except* where you were looking, so every time you looked at something you lost sight of it. That is exactly what happens if a region of the retina called the **macula** is damaged. The macula is an area about 5 mm in diameter that surrounds and includes the cone-rich fovea (itself only slightly larger than one of the periods on this page). If the macula degenerates, blindness results in the center of vision, as in Figure 10.12. This condition is extremely debilitating because, although peripheral vision remains intact, the elimination of central vision makes reading impossible.

There are a number of forms of **macular degeneration,** but the most common is called **senile**

- Macular degeneration is the second leading cause of blindness, accounting for 60,000 cases.
- Macular degeneration is the leading cause of blindness of people over 75 years old.

F I G U R E   10. 12   Macular degeneration causes a loss of central vision, as shown above.

macular degeneration because it occurs, without obvious reason, in older people. In its mild form, there is a slight thinning of the cone receptors and the formation of small white or yellow lumps on the retina. This form of macular degeneration usually progresses slowly and may not cause serious visual problems. In 5–20 percent of the cases, however, small new blood vessels, similar to those in diabetic retinopathy, grow underneath the macula area of the retina. These new blood vessels form very rapidly—over a period of only 1–2 months—and leak fluid into the macula, killing the cone receptors.

Until recently, there was no treatment for senile macular degeneration. However, a recent study by the National Eye Institute indicates that if the problem can be caught at an early stage in many patients with the more severe form of the disease, laser photocoagulation can stop or greatly reduce leakage of the newly formed vessels. This study, which was originally intended to last 5 years, was termed a success after only 3 years, and in 1982 the Eye Institute held a press conference to alert

ophthalmologists to this new way of treating this form of senile macular degeneration.

Dr. Carl Kupfer, director of the Eye Institute, stated at the press conference, "We believe that these findings may save as many as 13,000 Americans from going blind in the next year. That would mean that the expected nationwide incidence of blindness can be reduced by almost 14 percent over the next year." To achieve such dramatic results, however, laser treatment should be started as soon as the abnormal blood vessels begin forming and must be started before the disease progresses to where the fovea, at the macula's center, becomes damaged by the leaking vessels.

Detached Retina

Before I came to Pittsburgh, I lived in Boston for 2 years. I was lucky enough to be there in 1967 when the Boston Red Sox won the American League pennant for the first time since 1946. One of the star players on that team, Tony Conigliaro, was hit by a pitch the following year and began complain-

B O X 10. 2 / *Art of the Eye I: Artists with Visual Disabilities*

The loss of vision caused by accidents or disease is especially difficult for people who rely on vision for their livelihood. To a visual artist, losing vision is particularly devastating since it threatens their ability to continue as artists. Many artists have, however, had severe visual problems. Claude Monet became legally blind due to cataracts (Ravin, 1985) and Edgar Degas' legal blindness may have been due to macular degeneration (Forecast, 1986). These visual losses did not, however, stop Monet or Degas from painting.

Recently a group of contemporary American artists with various visual disabilities has displayed its works in a traveling exhibit called "Art of the Eye." The beauty of this exhibit is that it provides an opportunity for these artists to communicate, both through their art and their words, something about the perceptual changes caused by their eye problems. In this box, and the next one, we will present some of the works in this exhibit and the artists' descriptions of their visual problems.

Mary Solbrig, who is blind in one eye and has lost most of her central vision in the other eye due to macular degeneration, describes her vision as follows:

> Glare is a severe problem, but fortunately form and color remain. As I look around me, things are out of focus and distorted. Doorways have strange lines; glare obliterates objects completely; and there is a constant movement and quivering like a bed of worms, or the ground when a mole crawls through. The yellow line on the highway moves up and down like a snake crawling. Windows change from convex to concave. Houses and high buildings become crooked or wavy (Forecast, 1986, p. 31).

Her painting, shown below, reflects some of the distortions of vision she describes.

Nancy Luomala suffers from double vision due to head injuries sustained in an automobile accident. She depicts her visual experience in the mixed-media light box shown in Color Plate 10.1.

Mary Solbrig, *Our Home*, 1985 (watercolor).

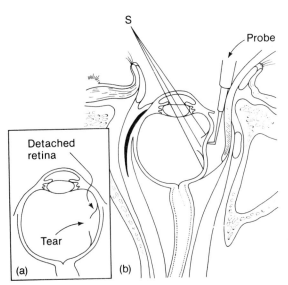

S

Probe

Detached
retina

Tear

(a)   (b)

F I G U R E   10. 13   (a) A detached retina. (b)
Procedure for reattaching the retina. To locate the site
of detachment, a probe pushes the eyeball from outside
while the surgeon, at S, looks into the eye. Once the
site of the detachment is located, the outside of the
eye is marked and a cooling or heating probe is applied
at the marked point.

ing that he could not see well—he had fuzzy vision
and found it difficult to catch what would have
been routine fly balls. What followed was a debate
between Dick Williams, the Red Sox manager, who
claimed that Conigliaro was actually all right, and
Conigliaro, who insisted that he couldn't see well.
Tests at the Massachusetts Eye and Ear Infirmary
confirmed that Conigliaro did, indeed, have a serious problem: His retina had become detached from
the underlying pigment epithelium, as shown in
Figure 10.13, and although attempts were made to
reattach his retina, Conigliaro's vision never
returned to normal and his baseball career was
ended. More recently, the detached retina suffered

- 25,000 cases of detached retina are reported
  each year.
- 6,000 people lose vision in one eye due to
  detached retina each year.

by Sugar Ray Leonard, the welterweight boxing
champion, caused him to retire temporarily from
boxing. His return to boxing a number of years
later occurred amid much discussion as to whether
returning to the ring was worth the risk of losing
sight in one eye. As it turned out, Leonard won
both the fight and the gamble with his sight, apparently escaping without damaging his eye.

A **detached retina** affects vision for two reasons: (1) For good image formation, the retina must
lie smoothly on top of the pigment epithelium, and
(2) more important, when the retina loses contact
with the pigment epithelium, the visual pigments
in the detached area are separated from enzymes
in the epithelium necessary for pigment regeneration. When the visual pigment can no longer
regenerate, that area of the retina becomes blind.

The treatment for a detached retina is an
operation that attempts to reattach it. The basic
idea of this operation is to cause the formation of
scar tissue inside the eye that will attach itself to
the retina and anchor it in place. This is accomplished by applying either a cooling or a heating
probe to exactly the right place on the outside of
the eyeball. Figure 10.13(b) shows the procedure
used to determine where to apply the probe. While
looking into the eye with a special viewing device,
the surgeon presses on the outside of the eyeball,
which causes an indentation that can be seen inside
the eye. The surgeon presses at a number of points,
until the indentation inside the eyeball matches
the location of the tear or hole in the retina, where
the detachment originated. Once the correct point
is located, it is marked on the outside of the eyeball, and that point is cooled or heated to create
an inflammatory response. The retina must then
be pushed flush with the wall of the eyeball. This
is accomplished by placing a band around the outside of the eyeball that creates a dumbbell-shaped
eye. Then, with the retina pressed against the wall
of the eye, the inflammation causes scarring that
"welds" the retina back onto the pigment epithelium. If the area of detached retina is not too big,
there is a 70–80 percent chance that this procedure will work. In most cases it restores vision,
although vision is sometimes not restored even
though the retina is successfully reattached. The

larger the detached area, the less likely it is that this operation (or others, which we will not describe here) will work.

Hereditary Retinal Degeneration

The most common form of retinal degeneration is a disease called **retinitis pigmentosa**, a **hereditary retinal degeneration** that is passed from one generation to the next (although not always affecting everyone in a family). We know little about what actually causes the disease, although one hypothesis is that it is caused by a problem in the pigment epithelium.

- Retinitis pigmentosa accounts for 26,000 cases of blindness.

A person with retinitis pigmentosa usually shows no signs of the disease until reaching adolescence. At this time, the person might begin to notice some difficulty in seeing at night, since the disease first attacks the rod receptors. As the person gets older, the disease slowly progresses, causing further losses of vision in the peripheral retina. Then, in its final stages, which may occur as early as a person's 30s or as late as the 50s or 60s (depending on the strain of the disease), retinitis pigmentosa also attacks the cones, resulting in complete blindness.

OPTIC NERVE DAMAGE

Glaucoma

Glaucoma, the leading cause of blindness in the United States, causes nerve fibers in the optic nerve to degenerate, preventing the nerve impulses generated by the retina from being transmitted to the brain. Although the end result of glaucoma is damage to the optic nerve, the source of the problem is at the front of the eye.

Figure 10.14(a) is a cross section of the front

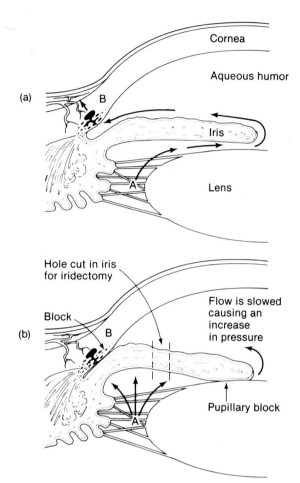

F I G U R E 10. 14   (a) Arrows indicate the flow of aqueous humor in the normal eye. The aqueous is produced at A and leaves the eye at B. In open-angle glaucoma, the aqueous cannot leave the eye, due to a blockage at B. (b) In closed-angle glaucoma, the raised iris causes a pupillary block that hinders the flow of aqueous from the eye. An iridectomy—cutting a hole in the iris—can be performed to provide a way for the aqueous to reach B.

of the eye. Under normal conditions, **aqueous humor**—the liquid found in the space between the cornea and lens—which is continuously produced at A, passes between the iris and lens following the path indicated by the arrows, then drains from the eye at B. In glaucoma the drainage of aqueous humor is partially blocked. In **closed-angle glaucoma** a **pupillary block** (Figure 10.14b) constricts the

- Glaucoma is the leading cause of blindness, accounting for 62,000 cases.
- 2 million people over 35 have glaucoma.
- 178,000 new cases of glaucoma are reported each year.
- Over $30 million per year is spent just for one type of eyedrop used to treat glaucoma.

opening between the iris and lens, making it more difficult for the aqueous to get through the opening and causing a pressure buildup behind the iris. This pressure buildup pushes the iris, thereby "closing the angle" between the cornea and iris and blocking the area at B where the aqueous leaves the eye. In **open-angle glaucoma** the eye looks normal as in Figure 10.14(a), but the drainage area at B is partially blocked, making it more difficult for the aqueous to leave the eye. The blocks that occur in both closed- and open-angle glaucoma result in a large resistance to the outflow of aqueous humor, and, since the aqueous continues to be produced inside the eye, the **intraocular pressure**—the pressure inside the eyeball—rises. This increase in intraocular pressure has two effects: (1) It compresses the blood vessels that provide nourishment to the retina, and (2) it presses on the head of the optic nerve at the back of the eye. These effects result in degeneration of the optic nerve fibers, and this degeneration results in blindness.

The increase in pressure that occurs in closed-angle glaucoma usually happens very rapidly and is accompanied by pain. The treatment for this type of glaucoma is an operation called an **iridectomy,** in which a small hole is cut in the iris, as shown in Figure 10.14(b). This hole opens a channel through which the aqueous can flow, thereby releasing the pressure on the iris. With the pressure gone, the iris flattens out and uncovers the area at B so the aqueous can flow out of the eye.

Intraocular pressure increases more slowly in open-angle glaucoma, which can often be treated by medication that brings down the pressure either by slowing the production of aqueous or by opening the blockage at B. Fortunately, open-angle glau-

coma (by far the most common type, accounting for about 85 percent of all glaucoma) progresses slowly enough that, if it is diagnosed in time, medication will usually decrease the pressure. In 5–10 percent of the cases of open-angle glaucoma, medications do not decrease the pressure, and an operation becomes necessary. The goal of this operation is to cut an opening at B that enables the aqueous to flow out.

THE EYE EXAMINATION

So far, we have described some of the things that can go wrong with the eye and how these problems are treated. In this part of the chapter, we will describe the procedures used to uncover some of these problems. Before describing the eye examination, however, we should consider who examines the eye.

Who Examines Eyes?

There are three types of professionals involved in eye care: ophthalmologists, optometrists, and opticians. We will consider each in turn.

(1) An **ophthalmologist** is an M.D. who has completed undergraduate school and 4 years of medical school, which provide general medical training. In order to become an ophthalmologist, a person needs 4 or more years of training after graduation from medical school to learn how to medically and surgically treat eye problems. Some ophthalmologists receive even further training, then specialize in specific areas such as pediatric ophthalmology (practice limited to children), diseases of the cornea, retinal diseases, or glaucoma. Most ophthalmologists, however, treat all eye problems, as well as prescribing glasses and fitting contact lenses.

(2) An **optometrist** has completed undergraduate school and, after four years of additional study, has received a doctor of optometry (O.D.) degree. Optometrists can examine eyes and fit and prescribe glasses or contact lenses, but if they find eye disease, they refer patients to an ophthalmologist.

BOX 10. 3 / *Art of the Eye II: Artists with Retinitis Pigmentosa and Retinal Detachment*

Don Pearson describes the effect of retinitis pigmentosa (RP) on his vision as follows:

> RP has had quite an impact on my vision. Tunnel vision makes things especially difficult at times. For example, when introduced to a person for the first time, I was accustomed to looking at his/her face. I would often notice a look of bewilderment, not realizing that the person was offering his/her hand for me to shake. Now I check to see whether the hand is extended.
>
> Nightblindness, another symptom, doesn't occur just at night. Entering a darkened room or walking under a shade tree can cause the same effect. I enjoy going dining and dancing with friends, but most places are so dark I can barely make out the candle on the table. I am always sticking my fingers in my dinner to find out where the food is. On the dance floor I can't make out much of what's going on around me. As long as I keep hand contact, I know I'm doing fine (Forecast, 1986, pp. 70–71).

Scott Nelson, the organizer of the exhibition, produced the apparatus shown here to illustrate the tunnel vision experienced by victims of RP. Looking through the viewing tubes (at left atop the tripod) narrows the field of view to the 15 degrees of visual angle experienced by Nelson. You can simulate this for yourself by looking through a standard toilet paper tube (4$\frac{1}{2}$ inches long and 1$\frac{1}{2}$ inches in diameter), which will narrow your field of view to about 19 degrees.

Nelson describes his work and his experience with tunnel vision as follows:

> Glance #2,672,493 is my contribution to an understanding of tunnel vision caused by retinitis pigmentosa. Made of welded and painted steel, this work attests to the fact that I seldom take a leisurely stroll. Seeing, for me, is a

Scott Nelson, *Glance #2,672,493,* 1985

highly complex activity that involves a myriad of calculated decisions about shape, depth, spatial arrangements and movement. Although my combined visual field is restricted to 15 degrees, I am able to assemble fragments of the visual field into complete images through scanning and tracking.

> It takes but a mere second for me to obtain four or five views of a complete field. This, together with a weak sensation of light entering from the periphery, convinces me that my field is complete and the world is there (Forecast, 1986, pp. 22–23).

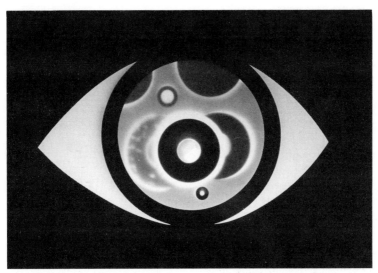

Carmello Ganello, *Retinal Detachment*, 1985 (mixed media light box)

Carmelo Gannello, whose art stems directly from his visual condition, describes his condition and the work inspired by it as follows:

I slipped and fell on the ice on the way to work one morning. My head didn't hit anything, but the following morning I noticed a veil over my eyes which kept coming and going. During the day the veil became worse and began to obstruct my vision. So I went to the eye doctor who told me that I had a retinal detachment. I was only 36 years old. It was already very difficult for me to see properly and, as I was an artist, this news was especially distressing to me; I wept bitterly.

. . . I had a second retinal detachment in the same eye and had to be hospitalized again. I lost more vision. Now . . . I experienced eye floaters.*

. . . At about this time, both my teacher . . . and my eye doctor encouraged me as I described my eye floaters. "Paint what you see," they said, and I did. . . . I started to make circles and other shapes I see in my eyes. However, I was keenly aware of one problem with my circles: they tended to appear medical, and I wanted them to be a form of art, directly related to my experience. I wanted to use my vision to create a living statement about how a visually impaired person sees the world around him. My shadows and floaters come in all shapes and sizes, from very large to small, and they travel all around my field of vision. Everywhere I look, the floaters are there. They are intensely black and some have bright flashing lights. This is what I use in my art—literally art of the eye (Forecast, 1986, pp. 54–55).

*Floaters are caused by opaque particles floating inside the vitreous humor, the jelly-like substance that fills the eyeball. Gannello's floaters are probably due to pieces of retinal material and blood inside the eyeball. It is common for people with normal vision to sometimes see small floaters. If you see them, don't worry. Floaters only become a problem when they are due to other more serious visual problems such as retinal detachment or hemorrhaging.

In general, optometrists cannot prescribe drugs, although this is a controversial issue, and bills have been passed in some state legislatures that allow optometrists to make limited use of some drugs.

(3) An **optician** is trained to fabricate and fit glasses and, in some states, contact lenses, on the prescription of an ophthalmologist or an optometrist.

What Happens During an Eye Exam?

The basic aims of an eye exam are (1) to determine how well the patient can see, (2) to correct vision if it is defective, (3) to determine the causes of defective vision by examining the optics of the eye and checking for eye diseases, and (4) to diagnose diseases that the patient may not even be aware of. To accomplish these aims, an eye specialist usually performs the following procedures:

Taking a medical history. The first step in an eye exam is to take a medical history. This history focuses on any eye problems that the patient may have had in the past, on any current eye problems, and on any general medical problems that may be related to the patient's eye vision.

Measuring visual acuity. This is the familiar part of the eye exam, in which you are asked to read letters on an eye chart like the one in Figure 10.15. The E at the top of the chart is usually the 20/400 line, which means that a person with normal vision should be able to see the E from a distance of 400 feet. Since the eye chart is usually viewed from about 20 feet, people with normal vision see the E easily. When asked to read the smallest line he or she can see, the patient usually picks a line that is easily read. With a little encouragement, however, most patients find that they can see lines smaller than the one they originally picked, and the examiner has the patient read smaller and smaller lines until letters are missed. The smallest line a person can read indicates his or her visual acuity, with normal vision defined as an acuity of 20/20. A person with worse than normal acuity, say 20/40, must view a display from a distance of 20 feet to see what a person with normal acuity can see at 40 feet. A person with better than normal acuity, say

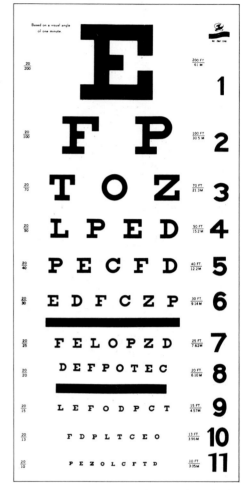

F I G U R E 10. 15 Snellen eye chart used to test visual acuity.

20/10, can see from a distance of 20 feet what a person with normal vision must view from 10 feet.

It is important to realize that the visual acuity test described above tests only foveal vision. When you read an eye chart you look directly at each letter, so the image of that letter falls on your fovea. Thus, as mentioned earlier, a person who scores 20/20 on a visual acuity test can still be classified as being legally blind if he or she has little or no vision in the periphery. Testing peripheral vision is usually not part of a routine eye exam, so we will describe how this is done at the end of the chapter.

In addition to testing far vision, it is also cus-

No. 1
In short-sighted persons the eye-ball is too long, and the light rays come to a focus in front of the retina,

No. 2
while in far-sighted persons the eye-ball is too short, and the focal point, therefore, falls be-

No. 3
hind the retina. In either case a blurred image is received upon the retina. In order

No. 4
to overcome this blurring, and thus correct the optical defect, the eye un-

No. 6
consciously makes an effort by which the ciliary muscle acts on

No. 8
the lens. This effort explains why eye-strain may cause

No. 10
pain and discomfort. An optical correction for

No. 12
the refractive error is found in specta-

F I G U R E 10. 16 Card for testing close vision. The patient's close vision is measured by determining the smallest line that he or she can read from a comfortable reading distance.

tomary to test near vision, especially in older patients who may be experiencing the effects of presbyopia (see p. 73). This is done by having them read the smallest line of a card like the one in Figure 10.16 from a comfortable reading distance.

Refraction. A score of 20/60 on a visual acuity test indicates worse than normal acuity but does not indicate what is causing this loss of acuity. Acuity could be decreased by one of the diseases described earlier or by a problem in focusing—myopia, hyperopia, or astigmatism. If the problem lies in the focusing mechanism of the eye, it is usually easily corrected by glasses or contact lenses. **Refraction** is the procedure used to determine the power of the corrective lenses needed to achieve clear vision.

The first step in refraction is a **retinoscopy exam**—an examination of the eye with a device called a retinoscope. This device projects a streak of light into the eye that is reflected into the eye of the examiner. The examiner moves the retinoscope back and forth and up and down across the eye, noticing what the reflected light looks like. If the patient's eye is focusing the light correctly, the examiner sees the whole pupil filled with light, and no correction is necessary (in this case, the patient usually will have tested at 20/20 or better in the

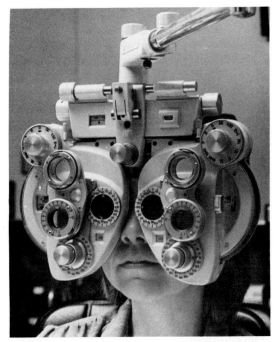

F I G U R E 10. 17 A device for placing different corrective lenses in front of the patient's eyes. Different lenses are placed in front of the eye during the retinoscopy exam and again as the patient looks at the eye chart.

visual acuity test). If, however, the patient's eye is not focusing the light correctly, the examiner sees a streak of light move back and forth across the pupil as the streak of light from the retinoscope is moved across the eye.

To determine the correction needed to bring the patient's eye to 20/20 vision, the examiner places corrective lenses in front of the eye while still moving the streak of light from the retinoscope back and forth. One way of placing these lenses in front of the eye is to use a device like the one shown in Figure 10.17. This device contains a variety of lenses that can be changed by turning a dial. The examiner's goal is to find the lens that causes the whole pupil to fill up with light when the retinoscope is moved back and forth. This lens brings light to a focus on the retina and is usually close to the one that will be prescribed to achieve 20/20 vision.

The retinoscopy exam results in a good first

approximation of the correct lens to prescribe for a patient, but the ultimate test is what the patient sees. To determine this, the patient looks at the eye chart while the examiner places first one lens and then another in front of the patient's eyes and asks which one results in the clearest vision. When the examiner determines which lens results in 20/20 vision, he writes a prescription for glasses or contact lenses. To fit contact lenses after determining the prescription, the examiner must match the shape of the contact lens to the shape of the patient's cornea.

The procedure described above, which is called refraction, is used to determine the correction needed to achieve clear far vision. Using a procedure we will not describe here, the examiner also determines whether a correction is needed to achieve clear near vision. This is particularly important for patients over 45 years old, who may experience reading difficulties due to presbyopia.

External eye exam. In an **external eye exam,** the examiner uses a variety of tests to check the condition of the external eye. He checks pupillary reaction by shining light into the eye, to see if the pupil responds by closing when the light is presented and opening when the light is removed. He also checks the color of the eye and surrounding tissues. "Red eye" may indicate that an inflammation is present. The examiner checks eye movement by having the patient follow a moving target, and he checks the alignment of the eyes by having the patient look at a target. If they are aligned correctly, both eyes will look directly at the target, but if the eyes are misaligned, one eye will look at the target, and the other will veer off to one side.

Slit lamp examination. The **slit lamp examination** checks the condition of the cornea and lens. The slit lamp, shown in Figure 10.18, projects a narrow slit of light into the patient's eye. This light can be precisely focused at different places inside the eye, and the examiner views this sharply focused slit of light through a binocular magnifier. This slit of light is like the sharp edge of a knife that cuts through the eye.

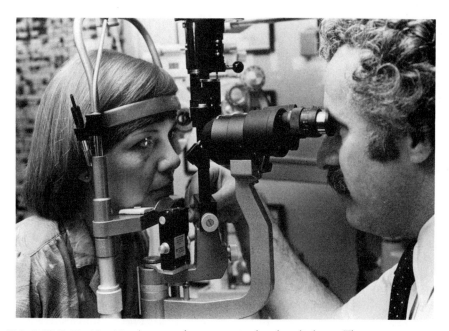

F I G U R E 10. 18 A patient being examined with a slit lamp. The examiner is checking the condition of the lens and cornea by viewing the slit of light through a binocular magnifier.

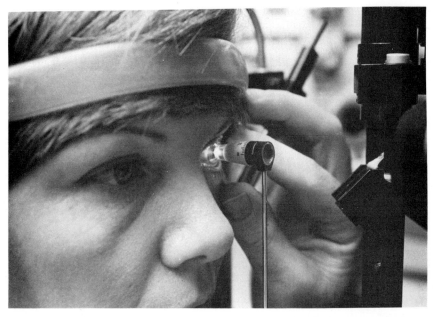

F I G U R E 10. 19 An applanation tonometer being applied to a patient's cornea.

What does the examiner see as he looks at the "cutting edge" of light from the slit lamp? By focusing the light at different levels inside the cornea and lens, the examiner can detect small imperfections—places where the cornea or lens is not completely transparent—which cannot be seen by any other method. These imperfections may indicate corneal disease or injury or the formation of a cataract.

Tonometry. Tonometry measures the intraocular pressure, the pressure inside the eye, and is therefore the test for glaucoma. Nowadays, an instrument called a **tonometer** is used to measure intraocular pressure. But before the development of this device, it was known that large increases of intraocular pressure, which accompany severe cases of glaucoma, cause the eye to become so hard that this hardness could be detected by pushing on the eyeball with a finger.

There are several types of tonometers, which measure the intraocular pressure by pushing on the cornea. The Schiotz tonometer is a hand-held device that consists of a small plunger attached to a cali- brated weight. The weight pushes the plunger and indents the cornea. If the intraocular pressure is high, the plunger causes a smaller indentation than if the intraocular pressure is normal. Thus, intraocular pressure is determined by measuring the indentation of the cornea. (Though this procedure may sound rather painful, it is not, because the examiner applies a few drops of anesthetic to the cornea before applying the tonometer.)

The applanation tonometer, shown being applied to a patient's cornea in Figure 10.19, is a more sophisticated and accurate instrument than the Schiotz tonometer. After a few drops of anesthetic are applied to the cornea, the flat end of a cylindrical rod, called an **applanator,** is slowly moved against the cornea by the examiner, who watches the applanator's progress through the same magnifiers used for the slit lamp exam (Figure 10.18). The examiner pushes the end of the applanator against the cornea until enough pressure is exerted to flatten a small area on the cornea's curved surface. The greater the force that must be exerted to flatten the cornea, the greater the intraocular pressure.

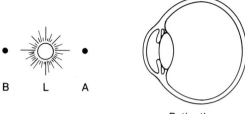

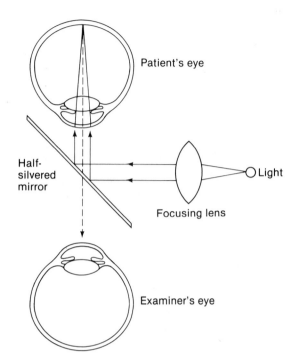

FIGURE 10.20 Ways to light up the inside of the eye that won't work. The light at L is blocked if the examiner's eye is positioned at A, and it blinds the examiner's eye positioned at B.

Ophthalmoscopy. So far, we have looked at the outside of the eye (external eye exam), examined the lens and cornea (slit lamp exam), and measured the intraocular pressure (tonometry), but we have yet to look at perhaps the most important structure of all—the retina. Since there is a hole in the front of the eye, it should be simple to see the retina; we only have to look into the hole. Unfortunately, it's not that simple; if you've ever looked into a person's pupil, you realize that it's dark in there. In order to see the retina, we must find some way to light up the inside of the eye.

We might try placing a light at L, as shown in Figure 10.20. This seems like a good idea until we try to look into the patient's eye. If I place my eye at A, my head blocks the light from L, and if I place my eye at B, I am blinded by the light at L. Clearly, neither of these methods will work.

It was not until 1850 that Hermann von Helmholtz, of the Young-Helmholtz theory of color vision (Figure 4.7), invented a device called the **ophthalmoscope.** The principle underlying Helmholtz' ophthalmoscope is shown in Figure 10.21. Helmholtz solved the problem of the blocked or blinding light of Figure 10.20, by placing the light off to the side and directing it into the patient's eye with a half-silvered mirror. The important property of a half-silvered mirror is that it reflects some of the light and transmits the rest, so an examiner positioned as shown in Figure 10.21 can see through the mirror and into the patient's eye. Actual ophthalmoscopes are much more complicated than the one diagrammed in Figure 10.21, consisting of numerous lenses, mirrors, and filters, but the basic

FIGURE 10.21 Principle behind the opthalmoscope. Light is reflected into the patient's eye by the half-silvered mirror. Some of this light is then reflected into the examiner's eye (along the dashed line), allowing the examiner to see the inside of the patient's eye.

principle remains the same as the original ophthalmoscope designed by Helmholtz in 1850.

Figure 10.22 is a patient's-eye view of an examination with an ophthalmoscope. (See also Figure 10.1, which shows a patient being examined with an ophthalmoscope.) Color Plate 10.2 shows what the ophthalmologist sees if the patient has a normal retina. The most prominent features of this view of the retina are the place where the optic nerve leaves the eye (called the **optic disc,** or blind spot), and the arteries and veins of the retina. In his examination, the ophthalmologist focuses on these features, noting any abnormalities in the appearance of the optic disc and retinal circulation. For example, the ophthalmologist could detect the presence of diabetic retinopathy by noticing a number of very small blood vessels (neovascularization). In fact, all the retinal injuries and diseases described above cause some change in the appear-

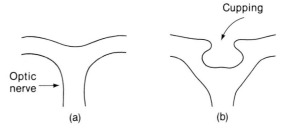

F I G U R E 10. 23 Side view of the optic nerve where it leaves the eye. (a) Normal optic nerve. (b) Optic nerve in eye with glaucoma, which shows "cupping" of optic disc.

gested by the routine tests. For example, a technique called **fluorescein angiography** is used to examine more closely the retinal circulation in patients with diabetic retinopathy. A fluorescent dye is injected intravenously into the arm, and when this dye reaches the retina, it sharply outlines the retinal arteries and veins, as shown in Figure 10.24. Only by this technique can we clearly see the small arteries formed by the neovascularization that accompanies diabetic retinopathy.

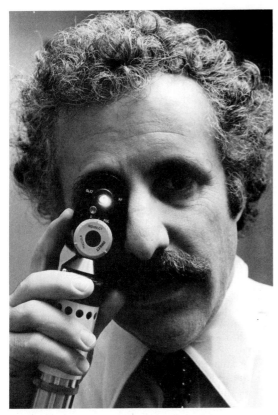

F I G U R E 10. 22 An ophthalmologist looking into your eye.

ance of the retina, which can be detected by looking at the retina with an ophthalmoscope.

Color Plate 10.3 shows the effect of glaucoma on the appearance of the retina. Compare the blood vessels near the optic discs in Color Plates 10.2 and 10.3. Notice that the blood vessels in the normal retina remain visible until they leave the eye in the middle of the optic disc, whereas the vessels in the eye with glaucoma vanish for a short distance, near the rim of the optic disc, and then reappear before leaving the eye. This effect results from the optic disc having been pushed in or "cupped" by the high pressure inside the eye, as shown in Figure 10.23.

Our description of an eye examination has covered most of the tests included in a routine exam. The examiner might decide to carry out a number of other tests if some problem were sug-

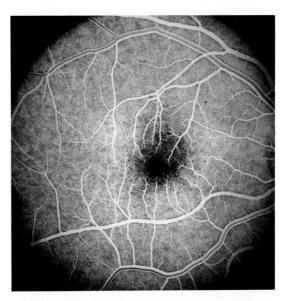

F I G U R E 10. 24 Fluorescent angiogram of a normal eye. In the normal eye, the blood vessels stand out in sharp contrast to the background. (Photograph courtesy of Eye and Ear Hospital of Pittsburgh.)

Other tests, which we will not describe in detail here, include the **electroretinogram,** which measures the electrical response of the rod and cone receptors (useful in diagnosing retinal degenerations such as retinitis pigmentosa), and the **visual field test,** which measures a person's ability to see in both the fovea and the periphery. This test locates blind spots (called "scotoma") that might be caused by retinal degeneration, detachment of the retina, or diseases such as glaucoma.

Summary

1. There are four major types of problems that can cause poor vision: (1) Light is not focused clearly on the retina; (2) light is blurred as it enters the eye; (3) the retina is damaged; and (4) the optic nerve is damaged.
2. Myopia is the inability to see distant objects clearly. In the myopic eye, parallel light rays come to a focus in front of the retina. The blurred vision of myopia can be corrected by glasses or contact lenses.
3. Hyperopia is the inability to see nearby objects clearly. In the hyperopic eye the focus point for parallel light is in back of the retina. Hyperopia can be corrected with glasses or contact lenses.
4. Astigmatism, which is caused by a misshapen cornea, results in blurring of some objects but not others. This condition can be corrected by glasses.
5. A person is considered legally blind if, after correction with glasses or contact lenses, he or she has a visual acuity of 20/200 or less in the better eye. A person with good central (foveal) vision but little peripheral vision can also be considered legally blind.
6. Disease or injury can decrease the transparency of the cornea and cause a blurred image on the retina. Corneal problems can be treated with drugs or can be corrected by a corneal transplant operation.
7. The most common cause of clouding of the lens, or cataract, is old age. In severe cases of cataract, the lens is removed and often replaced with an intraocular lens, which is implanted inside the eye.
8. Diabetic retinopathy is a condition that causes damage to the retina of some people with diabetes. Loss of vision can often be prevented by an operation called laser photocoagulation.
9. Macular degeneration is a degeneration of the macula, the area surrounding the fovea. Laser photocoagulation can often decrease the loss of sight caused by a severe form of macular degeneration.
10. Detached retina, the detachment of the retina from the underlying pigment epithelium, causes a loss of vision in the area of the detachment. The retina can often be reattached by heating or cooling the area on the outside of the eyeball that is adjacent to the detachment.
11. Retinitis pigmentosa is a hereditary disease which causes degeneration of the retina. There is no known treatment for this disease.
12. Glaucoma, the leading cause of blindness in the United States, causes nerve fibers in the optic nerve to degenerate due to a buildup of pressure inside the eye. This buildup of pressure can usually be decreased by means of drugs or surgery.
13. The three types of professionals involved in eye care are ophthalmologists, optometrists, and opticians.
14. A basic eye exam consists of the following procedures: taking a medical history, measuring visual acuity, refraction, external eye exam, slit lamp examination, tonometry, and ophthalmoscopy.
15. Visual acuity, a test of foveal vision, is measured by having a person read an eye chart.
16. The eye is refracted using a device called a retinoscope. The result of this procedure is an estimate of the correction needed to bring a person's eye to 20/20 vision.
17. The slit lamp examination checks the condition of the cornea and the lens.
18. Tonometry, which measures the intraocular pressure, is used to detect glaucoma.
19. A device called an ophthalmoscope enables an examiner to see the optic disc, as well as the arteries, veins, and other features of the retina.
20. Fluorescein angiography is used to examine the retinal circulation in patients with diabetic retinopathy and other conditions that affect the retinal circulation.

Boxes

1. Statistics show that blindness and visual disability affect a large number of people in the United States.
2. Artists of the past and present have continued their work even when stricken with visual disabilities.

Study Questions

1. What are the four major types of problems that cause poor vision? (375)
2. What is myopia? How are parallel rays of light brought to a focus in the myopic eye? What are the two possible causes of this incorrect focusing? (356)
3. How can we cause the point of focus to fall on the retina of a myopic eye without using corrective lenses? (357)
4. What is the far point? Where does the focus point fall if an object is farther from the eye than the far point? At the far point? Closer to the eye than the far point? Can a myope bring faraway objects into focus by accommodation? (357)
5. How must a corrective lens bend light so that a myope can see clearly? (358)
6. What is a diopter? Be able to calculate the correction in diopters if you are given the distance of the far point. (358)
7. What is hyperopia? How are parallel rays of light brought to a focus in the hyperopic eye? How is this condition corrected? (358)
8. What is astigmatism? What is it due to? How is this condition corrected? (359)
9. What is the legal definition of blindness? Can a person who is legally blind have 20/20 vision? (Explain your answer.) (360)
10. The cornea is responsible for about _____ percent of the eye's focusing power. (360)
11. What are the most common causes of eye injuries? What is the first treatment for corneal disease or injury? If that treatment fails, what is the second treatment? (360)
12. Describe a corneal transplant operation. Exactly what is transplanted in this operation? What is cryopreservation? What is the success rate of corneal transplants? (361)
13. What is a cataract? What is the frequency of cataracts in people over 65? What percentage of cataracts are serious enough to interfere with a person's normal activities? What percentage require surgery? (361)
14. Describe a cataract operation. (362)
15. When we remove the lens in a cataract operation, we decrease the focusing power of the eye. Why are glasses an unacceptable solution to this problem? What recent development solves this problem? (362)
16. What is the tissue upon which the retina rests? (362)
17. Describe what happens to the retinal circulation in mild and severe cases of diabetic retinopathy. (363)
18. Describe two procedures which have been used to stop neovascularization. (364)
19. What is a vitrectomy operation? What does it accomplish? (364)
20. What is the second leading cause of blindness in the United States? (364)
21. Describe the mild and severe types of macular degeneration. What new treatment for the severe form of macular degeneration looks promising? (365)
22. What is a detached retina? What are two reasons that a detached retina affects vision? (367)
23. Describe the procedure used to reattach a detached retina. (367)
24. What is retinitis pigmentosa? (368)
25. What is the leading cause of blindness in the United States? (368)
26. Describe the two types of glaucoma. How are these two types of glaucoma treated? (369)
27. Describe the training and capabilities of ophthalmologists, optometrists, and opticians. (369)
28. What are the four basic aims of an eye examination? (372)
29. How is visual acuity determined? What does it mean to say that someone has 20/100 vision? (372)
30. What is the purpose of the refraction part of the eye examination? What are the two steps in the refraction exam? (373)
31. What is the purpose of the external eye exam? (374)
32. What is the purpose of the slit lamp exam? (374)
33. What does the tonometry exam measure? What disease is it a test for? What is the basic principle behind the tonometry exam? (375)
34. What is the basic principle behind an ophthalmoscope? Be able to draw a diagram of an ophthalmoscope. (376)
35. What does the examiner look for in an ophthalmoscopy exam? (376)
36. What is cupping of the optic disc? What does it indicate? (377)
37. What is fluorescein angiography? (377)

Boxes

1. What are some of the major statistics that indicate the impact of vision problems in the United States? (357)
2. What vision problems are common in patients with retinitis pigmentosa? (370)

Glossary

Applanator. The part of an applanation tonometer that is pushed against the patient's cornea to determine the intraocular pressure. (375)

Aqueous humor. The liquid in the space between the cornea and lens of the eye. (368)

Astigmatism. A condition in which vision is blurred in some orientations due to a misshapen cornea. (359)

Blindness. A person is considered legally blind if he or she has visual acuity of 20/200 or less after correction or little peripheral vision. (360)

Cataract. A lens that is clouded. (361)

Cataract, congenital. A cataract present at birth. (361)

Cataract, secondary. A cataract caused by another eye disease. (361)

Cataract, senile. A cataract due to old age. This is the most common form of cataract. (361)

Cataract, traumatic. A cataract caused by injury. (361)

Cornea. The transparent structure at the front of the eye that is the eye's major focusing element. (360)

Corneal disease and injury. Any disease or injury which damages the cornea, causing a loss of transparency. (361)

Corneal transplant. The replacement of a damaged piece of cornea with a piece of healthy cornea taken from a donor. (361)

Cryopreservation. A technique in which a donor cornea is preserved by slowly bringing it down to a temperature of −190 °F. (361)

Detached retina. A condition in which the retina is detached from the back of the eye. (367)

Diabetes. A condition in which the body doesn't produce enough insulin. One side effect of diabetes is a loss of vision due to diabetic retinopathy. (362)

Diabetic retinopathy. Damage to the retina caused as a side effect of diabetes. This condition causes neovascularization—the formation of abnormal blood vessels which do not supply the retina with adequate oxygen and which bleed into the vitreous humor. (362)

Diopter. The strength of a lens. Diopters = 1/far point in meters. See Figure 10.4. (357)

Electroretinogram. An electrical response of the visual receptors that is used in diagnosing retinal degenerations. (378)

External eye exam. Examination of the condition of the outer eye. This exam includes, among other things, examination of the reaction of the pupil to light, the color of the eye, and alignment of the eyes. (374)

Far point. The distance at which the rays from a spot of light are focused on the retina of the unaccommodated eye. For a person with normal vision the far point is at infinity. For a person with myopic vision the spot must be moved closer to the eye to bring the rays to a focus on the retina. (357)

Farsightedness. See Hyperopia.

Fluorescein angiography. A technique in which a fluorescent dye is injected into a person's circulation. The outline of the retinal arteries and veins produced by this dye is observed to determine the condition of the retinal circulation. (377)

Glaucoma. A disease of the eye which results in an increase in intraocular pressure. (368)

Glaucoma, closed-angle. A form of glaucoma in which the iris is pushed up so that it closes the angle between the iris and the cornea and blocks the area through which the aqueous humor normally drains out of the eye. (368)

Glaucoma, open-angle. A form of glaucoma in which the area through which the aqueous normally drains out of the eye is blocked. In this form of glaucoma, the iris remains in its normal position so that the angle between the iris and cornea remains open. (369)

Hereditary retinal degeneration. A degeneration of the retina that is inherited. Retinitis pigmentosa is an example of a hereditary retinal degeneration. (368)

Hyperopia (farsightedness). Inability to see near objects clearly because the focus point for parallel rays of light is behind the retina. (358)

Intraocular lens. A corrective lens that is permanently implanted in the eye to replace the lens removed in a cataract operation. (362)

Intraocular pressure. Pressure inside the eyeball. (369)

Iridectomy. A procedure used to treat closed-angle glaucoma, in which a small hole is cut in the iris. This hole opens a channel through which aqueous humor can flow out of the eye. (369)

Laser photocoagulation. A procedure in which a laser beam is aimed at blood vessels that are leaking due to neovascularization. This laser beam photocoagulates—seals off—the blood vessels and stops the leaking. (364)

Lens. The focusing element of the eye, which light passes through after passing through the cornea and the aqueous humor. (361)

Macula. An area about 5 mm in diameter which surrounds and includes the fovea. (364)

Macular degeneration. A degeneration of the macula. (364)

Macular degeneration, senile. The most common form of macular degeneration, occurring in older people. (364)

Myopia (nearsightedness). Inability to see distant objects clearly because parallel rays of light are brought to a focus in front of the retina. (356)

Myopia, axial. Myopia caused by the fact that the eyeball is too long. (356)

Myopia, refractive. Myopia caused by the fact that the cornea and lens bend light too much (they have too much focusing power). (356)

Neovascularization. The formation of abnormal small blood vessels that occurs in patients with diabetic retinopathy. (363)

Ophthalmologist. A person who has specialized in the medical treatment of the eye by completing 4 or more years of training after receiving the M.D. degree. (369)

Ophthalmoscope. A device that enables an examiner to see the retina and retinal circulation inside the eye. (376)

Ophthalmoscopy. The use of an ophthalmoscope to visualize the retina and retinal circulation. (381)

Optic disc. The disc-shaped area at the back of the eye where the optic nerve leaves the eye. (376)

Optician. A person who is trained to fit glasses and, in some cases, contact lenses. (372)

Optometrist. A person who has received the doctor of optometry (O.D.) degree by completing 4 years of postgraduate study in optometry school. (369)

Panretinal coagulation. A procedure used to stop the bleeding caused by neovascularization, in which a laser is used to scatter 2,000 or more tiny burns on the retina. (364)

Phacoemulsification. A technique for removing a cataract by breaking up the lens with ultrasonic vibrations and then sucking the pieces of lens out of the eye through a hollow needle. (362)

Pigment epithelium. A layer of cells that lines the inside of the eyeball under the retina. (362)

Pupillary block. A blockage that constricts the opening between the iris and lens of the eye, making it difficult for aqueous humor to leave the eye. It is caused by the pushed-up iris that is characteristic of closed-angle glaucoma. (368)

Refraction. A procedure used to determine the power of corrective lenses needed to achieve clear vision. (373)

Retinitis pigmentosa. A hereditary retinal disease that causes a gradual loss of vision. (368)

Retinoscopy exam. Examination with a device called a retinoscope that indicates the power of corrective lenses needed to achieve normal vision. (373)

Slit lamp examination. An examination that checks the condition of the cornea and lens. (374)

Tonometer. A device for measuring the eye's intraocular pressure. (375)

Tonometry. An examination that determines the pressure inside the eye. (375)

Tunnel vision. Vision that results when there is little peripheral vision. (360)

Visual field test. A test that measures a person's ability to see both in the fovea and in the periphery. (378)

Vitrectomy. A procedure in which a hollow needle placed inside the eye sucks out vitreous humor and replaces it with a salt solution. This procedure is used if the vitreous is filled with blood, usually resulting from neovascularization. (364)

Vitreous humor. The jelly-like substance that fills the eyeball. (363)

CHAPTER 11

Hearing I: Psychophysics

A WORLD OF SOUND

Our perceptual world has been, so far in this book, almost exclusively visual. We have devoted many pages to vision both because of its importance and because we know much more about vision than any of the other senses. But hearing, to which we will devote the next three chapters, has functions that rival those of vision in importance. Hearing distinguishes humans from other species by enabling them to communicate ideas and concepts by means of oral language. Hearing adds a richness to our emotional lives through music. And hearing creates a world of sound that provides information about what is happening around us. We usually take this world of sound for granted. But consider, for a moment, this description of one man's experience while sitting in his backyard:

One day last spring . . . my wife and I were sitting in the garden drinking coffee and enjoying the morning sunlight. I suddenly realized as my wife and I talked that I was at that moment hearing her voice and following her conversation and that at the same time I could be aware that the radio inside was playing music, that two dogs in the next yard (out of sight) were playing together (and that one was a puppy and the other a mature, large dog), that the breeze was rustling the leaves in the tree overhead, that a variety of birds were singing and chirping, that an airplane was approaching overhead from the northwest, that the dog in the yard behind me was complaining about something, that a lawn mower was running somewhere in the neighborhood, and that traffic was cruising past on the main road a half a block away. And, I protest, I was still following the meaning of our conversation! All of this via variations of air pressure sensed at two little holes in my head. I was again reminded of the truly marvelous capacity of the auditory system to pick up acoustic information and identify its coherent aspects. (Jenkins, 1985, p. 115)

F I G U R E 11. 1 Jenkins' auditory world. The concentric circles symbolize the many sound stimuli, described in the text, that are reaching Jenkins' ear.

Jenkins' sound-filled environment is not that unique—he simply took the time to pay attention to the sounds around him. Though my first impression, as I sit at my desk on this Saturday morning, is of relative quiet, if I listen more intently I realize that I can hear birds chirping, a car door slamming in the parking lot outside my window, an air conditioner running upstairs, and the scratching sound of my pen as I write these words. Reflect for a moment on the variety of sounds you can hear right now, and consider what these sounds tell you about the nature of your environment.

What kinds of information does sound provide about our environment? To answer this question we need to realize that we hear because of changes in air pressure, or "vibrations" in the air. These air vibrations are usually created by the movement of objects—the movement of a bird's vocal folds, of a car door slamming, of the mech-

anism of an air conditioner motor, or of my pen scraping across the paper. With the exception of the sounds produced by forces of nature, such as wind blowing, the flowing of water, or waves pounding on the beach, most sounds are produced either by the movement of living things or machines.

Since most movement, as we saw in Chapter 8, is closely tied to the occurrence of events in the environment, to hear a sound is to know that events are happening. And, unlike the situation for vision, these events can be detected even if they are hidden from view. Birds chirping in a tree, a person's approaching footsteps in the dark, or a malfunctioning automobile engine may all be unseen, but nonetheless, the sound vibrations produced by these events signal their presence just as surely as if we had seen them.

In this chapter we will describe what these sound vibrations are like and what it is about these

B O X 11. 1 / *Sonar System of the Blind*

In 1749, Diderot reported the "amazing ability" of a blind acquaintance to perceive the presence of objects and their distance from him. Since that first published report, many people have confirmed this phenomenon and have speculated as to how it might occur. Explanations for this effect have ranged from **facial vision**—a hypothesized ability of blind people to detect obstacles by sensing pressure or temperature changes on their faces—to mystical explanations depending on magnetism, electrical fields, or the subconscious. Recent experiments, however, have shown that the primary mechanism appears to be auditory; blind people can judge the presence of objects by paying attention to the sounds of their own footsteps or vocalizations.

In an ingenious experiment, which showed that the sound of a person's footsteps can be used to detect his approach to an object, the experimenter carried a microphone at shoulder height and walked toward a wall. The subjects, who were isolated in a soundproof room and could hear only the sounds picked up by the microphone, were told to state when they first "perceived" the wall. Because the pitch of the experimenter's footsteps appeared to rise as he approached the wall, the subjects in the booth were able to perceive the wall at distances between 3 and 10 inches (Supa, Cotzin, & Dallenbach, 1944).

In another experiment, blindfolded subjects walked toward an obstacle positioned at a distance of 6, 12, 18, 24, or 30 feet, until they perceived it (and stopped) or collided with it. With some practice, all these subjects were able to stop before colliding with the obstacle; however, if they were both blindfolded *and* wore earplugs, their performance decreased and they collided with the object more frequently (Ammons, Worchel, & Dallenbach, 1953).

Perhaps the most impressive demonstration of how sound can be used to detect objects is provided by an experiment inspired by the way bats and dolphins use sonar, or "echo ranging," to determine the distances and sizes of objects. It was reasoned that if a dolphin can judge an object's distance by emitting a sound and sensing the echo reflected from the object, perhaps people can do the same thing. Two blind college students were asked to judge which of two objects was farther away. They were told that to aid them in making this judgment, they could produce any sound they wished. The subjects produced sounds in a variety of ways. They snapped their fingers, hissed, whistled, and, most often, repeated words such as "now, now, now. . . ." By judging the echo produced by these sounds, they were able to tell which of the two objects was closer. In fact, their performance was so impressive that it was possible to vary the separation between the objects and, using the method of constant stimuli (see Appendix A), to determine the psychophysical function in the figure. This function, which looks very much like other functions determined by the method of constant stimuli, is an impressive demonstration of the capacity of blind people to "see" with their ears (Kellogg, 1962; also see Rice, 1967).

vibrations that causes us to hear various qualities of sound. One goal of this chapter is to answer the question, "What is the relationship between the characteristics of sound stimuli and our experience?" We answer this question by taking a psychophysical approach to five basic qualities of sound: (1) pitch, (2) loudness, (3) location, (4) consonance and dissonance, and (5) timbre. In addition, we will describe how sequences of tones become organized perceptually so we hear certain tones as belonging together.

To begin our consideration of the psychophysical approach to hearing, we will describe the air vibrations that create sound.

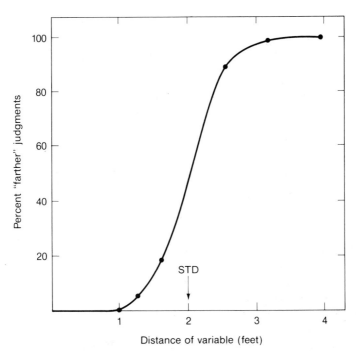

B O X 11. 1   The results of an experiment in which a blind observer was presented with two 1-foot diameter plywood discs, a standard disc which was always two feet away, and a variable disc which was either closer or farther than the standard. The observer judged whether each variable was closer or farther than the standard, making 100 judgments for each disc. That this blind observer was able to judge distance based on echo ranging is indicated by the fact that changing the distance of the variable by less than a foot (from 1.59 to 2.55 feet) resulted in a change from 19 to 89 percent "farther" responses. (Graph plotted from data in Kellogg, 1962.)

THE STIMULUS FOR HEARING

Sound as Vibrations of the Air

We begin by considering your radio or stereo system's loudspeaker, which is really a device for producing vibrations to be transmitted to the surrounding air. People have been known to turn their stereos up loud enough so these vibrations can be felt through a neighbor's wall, but even at softer levels, these vibrations are there. (Turn on your radio or stereo and feel the vibrations by placing your hand on the speaker. This technique is often used by deaf people to "listen" to music.)

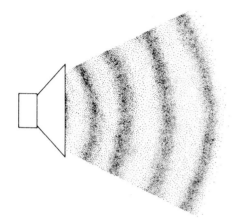

F I G U R E 11. 2 The effect of a vibrating speaker diaphragm on the surrounding air. Dark areas represent regions of high air pressure and light areas represent areas of low air pressure.

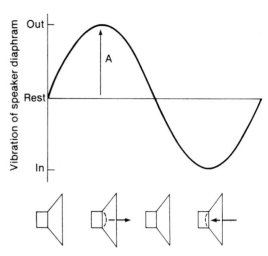

F I G U R E 11. 3 The motion of a speaker diaphragm in response to a sine-wave stimulus from an oscillator. The sine-wave motion of the diaphragm results in a pure tone. The amplitude (A) represents the maximum deflection of the speaker diaphragm from its rest position.

The vibrations you feel when you place your hand on the speaker affect the surrounding air, as shown in Figure 11.2. When the diaphragm of the speaker moves out, it pushes the surrounding air molecules together and increases the density of molecules near the diaphragm. This increased density increases the air pressure. Then, when the speaker diaphragm moves back in, it creates a partial vacuum, decreasing the density of molecules near the diaphragm, and decreases the air pressure. By repeating this process many hundreds or even thousands of times a second, the speaker creates a pattern of alternating high and low pressure in the wave that travels outward from the speaker, in much the same way that ripples travel outward from a pebble dropped in a quiet pool of water. This pattern of air pressure changes is called a **sound wave;** we will see later in this chapter that the nature of the sounds we hear, particularly a sound's pitch and loudness, is related to the form of this sound wave.

Pure tones. We will first consider a very simple kind of sound wave called a pure tone. **Pure tones** are not often found in our everyday environment but are used extensively in the laboratory to study the basic mechanisms of hearing. One way to produce a pure tone is to connect an electronic device called an **oscillator** to our speaker diaphragm. This

oscillator causes the diaphragm to vibrate in and out with a sine-wave motion, as shown in Figure 11.3. We can adjust the oscillator so that it causes the diaphragm to vibrate with a certain **amplitude**—the distance the diaphragm moves from its rest position—labeled A in Figure 11.3. We can also adjust the oscillator so that it causes the speaker to vibrate with a certain **frequency**—the number of times per second that the speaker diaphragm goes through the cycle of moving out, back in, and then out again, as shown in the figure.

The sine-wave vibration of the diaphragm causes changes in the pressure of the surrounding air, as shown in Figure 11.4. The air pressure increases and decreases in response to the sine-wave vibration of the speaker diaphragm. This sinusoidal change in pressure results in a pure tone, which is described by indicating its amplitude, as shown in the figure, and its frequency in units called **Hertz (Hz),** where one Hertz is the same as one cycle per sound. Thus, a 1,000-Hertz tone is a pure tone that goes through 1,000 cycles per second.

Complex sounds. The simplicity of pure tones makes them the starting place for much auditory

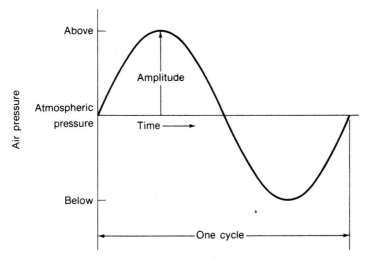

F I G U R E 11. 4 The sinusoidal vibration of the speaker diaphragm results in a sinusoidal change in the air pressure, as shown above.

research, as we will see both in this chapter and the next. Most of our experience, however, is not with pure tones but with more complex sounds such as speech, music, and various other sounds produced by nature and machines. Because of the importance of these complex sounds, we will devote considerable attention to the nature of musical tones in this chapter, and will devote all of Chapter 13 to speech.

We begin our description of musical tones with the piano keyboard of Figure 11.5. As we move from left to right on the keyboard, the frequency of the notes increases from 27.5 Hz for the lowest note on the keyboard to 4,186 Hz for the highest note. Although each note on the keyboard is associated with a single frequency, each tone produced by the piano and other musical instruments actually contains a large number of frequencies, and is, therefore, much more complex than the pure single frequency tones produced by our oscillator and loudspeaker of Figure 11.3.

Figure 11.6 shows the waveform of a typical musical tone. This waveform is more complicated than the sine wave of a single pure tone, but it has an important property that enables us to break it down into a number of sine-wave components. This property is **periodicity**—the waveform repeats itself over and over. This property of periodicity enables

us to use a technique called **Fourier analysis** to analyze this waveform into simpler components. (There are also nonperiodic sounds, like those produced by speech, slamming a door, or crumpling paper. We will focus on periodic sounds in this chapter and Chapter 12 and will describe speech in Chapter 13.)

Fourier analysis, which was developed in the 1800s by the French mathematician Joseph Fourier, is based on **Fourier's theorem,** which states that any periodic waveform can be reproduced by adding a number of sine-wave components. For example, by using Fourier's mathematical formula (described in Appendix D), we can determine that the waveform in Figure 11.6 can be reproduced by adding the 2 sine waves shown in Figure 11.7.

Another way of describing the components of the complex tone is shown in Figure 11.8. This figure, which is called a **Fourier spectrum,** indicates each sine wave's frequency by each line's position on the horizontal axis, and its amplitude by the height of each line. The line representing the lowest frequency, marked "f," is called the **fundamental frequency** of the tone, and corresponds to the frequency marked on the piano keyboard (in this case the 440 Hz of A above middle C). The other frequencies, which are all multiples of the fundamental frequency, are called the **harmonics**

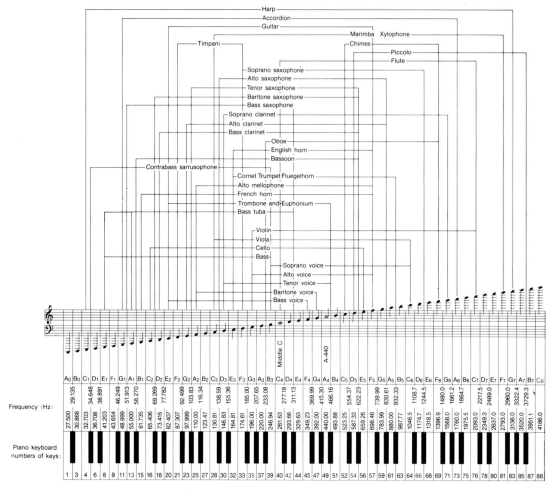

F I G U R E   11. 5   The piano keyboard showing the fundamental frequencies associated with each note and the ranges of various instruments. (From Conn, Ltd.)

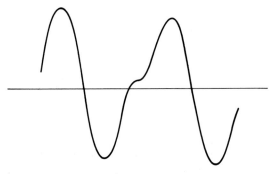

F I G U R E   11. 6   Pressure changes as a function of time for a musical tone.

or **overtones** of the fundamental frequency. In this example, the second harmonic has a frequency of $440 \times 2 = 880$ Hz, the third harmonic has a frequency of $440 \times 3 = 1320$ Hz, and so on. These harmonics add a richness to musical tones that is lacking in the thinner-sounding pure tones. Later in this chapter, we will see that the relative height and location of the harmonics help us to distinguish different musical instruments from one another and to determine how different tones sound when played together.

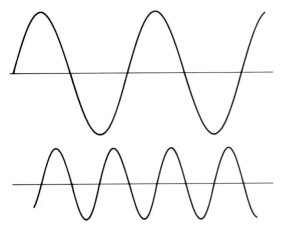

F I G U R E 11. 7 The musical tone of Figure 11.6 can be broken down into these two sine waves. This can be accomplished for any periodic waveform by using a procedure called Fourier analysis.

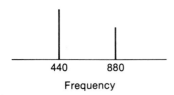

Frequency

F I G U R E 11. 8 Fourier spectrum for the tone of Figure 11.6. The spectrum indicates the tone is made up of one component with a frequency of 440 Hz and another component with a frequency of 880 Hz. The fact that the 440-Hz component is higher means that there is more energy at that frequency.

We will now briefly introduce the basic perceptual qualities of sound and, following this introduction, will describe each quality in more detail.

PERCEPTUAL DIMENSIONS OF HEARING

Loudness

Though **loudness** is difficult to define, we all know what it means to say that a jet plane taking off is loud or that a whisper is soft. If we hold a tone's frequency constant and increase its amplitude, the tone's loudness increases. We will see below, however, that other factors in addition to amplitude also determine loudness.

Pitch

A tone's **pitch** is related to the frequency of a pure tone, with lower frequencies causing low pitches and high frequencies causing high pitches. Although there are exceptions, as we will note later, the pitch of a musical tone is usually determined by its fundamental frequency.

Timbre

Timbre (pronounced tam′bre) is defined as "that attribute of sensation in terms of which a listener can judge that two sounds having the same loudness and pitch are dissimilar" (Erickson, 1975). One way to understand timbre is to compare the sound of a note of the same fundamental frequency played on two different strings of the violin. Although these two tones are the same note on the scale and have the same fundamental frequency and pitch, they sound slightly different when played on different strings; that is, they have different timbres.

A more striking example of tones with the same pitch but different timbres is provided by different musical instruments. Thus, when a trumpet and an oboe play the same note they sound very different. We might describe the sound of the trumpet as "bright" or "brassy" and the sound of the oboe as "nasal" or "reedy." We will see that one factor that determines these differences in the quality of tones produced by different instruments is the relative strength of the tone's various harmonics.

Consonance and Dissonance

When we hear a chord on the guitar or piano, a symphony played by an orchestra, or two people singing together, we are listening not to single, isolated tones but to two or more tones played simultaneously. When we listen to tones played simultaneously, we can judge whether these combinations are consonant or dissonant. **Consonance** and **dissonance** refer to the pleasingness of a combination of two or more tones, with combinations of tones that are consonant being perceived as harmonious or pleasing and combinations of tones that are dissonant being perceived as harsh or displeasing.

Perceptual Organization

Our discussion of perceptual organization in vision focused on how we perceive some components of a visual stimulus as being grouped together and on how we separate figure from ground. We can apply the same analysis to hearing by asking what causes a particular sequence of tones to be perceived as being grouped together. Hearing a melody over a background or being able to separate a number of different themes in a piece of music are examples of perceptual organization.

Localization

Most sounds are related to events, and events have specific locations—in front of us, behind us, or off to the side. **Localization** refers to our ability to determine from where a sound originates.

LOUDNESS AND THRESHOLDS

Amplitude, Decibels, and Loudness

Increasing a tone's amplitude increases its loudness. For example, if we increase the amplitude of a 1,000-Hz tone, starting near threshold, the tone is at first difficult to hear, but eventually, if we increase the amplitude enough, becomes ear-splittingly loud. This change in perception from inaudibility to ear-splitting loudness is accomplished by increasing the sound pressure by a factor of 10 million! Since it is rather unwieldy to deal with such large numbers when specifying a tone's amplitude, auditory researchers have developed a scale that converts amplitude into a much more manageable quantity, called the **decibel.**

Decibels are defined by the following equation:

$$dB = 20 \log(p/p_o)$$

TABLE 11.1 / *Some Common Sound Pressure Levels (in decibels)*

Sound	SPL (dB)
Barely audible sound (threshold)	0
Leaves rustling	20
Quiet residential community	40
Average speaking voice	60
Loud music from radio/heavy traffic	80
New York express subway	100
Overamplified rock group	120
Jet engine at takeoff	140

where p is the amplitude of the sound wave, and p_o is a reference pressure set by the experimenter. Most researchers set the reference pressure at 2×10^{-5} Newtons/m^2, a pressure close to the threshold for hearing in the most sensitive frequency range (1,000–4,000 Hz); to indicate that this is the chosen reference pressure, we use the term **sound pressure level (SPL).** Thus, in our discussion below, when we say that the SPL of a tone is 50 dB, you will know that this value was calculated based on a reference pressure of 2×10^{-5} Newtons/m^2.

To move decibels from the realm of numbers into real life, look at Table 11.1, which shows sound pressure levels in decibels for sounds ranging from threshold to a jet engine at takeoff.

The nice thing about the decibel scale is that it converts a sound pressure range of 1 to 10 million (extending from 0.0002, the sound pressure near threshold, to 2,000, the sound pressure of a jet at takeoff) into the much more manageable range of 0 to 140 dB.

Although it is tempting to equate loudness with SPL, especially when we look at Table 11.1, we should not fall into the trap of confusing the two. It is important to remember that SPL is a *physical quantity* that depends on the sound pressure, whereas loudness is a *psychological response* to the sound, and that while increasing the SPL often increases a tone's loudness, SPL and loudness are

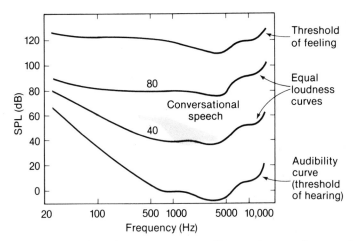

F I G U R E   11. 9   The auditory response area. Hearing functions between the lower curve, which represents the threshold for hearing, and the upper curve, which represents the threshold for feeling. Tones with SPLs below the threshold curve cannot be heard; tones with SPLs above the feeling curve result in pain and eventually cause damage to the ear. The shaded area indicates the frequency and intensity range for conversational speech. (From Fletcher & Munson, 1933.)

not the same thing. One way to show this is to consider the results of magnitude estimation experiments.

Magnitude Estimation of Loudness

If we use S. S. Stevens' magnitude estimation procedure (see page 13, Chapter 1) to determine the relationship between loudness and sound pressure, we find that there is *not* a one-to-one relationship between the two. At moderate intensities loudness and sound pressure are related by a power law with an exponent of about 0.4–0.6 (depending on the conditions of measurement and the frequency of the tone). This means that in hearing, as in vision, response compression occurs in the relationship between perception and the physical measurement of the stimulus. That is, large increases in sound pressure cause small increases in loudness. Increasing the sound pressure by a factor of 10 (which is the same as increasing SPL by 20 dB) increases the loudness by only a factor of about 2.5–4.0.

Another way to differentiate between the physical and psychological properties of sound is to consider the auditory response area, shown in Figure 11.9.

The Auditory Response Area

The area between the bottom and top curves of Figure 11.9 is called the **auditory response area,** because it defines the frequencies and the SPLs over which hearing functions. The bottom curve, marked "audibility curve," indicates the threshold SPL for frequencies throughout the range of hearing, whereas the top curve, marked "threshold of feeling," indicates the SPL at which sound is felt rather than heard. It is between these two extremes that we experience sound: At SPLs below the audibility curve, we can't hear sound; at SPLs above the threshold of feeling, we experience pain, and continued exposure to SPLs near or above this level is damaging to the ear.

The audibility curve. The **audibility curve** shows the minimum sound pressure level in decibels needed to just detect a tone, as a function of the tone's frequency. The audibility curve is analogous to the spectral sensitivity curve for vision, which we described in Chapter 3 (page 80). Remember that we determined the spectral sensitivity curve by measuring the light intensity necessary to just see a light, at wavelengths across the visible spectrum.

B O X   11. 2   /   *Infrasound Detection by the Homing Pigeon*

Just as we can see only a limited band of the electromagnetic spectrum, so we can hear only a limited band of frequencies. We can hear the vibrations we call sound in the frequency range from about 20 Hz to 20,000 Hz. Vibrations occurring below 20 Hz and above 20,000 Hz are silent to us, though some animals can hear these sounds. Dogs, for example, can hear higher frequencies than we can. Blowing a dog whistle has little effect on us but may get the attention of every dog on the block. At the other end of the frequency spectrum, below about 10 Hz, are sounds called **infrasounds,** which we can't hear but which are clearly audible to homing pigeons.

Infrasounds are fascinating because they are very prevalent and travel over long distances. Thunderstorms, earthquakes, ocean waves, and the wind coursing through mountain ranges produce infrasounds that can travel for hundreds or even thousands of miles, because low-frequency sounds are attenuated only slightly by the atmosphere (Cook, 1969; Gossard & Hooke, 1975). An example of the ability of infrasounds to travel long distances is shown in the figure above, which shows the locations of four tracking stations (circles) that picked up infrasounds generated by a severe thunderstorm (square).

Melvin Kreithen and Douglas Quine (1979) became interested in infrasound, because it had been suggested that birds might use these sounds as an aid to navigation (Griffin, 1969). They measured the bird's ability to detect infrasounds, by using a behavioral technique called *cardiac conditioning.* A 10-second burst of infrasound, followed by a mild shock, was presented at random intervals to a bird. After a number of these sound-shock presentations, the bird's heart rate speeded up when it heard the sound. Thus,

by presenting sounds and monitoring the bird's heart rate, the investigators could tell when the bird heard a sound. Using this method, Kreithen and Quine found, much to their surprise, that homing pigeons can detect sound vibrations as low as 0.05 Hz—0.05 cycles of vibration per second, or 3 cycles of vibration per *minute*!

By listening to these infrasounds, homing pigeons may be able to detect oncoming weather patterns or even use the sounds generated by faraway mountains and valleys to locate their position as they fly. Whether the pigeons actually use this information is unknown, but it is fascinating to think that a bird flying far overhead may, as it flies, be listening to a thunderstorm hundreds of miles away.

We determine the audibility curve by measuring the sound pressure level necessary to just hear a tone, at frequencies across the range of hearing. The audibility curve indicates that when a listener adjusts a 30-Hz tone to an SPL of about 65 dB, he or she can just hear it—it is at threshold. As we increase the frequency above 30 Hz, the threshold decreases until it reaches a minimum at about 2,000–4,000 Hz; then, above 4,000 Hz, the threshold increases with increases in frequency. It is interesting to note that the frequency range between about 400 and 3,000 Hz falls near the range of frequencies to which we are most sensitive and is also the range most important for understanding speech.

The audibility curve tells us some interesting things about the relationship between SPL (physical property) and loudness (psychological response) for pure tones. The audibility curve tells us that two tones with *different SPLs* can result in the *same loudness.* We can see how this works by looking up the thresholds for hearing a 30-Hz tone and a 1,000-Hz tone. The audibility curve indicates that the threshold for hearing the 30-Hz tone is 65 dB SPL

and the threshold for hearing the 1,000-Hz tone is 0 dB SPL. Thus, while these tones have vastly different SPLs, their loudnesses are the same—near zero—since these tones are both at threshold. This equal loudness of two tones with different SPLs is indicated by the solid arrows in Figure 11.10.

The audibility curve also shows that two tones of the *same SPL* can have quite *different loudnesses.* Consider, for example, our 30- and 1,000-Hz tones, which at threshold have SPLs of 65 and 0 dB, respectively. If we increase the SPL to 70 dB for both tones, the 30-Hz tone will be very soft, since it is just barely above its threshold (left dashed arrow, Figure 11.10). However, the 1,000-Hz tone will be very loud since it is far above threshold (right dashed arrow in Figure 11.10).

The above examples should convince you that although increasing SPL at a given frequency does increase loudness, loudness depends on both a tone's SPL *and* its frequency.

Equal loudness curves. That different SPLs can result in the same loudness is also indicated by the curves marked "40" and "80." These curves are **equal loudness curves,** which are determined by finding the SPL that causes the same loudness at each frequency. We do this by designating the 1,000-Hz tone as a standard and matching the loudness of all other tones to it. For example, the curve marked "40" in Figure 11.9 is the result of matching the loudness of all other frequencies to a 1,000-Hz tone that has an SPL of 40 dB.

Notice that the equal loudness curve marked "40" looks similar to the audibility function, in that it curves up at high and low frequencies. However, the equal loudness curve marked "80" is considerably flattened, indicating that at 80 dB all tones from 30–5,000 Hz have about the same loudness. The difference between the flat "80" curve and the upward-curving audibility function and "40" curve explains something that happens as you adjust the volume control on your stereo system.

If you are playing music at a fairly loud level, say 80 dB SPL, you should be able to easily hear all the frequencies in the music because, as the equal loudness curve for "80" indicates, all fre-

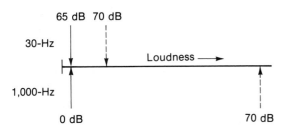

F I G U R E 11. 10 The far left side of the horizontal line represents zero loudness (just below threshold), and loudness increases as we move to the right. The arrows above the scale indicate the loudness and SPL in dB of two 30-Hz tones and the arrows below the scale indicate the loudness and SPL of two 1,000-Hz tones. The solid arrows indicate that 30-Hz and 1,000-Hz tones with the same loudness (just above zero) have different SPLs (65 dB and 0 dB, respectively). The dashed arrows indicate that 30-Hz and 1,000-Hz tones with the same SPL (70 dB) have different loudness, with the 1,000-Hz tone sounding much louder.

quencies sound equally loud at 80 dB SPL. What happens, however, when you turn down the loudness so that the music is very soft, say 10 dB SPL? Now all frequencies don't sound equally loud. In fact, some very high and very low frequencies are totally inaudible. You can see from the audibility curve that frequencies below about 500 Hz and above 10,000 Hz are inaudible at 10 dB SPL. (Be sure you understand how to determine this. Find 10 dB on the SPL scale and draw a horizontal line across to the right. You should notice that the 10-dB line intersects the audibility curve at a frequency just slightly over 500 Hz and under 10,000 Hz. Thus, the thresholds for frequencies below 500 Hz fall above the 10-dB line, which means that these frequencies are inaudible at 10 dB SPL.)

This is certainly a bad situation, because it means that when you play music softly, you won't hear the very low or very high pitches. Fortunately, most stereo receivers have a button or switch labeled "loudness" that, when activated, selectively boosts the level of very high and very low frequencies so that you can hear them, even when you are playing your stereo very softly.

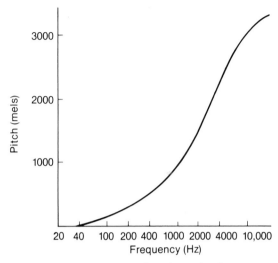

F I G U R E   11. 11   The relationship between frequency and pitch. The pitch scale on the left is in mels. A 2,000-mel tone sounds twice as high in pitch as a 1,000-mel tone. (Stevens & Volkman, 1940.)

PITCH

Tone Height and Tone Chroma

A tone's pitch is related to its frequency, with higher frequencies having higher pitches (Figure 11.11). This relation between pitch and frequency is seen in our piano keyboard of Figure 11.5. As we move from left to right across the keyboard, the fundamental frequency increases and pitch becomes higher. This increase in pitch with increasing frequency reflects an increase in **tone height** as we go up the scale.

But in addition to this increase in tone height that occurs as we move towards higher frequencies on the piano keyboard, something else happens: The letters of the notes A, B, C, D, E, F, and G repeat themselves. This repetition of notes reflects a quality called **tone chroma.** Notes with the same letters sound similar, even though they have different fundamental frequencies. These similar-

sounding tones are separated by intervals of one or more **octaves,** where tones separated by octaves have fundamental frequencies that are binary multiples of one another (x2, x4, x8, etc.). Thus A_5 on the piano keyboard has a fundamental frequency of 440 Hz, A_6 has a frequency of 880 Hz, and so on. Tones in this octave relation to one another have the same chroma.

These two concepts of tone height and tone chroma are combined in the spiral of Figure 11.12. Moving up the spiral increases tone height (pitch gets higher), and the places where the spiral crosses vertical lines have the same tone chroma (these tones are indicated by the same letter). Tone chroma is important because two notes with the same chroma are psychologically similar. Thus, a male and female can be considered to be singing "in unison" even if their voices are separated by an octave or more. This similarity between the same notes in different octaves also makes it possible for a singer on the verge of overreaching his or her voice range to shift the melody down to a lower octave.

The perceptual similarity of tones separated by an octave was demonstrated in an experiment by Diana Deutsch (1973). As shown in Figure 11.13,

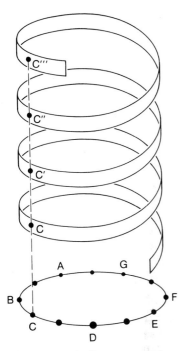

FIGURE 11. 12 Representing the notes of the scale on an ascending spiral graphically depicts the perceptions of tone height and tone chroma. As we move up along a vertical line, we encounter notes with the same letter. These notes, which are separated by octaves and therefore sound similar to each other, have the same *tone chroma*. As we move from one note to another, ascending the spiral, each note sounds higher than the note preceding it. This property is called *tone height*. Thus, two Cs separated by an octave or more would have different tone heights but the same tone chroma.

she presented a standard tone followed by a series of six intervening tones followed by a test tone. The listeners' task was to indicate whether the standard and test tones were the same or different. Even though Deutsch's subjects were told to ignore the intervening tones, their ability to detect the difference between the standard and test tones decreased if one of the six intervening tones was either the same as the test tone *or* if it was one octave higher or lower than the test tone. This effect, which Deutsch calls **octave generalization,** is due to the perceptual similarity of tones with the same chroma.

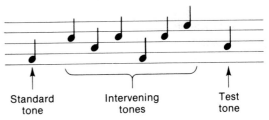

FIGURE 11. 13　Stimuli for Deutsch's (1973) octave generalization experiment.

Periodicity Pitch (The Effect of the Missing Fundamental)

We have seen that musical tones have a fundamental frequency and harmonics that are multiples of the fundamental frequency. We noted that the fundamental frequency determines the tone's pitch, so the tone in Figure 11.14(a) with a 400-Hz fundamental frequency sounds lower than the tone in Figure 11.14(b) with an 800-Hz fundamental frequency. Having said that, let's ask what happens if we eliminate the 400-Hz tone's fundamental frequency and leave the harmonics, as in Figure 11.14(c). You might think that doing this will cause the 400-Hz tone to sound higher, because its lowest frequency is now 800 Hz. But this is not what happens. Removing the fundamental changes the tone's timbre slightly but has no effect on the tone's pitch. The tone in Figure 11.14(c) still has the pitch of the 400-Hz tone and therefore sounds lower than the tone in Figure 11.14(b). The fact that pitch does not change when we remove the fundamental is called **periodicity pitch** or the **effect of the missing fundamental.** This effect poses a problem for the theories of pitch perception that we will discuss in the next chapter.

Though periodicity pitch poses a problem for theories of pitch perception, it has a number of practical consequences for the reproduction of music. Consider, for example, what happens as you listen to music on a cheap radio that can't reproduce frequencies below 300 Hz. If you're listening to music which contains a tone with a fundamental frequency of 100 Hz, your radio can't reproduce the fundamental frequency of the 100-Hz tone or of the 200-Hz second harmonic of that tone. Even

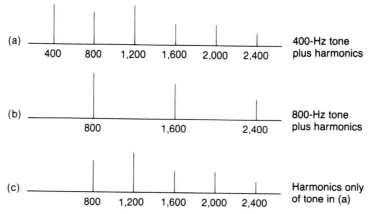

FIGURE 11.14 Fourier spectra of (a) a 400-Hz tone plus its harmonics, (b) an 800-Hz tone plus its harmonics, and (c) the tone in (a) minus its 400-Hz fundamental. See text for details.

though the radio reproduces only the third (300 Hz) and higher (400, 500, 600, etc.) harmonics of this tone, periodicity pitch comes to the rescue and causes you to perceive a pitch equivalent to that produced by a 100-Hz tone.

Periodicity pitch has also been used to overcome the following problem in the construction of pipe organs: An organ designer wants to produce a pitch corresponding to a 55-Hz tone. However, the longest organ pipe he can use is 1.5 m long, a length that produces a pitch of 110-Hz fundamental frequency. A longer pipe would be needed to produce the 55-Hz tone. The solution: Use the 1.5 m pipe, with its 110-Hz fundamental and a 1.0 m pipe, which produces a 165-Hz fundamental. Since 110 Hz and 165 Hz are the second and third harmonics of a 55-Hz tone ($55 \times 2 = 110$; $55 \times 3 = 165$), these two pipes, when sounded together, produce a tone with a pitch corresponding to 55 Hz (Dowling & Harwood, 1986).

TIMBRE

What causes the same note to sound different when played on different strings of a violin or on different instruments? One factor which causes these differ-

ences in timbre is the relative strengths of the harmonics. Figure 11.15 shows the heights of the harmonics for the A_4 note (fundamental frequency = 440 Hz) played on the A and D strings of the violin. Note that while the frequencies at which the harmonics occur are identical, the relative height of each harmonic is different.

Figure 11.16 compares the harmonics of the guitar, bassoon, and alto saxophone playing the note G_3 with a fundamental frequency of 196 Hz. Both the relative heights of the harmonics and the number of harmonics are different in these instruments. For example, the guitar has more harmonics than either the bassoon or the alto saxophone at high frequencies. Although the frequencies of the harmonics are always multiples of the fundamental frequency, harmonics can be absent, as is the case for some of the high-frequency harmonics of the bassoon and alto saxophone. The best example of an instrument which produces a tone with few harmonics is the flute. You can see from Figure 11.17 that for a 1,568-Hz tone (G_6) the flute has only one harmonic in addition to the fundamental, and this harmonic has very little energy. Because the fundamental contains most of the energy for this tone, the flute has the thinnest and purest tone of all of the musical instruments; the tone of the flute is the closest we can come to a pure tone. At

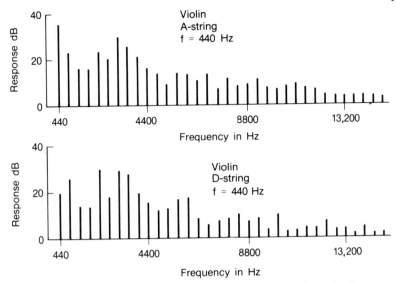

F I G U R E 11. 15 Fourier spectra for the A and D strings of a violin for a tone with a fundamental frequency of 440 Hz. (Olson, 1967.)

the other extreme, instruments like the guitar and the lower notes on the piano, which have many harmonics, have much fuller, richer tones than the flute.

Timbre does not, however, depend only on harmonic structure. Jean-Claude Risset and Max Mathews (1969) have synthesized tones with a computer using Fourier spectra such as those shown in Figure 11.15–11.17 and have found that the resulting tones do not resemble the appropriate musical instruments. For example, when they synthesized a tone with the harmonic content of a trumpet and presented this tone to a number of people, the tone was unanimously judged *not* to sound like a trumpet.

This result can be explained by studies which show that timbre is affected not only by the harmonic content of the tone but also by the time course of the tone's **attack,** the buildup of sound at the beginning of the tone; and by the time course of the tone's **decay,** the decrease in sound at the end of the tone. This is illustrated by the fact that it is easy to tell the difference between a tape recording of a high note played on the clarinet and a

recording of the same note played on the flute if the attack, the decay, and the sustained portion of the tone are heard; but if the tone's attack and decay are eliminated by erasing the first and last one-half second of the recording, it becomes very difficult to distinguish between the two instruments (Berger, 1964). Another way to make it difficult to distinguish one instrument from another is to play a tape of an instrument's tone backward. This changes the tone's original decay into the attack and the original attack into the decay but does not affect the harmonic structure of the tone. In spite of the fact that the harmonic structure is unaffected, a piano tone played backward does not sound like a piano (Berger, 1964; Erickson, 1975).

With these results in mind, Risset and Mathews decided to determine not only the harmonic structure of a trumpet tone but the way the harmonic structure changes with time. They did this by playing a recording of a trumpet tone into a computer which analyzed the the tone's harmonic structure. The result of this analysis for a 0.20-second tone is shown in Figure 11.18. In this figure, the buildup and decay of each harmonic is indicated by a line,

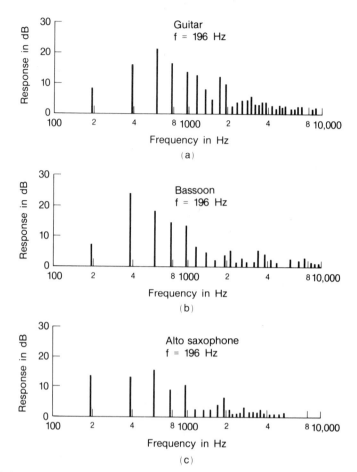

F I G U R E   11. 16   Fourier spectra for a guitar, a bassoon, and an alto saxophone playing a tone with a fundamental frequency of 196 Hz. Note that in this figure the frequency scale is compressed compared to Figure 11.16. (Olson, 1967.)

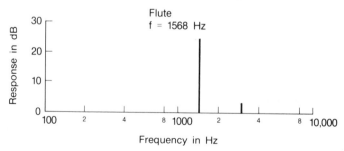

F I G U R E   11. 17   Fourier spectrum of a flute playing a tone with a fundamental frequency of 1,568 Hz. (Olson, 1967.)

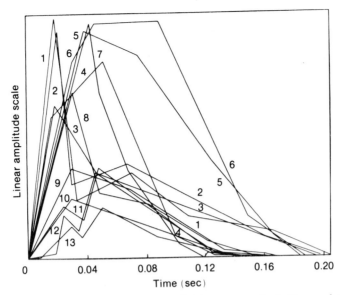

F I G U R E 11. 18 Buildup and decay of 13 harmonics of a 0.20 second trumpet tone with a fundamental frequency of 294 Hz. (From Risset and Mathews, 1969.)

and we can see that low harmonics build up faster than high harmonics. For example, the first harmonic reaches peak intensity in about 0.02 seconds, whereas the fifth harmonic reaches peak intensity in 0.04 seconds. Differences in the decay rates of the various harmonics also occur, with lower harmonics having longer decays. Risset and Mathews also analyzed longer tones and found that the harmonic structure is relatively constant during the sustained portion of the tone.

By using the data in Figure 11.18, Risset and Mathews synthesized a tone that sounded like a trumpet. When they interspersed five of their synthesized trumpet tones with five actual trumpet tones, nonmusicians could pick the actual tones with only chance accuracy, and even highly trained musicians were able to detect the real trumpet tones with only slightly better than chance accuracy.

Thus, timbre, the quality of a tone that enables us to distinguish between two tones having the same pitch and loudness, depends both on the tone's steady-state harmonic structure and on the time course of the attack and decay of the tone's harmonics.

CONSONANCE AND DISSONANCE

Combining Pure Tones

In discussing consonance and dissonance we will be describing how two tones of different frequencies sound when played simultaneously. However, before we can explain consonance and dissonance we need to understand a concept called critical bandwidth. We introduce this concept by describing a loudness matching experiment: We begin with a pair of tones—a 500 Hz tone and a 520 Hz tone. We present this pair simultaneously and determine the intensity of a 1,000 Hz tone that matches the loudness of this pair. Let's assume that a loudness match occurs when the 1,000 Hz tone is set at 40 dB SPL, as indicated in Table 11.2. We now replace the 520 Hz tone with a 540 Hz tone, being careful *not to change the SPL of the pair*, and redetermine the loudness match. When we do this, we get the same answer as before—40 dB. This indicates that the loudness of our pair of tones has remained constant. When we repeat this procedure for a 500 +

TABLE 11.2 / *Results of a Hypothetical Loudness Matching Experiment*

Tone Combination (SPL = Constant)	dB SPL for 1,000 Hz Tone to Match Loudness
500 + 520 Hz	40 dB
500 + 540 Hz	40 dB
500 + 560 Hz	40 dB
500 + 580 Hz	44 dB
500 + 600 Hz	49 dB

560 Hz pair we again get the same match. However, as we can see from Table 11.2, the match changes for the 500 + 580 Hz and 500 + 600 Hz pairs. For these pairs we must now increase the SPL of the 1,000 Hz tone to achieve a match. The frequency separation between the 2 tones at which loudness begins to increase—about 80 Hz in our example—is called the **critical bandwidth** (Zwicker, Flottorp, & Stevens, 1957).

What is happening here? The results of this loudness matching experiment, plus many others, have led researchers to conclude that when two tones are close in frequency they interfere with each other, and this interference decreases the loudness of the pair. But when the two tones are separated by more than the critical bandwidth, the tones stop interfering with one another and the loudness of the pair increases. Thus, the loudness of a combination of pure tones depends on the spacing between the frequencies of the tones, with two tones separated by more than the critical bandwidth sounding louder than two tones with the same overall SPL which are within the same critical band.

Now that we know what the critical band is, we can begin our discussion of consonance and dissonance by considering how we perceive combinations of pure tones. We will start with two pure tones of the same frequency, and observe how our perception changes as we slowly increase the frequency of one of the tones. When the difference in frequency between the two tones is less than about 10–15 Hz, we hear a single "fused" tone with a pitch midway between the two tones, and this tone's loudness oscillates (increases and decreases) rapidly with a rate equal to the difference in frequency between the two tones. Thus, if we simultaneously present a 400-Hz tone and a 410-Hz tone, we hear a fused tone with a pitch equivalent to a 405-Hz tone, and the loudness of this tone oscillates 10 times per second. This oscillation of loudness is called **beats** or **beating.**

As we increase the frequency difference between the two tones so that the difference is greater than 10–15 Hz, the beating stops and is replaced by a sensation of roughness. Increasing the separation between the two tones further changes our perception from one rough tone to two separate rough tones. Finally, at frequency separations greater than the critical bandwidth, the sensation of roughness disappears and we hear two separate smooth tones. For our 400-Hz tone the critical bandwidth is about 100 Hz, so we must increase the frequency of the variable tone to about 500 Hz to perceive two smooth-sounding tones. Since the critical bandwidth is larger at higher frequencies, two high-frequency tones must be spaced farther apart to obtain a perception of smoothness. For example, at 4,000 Hz the frequency of the variable tone must be increased to about 4,800 Hz to be outside the critical bandwidth and, therefore, to be perceived as smooth.

The relationship between consonance and critical bandwidth has been demonstrated by Reinier Plomp and W. J. M. Levelt (1965), who varied the difference in frequency between two pure tones and asked listeners to rate these tones on a seven-point scale, with a rating of "1" indicating that the two tones sounded very dissonant and a rating of "7" indicating that the two tones sounded very consonant. The results, shown in Figure 11.19, indicate that when two 400-Hz tones are played in unison they are judged to be very consonant, but as the frequency of one of the tones is increased, the tones are judged more and more dissonant until, when the higher tone reaches about 435 Hz, the pair of tones is judged to be very dissonant. Increasing the separation between the two tones further increases the consonance until, when the tones are

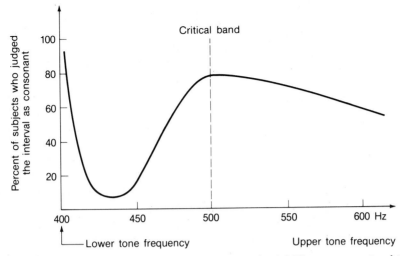

F I G U R E 11. 19 The results of Plomp and Levelt's (1965) experiment, in which subjects were presented with a 400-Hz tone paired with a tone of another frequency, indicated on the horizontal axis, and were asked to judge the consonance of the pair, indicated on the vertical axis.

separated by the critical bandwidth, consonance reaches a maximum. Thus, two pure tones are judged to be the most consonant when they either are played in unison or are separated by the critical bandwidth, and tones are judged to be most dissonant when they are separated by about 25–50 percent of the critical bandwidth. We will now show how these results for pure tones can be used to explain the consonance and dissonance observed when we combine complex tones.

Combining Complex Tones

In discussing the consonance or dissonance of complex tones, such as those produced by musical instruments, we usually refer to a system of **musical intervals** that has been devised to enable us to indicate the distance between two tones in a pair. We can understand this system by referring to the piano keyboard of Figure 11.5. Intervals are defined by simply counting the number of keys between two notes in a scale, including both the first and last notes. (To simplify our discussion we will stay in the key of C, which has no sharps or flats.) For example, if we go from C to D two keys are involved, so the interval C to D is called a major second.

Similarly, C to E is a major third, C to F is a major fourth, and so on until we reach the next C, which defines the interval of a octave.

Although little experimental work has been done on the consonance and dissonance of musical tones, it is generally agreed that tones played in unison and tones separated by octaves are the most consonant, closely followed by tones separated by a major fifth,* with the other intervals being less consonant (Geldard, 1972; Roederer, 1975). The results of Plomp and Levelt's experiments with pure tones can be used to explain why some intervals of complex tones are more consonant than others by considering how harmonics of pairs of complex tones interact. For example, look at the two Fourier spectra in Figure 11.20. Tone A has a fundamental frequency of 400 Hz and tone B has a fundamental frequency of 800 Hz, so the two tones are one octave apart. Comparison of the harmonics indicates that the fundamental and harmonics of tone B exactly match the harmonics of tone A. This exact matching is the reason that octaves sound so similar and are so consonant.

---

*In musical notation, "major fourths" and "major fifths" are also called "perfect fourths" and "perfect fifths."

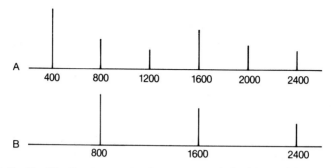

F I G U R E 11. 20 Fourier spectra of two tones with fundamental frequencies separated by an octave.

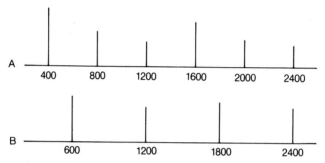

F I G U R E 11. 21 Fourier spectra of two tones with fundamental frequencies separated by a major fifth.

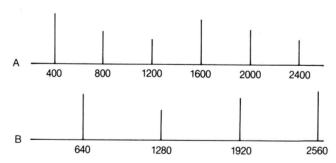

F I G U R E 11. 22 Fourier spectra of two tones with fundamental frequencies separated by a minor sixth.

Let's now consider two tones a major fifth apart, tone A with a fundamental frequency of 400 Hz and tone B with a fundamental frequency of 600 Hz (Figure 11.21). In this case the second and fourth harmonics of B match the harmonics of A, but the third harmonic of B (1,800 Hz) falls within 200 Hz of the 1,600-Hz fourth and 2,000-Hz fifth harmonics of A. Since the critical bandwidth at 1,800 Hz is about 300 Hz, this means that the 1,600- and 2,000-Hz harmonics of A fall within the critical bandwidth of the 1,800-Hz harmonic of B. This interaction between harmonics results in "roughness" and a decrease in consonance compared with tones separated by an octave.

Finally, let's consider two tones a minor sixth apart, tone A with a fundamental frequency of 400 Hz and tone B with a fundamental frequency of 640 Hz (Figure 11.22). Here we find that the second, third, and fourth harmonics of B fall within the critical bandwidth of the third, fifth, and sixth harmonics of A, so we would expect an increase in roughness and therefore a decrease in consonance for this interval compared with the two above.

The analysis above explains consonance and dissonance on the basis of the physical relationships between the harmonics. Jean-Claude Risset (1978) points out, however, that although this type of explanation is useful in evaluating the smoothness or roughness of a combination of tones, it does not completely explain musical consonance. Risset bases this statement on the fact that the consonance of combinations of tones is affected by the context in which these combinations appear. That is, the consonance or dissonance of a particular combination of tones depends to some extent on the preceding or following tones.

Learning and cultural factors also affect consonance. For example, Indian music, which is based on a scale different from Western music, may sound strange to listeners used to Western music but is pleasing to Indians. Another example of the effects of learning on the perception of consonance is provided by modern composers such as Stravinsky, whose music was initially equated to noise when it was introduced in the 1920s but is now accepted by many as being pleasing to hear. Similarly, listeners in 1800 reacted with discomfort to the opening chord of Beethoven's First Symphony, one which we consider very conventional today (Dowling & Harwood, 1986). The physical effects of interactions between harmonics *and* the effects of context and learning combine to help determine our perception of consonance.

PERCEPTUAL ORGANIZATION

Just as visual stimuli are perceptually organized so that certain elements of a scene appear to "belong together," so are tones. And some of the rules for grouping tones are similar to the "Gestalt laws" that describe the grouping of visual stimuli. In this section we will consider some of the principles that apply to the grouping of tones.

Similarity

"Tones that are similar to one another tend to be perceived as belonging together" is a statement of the law of similarity for hearing. The dimension of tones that contributes most to perceptual grouping by similarity is pitch, with tones more similar in pitch being more likely to be perceived as belonging together. The importance of this principle is reflected in the fact that music of all cultures uses small pitch separations between notes of melodies (Dowling & Harwood, 1986).

George Heise and George Miller (1951) showed that if a tone is separated in pitch from others in a sequence, it will, when the separation becomes great enough, be perceived as separate from the other tones. To show this they played a sequence of tones like the one in Figure 11.23(a) and increased the frequency of the middle tone of the sequence, indicated by the arrow. When the tone's frequency is increased only slightly, it remains perceptually grouped with the other tones. However, when the separation is increased farther, as in (b), the tone perceptually separates from the rest of the sequence and is heard as an isolated "pop" or figure superimposed on the melodic pattern in the background. Thus, grouping by similarity occurs as long as the pitch differences between adjacent tones are not too great. Increasing these differences beyond

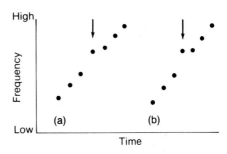

F I G U R E   11. 23   A tone sequence used in Heise and Miller's (1951) experiment.

F I G U R E   11. 24   Four measures of a composition by J. S. Bach (*Choral Prelude on Jesus Christus unser Heiland,* 1739) that result in auditory stream segregation.

a certain point causes grouping by similarity to break down and one note is perceived as separate from the rest.

Grouping by similarity was used by composers long before psychologists began studying it. Composers in the Baroque period (1600–1750) knew that if notes alternate rapidly between high and low tones, the listener doesn't hear them as alternating but perceives two separate melodies, with the high tones perceived as being played by one instrument and the low tones as being played by another. An excerpt from a composition by J. S. Bach that uses this device is shown in Figure 11.24. When this passage is played rapidly, the low notes sound as if they are a melody played by one instrument and the high notes sound like a different melody played by another instrument. This effect has been called *implied polyphony* or *compound melodic line* by musicians, and has been called **auditory stream segregation** by psychologists Albert Bregman and Jeffry Campbell (1971).

Bregman and Campbell demonstrated auditory stream segregation experimentally by alternating high and low tones, as shown in the sequence in Figure 11.25. When the high-pitched tones are slowly alternated with the low-pitched tones, as in Figure 11.25(a), the tones are heard in one stream— one after another—hi-lo-hi-lo-hi-lo, as indicated by the dashed line. If, however, the tones are alternated very rapidly, as in Figure 11.25(b), the high and low tones become perceptually grouped into two auditory streams so that the listener perceives two separate streams of sound, one high pitched and one low pitched, occurring simultaneously.

This grouping of tones into streams by similarity of pitch is also demonstrated by an experiment done by Bregman and Alexander Rudnicky (1975), diagrammed in Figure 11.26. The listener is first presented with two standard tones, A and B (11.26a). When these tones are presented alone, it is easy to perceive their order (AB or BA). However, when these tones are sandwiched between

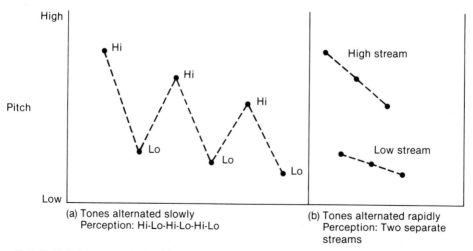

F I G U R E   11. 25   (a) Slow alternation of high and low tones does not result in auditory stream segregation. (b) Faster alternation results in segregation into high and low streams.

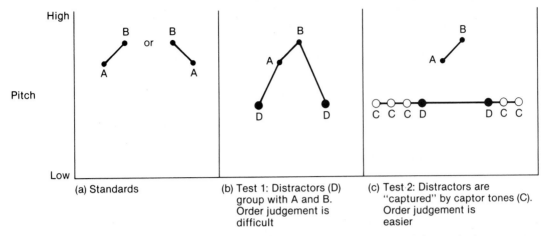

F I G U R E 11. 26 Bregman and Rudnicky's (1975) experiment. (a) The standard tones; (b) Test 1: the distractor (D) tones group with A and B, making it difficult to judge the order of A and B; (c) Test 2: the addition of captor (C) tones with the same pitch as the distractor tones causes the distractor tones to form a separate stream (law of similarity) and makes it easier to judge the order of tones A and B.

two distractor (D) tones (11.26b), it becomes very hard to judge their order. The name "distractor tones" is well taken—they distract the listener, making it difficult to judge the order of tones A and B.

But the distracting effect of the D tones can be eliminated by using the law of similarity. To do this, Bregman and Rudnicky added a series of "captor" tones (C) with the same pitch as the distractors (Figure 11.26c). Since these captor tones have the same pitch as the distractors, they "capture" the distractors and form a stream that separates them from tones A and B. This causes A and B to be perceived as belonging to a separate stream and makes it much easier to perceive their order.

A final example of how similarity of pitch can affect perception is an effect called the **scale illusion** or **melodic channeling.** Diana Deutsch (1975) demonstrated this effect by presenting two scales simultaneously, one ascending and one descending (Figure 11.27a). The subject listened to these scales through earphones that presented successive notes from each scale alternately to the left and right ears, as shown in Figure 11.27(b). From Figure 11.27(b) you can see that the first three notes presented to each ear jump up and down, high-low-high in the right ear, and low-high-low in the left

ear. But this is not what the subjects perceived. They perceived the smooth sequence of notes shown in Figure 11.27(c), with a high melodic line perceived in the right ear and a lower melodic line perceived in the left ear.

The scale illusion illustrates grouping by similarity, since tones with similar pitches are grouped in the same ear. In addition, this illusion illustrates an important function of perceptual grouping: Perceptual grouping helps us to interpret the environment effectively. It is most effective to perceive similar sounds as coming from the same source, because this is what usually happens in the environment. When psychologists create abnormal stimuli, as in Deutsch's experiment, the perceptual system applies the rule of grouping by similarity and is fooled into assigning similar pitches to the same ear. But in the normal environment (when psychologists aren't controlling the stimuli), this rule of similarity helps us to correctly perceive where sounds are coming from.

Proximity

Auditory stream segregation provides an example of how proximity affects our perception of tones. Stream segregation requires not only that one series

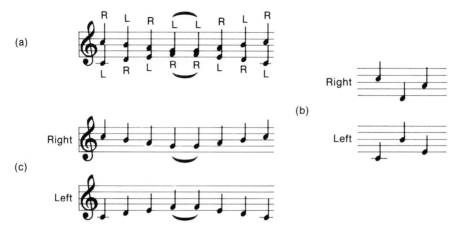

F I G U R E 11. 27   (a) Stimuli presented simultaneously to the subject's left and right ears in Deutsch's (1975) "scale illusion" experiment. (b) The first three notes presented to the left and right ears in Deutsch's experiment. The notes presented to each ear do not form a scale—they jump up and down. (c) What the subject hears. Although the notes in each ear jump up and down, the subject perceives a smooth sequence of notes in each ear. This is called the scale illusion or melodic channeling.

of tones be high pitched and the other low pitched but also that these tones occur close together in time. This is the law of proximity: Tones must follow each other rapidly to be perceived together. If the tones are too far apart in time, as in Figure 11.25(a), streaming will not occur, even if the tones are similar in pitch.

Good Continuation

Auditory good continuation has been demonstrated by Richard Warren, C. J. Obuseck, and J. M. Acroff (1972). When they presented bursts of tone interrupted by gaps of silence, as in Figure 11.28(a), listeners perceive both the tones and the silence between the tones. If, however, the silent gaps are filled in with a hissing sound, called "noise," as in Figure 11.28(b), the listeners perceive the tone as continuing under the noise, as shown in Figure 11.28(c). This demonstration is analogous to the demonstration of visual good continuation in Pissarro's painting in Figure 6.17. Just as Pissarro's smokestack is perceived as continuous even though it is twice interrupted by smoke, an inter-

rupted tone can be perceived as continuous even though it is interrupted by bursts of noise.

Melody Schema

Just as vision is influenced by our past experiences and by our expectations caused by these experiences (see pp. 17 and 26), so is hearing. The effect of expectation on our perception of melodies is demonstrated by an experiment done by W. Jay Dowling (1973). Dowling had his subjects listen to two **interleaved melodies,** as shown in Figure 11.29(a); notes of "Three Blind Mice" are alter-

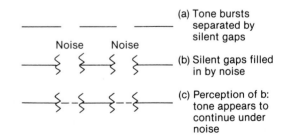

F I G U R E 11. 28   A demonstration of good continuation, using tones.

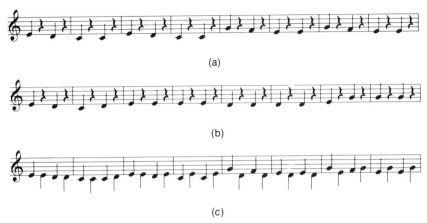

FIGURE 11. 29 (a) "Three Blind Mice," (b) "Mary Had a Little Lamb," and (c) both melodies interleaved ("Three Blind Mice": stems up; "Mary Had a Little Lamb": stems down).

nated with notes of "Mary Had a Little Lamb." When subjects listen to these combined melodies, they report hearing a meaningless jumble of notes. However, when they are told the names of the songs, they are able to hear either melody, depending on which one they pay attention to.

What listeners are doing, according to Dowling and Dane Harwood (1986), is applying a **melody schema** to the interleaved melody. A melody schema is a representation of a familiar melody that is stored in the person's memory. When a person doesn't know that melody is present, she has no access to the schema and therefore has nothing to compare the unknown melody to. But if the person is told which melody is present, she compares what is heard to the "Three Blind Mice" or "Mary Had a Little Lamb" schema and perceives the melodies.

I demonstrate to my classes the effect of schemas on hearing words by playing a Rolling Stones recording and asking the class to try to identify the lyrics. This task is extremely difficult, both because of the loud instrumental backing and Mick Jagger's less-than-precise enunciation. But when I play the song a second time, accompanied by the words projected onto a screen, the previously difficult-to-understand words become easy to perceive. In the chapter on speech we will describe additional examples of how our expectations influence our perception of words.

LOCALIZATION

Auditory Space

Standing on a hill overlooking a neighborhood in Pittsburgh, at the beginning of our discussion of depth perception in Chapter 7, we were able to see from the cars and houses directly in front of us to the houses and trees lining a ridge in the distance. Our ability to see objects in the visual space around us is something we are usually much more aware of than the other kind of space that surrounds us—the auditory space created by trees overhead rustling in the wind, the sound of cars approaching from the right, and the sound of a dog barking a block away. We can think of these sounds as making up an auditory space because, when we hear them, we can usually tell where they are coming from.

In Chapter 7 we saw that we can perceive depth with just one eye by using monocular depth cues; depth perception is improved, however, if we are able to make use of the depth information provided by binocular disparity. In hearing, the use of two ears is very important if we are to accurately localize sounds in our environment. You can prove this to yourself by blocking the sound from one ear and noticing how well you can tell where the sounds

BOX 11. 3 / *Perceiving Sound in Rooms: Reverberation Time*

We've seen that your perception of light depends not only on the nature of the light source but also on what happens to the light between the time it leaves its source and the time it enters your eyes. If light encounters haze on its way from an object to your eyes, the object may seem bluer or fuzzier than it would if the haze were not there. In a similar way, your perception of sound also depends not only on the sound produced at the source but also on what happens to the sound between the time it leaves the source and the time it enters your ears.

What happens to a sound between the time it is produced and the time it reaches your ears? We can see from the figure that the answer to this question depends on the environment in which you hear the sound. If you are sitting outdoors next to someone playing a guitar, most of the sound you hear travels in a straight line and reaches your ears directly. If, however, you are listening to the same guitar in an enclosed room, then only some of the sound you hear travels directly to your ears; the rest of the sound you hear travels from the guitar to the room's walls, ceiling, and floor before reaching your ears. The sound reaching your ears directly, along path a,

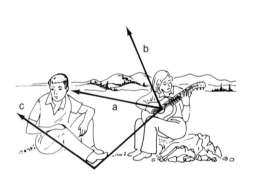

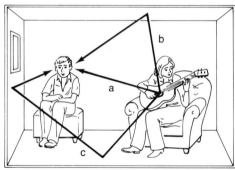

around you are coming from. You will probably notice that it is much more difficult to localize sounds with one ear than it is with two, and you end up moving your head around a lot to compensate for the loss of information from the blocked ear. Sounds are localized much less accurately with **monaural** (one-eared) **hearing** than with **binaural** (two-eared) **hearing.**

Just as we can locate objects in visual space because our two eyes receive slightly different images, sound localization in auditory space depends on our having two ears that receive slightly different sounds. In the remainder of this chapter we will describe these differences in the information we take in with the left and right ears.

Interaural Time Difference

The basis for the idea that the two ears receive different sounds is illustrated in Figure 11.30. We can see from this figure that when a sound originates from directly in front of the listener, at A,

is called **direct sound,** and the sound reaching your ears later, along paths like b and c, is called **indirect sound.**

The science of architectural acoustics is largely concerned with how this indirect sound changes the quality of the sounds we hear in rooms. The major factor affecting indirect sound is the amount of sound absorbed by the walls, ceilings, and floors of the room. If most of the sound is absorbed, then there are few sound reflections and we hear little indirect sound. If little of the sound is absorbed, however, then there are many sound reflections and we hear much indirect sound. The amount of indirect sound produced by a room is expressed as the **reverberation time** of the room, where reverberation time is the time it takes for the sound to decrease to one-thousandth its original pressure.

What is the relationship between reverberation time and our perception of music? If the reverberation time is short, music will sound "dead," because most of the sound is absorbed by the room and it is difficult to produce sounds of very high intensity. If the reverberation time is long, music sounds "muddled," because most of the sound is reflected by the room and the sounds overlap each other. Thus, the job of the acoustical engineer is to design a room in which the reverberation time is neither too short nor too long. The optimal reverberation time for a room depends on the size of the room, with most average-sized concert halls needing a reverberation time of about 1.5–2.0 seconds.

However, reverberation time is apparently not the only factor that affects our perception of music in concert halls. This is illustrated by the problems associated with the design of New York's Philharmonic Hall. When it opened in 1962, Philharmonic Hall had a reverberation time of close to 2.0 seconds, a value comparable to the reverberation times of many of the most successful concert halls in the world. Even so, the hall was criticized for sounding as though it had a short reverberation time, and musicians in the orchestra complained that they could not hear each other. These criticisms resulted in a series of alterations to the hall, made over many years, until eventually, when none of the alterations proved satisfactory, the entire interior of the hall was destroyed and the hall was completely rebuilt. Finally, in 1976, 14 years after it opened, Philharmonic Hall had good acoustics. Based on this experience with Philharmonic Hall, it is safe to say that the acoustics of concert halls is not an exact science (Backus, 1977).

the distance to each ear is the same, but if a sound originates from the side, as in B, the sound must travel farther and therefore takes longer to get to the left ear than to the right ear. This difference in the time it takes for the sound to get to the left and right ears is called the **interaural time difference.**

We can measure how the interaural time difference changes with a sound's location by placing microphones in a person's ears and measuring the arrival time of sounds originating from sources located at different positions in space relative to the person. The results of these measurements indicate that the interaural time difference is zero when the source is directly in front of or directly behind the listener; however, as the source is moved to the side, there is a delay between the time the sound reaches the near ear and the time it reaches the far ear, with this difference reaching a maximum of about 600 microseconds (6/10,000 sec) when the sound is located directly opposite one of the ears, as in B of Figure 11.30 (Feddersen, Saudel, Teas, & Jeffress, 1957). Although time differ-

---

B O X 11. 4 / *The Precedence Effect*

The reverberation that occurs when you listen to music, or to someone talking in an enclosed room, means that your ears first receive sound waves directly from the sound source and then receive indirect sounds, which are reflected from the ceiling, floor, and walls of the room. Since your ears receive a sequence of sounds, why do you perceive only a single sound? The answer to this question is that, for reasons still not completely understood, your auditory system suppresses the sound waves that reach your ears indirectly and attends only to the first sound waves reaching your ears. This effect, which is called the **precedence effect,** was extensively studied by Hans Wallach and coworkers (1949).

Wallach demonstrated the precedence effect by having a subject listen to music coming from two speakers located an equal distance away. When the music came from both speakers simultaneously, the subject heard the music coming from a point between the two speakers. However, if Wallach caused the sound from one speaker to precede the sound from the other by having two phonograph pickups play the same record—the needle of one pickup following in the same groove as the needle of the other—the subject reported that the sound appeared to come only from the speaker that first produced the sound. On the basis of this result and those of other experiments, Wallach concluded that the first sound reaching our ears is heard, and sounds arriving within about 70 msec of this first sound are suppressed.

You might think that this effect is due to the fact that moving toward one speaker makes the

D E M O N S T R A T I O N

Experiencing the Precedence Effect

To demonstrate the precedence effect to yourself, turn your stereo system to monaural (or "mixed") so that both speakers play the same sounds, and position yourself between the speakers, so you hear the sound coming from both speakers or from a point between them. Then move a small distance to the left or right. When you do this, the sound suddenly appears to be coming from only the nearer speaker.

---

sound from that speaker louder. However, Wallach showed that the small increase in loudness that would occur from moving slightly closer to one speaker cannot cause you to hear only that speaker; you hear only the nearer speaker because the sound from that speaker reaches your ears first.

When you hear the sound coming from the near speaker, does this mean you no longer hear the far speaker? You can answer this question by positioning yourself closer to one speaker and having a friend disconnect the other speaker. When this happens, you will notice a difference in the quality of the sound. Even when you think you are listening to only the near speaker, you are also hearing the far speaker, and the contribution from this speaker gives the sound a fuller, more expansive quality (Green, 1976).

---

ences on the order of microseconds are very small, it has been shown that we can detect differences in arrival time as short as 10 microseconds (Durlach & Colburn, 1978).

While the interaural time difference provides

information about the location of a tone, it does not do so unambiguously, because a number of points in space can result in the same interaural time difference. Any point lying on a surface called the **cone of confusion,** shown in Figure 11.31, results

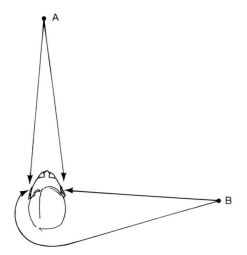

F I G U R E 11. 30 The principle behind interaural time difference. The tone directly in front of the listener at A reaches the left and right ears at the same time. However, if the tone is off°to the side at B, it reaches the listener's right ear before it reaches his left ear.

in the same interaural time difference, so it is difficult to tell exactly where on the cone a sound is coming from. The solution to this problem is simple: When the observer moves his or her head, tones that were difficult to localize with the head stationary can be localized much more easily. Our ability to accurately localize tones in everyday experience can be largely attributed to the effect of these head movements.

Interaural Intensity Difference

In addition to a difference in the arrival time of sound at the two ears, there is also a difference in the intensity of the sound reaching the two ears. This occurs because the head casts a "shadow," which decreases the intensity of the sound reaching the far ear. This difference in the intensity reaching the two ears, which is called the **interaural intensity difference,** has been measured by recording the sound intensity reaching each ear with microphones and a movable sound source. The results of these measurements indicate that the magnitude of this shadow depends on the frequency of the tone. There is essentially no shadow for low-frequency tones, but there is a large shadow for high-frequency tones. Thus, when a 200-Hz tone is moved to different locations, the sound intensities reaching both ears stay equal, but when a 6,000-Hz tone is moved there are locations where the intensity reaching the far ear is up to 20 dB less than the intensity reaching the near ear.

The difference between the interaural intensity differences for high and low frequencies is caused

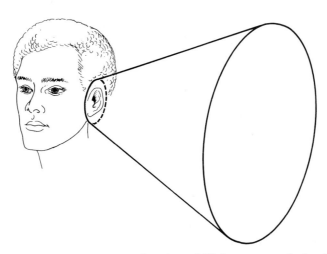

F I G U R E 11. 31 The "cone of confusion." Without moving the head it is difficult to localize tones originating from locations on the surface of this cone.

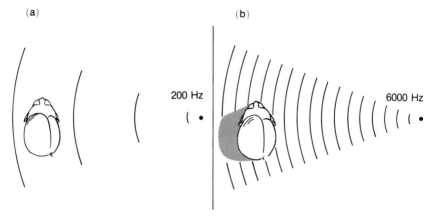

F I G U R E 11. 32 The principle behind interaural intensity difference. Low-frequency tones are not affected by the listener's head so the intensity of the 200-Hz tone is the same at both ears. High-frequency tones are affected by the presence of the listener's head, resulting in a sound "shadow" that decreases the intensity of the tone reaching the listener's far ear.

by differences in the wavelengths of the tones. The wavelength of the 200-Hz tone is large compared to the size of the head, as shown in Figure 11.32(a); so the head does not interfere with the sound wave, and the intensity is unaffected. The wavelength of the 6,000-Hz tone, however, is very small compared to the size of the head, as shown in Figure 11.32(b); so the wave casts a shadow on the far side of the head, and then intensity at the far ear is decreased. Because of this effect of the tone's wavelength, the interaural intensity difference is an effective cue for sound location only at high frequencies.

Sound Reflections by the Pinna

Finally, we consider how the **pinna**, or **earlobe** (Figure 11.33) affects localization. Gardner and Gardner (1973) inserted plugs of various shapes into people's ears and found that as they increasingly smoothed out the pinna by inserting different plugs, their listeners had more and more difficulty in localizing sounds. One possible reason for this result is that high-frequency tones are reflected back and forth inside the whorls of the pinna, causing "echoes" with different patterns for different distances and directions of the sound source (Batteau, 1967; Scharf, 1975; Butler & Belendiuk, 1977).

THE PSYCHOPHYSICAL APPROACH TO HEARING

In describing the relationship between the stimulus for hearing and perception, we have identified which aspects of stimuli affect specific perceptions. We have seen that pitch depends on frequency, loudness depends on amplitude, the consonance and dissonance of complex tones depends on the frequency relations between tones' harmonics, and our ability to localize sounds in space depends on the time and intensity relations of the sounds reaching our two ears.

In this chapter we have not focused on describing mechanisms. That is, we have presented no theory about how we hear pitch or how we hear loudness. In the next chapter we will focus on mechanisms, with our central concern being to answer the question: What physiological mechanisms are responsible for our perception of pitch and sound location?

Although in answering this question we will be describing the physiological mechanisms of hearing, we will see that our understanding of these physiological mechanisms is based on a foundation of psychophysical results. It is appropriate to repeat here a statement we made in the first chapter: "The

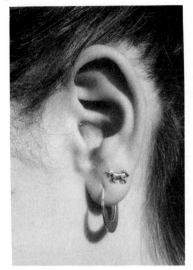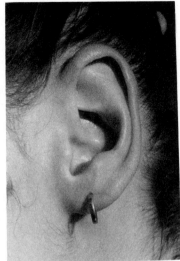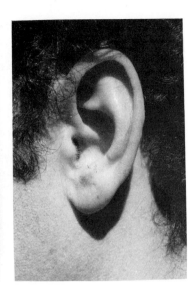

F I G U R E   11. 33 Different people have pinnas with very different shapes. These shapes affect the way the sound bounces around in the pinna, and this "bouncing" provides information for sound localization.

results of physiological experiments must be combined with the results of behavioral tests for the physiological results to have meaning for perception" (p. 19). Thus, although we will focus on physiology in the next chapter, it is important to remember that to begin searching for a physiological mechanism we need to know what aspect of the stimulus controls a specific perception. Thus, the links between frequency and pitch; amplitude and loudness; time and intensity relations and localization are crucial to our search for physiological mechanisms. (Remember that we made the same point in describing color vision in Chapter 4. We needed to know that there is a link between hue and wavelength before progress could be made in understanding the mechanisms for color vision.)

We will also see that psychophysical results pose problems for physiological theories to answer. For example, we will see that there are theories that explain how nerve impulses can signal the presence of different frequencies. However, we will also see that these theories have difficulty explaining why we continue to hear the same pitch even if we eliminate the fundamental frequency of a complex tone. Psychophysics, therefore, provides both the starting point and the testing ground for the physiological theories of hearing that we will describe in the next chapter.

Summary

1. An object generates sound when its vibrations result in pressure waves in the medium surrounding the object. When these vibrations are sinusoidal, a pure tone results. Two basic characteristics of pure tones are the frequency and amplitude of the wave.

2. Musical tones are more complex than pure tones, but by using Fourier analysis we can break these tones down into a number of sine-wave components. We can represent these components with a Fourier spectrum showing the energy in the tone's fundamental frequency and harmonics.

3. The unit used to designate the amplitude of a tone is the decibel (dB). $dB = 20 \log(p/p_o)$. When the reference pressure, p_o, is set at 2×10^{-5} Newtons/meter^2, this amplitude measure is called sound pressure level (SPL).

4. Loudness is closely related to SPL. The power function relating loudness and pressure has an exponent

of 0.4–0.6, depending on the frequency and the conditions of measurement.

5. The auditory response area defines the frequencies and the SPLs over which hearing functions. The audibility curve indicates the threshold SPL for frequencies throughout the range of hearing. The range of hearing extends from 20 Hz to 20,000 Hz, with the lowest threshold at 2,000–4,000 Hz. The audibility curve tells us that two tones with different SPLs can both be at threshold.

6. An equal loudness curve is a plot of the SPL which results in the same loudness as a 1,000-Hz reference tone for frequencies across the range of hearing. Equal loudness curves tell us that two tones with the same SPLs can result in different loudnesses and that two tones with different SPLs can result in the same loudness.

7. A tone's pitch is related to its frequency. The increase in pitch with increasing frequency reflects the quality of tone height, and the similarity of sounds an octave apart reflects the quality of tone chroma.

8. Periodicity pitch, or the effect of the missing fundamental, refers to the fact that eliminating the fundamental frequency of a musical tone does not change its pitch.

9. Timbre refers to the quality of a tone. Two identical notes played by different instruments have different timbres. This difference is caused by differences in the harmonic structure and timing of the tone's attack and decay.

10. The critical bandwidth of the frequency band within which two tones interfere with one another. Two tones separated by more than the critical band sound louder than two tones that have the same overall level that are not separated by a critical bandwidth.

11. Consonance and dissonance refer to the pleasingness of a combination of two or more tones. Pure tones with frequencies within their critical bandwidth tend to sound rough, or dissonant. When the separation is increased so it is greater than the critical bandwidth, the combination sounds smoother, or more consonant. The consonance or dissonance of combinations of complex musical tones can be explained in terms of interactions between their Fourier components; dissonance increases when pairs of harmonics fall within the critical band.

12. Just as visual stimuli are perceptually organized so that certain elements of a scene appear to "belong together," so are tones. There are many examples of how sequences of tones become grouped by similarity, one of which is auditory stream segregation. The Gestalt laws of proximity and good continuation can also be demonstrated with auditory stimuli.

13. Melody schemas illustrate the effect of the listener's past experience on auditory perception.

14. Sound is localized by means of interaural time and intensity differences and by head movements.

Boxes

1. Blind people can judge the presence of objects by paying attention to the sounds of their own footsteps or vocalizations.

2. Homing pigeons can detect infrasounds—frequencies below 10 Hz. It has been hypothesized that this ability may be used as an aid in navigation.

3. The quality of sound heard in rooms depends on the amount of sound absorbed by the surfaces in the room. Concert halls with short reverberation times can cause music to sound "dead," whereas concert halls with long reverberation times can cause music to sound "muddled."

4. The auditory system suppresses sound waves that reach the ears indirectly. This is called the precedence effect.

Study Questions

1. What kinds of information does sound provide about our environment? (383)

2. What do we mean when we say that sounds are air vibrations? (385)

3. What is a pure tone? What is frequency? amplitude? (386)

4. Describe the properties of musical tones. What does Fourier analysis accomplish and how is it applied to the description of musical tones. What is the fundamental? harmonics? (387)

5. What physical property of sound determines its loudness? What is a decibel? What is sound pressure level (SPL)? Why do we use decibels? (389)

6. What is the relationship between SPL and loudness? Why do we say that loudness and SPL are not the same thing? (390)

7. What is the auditory response area? What is the audibility curve? According to the audibility curve, the threshold for hearing is lowest at _____ Hz. How is the audibility curve measured? (391)

8. How can we use the audibility curve to show that loudness and decibels (SPL) are not the same thing?

Using Figure 11.9 show how different SPLs can result in the same loudness and how the same SPLs can have different loudnesses. (393)

9. What is an equal loudness curve? How is it measured? (393)
10. What is the principle behind the "loudness" button on your stereo? (394)
11. What physical property of sound determines its pitch? What is tone height? tone chroma? octave generalization? What is special about octaves? (394)
12. What is periodicity pitch (the effect of the missing fundamental)? What practical consequences does periodicity pitch have for the reproduction of music? (395)
13. What is timbre? What aspects of the stimulus cause differences in timbre? (396)
14. What is the critical bandwidth? What does it show? (400)
15. What is consonance? dissonance? Describe how they change as we increase the frequency difference between two tones. (399)
16. Some combinations of complex tones are more dissonant than others. How do the Fourier spectra of these tones explain this? (401)
17. Give some examples of how tones become perceptually grouped by similarity of pitch. What is auditory stream segregation? the scale illusion? (403)
18. Give an example of how tones become perceptually grouped by proximity. (405)
19. Give an example of auditory good continuation. (406)
20. What is melody schema? (407)
21. What is interaural time difference? How does it change with the position of the sound source? How brief a time difference can we resolve? (408)
22. What is the cone of confusion? Why does moving the head make it easier to localize tones? (410)
23. What is interaural intensity difference? Does it occur for both high and low frequencies? (411)
24. What role do sound reflections by the pinna play in sound localization? (412)

Boxes

1. What is the basis of some blind persons' ability to detect objects before they bump into them? (384)
2. What is infrasound? How did Kreithen and Quine show that pigeons can hear infrasounds? (392)
3. What is direct sound? indirect sound? reverberation time? What is the relationship between reverberation time and the perception of music in concert halls? (409)
4. What is the precedence effect? How can you demonstrate this effect using your stereo system? (410)

Glossary

Amplitude. In the case of a repeating sound wave, such as the sine wave of a pure tone, amplitude represents the pressure difference between atmospheric pressure and the maximum pressure of the wave. (386)

Attack. The buildup of sound at the beginning of a tone. (397)

Audibility curve. Curve that indicates the sound pressure level (SPL) at threshold for frequencies across the audible spectrum. (391)

Auditory response area. The area that defines the frequencies and SPLs over which hearing functions. This area extends between the audibility curve and the curve for the threshold of feeling. (391)

Auditory stream segregation. When a series of tones that differ in pitch are played so that the high- and low-pitched tones alternate rapidly, the high and low pitches become perceptually separate into simultaneously occurring independent streams of sound. (404)

Beating. An oscillation of loudness that occurs when two tones with slightly different frequencies are presented simultaneously. (400)

Beats. See beating.

Binaural hearing. Hearing with two ears. (408)

Cone of confusion. The cone-shaped surface that is defined by all of the points in space that are the same distance from both ears. (410)

Consonance. A pleasing or harmonious combination of two or more tones. (389)

Critical bandwidth. The band of frequencies within which tones interact with each other. Thus, two tones that are separated by a frequency difference smaller than the critical bandwidth do not sound as loud as two tones, with the same combined SPL, that are separated by a frequency difference larger than the critical bandwidth. (400)

Decay. The decrease in sound at the end of a tone. (397)

Decibel (dB). A unit that indicates the presence of a tone relative to a reference pressure. $dB = 20 \log(p/p_o)$, where p is the pressure of the tone and p_o is the reference pressure. (390)

Direct sound. Sound that is transmitted to the ears directly from a sound source. (409)

Dissonance. A displeasing or harsh combination of two or more tones. (390)

Earlobe. See pinna.

Equal loudness curve. A curve that indicates the SPLs which result in a perception of the same loudness at frequencies across the audible spectrum. (393)

Facial vision. A hypothesized ability of blind people to detect obstacles by sensing pressure or temperature changes on their faces. (384)

Fourier analysis. A mathematical technique that analyzes complex periodic waveforms into a number of sine-wave components. (387)

Fourier spectrum. The sine-wave components that make up a periodic waveform. Fourier spectra are usually depicted by a line for each sine-wave frequency, with the height of the line indicating the amount of energy at that frequency. (387)

Fourier's theorem. Any periodic waveform can be reproduced by adding a number of sine-wave components. (387)

Frequency. In the case of a sound wave that repeats itself like the sine wave of a pure tone, frequency is the number of times per second that the wave repeats itself. (386)

Fundamental frequency. The fundamental frequency is usually the lowest frequency in the Fourier spectrum of a complex tone. The tone's other components, called harmonics, have frequencies that are multiples of the fundamental frequency. (387)

Harmonics. Fourier components of a complex tone with frequencies that are multiples of the fundamental frequency. (387)

Hertz (Hz). The unit for designating the frequency of a tone. One Hertz equals one cycle per second. (386)

Indirect sound. Sound that reaches the ears after being reflected from a surface such as a room's walls. (409)

Infrasound. Vibrations below 10 Hertz. (392)

Interaural intensity difference. When a sound source is positioned closer to one ear than to the other, the intensity of the sound is greater at the closer ear. This effect is most pronounced for high-frequency tones. (411)

Interaural time difference. When a sound source is positioned closer to one ear than to the other, the sound reaches the close ear slightly before reaching the far ear. (409)

Interleaved melodies. The stimulus produced when the notes of two different melodies are presented alternately. (406)

Localization. In audition, the capacity to locate a sound in space. (390)

Loudness. The quality of sound that ranges from soft to loud. For a tone of a particular frequency, loudness usually increases with increasing decibels. (389)

Melodic channeling. See Scale illusion.

Melody schema. A representation of a familiar melody that is stored in a person's memory. (407)

Missing fundamental, effect of. See Periodicity pitch.

Monaural hearing. Hearing with one ear. (408)

Musical interval. The distance between two tones on the musical scale. For example, the interval between two Cs on the scale is one octave. (401)

Octave. Tones that have frequencies that are binary multiples of each other ($x2$, $x4$, etc.) are separated by octaves. For example, an 800-Hz tone is one octave above a 400-Hz tone. (394)

Octave generalization. An effect observed in an experiment by Deutsch in which two tones separated by an interval of an octave had perceptual effects similar to two identical tones. These similar effects are caused by the perceptual similarity of tones separated by octaves. (395)

Oscillator. An electronic device used to produce pure tones. (386)

Overtone. See Harmonics.

Periodicity. The repetition of a sound wave's pattern. (387)

Periodicity pitch. The fact that a complex tone's pitch remains the same even if we eliminate the fundamental frequency. (395)

Pinna. The part of the ear that is visible on the outside of the head. (412)

Pitch. That quality of sound ranging from low to high which is most closely associated with the frequency of a tone. (389)

Precedence effect. If two identical or very similar sounds reach your ears separated by a time interval of less than about 50–100 msec, you hear the sound that reaches your ears first and the auditory system suppresses the sounds that reach your ears within this 50–100-msec time interval. (410)

Pure tone. A tone with pressure changes that can be described by a single sine wave. (386)

Reverberation time. Reflection of sound by the walls, ceiling, or floor of a room increases the duration of the sound. The reverberation time of a room is the time it takes for a sound to decrease to 1/1,000 of its original pressure. (409)

Scale illusion. An illusion that occurs when successive notes from a scale are presented alternately to the left and right ears. Even though each ear receives notes that jump up and down in frequency, smoothly ascending or descending scales are heard in each ear. (405)

Sound pressure level (SPL). A designation used to indicate that the reference pressure used for calculating a tone's decibel rating is set at 2×10^{-5} Newtons/m^2, near the threshold in the most sensitive frequency range for hearing. (390)

Sound waves. Pressure changes in a medium. Most of the sounds we hear are due to pressure changes in the air. (386)

Timbre. The quality of a tone. Different musical instruments have different timbres, so when we play the same note on different instruments, the notes have the same pitch but sound different. (389)

Tone chroma. The perceptual similarity of notes separated by octaves reflects the fact that these notes have the same tone chroma. (394)

Tone height. The increase in pitch that occurs as frequency is increased. (394)

Hearing II: Physiological Mechanisms

In Jenkins' description of his auditory environment that opened the last chapter, he marvels at the fact that variations of air pressure sensed at two little holes in his head can cause him to perceive, among other things, his wife's conversation, birds chirping, dogs barking, leaves rustling in a tree, and an airplane overhead.

In this chapter we will consider how the variations in air pressure that enter those "two little holes" signal qualities of the auditory environment to the brain. To do this we will focus not on the complex sounds described by Jenkins but on two basic qualities of simple pure tones: (1) pitch and (2) location. We focus on these two qualities because of the large amount of research devoted to them and because, in the case of pitch, we can describe two physiological theories which, in combination, explain many of the facts of pitch perception.

Our major concern will be to answer the question: What is the neural code for pitch and for sound location? That is, how do nerve impulses signal these qualities to the brain? (Figure 12.1). The first step in answering this question is to describe the structure of the auditory system.

STRUCTURE AND FUNCTIONING OF THE AUDITORY SYSTEM

Our first task in describing the structure of any sensory system is to describe how energy from the environment reaches the receptors. This was easy for vision—light enters the pupil and strikes the rods and cones that line the back of the eyeball. Audition, however, is a more complicated story. The stimulus for hearing—pressure changes in the air—follows a complex path between the time it enters the auditory canal (see Figure 12.2) until it reaches its goal—receptors called **hair cells**—inside a snail-shaped structure called the **cochlea.**

These hair cells, shown in Figure 12.3, contain tiny structures called cilia, which, when they are bent, generate the electrical signals that eventually result in our perception of sound. Our problem is to describe how sound vibrations entering the ear cause these hair cells to vibrate. To do this, we will begin with sound waves entering the ear and follow their effect as they travel through the ear's various structures.

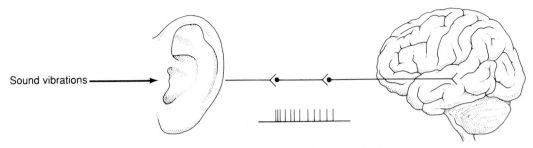

Neural code for pitch? For location?

F I G U R E 12. 1 In vision, light energy is transformed into neural impulses that carry a code representing various visual qualities. In hearing, sound vibrations are transformed into neural impulses that carry a code representing various auditory qualities. Our major concern in this chapter is to identify this code for pitch and location.

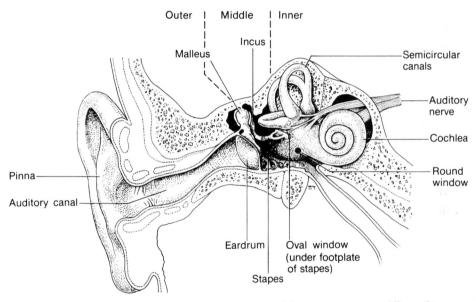

F I G U R E 12. 2 The ear, showing its three subdivisions—outer, middle, and inner.

The Outer Ear

When we talk about the "ear" in everyday conversation, we are usually referring to the pinnae, the funny-looking structures that stick out from the sides of our head (Figure 11.33). While this most obvious part of the ear is of some importance in helping us locate sounds and is of great importance for those of us who wear eyeglasses or earrings, it is the part of the ear we could most easily do without. The major workings of the ear are found inside the head, hidden from view.

It is to these hidden places inside the head that sound waves must travel before they are heard, and in the first stage of their journey they pass through the **outer ear,** which consists of the pinna and the **auditory canal** (Figure 12.2). The auditory canal is a tubelike structure about 3 cm long whose

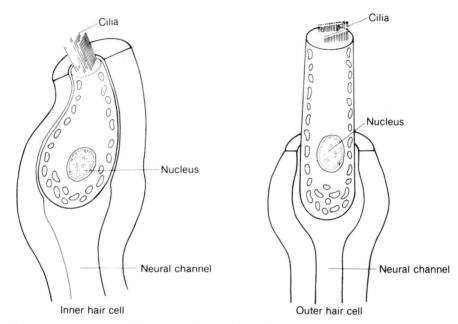

F I G U R E 12. 3 The inner and outer hair cells. Vibration of the cilia, or hairs, generates an electrical signal. (Adapted from Gulick, 1971.)

function is to protect the delicate structures of the middle ear from the hazards of the outside world. The auditory canal's 3-cm recess, along with its wax, which has an apparently unpleasant effect on curious insects (Schubert, 1980), protects the delicate **tympanic membrane,** or **eardrum,** at the end of the canal and helps keep this membrane and the structures in the middle ear at a relatively constant temperature.

In addition to its protective function, the outer ear has another role: to enhance the intensities of some sounds by means of a mechanism called **resonance.** Resonance occurs when sound waves near the **resonant frequency** of the auditory canal are reflected from the closed end of the canal and reinforce the incoming sound waves of the same frequency. The resonant frequency of the auditory canal, which is determined by the length of the canal, is about 3,400 Hz, and measurements of the sound pressures inside the ear indicate that the auditory canal has a slight amplifying effect on frequencies between about 2,000 and 5,000 Hz.

The Middle Ear

Airborne sound waves reach the **middle ear** when they set the tympanic membrane into vibration. The middle ear is a small cavity, about 2 cubic cm in volume, bounded on one side by the tympanic membrane and on the other by the cochlea. Inside this cavity are the **ossicles,** the three smallest bones in the body. The first of these bones, the **malleus** (or **hammer**), is set into vibration by the tympanic membrane and transmits its vibrations to the **incus** (or **anvil**) which, in turn, transmits its vibrations to the **stapes** (or **stirrup**). The stapes then transmits its vibrations to the cochlea through the **oval window** (see Figures 12.2 and 12.4).

Why are the ossicles necessary? We can understand why by noting that both the outer ear and middle ear are filled with air but the inner ear contains a watery liquid called cochlear fluid, which is much denser than the air (Figure 12.5). The high density of the cochlear fluid compared to the air creates a problem: Airborne vibrations are

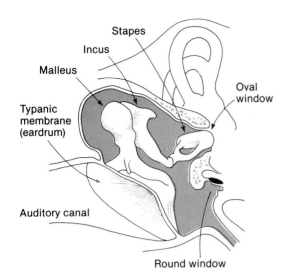

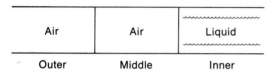

FIGURE 12. 4 The middle ear. The three bones of the middle ear transmit the vibrations of the tympanic membrane to the inner ear.

FIGURE 12. 5 Environments inside the outer, middle, and inner ears. The fact that liquid fills the inner ear poses a problem for the transmission of sound vibrations from the air of the middle ear.

transmitted poorly to the much denser cochlear fluid, so if these vibrations had to pass directly from the air to the fluid, only about 3 percent of the vibrations would be transmitted (Durrant & Lovrinic, 1977). The ossicles help solve this problem by amplifying the vibrations in two ways:

1. The ossicles concentrate the vibration of the large tympanic membrane onto the smaller stapes. The tympanic membrane has an area of about 0.6 square centimeters, whereas the stapes footplate has an area of about 0.032 square centimeters—a ratio of about 17 to 1. Concentrating the vibration of the large tympanic membrane onto the smaller stapes, as shown in Figure 12.6, increases the pressure per unit area in the same way that a 110-lb woman wearing shoes with 1-cm spiked heels can generate a pressure of 110,000 pounds per square foot by concentrating all of her weight on one heel.

2. The ossicles act according to the lever principle. Figure 12.7 illustrates this principle. If a board is balanced on a fulcrum, a small weight

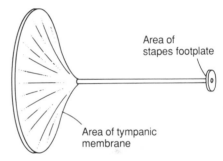

FIGURE 12. 6 A diagrammatic representation of tympanic membrane and the stapes showing the difference in size between the two. (From Schubert, 1980.)

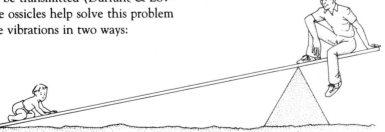

FIGURE 12. 7 The lever principle. The baby on the long end of the board can overcome the weight of the man on the short end. (The baby will, however, be in for a surprise if it crawls very far toward the man.)

on the long end of the board can overcome a larger weight on the short end of the board. Though it is not obvious from looking at the ossicles, they are hinged so that they increase the vibration by a factor of about 1.3 by means of this lever principle.

These two amplification mechanisms increase the vibrations by a factor of at least $(1.3 \times 17) = 22$ (Durant & Lovrinic, 1977), with some calculations setting this value as high as a factor of 100 (Schubert, 1980). In any case, without the middle ear it would be much more difficult for us to hear. In fact, the effect of losing the ossicles has been measured in patients whose ossicles have been damaged beyond surgical repair. In such cases an operation is sometimes performed so that sound is transmitted directly to the cochlea through the air. When the ossicles are absent, the sound pressure must be increased by a factor of $10-50$ to achieve the same hearing ability as when the ossicles were present.

The Inner Ear

Vibrations enter the liquid-filled cochlea of the **inner ear** through the oval window. The cochlea, which is a bony snail-like structure, is difficult to visualize because it is rolled into 2 ¾ turns. But if we uncoil the cochlea so it becomes a long straight tube, as in Figure 12.8(a) and (b), we can more easily describe the structure inside. The most obvious feature of the uncoiled cochlea is that it is divided in half by a structure called the **cochlear partition,** extending almost the entire length of the cochlea, except for a small opening at the end called the **helicotrema,** which connects the top and the bottom of the cochlea. (It should be noted that diagrams such as this one, which are not to scale, do not indicate the cochlea's true shape. In reality, the diameter of the uncoiled cochlea forms a cylinder 2 mm in diameter and 35 mm long.)

The cochlear partition is best seen if we look at the cochlea end-on and in cross section, as in Figure 12.9. When we look at the cochlea in this

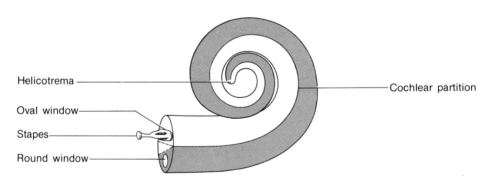

(a) Partially uncoiled cochlea

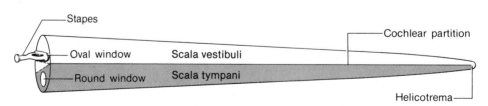

(b) Fully uncoiled cochlea

F I G U R E   12. 8   (a) A partially uncoiled cochlea. (b) A fully uncoiled cochlea.

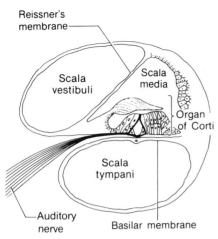

F I G U R E 12. 9 A cross section of the cochlea.

way, we see that it is divided into three compartments, the *scala vestibuli,* the *scala tympani,* and the *scala media,* and that the cochlear partition contains a large structure called the **organ of Corti.** Details of the organ of Corti are shown in side view in Figure 12.10 and in perspective in Figure 12.11. Its three structures of primary importance are the

basilar membrane, the tectorial membrane, and the hair cells.

The hair cells, which are the receptors for hearing, are shown in Figure 12.3. There are two types of hair cells, the inner hair cells and the outer hair cells (Figures 12.10 and 12.11), with the outer hair cells being by far the most numerous and carrying most of the signals generated in the cochlea. Although the inner and outer hair cells may serve different functions (Dallos, Billone, Durrant, Waug, & Raynor, 1972), they share a very important structure—small cilia (or hairs) which protrude from the cell body. These hairs are the target of the vibrations we have been following through the ear, because when they bend, they cause the release of a chemical transmitter onto a nerve fiber, which then generates electrical signals that are transmitted toward the brain in the auditory nerve.

But what causes the hair cells to bend? To answer this question let's return to the oval window, where the stapes is vibrating. When the stapes pushes in on the oval window, it transmits pressure to the liquid inside the cochlea. From Figure 12.8(b), we might think this pressure would be transmitted down the scala vestibuli, around the opening at the helicotrema, and down the scala tympani to

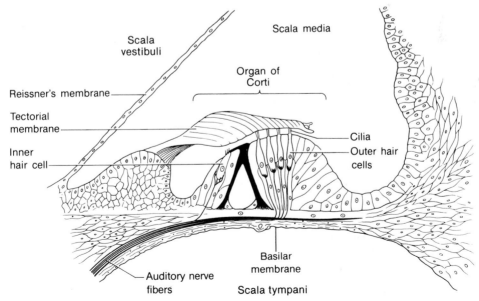

F I G U R E 12. 10 The organ of Corti. (Adapted from Gulick, 1971.)

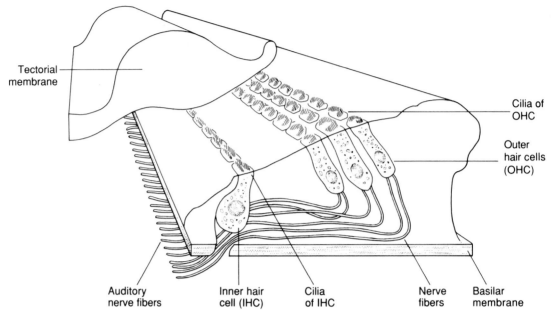

Tectorial membrane

Cilia of OHC

Outer hair cells (OHC)

Auditory nerve fibers

Inner hair cell (IHC)

Cilia of IHC

Nerve fibers

Basilar membrane

F I G U R E 12. 11   Perspective view of the organ of Corti. The tectorial membrane is actually closer to the hair cells than shown here (see Figure 12.10). (Adapted from Kiang, 1986.)

the **round window.** This is not, however, what happens. Very little pressure is transmitted around the end of the cochlear partition; the helicotrema acts almost as if it were closed. Rather than transmit pressure through the helicotrema, the liquid in the scala vestibuli pushes on the cochlear partition. This push, which causes the elastic cochlear partition to move downward, is followed by a pull which causes the cochlear partition to move upward. This pull occurs when the stapes pulls back from the oval window, decreasing the pressure inside the scala vestibuli. This pushing and pulling sets the cochlear partition into an up-and-down motion, vibrating with exactly the same frequency as the stapes.

The vibration of the cochlear partition sets the organ of Corti into an up-and-down motion and causes some of the cilia of the hair cells to be bent by rubbing against the tectorial membrane (notice the close relationship between the cilia and the tectorial membrane illustrated in Figures 12.10 and 12.11), and others to be bent by the vibration of the surrounding liquid. This bending of the cilia causes the hair cells to release a chemical trans-

mitter that generates nerve impulses in the auditory nerve.

Central Structures

Just as the pathway from the stimulus in the environment to the receptors is much more complex for the auditory than for the visual system, so is the pathway from the receptors to the brain. Remember that most of the neurons leaving the eye in the optic nerve synapse in the lateral geniculate nucleus of the thalamus and from there go to the visual cortex. Nerve fibers in the auditory nerve also synapse in the thalamus, but before reaching it, they synapse in three other nuclei.

Figure 12.12 shows the pathway from the cochlea to the auditory cortex. The route is quite complex, and we do not yet know many of its details. Figure 12.12, however, does identify the most important structures through which signals pass on their way to the cortex. Nerve fibers from the cochlea first synapse in the **cochlear nucleus,** then in the superior olivary nucleus, and finally in the

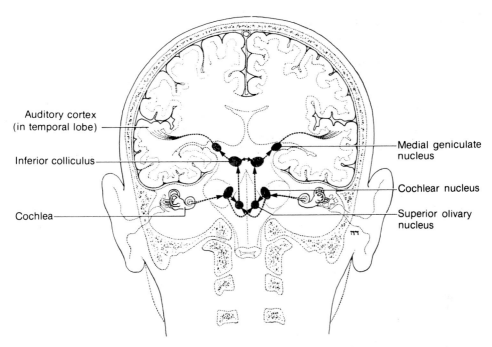

FIGURE 12.12 Simplified diagram of the auditory pathways. (Adapted from Wever, 1949.)

inferior colliculus of the midbrain, before reaching the medial geniculate nucleus of the thalamus. From the medial geniculate nucleus, fibers then go to the primary **auditory receiving area,** which is located in the temporal lobe of the cortex.

The complexity of the auditory system becomes apparent when we consider that, in addition to the pathway from the cochlea to the cortex, there are also connections between nuclei on the opposite sides. For example, the cochlear nucleus of the right ear sends axons to the superior olivary nucleus and the inferior colliculus of the left ear, and the left and right inferior colliculi communicate with each other. In addition to these fibers, which send signals from the cochlea toward the brain, other fibers send signals from the brain back to the cochlea.

Now that we have described the auditory system, we are going to ask how the structure of this system enables us to perceive two qualities of auditory experience: (1) pitch and (2) location in space. In the last chapter we described some of the psychophysical research on these qualities. Here we

focus on physiological research that asks the following question: What is the neural code for pitch and for location in space?

In describing what we know about the neural code, we will focus our attention on the simplest type of sound stimuli—pure tones. We do this because using these simple stimuli has proved to be a good way to begin unraveling the complexities of the auditory process. We begin our description of the physiology of hearing by asking the question that has occupied the majority of auditory researchers: What is the physiological mechanism for pitch perception?

INTRODUCTION TO THE PHYSIOLOGY OF PITCH PERCEPTION

Our problem in trying to understand the physiology of pitch perception is the problem of neural coding: How does the firing of neurons signal different pitches? This question is analogous to one we considered in the chapter on color vision when we asked: How does the firing of neurons signal different colors? We saw that the first step in answering this question for color vision was to identify wavelength as the physical property of the stimulus that is most closely associated with our perception of color. Our initial task in this chapter is the same: to identify the physical property of the stimulus that is most closely associated with our perception of pitch. In Chapter 11 we saw that this property is *frequency*. As shown in Figure 11.11, high frequencies are associated with high pitches and low frequencies with low pitches. Knowing this connection, we can now state our problem as follows: How is *frequency* coded in neural impulses?

The following two answers to this question have been proposed:

1. There is a **place code** for frequency. Different frequencies are signaled by activity in neurons that are located at different *places* in the auditory system. According to this idea, neurons connected to receptors in different places in the cochlea signal different frequencies, as shown in Figure 12.13.

2. There is a **temporal code** for frequency. Different frequencies are signaled by the *timing* of nerve impulses. For example, low frequencies could be signaled by low firing rates and higher frequencies by higher firing rates, as illustrated in Figure 12.14.

As we discuss these two approaches to pitch perception in the pages that follow, we will see parallels to our discussion of color vision in Chapter 4. In the early days of research on color vision two theories—trichromatic and opponent-process—competed for recognition. For a long time trichromatic theory was considered to be the correct one by most researchers. But when modern research provided electrophysiological evidence for opponent-process theory, it gained adherents, and eventually it became clear that both trichromatic and opponent-process theories were correct.

A similar situation has occurred for pitch perception. Place theory initially dominated research

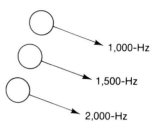

F I G U R E 12. 13   The idea behind a place code for frequency is that different frequencies are signaled by neurons located in different places in the auditory system. This drawing, which doesn't represent any particular structure in the auditory system, shows three different neurons located in different places that fire best to different frequencies.

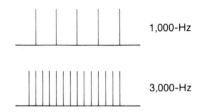

F I G U R E 12. 14   The idea behind the temporal code for frequency is that different frequencies are signaled by the timing of nerve impulses. Here, the rate of firing to a 3,000-Hz tone is higher than the rate of firing to a 1,000-Hz tone.

on pitch perception, until recent research made it clear that both place *and* temporal approaches were correct. We will begin by considering place theory, we will then describe temporal theory, and, finally, we will show how both mechanisms work together to explain the physiology of pitch perception.

THE PLACE CODE FOR FREQUENCY

Place theories of pitch perception focus on the basilar membrane—the structure that extends the 35-mm length of the cochlea, supporting the organ of Corti and, therefore, the receptors for hearing. Two different versions of place theory have been

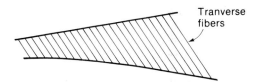

F I G U R E 12.15 Helmholtz hypothesized that the basilar membrane was made up of loosely connected transverse fibers. According to Helmholtz, vibration of long fibers signaled low frequencies and vibration of short fibers signaled high frequencies.

proposed: Hermann von Helmholtz' resonance theory, which we will describe only briefly because it is mainly of historical interest, and Georg von Békésy's traveling wave theory, which we will describe in detail.

Helmholtz' Resonance Theory

An early place theory was proposed by Hermann von Helmholtz (1863), who also championed the trichromatic theory of color vision. Helmholtz' proposal was called **resonance theory.** This theory proposed that the basilar membrane is made up of a series of loosely connected transverse fibers, as shown in Figure 12.15, each tuned to resonate to a specific frequency. Helmholtz knew that the basilar membrane was wider at one end than at the other, so he hypothesized that low frequencies would set the longer fibers into vibration and high frequencies would set the shorter fibers into vibration, just as long strings on the harp or piano correspond to low pitches and short strings to high pitches.

According to this idea, a particular frequency would stimulate only the basilar membrane fiber sensitive to this frequency, and this fiber's vibration would cause the neurons at this area of the basilar membrane to fire. Resonance theory has been rejected, however, because we now know that the basilar membrane's fibers are connected to each other so that one cannot resonate independently of the others, as Helmholtz proposed. As we will see next, large portions of the basilar membrane vibrate in response to sound.

Békésy's Traveling Wave

Georg von Békésy established the modern era of research on the ear with a series of studies which he began in 1928 and which culminated in the Nobel prize in physiology and medicine in 1961. Békésy proposed that each frequency maximally stimulates hair cells at a particular place along the cochlear partition. Low-frequency tones stimulate hair cells near the helicotrema end of the cochlear partition, whereas high-frequency tones stimulate hair cells near the stapes end. Frequency is therefore signaled by the *place* along the cochlear partition that is maximally stimulated.

This may sound similar to Helmholtz' resonance theory because both theories postulate that a specific frequency stimulates a specific place along the cochlear partition. The two theories differ, however, in the mechanisms that they propose to explain how these specific places are stimulated. Whereas Helmholtz proposed that different places were stimulated because of the existence of tuned resonators along the basilar membrane, Békésy proposed that different places were stimulated because the basilar membrane vibrates with a wave-like motion.

The first step in reaching this conclusion was Békésy's determination that the vibration of the

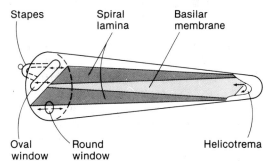

F I G U R E 12.16 A perspective view of an uncoiled cochlea, showing how the basilar membrane gets wider at the helicotrema end of the cochlea. The spiral lamina is a supporting structure which makes up for the basilar membrane's difference in width at the stapes and helicotrema ends of the cochlea. (From Schubert, 1980.)

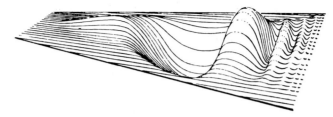

FIGURE 12.17 A perspective view showing the traveling wave of the basilar membrane. (From Tonndorf, 1960.)

cochlear partition is controlled largely by the properties of the basilar membrane. (Notice in Figures 12.9 and 12.10 that the organ of Corti sits on top of the basilar membrane.) He then analyzed the properties of the basilar membrane, taking note of two important facts: (1) The basilar membrane is three or four times wider at the helicotrema end than at the stapes end (see Figure 12.16), and (2) it is about 100 times stiffer at the stapes than at the helicotrema. Using these facts, Békésy constructed models of the cochlea, which enabled him to show that the pressure waves in the cochlear fluid set up a **traveling wave** on the basilar membrane. He later observed this traveling wave by drilling a hole in the cochlea of a human cadaver and observing the vibrations of the basilar membrane with a microscope (Békésy, 1960).

Figures 12.17 and 12.18 show what a traveling wave looks like. The horizontal line in Figure 12.18 represents the basilar membrane at rest, with

the end marked S being near the stapes and the end marked H being near the helicotrema. Curve 1 shows the position of the basilar membrane at one point in time during its vibration, and curves 2 and 3 show the position of the membrane at two later instants. Figure 12.17 shows a perspective view of the traveling wave at one point in time. In both figures a wave is traveling down the basilar membrane from the stapes to the helicotrema. *

Since the shape of the traveling wave changes with each instant of time, it is difficult to visualize its overall effect on the basilar membrane. We can, however, visualize its overall effect more easily by determining the maximum displacement that the wave causes at each point along the membrane. This maximum displacement, which is indicated by the dashed line of Figure 12.18, is called the **envelope of the traveling wave.** The envelope helps us to determine the effect of the basilar membrane's vibration on the hair cells, because the degree to which the hair cells are bent, and the resultant rate of firing in the fibers of those hair cells, depends on the amount that the basilar membrane is displaced, with greater displacement resulting in greater firing rates.

Békésy's (1960) observations of the basilar membrane's vibrations led him to conclude that the envelope of the basilar membrane has two important properties: (1) The envelope is peaked at one point on the basilar membrane. The envelope of Figure 12.18 indicates that point A on the basilar membrane is displaced the most by the traveling wave. This means that hair cells near point

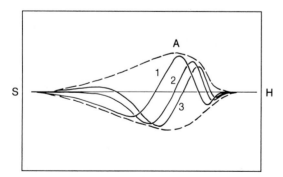

FIGURE 12.18 Vibration of the basilar membrane, showing the position of the membrane at three points in time, indicated by the solid lines, and the envelope of the vibration, indicated by the dashed lines. (Adapted from Békésy, 1960.)

*It is important to note that in both of these figures the amplitude of the wave is exaggerated. The wave actually displaces the 35-mm-long basilar membrane by only a few microns, where 1 micron = $\frac{1}{1,000}$ mm.

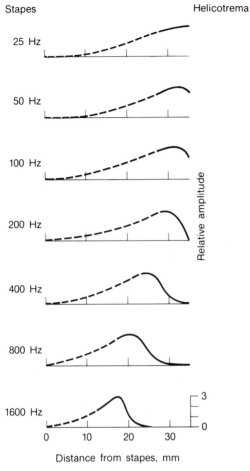

F I G U R E 12. 19 The envelope of the basilar membrane's vibration at frequencies ranging from 25 to 1,600 Hz. (From Békésy, 1960.)

cotrema (note, however, that at low frequencies, most of the membrane vibrates), and (2) as we increase the frequency, maximum hair cell activity moves toward the stapes. This connection between place of maximum basilar membrane vibration and frequency is supported not only by Békésy's calculations and direct observations of the membrane but also by additional evidence.

Additional Evidence for Békésy's Place Theory

Mapping the cochlea. A frequency map of the cochlea can be constructed by placing electrodes at different locations on the cochlea and determining the stimulus frequency that causes the largest response at each location. Such a map, shown in Figure 12.20, confirms the idea that the helicotrema end of the cochlea is stimulated best by low frequencies and the stapes end by high frequencies.

The relation between position on the cochlea and stimulus frequency has also been demonstrated

A will send out stronger signals than those near other parts of the membrane. (2) The position of this peak on the basilar membrane is a function of the frequency of the sound. We can see in Figure 12.19, which shows the envelopes of vibration for stimuli ranging from 25 to 1,600 Hz, that low frequencies cause maximum vibration near the helicotrema, while high frequencies cause maximum vibration near the stapes.

The change in the peak of the basilar membrane displacement with frequency means that (1) when we present a low-frequency tone, there will be greater activity in the hair cells near the heli-

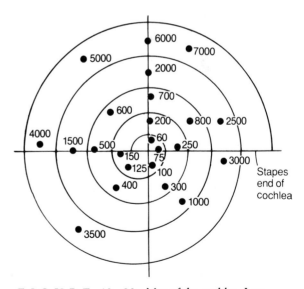

F I G U R E 12. 20 Map of the cochlea. Low frequencies cause the largest response near the helicotrema and high frequencies cause the largest response near the stapes. (From Culler, Cookley, Lowy, & Gross, 1943.)

B O X   1 2 . 1   /   *Environmental Noise and Hearing Loss*

The results of studies such as those presented in Figure 12.21 show that continuous exposure to high-intensity tones can damage the cochleas of animals. Does this mean that environmental noise might damage the cochleas of people, resulting, perhaps, in permanent hearing loss? the answer to both parts of this question appears to be "yes."

Some people who have worked in noisy environments have willed their ear structures to medical research, and, in a number of these cases, clear damage to the organ of Corti has been observed. For example, examination of the cochlea of a man who worked in a steel mill indicated that the organ of Corti had collapsed and that no receptor cells remained (Miller, 1974).

There are also psychophysical measurements of the hearing of people who work in noisy environments. One study found that jute weavers exposed to mill noises of 98 decibels (dB), 8 hours per day for 10 years or more, experienced a 35-dB rise in their threshold for hearing a 4,000-Hz tone.

The permanent hearing loss suffered by the jute weavers was caused by long-term exposure to noise; however, hearing can also be permanently impaired by impulsive noises intense enough to rip or tear the structures of the inner ear. One example is provided by a 21-year-old

college student who was in the process of raiding a rival fraternity house when a firecracker exploded in his hand, 15 inches from his right ear. As shown in the figure this mishap caused a rise in his threshold of over 50 dB, at frequencies between 3,000 and 8,000 Hz. But even more serious than this large rise in threshold, the student also experienced a ringing sensation in his ear that was still present 2 years after the accident (Ward & Glorig, 1961).

Ringing in the ears, which is known as **tinnitus** (ti-NEYE-tus, from the Latin for "tinkling"), affects more than 36 million Americans, nearly 8 million of them severely. The most common cause of tinnitus is exposure to loud sounds, although this condition can also be caused by certain drugs, ear infections, or food allergies. Whatever the cause, tinnitus is an extremely debilitating condition. According to Dr. Jack Vernon, director of the Kresge Hearing Research Laboratory at the University of Oregon, tinnitus is the third worst thing that can happen to us, ranking only below intractable severe pain and intractable severe dizziness. In its most serious form, the constant noise of tinnitus is totally incapacitating, making it impossible for people to maintain their concentration long enough to complete a task, and in some cases even driving people to suicide.

---

by **stimulation deafness** experiments, in which the structures of the cochlea are examined after an animal has been exposed to loud tones. The results of such an experiment are shown in Figure 12.21. In this experiment, guinea pigs were exposed to high-intensity tones for four minutes, the animals were sacrificed, and their cochleas were examined. In Figure 12.21, the light areas indicate the extent of damage to the organ of Corti for tones of different frequencies. The 300-Hz tone causes damage to a large area near the helicotrema, and as the fre-

quency of the tone is increased, the damage moves toward the stapes and also becomes more localized, with high-frequency tones causing damage to much smaller areas than low-frequency tones (Smith, 1947).

Békésy's observations of the traveling wave, the map of the cochlea in Figure 12.20, and the stimulation deafness experiments of Figure 12.21 all indicate a correspondence between stimulus frequency and the maximally stimulated place on the cochlea. However, for a place code such as this to

Is there a cure for this condition? Unfortunately, for most people the answer to this question is "no." Some people, however, can gain relief by using a device called a **tinnitus masker.** The masker, which is worn in the ear like a hearing aid, produces a sound like a waterfall or the hiss of an FM radio tuned between stations. This externally produced noise masks the internal noise of tinnitus, making life bearable for some tinnitus sufferers.

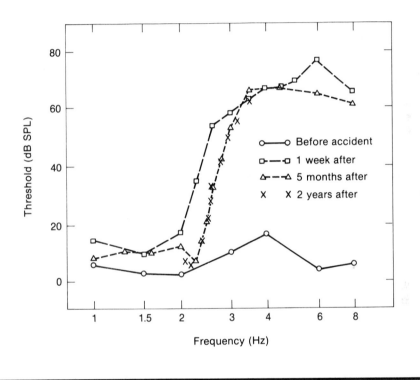

work, the place information contained in the cochlea must be transmitted to more central stations in the auditory system. We can show that this does, in fact, occur by looking at how neurons on these more central structures respond to different frequencies.

Place information past the cochlea. One way to show that the place information that leaves the cochlea is transmitted to other structures along the auditory pathway is to show that there are maps of frequencies on these structures, just as there are maps of frequencies on the cochlea. Such maps are called **tonotopic maps,** because they are maps that indicate the locations on these structures of the activity caused by tones of different frequencies. (Remember in Chapter 3 we discussed topographic maps of the retina, which indicated the locations on the LGN and visual cortex of the activity caused by stimulating different places on the retina.)

The first step in determining a tonotopic map is to find the frequencies to which a neuron responds.

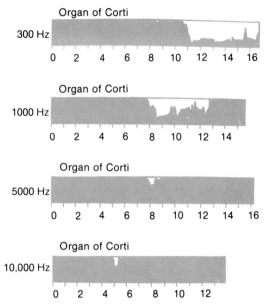

FIGURE 12. 21 The effects of overstimulation on the organ of Corti. Degeneration of the organ of Corti is indicated in white. The stapes end of the organ of Corti is on the left. (From Smith, 1947; Smith & Wever, 1949.)

We do this by determining the neuron's **tuning curve,** a curve that indicates the intensity necessary to elicit a threshold response at frequencies covering the audible range. Figure 12.22 shows tuning curves for three auditory nerve fibers. The frequency at which each neuron has the lowest threshold, indicated by the arrows, is called the "best frequency" or **characteristic frequency** of the neuron.

To determine a tonotopic map, we determine the characteristic frequencies of a number of neurons and their locations. Figure 12.23 shows the result of such determinations on the surface of the auditory cortex of the cat. The characteristic frequencies of neurons in this area of the cortex are arranged in an orderly way, with neurons responding best to high frequencies located to the left and neurons responding to lower frequencies to the right. In addition to the surface map shown in Figure 12.23, there is also a **columnar arrangement** similar to that observed in the visual and cutaneous systems (see page 96, in Chapter 3). If we record along an electrode track which is perpendicular to

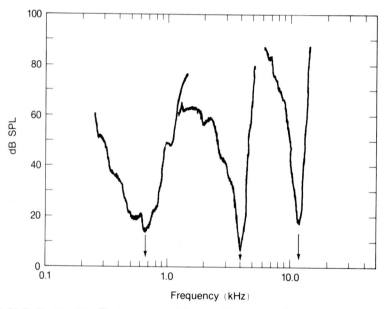

FIGURE 12. 22 Tuning curves of three auditory nerve fibers in one animal. The characteristic frequency of each fiber is indicted by the arrows along the frequency axis. (From Kiang, 1975.)

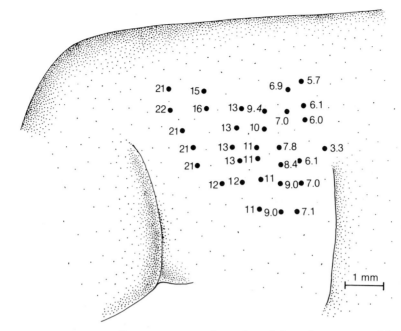

F I G U R E 12. 23 Tonotopic map on the surface of the auditory cortex of the cat. Each large dot represents a single neuron, and the number beside each dot represents the characteristic frequency of that neuron in thousands of Hz. (From Abeles & Goldstein, 1970.)

the surface of the cortex, we find neurons with the same characteristic frequency (Abeles & Goldstein, 1970).

This type of tonotopic map has been found in all of the nuclei shown in Figure 12.12, and the presence of such maps supports the idea that the frequency of a tone can be indicated by the place where activity is occurring.

We can summarize the evidence for Békésy's place theory as follows:

1. The maximum displacement of the traveling wave generated by sound moves from the helicotrema to the stapes end of the basilar membrane as the frequency of the stimulus is increased.
2. Maps determined by recording the electrical response of the cochlea show that low-frequency tones generate a larger response near the helicotrema and high-frequency tones generate a larger response near the stapes.
3. Stimulation deafness experiments show a similar separation of high- and low-frequency tones along the cochlea.
4. There are tonotopic maps in the central structures of the auditory system.

There is, therefore, strong support for Békésy's theory. We will now see that there is also evidence for a temporal theory of pitch perception.

THE TEMPORAL CODE FOR FREQUENCY

We will describe temporal theory by describing the development of this theory in chronological order, beginning with a theory proposed by Rutherford in 1886 and ending with more recent experimental measurements of neural firing.

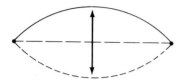

F I G U R E 12. 24 Rutherford's conception of how the basilar membrane vibrates. The horizontal line indicates the resting level of the membrane and the curved lines show the membrane at its maximum up position and its maximum down position.

Rutherford's Frequency Theory

In 1886, Rutherford proposed that the basilar membrane vibrates as a whole, as shown in Figure 12.24, and that the rate of this vibration matches the frequency of the stimulus. According to his **frequency theory,** the frequency of the stimulus is signaled by the frequency of nerve firing. Thus, if a 10,000-Hz tone causes the basilar membrane to vibrate 10,000 times per second, this vibration would cause nerve fibers in the auditory nerve to fire at 10,000 impulses per second.

Although we now know that the basilar membrane does not vibrate as a whole as Rutherford proposed, this is not a serious problem for frequency theory because if we observe one point on the vibrating membrane, we see that the frequency of vibration of that point does match the frequency of the stimulus. A 400-Hz tone causes a particular point to move up and down 400 times a second, a 3,000-Hz stimulus causes the point to move up and down 3,000 times a second, and so on.

The flaw in Rutherford's theory is that nerve fibers have a refractory period which limits their maximum rate of firing to about 1,000 impulses per second (see p. 40 in Chapter 2). Thus, while the *basilar membrane* may vibrate 3,000 times in response to a 3,000-Hz tone, a single *nerve fiber* cannot fire at 3,000 impulses per second. In order to deal with this problem, E. Glen Wever (1949) proposed a modification of frequency theory called the **volley principle.**

Wever's Volley Principle

E. G. Wever's (1949) volley principle states that high rates of nerve firing can be accomplished if nerve fibers work in the manner illustrated in Figure 12.25. In this illustration five fibers work

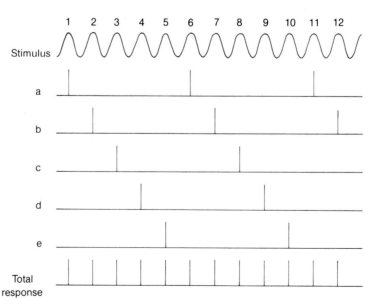

F I G U R E 12. 25 How a number of nerve fibers work together, according to Wever's volley principle.

together, with each fiber firing every fifth period of the sound wave. Fiber a fires to the first period and then becomes refractory. While a is refractory, fibers b, c, d, and e fire to the second, third, fourth, and fifth periods, respectively, and then a, which has now recovered from being refractory, fires to the sixth period, and so on. Thus, although the rate of firing of each individual fiber is limited by its refractory period, groups of fibers can work together to signal high frequencies of stimulation, as indicated by the bottom record of Figure 12.25.

Wever's proposal that a temporal code for frequency can be achieved by groups of nerve fibers found support in the results of experiments published almost 20 years after his original proposal. These results provide evidence for a phenomenon called phase locking.

Phase Locking

Measurements of the way auditory nerve fibers respond show that they fire in synchrony with the phase of the stimulus. (Rose, Brugge, Anderson, & Hind, 1967). This firing in synchrony with the phase of the stimulus is illustrated in Figure 12.26, which shows the relationship between a pure tone stimulus and the firing of three auditory nerve fibers. Looking at the response of fiber a, we can see that it fires in an irregular manner, but that when it does fire, it fires only when the pure tone stimulus is at the same point in the cycle as before. This synchronization of nerve firing with the same point

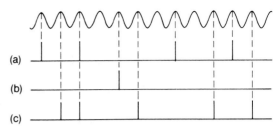

F I G U R E 12. 26   The response of three nerve fibers that are phase locked to the stimulus.

in the cycle of a pure tone stimulus is called **phase locking**. Similar results for two more fibers are also shown in this figure. Note that although the rates and patterns of firing are different for each fiber, when they do fire they are phase locked to the stimulus.

When large groups of fibers are phase locked to a stimulus, a firing pattern like the one shown in Figure 12.27 is created. This figure shows that if we measure the firing for a large number of fibers in response to a tone of a particular frequency, fibers fire in bursts separated by silent intervals and the timing of these bursts depends on the frequency of the stimulus.

Most of the evidence that phase locking is important in signaling the frequency of the stimulus comes from records like those of Figure 12.26 obtained from auditory nerve fibers. The evidence for phase locking becomes weaker, however, at higher centers in the auditory system because as we move toward the cortex, it becomes harder to

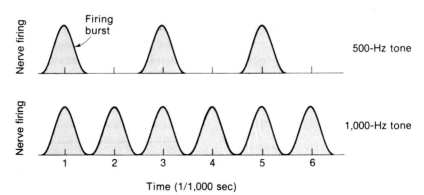

F I G U R E 12. 27   Phase locking causes large numbers of nerve fibers to fire in bursts separated by silent intervals.

find neurons that will phase lock to frequencies above about 1,000 Hz. And even early in the system, in the auditory nerve, phase locking becomes very weak by about 5,000 Hz. Thus, phase locking signals stimulus frequency for low-frequency tones but not for high-frequency tones.

WHAT THE PLACE AND TEMPORAL THEORIES CAN AND CANNOT EXPLAIN

How Place and Timing Work Together

It is clear that both the place and temporal theories show how information signaling frequency is contained in the neural signal. The present situation in hearing is, therefore, similar in some ways to the situation in color vision, in which there are two theories that explain how information signaling wavelength is created in the visual system. Just as it is now accepted that trichromatic and opponent-process theories work together to determine color vision, it is also accepted that place and timing theories work together to determine pitch perception.

We can see how the place and timing mechanisms may work together by considering how they operate in different frequency ranges. Place mechanism is weak at frequencies below 1,000 Hz because of the broad pattern of vibration on the basilar membrane at these frequencies; however, the timing mechanism works best at these frequencies because fibers can phase lock most easily below 1,000 Hz. On the other hand, timing is weak at frequencies above about 5,000 Hz because cells lose their ability to phase lock above this frequency; however, the place mechanism is at its best at these high frequencies because the basilar membrane's vibration pattern is more narrowly tuned at high frequencies.

Thus, a number of results suggest that the timing of nerve impulses is important at low frequencies (below 500–1,000 Hz), that place is important at high frequencies (above 4,500–5,000 Hz), and that both mechanisms operate at frequencies

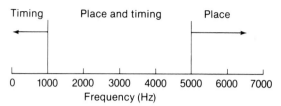

F I G U R E 12. 28 Pitch perception is determined by the timing of nerve firing below 1,000 Hz, by the place of stimulation along the basilar membrane above 5,000 Hz, and by both timing and place mechanisms between 1,000 and 5,000 Hz.

in between (see Figure 12.28). An interesting fact that supports the idea that there is a change in mechanism of pitch perception at about 4,000–5,000 Hz is that tones above about 5,000 Hz lack the musical quality of tones below that frequency. That is, a sequence of tones with frequencies above 5,000 Hz does not result in a sense of melody (Attneave & Olson, 1971). (Remember that the highest note on the piano has a frequency of 4,186 Hz.)

Although the combination of the place and timing mechanisms seems to explain what we know about pitch perception better than either of these mechanisms alone, this does not mean that we have solved all of the problems of pitch perception. There are still a number of phenomena we cannot completely explain. Let's briefly consider two of them.

The Effect of Increasing Stimulus Intensity

According to place theory, a tone's frequency is indicted by a high rate of firing in a small group of neurons that are stimulated best by a particular frequency and by lower rates in other neurons. For example, a 1,000-Hz tone will be signaled by a high firing rate in neurons with a characteristic frequency of 1,000 Hz combined with lower rates in neurons with characteristic frequencies above and below 1,000 Hz. But let's consider what happens when we increase the stimulus intensity. At high stimulus intensities the difference in firing rates between neurons with different characteristic frequencies becomes smaller, as illustrated in Figure

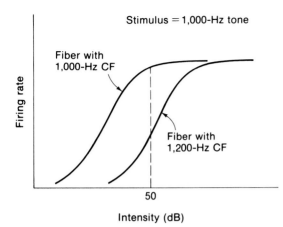

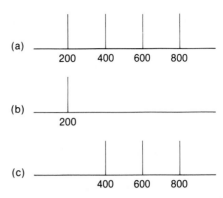

F I G U R E 12. 29 The relationship between the intensity of a 1,000-Hz tone and the response of two nerve fibers, one with a characteristic frequency of 1,000 Hz and another with a characteristic frequency of 1,200 Hz. This graph shows that at low intensities the 1,000-Hz fiber fires better than the 1,200-Hz fiber to the 1,000-Hz tone. However, at high intensities both fibers fire at the same rate to this tone.

F I G U R E 12. 30 Fourier spectra for three different tones that would have the same pitch. (a) A tone with a 200-Hz fundamental plus 400-, 600-, and 800-Hz harmonics; (b) the fundamental alone; and (c) the harmonics alone. These three tones differ in timbre but would have the same pitch (see Chapter 11).

12.29. We can see from this figure that increasing intensity increases the rate of firing of a 1,000-Hz fiber until, at 50 dB, the fiber **saturates**—that is, it reaches its maximum response so that further increases in intensity cause no further increase in response. But as we increase the intensity above 50 dB, other fibers, like the one marked 1,200 Hz, that are less sensitive to a 1,000-Hz tone, increase their firing rate and also eventually saturate. Thus, at very high intensity levels both the 1,000- and 1,200-Hz fibers are firing equally rapidly. Yet, we still perceive the tone as having a pitch corresponding to 1,000 Hz.

Place theory has a difficult time explaining this result. Apparently the place mechanism must be aided at very high intensities by some form of timing code, although the exact nature of this code remains to be determined.

Periodicity Pitch

Complex tones pose another problem for theories of pitch perception. For example, let's consider periodicity pitch, or the effect of the missing fun-

damental, which we discussed in Chapter 11 (see p. 395). Removing the fundamental frequency from a complex tone so only the harmonics remain does not affect the tone's pitch. For example, a complex tone with a fundamental frequency of 200 Hz and harmonics at 400, 600, and 800 Hz still has a pitch that corresponds to 200 Hz, even after we eliminate the 200-Hz component of the tone. Thus, as we can see from Figure 12.30, tones with different Fourier spectra can have the same pitch.

The problem this poses for place theory is that combinations of frequencies that result in different patterns of vibration on the basilar membrane can have the same pitch. Therefore, most explanations of periodicity pitch do not focus on the basilar membrane but look to activity in more central structures of the auditory system. One piece of evidence that supports the idea of looking more centrally is the finding that periodicity pitch is perceived even if the harmonics are presented to different ears. Presenting a 1,600-Hz tone to one ear and a 1,700-Hz tone to the other results in a perception of pitch that corresponds to 100 Hz (Houtsma & Goldstein, 1972). (Remember that since harmonics are always multiples of the fundamental frequency, the *difference* between two adjacent harmonics corresponds to the fundamental frequency.) The perception of periodicity pitch under these conditions must, therefore, be determined by a structure in which the signals from the two ears are combined.

The results of many psychophysical experiments have led to the proposal that periodicity pitch is the result of a **central pitch processor**—a central mechanism that analyzes the *pattern* of harmonics and selects the fundamental frequency that is most likely to have been part of that pattern (Evans, 1978; Getty & Howard, 1981; Goldstein, 1978; also see Wightman, 1973 for another type of central processor). Although this idea is supported by psychophysical results, it remains simply a hypothesis about how the physiology might operate. Thus, this is an example of psychophysical results that suggest a possible physiological mechanism that remains to be proven by the physiologists.

It should be clear from our discussion of the evidence for and against the place and temporal theories of pitch perception that neither theory can stand on its own and that even if we combine the two there are still phenomena that we can't explain. This has not, however, led to the rejection of these theories. The auditory system clearly uses both place *and* timing information in signaling pitch. Place and temporal theories are, therefore, not wrong—we simply do not understand the details of how the nervous system uses place and timing information to distinguish one frequency from another.

THE CODE FOR THE LOCATION OF SOUNDS IN SPACE

Neurons That Respond to Binaural Cues

In our discussion of the psychophysics of hearing, we saw that there are a number of cues that help us to localize sounds in space. The most important of these cues are (1) *interaural time difference*, the difference in the time it takes for a sound to get to the left and right ears, and (2) *interaural intensity difference*, the difference in the intensity of sound

reaching the left and right ears. We will show that there is physiological evidence for neurons that are sensitive to the interaural time difference cue, and for neural responses that are affected by the intensities of sound reaching the left and right ears.

We begin our consideration of the physiology of sound localization by describing neurons in the monkey's cortex that respond best to specific interaural time differences. Such a cell fires best when there is a specific delay between when a sound is presented to the left ear and to the right ear. For example, one of these cells fires best when a sound reaches the left ear 800 microseconds before it reaches the right ear (Brugge & Merzenich, 1973). This cell, which could be called an **interaural time difference detector,** is similar to the binocular depth cells described in Chapter 7 that respond best to specific degrees of disparity between the two eyes. These interaural time difference cells have been recorded not only from the cortex but also from nuclei as early in the auditory system as the superior olivary nucleus, the first nucleus in the system to receive inputs from both ears (Hall, 1965).

The existence of cells like the interaural time difference detectors shows that the auditory system has a way of detecting specific *cues* for location in auditory space. But detecting a cue is not the same thing as detecting a particular location in space. Is there any evidence for neurons that respond only to sounds that originate from a particular location?

Neurons That Have Receptive Fields in Space

Recent research indicates that there are, in fact, cells that respond only when a sound source is located at a particular area of space relative to an animal's head. One of the earliest reports of these neurons came from recordings from cells located in the barn owl's **mesencephalicus lateralus dorsalis (MLD),** a nucleus equivalent to the inferior colliculus of mammals. These cells have been studied by Eric Knudsen and Masakazu Konishi (1978a, b) using the apparatus shown in Figure 12.31. By recording from a cell while stimulating from different posi-

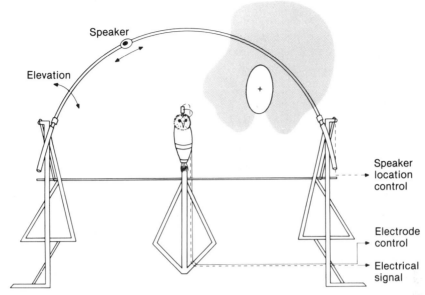

F I G U R E 12. 31 The apparatus used by Knudsen and Konishi (1978) to map auditory receptive fields in space. The sound can be moved to different positions in space by sliding the speaker along the curved rod and by moving the rod around the owl. The elliptical area marked with a "+" is the excitatory area of a typical receptive field and the shaded area is the inhibitory area.

tions in space, they found cells that respond only when the sound originates from a small elliptical area in space, the receptive field of the cell. Furthermore, they found that some of these receptive fields have excitatory centers and inhibitory surrounds; so an excitatory response elicited by a sound in the center of the receptive field could be inhibited by presentation of another sound presented to the side or above or below the center. This property of the MLD cells means that center-surround receptive fields exist not only on the retina (Figures 2.19 and 3.29), but also in space!

Knudsen and Konishi not only found cells with receptive fields at particular locations in space but they also discovered that these cells are arranged so that there is a map of auditory space on the MLD. That is, each cell on the MLD responds to a specific area in space (relative to the position of the head), and adjacent cells respond to adjacent areas of space (Figure 12.32). We can compare this mapping of space on the MLD to other maps in

the nervous system: Each point on the cochlea is represented by a small area on the auditory cortex (Figure 12.23) and each point on the retina is represented by a small area on the visual cortex. (And we will see in Chapter 14 that a similar situation also exists for points on the skin.) Thus, this point-to-point mapping of space that occurs in the owl's MLD is similar to the point-to-point mapping that occurs in the auditory and visual cortex.

There is, however, an important difference between the mapping of space in the owl's MLD and the mapping of the retina and cochlea in the visual and auditory cortex. Consider, for example, the principle behind the map of the retina on the cortex. This map occurs because sequences of neurons connect points on the retina to areas on the visual cortex, as shown in Figure 12.33(a). But where is the connection between points in space and the owl's MLD? Clearly, no connections exist (Figure 12.33b). The map of space in the MLD is created not by anatomical connections formed

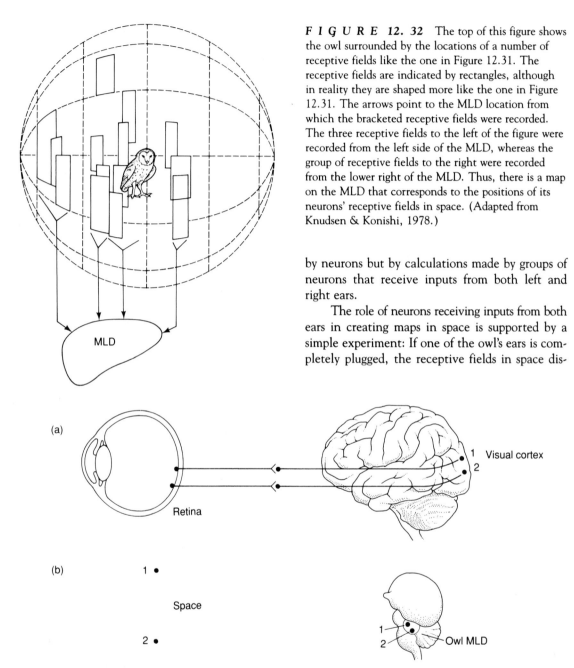

F I G U R E 12. 32 The top of this figure shows the owl surrounded by the locations of a number of receptive fields like the one in Figure 12.31. The receptive fields are indicated by rectangles, although in reality they are shaped more like the one in Figure 12.31. The arrows point to the MLD location from which the bracketed receptive fields were recorded. The three receptive fields to the left of the figure were recorded from the left side of the MLD, whereas the group of receptive fields to the right were recorded from the lower right of the MLD. Thus, there is a map on the MLD that corresponds to the positions of its neurons' receptive fields in space. (Adapted from Knudsen & Konishi, 1978.)

by neurons but by calculations made by groups of neurons that receive inputs from both left and right ears.

The role of neurons receiving inputs from both ears in creating maps in space is supported by a simple experiment: If one of the owl's ears is completely plugged, the receptive fields in space dis-

F I G U R E 12. 33 The map of retinal locations in the visual cortex and the map of locations in space in the owl's MLD are constructed according to different principles. The retinal map on the cortex occurs because there are neural connections linking points on the retina with neurons in the cortex. There is, however, no such anatomical connection between neurons in the owl's MLD and its receptive fields in space. The map in the MLD is constructed from information received by the left and right ears rather than from anatomical connections.

appear. And if one ear is partially plugged, so it receives less sound than it ordinarily would, the location of the receptive field shifts, so the sound source must be moved to a new location to excite the neuron (Konishi, 1984).

Receptive fields that respond to specific locations in space have also been recorded from neurons in the cat's auditory cortex. John Middlebrooks and John Pettigrew (1981) found that about 25 percent of the neurons in the primary auditory cortex respond only when a speaker is positioned in a particular place in space. These cells are, therefore, like those recorded from the owl, although Middlebrooks and Pettigrew did not observe the precise mapping that Knudsen and Konishi found in the owl.

THE ROLE OF THE AUDITORY CORTEX

What is the role of the auditory cortex in hearing? Although this may not sound like a question to be taken seriously, since we usually think of the cortex as the place where perceptions are determined, the answer to this question is not necessarily what we might expect. Contrary to our expectations, animals can hear some qualities of sound perfectly well without an auditory cortex. One of these qualities is pitch.

The Perception of Pitch

Does the auditory cortex play a role in the perception of pitch? We might answer this question affirmatively, especially since we know that there is a tonotopic map of frequencies on the cortex (FIgure 12.23) and that cells with the same characteristic frequency are organized in cortical columns. However, contrary to our expectations, there is evidence that the cortex is probably not involved in our perception of pitch. This evidence comes from behavioral experiments in which cats are trained to respond to changes in the frequency of a tone, their auditory cortex is then removed, and

they are then retrained on the same task. For example, Jerry Cranford and coworkers (1976) trained cats to cross to the opposite side of a box in response to two tones alternating between 1,000 and 1,200 Hz. (If they didn't cross after hearing this alternation for 12 seconds, they were shocked, a condition that encourages them to learn the task.) Once the cats had learned this task, their auditory cortex was removed, and although immediately after the operation they behaved like untrained cats, they were able to relearn the task when given new training.

The fact that cats with no auditory cortex can learn to discriminate between two different frequencies has led researchers to conclude that the ability to perceive pitch is not determined by the auditory cortex and that lower centers prior to the cortex may be involved (Durrant & Lovrinic, 1977).

The Perception of Location

Although removal of the cortex does not affect a cat's ability to respond to the difference between two frequencies, it does affect its ability to respond to a sound's location in space. In experiments similar to the one described above, it has been shown that after a cat's auditory cortex is removed, it cannot learn to approach the source of a sound, something it can learn when its cortex is intact (Neff, Fisher, Diamond, & Yela, 1956). This has led to the conclusion that the auditory cortex is necessary for sound localization, and this conclusion is supported by the fact that there are cells in the cortex that respond to cues for sound location and to sounds coming from a particular area of space.

However, new results have led some researchers to suggest that the auditory cortex may not, in fact, be necessary for locating sounds in space. In these studies, monkeys with no auditory cortex could be trained to press one response lever when sound came from the left and another lever when sound came from the right (Heffner, 1978; Cranford, 1979). Thus, while the earlier studies showed that animals without an auditory cortex are unable to *approach* the location of a tone, these newer studies show that animals without an auditory cortex can

F I G U R E 12. 34 Cats can tell the difference between these two patterns of stimulation before their cortex is removed but can no longer discriminate between the two after their cortex is removed.

differentiate between tones at different locations by pressing levers. It is difficult to know what these results mean, because we do not know what the animals are experiencing. Perhaps animals without an auditory cortex can experience "left" and "right" but may not experience the specific place from which the tones are originating. I. C. Whitfield (1979) has suggested that cats without an auditory cortex may not be able to experience "thereness." Clearly, further research is needed to determine exactly what role the cortex plays in localizing sounds.

The Perception of Pattern

Removal of the cortex eliminates a cat's ability to respond to the *pattern* of tones. To understand what we mean by this, let's consider an experiment by Irving Diamond and Dewey Neff (1957). Diamond and Neff trained cats to perform the discrimination diagrammed in Figure 12.34. In this discrimination, the cat had to learn to distinguish between a sequence in which the pattern was 800–1,000–800 (low-high-low) and a sequence in which the pattern was 1,000–800–1,000 (high-low-high). As in Cranford's pitch discrimination study, cats can learn this task before their cortex is removed. However, unlike the pitch study, the cats cannot relearn this task after their cortex is removed. Thus, while the cortex may not be necessary for the perception of pitch, it is necessary for the perception of patterns.

Cortical Responses to Complex Stimuli

From the limited research that has been done on the auditory cortex and other higher auditory centers, it appears that we can draw an analogy between the auditory and visual systems. Remember that cells early in the visual system respond primarily to simple stimuli, such as spots of light, whereas cells in the visual cortex respond to more complex stimuli, such as corners that move in a particular direction. A similar situation apparently exists in the auditory system. Early in the system, cells respond well to pure tones; as we move up the auditory pathways, however, we find cells that respond only to more complex stimuli. For example, cells have been found that respond neither to pure tones nor to combinations of tones but do respond to noises like keys jangling or paper tearing. Whitfield and Evans (1965) found cortical cells in the cat that responded only to smooth changes in the frequency of a tone: Some cells responded only when the tone was swept from low to high frequencies, and others responded when the tonal frequency was swept from high to low. These cells are called **frequency sweep detectors,** because they respond well to changes in frequency but poorly or not at all to steady tones of a single frequency.

Based on results such as those described above, it has been suggested that "the greater the complexity of the sound and the more information contained within the sound, the greater the extent to which the cortex is expected to be involved in the processing of auditory information" (Durrant and Lovrinic, 1977, p. 134). (Also see Whitfield, 1980).

The cortex is undoubtedly heavily involved in the perception of speech—a type of complex sound we will discuss in the next chapter—and cortical areas beyond the primary auditory cortex are involved in dealing with the complexities of meaning and memory, critical components for the accurate perception of speech.

Summary

1. The ear consists of three divisions: (1) Outer ear—pinna, auditory canal, tympanic membrane. The tympanic membrane vibrates in response to sound. The outer ear amplifies frequencies between 2,000 and 5,000 Hz by resonance. (2) Middle ear—ossicles: malleus, incus, and stapes. The lever action of the ossicles and the difference in area between the tympanic membrane and the footplate of the stapes amplify the vibrations as they are transmitted to the inner ear. (3) Inner ear—cochlea, cochlear partition, helicotrema, organ of Corti, basilar membrane, tectorial membrane, hair cells. Vibration is transmitted from the cochlear fluid to the basilar membrane and hair cells. The bending of the hair cells against the tectorial membrane that occurs in response to vibration causes transduction.

2. The pathway from the cochlea to the brain is complex, passing through many nuclei before reaching the auditory receiving area in the temporal lobe.

3. Helmholtz' resonance theory of pitch perception proposed that fibers on the basilar membrane act like independently tuned resonators. This idea was later shown to be incorrect.

4. Békésy showed that the basilar membrane vibrates in a traveling wave. The peak of the envelope of the traveling wave depends on frequency, with low frequencies causing peak vibration near the helicotrema and high frequencies causing peak vibration near the stapes. This correlation between the location of the peak of the basilar membrane's vibration and frequency is the basis of Békésy's place theory of pitch perception.

5. Additional evidence for place theory is provided by electrical maps of the cochlea, stimulation deafness experiments, and the presence of tonotopic maps in the nuclei of the auditory system. Tonotopic maps are determined by measuring tuning curves to determine a neuron's characteristic frequency and then mapping the locations of each characteristic frequency onto the surface of each nucleus.

6. Rutherford proposed that the basilar membrane vibrates as a whole and that the stimulus frequency is signaled by the frequency of nerve firing of single nerve fibers. This idea cannot be correct, however, because nerve fibers have a refractory period which limits their rate of firing to about 1,000 impulses per second.

7. Wever's volley principle states that stimulus frequency is signaled by groups of fibers firing in volleys. Later research showed that fibers in the auditory nerve fire in synchrony with the stimulus. This synchronization of nerve firing with the peak of a pure tone stimulus is called phase locking.

8. The place and timing mechanisms work best in different frequency ranges. The timing mechanism works best at low frequencies (below 1,000 Hz) and the place mechanism works best at high frequencies (above 4,000–5,000 Hz). Both mechanisms operate at frequencies in between.

9. Facts that pose challenges for our understanding of pitch perception are (1) we can perceive pitch at intensity levels high enough to cause fibers all along the cochlea to fire, and (2) the phenomena of periodicity pitch.

10. There are neurons in the auditory system that respond best to specific time differences between the time of arrival of sounds at the left and right ears. These neurons probably play a role in our ability to localize sounds in space.

11. There are neurons in the owl's auditory system that respond only when a sound source is located at a particular area of space relative to the owl's head. These neurons have center-surround receptive fields similar to those found in the visual system. In contrast to the situation for vision, however, there are no anatomical connections between these neurons and their receptive field.

12. The auditory cortex is not necessary for pitch perception but is important for discriminating the temporal patterns of tones and the location of tones, although the exact role of the cortex in sound localization is controversial. The cortex also contains neurons that respond to complex stimuli.

Box

1. Noise in the environment can damage the cochlea and can cause permanent hearing loss. Loud noise and other causes can result in a condition called tinnitus.

Study Questions

1. Be able to identify the following structures on a diagram of the ear and describe their functions: outer ear, middle ear, inner ear, auditory canal, tympanic membrane, ossicles, hammer, anvil, stirrup, oval window, helicotrema, organ of Corti, basilar membrane, tectorial membrane, hair cells. (419)

2. What is resonance? How does resonance in the auditory canal play a role in the process of hearing? (420)

3. How do the bones of the middle ear amplify the vibrations as they are transmitted to the inner ear? (421)

4. What effect do the vibrations that are transmitted to the liquid in the inner ear have on the structures in the inner ear? What causes the hair cells to bend? (424)

5. What is the first nucleus where synapses occur after the cochlea? Where is the cortical receiving area for hearing? (425)

6. What is Helmholtz' resonance theory of pitch perception and why is it invalid? (427)

7. What is the basic idea behind Békésy's place theory? (427)

8. What properties of the basilar membrane did Békésy take into account to determine that the membrane vibrates in a traveling wave? (428)

9. What does a traveling wave look like? What is the envelope of the traveling wave? (428)

10. How does the envelope of the traveling wave change as frequency changes? How does this affect the firing of the hair cells? (429)

11. What does the map of frequencies look like on the cochlea? Which frequencies are near the stapes end and which are near the helicotrema? How was this map determined? (429)

12. What do stimulation deafness experiments show? (430)

13. What is a tonotopic map? How is a tonotopic map determined? Do tonotopic maps exist in the auditory system? (431)

14. What is a tuning curve? a neuron's characteristic frequency? (432)

15. Describe the columnar arrangement of neurons in the auditory cortex. (432)

16. Describe Rutherford's frequency theory of pitch perception. What was the flaw in his theory? (434)

17. Describe Wever's volley principle. (435)

18. What is phase locking? How is it related to the volley principle? At what frequencies does phase locking work? (435)

19. How might the place and timing mechanisms work together? At what frequencies does each theory work best? (436)

20. Describe two aspects of auditory functioning that are difficult to explain based on our present knowledge of the auditory system. (436)

21. What is a central pitch processor? Why has it been proposed? (438)

22. What is an interaural time difference detector? Where are these cells located? (438)

23. Describe the auditory center-surround receptive fields that exist in space. (438)

24. What is a difference between the "maps" of space in the auditory system and other maps in the nervous system? (439)

25. What tasks can a cat perform without its auditory cortex? Is the ability to perceive pitch determined by the auditory cortex? (441)

26. Under what testing conditions can monkeys without an auditory cortex respond to a tone's location in space? Under what conditions can't they respond to the tone's location? What can we conclude from these results? (441)

27. Describe Diamond and Neff's experiment in which they showed that the auditory cortex is necessary for discriminating patterns of tones. (442)

28. Are there neurons in the auditory system that respond only to complex tones? What is a frequency sweep detector? (442)

29. The auditory cortex is involved in the processing of what kinds of sounds? (442)

Box

1. What is the effect of long-term and short-term environmental noise on hearing? Is the major hearing loss at high or low frequencies? What is tinnitus? Is there a cure for tinnitus? (430)

Glossary

Auditory canal. The canal through which air vibrations travel from the environment to the tympanic membrane. (419)

Auditory receiving area. The area of the cortex, located in the temporal lobe, that is the primary receiving area for hearing. (425)

Basilar membrane. A membrane that stretches the length of the cochlea and controls the vibration of the cochlear partition. (423)

Central pitch processor. A hypothetical central mechanism that analyzes the pattern of a tone's harmonics and selects the fundamental frequency that is most likely to have been part of that pattern. (438)

Characteristic frequency. The frequency at which a neuron has its lowest threshold. (432)

Cochlea. The snail-shaped, liquid-filled structure that contains the structures of the inner ear, the most important of which are the basilar membrane, the tectorial membrane, and the hair cells. (418)

Cochlear nucleus. The nucleus where nerve fibers from the cochlea first synapse. (424)

Cochlear partition. A partition in the cochlea, extending almost its full length, that separates the scala tympani and the scala vestibuli. (422)

Columnar arrangement. Neurons in the auditory cortex are arranged in columns, with neurons in each column having the same characteristic frequency. (433)

Envelope of the traveling wave. A curve which indicates the maximum displacement at each point along the basilar membrane caused by a traveling wave. (428)

Frequency sweep detector. A neuron in the auditory cortex that fires only when frequencies are smoothly increased or decreased. (442)

Frequency theory. Rutherford's theory of pitch perception, which proposes that the basilar membrane vibrates as a whole and that the rate of this vibration matches the frequency of the stimulus. (434)

Hair cells. Small hairs, or cilia, that are the receptors for hearing. There are two kinds of hair cells—inner and outer. (418)

Helicotrema. A small opening at the end of the cochlear partition which connects the scala vestibuli and the scala tympani. (422)

Incus (anvil). The second of the three ossicles of the middle ear. It transmits vibrations from the malleus to the stapes. (420)

Inner ear. The innermost division of the ear, containing the cochlea. (422)

Interaural time difference detector. A neuron that fires only when a stimulus is presented first to one ear and then to the other, with a specific delay between stimulation of the two ears. (438)

Malleus (hammer). The first of the ossicles of the middle ear. Receives vibrations from the tympanic membrane and transmits these vibrations to the incus. (420)

Mesencephalicus lateralus dorsalis (MLD). A nucleus in the owl that contains cells that respond only when the sound source is located in a particular area of space relative to an animal's head. (438)

Middle ear. The small air-filled space between the auditory canal and cochlea that contains the ossicles. (420)

Organ of Corti. The major structure of the cochlear partition, the organ of Corti contains the basilar membrane, the tectorial membrane, and the receptors for hearing. (423)

Ossicles. Three small bones in the middle ear that transmit vibrations from the outer to the inner ear. (420)

Outer ear. The pinnae and the external auditory meatus. (419)

Oval window. A small membrane-covered hole in the cochlea that receives vibrations from the stapes. (420)

Phase locking. Occurs when nerve firing is synchronized with the peak of a pure tone stimulus. (435)

Place code. The idea that the frequency of a tone is signaled by the place in the auditory system that is maximally stimulated. (426)

Resonance. A mechanism that enhances the intensity of certain frequencies due to reflection of sound waves in a closed tube. Resonance occurs in the auditory canal. (420)

Resonance theory. Helmholtz' theory of pitch perception, which proposes that the basilar membrane is made up of a series of transverse fibers, each tuned to resonate to a specific frequency. (427)

Resonant frequency. The frequency which is most strongly enhanced by resonance. The resonance frequency of a closed tube is determined by the length of the tube. (420)

Round window. A small membrane-covered opening at the end of the scala tympani. (423)

Saturation. The intensity at which a nerve fiber reaches its maximum response. Once saturated, further increases in intensity cause no further increase in the fiber's firing rate. (437)

Stapes (stirrup). The last of the three ossicles in the middle ear. It receives vibrations from the incus and transmits these vibrations to the oval window of the inner ear. (420)

Stimulation deafness. Deafness caused by intense auditory stimulation that damages structures in the cochlea. (430)

Tectorial membrane. A membrane that stretches the length of the cochlea and is located directly over the hair cells. Vibrations of the cochlear partition cause the tectorial membrane to stimulate the hair cells by rubbing against them. (423)

Temporal code. A code in which frequency is signaled by the timing of nerve impulses. One example of a temporal code is one in which high rates of nerve firing signal high frequencies and low rates of nerve firing signal low frequencies. (426)

Tinnitus. A persistent ringing in the ears, often caused by exposure to loud sounds. (430)

Tinnitus masker. A device that produces a hissing sound, which in some patients masks, or covers up, the ringing produced by tinnitus. (431)

Tonotopic map. When neurons with the same characteristic frequency are grouped together and neurons with nearby characteristic frequencies are found near each other. (431)

Traveling wave. The basilar membrane vibrates in a traveling wave, in which the peak of the membrane's vibration travels from the stapes to the helicotrema. (428)

Tuning curve. A curve that indicates the intensity necessary to elicit a threshold response from a neuron at different frequencies along the audible range. (432)

Tympanic membrane (eardrum). A membrane at the end of the auditory canal that vibrates in response to vibrations of the air and transmits these vibrations to the ossicles in the middle ear. (420)

Volley principle. Wever's idea that groups of nerve fibers fire in volleys, with some fibers firing while others are refractory. In this way, groups of fibers can effect high rates of nerve firing. (434)

CHAPTER 13

The Stimulus for Speech
Production of the Speech Stimulus
The Theory of Acoustic Invariance
Categorical Perception
Neural Mechanisms of Speech Perception
Conversational Speech

Perceiving Speech

Despite the complexity of visual perception we have few problems in seeing form, color, and depth, unless viewing conditions are poor or the stimuli are particularly ambiguous. The same is true for speech perception. Unless noise or extremely slurred speech interferes, we easily understand people when they talk to us. But this ease of speech perception masks underlying mechanisms that are extremely complex and still not completely understood.

One of the most complex things about speech perception is the speech stimulus, a constantly changing pattern of frequencies of much greater complexity than the pure tones and musical notes of the previous two chapters. To understand speech perception, therefore, we need to understand the nature of the stimulus for speech.

THE STIMULUS FOR SPEECH

The Phoneme

Our first task in studying speech perception is to break speech sounds into units that are small enough to work with. What are these units? The flow of a sentence? A particular word? A syllable? The sound of a letter? A sentence is too large a unit for easy analysis, and some letters have no sounds at all. Much speech research has been based on a unit called the phoneme. A **phoneme** is the shortest segment of speech which, if changed, would change the meaning of a word. The phonemes of English, listed in Table 13.1, are represented by phonetic symbols that stand for speech sounds, with 15 phonemes having vowel sounds and 23 phonemes having consonant sounds. To illustrate our definition of *phoneme,* consider the word "bit," which contains the phonemes /b/, /I/, and /t/*. We know that /b/, /I/, and /t/ are phonemes, because we can change the meaning of the word by changing each phoneme individually. Thus, "bit" becomes "pit" if the /b/ is changed to /p/, it becomes "bet" if the /I/ is changed to /ɛ/, and it becomes "bid" if the /t/ is changed to /d/.

Phonemes, then, stand for specific sounds. When these sounds are produced each generates a different pattern of frequencies in the air. This pattern of frequencies is called the **acoustic signal.** One way to visualize this signal is by means of the sound spectrogram.

---

*Single phonemes and pairs of phonemes are set off from the text by slashes.

447

TABLE 13. 1 / *Major consonants and*
vowels of English and
their phonetic symbols

Consonants				Vowels	
p	pull	s	sip	i	heed
b	bull	z	zip	I	hid
m	man	r	rip	e	bait
w	will	š	should	ɛ	head
f	fill	ž	pleasure	æ	had
v	vet	č	chop	u	who'd
θ	thigh	ǰ	gyp	U	put
ð	thy	y	yip	ʌ	but
t	tie	k	kale	o	boat
d	die	g	gale	ɔ	bought
n	near	h	hail	a	hot
l	lear	ŋ	sing	ə	sofa
				ɨ	many

The Sound Spectrogram

The **sound spectrogram** in Figure 13.1 shows the pattern of frequencies for the words "shoo cat." Frequency is plotted on the vertical axis and time on the horizontal axis, with the amount of sound energy indicated by the degree of darkness.

The best way to understand the spectrogram is to read it from left to right, trying to correlate the sound produced at each point on the time axis with the frequencies indicated above those points. Starting at the left of Figure 13.1, we first encounter the /š/ (sh) sound of the word "shoo." Notice that the /š/ lasts about 0.2 seconds, and during that time it generates a lot of energy between 2,000 and 3,500 Hz (indicated by the dark area on the spectrogram) and also some energy between 3,500 and 6,000 Hz. /š/ is a high-pitched sound so the spectrogram shows frequencies only above about 2,000 Hz.

The /u/ (oo) sound that follows is lower pitched in this speaker, so it creates a spectrogram with energy only below 2,000 Hz. The energy caused by /u/ occurs primarily in two bands, one at the very bottom of the spectrogram, below 500 Hz (marked F1), and the other (marked F2) at about 1,000 Hz. These horizontal (or nearly horizontal) bands of energy, called **formants,** are characteristic of vowels. The band with the lowest frequency is called the first formant; the next highest frequency, the second formant; and so on. Notice that three formants (marked F1, F2, and F3) are visible for the /ae/ sound of "cat."

Now that we know what a phoneme is and have seen how the frequencies associated with phonemes can be displayed on the spectrogram, we are ready to tackle the basic problem of speech perception: What is the information that signals the presence of each phoneme?

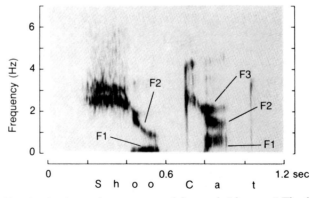

F I G U R E 13. 1 A sound spectrogram of the words "shoo cat." The formants, horizontal bands of energy characteristic of vowels, are marked. F1 is the first formant (lowest frequency), F2, the second formant, and F3, the third. (From Kiang, 1975.)

The Information Associated with Phonemes

One of the first problems to be solved when studying any perceptual quality is identifying the physical stimulus associated with that quality. We have seen that the first step in studying color vision was to show that different hues are associated with different wavelengths of light, and that the first step in studying pitch perception was to show that our perception of pitch is associated with the frequency of pressure changes in the air. To take a similar step for speech perception, we want to identify the **acoustic cue** for each phoneme—the specific part of the acoustic signal that is associated with each phoneme.

How can we identify the acoustic cue for a phoneme? One approach would be to look at the spectrogram and determine the pattern of frequencies located directly above the phoneme. In doing this, we would hope to find the same pattern of frequencies every time a particular phoneme occurs. If we succeeded in doing this, we could say that the acoustic cue for that phoneme is *invariant*. An **invariant acoustic cue** is a pattern of frequencies that *remains constant* when the phoneme appears in different contexts.

It's easy to understand why discovery of an invariant acoustic cue for each phoneme would make it much easier for us to understand speech perception. If the same acoustic signal is always associated with a particular phoneme, then the presence of that acoustic signal will always signal the presence of that phoneme. One of the goals of research on speech perception has, therefore, been to identify an invariant acoustic cue for each phoneme. In searching for these invariant acoustic cues, early researchers looked at spectrograms and tried to identify the patterns of frequencies always associated with a particular phoneme. What these researchers found, however, was not a constant acoustic cue for each phoneme but, instead, that the acoustic signal associated with each phoneme changes when the phoneme appears in different contexts. To understand the basis for this conclusion, let's consider some research done at a laboratory responsible for many pioneering discoveries

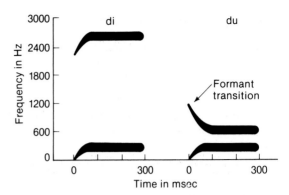

F I G U R E   13. 2   Hand-drawn spectrograms for /di/ and /du/. (From Liberman, Cooper, Shankweiler, & Studdert-Kennedy, 1967.)

in speech perception, the Haskins Laboratory in New Haven, Connecticut.

Demonstrations of Acoustic Variability

The Haskins researchers, led by Alvin Liberman, used the speech spectrogram to show that the acoustic cue for a particular phoneme changes when the phoneme is in different contexts. An example of this variability is shown in Figure 13.2, which shows idealized spectrograms for the sounds /di/ and /du/. We say that these spectrograms are idealized because they are hand-drawn and do not show many of the irregularities obvious in the spectrogram in Figure 13.1. These hand-drawn spectrograms do, however, accurately show the two most important characteristics of the sounds /di/ and /du/: the formants and the formant transitions. The formants are the horizontal bands of energy at about 200 and 2,600 Hz for /di/ and at 200 and 600 Hz for /du/. Remembering that formants are characteristic of vowels, we conclude that the formants at 200 and 2,600 Hz are the acoustic cue for the sound /i/ and the formants at 200 and 600 are the acoustic cue for the sound /u/.

The rapid shifts in frequency preceding each formant are called **formant transitions.** The formant transitions are the acoustic cues for the sound /d/. We can see that the formant transitions associated with the first formants of /di/ and /du/ are the same. However, the formant transition for the second formant in /di/ is different from the formant transition for the second formant in /du/, even though in each case we hear the same /d/ sound. This illustrates the variability of the acoustic cue for /d/. The acoustic cue that signals the consonant /d/ depends on the vowel following the /d/, with the /d/ sound being associated with a different acoustic cue when followed by /i/ than when followed by /u/.

Another illustration of the fact that a given phoneme may be associated with different acoustic cues is that subjects perceive the /p/ sound in the word "split' when the acoustic energy for the /p/ sound is present *or* if this energy is replaced with a 100-msec interval of silence between the /s/ and /lit/ parts of the word (Fitch, Halwes, Erickson, & Liberman, 1980; Jusczyk, 1986).

The two examples above show that the same phoneme can have more than one acoustic cue. But we can also show that the same acoustic cue can be associated with different phonemes. Inserting a brief period of silence between the phoneme /s/ and /i/ results in the perception "ski," whereas inserting the same silence between /s/ and /u/ results in the perception "spu" (Jusczyk, 1986).

It should be clear from the examples above that the speech stimulus is extremely variable. And this variability occurs not only when phonemes are placed in different contexts but also when different people speak. For example, the frequencies of the formants that signal vowels depend on the speaker, with the frequencies for male speakers generally being lower than the frequencies for female speakers. Thus, although the sound /u/ for the speaker who produced the spectrogram in Figure 13.1 is signaled by F1 at 300 Hz and F2 at 1,000 Hz, these frequencies would probably be different for another speaker.

However, in spite of the variability caused by differing contexts, by voices that are high pitched or low pitched, accents that are southern, midwestern, down'east, or foreign, and by rapid speakers and s—l—o—w speakers, we still are able to understand most people when they speak to us. Our ability to understand speech in the face of this extreme variability is one of the major puzzles of speech perception.

The Haskins researchers' answer to this puzzle was to propose that although the cues for each phoneme may change in different contexts, we are able to take these changes in context into account. This "taking context into account" involves a mechanism that we won't describe here (see Liberman et al., 1967; Goldstein, 1984; Liberman & Mattingly, 1985), both because it is complicated and because an alternative answer has recently been proposed. This alternative answer is based on a new method of displaying the speech stimulus which suggests that invariant acoustic cues for phonemes do, in fact, exist. To describe this research, we need to first describe how the speech stimulus is produced.

PRODUCTION OF THE SPEECH STIMULUS

All speech sounds begin as pressure generated by the lungs that pushes air through the vocal tract (Figure 13.3). The sound produced depends on the state of the vocal tract as the air is pushed through it (Figure 13.4).

Vowels are produced with the vocal tract in a relatively open state, with the shape of the opening determining the frequency of the formants, which we saw in Figure 13.1 are bands of relatively constant frequencies. You can demonstrate this relation between the shape of the vocal tract and specific vowels by noticing how the opening in your mouth changes as you say different vowels. (Try it: a, e, i, o, oo.)

The consonants, on the other hand, are produced by constricting or closing the vocal tract. Instead of the continuous stream of energy characteristic of vowels (notice that you can hold a vowel until you run out of breath), consonants are characterized by rapidly changing bursts of energy and periods of silence.

To illustrate the differences between how different consonants are produced, let's focus on the sounds /d/ and /f/. Make these sounds, and notice what your tongue, lips, and teeth are doing. As you produce the sound /d/, you place your tongue

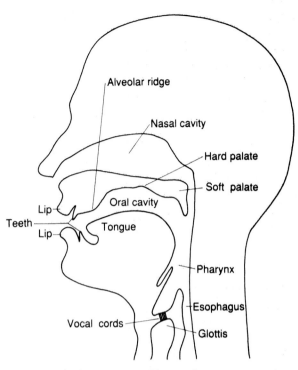

F I G U R E 13. 3 The vocal tract.

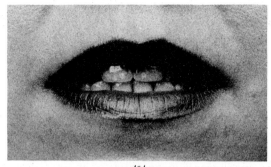

/s/

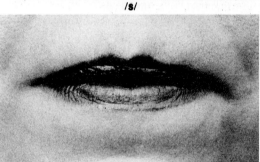

/p/

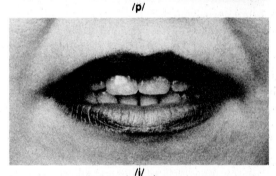

/i/

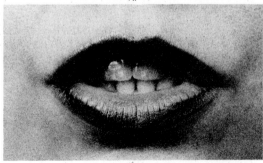

/č/

F I G U R E 13. 4 The shape of the lips while producing the word "speech." The differences in these shapes is one indication of the differences in the configuration of the vocal tract during the production of different phonemes.

against the ridge above your upper teeth (the alveolar ridge of Figure 13.3) and then release a slight rush of air as you move your tongue away from the alveolar ridge (try it). As you produce the sound /f/, you place your bottom lip against your upper front teeth and then push air between the lips and the teeth.

From these examples you can see that there are large differences in the way /d/ and /f/ are produced. In fact, when we consider all of the phonemes, we find that *no two phonemes are produced in exactly the same way.* (That's why they sound different!) To describe these differences in the way different phonemes are produced, we need to introduce the concept of the **phonetic feature**—physical movements in the vocal tract that accompany the production of every phoneme. The production of a consonant can be described in terms of three types of phonetic features: (1) voicing, (2) place of articulation, and (3) manner of articulation. Let's look at each, in turn.

Voicing refers to whether or not producing the

sound causes the vocal cords (see Figure 13.3) to vibrate. Place your fingers on either side of your neck and say the words "sip" and "zip." The vibration you feel when you say the /z/ of "zip" is due to vibration of the vocal cords. That you feel no vibration when you say the /s/ of "sip" means that the vocal cords are not vibrating. Consonants that cause vibration of the vocal cords are called *voiced,* whereas consonants that cause no vibration are called **unvoiced.** The consonant /d/ is voiced and the consonant /f/ is unvoiced.

Place of articulation refers to the fact that the airstream is obstructed in some way during the production of all consonants. The place of articulation is the place at which this obstruction occurs. For the sound /d/, the place of articulation is the alveolar ridge; therefore, the place of articulation for /d/ is called *alveolar.* For the sound /f/, the place of articulation—the bottom lip and the upper front teeth—is called *labiodental.*

Manner of articulation refers to the mechanical means by which the consonants are produced and most often to the way air is pushed through an opening. To produce the sound /d/, we completely close off the place of articulation, by placing the tongue on the alveolar ridge and then releasing a slight rush of air. This manner of articulation is called *stop.* To produce the sound /f/ we push air between the small space between the lips and the upper teeth. This manner of articulation is called *fricative.*

The three types of phonetic features—voicing, place of articulation, and manner of articulation—provide a way to distinguish between the different phonemes. In English there are two types of voicing, seven different places of articulation, and six different manners of articulation (see Appendix E), so there are enough combinations of features to enable each phoneme to have its own unique set of phonetic features. For example, we can describe /d/ as a *voiced* (voicing), *alveolar* (place of articulation) *stop* (manner of articulation), and /f/ as an *unvoiced, labiodental fricative.* If we consider all of the other phonemes, we see that each one has its own unique set of phonetic features. Thus, if we can identify a phoneme's phonetic features we will have identified the phoneme.

The fact that phonemes can be identified by their phonetic features, plus the development of a new way of displaying the speech stimulus, has led to the **theory of acoustic invariance,** the idea that our perception of phonemes is based on information provided by invariant acoustic cues associated with that phoneme (Stevens & Blumstein, 1981).

THE THEORY OF ACOUSTIC INVARIANCE

A development that led to the proposal that invariant acoustic cues may, in fact, exist was the use of the **short-term spectrum** in place of the sound spectrogram. Whereas the spectrogram shows the pattern of frequencies during the time course of a whole phoneme, or, in the case of Figure 13.1, two words consisting of five phonemes, the short-term spectrum shows, in detail, which frequencies are produced during a short period of time.

A short-term spectrum for the sound /ga/ is shown in Figure 13.5(a), along with the sound spectrogram for /ga/. This short-term spectrum indicates which frequencies occur during the first 26 msec of the sound /ga/. Notice that the short-term spectrum in Figure 13.5(a) indicates a peak of energy just below 2,000 Hz. This peak in the short-term spectrum corresponds well with the dark area below 2,000 Hz in the first 26 msec of the spectrogram in Figure 13.5(b). Also notice that there is a minimum in the short-term spectrum, just below 3,000 Hz, which is visible as the light area below 3,000 Hz in the first 26 msec of the spectrogram. One advantage of the short-term spectrum over the spectrogram is that it indicates with much more precision exactly how much energy is present at each frequency. The disadvantage of the short-term spectrum is that it gives us information only about the frequencies present during a very brief period of time. However, by combining a sequence of short-term spectra into **running spectral displays,** as shown in Figure 13.6, we can see not only which frequencies are present at one point in time but can see how these frequencies change as time progresses.

(a)

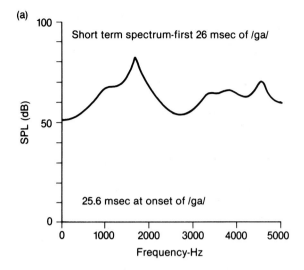

(b)

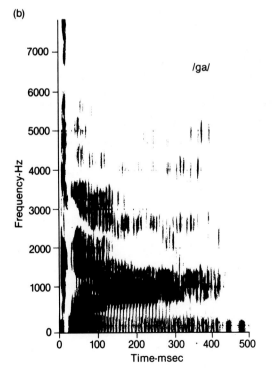

F I G U R E 13. 5 (a) A short-term spectrum of the acoustic energy in the first 26 msec of the phoneme /ga/. (b) Sound spectrogram of the phoneme /ga/. (Courtesy of James Sawusch.)

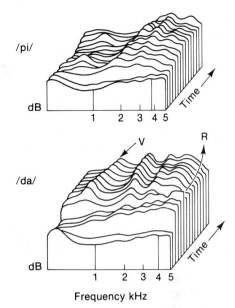

F I G U R E 13. 6 Running spectral displays for /pi/ and /da/. These displays are made up of a sequence of short-term spectra like the one in Figure 13.5. Each of these spectra is displaced 5 msec on the time axis so each step we move along this axis indicates the frequencies present in the next 5 msec. The low-frequency peak (V) in the /da/ display is a cue for voicing, and the rising high-frequency peak (R) is a cue for alveolar place of articulation. (From Kewley-Port & Luce, 1984.)

A number of researchers have begun to use short-term spectra and running spectral displays to try to identify invariant acoustic cues that specify phonetic features (Blumstein & Stevens, 1979; Stevens & Blumstein, 1978, 1981; Kewley-Port, 1983; Kewley-Port & Luce, 1984; Searle, Jacobson, & Rayment, 1979). To understand how these spectral displays might contain invariant acoustic cues, let's consider the running spectral displays in Figure 13.6. Diane Kewley-Port and Paul Luce (1984) have hypothesized that specific properties of these displays are correlated with specific phonetic features. Two of these properties are as follows:

1. Onset of a prominent low-frequency peak that is continuous in succeeding frames. This continuous low-frequency peak, which signals the presence of voicing, is marked "V" in the dis-

play for /da/ but does not occur in the display for /pi/. From this information we can conclude that /d/ is voiced but that /p/ is not.

2. The relative tilt of high-frequency peaks. A rising tilt, indicated by the "R" for the /da/ spectra, is one cue for an alveolar place of articulation.

The beauty of the information contained in the running spectral displays is that it remains relatively invariant in different contexts. This has been demonstrated by measuring how well people can identify phonetic features by looking at properties of the running spectra like the two described above. Voicing and place of articulation can be identified correctly about 80–90 percent of the time (Kewley-Port & Luce, 1984). These results suggest that perhaps there are invariant acoustic cues that can be used by the auditory system to identify phonemes. It is important to note, however, that this work, although extremely promising, is also very recent, and that more research needs to be done before we can be sure that the information contained in these running spectra is actually used by people to perceive speech (Stevens & Blumstein, 1981).

It is also important to realize that, in addition to these invariant acoustic cues, the variable information in the acoustic signal may also help us to perceive speech. Some researchers have suggested that variations in the speech signal may follow specific rules that make it possible for us to use certain cues when they appear in specific contexts (Elman & McClelland, 1983).

Another way of thinking about this variable information is to draw an analogy with the process of depth perception. We perceive an object's depth by taking many cues into account, both monocular and binocular. A particular depth cue may not unambiguously indicate an object's depth in a particular situation, but, by combining all of the available information, we can accurately perceive the object's depth. Perhaps a similar situation exists for the variable information in the acoustic signal. Although the same information may not always be associated with a particular phoneme, the infor-

mation that is present may help us to perceive the phoneme.

Our discussion so far in the chapter has focused on one of the central questions of speech perception: What information is available to the auditory system to signal individual phonemes? We have seen that early research, based on the sound spectrogram, demonstrated the great variability of the acoustic signal and suggested that phonemes are not signaled by invariant acoustic cues. We have also seen that more recent research, based on short-term spectra and running spectral displays, has shown that invariant acoustic cues may exist for the phonetic features on which each phoneme is based. This invariant information, combined with variable information in the acoustic signal, provides the information necessary for the auditory system to transform the complex and constantly changing pattern of frequencies of speech into meaningful sounds.

It should be clear, however, that much research remains to be done before we are able to precisely specify the information that signals phonemes. And once we have succeeded in doing this, we also must deal with another question: How is this information transformed into the perception of meaningful speech? When we look at how researchers have dealt with this question, we find that they have arrived at two different conceptions about the nature of this process:

1. Speech is special. The process of transforming information into the perception of speech is accomplished by a processor that is specialized to process only speech stimuli. Speech is "special" since it has its own processing mechanism.

2. Speech is simply a complex auditory stimulus. The process of transforming information into the perception of speech is accomplished by the same mechanisms that process other complex auditory stimuli.

The first idea, that speech is "special," was proposed by researchers at the Haskins Laboratory based on a phenomenon called **categorical perception,** which seemed to show that listeners categorized speech sounds in a different way than other sounds (Liberman et al., 1967). To understand what we mean by this, let's describe the procedure of a typical categorical perception experiment.

CATEGORICAL PERCEPTION AND THE "SPECIALNESS" OF SPEECH

To describe a categorical perception experiment, we need to understand a characteristic of the acoustic signal called **voice onset time (VOT)**. Voice onset time is the time delay between the beginning of a sound and the beginning of the vibration of the vocal cords that accompanies voicing. We can illustrate this by considering the consonants /d/, which is voiced, and /t/, which is unvoiced. This difference between /d/ and /t/ causes a difference in VOT that is illustrated by the spectrograms in Figure 13.7.

We can see from these spectrograms that the time between the beginning of the sound /da/ and the beginning of voicing (indicated by the presence of vertical striations in the spectrogram) is 17 msec for /da/ and 91 msec for /ta/. Thus, the voiced /d/ causes /da/ to have a short VOT, and the unvoiced /t/ causes /ta/ to have a long VOT.

There are two parts to a categorical perception experiment: (1) categorization and (2) discrimination. The categorization part of the experiment is based on our ability to use a computer (1) to synthesize a sound with VOT = 0 msec that is perceived as /da/ and (2) to increase the VOT in small steps until at longer VOTs the sound is perceived as /ta/. In the experiment, the computer varies the VOT in small steps between about 0 and 80 msec, and the listener's task is to indicate whether they hear /da/ or /ta/ at each step. The results of such an experiment are shown by the solid line in Figure 13.8 (Eimas & Corbit, 1973). When the VOT is 0 msec, 100 percent of the stimuli are identified as /da/, and increasing VOT has no effect until the VOT reaches about 35 msec. At this point, which is called the **phonetic boundary,** listeners suddenly begin hearing /ta/, and when the VOT

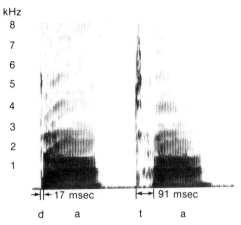

F I G U R E   13. 7 Spectrograms for /da/ and /ta/. The voice onset time—the time between the beginning of the sound and the onset of voicing—is indicated at the beginning of the spectrogram for each sound. (Spectrogram courtesy of Ron Cole.)

is increased just a little more to 40 msec, most of the stimuli are identified as /ta/. Even though the VOT is changed in many steps, the listener perceives only two categories, /da/ and /ta/.

In the discrimination part of the categorical perception experiment, we determine how well a listener can discriminate between two stimuli that differ in VOT. When we do this, we find that a listener cannot tell the difference between two stimuli that are in the same category but can tell the difference between two stimuli that are in different categories. For example, a listener can't tell the difference between two stimuli with VOTs of 0 and 30 msec (both are perceived as /da/) but can tell the difference between two stimuli with VOTs of 30 and 50 msec (one is perceived as /da/, the other as /ta/). Categorical perception occurs (1) when we perceive stimuli in categories, as in the categorizing part of the experiment, and (2) when we can discriminate between stimuli from different categories but can't discriminate between stimuli in the same category.

The discovery of categorical perception led the Haskins researchers to conclude that speech is special. They concluded this because categorical perception had not been observed for other types

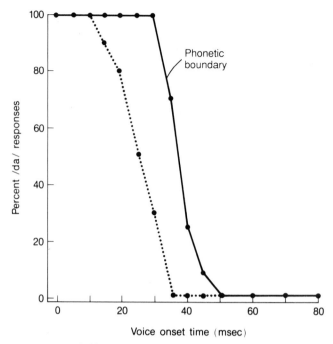

F I G U R E 13. 8 Solid line: the percent of sounds identified as /da/ as voice onset time is varied from 0 to 80 msec. Dotted line: the percent of sounds identified as /da/ after adaptation to /ba/ for two minutes. The phonetic boundary's shift to the left indicates that /da/ is heard less often after adaptation. (From Eimas & Corbit, 1973.)

of sounds. For example, consider what happens when we start with a low-frequency pure tone and slowly increase the frequency. If pitch were perceived categorically, then we might expect that all low-frequency tones would sound the same and all high-frequency tones would sound the same, with an abrupt change in pitch occurring at some intermediate frequency. This is not, however, what happens. As we increase the frequency of a pure tone, we hear continuous changes in the tone's pitch. We perceive hundreds of different pitches.

The Haskins researchers' conclusion that categorical perception is unique only to speech seemed to indicate that speech is special, but later research demonstrated categorical perception for nonspeech sounds like buzzes, noises, and musical stimuli (Miller, Wier, Pastore, Kelly, & Dooling, 1976; Pisoni, 1977; Zatorre & Halbern, 1979). The finding that categorical perception occurs for non-

speech sounds plus the demonstration of categorical perception in monkeys and chinchillas (Kuhl, 1986) and even quail (Kluender et al. 1987) has convinced many researchers that speech is not processed by a special speech processor but, rather, is processed in the same way that other complex signals are processed by the auditory system.

Does the fact that the categorical perception results cannot be interpreted to support the idea that speech is "special" mean that all of the research on categorical perception was done for no purpose? Not at all. Categorical perception serves an important purpose in speech perception. It simplifies our perception of the speech signal. Consider how many different sounds there would be if our perception were changed every time we even slightly changed the VOT. The large number of sounds that would result might make perception more complicated. Instead, categorical perception reduces the number of discriminable sounds, a result that becomes particularly important when we are faced with the rapid-fire sequence of phonemes we hear in normal speech.

NEURAL MECHANISMS OF SPEECH PERCEPTION

What are the neural mechanisms underlying the perception of speech? One answer to this question was proposed by Peter Eimas and John Corbit (1973) on the basis of a **selective adaptation** experiment analogous to the visual grating experiment of Figure 3.38. In the visual experiment, adaptation to a grating of a particular orientation dims our perception of gratings with that orientation but has little effect on gratings with other orientations. We explain this selective dimming effect by assuming that adaptation to a particular orientation fatigues feature detectors sensitive to that orientation but does not affect feature detectors sensitive to other orientations.

Following this idea, Eimas and Corbit reasoned that perhaps it would be possible to use a similar adaptation procedure to demonstrate the existence of detectors that respond to particular phonetic features. We have already described the first part of Eimas and Corbit's experiment—they are the researchers who produced the solid curve in Figure 13.8. That curve indicates that the phonetic boundary between /da/ and /ta/ is at 35–45 msec. At VOTs shorter than 35 msec, Eimas and Corbit's subjects always perceived /da/, and at VOTs longer than 50 msec, their subjects always perceived /ta/.

Having determined the solid curve in Figure 13.8, Eimas and Corbit then adapted their subjects to the voiced syllable /ba/ by repeating it for 2 minutes. They reasoned that if this repetition fatigues a phonetic detector that responds to voicing, then after adaptation subjects should be less able to perceive voiced syllables such as /da/, and this decrease in the perception of /da/ should be

reflected in a shift in the phonetic boundary. This is exactly what Eimas and Corbit found. When they asked their adapted subjects to label stimuli as they changed VOT, they obtained the dashed curve in Figure 13.8.—/da/ was now heard on 100 percent of the trials only at VOTs below about 10 msec.

The results of Eimas and Corbit's selective adaptation experiment support the idea that detectors for phonetic features exist, just as the results of visual selective adaptation experiments support the idea that detectors for visual features exist. In both cases, presenting an adapting stimulus with a specific property (such as orientation for vision and voicing for speech) decreases the response of the feature detector that responds to that property.

This idea of phonetic feature detectors was extremely popular when it was first proposed. One reason for this popularity was that these phonetic detectors were proposed at a time when more and more specialized feature detectors were being discovered for vision. However, recent experiments have led to a reinterpretation of Eimas and Corbit's selective adaptation results. One of these experiments, by Martin Roberts and Quentin Summerfield (1981), makes use of a phenomenon called **audiovisual speech perception.** We will first describe this phenomenon and will then show how Roberts and Summerfield used it in their experiment.

Audiovisual speech perception was first demonstrated by John MacDonald and Harry McGurk (1978), using the following procedure:

1. They videotaped a person repeating the sounds /ga-ga/.
2. When playing the videotape back, they turned off the /ga-ga/ sound and substituted the sound /ba-ba/. Thus, the *visual image* on the screen showed a woman making the lip movements for /ga-ga/, but the *acoustic signal* coming from the loudspeakers was for /ba-ba/ (Figure 13.9).
3. When they showed this display to subjects, they *heard* the sound /da-da/! Thus, when visually perceived lip movements didn't match the acoustic signal, the subject perceived a sound different from the sound usually per-

---

B O X   13. 1.   /   *Can Infants Perceive Speech?*

Peter Eimas and coworkers (1971) have shown that very young infants may be able to perceive speech. The evidence for this early perception of speech comes from the results of categorical perception experiments similar to those run on adults. Eimas found that infants as young as 1 month old perform similarly to adults in these categorical perception experiments, in that they perceive the difference between two sounds with voice onset times (VOTs) that span a phonetic boundary and therefore sound different to adults (VOTs = +20 and +40 msec, which sound like /ba/ and /pa/, respectively), but they perceive little or no difference between two sounds with VOTs that are on the same side of the phonetic boundary and therefore sound the same to adults (VOTs = +60 and +80 msec, which both sound like /pa/).

How is it possible to tell whether or not a 1-month-old infant can tell the difference between sounds? Eimas made use of the fact that an infant will suck on a nipple in order to hear a series of brief speech sounds. If, however, the same speech sounds are repeated over and over, the infant eventually habituates to these sounds (see pp. 320–321 in Chapter 9) and the rate of sucking decreases. By presenting a new stimulus when the rate of sucking has decreased, we can determine whether the new stimulus sounds the same or different to the infant. If the new stimulus sounds different, dishabituation will occur and the rate of sucking will increase. If the new stimulus sounds the same, however, habituation will continue and the rate of sucking will either stay the same or decrease further.

Look at the results in the left graph on the next page. The number of sucking responses made when no sound was presented is indicated by the point at B. When sucking results in the presentation of a sound with a VOT of +20 msec sounds like /ba/ to an adult), the number of sucking responses increases to a high level; then, after 3 minutes, the number of sucking responses begins to decrease. When the VOT is changed to +40 msec (sounds like /pa/ to an adult), the number of sucking responses increases, as indicated by the points to the right of the dashed line. This result means that the infant perceives a difference between sounds with VOTs of +20 and +40 msec. The center graph, however, shows that changing the VOT from +60 to +80 msec (both sound like /pa/ to an adult) has only a small effect on sucking, indicating that the infants perceive little, if any, difference between the two sounds. Finally, the results for a control group (the right graph) show that when the sound is not changed, the number of sucking responses decreases throughout the experiment.

These results show that when the VOT is shifted across the phonetic boundary (left graph), the infants perceive a change in the sound, and when the VOT is shifted on the same side of the phonetic boundary (center graph), the infants perceive little or no change in the sound. That infants as young as 1 month of age are capable of categorical perception is particularly impressive, considering that these infants have had virtually no experience in producing

---

ceived in response to the acoustic signal (McGurk & MacDonald, 1976; MacDonald & McGurk, 1978; Summerfield, 1979).

Now that we know what audiovisual speech perception is we can describe Roberts and Sum-

merfield's experiment. They began by determining a curve like the one in Figure 13.8 with stimuli that caused subjects to perceive /bɛ/ on one side of the phonetic boundary and /dɛ/ on the other side. Then they adapted their subjects with the acoustical signal for /bɛ/, while their subjects watched

speech sounds and only limited experience in hearing them. We can, in fact, draw an analogy between young kittens, whose adultlike receptive fields indicate that they have feature detectors for visual stimuli by 6 weeks of age (see pp. 337–338, in Chapter 9), and Eimas' infants, whose adultlike categorical perception indicates that they have mechanisms for detecting speech stimuli at a very early age.

A word of caution, however, is in order regarding the interpretation of Eimas' results. That infants may possess mechanisms for detecting speech sounds does not necessarily mean that infants recognize these sounds as speech. That capacity probably develops later—the result of learning gained as the infant listens to the speech of those around him (Aslin & Pisoni, 1980; Walley, Pisoni, & Aslin, 1981).

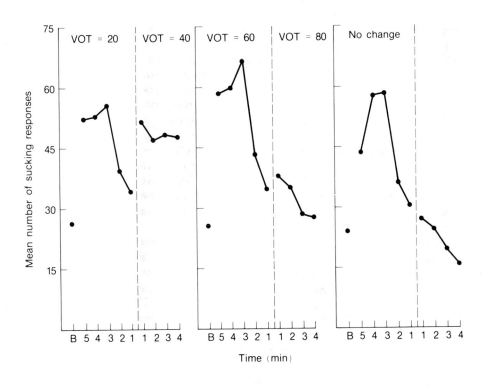

a TV monitor of a person making the lip movements for /gɛ/, which caused them to perceive /dɛ/. According to the theory of phonetic feature detectors, the subjects' perception of /dɛ/ means that a phonetic detector associated with /dɛ/is being activated. If the /dɛ/ detector is acti-

vated by the perception of /dɛ/ during adaptation, this should decrease the perception of /dɛ/ when a curve like the one in Figure 13.8 is remeasured following adaptation.

What happened? Just the opposite of the feature detector prediction. After adaptation Roberts

F I G U R E 13. 9 Audiovisual speech perception. The woman's lips are moving as if she is saying /ga-ga/, but the actual sound is /ba-ba/. The listener, however, reports hearing the sound /da-da/.

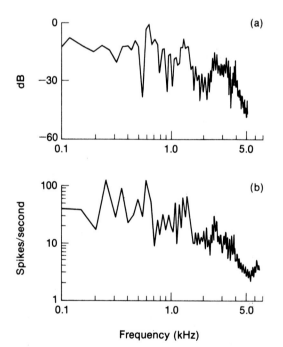

Frequency (kHz)

F I G U R E 13. 10 (a) Short-term spectrum for /da/. This curve indicates the energy distribution in /da/ between 20 and 40 msec after the beginning of the signal. (b) Nerve firing of a population of cat auditory nerve fibers to the same stimulus. (From Sachs, Young, & Miller, 1982.)

and Summerfield's subjects were *more likely* to perceive /dɛ/, the sound they should *not* have been able to hear well if the /dɛ/ detector were being fatigued by adaptation. Adaptation instead decreased the subject's ability to hear /bɛ/, the sound associated with the acoustic signal to which they were being adapted. Adaptation is, therefore, controlled not by what the subject *perceives* but by the *nature of the acoustic stimulus* entering the subject's ears.

If the results of selective adaptation experiments aren't caused by fatiguing of a specialized phonetic detector, what is causing the phonetic boundary to shift? Although we can't answer this question precisely, it is likely that adaptation is fatiguing neurons that respond to the frequencies contained in the adapting stimulus (Sawusch & Jusczyk, 1981). These neurons do not have to be phonetic detectors specialized for speech but can be the same neurons responsible for hearing sounds in general.

This idea that speech perception is the product of normal auditory mechanisms is consistent with the idea that we expressed earlier, that speech is *not* special, and is also reflected in recent research on the physiological basis of speech perception. Although this research is still in its infancy, it has been possible to demonstrate some striking parallels between the speech stimulus and the firing of auditory neurons. For example, Figure 13.10 shows the short-term spectrum for the sound /da/ and the firing pattern for a representative population of cat auditory nerve fibers with low, medium, and high characteristic frequencies. (Remember from Chapter 12, p. 432, that the neuron's characteristic frequency is the frequency to which this neuron responds best.) The match between the speech stimulus and the firing of neurons in the auditory nerve indicates that information in the speech stimulus is represented by the pattern of firing of auditory nerve fibers.

Up till now we have focused almost entirely on how we perceive phonemes and have taken a bottom-up approach to speech perception. That is, we have looked at the relationship between the perception of phonemes and the *acoustic signal*. But our perception of speech is influenced not only by the acoustic signal but also by the meanings of the words and sentences of everyday speech. After all, when we listen to someone talking we don't just hear phonemes; we hear words, sentences, and thoughts. We will, therefore, complete our discussion of speech perception by taking a top-down approach. That is, we will consider how *meaning* influences our perception of conversational speech. (See p. 216 to review bottom-up and top-down processing.)

CONVERSATIONAL SPEECH

Two Problems of Conversational Speech

When we consider the problem of conversational speech—speech that occurs in words, sentences, and connected thoughts—we are faced with the following two facts which need to be explained. (1) No physical boundaries exist between words, but we hear individual words. (2) Conversational speech is so sloppy that about half of the words are unintelligible when taken out of context. Let's consider each of these problems in turn.

No physical boundaries exist between words.

Though it may seem that there is a slight break between each word in a conversation, a sound spectrogram shows that it is often difficult to tell where one word ends and the next begins in conversational speech. A good example of this lack of boundaries between words is shown in the spectrogram of "I owe you a yo-yo" in Figure 13.11. From this spectrogram, it is not at all obvious where one word ends and the other begins, and even an experienced spectrogram reader would find it extremely difficult to locate the individual words.

It becomes obvious that there are no spaces between words when you consider how a foreign language sounds. To someone unfamiliar with a language, the sounds of that language seem to speed by in an unbroken string; however, to a speaker of that language, the words seem separated just as the words of English seem separated to you. Since these separations are not contained in the acoustic signal, our knowledge of the language must help us perceive them.

Speech is sloppy. The sloppy pronunciation of most words in conversational speech makes about half of the words unintelligible when taken from their fluent context and presented alone. Irwin Pollack and J. M. Pickett (1964) experimentally demonstrated this difficulty in understanding words isolated from conversational speech. They recorded the conversations of subjects who sat in a room,

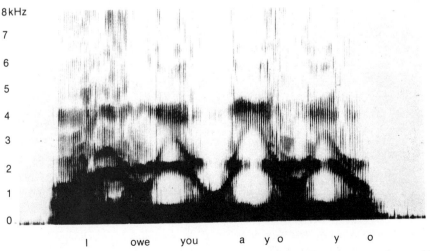

F I G U R E 13. 11 Spectrogram of "I owe you a yo-yo." (Spectrogram courtesy of Ron Cole.)

waiting for the experiment to begin. When the subjects were then presented with recordings of single words from their own conversations, they could identify only half the words, even though they were listening to their own voices!

You might think at first that Pollack and Pickett's subjects were particularly sloppy speakers. But try saying the following sentence at the speed you would use in talking to a friend: "This was a best buy." How did you say "best buy"? Did you pronounce the /t/ of "best," or did you say "bes buy"? What about "She is a bad girl"? While saying this rapidly, notice whether your tongue hits the top of your mouth as you say the /d/ of "bad." Many people omit the /d/ and say "ba girl." Finally, what about "Did you go to the store?" Did you say "did you" or "dijoo"?

That people speak differently in conversational speech than when speaking slowly is also shown by the spectrograms of Figures 13.12(a) and (b). The spectrogram in Figure 13.12(a) is for the question, "What are you doing?", spoken slowly and distinctly, whereas the spectrogram in Figure 13.12(b) is for the same question taken from conversational speech. "What are you doing?" becomes "Whad'aya doin?" in conversational speech, and this difference is easily seen in the spectrogram. While the patterns for the first and last words ("What" and "doing") are similar in both spectrograms, the pauses between words are absent or much less obvious in the spectrogram of Figure 13.12(b), and the middle of this spectrogram is completely changed, with a number of speech sounds missing.

Though there are often no breaks between words in conversational speech, and though speech is sloppy, we somehow understand what people are saying. We do this by taking context into account. In the next sections, we will consider some experiments that show how the presence of context helps make conversational speech intelligible.

Putting Breaks Between Words

If there are no breaks between words in normal speech, what puts the breaks there? The answer to this question is *meaning*. Our knowledge of the language gives meaning to the sounds we hear, which helps us to carry out the process of **segmentation**— putting breaks between words. With a few examples we can illustrate how meaning results in segmentation.

DEMONSTRATION

Segmentation and Meaning

Try the following two demonstrations:

1. Read the following words: Anna Mary Candy Lights Since Imp Pulp Lay Things. Now that you've read the words, what do they mean? If you think that this is a list of unconnected words beginning with the names of two women, Anna and Mary, you're right; but if you read this series of words a little faster, ignoring the spaces between the words on the page, you may hear a connected sentence that does not begin with the names Anna and Mary.

2. Read the following phrase fairly rapidly to a few people: "In mud eels are, in clay none are," and ask them to write the phrase.

If you succeeded in creating a new sentence from the series of words in the first demonstration, you did so by changing the segmentation, and this change was achieved by your knowledge of the meaning of the sounds. (For the answer see the bottom of page 464—but don't peek until you've tried reading the words rapidly.)

When Raj Reddy (1976) asked subjects to write their perception of "In mud eels are, in clay none are," he obtained responses like, "In muddies, sar, in clay nanar"; "in may deals are, en clainanar"; "In madel sar, in claynanar." In the absence of any context, Reddy's listeners clearly had difficulty figuring out what the phrase meant and, therefore, forced their own interpretation on the sounds they heard. Had the listeners known that the passage was taken from a book about where amphibians live, their knowledge about possible meanings of the words would facilitate segmentation and increase their probability of decoding the sentences correctly.

Pairs of words that flow together in speech also exemplify how segmentation results from meaning:

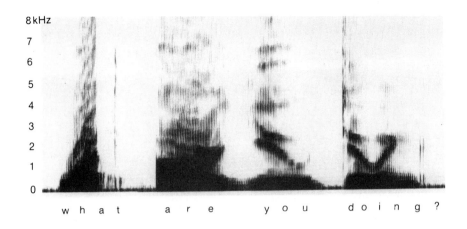

w h a t   a r e   y o u   d o i n g ?

(a)

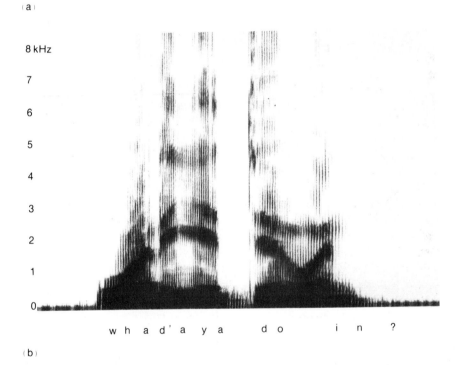

w h a d'a   y a   d o   i n   ?

(b)

F I G U R E 13. 12   (a) Spectrogram of "What are you doing" pronounced slowly and distinctly. (b) Spectrogram of "What are you doing" as pronounced in conversational speech. Note that (b) has been enlarged so it is almost as wide as (a). However, (a) lasts about 2.1 seconds, and (b) lasts only about 0.9 seconds. (Spectrograms courtesy of Ron Cole.)

"Big girl" can be interpreted as "big Earl," and the interpretation you pick probably depends on the overall meaning of the sentence in which these words appear. This example is similar to the familiar "I scream, you scream, we all scream for ice cream" that many people learn as children. The different segmentations of "I scream" and "ice cream' are put there by the meaning of the sentence. In the next section, we will look at another example of how meaning influences perception.

F I G U R E 13. 13   Archie is experiencing a problem in speech segmentation.

Semantics, Syntax, and Speech Perception

Some experiments have shown that words are more intelligible when heard in the context of a grammatical sentence than when presented as items in a list of unconnected words. An experiment by George Miller and Stephen Isard (1963) investigated how semantics and syntax affect the perception of speech. **Semantics** specifies whether or not it is appropriate to use a word in a sentence based on the word's meaning, and **syntax** specifies which structures of a sentence are allowed. Let's illustrate what we mean by semantics and syntax with some examples. "The boy spoke a word" is a perfectly good sentence semantically and syntactically. If, however, we change the sentence to "The boy spoke a triangle," it makes no sense. The use of the word "triangle" is semantically incorrect, because the meaning of the word "triangle" does not fit into this sentence; therefore, we call this a *semantically anomalous* sentence. Note that a semantically anomalous sentence is still grammatically and syntactically correct; however, we can change the sentence further to make it syntactically incorrect by changing the order of the words. Changing the sentence to "Spoke triangle boy the a" turns it into a grammatically and syntactically incorrect string of words, because the various parts of speech (nouns, verbs, etc.) are not in the correct order.

Miller and Isard constructed sentences that

Answer: An American delights in simple playthings.

fell into three classes: (1) normal grammatical sentences, (2) anomalous sentences (semantically incorrect), and (3) ungrammatical strings of words (syntactically incorrect). Five examples of normal sentences they used are

Gadgets simplify work around the house.
Accidents kill motorists on the highways.
Trains carry passengers across the country.
Bears steal honey from the hive.
Hunters shoot elephants between the eyes.

These normal grammatical sentences were then changed into the following five semantically anomalous sentences, by taking one word from each normal sentence.

Gadgets kill passengers from the eyes.
Accidents carry honey between the house.
Trains steal elephants around the highways.
Bears shoot work on the country.
Hunters simplify motorists across the hive.

Finally, five ungrammatical strings of words were produced by haphazardly rearranging the words as follows:

Around accidents country honey the shoot.
On trains have elephants the simplify.
Across bears eyes work the kill.
From hunters house motorists the carry.
Between gadgets highways passengers the steal.

Miller and Isard constructed 50 sentences of each type and recorded the resulting 150 sentences in a random order on a tape. Subjects then listened to the tape through earphones and were asked to repeat aloud what they heard as they were hearing it. This technique, which is called **shadowing,** results in a record of what the subjects heard. The subjects' responses were tape recorded and later scored for the number of complete sentences or strings of words repeated exactly. The results of this scoring showed that 89 percent of the normal sentences, 79 percent of the anomalous sentences, and 56 percent of the ungrammatical strings were repeated exactly. This result indicates that subjects must be making use of semantic *and* syntactic information when perceiving speech because when semantic information is lost, as was the case in the anomalous sentences, performance drops; and when syntactic information is lost, as was the case in the ungrammatical strings of words, performance drops even further. In fact, these differences among the three types of stimuli became even greater when the subjects heard the stimuli in the presence of a background noise. For example, at a moderately high level of background noise, 63 percent of the normal sentences, 22 percent of the anomalous sentences, and only 3 percent of the ungrammatical strings were perceived correctly. This is impressive evidence that listeners use both semantic and syntactic information in their perception of sentences.

In the next section, we will describe some experiments that show that the meaning of a sentence can cause us to hear sounds that aren't even there.

The Phonemic Restoration Effect

Richard Warren (1970) did an experiment in which subjects listened to a tape recording of the passage: "The state governors met with their respective legislatures convening in the capital city," in which the first /s/ in "legislatures" was replaced by the sound of a cough. The subjects were told that there would be a cough somewhere in the sentence and that they should indicate where in the sentence the cough occurred. The result of this experiment was that no subject identified the correct position of the cough, and, even more interesting, none of the subjects noticed that the /s/ in "legislatures" was missing. This effect, which Warren calls the **phonemic restoration effect,** was even experienced by students and staff in the psychology department who knew that the /s/ was missing.

Warren not only demonstrated the phonemic restoration effect but also showed that it can be influenced by the meaning of words *following* the missing phoneme. For example, the last word of the phrase "There was time to •ave . . ." (where the • indicates the presence of a cough or other sound) could be "shave," "save," "wave," or "rave," but subjects heard the word "wave" if the remainder of the sentence had to do with saying goodbye to a departing friend.

The phonemic restoration effect tells us something important about how speech perception works. We can appreciate this by considering some experiments in which Arthur Samuel (1981) used the phonemic restoration effect to show that speech perception is determined by a person's *expectations* (top-down processing) combined with the nature of the *acoustic signal* (bottom-up processing).

Samuel varied the characteristics of the words and phonemes, upon which he superimposed a white noise masking stimulus. (This white noise, which was used instead of the cough in Warren's experiment, was a hiss like the sound produced by a TV set turned to a nonbroadcasting channel.) Samuel found that phonemic restoration is influenced by the length of the word in which the masked phoneme appears and by whether the word is meaningful. The phonemic restoration effect is more likely to occur when the phoneme appears in a long word. The reason for this is that the subject is able to use the additional context provided by the longer word to determine the identity of the masked phoneme. Also supporting the idea that context is important is Samuel's finding that more restoration occurs for a real word like "prOgress" (where the capital letter indicates the masked phoneme) than for a similar "pseudoword" like "crOgress."

But speech perception also depends on the nature of the acoustic signal. Thus, Samuel found that restoration is better if the masking sound and the masked phoneme sound similar. What's happening in phonemic restoration, according to Samuel, is that we use the context to develop some expectation for what a sound will be. But before we actually perceive the sound, its presence must be *confirmed* by the presence of a sound that is similar to it. If the white noise mask has a sound similar to the phoneme we are expecting, we hear it. If the mask does not sound similar, phonemic restoration does not occur.

From the results of the experiments discussed above, we can conclude that speech perception depends both on the bottom-up information provided by the acoustic signal and on the top-down information provided by the meanings of words and sentences. We can appreciate the interdependence of the acoustic and contextual units of speech when we realize that, although we use the context to help us to understand the acoustic signal, the acoustic signal is the starting point for determining the context. Look at it this way: There may be enough information in my sloppy handwriting so that a person can decipher it, using bottom-up processing, solely on the basis of the squiggles on the page; but my handwriting is much easier to decipher if, using top-down processing, the person takes the meanings of the words into account. Speech perception apparently works in a similar way. Although most of the information is contained in the acoustic signal, taking meaning into account makes understanding speech much easier.

Summary

1. A phoneme is the shortest segment which, if changed, would change the meaning of a word.
2. The sound spectrogram, which is a plot of frequency versus time, provides a visual picture of the speech stimulus.
3. The acoustic cue for a phoneme is the specific part of the acoustic signal that is associated with the phoneme. Research in which the frequency pattern on the spectrogram was correlated with specific phonemes seemed to indicate that the acoustic cue for a phoneme can change with context.
4. The production of consonants can be described in terms of phonetic features—physical movements of the vocal tract that accompany the production of phonemes. A particular phoneme can be described by its voicing, place of articulation, and manner of articulation.
5. According to the theory of acoustic invariance, our perception of phonemes is based on information provided by invariant acoustic cues associated with that phoneme. Evidence for the existence of these invariant cues has been provided by experiments using the short-term spectrum and running spectral displays to describe the phoneme's acoustic signal. In addition to invariant acoustic cues, variable information in the acoustic signal may also help us to perceive speech.
6. The idea that speech has its own special processing mechanism was initially supported by the phenomenon of categorical perception, which seemed to be exclusive to speech. Later research, however, showed that categorical perception also occurs for non-speech sounds. Many researchers, therefore, feel that speech is not processed by a special mechanism.
7. The idea that speech perception is determined by detectors that respond to particular phonetic features was initially supported by the results of selective adaptation experiments. Later research, using the phenomenon of audiovisual speech perception, has led to the rejection of this idea. There is evidence, however, that demonstrates parallels between the speech stimulus and the firing of auditory neurons.
8. To understand speech perception we must take into account the fact that in conversational speech there are no breaks between words, and speech is so sloppy that we can only recognize half the words when they are presented alone. The process of segmentation—putting breaks between words—is a top-down process that is aided by our knowledge of the meanings of the words.
9. Sentences are easier to understand if they are semantically and syntactically correct. Making sentences semantically anomalous reduces a listener's ability to identify the words in the sentence correctly, and changing sentences into ungrammatical strings of words by eliminating syntax further decreases the listener's ability to identify the words.
10. The phonemic restoration effect shows that the context in which a phoneme appears can cause us

to hear that phoneme even if its sound is obscured by noise. Research on the phonemic restoration effect shows that speech perception is determined by a person's expectations (top-down processing) combined with the nature of the acoustic signal (bottom-up processing).

Box

1. Infants as young as 1-month old perform similarly to adults in categorical perception experiments. This result suggests that infants may possess mechanisms for detecting speech sounds.

Study Questions

1. What is a phoneme? (447)
2. What is a sound spectrogram? What is plotted on the vertical and horizontal axes of the spectrogram? What does a formant look like on the spectrogram? (448)
3. Define: acoustic cue; invariant acoustic cue. (449)
4. How did researchers at the Haskins Laboratory use the spectrogram to demonstrate the acoustic variability of phonemes? (449)
5. What is a phonetic feature? What is place of articulation? manner of articulation? voicing? (451)
6. What is the theory of acoustic invariance? (452)
7. What is plotted in a short-term spectrum? in a running spectral display? How is the running spectral display used to support the theory of acoustic invariance? (452)
8. What is categorical perception? voice onset time (VOT)? Describe a typical categorical perception experiment. What is the phonetic boundary? How well can a listener discriminate between two sounds on the same and on different sides of the phonetic boundary? (455)
9. Why did the discovery of categorical perception lead the Haskins researchers to conclude that speech is "special"? What evidence argues against this conclusion? (455)
10. Describe Eimas and Corbit's selective adaptation experiments. Why do these experiments support the idea that feature detectors may be involved in the perception of speech? (457)

11. What is audiovisual speech perception? How do the results of Roberts and Summerfield's experiments lead to a reinterpretation of the Eimas and Corbit results? (457)
12. What is the basis for the idea that speech perception is the product of normal auditory mechanisms? (460)
13. Are there boundaries between words in conversational speech? (461)
14. What percentage of words in conversational speech are intelligible when taken from their speech context? (461)
15. What is segmentation? What is the principal factor responsible for segmentation? (462)
16. What is semantics? syntax? shadowing? What do the results of Miller and Isard's experiment tell us about the contribution of context to our understanding of speech? (464)
17. What is the phonemic restoration effect? What does it tell us about speech perception? How do top-down and bottom-up processes contribute to speech perception? (465)

Box

1. Describe Eimas' experiments which show that infants are capable of categorical perception. What does this result tell us about an infant's ability to recognize speech sounds? (458)

Glossary

Acoustic cue. A pattern of frequencies-over-time associated with a particular phoneme. (449)

Acoustic signal. A sound's pattern of frequencies-over-time. (447)

Audiovisual speech perception. A person views a speaker on a videotape in which the accompanying sound track does not match the speaker's lip movements. Audiovisual speech perception refers to the changes in the person's perception of the sound track caused by viewing the speaker's lip movements. (457)

Categorical perception. As voice onset time is changed over a large range, a listener perceives only two discriminable phonemes, one on one side of the phonetic boundary and another on the other side of the phonetic boundary. (454)

Formant. A band of energy, characteristic of vowels, that shows up as a horizontal band on the sound spectrogram. (448)

Formant transition. A rapid shift in frequency immediately preceding a formant. (449)

Invariant acoustic cue. A pattern of frequencies that remains constant when a phoneme appears in different contexts. (449)

Manner of articulation. The mechanical means by which a consonant is produced. (452)

Phoneme. The shortest segment of speech which, if changed, changes the meaning of a word. (447)

Phonemic restoration effect. If a phoneme in a meaningful statement is obscured by noise, the auditory system "fills in" the phoneme so that a listener is not aware that the phoneme is missing. (465)

Phonetic boundary. The voice onset time at which perception abruptly changes from one phoneme to another. A listener cannot tell the difference between two phonemes on the same side of the phonetic boundary, but can tell the difference between two phonemes on opposite sides of the boundary. (455)

Phonetic feature. The physical movements of the vocal tract that accompany the production of each phoneme. (451)

Place of articulation. The place in the airstream obstructed during production of a consonant. (452)

Running spectral display. A series of short-term spectra that indicate the frequencies present in the acoustic signal at a sequence of points in time. (452)

Segmentation. The process of dividing a speech signal into individual words by creating perceptual breaks between each word. (462)

Selective adaptation. In speech, selective adaptation refers to a procedure in which (1) a listener's phonetic boundary is determined, (2) the listener is selectively adapted by being repeatedly exposed to a particular syllable, and (3) the phonetic boundary is redetermined. The selective adaptation procedure, if effective, causes a change in the phonetic boundary. (457)

Semantics. Specifies whether or not it is appropriate to use a word in a sentence, based on the word's meaning. (464)

Shadowing. A procedure in which a listener is asked to repeat a message aloud as he or she hears it. (465)

Short-term spectrum. A display indicating the amount of energy present at each frequency in the acoustic signal over a short period of time. (452)

Sound spectrogram. A display that shows the amount of energy present at different frequencies during the entire time course of a speech stimulus. (448)

Syntax. Specifies which structures of a sentence are allowed. (464)

Theory of acoustic invariance. The idea that our perception of phonemes is based on information provided by invariant acoustic cues associated with that phoneme. (452)

Vocal tract. The pathway along which air travels, from the lungs to the mouth, as speech is produced. (450)

Voice onset time (VOT). The time delay between the beginning of a sound and the beginning of voicing. (455)

Voicing. Refers to the state of the vocal cords during production of a phoneme. Phonemes that cause vibrations of the vocal cord are voiced and phonemes that cause no vibrations are unvoiced. (451)

CHAPTER 14

The Skin and Its Receptors
Receptors and Perception
Neural Processing
Central Influences on Perception
The Role of the Active Observer

The Cutaneous Senses

The skin—the largest receptor surface of any of the senses—is the staging ground for perceptual qualities as varied as touch, warmth, cold, pain, tickle, and itch. This multiplicity of perceptions has led to the use of the term **cutaneous senses** to refer to the many qualities we sense through the skin. This term implies that a number of different *senses* are associated with the skin, a touch (or pressure) sense, a temperature sense, a pain sense, and tickle and itch senses. For our purposes, however, the issue of whether these are distinctly different senses or are simply different qualities sensed through the skin is not important. Our task will be to explain how different types of stimulation elicit this varied array of qualities, focusing on three of these qualities: touch, temperature, and pain.

As is the case for other kinds of perception, we often take the perceptions sensed by the skin for granted. But imagine how your ability to write might change if your hand were anesthetized. Would you know how firmly to grasp your pen if you had no feeling in your hand? Consider, also, all of the other things you do with your hands. How would losing feeling in your hand affect your ability to do these things? We know that a complete loss of our ability to feel with the skin is dangerous, as demonstrated by people who, because of this problem, suffer constant bruises and burns in the absence of

the warnings provided by touch and pain. And consider for a moment what sex would be like without the sense of touch. Or perhaps a better way to put this is to ask if sex without the sense of touch is something people would care about at all.

When we consider that the perceptions we experience through our skin are crucial for protecting ourselves from injury and for motivating sexual activity, we can see that these perceptions are crucial for our survival, and for the survival of our species. We could, in fact, make a good case for the idea that perceptions felt through the skin are as important for survival as those provided by vision and hearing.

One of the purposes of this chapter is to describe some of the special properties of the skin and its receptors. Another purpose is to show that the mechanisms that result in perceptions from stimulation of the skin are similar to the mechanisms that result in perceptions from stimulation of our other senses. We can find parallels between the cutaneous senses and all of our other senses, but to keep things simple our major comparison will be between the cutaneous senses and the sense of vision.

In making this comparison we will see that despite the vast differences in how we *experience* stimulation of the skin and stimulation of the retina, there are many similarities in the underlying

---

B O X   14. 1   /   *Seeing with the Skin*

The person sitting in the chair has her back resting against an array of 400 small vibrators. This person is blind, but by means of this **mechanical substitution system** developed by Paul Bach-y-Rita and co-workers (1969, 1970, 1972; White, Saunders, Seadden, Bach-y-Rita, & Collins, 1970), the person can "see with her skin."

A television camera controlled by the subject takes a picture of the scene, which is translated into signals that control the vibrators in the back of the chair. Light areas of the scene cause more vibration than dark areas. After an initial period of training, subjects can learn to interpret these vibrations as representing simple objects. With further training, subjects can learn to perceive both the identities of objects and their locations relative to each other in space. Subjects are able to determine the locations of objects in space, using information provided by depth cues. For example, subjects learn that vibration higher on the back often corresponds to objects that are farther away (relative height), that the area of

vibration increases as an object moves closer (relative size), and that when the vibration from one object partially obscures the vibration from another, the object with part of its vibration covered is farther away (overlap).

That subjects could tell that one object overlapped another means that they segregated the vibrations representing the foreground object from those representing the object in the background. In addition to being able to identify single objects and make depth judgments, some subjects can "see" remarkable details, as indicated by the following statements from an experienced subject: "That is Betty; she is wearing her hair down today and does not have her glasses on. Her mouth is open, and she is moving her right hand from her left side to the back of her head." This impressive demonstration of the skin's ability to "see" has led to work on more portable "mechanical substitution systems" that could be used by a blind person as he or she walks through the environment.

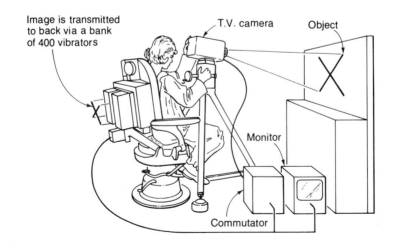

Image is transmitted to back via a bank of 400 vibrators

T.V. camera

Object

Monitor

Commutator

mechanisms. We will consider these similarities under four headings: (1) receptors and perception; (2) neural processing; (3) central influences; and (4) the role of the active observer. In each case, we will begin by briefly reviewing the relevant visual phenomena and will then consider the analogous phenomena and mechanisms for the skin. However, before we begin these comparisons, we need to briefly describe the skin and its receptors.

THE SKIN AND ITS RECEPTORS

When you look at your skin you see the skin's outer layer, the **epidermis,** which is actually several layers of tough dead skin cells. Hairy skin covers most of the body, but hairless (glabrous) skin (Figure 14.1) is found on the fingers and palms of the hands, and on the toes and soles of the feet. Both hairy and glabrous skin serve a number of functions. Skin protects us by keeping dirt and moisture from penetrating our bodies while at the same time allowing sweat to escape to help the body maintain its proper temperature.

Another function of the skin—the one we are concerned with—is to provide information about the various stimuli that contact it. The sun's rays heat our skin and we feel warm; a cold wind causes us to shiver; a pinprick hurts us, and a backrub feels great. To understand how these perceptions originate, we must look at the skin's inner layer, the **dermis,** which contains numerous nerve endings and receptors, some of which are shown in Figure 14.2. Nineteenth-century anatomists gave names to the wide variety of receptor structures found in the skin. Figure 14.2 shows some of the more important ones: The **Ruffini endings, Krause end bulbs, Pacinian corpuscles, Merkel discs,** and **Meissner corpuscles** are all specialized end organs that surround the ends of nerve fibers. In addition, there are **free nerve endings,** nerve fibers with no end receptor, that are wrapped around the bases of hairs and are also found elsewhere in the dermis.

Nerve fibers travel from the skin to synapse in the spinal cord, in which they travel to the

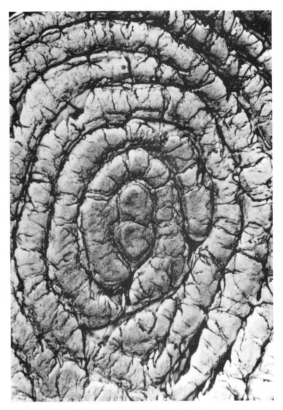

F I G U R E 14. 1 Scanning electron micrograph of the hairless skin on the tip of the finger, magnified 27 times. (From Shih & Kessell, 1982.)

sensory area of the thalamus at the base of the brain. (Remember that visual and auditory neurons also synapse in the thalamus.) From the thalamus, fibers travel to the **somatosensory area** in the parietal lobe of the cortex (see Figure 2.9). As we will see later, signals from different parts of the body reach specific locations in the somatosensory cortex.

RECEPTORS AND PERCEPTION

Let's return for a moment to the discussion at the beginning of this book in which we considered the role of the visual receptors in perception. One of the main messages of Chapter 3 was that much of

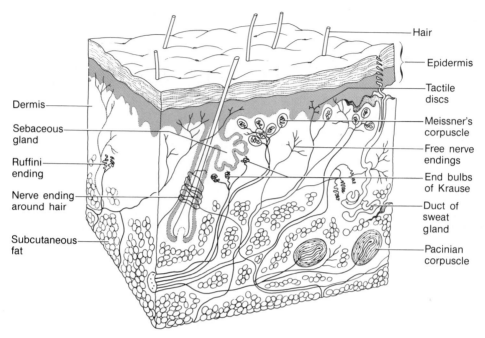

FIGURE 14.2 A cross section of the skin, showing the layers of the skin and some of the receptors in the dermis layer. (From Gardner, 1975.)

our visual experience can be traced to the properties of the rod and cone receptors. Since rod visual pigments absorb light best at short wavelengths, we see best at short wavelengths when the rods are active. Since cone visual pigments regenerate more rapidly than rod visual pigments in the dark, cone vision increases its sensitivity much more rapidly than rod vision during dark adaptation. In addition, the rods' extensive convergence makes them more sensitive than the cones when dark adapted, and the cones' small amount of convergence makes them able to detect fine details better than the rods.

The receptors, as the initial elements in any sensory system, have the potential to play an important role in determining our perceptions. This is certainly the case in vision and, as we will see, for the cutaneous senses. To begin our discussion of this connection between cutaneous receptors and perception, let's look at evidence for a number of different types of receptors in the skin.

Cutaneous Receptor Types

One way to differentiate between different types of cutaneous receptors is on the basis of their structure. It has, however, been more profitable to differentiate between cutaneous receptors by recording from their nerve fibers and determining how these fibers respond to different types of stimuli. Using this procedure, it has been possible to differentiate three classes of cutaneous receptors: (1) mechanoreceptors, (2) thermoreceptors, and (3) nociceptors.

Mechanoreceptors. **Mechanoreceptors** respond to indentation of the skin. There are two kinds of mechanoreceptors, **rapidly adapting (RA) mechanoreceptors** and **slowly adapting (SA) mechanoreceptors.*** RA receptors respond only as pressure

---

*There are also a number of subtypes of mechanoreceptors under these two broad classes. See Burgess and Perl (1973) and Iggo (1982) for descriptions of these subtypes.

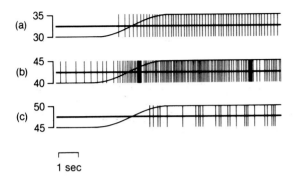

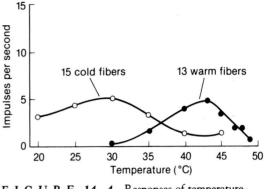

F I G U R E 14. 3 The response of a "warm" fiber in the monkey. Record A indicates that the fiber does not fire at a temperature of 30°C, but as the temperature is increased to 35°C (indicated by the sloping line), the firing rate increases, and the fiber continues to fire when the temperature is held at 35°C. Record B shows a large increase in firing when the temperature is increased from 40 to 45, but record C shows only a small response to an increase from 45 to 50. (From Duclaux & Kenshalo, 1980.)

F I G U R E 14. 4 Responses of temperature-sensitive fibers in the monkey to constant temperatures. The curve on the left (open circles) shows the average response of a group of 15 "cold" fibers that respond best at about 30°C. The curve on the right (filled circles) shows the average response of a group of 13 "warm" fibers that respond best at about 44°C. (From Kenshalo, 1976.)

indents the skin, and generally fire more rapidly to faster velocities of indentation. These receptors adapt rapidly and cease responding when constant pressure is applied to the skin. SA receptors also respond to stimulus indentation but, unlike RA receptors, continue responding to steady indentation.

Thermoreceptors. **Thermoreceptors** respond to specific temperatures and to changes in temperature. There are two kinds of thermoreceptors: warm receptors and cold receptors. Figure 14.3 shows how a **warm fiber** responds to increases in temperature. This neuron is typical of warm fibers since (1) it increases its firing rate when the temperature is increased—firing most rapidly during an increase from 40 to 45 degrees C, (2) it continues to fire as long as the higher temperature is kept on, (3) it decreases its firing rate when the temperature is decreased, and (4) it does not respond to mechanical stimulation (Kenshalo, 1976; Duclaux & Kenshalo, 1980). **Cold fibers,** on the other hand, increase their firing rate when the temperature is

decreased and continue to fire at low temperatures. The different ways that cold and warm fibers respond to steady temperatures are shown in Figure 14.4. Cold fibers respond in the 20–45 degree C range, with the best response at about 30 degrees. Warm fibers respond in the 30–48 degree range, with the best response at about 44 degrees.

Nociceptors. **Nociceptors** respond to stimulation such as intense pressure, high heat, or burning chemicals that can potentially damage the skin. Figure 14.5 shows the response of a cat's nociceptor, which begins firing when the temperature reaches about 45°C, the same temperature at which a human begins to feel pain (Beck, Handwerker, & Zimmerman, 1974; Zimmerman, 1979).

We will now ask two important questions about these different types of receptors: (1) Is there a relationship between these receptor *types* and the different receptor *structures* found in the skin? and (2) What is the connection between these receptor types and *perception*? Let's consider each of these questions.

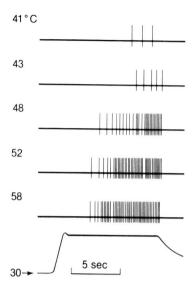

41°C

43

48

52

58

30→   5 sec

F I G U R E   14. 5   The response of a "nociceptor" in the cat to heating of the skin. This fiber begins firing at temperatures above about 45°C and reaches maximum firing rates above about 55°C. (From Beck et al., 1974.)

Is There a Relationship Between Receptor Type and Structure?

Though it has been possible to classify cutaneous receptors based on how they respond to stimuli, it has not always been possible to match these differing responses to specific end organs in the skin. For example, we cannot say whether specific end organs are associated with thermoreceptors or nociceptors. We do know that Pacinian and Meissner corpuscles are RA mechanoreceptors (with the

Pacinian corpuscle responding best to rapid vibration and the Meissner corpuscle responding best to slower movement). And we know that Merkle cells and Ruffini endings are SA mechanoreceptors (Iggo & Andres, 1982; Iggo, 1982).

However, the important fact for our purposes is not to know which end organ goes with which type of response but, rather, to understand how properties of an end organ can influence a fiber's response. Do end organs have properties that determine how their nerve fibers respond? If we could exchange the end organs on two different fibers, would that change the stimuli to which the fibers respond best? Based on the results of research on the Pacinian corpuscle, we can conclude that the answer to each of these questions is "yes": It does appear that properties of the end organs do influence the types of stimuli "preferred" by a nerve fiber.

The Pacinian corpuscle, shown in Figure 14.6, has been studied extensively because of its distinctive elliptical shape (which makes it easy to identify), its large size (about 1 mm long and 0.6 mm thick), and its accessibility (it is found in the skin, muscles, tendons, and joints, and also in the cat's mesentery, a readily accessible membrane attached to the intestine, from which Pacinian corpuscles can easily be removed).

By taking into account the physical properties of the corpuscle, Werner Lowenstein and R. Skalak (1966) were able to calculate how a push on the corpuscle at A (Figure 14.6) is translated into pressure on the nerve fiber at B. They found that the Pacinian corpuscle modifies the pressure stim-

Push at A

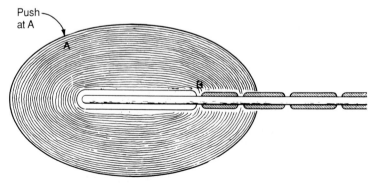

F I G U R E   14. 6   A Pacinian corpuscle. (From Lowenstein, 1960.)

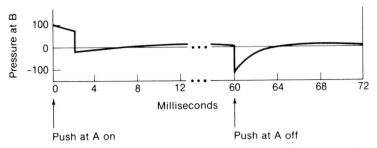

F I G U R E 14. 7 Record of the pressure at B in the Pacinian corpuscle of Figure 14.6 caused by pushing the corpuscle at A. (From Lowenstein & Skalak, 1966.)

ulus on its way to the nerve fiber, so that a push at A causes the pressure to change at B only at the beginning or end of the push. According to their calculations, continuing to push with constant pressure should cause no effect at B. So as far as the nerve fiber is concerned, no stimulus is present until the pressure at A is released, at which time a brief change occurs in the pressure at B. Their prediction, therefore, was that the Pacinian corpuscle transmits pressure to the nerve fiber when the stimulus is applied or removed, but it does not transmit pressure that is continuous. Thus, the effect of the corpuscle on the nerve fiber should be to cause it to fire only when the stimulus is applied or removed.

To check their prediction, Lowenstein and Skalak measured the response of the nerve fiber under two conditions: (1) when the corpuscle was dissected away so pressure could be applied directly to the nerve fiber, and (2) when the corpuscle remained so pressure could be applied to the corpuscle. Their results were exactly as predicted in their calculations; when pressure was applied directly to the fiber, it responded when the pressure was first applied, during the time the pressure continued, and when the pressure was removed. However, when pressure was applied to the intact corpuscle, the fiber responded only when the pressure was first applied and when it was removed. Thus, the presence of the Pacinian corpuscle critically affects how the nerve fiber fires and endows its nerve fiber with the properties of an RA mechanoreceptor—a receptor that adapts rapidly to constant stimulation and, therefore, responds poorly to sustained pressure on the skin.

Is There a Relationship Between Receptor Type and Perception?

So far we have focused on the stimuli to which cutaneous fibers respond. But what about perception? Does the firing of a particular type of fiber result in a particular perception?

The 19th-century physiologist Max von Frey thought it was possible to match specific end organs with specific perceptions. Between 1894 and 1895 he published a series of papers in which he proposed that stimulation of the Ruffini endings was responsible for the sensation of warmth, the Krause end bulbs for cold, the Meissner corpuscles for touch, and the free nerve endings for pain (Figure 14.8).

Supporting evidence for von Frey's idea was supplied by experiments in which **sensory spots** were mapped on the skin by applying stimuli to very small spots and noting the resulting sensations. The results for cold and warm stimuli are shown in Figure 14.9. Stimulation with cold results in the sensations of cold at the locations shown by

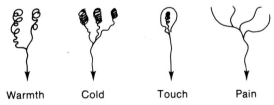

Warmth   Cold   Touch   Pain

F I G U R E 14. 8 Max von Frey (1894) proposed that the perceptions of warmth, cold, touch, and pain could be linked to stimulation of specific receptor end organs. This idea was not, however, confirmed by later experiments.

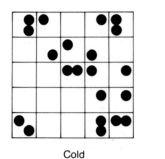
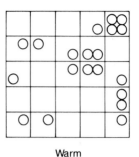

Cold   Warm

F I G U R E 14. 9 Cold and warm sensory spots on the skin. (From Dallenbach, 1927.)

the filled circles, while stimulation with heat results in the sensation of warmth at the locations shown by the open circles. Note that the cold and warm spots do not usually overlap and that many spots on the skin result in neither cold nor warm sensations. Similar results are obtained for touch and pain stimuli. Von Frey interpreted these results to mean that specialized receptors must be located under each sensory spot: Krause end bulbs should be found under cold spots, Ruffini endings under warm spots, and so on.

Von Frey's hypothesis, however, did not withstand the test of further experimentation. Later investigators mapped sensory spots on their skin and then dissected the skin (ouch!) to see which receptors are located under each spot (Burgess & Perl, 1973). These experiments found little correlation between the type of sensory spot and the receptor structure located under it. In fact, Krause end bulbs and Ruffini endings rarely have been found under cold or warm spots. Additional evidence that argued against von Frey's theory was provided by P. P. Lele and G. Weddell (1956), who showed that stimulation of the cornea of the eye, which contains only free nerve endings, can result in all four of von Frey's primary sensations.

Though von Frey's proposed linkages between specific *receptor end organs* and perception was not correct, linkages have been proposed, based on modern data, which suggest linkages between specific *receptor types* and perception. It has, for example, been proposed that since nociceptors respond only to stimuli that cause tissue damage, they are

responsible for our perception of pain. It is also likely that thermoreceptors are important for our perception of temperature, and since Pacinian corpuscles respond best to rapidly changing stimuli, they may be responsible for our perception of vibration.

You may recognize von Frey's proposal, as well as the proposed modern links between receptor types and perception, as a form of *specificity theory*—the idea that the sensory code for specific perceptions is the firing of specific nerve fibers (see Chapter 2, p. 52). The finding that most cutaneous fibers respond best to a specific kind of stimulus does support specificity theory. However, the fact that most stimuli elicit responses from a number of different types of fibers means that specificity is not the entire answer to coding in the cutaneous system. Consider, for example, what happens when we touch the skin. Touching the skin activates a number of receptor types: (1) bending hairs activates RA mechanoreceptors that are connected to hair cells, (2) indentation of the skin with some velocity activates other RA mechanoreceptors, and (3) sustained pressure activates SA mechanoreceptors. Thus, a number of different fibers fire in response to a touch—each one signaling a different aspect of the stimulus (Figure 14.10). Or consider what happens when a potentially damaging stimulus is applied to the skin. Nociceptors fire most vigorously to such a stimulus, but mechanoreceptors and thermoreceptors may also fire, though at a lower rate. Even though the major pain signal may come from the nociceptor, it is likely that the

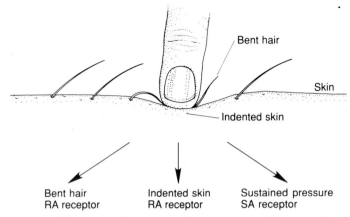

FIGURE 14. 10 An object pushing on hairy skin activates a number of different types of receptors.

firing of these other receptors also contributes in some way to the quality of the pain experienced (Iggo, 1982).

Thus, though fibers may respond best to specific stimuli, a number of these specific fibers are probably activated by a particular stimulus. Sensory quality on the skin is, therefore, probably determined by the firing *pattern* of numerous fibers that respond best to *specific* stimuli. This suggested combination of specificity and pattern theories is analogous to our conclusion in Chapter 2, that to precisely specify a stimulus the visual system must consider the overall pattern of firing of a large number of fairly specific feature detectors (see p. 53).

NEURAL PROCESSING

Now that we have considered the role of the receptors in cutaneous perception, let's consider how the signals from the receptors are processed by the nervous system. In Chapters 2 and 3 we saw that neural convergence endows every nerve fiber with a *receptive field*—an area on the retina that, when stimulated, changes the fiber's firing rate. We saw that the addition of inhibition creates the center-surround receptive fields (see Figure 2.19) of retinal and lateral geniculate neurons and creates the sim-

ple, complex, and hypercomplex receptive fields of cortical neurons. As we describe the receptive field properties of cutaneous neurons, we will see that these receptive fields share many properties with the receptive fields of visual neurons.

Receptive Fields on the Skin

Figure 14.11 shows the receptive field of a neuron in the monkey's thalamus that receives signals from receptors in the skin of the monkey's arm. This is

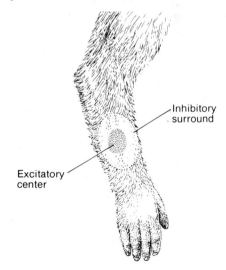

FIGURE 14. 11 An excitatory center, inhibitory-surround receptive field on a monkey's arm.

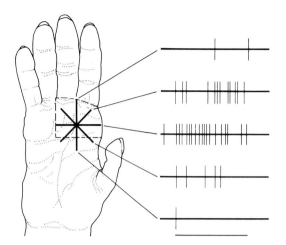

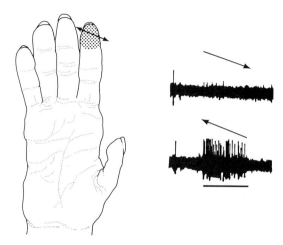

FIGURE 14.12 The receptive field of a neuron in the monkey's parietal cortex that responds when a metal edge is placed on the hand. This cell responds well when the edge is oriented horizontally but responds less well to other orientations. (From Hyvärinen & Poranen, 1978.)

FIGURE 14.13 The receptive field of a neuron in the monkey's parietal cortex which responds to movement across the fingertip from right to left but does not respond to movement from left to right. (From Hyvärinen & Poranen, 1978.)

an excitatory-center, inhibitory-surround receptive field similar to the center-surround receptive fields of visual neurons in the retina and lateral geniculate nucleus (Mountcastle & Powell, 1959). (Remember that the receptive field of a cutaneous nerve fiber is *always* on the receptor surface—in this case, the skin.)

If we move up to the cortex, we find neurons that respond to more specialized stimulation of the skin. Figures 14.12 and 14.13 show the receptive fields of neurons in the monkey's somatosensory cortex in the parietal lobe; these are quite similar to the receptive fields of simple and complex cells in the visual cortex. The cell in Figure 14.12 responds to a metal edge oriented horizontally but responds less well to other orientations. Figure 14.13 shows a cell that responds to movement across the skin in a specified direction (Hyvarinin & Poranen, 1978; see also Whitsel, Roppolo, & Werner, 1972; Costanzo & Gardner, 1980). In Chapter 8 we proposed a neural circuit to explain how visual neurons could respond selectively to movement in one direction (see Figure 8.9). It is likely that a similar type of circuit is behind the firing of cutaneous neurons like the one in Figure 14.13.

The similarity between these neurons and neurons in the visual system is striking. In both vision and touch, neurons near the receptors respond to a wide range of stimuli, whereas neurons in the cortex respond only to more specific stimuli. Similar principles of information processing apparently operate for both of these senses.

One of the more exciting developments in the physiology of touch is the recent finding that some cells in the monkey cortex respond only when the monkey grasps three-dimensional objects with specific shapes. These experiments, carried out in awake, behaving monkeys with implanted electrodes, have uncovered neurons like the one in Figure 14.14, which does not respond when the experimenter stimulates the skin, but does respond when the monkey grasps certain objects. This cell responds when the monkey grasps a ruler or a block of wood but does not respond if the monkey grasps a cylinder. The cell in Figure 14.15, on the other hand, responds when the monkey grasps round objects but not when it grasps objects with straight edges. Neurons like these may play a role in what has been called active touch—touch in which the subject plays an active role in searching out and

B O X 14. 2. / *Lateral Inhibition on the Skin*

Lateral inhibition, which plays such an important role in determining the nature of electrophysiologically determined receptive fields on both the retina (p. 43) and the skin (p. 477), has been demonstrated psychophysically on the skin by Georg von Békésy (1958, 1959, 1967).

The procedure for this demonstration is simple: two small pointers attached to fine hairs are touched to the skin, as shown on the hand at the top of the figure. The points stimulated on the skin are separated by different distances, by varying the separation between the pointers, and the observer is asked to describe the distribution of the pressure sensation at each separation.

The results of this experiment, shown to the right of the hand, indicate that the observer feels a single pressure distribution both when a single hair is pushed into the skin and at separations of 1.5, 2.0, and 2.5 cm. When the two hairs are separated by 3.0 cm, however, the perceived pressure distribution splits in two and is greatly decreased in magnitude. When the separation between the hairs is increased further, to 3.5 cm, the perceived pressure grows so that each point is perceived to be similar to the pressure resulting from the single stimulation.

The large decrease in sensation at the 3.0-cm separation is due to lateral inhibition. We can understand how this works by looking at diagrams (a), (b), and (c). Diagram (a) shows that pressing on the skin causes an area of excitation near the point of stimulation, and an area of inhibition surrounding the area of excitation. Diagram (b) shows what happens when two points are separated by 3.0 cm. At this separation, the inhibitory areas fall under the excitatory areas and subtract from the excitation, causing a decrease in the sensation of pressure. When the separation between the two points is increased above 3.0 cm, as shown in (c), the inhibitory

areas no longer subtract from the excitatory areas, and the sensation of pressure increases. Thus, the perception of pressure on your skin depends on two things: (1) the excitation that surrounds the point of stimulation and (2) the lateral inhibition that surrounds this excitation.

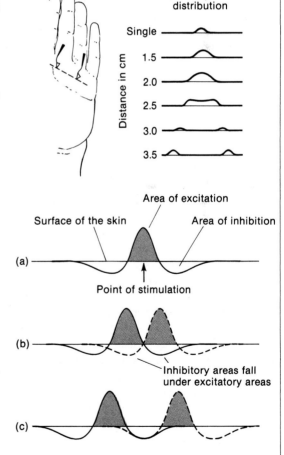

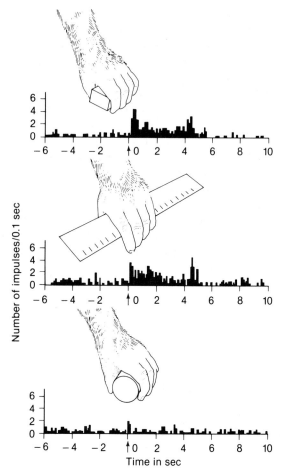

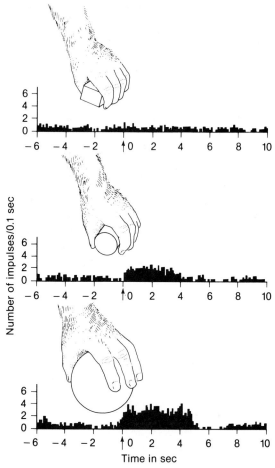

F I G U R E 14. 14 The response of a neuron in a monkey's parietal cortex that fires when the monkey grasps a rectangular block or a ruler, but does not fire when the monkey grasps a cylinder. The neuron's rate of firing is indicated by the height of the bars. The monkey grasps the objects at time = 0. (From Sakata & Iwamura, 1978.)

F I G U R E 14. 15 The response of a neuron in a monkey's parietal cortex that fires when the monkey grasps a cylinder or a ball, but does not fire when the monkey grasps a rectangular block. (From Sakata & Iwamura, 1978.)

touching stimuli. We will consider some of the psychophysical aspects of active touch at the end of this chapter.

The Relation Between Physiology and Cutaneous Acuity

In Chapter 3 we saw that differences in neural processing between the rod and cone receptors can explain differences in rod and cone *visual acuity*.

Visual acuity—the ability to detect fine details—is sharpest when an object is imaged on the fovea, the area of the retina that contains only cones. One reason for the foveal cones' greater visual acuity is that they are densely packed in this area, creating a fine "grain." Another reason is that signals from the foveal cones show little convergence onto other neurons. The highly converging rod system, on the other hand, sends signals from many receptors to a single neuron, thereby limiting the rod system's ability to resolve details.

Just as there is an area of retina that has higher acuity than other areas, there are areas on the skin that have higher acuity than others. We can demonstrate this by measuring acuity on different areas of the body. We measure this acuity by determining the **two-point threshold**—the smallest separation between two points on the skin that is perceived as two points.

DEMONSTRATION

Comparing Two-Point Thresholds

Hold two pencils side by side, so that their points are about 12 mm (½ inch) apart; then touch both points simultaneously to the tip of your thumb and see if you feel two points. If you feel only one, increase the distance between the pencil points until you feel two; then note the distance between them. Now move the pencil points to the underside of your forearm. With the points about 12 mm apart (or at the smallest separation you felt as two points on your thumb), touch them to your forearm and note whether you feel one point or two. If you feel only one, how much must you increase the separation before you feel two? If your results match those from the laboratory, you will find that the two-point threshold on your forearm is much larger than the two-point threshold on your thumb. Figure 14.16, which shows how the two-point threshold varies at different parts of the body, indicates that the two-point threshold is over 10 times smaller on the forearm than on the thumb. This result, therefore, is analogous to the results for the visual system. Areas that are responsible for making fine

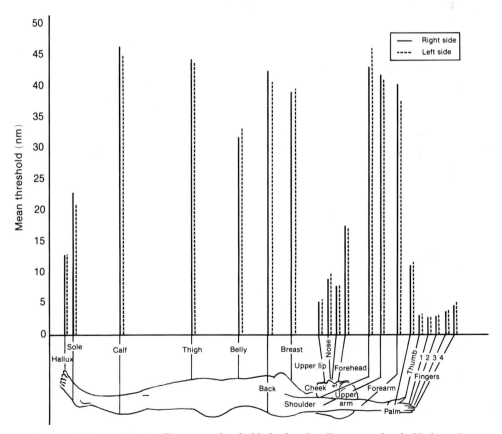

F I G U R E 14. 16 Two-point thresholds for females. Two-point thresholds for males follow the same pattern. (From Weinstein in D. R. Kenshalo (ed.) *The Skin Senses*, 1968. Courtesy of Charles C. Thomas, Publisher, Springfield, Ill.)

spatial discriminations—the fovea for vision and the fingers for touch—have high acuity, whereas other areas have lower acuity.

We can see a relationship between the two-point threshold and physiology by using the technique of **microneurography** (see Chapter 2, page 58), which allows us to record the activity of a single neuron in the skin of an awake human. Using this technique, A. B. Vallbo and R. S. Johansson (1978) determined the receptive fields of neurons that are connected to receptors in the hand and fingers. Some receptive fields were small, like those in Figure 14.17(a), and others were large, like those in Figure 14.17(b). Vallbo and Johansson found a higher density of small receptive fields on the fingertips than on the hand—exactly what we would expect, since the two-point threshold is smaller on the fingertips than on the hand. In fact, Vallbo and Johansson found a direct relationship between the size of the two-point threshold and the density of neurons with small receptive fields (Figure 14.18). Parts of the body with small two-point thresholds also have small receptive fields.

This relation between cutaneous acuity and physiology observed in neurons in the skin is trans-

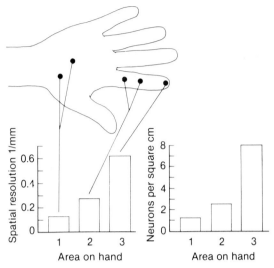

FIGURE 14. 18   Left: The bar graph shows the spatial resolution at three places on the hand and fingers. Spatial resolution, which is determined by taking the inverse of the two-point threshold (so a small two-point threshold results in high spatial resolution), increases as we move from the hand to the fingertip. Right: The density of neurons with small receptive fields at the same three locations. These data indicate that areas that have high spatial resolution have high densities of neurons with small receptive fields. (From Vallbo and Johansson, 1978.)

lated into a dramatic relationship between acuity and the space on the cortex devoted to different areas of the body, a relationship that is similar to the situation in the visual system. Remember our discussion on pages 97–98 of the *magnification factor* in vision. We saw that each part of the retina is not represented by an equal area on the visual cortex. The fovea is represented by a cortical area far out of proportion to its size. The area of visual cortex devoted to the fovea is *magnified* to provide the extra neural processing needed to perceive the fine details of objects imaged on the fovea.

We can show that there is a similar situation in the cutaneous system by measuring the area on the cortex that corresponds to each area of the body. When we do this we see that for each point on the skin there is a corresponding point or small area on the surface of the somatosensory cortex,

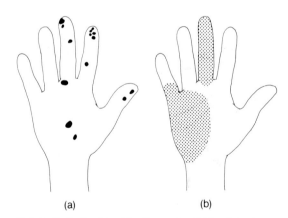

(a)   (b)

FIGURE 14. 17   Receptive fields of single neurons in the human that are sensitive to touch. A number of small receptive fields are shown in (a) and two large receptive fields are shown in (b). (From Vallbo & Johansson, 1978.)

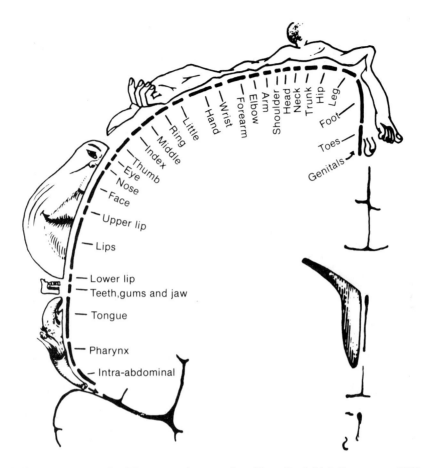

Labels in figure: Little, Ring, Middle, Index, Thumb, Eye, Nose, Face, Upper lip, Lips, Lower lip, Teeth,gums and jaw, Tongue, Pharynx, Intra-abdominal, Hand, Wrist, Forearm, Elbow, Arm, Shoulder, Head, Neck, Trunk, Hip, Leg, Foot, Toes, Genitals

F I G U R E 14. 19   The sensory homunculus. (From Penfield & Rasmussen, 1950.)

as shown in Figure 14.19. This strangely shaped representation of a person on the cortex is called a **homunculus,** for "little man." Let's first describe how the homunculus is determined and then relate this strange-looking little man to the two-point threshold.

One way to chart the shape of the homunculus is by surgically placing a recording electrode on the brain and then stimulating small points on the body to locate the area which, when stimulated, causes electrical activity under the electrode. This method, called the **evoked potential** method, was used by Clinton Woolsey, Wade Marshall, and Philip Bard (1942) to determine the body map on the cortex of the rhesus monkey. By gently stroking the monkey with a camel's hair brush and recording the evoked potentials from the cortex,

they created a map similar to the one for the human in Figure 14.19. However, the evoked potential method is very time consuming, requiring 15–40 minutes for each of the many locations on the brain, and is therefore difficult to use with humans. Thus, for humans, the relationship between points on the brain and points on the body was determined by applying a mild shock to a small area of the brain and asking the person to describe where he or she felt a sensation.

The people who allowed their brains to be electrically stimulated to produce Figure 14.19 were patients of neurosurgeons Wilder Penfield and Theodore Rasmussen (1950). Penfield and Rasmussen were operating on these patients to remove brain tumors suspected of causing epileptic seizures. A major problem in this surgery is to remove the tumor without damaging the sensory or motor areas of the brain, which are located right next to each other on either side of the central fissure (see Figure 2.9). Damage to the sensory area would cause a loss of sensation from a part of the body, and damage to the motor area would cause paralysis. Before removing the tumor, therefore, it is necessary to map the sensory and motor areas of the brain in each patient.

The mapping of the sensory and motor areas is done by opening the skull under local anesthesia and stimulating the surface of the brain with low-voltage electricity. The person experiences a sensation such as tingling, tickling, or numbness on a body part when stimulation is applied to the sensory area of the cortex, and he or she moves some body part when stimulation is applied to the motor area of the cortex. Only a local anesthetic is used because the patient must be awake to report the location and type of sensation or muscle contraction resulting from stimulation. Since the anesthesia is applied where the skull is cut and since there are no pain receptors in the brain itself, the patient feels no pain when the brain is stimulated.

Our homunculus of Figure 14.19, the result of numerous operations performed over a 20-year period, shows that some areas on the skin are represented by a disproportionately large area on the brain. The area devoted to the thumb, for example, is as large as the area devoted to the entire forearm. As with the magnification factor for foveal vision, the apparent overrepresentation of various body parts on the sensory cortex is related to the functioning of these areas. By comparing Figures 14.19 and 14.16, we can note the close relationship between the two-point threshold on the skin and the cortical representation of the skin: Areas on the skin with small two-point thresholds are represented by large areas on the cortex. Thus, the map of the body on the brain may look distorted, but the distortions provide the extra neural processing that enables us to accurately sense fine details with our fingers and other parts of the body.

Before leaving our discussion of the homunculus, we should note that recent experiments, in which the homunculus was determined by recording from single neurons in the brains of monkeys,

indicate that there is actually more than one map of the body on the brain. R. J. Nelson and coworkers (1980) found that there are at least two, and probably four, separate maps of the monkey's body in the sensory area of its brain. The apparent reason for these multiple representations is that different areas within the sensory cortex have different functions. For example, one area might be specialized for the discrimination of forms and another for the discrimination of textures. Whatever their function, these multiple maps of the body on the brain exhibit the same distortions as our simple homunculus in Figure 4.20—areas of the body that discriminate fine details are allotted large areas on the cortex.

CENTRAL INFLUENCES ON PERCEPTION

We have considered the somatosensory cortex twice in this chapter—first to show that there are central neurons that respond to specific orientations and directions of movement on the skin, and second to show that the homunculus is distorted to correspond to the acuity of different areas on the skin. In both cases, these properties of the cortex reflect the neural processing that occurs as nerve signals travel from the skin to the cortex and the neural processing that occurs in the cortex itself. In this section we are going to consider not the signals that travel toward the cortex or within the cortex but, rather, the signals that the cortex sends back *toward* the skin. We will see that far from being only a receiver of signals from "below," the somatosensory cortex can send out its own signals to influence the neural messages that reach it.

Before considering the neural evidence for this idea, let's discuss some psychophysical observations relevant to this cortical "feedback." These observations show that our perception of pain can be affected by factors other than the stimulation of pain receptors in the skin. Pain can also be affected by factors such as the general situation in which the pain stimulus occurs, and by the person's culture and previous experiences. If this sounds familiar, it is because we have encountered similar

B O X 14. 3. / *Kinesthesis*

Where are your arms right now? your legs? Are you moving part of your body? Your ability to answer these questions attests to the existence of **kinesthesis**—the ability to feel the motions and positions of our limbs and body. We owe this ability to receptors located in the joints. Esther Gardner and Richard Costanzo (1981) have measured the responses of neurons in the soma-tosensory cortex in the monkey's parietal lobe that receive inputs from these joint receptors. They found three different types of **kinesthetic neurons:**

(1) Rapidly-adapting neurons. These neurons respond only when a limb is moved in a particular direction. Some fire when the limb is flexed and others fire when the limb is extended. The higher the velocity of movement the better the firing.

(2) Slowly-adapting neurons. These neurons respond when a limb is moving *and* when the limb is held in a static position. The size of these responses to static position depends on the limb's state of extension and flexion, with larger responses being generated by greater exten-sions and flexions.

(3) Neurons that fire maximally to maintained limb positions. These neurons are called **posi-tional neurons** because they fire best to static position rather than to movement.

Most of the above neurons respond to the movement of a particular joint. In addition, how-ever, Costanzo and Gardner (1981) also found **multiple-joint neurons** that respond best to the flexion of a number of joints. For example, the figure below shows that one of these neurons responds to flexion of the wrist (a) but responds even better to combined flexion of the wrist and fingers (b). These neurons are concerned more with postural information than with movement.

These recordings from single neurons show that information about the positioning and movement of our joints is transmitted to neurons in the parietal cortex. We can imagine the mas-sive amount of information provided by these neurons when we consider that there are over 60 joints in our body, all of which must be sending information to the cortex regarding their position and movement. But kinesthesis is more than sim-ply our ability to sense joint position and veloc-ity. It also enables us to sense a picture of our entire body in space. Thus, we not only need to know the position of each joint, but where each one is *relative to the others*. In other words, the information from single joints must be *integrated* to create an image of the position of the body as a whole. The multiple-joint neurons, which receive inputs from groups of joints, may help accomplish this integration.

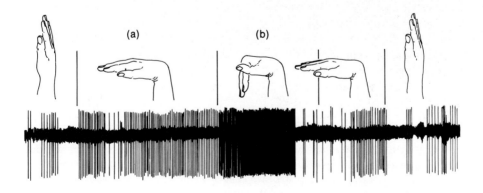

(a)   (b)

observations for the sense of vision. Remember the idea of *top-down processing* from Chapter 6 (p. 217)—the idea that our knowledge of the world can influence our visual perceptions (see also page 465 for examples of top-down processing in hearing). For example, consider the rat–man demonstration of Figure 1.13. By first presenting the picture in Figure 1.13, we cause people to perceive Figure 1.17 as a rat, whereas first presenting Figure 1.18 causes people to perceive it as a man. This demonstration, and many others, show that our visual perceptions can be affected by more than simply how our receptors are stimulated. Let's consider evidence that this also occurs for the perception of pain.

The Effect of Culture and Experience on Pain Perception

The effect of culture on pain perception is most graphically demonstrated by rituals such as the hook-swinging ceremony practiced in some parts of India (Kosambi, 1967). This ritual is described as follows by Ronald Melzak (1973) in his highly readable book *The Puzzle of Pain.*

The ceremony derives from an ancient practice in which a member of a social group is chosen to represent the power of the gods. The role of the chosen man (or "cel-ebrant") is to bless the children and crops in a series of neighboring villages during a particular period of the year. What is remarkable about the ritual is that steel hooks, which are attached by strong ropes to the top of a special cart, are shoved under his skin and muscles on both sides of his back [Figure 14.20]. The cart is then moved from village to village. Usually the man hangs on to the ropes as the cart is moved about. But at the climax of the ceremony in each village, he swings free, hanging only from the hooks embedded in his back, to bless the children and crops. Astonishingly, there is no evidence that the man is in pain during the ritual; rather, he appears to be in a "state of exaltation." When the hooks are later removed, the wounds heal rapidly without any medical treatment other than the application of wood ash. Two weeks later the marks on his back are scarcely visible.

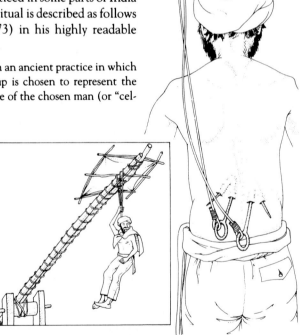

F I G U R E 14. 20 Top: Two steel hooks in the back of the "celebrant" of the Indian hook-swinging ceremony. Bottom: The celebrant hangs onto the ropes as a cart takes him from village to village. After he blesses each child and farm field in the village he swings freely, suspended by the hooks in his back. (From Kosambi, 1967.)

It seems unbelievable that a person could feel little or no pain while hanging from steel hooks embedded in his back, but this is apparently what happens during the hook-swinging ceremony. Perhaps the ceremony has some effect on the celebrant's mental state that prevents him from feeling pain. There are, in fact, many examples of situations in which a person's mental state affects pain perception. For example, H. K. Beecher (1972) found that morphine reduces pathologically produced pain that is accompanied by anxiety but doesn't reduce experimentally produced pain that is unaccompanied by anxiety. "Thus," according to Beecher, "we can state a new principle of drug action: some agents are effective only in the presence of a required mental state."

Further evidence that a person's mental state affects his or her perception of pain is provided by Beecher's observation that 25 percent of men seriously wounded in battle requested a narcotic for pain relief, whereas over 80 percent of civilians about to undergo major surgery requested pain relief. The difference in these percentages can be traced to the mental states of the patients. The civilians were upset about their surgical wounds because they associated these wounds with disturbing health problems. The soldiers, on the other hand, were not upset about their battle wounds because they knew that their wounds would provide escape from a hazardous battlefield to the safety of a behind-the-lines hospital.

In a hospital study, when surgical patients were told what to expect and were instructed to relax to alleviate their pain, they requested fewer pain killers following surgery and were sent home 2.7 days earlier than patients who were not given this information. Studies have also shown that up to 35 percent of patients with pathological pain get relief from taking a **placebo,** a pill which they believe contains pain killers but which, in fact, contains no active ingredients (Weisenberg, 1977).

The above examples indicate that just as visual perception is affected by central influences, so is pain perception. Although we have few clues regarding the neural mechanisms responsible for these central effects in vision, we do have some

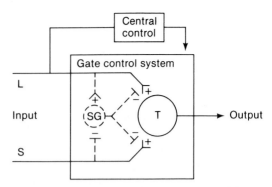

F I G U R E   14. 21   The circuit proposed by Melzak and Wall (1965) for their gate control theory of pain perception. See text for details.

idea of how this might work for pain. This explanation takes the form of gate control theory.

Gate Control Theory

Gate control theory, which was proposed by Ronald Melzak and Patrick Wall (1965), proposes that pain perception is controlled by a neural circuit like the one in Figure 14.21. In this circuit, activity in the **transmission (T) cell** causes pain, but some of the signals that feed into the T-cell are processed by the gate control system indicated by the dashed structures. Two kinds of fibers send signals to the T-cell, **small-diameter (S) fibers** and **large-diameter (L) fibers.** Ignoring for a moment the dashed structures, we can see that activation of either the S-fibers or the L-fibers increases activity in the T-cell.

The dashed structures, however, are the most important part of the circuit, because they control the "gate." We saw that activity in the L-fibers excites the T-cell, but it also does something else. It closes the gate by activating a structure in the spinal cord called the **substantia gelantinosa (SG),** which, in turn, sends inhibition to the T-cell. Consequently, the net effect of activity in the L-fibers is to decrease the activity of the T-cell and thus decrease the perception of pain.

Activity in the S-fibers has the opposite effect—it opens the gate by inhibiting the SG, thereby decreasing the amount of inhibition sent by the SG to the T-cell. With the gate open, the activity of the T-cell, and thus the perception of pain, is increased. So, according to gate control theory, we should experience more pain with a lot of S-fiber activity (because the gate is opened) and less pain with a lot of L-fiber activity (because the gate is closed).

The idea that S-fiber activity increases pain by opening the gate makes sense, because small fibers are usually associated with the nociceptors described earlier. The gate control mechanism can also be influenced by signals sent down from the brain. These signals, represented in Figure 14.21 by the box labeled "central control," are transmitted in L-fibers, so their effect is to close the gate and reduce the perception of pain.

The idea that signals sent down from the brain can reduce the perception of pain is supported by the results of an experiment done by David Reynolds (1969). Reynolds first showed that a rat responded vigorously when he pinched its tail or paw. He then electrically stimulated an area in the rat's midbrain and showed that, while the stimulation was on, the animal no longer seemed to mind having its tail or paw pinched. In fact, Reynolds was even able to perform abdominal surgery on rats with no anesthesia other than the electrical stimulation. This effect of brain stimulation, which has been confirmed in many experiments, is called **stimulation produced analgesia (SPA).**

The importance of gate control theory lies in its ability to take into account that pain is not simply determined by the activity of fibers connected to nociceptors. Gate control theory would explain some of the psychological effects we described above by saying that activity in L-fibers, or signals sent down from the brain, closes the gate. The pain reduction achieved by acupuncture is another effect that can be explained by gate control theory.

Acupuncture is the procedure practiced in China, in which fine needles are inserted into the skin at certain "acupuncture points" in the body (Figure 14.22). Twirling these needles, or passing electrical current through them, has been reported to produce a profound **analgesia** (elimination of

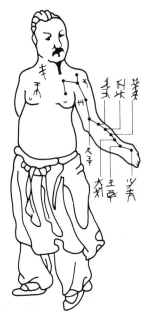

F I G U R E 14. 22 A Chinese acupuncture chart which shows the sites for insertion of acupuncture needles.

pain without loss of consciousness), which makes it possible to perform major surgery in a totally awake patient (Melzak, 1973). Gate control theory would suggest that the stimulating needles close the gate by activating L-fibers or fibers descending from the brain.

Although certain details of gate control theory are not accepted by everyone (Nathan, 1976), most researchers feel that the way this theory accounts for input from nonpain fibers is a great advance in our understanding of pain perception (Sherrick & Cholewiak, 1986). Another important development in our understanding of how central factors influence pain perception is the discovery that the nervous system contains endorphins, chemicals produced by the brain that have properties closely related to those of opiates such as morphine.

Endorphins

A family of substances called **endorphins,** *endogenous (naturally occurring in the body) morphine-like substances,* have recently been found in the nervous system, and a large body of evidence indicates that these substances have powerful analgesic (pain-reducing) effects (Cannon, 1978; Mayer, 1979; Watkins & Mayer, 1982). Some of the evidence supporting this idea is that:

1. Areas in the brain stem have been shown, using biochemical techniques, to be sites where opiates such as morphine act to produce their analgesic effects.
2. Endorphins are found at these **opiate sites.** This suggests that the naturally occurring endorphins act to reduce pain in the same way as do the opiates.
3. Stimulation produced analgesia (SPA, see above) is most effective when administered to the sites that contain endorphins. This suggests that SPA works by releasing endorphins into the nervous system.
4. Injecting **naloxone,** a substance known to inhibit the activity of opiates, into the brain decreases the effect of SPA. This suggests that naloxone inhibits the activity of the endorphins responsible for the effects of SPA.
5. Injecting naloxone into the brain also decreases the effect of acupuncture, thus supporting the idea that acupuncture works by stimulating nerve fibers to cause the release of endorphins.

This evidence strongly suggests that the brain uses endorphins to control pain.

Interestingly, it has also been shown that naloxone decreases the analgesic effect of placebos. Since placebos contain no active chemicals, their effects have always been thought to be "psychological." Now endorphins provide a physiological explanation for the psychological effect of placebos and, presumably, for some of the other psychological effects we have discussed. The discovery of endorphins also fits well with gate control theory. According to gate control theory, endorphins released by the brain stimulate L-fibers, which then close the gate and thus decrease the perception of pain.

We have seen that pain perception, perhaps more so than visual perception, is influenced by factors in addition to the signals triggered in the receptors. Many things influence these signals from

pain receptors during their journey toward the brain, including signals traveling down *from* the brain, perhaps caused by endorphins that respond to psychological influences.

In the final section of this chapter we will draw another analogy with vision, by discussing how perception is influenced by the observer's active participation in the perceptual process.

THE ROLE OF THE ACTIVE OBSERVER

In discussing the constructivist approach to the study of visual perception, we saw that to fully understand the perceptual process, we must consider the role of the active observer. We saw that observers are not passive recipients of visual information, but, rather, they actively make eye movements to scan visual stimuli (see page 25). We also saw that J. J. Gibson, as part of his ecological approach to perception, saw the importance for visual perception of the observer's movement through the environment.

Gibson has made a similar argument regarding the importance of movement for the sense of touch. In a paper entitled "Observations on Active Touch," Gibson draws a distinction between passive touch and active touch. In **passive touch** stationary skin is subjected to a stimulus. Most of the experiments we have described so far involve passive touch—a person's or animal's skin is stimulated by an experimenter. In **active touch** the person moves his or her skin to contact a stimulus. This is a common occurrence in our everyday experience, as we, for example, use our fingers to sense small details of objects or to feel textures (Loomis & Lederman, 1986).

Perhaps the difference between active and passive touch is best described in terms of our experience. We tend to relate passive touch to the sensation experienced in the *skin,* whereas we tend to relate active touch to the *object* being touched. For example, if someone stimulates your skin with a pointed object, you might say, "I feel a prickling sensation on my skin"; however, if you feel the tip of the pointed object yourself, you might say, "I

B O X   14. 4   /   *Reading Braille: The Limitations of Tactile Perception*

What would you perceive if you ran your fingers over raised dots arranged in the pattern shown at the right? A person who reads **braille** would perceive the words *active touch*. The ability of the blind to read by moving their fingers over braille is an impressive example of how information can be taken in by active touch. A braille *character* consists of a *cell* made up of from one to six dots. Different arrangements of dots and blank spaces are used to represent the alphabet, as shown, and in addition to characters for each letter of the alphabet, there are also characters for numbers, punctuation marks, and common speech sounds and words.

Braille was invented by a blind Frenchman, Louis Braille, in 1824. At that time, the only reading materials available to blind people were a few books that were printed by embossing the shapes of conventional letters onto the page. These books, however, were rarely read, because each letter had to be tediously scanned in order to synthesize its complete shape. The dots of braille eliminated this problem, and braille and other raised-dot-systems introduced during the 1800s gained wide popularity among the blind.

Braille is interesting not only because of its practical importance to blind people but also because of the comparison it affords between tactile and visual reading. The average visual reader reads at about 250–300 words per minute (wpm), whereas experienced braille readers typically read at around 100 wpm. Why is braille reading so much slower than visual reading? One answer is that reading braille is limited by the speed of hand movements, which are slower than eye movements. But there are more fundamental reasons, having to do with (1) differences in visual and tactile acuity and (2) differences in the way information is taken in by the eye and by the fingers.

To understand that visual acuity is much better than tactile acuity, we need only realize that if we moved the braille dots closer together we would be able to easily perceive the spaces between them visually, but it would become difficult to perceive the spaces tactually. Thus, for braille characters to be perceived by touch the dots must be widely spaced, making a character about the size of a person's fingertip. Thus, a braille reader can only perceive one character at a time. Compare this to visual reading, in which we take in whole words at a time, and, in fact, usually look a few words ahead as we read.

The importance of single characters as units of braille reading is supported by experiments in which Carson Nolan and Cleves Kederis (1969) determined the recognition times for individual characters and for words made up of a number of characters. They found that it takes 50–150 percent longer to identify a word than to identify all the individual characters making up the word; therefore, they concluded that the time needed for braille readers to identify a word is made up of the time needed to individually identify each character *plus* the time needed to integrate the information derived from the recognition of each character. Nolan and Kederis concluded, therefore, that the basic unit of braille perception is the individual braille character, a conclusion that has been confirmed by later studies (Foulke, 1982).

This character-by-character braille processing is very different from visual processing, in which readers typically identify whole words as units rather than identifying each letter singly and then combining them. In fact, if visual readers are forced to read single letters at a time by looking at print through a narrow tube, reading speed drops to 65–75 wpm, somewhat below that of an experienced braille reader (Foulke,

1982). The slowness of braille reading compared to visual reading appears, therefore, to be due primarily to limits on how tactile information can be taken in. Imagine how the rate of braille reading might be increased if our fingertip acuity were good enough to enable us to reduce the size of braille characters so that a fingertip could feel two or three characters at once. This is not possible, however, so braille readers must take in information a character at a time.

Braille readers do, however, make use of some information in addition to the individual characters. Familiar words and material are recognized more rapidly than are unfamiliar words and material, indicating that top-down processing, which depends on the reader's knowledge, is being used. Another example of the use of top-down processing is the fact that braille readers read nonsense words that follow the rules of English spelling (for example, *funts* and *lods*) more rapidly and accurately than words that violate these rules (for example, *ntsuf* and *dsol*) (Pick, Thomas, & Pick, 1966). Thus braille readers, like visual readers, use information in addition to individual letters to help them read faster (Kruger, 1982).

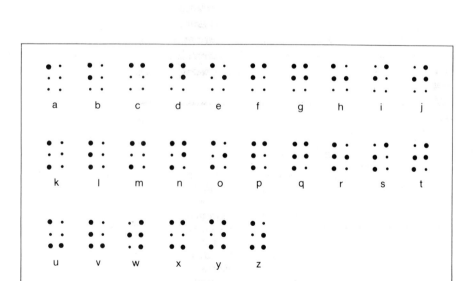

The braille alphabet

feel a pointed object" (Kruger, 1970). Another example: If you move your hand over the edges and surfaces of an object (active touch), you do not perceive the object as moving, even though it is moving relative to the skin. If, however, someone else moves an object across your skin (passive touch), you perceive the object moving across your skin.

Though we do not completely understand why these two types of touch result in such different experiences, a number of properties differentiate active from passive touch. An important property of active touch, according to Gibson, is that it is purposive; that is, when you feel something, especially an object with which you are unfamiliar, your purpose is to determine its shape. Just as you visually scan a scene by looking at its most interesting or important areas, you feel an object by touching the parts that contain information about its shape. This purposive character may be important in determining the experience of active touch.

In addition to its purposive aspect, active touch includes other properties absent from passive touch. As you feel something, you stimulate receptors not only in the skin but also in the joints and tendons that are activated as you move your fingers or hands over an object (see Box 14.3), whereas passive touch stimulates only the receptors in the skin. Furthermore, moving your fingers over an object enables you to perceive both the "touch" that occurs when a stimulus is applied to passive skin and the sounds that occur when skin moves actively over a surface.

DEMONSTRATION

The Sounds of Touching

Consider the different sounds that result from touching different materials, by gently moving your fingers over a smooth surface such as the top of your desk, and over a slightly rougher surface such as a page of this book or your clothes. You perceive a different sound from each material and combine this with your other perceptions to form an overall perception of the nature of the object you are touching (Taylor, Lederman, & Gibson, 1973).

According to Gibson, active touch is superior to passive touch in enabling us to gather information about objects in our environment. For example, in one experiment Gibson (1962) found that if subjects actively feel cookie cutters of various shapes, they are able to correctly identify the shape 95 percent of the time. However, if the cookie cutters are pushed onto the skin by someone else, the subjects can correctly identify the shape only 49 percent of the time.

However, a dissenting view was expressed by A. S. Schwartz and coworkers (1975), who repeated Gibson's cookie cutter experiment, with an additional passive condition. In one condition, they repeated Gibson's procedure, in which the cookie cutter was pressed onto the subject's palm, but in the additional condition, he had the subject stick out his finger and feel the shape as the experimenter moved the edges of the cookie cutter across his finger. Schwartz, like Gibson, found that subjects had a hard time identifying objects pushed into their palms by the experimenter; but Schwartz also found that when he moved the cookie cutter over the subjects' outstretched (but passive) fingers, they correctly identified the shape 93 percent of the time. Thus, Schwartz argues that although the subjective experiences of active and passive touch may be different, passive touch can provide information about a stimulus equal to that of active touch, as long as the stimulus is moved across the subject's skin. Movement across the skin, not purposiveness, is what is important for discriminating shapes, according to Schwartz.

Though the mechanisms involved in both active and passive touch are still not completely understood, there is no doubt that movement of a stimulus across the skin does provide more information about an object than do stationary stimuli. We have seen that movement is a powerful source of visual information and that most neurons in the visual cortex respond best to moving stimuli. A similar situation exists for the cutaneous senses: "Neural information," according to Kenneth Johnson (1983), "is richer and more intense when skin movement is involved." For example, when Johnson measured the responses of neurons to the movement of braille dots across a monkey's skin, he found SA mechanoreceptors, the receptors best suited to detect the fine details of the braille dot patterns, fired 10 times more strongly to this movement than when stationary braille dots were presented to the skin. The importance of movement in both touch and vision adds yet another parallel to the many that exist between the cutaneous senses and vision.

Summary

1. The skin serves a number of functions, of which the most important to us is to provide information about stimuli that contact the skin. This information is provided by receptors in the dermis.
2. There are three classes of cutaneous receptors that fire to specific types of stimuli: (1) mechanoreceptors, (2) thermoreceptors, and (3) nociceptors. It has, however, not always been possible to match these receptors to specific end organs in the skin.
3. Properties of the Pacinian corpuscle end organ cause its nerve fiber to fire only to the onset and offset of stimulation.
4. Von Frey proposed that specific receptor structures are responsible for our perception of warmth, cold, touch, and pain. This pairing of receptor *structures* with perception has not been supported by experiments. However, modern electrophysiological research suggests that we can propose links between specific receptor *types* and perception. Von Frey's theory and these proposed modern links between receptor types and perception are forms of specificity theory. However, since many different types of receptors fire to a particular stimulus, sensory quality on the skin is probably determined by the pattern of firing of many neurons.
5. Neurons in the monkey's thalamus have center-surround receptive fields on the skin similar to those found in the visual system. Cortical neurons respond to more specialized stimuli such as movement across the skin in a particular direction.
6. There are areas of the skin that have higher acuity, as measured by the two-point threshold, than other areas. These differences have been related to receptive field size (higher acuity is associated with smaller receptive fields) and the area devoted to different parts of the body on the cortex (high acuity is associated with greater area on the cortex).
7. The perception of pain is determined not only by the firing of pain receptors but also by factors such as the person's culture, previous experience, and the general situation in which the pain stimulus occurs.
8. Gate control theory proposes that the neural signals that cause the perception of pain must pass through a neural circuit called a gate control system before being transmitted to the brain.
9. Electrical stimulation of specific areas in the brain can cause a reduction of pain perception called stimulation produced analgesia.
10. Gate control theory can explain the reduction in pain caused by acupuncture.
11. Endorphins are chemicals in the brain that have powerful analgesic effects. Thus, the brain has an internal mechanism for controlling pain and this mechanism may be responsible for the pain reduction caused by placebos and acupuncture. Also, endorphins may be involved in the operation of the gate control mechanism.
12. Most laboratory experiments involve passive touch in which stimuli are applied to the skin of a passive observer. In contrast, active touch involves an active observer who seeks out stimuli in the environment. The subjective experiences resulting from passive and active touch are different. Though the mechanisms involved in both active and passive touch are still not completely understood, there is no doubt that movement of a stimulus across the skin provides more information about an object than do stationary stimuli.

Boxes

1. A mechanical substitution system has been developed that enables blind people to detect environmental properties by sensing vibrational patterns on the skin.
2. The perception of pressure on the skin is affected by lateral inhibition.
3. Kinesthesis, the ability to feel the motions and positions of the limbs and body, is determined by a number of different neurons that receive inputs from receptors in the joints.
4. Braille is a system of raised dots that enables blind people to read. Comparing tactile to visual reading indicates that tactile reading, via braille, is slower because of limitations in tactile acuity and because of the way information is taken in by the fingers.

Study Questions

1. Describe the two layers of the skin. (471)
2. What are the three types of cutaneous receptors, as determined by measuring how they respond to different types of stimuli? Be sure you know which stimuli cause each receptor type to respond. (472)
3. Are there specific end organs that are associated with the receptor types in question 2? (474)
4. How does the Pacinian corpuscle modify a pressure stimulus as it is transmitted to the nerve fiber within the corpuscle? What effect does the Pacinian corpuscle have on the response of the nerve fiber? (474)
5. Describe von Frey's specificity theory. How did he use the results of experiments in which sensory spots were mapped on the skin to support his theory? (475)
6. How do modern experiments on sensory spots argue against von Frey's theory? What other evidence argues against von Frey's theory? (475)
7. What is the reasoning behind the idea that sensory quality on the skin is determined by the firing pattern of numerous fibers that respond best to specific stimuli? (476)
8. Describe the different types of receptive fields that have been recorded from neurons in the cutaneous system. How do these neurons compare to neurons in the visual system? (477)
9. What is the relationship between cutaneous acuity as measured by the two-point threshold and (a) receptive field size and (b) the area devoted to different body parts in the cortex? How does this relationship compare to similar relationships in the visual system? (480)
10. Describe the evoked potential and stimulation methods of determining the homunculus in Figure 14.19. (483)
11. Describe evidence which shows that the perception of pain is determined not only by the firing of pain receptors but also by factors such as the person's culture, previous experience, and the general situation in which the pain stimulus occurs. (484)
12. Describe how gate control theory works. By referring to the circuit in Figure 14.21, show how stimulating L-fibers closes the gate and stimulating S-fibers opens the gate. (487)
13. What is stimulation produced analgesia (SPA)? acupuncture? How does gate control theory deal with these two phenomena? (488)
14. What are endorphins? Cite five pieces of evidence that support the idea that endorphins have powerful analgesic effects. (489)
15. What is the relationship between placebos, acupuncture, endorphins, and gate control theory? (489)
16. What is the difference between active and passive touch? Be able to tell whether a given experience (for example, "I feel a tickling sensation on my skin") is due to active or passive touch. (489)
17. Describe Gibson's "cookie cutter" experiment. Describe Schwartz' active touch experiment and compare his conclusions regarding active touch to Gibson's conclusions. (492)

Boxes

1. Describe the mechanical substitution system which enables blind people to "see" by stimulating the skin. (470)
2. Why does a person feel only one pressure distribution when two points that are close together on the skin are stimulated? How does the idea of lateral inhibition on the skin explain why the perceived pressures for two spots separated by 3.0 mm are smaller than the perceived pressures for two spots separated by 3.5 mm? (479)
3. What is kinesthesis? Describe the different types of neurons that are responsible for kinesthesis. (485)
4. Describe a braille character. What is the basic unit of braille perception? What factors, in addition to the nature of the braille character, are involved in braille reading? What factors cause braille reading to be slower than visual reading? (490)

Glossary

Active touch. Touch in which the observer plays an active role in touching an object, usually with his or her hands. (489)

Acupuncture. A procedure in which fine needles are inserted into the skin at specific points. Twirling these needles or passing electrical current through them can cause analgesia. (488)

Analgesia. The elimination of pain without loss of consciousness. (488)

Braille. A system of raised dots in which different patterns of dots stand for different letters of the alphabet. Blind people can read by feeling these dots with their fingertips. (490)

Cold fiber. A nerve fiber that responds to decreases in temperature or to steady low temperatures. (473)

Cutaneous senses. The senses that serve the qualities sensed through the skin. (469)

Dermis. The inner layer of skin that contains nerve endings and receptors. (471)

Endorphins. Chemicals that are naturally produced in the brain which cause analgesia. (488)

Epidermis. The outer layer of the skin, actually several layers of dead skin cells. (471)

Evoked potential. The electrical response of the brain, recorded by relatively large electrodes that pick up activity from large numbers of neurons. (483)

Free nerve endings. Nerve endings without receptors which, according to Max von Frey, signal the sensation of pain. (471)

Gate control theory. Melzak and Wall's idea that our perception of pain is controlled by a neural circuit which takes into account the relative amount of activity in large (L) fibers and small (S) fibers. (487)

Homunculus. "Little man." Refers to the map of the body in the somatosensory cortex. (483)

Kinesthesis. The sense that enables us to feel the motions and positions of the limbs and body. (485)

Kinesthetic neurons. Cortical neurons that receive inputs from the joints. (485)

Krause end bulb. A receptor which, according to Max von Frey, signals the sensation of cold. (471)

Large-diameter fiber (L-fiber). According to gate control, theory activity in L-fibers closes the gate control mechanism and therefore decreases the perception of pain. (487)

Lateral inhibition. In the skin, stimulation at one point causes an area of excitation immediately surrounding that point and an area of inhibition surrounding the area of excitation. (479)

Mechanical substitution system. A system which translates the pattern of light and dark in the environment into patterns of tactile stimulation on a person's back. (470)

Mechanoreceptor. Receptor that responds to indentations of the skin. (472)

Meissner corpuscle. A receptor which, according to Max von Frey, signals the sensation of touch. (471)

Merkel disc. A receptor in the epidermis. (471)

Microneurography. A procedure for recording the activity of single neurons in the skin of awake humans. (482)

Multiple-joint neurons. Kinesthetic neurons that respond best to simultaneous flexion of a number of joints. (485)

Naloxone. A substance that inhibits the activity of opi-

ates. It is hypothesized that naloxone also inhibits the activity of endorphins. (489)

Nociceptor. A receptor that responds to stimuli that are damaging to the skin. (473)

Opiate sites. Sites in the brain stem where opiates like morphine act to produce analgesic effects. (489)

Pacinian corpuscle. A receptor with a distinctive elliptical shape; it transmits pressure to the nerve fiber inside it only at the beginning or end of the pressure stimulus. (471)

Passive touch. When stationary skin is subjected to a stimulus. (489)

Placebo. A substance that a person believes will relieve symptoms such as pain but which, unknown to the person, contains no chemicals that actually act on these symptoms. (487)

Positional neurons. Kinesthetic neurons that fire best to the static position of a limb. (485)

Rapidly adapting (RA) mechanoreceptors. Fibers that respond as pressure indents the skin, generally firing more rapidly to faster velocities of indentation. These neurons do not fire to constant pressure. (472)

Ruffini ending. A receptor which, according to Max von Frey, signals the sensation of warmth. (471)

Sensory spots. Spots on the skin, stimulation of which results in one specific sensation. For example, stimulation of a "warm spot" results only in the sensation of warmth. (475)

Slowly adapting (SA) mechanoreceptors. Fibers that respond to indentation of the skin and continue to respond during constant indentation. (472)

Small-diameter fiber (S-fiber). According to gate control theory, activity in S-fibers opens the gate control mechanism and therefore increases the perception of pain. (487)

Somatosensory area. Area in the parietal lobe of the cortex that receives inputs from the skin. (471)

Stimulation produced analgesia (SPA). Brain stimulation which eliminates or strongly decreases the perception of pain. (488)

Substantia gelantinosa (SG). A nucleus in the spinal cord that, according to gate control theory, receives inputs from S-fibers and L-fibers and sends inhibition to the T-cell. (487)

Thermoreceptor. Receptor that responds to specific temperatures or changes in temperature. (473)

Transmission cell (T-cell). According to gate control theory, the transmission cell receives input from the L- and S-fibers. Activity in the T-cell determines the perception of pain. (487)

Two-point threshold. The smallest separation between two points on the skin that is perceived as two points. A measure of acuity on the skin. (481)

Warm fiber. A nerve fiber that responds to increases in temperature or to steady high temperatures. (473)

CHAPTER **15**

The Chemical Senses

In this, the last chapter of the book, we consider the chemical senses, taste and smell. These senses respond to chemical stimuli—invisible molecules in the air in the case of smell and liquid solutions in the case of taste—and have been called "molecule detectors," because they endow different molecules with distinctive smells and tastes (Cain, 1988; Kauer, 1987). We first consider the sense of smell, or olfaction, as it is usually called in the scientific literature.

OLFACTION

Olfaction is essential for the survival of many animals and makes life much more interesting for humans. That many animals rely on their sense of smell for survival is reflected in the relative sizes of their olfactory organs. Dogs, for example, who spend a good portion of their waking hours sniffing, have olfactory mucosa much larger than a human's; and sheep, who rely on their noses to find food, have olfactory organs that take up a large portion of their skull.

Humans, on the other hand, could live without a sense of smell if they had to. But life would certainly be less interesting without good smells from the kitchen or the rain-freshened air after a spring shower, and life becomes a little more dangerous if we don't have smell to warn us of spoiled food, leaking gas, or smoke from a fire.

Many writers, commenting on our attitude toward smells, have pointed out that in our society we tend to avoid many smells. As William Cain (1978), a leading researcher on smell, says,

There is a strong effort to manage man's olfactory environment. It is generally felt that, with few exceptions, both indoor and outdoor air should be odorless. Odors produced by warning agents, perfumes, and foods constitute permissible exceptions, but these may be welcome only at certain times, in certain places and for certain durations. It may be argued that we are too obsessed with, and hence strive to overmanage, some aspects of the olfactory environment. Do you take steps to ensure that your home does not have "house-itosis"? Do your clothes, hands, and armpits have just a hint of yummy lemon-fresh fragrance? Does your bathroom smell like the great outdoors?

And E. T. Hall, in his book *The Hidden Dimension* (1966), makes a similar point, with special reference to Americans:

In the use of the olfactory apparatus Americans are culturally underdeveloped. The extensive use of deodorants and the suppression of odor in public places results in a land of olfactory blandness and sameness that would be difficult to duplicate anywhere else in the world.

Why this obsession with smells? Perhaps people's feelings about smells have to do with the strong reactions that olfaction is capable of eliciting. To support the idea that no other sense elicits such a wide range of emotional reactions to simple stimuli, John Levine and Donald McBurney (1983) point out that it is implausible to imagine a color or a tone that can either empty a building of its occupants as rapidly as can the smell of smoke or command the high price of some perfumes.

Despite the powerful effects that smells can exert, the human olfactory system has a reputation for being deficient. Humans have, in fact, been called **microsmatic** (lacking a keen sense of smell), in contrast to many animals, who are called **macrosmatic** (having a keen sense of smell). Although many animals are more sensitive to smells than humans, calling humans microsmatic somewhat overstates the case. In fact, recent research indicates that the human olfactory system is quite a bit more impressive than it was once thought to be. Let's consider some of the evidence uncovered by this research.

SOME MYTHS ABOUT HUMAN OLFACTION

Myth #1: Human Olfactory Receptors Are Less Sensitive Than Other Animals'

The idea that human smell *receptors* are much less sensitive than those of other animals arose because some animals are much more sensitive to odors than are humans. The most familiar example of this is the dog, which deserves its reputation for being able to detect very faint smells. Mairico Burton (1972) relates the story of a dog the Cairo police used to find a stolen donkey that had walked across rocky ground four days earlier. The dog put its nose to the donkey's trail and followed the scent right up to the door of the house where the donkey was being hidden. This ability to follow very faint smells has been experimentally confirmed in the laboratory: Dogs can detect most substances in concentrations 100 times lower than concentrations humans can detect (Moulton, 1977).

But is this greater sensitivity of the dog evidence that the human's *receptors* are less sensitive than the dog's? Not necessarily. H. deVries and M. Stuiver (1961) have shown that human olfactory receptors can be excited by the action of just one molecule of odorant. Nothing can be more sensitive than one molecule per receptor, so the dog's greater sensitivity must be due to something else. That something else is the *number* of receptors: about 1 billion in the dog, compared to about 10 million for man (Moulton, 1977; Dodd and Squirrell, 1980).

Myth #2: Our Ability to Detect Differences in Smell Intensity Is Poor

The ability to detect differences in intensity is indicated by the difference threshold—the smallest difference between two stimuli that can be detected (see Appendix A), and in the past, olfaction has been reputed to have the largest difference threshold of all the senses, with typical values ranging from about 25 to 33 percent (Gamble, 1898; Stone & Bosley, 1965). That is, the concentration of an odorant must be increased by 25–33 percent before a person can detect an increase in odor intensity.

Recently, William Cain (1977) measured the difference threshold for a number of odorants, by presenting two odorants of different concentrations on each trial and asking subjects to judge which was more intense. He presented the odorants by placing a small amount of each substance onto an absorbent cotton ball, in a glass vessel designed for olfactory testing. His results were better than those of most other studies, with an average difference threshold for three odorants of 19 percent, and a relatively low difference threshold of 7 percent for one of the odorants, n-butyl alcohol.

But Cain didn't stop with these measurements, because an average difference threshold of 19 percent still seemed high to him. He next analyzed the stimuli he had presented to his human subjects using a **gas chromatograph,** a device that accurately measures the concentration of the vapor given off by each stimulus. Cain found what he had suspected: Stimuli that were supposed to have the same concentration actually varied considerably, apparently due to variations in adsorption by the walls of the glass vessel and to differences in the airflow pattern through the cotton in different samples.

If stimulus variability is responsible for the large difference thresholds reported for olfaction, then presenting the stimuli in a more precise way should decrease the difference threshold. Cain showed that this does, in fact, occur by presenting his stimuli with an **olfactometer,** a device that presents olfactory stimuli with much greater precision than cotton balls. When stimulus variability was decreased in this way, Cain found an average difference threshold of 11 percent, with n-butyl alcohol having an impressively low threshold of only 5 percent. These figures, which rival difference thresholds for vision and hearing, show that our ability to detect differences in smell intensity is, in fact, not poor compared to the other senses.

Myth #3: Our Ability to Identify Odors Is Poor

The idea that our ability to identify odors is poor comes from experiments in which people are presented with a series of odorants and are asked to tell the experimenter what they are. In a typical experiment, Trygg Engen and Carl Pfaffmann (1960) asked subjects to assign each of 36 different stimuli a label based on their smell. Each labeled odorant was then presented again, and each subject was asked to remember the label he or she had previously assigned to that odorant. Even though the subjects were given a number of trials and were reminded of the correct labels for stimuli they did not identify correctly, they were able to correctly identify only 17 of the 36 stimuli.

Why did people fail to identify over half of the odorants in the Engen and Pfaffman experiment? J. A. Desor and Gary K. Beauchamp (1974) thought that one reason might be that most of Engen and Pfaffmann's odorants were unfamiliar chemicals such as hexane and nitrobenzene. Perhaps, reasoned Desor and Beauchamp, familiar materials like coffee, bananas, and motor oil might be easier to identify. However, when confronted with these familiar substances, subjects could still only identify about half of them correctly—the same result as Engen and Pfaffmann obtained for unfamiliar chemicals. Apparently, however, there is something to be gained by using familiar stimuli, because if Desor and Beauchamp named the substances when they first presented them and then reminded subjects of the correct name if they failed to respond correctly on subsequent trials, their subjects could, after some practice, correctly identify 63 of 64 substances.

According to Cain (1979, 1980), the key to the good performance in Desor and Beauchamp's experiment is that their subjects were provided with the correct names, or labels, at the beginning of the experiment. In his own experiments, Cain showed that if subjects assign a correct label to a familiar object the first time they smell it (for example, labeling an orange "orange"), or if the experimenter provides the correct labels, they usually identify it correctly the next time it is pre-

---

B O X 1 5. 1 / *Odor Identification in the Blind*

Does the loss of one of our senses cause sharpening of the ones that remain? If we ask this question about olfaction we find that the answer depends on what aspect of olfaction we are talking about. Tests of odor sensitivity indicate that blind subjects have lower sensitivity to odors than do sighted subjects. Nonetheless, blind subjects are better at *identifying* odors.

Claire Murphy and William Cain (1986) blindfolded a group of sighted subjects and a group of blind subjects and asked them to identify 80 everyday odors, such as baby powder, cloves, cigarette butts, and mothballs. The blind group correctly identified an average of 33.6 odors, whereas the sighted group identified an average of 25.6 odors—a 31 percent advantage for the blind subjects.

Why are blind people better than sighted people at identifying odors? Better sensitivity is not the answer, since the blind subjects had worse sensitivity than the sighted subjects. Cain and Murphy point to the fact that practice improves the ability to identify odors. Perhaps, they suggest, the blind subject's superiority reflects their greater attention to odors in their environment. Cain and Murphy put it this way: "Like reading braille (see Box 14.4) or locating large objects from sound reflections (see Box 11.1), odor identification is a skill that offers distinct benefits for those who need it and choose to invest in it. The blind apparently make an investment, even to the point of overcoming certain minor olfactory limitations" (p. 179).

---

sented. If, however, they assign an incorrect label to an object the first time they smell it (for example, labeling machine oil "cheese"), they usually misidentify it the next time it is presented. Thus, according to Cain, when we have trouble identifying odors, this trouble results not from a deficiency in our olfactory system but from an inability to retrieve the odor's name from our memory.

The amazing thing about the role memory plays in odor identification is that knowing the correct label for the odor actually seems to transform our perception into that odor. Cain (1980) gives the example of an object initially identified by the subject as "fishy-goaty-oily." When the experimenter tells the subject that the fishy-goaty-oily smell actually comes from leather, the smell is then transformed into that of leather. I recently had a similar experience. A friend gave me a bottle of Aquavit, a Danish drink with a very interesting smell, for Christmas. As I was sampling this drink with some friends, we tried to identify its smell. Many odors were proposed ("anise," "orange," "lemon"), but it wasn't until someone turned the

bottle around and read the label on the back that the truth became known: "Aquavit ("Water of Life") is the Danish national drink—a delicious, crystal-clear spirit distilled from grain, with a slight taste of *caraway*." Upon hearing the word "caraway," the previous hypotheses of anise, orange, and lemon were instantly transformed into caraway. It seemed obvious as soon as we knew the answer.

DEMONSTRATION

Naming and Odor Identification

To demonstrate the effect of naming substances on odor identification, have a friend collect a number of familiar objects for you and, without looking, try identifying the odors. You will find that you can identify some but not others, and when your friend tells you the correct answer for the ones you missed, you will wonder how you could have failed to identify such a familiar smell. But don't blame your misses on your nose; blame your memory!

Myth #4: Animals Can Use Odors to Communicate but Humans Can't

We will see below, when we discuss pheromones, that the first part of this myth is correct: Animals are, in fact, very capable of communicating with odors and smell plays an important role in their lives. As McKenzie (1923) has remarked about the dog: "He can recognize his master by sight, no doubt, yet, as we know, he is never perfectly satisfied until he has taken stock also of the scent, the more precisely to do so bringing his snout into actual contact with the person he is examining. It is as if his eyes might deceive him, but never his nose." Humans, however, are constrained from behaving like dogs. Except in the most intimate situations, it is considered poor form to smell other people at close range. However, what if we lived in a society that condoned this kind of behavior? Could we identify other people based on their smell? A recent experiment suggests that the answer to this question might be "yes."

Michael Russell (1976) had subjects wear undershirts for 24 hours, without showering or using deodorant or perfume. The undershirts were then sealed in a bag and given to the experimenter, who, in turn, presented each subject with three undershirts to smell: One was the subject's own shirt, one was a male's, and one was a female's. About three-quarters of the subjects succeeded in identifying their own undershirt, based on its odor, and also correctly identified which of the other shirts were worn by males or females (see also McBurney, Levine, & Cavanaugh 1977, for a similar experiment). Similar results have also been reported for breath odors, which subjects can identify as being produced by a male or by a female (Doty, Green, Ram, & Yankell, 1982). These results certainly don't suggest that people can identify other people solely by their smell, but they do suggest that our ability to use smell in such situations might be underrated.

The phenomenon of **menstrual synchrony** also suggests a role for smell in interpersonal relations. Martha McClintock (1971) noted that women who live or work together often report that their menstrual periods begin at about the same time. For example, one group of seven female lifeguards had widely scattered menstrual periods at the beginning of the summer, but by the end of the summer, all began their periods within 4 days of each other. To investigate this phenomenon, McClintock asked 135 females, aged 17–22, living in a college dormitory, to indicate when their periods began throughout the school year. She found that women who saw each other often (roommates or close friends) tended to have synchronous periods by the end of the school year. After ruling out factors such as awareness of the other person's period, McClintock concluded that "there is some interpersonal physiological process which affects the menstrual cycle."

What might this physiological process be? Michael Russell and coworkers (1980) did an experiment which suggests that smell might have something to do with this physiological process. He had a "donor" woman wear cotton pads in her armpits for 24 hours, three times a week. The sweat extracted from these pads was then rubbed onto the upper lip of a woman in the "experimental group." A control group of women received the same treatment, but without the sweat. The results for the experimental group showed that prior to the experiment there was an average of 9.3 days between the onset of the donor's and subject's periods, but after 5 months, the average time between onset was reduced to 3.4 days. The control group showed no such synchrony. Since the donors and the subjects in the experimental group never saw each other, Russell concludes that odor must be the factor that causes menstrual synchrony.

The evidence above indicates that smell at least potentially plays some role in human communication. The evidence available to date, however, is only suggestive, and in our society the role of smell in human communication is surely small. To find strong evidence for odor as a method of communication we must turn to animals.

ODOR AND ANIMAL COMMUNICATION: PHEROMONES

Smell provides the dominant means of communication in many animals, but it does much more than that. Many animals release chemicals called **pheromones** which, when sensed by other animals of the same species, cause specific reactions (Karlson & Luscher, 1959). There are two major classes of pheromones, **primers** and **releasers**. Primers usually trigger a chain of long-lasting physiological (usually hormonal) effects in another animal. For example, Hilda Bruce (1959) found that if a female mouse which has just mated is exposed to the smell of a strange male mouse within 24 hours, the smell of the strange male mouse prevents the just-mated female mouse from becoming pregnant (the **Bruce effect**).

Releasers, on the other hand, usually trigger an immediate behavioral reaction in another animal. Examples of a few of the behaviors caused by releasers are discussed below.

Sex. Chemicals that control sexual behavior are the most powerful of the pheromones, with extremely small quantities effective over long distances. For example, the pheromone bombykol, released by the female silkworm moth, can attract a male from over 3 km away, and though a single female contains openly about .01 millionth gram of bombykol, this is enough chemical to potentially attract 1 billion males (Wilson, 1963)!

Many sexual pheromones have a dual function: They attract a mate, and they trigger the sequence of stereotyped behaviors necessary for mating. Sometimes this stereotyped mating response is triggered even if the pheromone is presented in the wrong context; male tortoises have been observed mounting such inappropriate objects as a head of lettuce over which a female has recently climbed (Shorey, 1977).

Aggression. Honeybee workers disturbed at the hive release an alarm pheromone (isopental acetate) from their sting chambers which attracts other bees and causes them to attack objects in the vicinity of the hive. When the bees sting the enemy, additional pheromone is released to cause more bees to attack the potential intruder. This pheromone effect is probably responsible for the phenomenon, well known to beekeepers, that more than one bee will often sting the same spot (Shorey, 1977).

Disposing of the dead. Within a few days after an ant dies, the chemical decomposition products of the dead ant stimulate worker ants to carry the corpse to the refuse pile outside the nest. When living ants are experimentally daubed with the chemical decomposition products, they are carried to the refuse pile. After being dumped on the refuse pile the ant promptly returns to the nest, only to be carried out again, and this process continues until the ant's "death smell" has worn off (Wilson, 1963).

All of the above are examples of how pheromones affect the behavior of nonmammals. There is also ample evidence that the sense of smell plays an important role in regulating the behavior of many mammals. For example, the scent marking practiced by many mammals has been linked to aggressive behavior. Animals mark either objects in the environment or other animals by rubbing the scent glands on their bodies against them, after which aggressive behavior often occurs (Ralls, 1971).

Pheromones also play an important role in regulating sexual behavior in many mammals.[*] For example, a vaginal discharge of the female golden hamster causes males to mate within seconds of being exposed to the female. The male will also attempt to mate with another male that is smeared with this discharge, but this same male loses all interest in mating if its olfactory bulbs (see "Structure of the Olfactory System," below) are removed (Devor, 1977). A similar effect occurs in dogs. Female dogs in heat give off a special odor that attracts male dogs. If this odor is smeared onto a female that is not in heat, a male will attempt to

[*] Many investigators object to applying the term "pheromone"—which was originally developed to deal with fairly stereotyped, genetically programmed insect behavior—to more complex mammalian behaviors, preferring instead to use the term "chemical signals" when referring to mammals (Beauchamp, Doty, Moulton, & Mugford, 1976).

mate with the female, even though the male showed no interest in mating minutes earlier, before application of the odor (Goodwin, Gooding, & Regnier, 1979).

But what about human sexual behavior? Is it influenced by chemical signals? In the early 1970s, research on our close relative, the monkey, seemed to show that chemical signals control the monkey's sexual and reproductive behavior (Michael & Kaverne, 1968; Michael, Kaverne, & Bonsall 1971). However, recent evidence (Goldfoot, Essock-Vitale, Asa, Thornton, & Leshner, 1978) indicates that olfaction may not, in fact, control reproductive behavior in monkeys, and a paper reviewing all the evidence on the role of pheromones in monkey sexual behavior concluded: "It is probable that olfaction . . . influences behavior, but it seems unlikely that chemical communication plays any significant role in the control of higher primate reproductive and sexual behavior" (Rogel, 1978).

Whether or not olfaction plays a significant role in reproductive and sexual behavior in monkeys or humans, the above discussion should convince you not only of the importance of olfaction in animal behavior but also of the impressive capabilities of the human olfactory system. Let's now consider how this system works.

STRUCTURE OF THE OLFACTORY SYSTEM

In Figure 15.1, stimuli from the rose enter the nose and find their way to the olfactory mucosa and the receptors in the mucosa (Figure 15.2). Molecules of odorant contact the cilia of the receptors and produce an electrical signal that travels along nerve fibers to the **olfactory bulb.** The olfactory bulb is analogous to the retina in that it is here that the

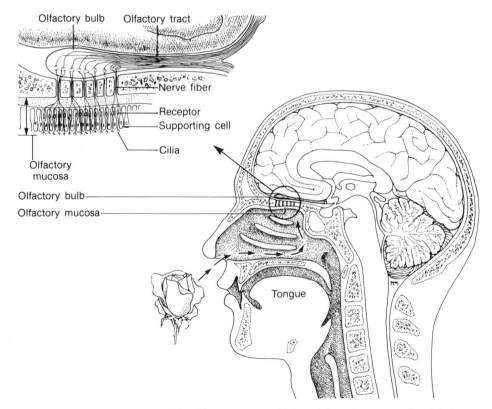

F I G U R E 15. 1   The olfactory system. (Adapted from Amoore et al., 1964.)

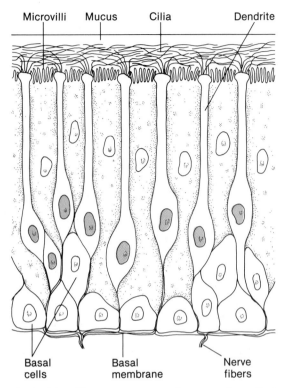

Microvilli   Mucus   Cilia   Dendrite

Basal
cells

Basal
membrane

Nerve
fibers

FIGURE 15.2 The olfactory receptors and mucosa. A smell stimulus is picked up by the mucus layer and stimulates the cilia attached to the olfactory receptors. Note that each receptor is separated from its neighbor by a thick supporting cell.

initial processing of the signals generated in the receptors takes place; the olfactory bulb is where fibers from the receptors first synapse, and it also contains many additional synapses and complex connections, as does the retina.

From the olfactory bulb, fibers travel in two circuits. One circuit passes through the thalamus, where all the other senses also synapse, and the other circuit passes through the amygdala, the hippocampus, and the hypothalamus, all structures deep inside the brain which play roles in the regulation of feeding, drinking, and reproductive behavior. It has been suggested that the pathway through the thalamus is the one primarily responsible for our perception of odors, whereas the pathway through the hypothalamus may help determine whether a particular odor smells "good" or "bad." Both of these circuits meet in the orbito-frontal cortex, an area in the frontal lobe just above the eyes (see Figure 2.9) (Cain, 1988; Takagi, 1980; Tanabe, Iino, & Takagi, 1975).

THE ODOR STIMULUS AND THE CODE FOR QUALITY

The stimuli for smell are molecules in the air. Thus, when you smell a rose, or anything else, you are smelling molecules that have left the substance and have traveled through the air to your nose. These molecules are drawn into the nose by breathing or active sniffing and contact the mucous membrane. This contact somehow triggers an electrical signal in the receptors and these signals are transmitted to the olfactory bulb and then to other structures in the olfactory system.

The key question in olfaction is: How are the qualities of the thousands of different odors we can smell indicated by the electrical signals that travel through the olfactory system? In other words, what is the sensory code for odor quality? In previous chapters we have dealt with the problem of sensory coding in vision, hearing, and the cutaneous senses; however, olfaction poses problems not encountered in these senses that make it more difficult to determine the sensory code for odor.

To appreciate these problems, we need first to consider how we went about determining the sensory code in vision and hearing. The first step in studying these senses was to identify the physical properties of the stimulus that, when changed, alter the perception of the stimulus. Thus, early researchers in color vision found that changing the physical property of wavelength changes the perception of hue. For example, increasing the wavelength of light from 400 to 650 nm changes our perception from blue to red. In fact, we can see all the hues of the spectrum as we increase the wavelength, and each hue is similar to the one that just precedes it. Similarly, early researchers in hearing found that changing the physical property of frequency changes the pitch of a sound. Increasing the frequency changes our perception from a low pitch to a high pitch, and when we do this, each tone seems to follow from the one preceding.

The psychophysically determined linkages between wavelength and hue and between frequency and pitch identified wavelength and frequency as important physical properties to study in vision and hearing, and enabled us to pose our questions about the sensory code in physical terms. Thus, "what is the code for hue?" becomes "what is the code for wavelength?" and "what is the code for pitch?" becomes "what is the code for frequency?"* Being able to pose our questions in this way has enabled us to do physiological experiments that have related wavelength and frequency to the

activity of the nervous system. Thus, a good deal of our knowledge of vision and hearing comes from the following three-step procedure:

1. Identification of the quality to be studied
2. Determination of the physical property of the stimulus linked to that quality
3. Determination of how changing this physical property changes the activity of the nervous system

One reason for our limited knowledge of olfaction compared to vision and hearing is that we have not yet been able to organize olfactory quality in any meaningful way and have not yet identified a physical property analogous to wavelength and frequency which is linked to olfactory quality. Let's consider these two problems:

Classifying Odor Qualities

One problem in dealing with odor quality is that it is difficult to adequately describe odors, because we lack a specific language for odor quality. For example, if you asked people to smell the chemical β-ionone they would probably say that it smells like violets. This description, it turns out, is fairly accurate, but if you compare β-ionone to real violets, they smell different. The perfume industry's solution is to use names such as "woody violet" and "sweet violet" to distinguish between different violet smells, but this hardly solves the problem we face in trying to determine how olfaction works.

A large number of attempts have been made to find a way to classify odors and so bring some order into this confusing situation. One of the best-known attempts is Henning's **odor prism,** shown in Figure 15.3. Henning's prism has six corners, at which the qualities putrid, ethereal, resinous, spicy, fragrant, and burned are located. Odors lying along an edge of the prism resemble the qualities at the four corners of the surface, in proportion to their nearness to each corner. For example, Figure 15.4 shows the face of the prism that has fragrant, ethereal, resinous, and spicy at its corners. From its location on the ethereal-resinous edge, we can see that lemon oil has both ethereal and resinous prop-

*These physically stated questions are useful only as long as the physical properties are correlated with perception. For example, in our discussion of color constancy in Chapter 4 we saw that hue is not always correlated with wavelength. When this occurs we need to revert to our perceptual question, "what is the code for hue?"

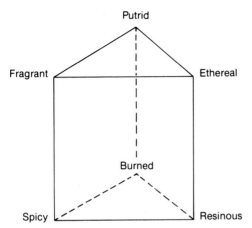

F I G U R E 15. 3 Henning's odor prism. (From Woodworth, 1938.)

us to understand olfaction, and the Henning prism is now only of historical importance (Bartoshuk, Cain, & Pfaffmann, 1985). Unfortunately, other classification schemes are not better than Henning's. Many schemes propose too few classifications, thereby making it impossible to find a class for some odors, and others propose categories so broad or ambiguous that some subjects might judge a particular odor to be in one category while others would judge the same odor to be in another category.

Further complicating the task of classifying odors is the possibility that any classification scheme can be influenced by the classifier's knowledge of objects in his or her environment. William Cain gives the following example of how cognitive factors can influence the classification of odors:

A neighbor drops in one morning and notices, quite accurately, the smells of coffee, toast, and fried bacon emanating from your kitchen. Such a sensory analysis

erties but that it is more like ethereal, since it is closer to the ethereal corner.

Although the geometry of Henning's odor prism is aesthetically appealing, this method of classifying odors has proven to be of little use in helping

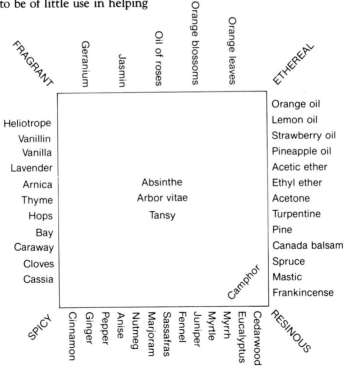

F I G U R E 15. 4 The face of Henning's odor prism that is facing us in Figure 15.3, showing the many smells that fall between the basic ones at the corners of the prism. (From Woodworth, 1938.)

would hardly be astonishing. But consider that the smell of coffee arises from the action of many, perhaps more than a hundred, chemical constituents. The smells of bacon and toast also arise from many constituents. Yet, from this vast array of airborne constituents, three rather unitary odors (coffee, bacon, toast) emerge. A person who had never smelled coffee, bacon, and toast would obviously find another set of qualities or perhaps a single unitary quality in the same array and could claim equal validity for the observation (Bartoshuk, Cain, and Pfaffmann, 1985, p. 251).

The lack of a good system of odor classification has led John Levine and Donald McBurney (1983) to sum up the situation in this way: "Of the many systems of classifying odors that have been proposed over the centuries, none has ever done much for the field except decorate textbooks."

The Connection Between Odor and Physical Properties

It has been said that olfaction behaves in part as a molecular shape detector (Cain, 1988). This idea that a molecule's shape is an important determinant of odor quality is the cornerstone of John Amoore's (1970) **stereochemical theory of odor.** This theory postulates that there are different molecular shapes for different odor qualities and that there are "sites" on the olfactory receptors shaped to accept only molecules with the correct shape. Figure 15.5 shows some molecular models and models of the olfactory receptor sites into which these molecules are supposed to fit.

Despite the appeal of this idea, Amoore was unable to find any evidence for the specific recep-

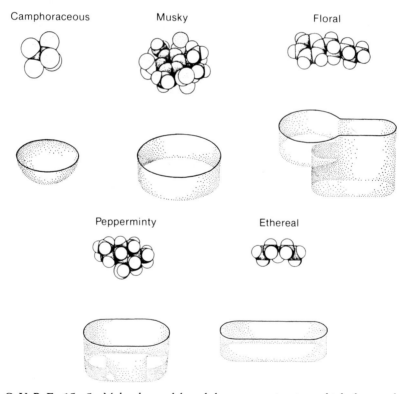

F I G U R E   15. 5   Molecular models and the receptor sites into which these molecules fit, according to Amoore (1964) and Amoore, Johnston, and Rubin's (1970) stereochemical theory of odor.

F I G U R E 15. 6 Two molecules with similar structures but with different odors.

tor sites that he proposed and therefore concluded that "the site-fitting model for olfaction is evidently of rather limited value" (Amoore, 1970, p. 138). Nonetheless, the idea that *molecular shape* is important in determining odor is still very much alive, and some connections have been demonstrated between molecular shape and odor quality. Molecular shape is not, however, the only determinant of odor quality, because many molecules with very similar shapes have very different odors. Odor quality is also affected by physical and chemical properties, such as chemical reactivity and the electrical charge of elements that make up a molecule. Especially for smaller molecules, making a small change in just one molecular group can cause large changes in odor. For example, when the CO group of the molecule on the left in Figure 15.6 is replaced by a CH_3 group, the odor changes from musk to odorless, even though the shapes of the two molecules are almost identical (Beets, 1978). Thus, while the search for the physical properties that correspond to odor quality has met with some success, we are far from being able to predict a substance's odor from its physical properties, and, as John Kauer (1987) notes in a recent review of olfactory research, "Odor quality cannot be defined simply on any easily characterized physiochemical continua, as can visual stimuli by wavelength or auditory pitch by frequency" (p. 208).

THE NEURAL CODE FOR ODOR QUALITY

Although we have not yet found a simple way to classify odor quality or to relate odor quality to the physical properties of molecules, this has not stopped researchers from searching for the neural code for quality. We will describe this research by first considering how chemicals affect the olfactory receptors and we will then describe how the olfactory bulb and other, more central, structures respond to different chemicals.

Coding at the Level of the Receptors

How do the receptors code odor quality? Are there receptors that respond to specific odorants or to groups of similarly smelling odorants? The answer to this question is "no"; most receptors respond to a number of different odors. Evidence that receptors fire to many odorants comes from Don Matthews' (1972) recordings from receptors in the tortoise olfactory mucosa. His results, illustrated in Figure 15.7, show how 19 receptors respond to 27 different odorants. Note that most of the receptors respond to more than one odorant, with the ones on the far right responding to more than 10 of the 27 odorants. Results similar to these, showing that individual receptors respond to a number of stimuli, have also been found in the frog (Blank, 1974; Holley, Duchamp, Revial, Juge, & Macleod, 1974) and the rabbit (Moulton, 1965).

If single receptors don't respond best to specific odorants, how do the receptors signal odor quality? The answer is that different odorants cause different *spatial patterns* of response in the sheet of receptors under the mucosa. In other words, one chemical might cause maximum receptor activity in the receptors at one end of the mucosa whereas another chemical might cause maximal activity at the other end. Two different mechanisms are responsible for these different patterns of activity: (1) the regional sensitivity effect and (2) the chromatographic effect.

The regional sensitivity effect. The idea behind the **regional sensitivity effect** is simple—different areas on the mucosa are sensitive to some odorants and are not as sensitive to others. John Kauer and David Moulton (1974) demonstrated this by using a small nozzle to present odorants to small areas of

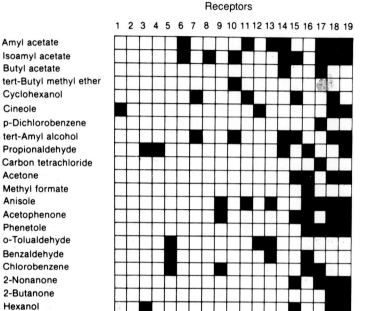

FIGURE 15. 7 The responses of 19 different olfactory receptors of the tortoise to various stimuli. The darkened squares indicate that a stimulus elicits a response from a receptor. The receptors that respond to the fewest stimuli are on the left and those that respond to the greatest number of stimuli are on the right. (From Matthews, 1972.)

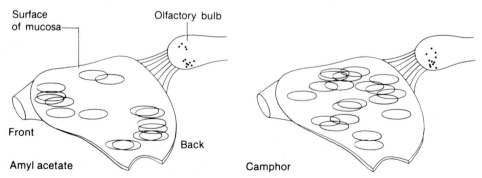

FIGURE 15. 8 The results of Kauer and Moulton's (1974) determination of the area on the mucosa that responds best to amyl acetate (left) and camphor (right). Each oval represents the area of mucosa which elicits the largest response from a different neuron in the olfactory bulb.

receptors on a salamander's olfactory mucosa. As they recorded from a neuron in the olfactory bulb, they moved the nozzle to different areas on the mucosa and found that although a particular olfactory bulb neuron responds to the stimulation of many different areas, it responds best to stimulation of one or two areas. Figure 15.8 shows the results of experiments on a number of neurons in the olfactory bulb for two stimuli, amyl acetate and camphor. Each oval indicates the area of mucosa that results in a maximal response to that chemical. Note that the distributions of these areas of maximal response are different for the two chemicals. Large amyl acetate responses result from stimulation of receptors on the front or back of the mucosa, while large camphor responses result from stimulation of receptors nearer the middle of the mucosa. Thus, since receptors in different areas are sensitive to different chemicals, each chemical causes a different pattern of receptor firing.

Alan MacKay-Sim, Paul Shaman, and David Moulton (1982) demonstrated this regional sensitivity in another way be presenting chemicals to small areas on the olfactory mucosa, as before, but by recording responses not from the olfactory bulb but from the olfactory mucosa itself. By stimulating with different chemicals and recording the **electroolfactogram,** a response that indicates the pooled electrical activity of thousands of receptors, they found that the size of the response depends on the chemical used and where on the mucosa this chemical is applied. Figure 15.9 shows their results for two chemicals, limonene and butanol, which have very different areas of maximum sensitivity on the mucosa.

The chromatographic effect. Max Mozell (1966; Mozell & Hornung, 1984, 1985) proposes that odorant molecules interact with the olfactory mucosa in a way similar to the way chemicals interact with a gas chromatograph, a device used to separate the different components of a chemical mixture. In gas chromatography, the mixture to be analyzed is transported by a carrier gas through a chromatographic column, which is filled with a material called the sorbent. As the mixture is carried through the column by the gas, some molecules travel

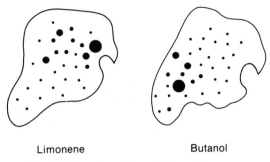

Limonene   Butanol

F I G U R E 15. 9 Size of electroolfactogram (EOG) response of olfactory mucosa to stimulation of the mucosa by limonene and butanol. The larger the dot, the larger the size of the EOG response. (From MacKay-Sim, Shamau, & Moulton, 1982.)

through the column slowly because they are attracted to the sorbent, and other molecules, less strongly attracted to the sorbent, travel through the column more rapidly. The different molecules of the mixture become separated as they flow through the column, with molecules that travel more slowly being deposited on the sorbent at the beginning of the column and molecules that travel more rapidly being deposited more uniformly across the column.

Mozell proposes that the olfactory mucosa behaves like the sorbent of the chromatograph. Thus, as odorant molecules flow over the mucosa, those that are strongly attracted to the mucosa flow slowly and stimulate receptors at the front of the mucosa more strongly, whereas molecules that are weakly attracted to the mucosa flow more rapidly and stimulate receptors more uniformly across the patch of mucosa. Therefore, each molecule results in a different pattern of receptor stimulation not because of differences in the sensitivity of the receptors but because of differences in the way the molecules *distribute themselves* on the receptors. This is called the **chromatographic effect.**

Mozell has demonstrated, in many different experiments, that odorant molecules do, in fact, distribute themselves differently on the mucosa (Mozell, 1964, 1966, 1970; Mozell & Jagodewiez, 1973; Hornung, Lansing, & Mozell, 1975; Hornung & Mozell, 1977). For example, Hornung and Mozell (1981) determined where odorants were deposited on a frog's olfactory mucosa by flowing

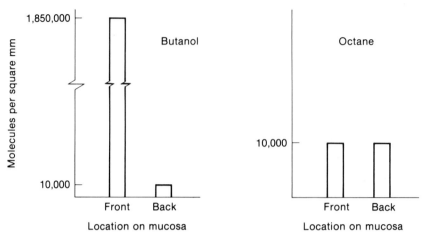

FIGURE 15. 10 How butanol and octane molecules distribute themselves on a frog's olfactory mucosa. Far more butanol is deposited on the front of the mucosa than on the back, but equal amounts of octane are deposited on the front and back of the mucosa. (Adapted from Hornung & Mozell, 1981.)

radioactively labeled odorants over the mucosa and then analyzing the pattern of activity. They found, for example, that large amounts of the chemical butanol were deposited on the front of the mucosa and only a small amount on the back, whereas octane was distributed fairly evenly over the whole mucosa (Figure 15.10).

The regional sensitivity effect and the chromatographic effect work together to create different patterns of receptor activity for different chemicals. Are these differing patterns of receptor activity translated into differing patterns of activity in other structures in the olfactory system? The answer to this question, as we will see below, is "yes."

Coding in the Olfactory Bulb and Beyond

If the distinctive patterns of receptor firing for different odorants are transmitted to the olfactory bulb, different odorants should cause different patterns of activity in the olfactory bulb. Recent experiments show that this appears to be the case.

K. B. Döving and A. J. Pinching (1973; Pinching & Döving, 1974) asked what would happen to an animal's olfactory bulb if the animal were exposed to one odorant for a long period of time. To

answer this question, they exposed each of a number of rats to a different odorant for 3 months and then examined the rats' olfactory bulbs. When they did this, they found that exposure to the odorants caused parts of the olfactory bulb to degenerate, and the pattern of degeneration was different for each odorant. Each odorant did not, however, have its own exclusive area on the olfactory bulb. Each odorant caused large areas to degenerate, thereby creating considerable overlap between the different patterns.

Why should long-term exposure to an odorant cause degeneration in the olfactory bulb? Two possible explanations are:

1. Overstimulation causes degeneration. Long-term exposure to an odorant overstimulates neurons that respond to that odorant and therefore causes them to degenerate. This explanation is analogous to the one proposed to explain *stimulation deafness* in hearing, in which long-term exposure to a particular frequency causes degeneration of local areas of the cochlear partition (see p. 430).

2. Understimulation causes degeneration. If only one odorant is presented, neurons that respond to other odorants are deprived of stimulation and this deprivation causes them to degener-

ate. This explanation is analogous to one of the mechanisms proposed to explain the results of *selective rearing experiments* in vision, in which exposure to vertical contours causes a decrease in neurons that respond to horizontal contours.

To determine which of these mechanisms is operating in Döving and Pinching's experiments, D. G. Laing and H. Panhuber (1978) exposed rats to either acetophenone or cyclohexanone for up to 4 months and then measured the rats' sensitivity to these odors and to other odors. They found that the sensitivity to acetophenone and cyclohexanone was not affected by this long exposure, but that the sensitivity to the other chemicals decreased. Laing and Panhuber therefore concluded that the neurons functioning after long-term odor exposure are those that respond to the odors presented during the exposure. Thus, the understimulation mechanism described above appears to be correct—neurons that are *not* stimulated degenerate and neurons that are stimulated survive (also see Laing and Panhuber, 1980).

A more recent experiment by William Stewart, John Kauer, and Gordon Shepherd (1979) used the 2-deoxyglucose (2-DG) technique to show that different patterns of neurons are activated by different odorants. We originally described the 2-DG technique in Chapter 2, but we've come a long way since then, so let's briefly review this procedure. 2-deoxyglucose has three important properties. (1) Since its structure is similar to glucose, a primary source of energy for neurons, it is taken up by neurons as though it were glucose. The more active the neuron, the more 2-DG is taken up by the neuron. (2) When 2-DG is taken up by a neuron it accumulates inside the neuron. (3) 2-DG can be labeled with a radioactive isotope, carbon 14. Therefore, by measuring the amount of radioactivity in various parts of the brain, we can determine which neurons are most active.

Stewart injected rats with radioactively labeled 2-DG and exposed them to either amyl acetate or camphor for 45 minutes, thereby activating neurons that would be stimulated by amyl acetate or camphor and causing them to take up 2-DG. After this 45-minute exposure, the rats were sacrificed, and their olfactory bulbs were examined to deter-

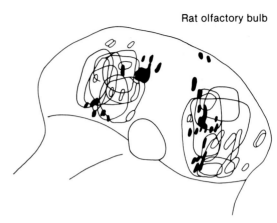

Rat olfactory bulb

F I G U R E 15. 11 Areas of highest activity in the rats' olfactory bulb caused by stimulation with camphor (dark areas) and by stimulation with amyl acetate (open areas), as determined by the 2-DG technique. (Stewart, Kauer, & Shepherd, 1979.)

mine the pattern of radioactivity. The results, shown in Figure 15.11, indicate that different patterns of neurons are activated by amyl acetate and camphor. Note, however, that although the patterns are different, each substance causes activity over a large area and there is considerable overlap between the areas activated.

The results of both the receptor and olfactory bulb experiments, described above, point to a much more diffuse type of coding in the olfactory system than in the other sensory systems. For example, a touch to your hand activates mechanoreceptors in the parts of the hand touched, which causes activity in a fairly well-defined area of cortex. In contrast, sniffing some amyl acetate activates a fairly diffuse pattern of receptors on your olfactory mucosa which causes widespread activity in your olfactory bulb. This activity may be different from that generated by sniffing some other substance, but it is not precisely localized, as is the response to having your hand touched. Somehow, even though the coding in the olfactory system appears to be fairly diffuse, we are capable of distinguishing tens of thousands of different odors.

Perhaps our ability to distinguish this large number of odors requires processing in centers higher than the olfactory bulb. We know little about the nature of this processing; however, some experiments by T. Tanabe and coworkers (1974, 1975) have uncovered an area of the brain that contains many neurons that respond to only a few odorant molecules. This area, which is called the **lateral postero-orbital frontal cortex (LPOF),** is located on the underside of the frontal lobe.

Tanabe showed by both behavioral and electrophysiological methods that the LPOF is important in olfaction. His behavioral test was simple. He impregnated two small pieces of bread with different odors and gave one of them a bitter taste. When each piece was given to a monkey, the monkey first smelled each piece and then ate it. But, after determining which smell was associated with the bitter taste, the monkey was able to avoid the bitter piece of bread, solely on the basis of its smell, 81 percent of the time. Removal of the LPOF, however, reduced this ability from 81 percent to 26 percent. This large decrease in performance did not occur with the removal of other cortical olfactory areas.

Tanabe's electrophysiological results, shown in Figure 15.12, are of particular interest to us because they show the degree to which eight different odorants caused neural responses in the olfactory bulb, amygdala, and LPOF. Each bar indicates the percentage of neurons responding to the number of odorants indicated on the horizontal axis. Note that few of the cells in the olfactory bulb and amygdala respond to only one odor, whereas half of the cells in the LPOF respond to only one odor. Neurons in the LPOF, then, are tuned to respond to much more specific odorants than are neurons in lower centers. From these results, it is tempting to draw an analogy between neurons in the LPOF and neurons such as the hypercomplex cells of the visual system that respond only to very specific visual stimuli. Such analogies cannot, however, be taken too seriously until we have more experimental evidence about information processing in the olfactory system.

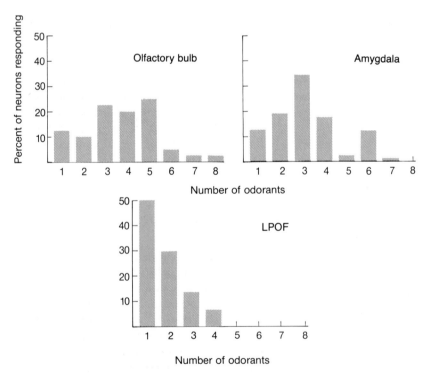

F I G U R E   15. 12 Histograms showing how cells in the olfactory bulb, the amygdala, and the LPOF respond to eight different odorants. (From Tanabe, Iino, & Takagi, 1975.)

TASTE

Taste is usually thought of as a partner to smell, since they work together at mealtimes. As we put food into our mouths, the nose, conveniently located just above, adds flavor to our food. To demonstrate this to yourself, you have only to hold your nose while eating. When you do this it becomes difficult to distinguish a piece of raw potato from an apple and much of the flavor of meats, fruits, butter, and coffee is eliminated (Geldard, 1972).

But taste is a sense in its own right, with its own properties, many quite different from smell, and the pleasure we derive from eating owes a lot to the taste receptors on our tongues and in our mouths. Adding a little salt or sugar to food may affect its smell only slightly but can have a large effect on its taste. Interestingly enough, taste is perhaps the most public of all our senses, in that people often taste things together and often share their taste experiences as they eat: "This chicken would taste better with a little more salt," "I can't stand liver," "Your apple pie is fantastic, Mom." When we share our taste experiences like this, we are emphasizing the *affective* aspect of taste; that is, we usually label tastes as pleasant or unpleasant and these labels affect which foods we choose to eat and which foods we avoid.

Many factors influence how foods taste to us: how much we've already eaten, our past experiences with different foods, our genetic makeup, the food we've just finished eating, and our nutritional state, among others. As we have for the other senses in this book, we want to consider the physiological workings of the sense of taste, but first let's consider some of the factors that influence which foods we seek out and which we avoid.

FACTORS INFLUENCING FOOD INTAKE

Internal State of the Organism

A restaurant near my house has fantastic banana cream pie. The first forkful is always great, and I find myself wishing they had given me a bigger piece. By the last forkful, however, the thrill is gone. I've had enough. This is a phenomenon that Cabanac (1971, 1979) calls **alliesthesia,** changed sensation. Our reaction to a taste stimulus may be positive when we first taste it, but this positive response may become negative after we've eaten for a while. To illustrate this effect, Cabanac describes an experiment in which he had people rate the pleasantness of a sugar solution. If they taste a sample and then spit it out, the sugar continues to get positive ratings over many samplings. If, however, people drink the sample each time they taste it, the originally pleasant sugar solution becomes unpleasant, and eventually the people refuse to drink any more. According to Cabanac, this experiment, and many others with similar results, illustrate that a given stimulus can be pleasant or unpleasant, depending upon signals from inside the body.

Genetics and Past Experience

It is generally assumed that many taste preferences are genetically determined. That is, people are born with a built-in preference for sweet foods, find bitter and sour foods unpleasant, and like salty foods at low concentrations but dislike them at high concentrations. There are good reasons for these built-in preferences. Sweetness usually indicates the presence of sugar, an important source of energy, whereas sourness or bitterness often indicates the presence of dangerous substances, such as poisons that result in sickness or death.

While people undoubtedly are born with built-in preferences for certain tastes, it is also true that not everyone likes the same foods. Could it be that different people taste things differently? In fact, there is evidence that people do taste things differently and that some of these differences could be due to genetic differences between people. One of the most well-documented genetic effects in taste involves people's ability to taste the bitter substance **phenyltiocarbamide (PTC).** Linda Bartoshuk (1980) describes the discovery of this PTC effect:

The different reactions to PTC were discovered accidentally in 1932 by Arthur L. Fox, a chemist working at the E. I. DuPont deNemours Company in Wilmington, Delaware. Fox had prepared some PTC, and when he poured the compound into a bottle, some of the dust escaped into the air. One of his colleagues complained about the bitter taste of the dust, but Fox, much closer to the material, noticed nothing. Albert F. Blakeslee, an eminent geneticist of the era, was quick to pursue this observation. At a meeting of the American Association for the Advancement of Science (AAAS) in 1934, Blakeslee prepared an exhibit that dispensed PTC crystals to 2,500 of the conferees. The results: 28 percent of them described it as tasteless, 66 percent as bitter, and 6 percent as having some other taste.

People who can taste PTC are described as *tasters* and those who cannot are called *nontasters* (or **taste blind** to PTC). Molly L. Hall, Bartoshuk, and coworkers (1975) have found that most people who can taste PTC also perceive a bitter taste in caffeine at much lower concentrations than do nontasters, and Bartoshuk (1979) has reported a similar result for the artificial sweetener saccharin. That some people are much more sensitive to the bitter tastes of caffeine and saccharin than others is particularly interesting, since these two substances are found in many common foods. Caffeine makes coffee taste bitter to tasters but has little effect on nontasters, and saccharin, in the concentrations used in soft drinks, tastes two to three times more bitter to tasters than to nontasters.

Another taste that some people experience but others don't is the sweet taste of water after eating artichokes. This is called the **artichoke effect.** At the same AAAS meeting where Blakeslee studied people's sensitivity to the bitter taste of PTC, he also did an informal experiment on the artichoke effect. A dinner at the AAAS meeting included a salad consisting solely of artichokes and mayonnaise. After eating the artichokes, 60 percent of the diners found that the taste of water was altered, in most cases to sweet, whereas the rest of the diners experienced no effect (Bartoshuk, 1980). According to Bartoshuk, that some people experience this effect while others do not suggests that genetics may be behind this difference.

While some individual differences in taste may be due to genetics, others may be due to people's past experiences with different foods. Many Mexicans, for example, like chili peppers that would cause great distress to Americans. I can vividly remember some of the meals an old roommate of mine from Nigeria used to cook; his liberal seasoning with red pepper seemed to enhance the taste for him but did little for me except greatly increase my consumption of water. Perhaps now that I've developed a taste for spicy Szechwan Chinese food, I would be more tolerant of my exroommate's red peppers.

Despite much anecdotal evidence that past experience with food can change people's food preferences, there is little experimental evidence that early experience with food results in permanent attachments to a particular food or flavor (Beauchamp & Maller, 1977). A recent experiment by Howard Moskowitz and coworkers (1975), however, does suggest that past experience may shape food preferences. Moskowitz first asked a group of Indian medical students to rate the pleasantness of various compounds and learned that they, like most other people, found sour compounds unpleasant. He then tested some Indians of the Karnataka province and learned that they found both citric acid and quinine to be pleasant tasting. This is quite different from the results with the Indian medical students, who had described the citric acid as having an unpleasant sour taste and quinine as having an unpleasant bitter taste. Moskowitz felt that past experience was the most likely explanation for the Karnataka Indians' strange preference for sour and bitter compounds. Their diet consisted of many sour foods, with the tamarind, a particularly sour fruit, making up a large portion of it. Being poor, they ate the tamarind out of necessity, and, from constant exposure to this fruit, probably acquired a taste for sour foods. (It should be noted, however, that a genetic explanation for this phenomenon cannot be ruled out.)

Conditioned Taste Aversion

Food preferences can be affected not only by the long-term exposure to foods that results from daily eating patterns, as appears to be the case for the Karnataka Indians, but also by a single pairing of

BOX 15.2 / *Green Mashed Potatoes?*

If, when you were younger, you discovered the magic of your mother's food coloring, you may have created, as I once did, such exotic foods as green mashed potatoes or blue applesauce. If you then tried to interest someone in eating your concoctions, you probably found that people are not enthusiastic about trying strangely colored foods.

The appearance of food plays an important role in people's attitudes about food, as evidenced by the large sums of money spent to produce appetizing-looking pictures of food to put on the cans, jars, and boxes that package the food. Another connection between vision and food is illustrated by the statement "That food looks good," which, translated, means, "That food looks as if it would taste good." This statement is interesting, because it implies that we can decide if a particular food tastes good, based only on its appearance. Though most people would not go so far as to agree with this statement, most would agree that the appearance of their food does influence its desirability. However, only a few studies have been published on how color, one of the most important aspects of a food's appearance, influences a food's flavor.

Karl Duncker (1939) (whose work on induced movement was discussed in Chapter 8) found that subjects think that white chocolate candy tastes "milkier" and "less chocolatey" than brown chocolate candy. Experiments on how color affects the taste of liquids have shown that the color of a liquid can influence a subject's ability both to identify the flavor of the liquid and to detect small differences in taste between two liquids. For example, when 200 pharmacy students were asked to identify the taste of various colored syrups, most of them were unable to accurately identify the actual flavor when the syrups were colorless, and most had an even more difficult time when inappropriate colors were added to the syrups (Kanig, 1955).

The influence of color on taste has also been demonstrated in an experiment in which subjects were presented with two solutions of pear nectar, one containing 5.0 percent sucrose and the other containing 5.2 percent sucrose, and were asked to judge which was sweeter. When the solutions had no color, 65 percent of the subjects' responses were correct, but when the solutions had different colors (red, yellow, green, or blue), the accuracy of the responses dropped to 50 percent.

Similar results occurred when citric acid was added to one sample and subjects were asked to judge which of two samples was more sour. In this test, subjects were correct 81 percent of the time for uncolored samples and 65 percent of the time for colored samples. These results indicate that it is easier to judge small differences in flavor when both samples are colorless than when they are two different colors (Pangborn & Hansen, 1963). Apparently, our sense of flavor is influenced not only by our tongue and nose but also by our eyes!

---

food with sickness. The first experiments to illustrate this effect were done by John Garcia and coworkers (Garcia, Ervin, & Koelling, 1966; Garcia & Koelling, 1966) on rats. In a typical experiment, Garcia first determined that a rat will drink a sugar solution that tastes sweet to humans. The rats were then fed sugar water containing a poison that made them sick. After recovering from the resulting sickness, the rats would drink little or none of the sugar solution that, before it was paired with sickness, they drank in large quantities. This avoidance of a taste after it is paired with sickness is called **conditioned taste aversion.**

Why do the rats avoid the sugar water after it is paired with sickness? One possibility is that pairing sugar water with sickness doesn't change the taste of the sugar water; instead, this pairing causes the rats to avoid the sugar taste because they have learned that sickness follows it. On the other hand, the rats may avoid the sugar water because it takes on an unpleasant taste after they become sick. We cannot answer this question for the rat, since the rat can't tell us what it experiences; however, reports from humans support the idea that conditioned taste aversion actually changes the taste of the substance paired with sickness. A number of years ago, I experienced such an effect when I got sick about a half an hour after drinking one of my favorite drinks, cream soda. Even though I knew that the sickness had no actual connection to the cream soda (I had the 24-hour flu), the taste of the cream soda became associated with feeling sick, and for many years afterward cream soda tasted terrible to me. Other people have made similar observations (Garcia, Hawkins, & Rusiniak, 1974), and some have shown that children made sick by chemotherapy treatments for cancer will avoid eating the ice cream they had eaten just before their chemotherapy injection (Bernstein, 1978).

Specific Hungers

We've already mentioned that people are born with a preference for certain tastes and that these genetically programmed taste preferences help people seek out foods that are high in energy (indicated by their sweet taste) and avoid foods that may be poisonous (indicated by their sour or bitter taste). In fact, taste appears to play a major role in regulating the intake of certain substances. For example, rats and people have a **specific hunger** for sodium, a necessary component of their diets (Beauchamp, 1987). Rats deprived of sodium will increase their sodium intake to make up the deficit, and they use taste to recognize foods that contain sodium (Rozin, 1976).

A most dramatic demonstration that taste regulates this hunger for sodium is M. Nachman's (1963) experiment in which he created a need for salt in a rat by performing an adrenalectomy (removal of the adrenal gland), thereby causing the rat to eat large amounts of lithium chloride, even though this substance is toxic and makes the rat ill. The rat does this because lithium chloride tastes identical to sodium chloride, the substance the rat actually needs to correct the salt deficit created by the adrenalectomy.

Specific hunger for salt, analogous to that found in Nachman's adrenalectomized rats, has been reported in people who suffer from various diseases. In the 1930s, before the condition of specific salt hunger was widely recognized, a child whose adrenal cortex was diseased craved large amounts of salt. In an attempt to find out what caused this craving, the child was hospitalized, only to die after being placed on a standard hospital diet, which didn't satisfy the child's increased need for salt. Addison's disease also increases hunger for salt. A 34-year-old man with this disease was reported to routinely half fill a glass with salt before adding tomato juice and to cover his steak with a one-inch-thick layer of salt (Liphovsky, 1977).

The above examples illustrate some of the genetic, environmental, and biological factors that influence our sense of taste. Undoubtedly, our decision whether or not to ingest a particular food results from a complex interaction of genetically determined, experiential, and physiological influences (Beauchamp, 1987; Rozin, 1976), and because of its role in food selection, taste is of great importance in our day-to-day lives. We will now consider the physiological workings of the sense of taste, beginning at the most logical starting place—the tongue.

STRUCTURE OF THE TASTE SYSTEM

The surface of the tongue, shown in Figure 15.13, contains many ridges and valleys due to the presence of structures called **papillae,** of which there are four kinds: (1) Filiform papillae, shaped like cones, are found over the entire surface of the tongue, giving it its rough appearance; (2) fungiform papillae, shaped like mushrooms, are found at the tip and sides of the tongue; (3) foliate papillae are a series of folds along the sides of the middle of the tongue; and (4) circumvallate papillae, shaped

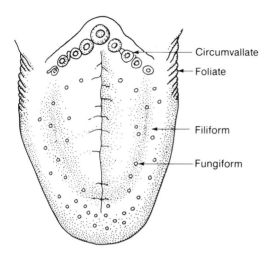

F I G U R E 15. 13 The tongue, showing the four different types of papillae.

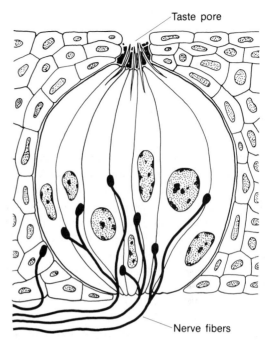

F I G U R E 15. 14 A taste bud of the foliate papillae. The taste bud is made up of a number of cells, some of which are taste cells and some of which are supporting cells. (Adapted from Murray & Murray, 1970.)

like flat mounds surrounded by a trench, are found at the back of the tongue.

All of these papillae except the filiform contain **taste buds,** with the human tongue containing a total of about 10,000 taste buds (Bartoshuk, 1971). Since the filiform papillae contain no taste buds, stimulation of the central part of the tongue, which contains only filiform papillae, causes no taste sensations. Figure 15.14 shows that each taste bud is made up of a number of receptor cells, each of which projects into a taste pore at the top of the bud. At this pore, the taste solution on the tongue contacts the taste cells to generate the electrical signals that are transmitted along the fibers leaving the taste bud.

Fibers from the front of the tongue travel toward the brain in the chorda tympani nerve, and fibers from the back of the tongue travel toward the brain in the glossopharyngeal nerve. These nerves transmit signals to the solitary nucleus in the medulla near the base of the brain (on top of the spinal cord), then to the thalamus and the parietal cortex. As is the case for olfaction, the cortical projections for taste are not precisely known; however, it appears that the central projections for taste are within or close to the tactile projection areas for the tongue in the somatosensory cortex (see Figure 2.9).

TASTE QUALITY

The Four Basic Tastes

Our description of odor quality led us to the conclusion that it is impossible to classify odors into a small number of categories. The situation for taste is different. Although some researchers feel that the evidence for a small number of basic tastes is not strong enough to warrant such a classification system (Erickson, 1982), most taste researchers favor the idea that there are four basic taste qualities: salty, sour, sweet, and bitter. Many lists of taste qualities have been proposed over the centuries, but almost all have included these four qualities. For example, Aristotle's list of qualities, proposed over 2,000 years ago, included salty, sour, sweet, and bitter plus the tastes astringent, pungent, and harsh, while Zotterman's (1956) list includes salty, sour, sweet, and bitter, plus the taste of water.

One reason for this general agreement about salty, sour, sweet, and bitter is that these qualities are consistently reported by subjects; when tastes such as metallic or alkaline are reported, it is usually found that they result from a combination of smell and taste, rather than from stimulation of the taste buds alone.

Donald McBurney (1969) has applied the method of magnitude estimation (see page 13, in Chapter 1 and Appendix A) to the analysis of taste quality. He first rinses the subject's tongue with water and then flows the taste solution over the tongue for 5 seconds. Subjects are instructed to give magnitude estimates of the intensity of each of the four taste qualities for each solution. When this procedure is followed, some substances have a predominant taste, but many others result in combinations of the four tastes. For example, each of the compounds sodium chloride (salty), hydrochloric acid (sour), sucrose (sweet), and quinine (bitter) is the closest we can come to a substance with only one of the four basic tastes, but the compound potassium chloride (KCl) has substantial salty and bitter components, as shown in Figure 15.15. Similarly, sodium nitrate ($NaNO_3$) results in a combined taste made up of a combination of salty, sour, and bitter.

Subjects, therefore, can describe their taste sensations based on these four qualities, and even if given the option of using additional qualities of their own choice, they will usually stay with the four basic tastes. Thus, salty, sour, sweet, and bitter appear to be adequate to describe the majority of our taste experiences.

The Taste of Water

Though it has been included in some people's lists of taste qualities, water has usually been considered to be tasteless. However, water can be given a taste by adapting the tongue to various other substances. For example, if water is flowed over the tongue after a salty solution, the water will taste sour or bitter. Adapting to sour or bitter causes a sweet **water taste,** and adapting to sweet causes a bitter

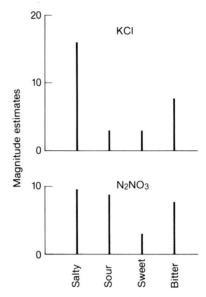

F I G U R E 15. 15 Contribution of each of the four basic tastes to the tastes of KC1 and $NaNO_3$ determined by the method of magnitude estimation. The height of the line indicates the size of the magnitude estimate for each basic taste. (McBurney, 1969.)

water taste (McBurney & Shick, 1971). It is interesting both that adaptation can cause water to have its own taste and that the taste the water takes on is always one or more of the four basic taste qualities. That no new water tastes appear further supports the idea that there is something special about salty, sour, sweet, and bitter.

Physical Properties and Taste Quality

Even though the connections between the physical properties of molecules and taste quality are not clear-cut, there is increasing evidence that specific physical and chemical properties are characteristic of each basic taste. Table 15.1 below lists each taste quality and the physical property associated with that quality (Beidler, 1978; Bartoshuk, 1985).

Despite good evidence that each quality depends on different physical properties, the exact physical properties involved for each quality are not precisely known. For one thing, the properties listed, especially for sweet and bitter, are very gen-

TABLE 15. 1 / *Physical Properties Associated with Taste Qualities*

Quality	Relevant Physical Property
Sour	Organic and inorganic acids that release a hydrogen ion (H+) in solution. However, not all acids are predominantly sour.
Salty	Organic and inorganic salts. The cation (positively charged component of a molecule; Na+ in NaCl) is most important.
Sweet	Complex organic molecules such as sugar.
Bitter	There is no good rule for bitter substances. Some are related to the structure of sweet molecules but with different molecular dimensions.

eral, and even for sour and salty, for which we have more information, there are unsolved problems. For example, although sourness usually depends on the presence of a charged hydrogen atom (H+), some compounds with large amounts of H+ can be less sour than other compounds with much less H+. This lack of correlation between the amount of H+ and taste quality means that some other property also determines sourness. Salt poses another interesting problem because it changes its quality as concentration changes. Thus, as the concentration of potassium chloride (KCl) is increased from low to high, this salt is perceived to be sweet, bitter, and, finally, salty.

We turn now from our discussion of physical properties and taste quality to taste coding.

THE NEURAL CODE FOR TASTE QUALITY

What is the neural code for taste quality? It is appropriate that we consider this question in the final pages of this book, because it brings up issues we have considered from the beginning. In Chapter 2, when we introduced the idea of sensory coding, we distinguished between *specificity theory*, the idea that quality is signaled by the activity in specific neurons, and *across-fiber-pattern theory*, the idea that quality is signaled by the pattern of activity in many fibers. In that discussion, and in others we have had throughout the book, we have favored an across-fiber-pattern theory of sensory coding. The situation for taste, however, is not clear-cut; there are good arguments for both types of coding.

Specificity (Labeled Line) Coding

According to specificity theory, different taste qualities are signaled by activity in specific nerve fibers. That is, the quality salty is signaled by activity in "salty fibers," sourness is signaled by activity in "sour fibers," and so on. This method of signaling taste quality is called **labeled lines,** because each nerve fiber is labeled as corresponding to a particular taste quality, in much the same way as different fibers in the skin correspond to specific qualities such as "warm," "cold," "touch," and "pain" (see page 472, in Chapter 14).

The strongest evidence for a labeled line theory of taste would be the existence of neurons that respond *only* to a particular class of taste stimuli. Such neurons are, however, rare. Most taste neurons fire to a number of the four basic tastes, as shown by their **response profiles,** plots like those in Figure 15.16 that show the neuron's response to each of the four basic taste qualities.

Although taste fibers usually respond to more than one taste quality, it has been suggested that we can group neurons based on the quality to which the neuron responds best. According to this idea, neurons that respond best to a particular quality signal the presence of that quality. Figure 15.16 shows the response profiles of five "NaCl-best" fibers and five "HCl-best" fibers in the hamster. Notice that the fibers within each group have similar profiles. Thus, the NaCl-best fibers respond best to NaCl, respond less well to HCl, and respond only slightly or not at all to sucrose and quinine. The HCl-best fibers respond best to HCl, less well to NaCl, slightly to quinine, and slightly or not at all

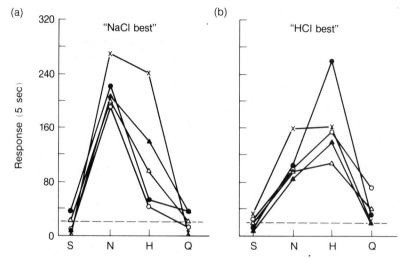

F I G U R E 15. 16 Response profiles of (a) five "NaCl-best" fibers and (b) five "HCl-best" fibers in the hamster. The letters on the horizontal axis stand for sucrose (S), sodium chloride (N), hydrogen chloride (H), and quinine (Q), and the numbers on the vertical axis indicate the number of nerve impulses generated by each of these stimuli during the first five seconds of the response. (From Frank, 1973.)

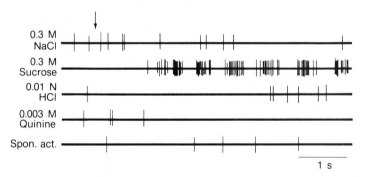

F I G U R E 15. 17 Response of a single fiber in the monkey's chorda tympani nerve to salt, sucrose, hydrochloric acid, and quinine. The bottom record indicates the rate of spontaneous activity. The arrow above the record for NaCl indicates the time of application of the stimuli. (Sato, Ogawa, & Yamashita, 1975.)

to sucrose. "Quinine-best" and "sucrose-best" fibers also have predictable response profiles.

The idea of labeled lines explains the fact, mentioned earlier, that many substances elicit a mixture of the four basic tastes. For example, a predominantly salty substance might also have some sour and some bitter taste. According to the labeled line theory, the salty substance would cause vigorous firing in the "salt-best" fibers, which would

result in a strong perception of saltiness. However, the salty substance would also cause smaller responses in the "sour-best" and "bitter-best" fibers, and the activity in these fibers would add slight sour and bitter tastes to the salty compound (Bartoshuk, 1978).

Proponents of the labeled line idea also point to the results of experiments that demonstrate selective effects on one type of fiber. For example,

Robert Contreras and Marion Frank (1979) found that depriving rats of sodium decreased the size of the response elicited from NaCl-best fibers but had little effect on other fiber types.

Additional evidence for the idea of labeled lines has come from recordings in higher animals such as the monkey, which appears to contain some fibers that respond only to specific stimuli, an example of which is shown in Figure 15.17 (Sato, Agoura, & Yamashita, 1975). This fiber responds poorly to sodium chloride, hydrochloric acid, and quinine but responds well to sucrose.

Although there is evidence for different types of taste neurons, this doesn't mean that neural coding must depend on labeled lines. We know, for example, that color vision depends on three types of cone receptors that are maximally sensitive to different regions of the spectrum. However, coding in this system depends not on the responses of individual neurons but on the *pattern of response* of the short-, medium-, and long-wavelength cones. Here we have a system in which neurons with different "best-wavelengths" participate in across-fiber-pattern coding. Some researchers argue that a similar situation occurs in taste.

Across-Fiber Patterning

We considered evidence for across-fiber coding in taste in Chapter 2 when we described Robert Erickson's experiment in which he showed that substances that taste alike to a rat have similar across-fiber patterns. This result, shown in Figure 15.18, shows that NH_4Cl and KCl, two substances that taste similar to the rat, have similar across-fiber patterns, which differ greatly from the pattern for NaCl, which tastes very different from either of these two substances.

More evidence in favor of across-fiber patterning comes from cross adaptation experiments. **Cross adaptation** is the reduction in the taste of one compound after adaptation to another compound. If the tongue is adapted to a compound with a predominant quality, such as sodium chloride (salt), this reduces the intensity of the taste resulting from stimulation by other compounds with the same quality. Thus, adapting the tongue to sodium chloride reduces the saltiness of other substances, while leaving other taste qualities unchanged.

David Smith and Marion Frank (1972) used

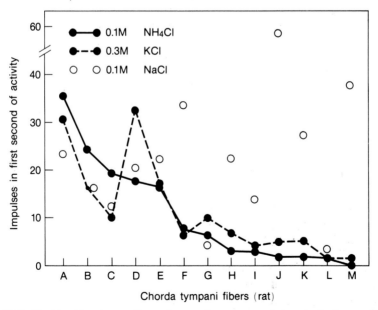

F I G U R E 15. 18 Across-fiber patterns of response to three salts in the rat. Each letter on the horizontal axis indicates a different single fiber. (From Erickson, 1963.)

an electrophysiological cross adaptation procedure to show that substances that are more similar, as measured by cross adaptation, have similar across-fiber patterns. They measured cross adaptation for a large number of salts by first determining the magnitude of the response of a rat's chorda tympani nerve to a test salt, then adapting the rat's tongue with an adapting salt, and, finally, remeasuring the nerve's response to the test salt.

Smith and Frank measured large amounts of cross adaptation between some compounds. For example, adapting with NaCl reduces the response to NaBr (sodium bromide) to zero. However, they found little cross adaptation between other compounds; adapting with NaCl had almost no effect on the response to KCl. Smith and Frank then compared their measured amount of cross adaptation for each pair of salts to the across-fiber patterns of nerve firing for the same salts, as measured by Erickson (1963). This comparison indicated that the greater the cross adaptation between the two salts, the more similar their across-fiber firing patterns; thus, similar substances cause similar patterns of firing (also see Smith, 1974).

Since there is evidence supporting both approaches to the coding of taste quality, we are left asking the question, "Which is correct?" Unfortunately we can't, at the present time, answer

this question. Each theory *could* be correct. David Smith and coworkers (1983) point out that there is good evidence that similar tasting compounds evoke highly similar across-fiber patterns. But they also point out that these patterns are dominated by activity in particular neurons. They found, for example, that sweet-tasting compounds produced highly similar across-fiber patterns in the hamster, primarily because of the high firing rates contributed by the "sucrose-best" neurons. Similarly, the similar across-fiber patterns they observed for salty-tasting compounds depended primarily on the firing of the "salt-best" neurons. The key question is: What information is *actually used* by the brain to determine our experience of taste quality? Is the key information contained in the activity of individual "sucrose-best" or "salt-best" neurons or is it contained in the patterns of firing of many types of neurons? At this point we don't know.

These questions, and many of the other still-to-be-answered ones we have posed in this book, will, however, eventually be answered. Some of them are being answered now, in the many laboratories doing research on the senses. Others of these questions will take longer to answer. Perhaps some of these will be answered by the next generation of researchers, which, hopefully, will even include some of the readers of this book.

Summary

Olfaction

1. In our society we tend to avoid many smells, perhaps because the sense of smell is capable of eliciting strong reactions.
2. The idea that human smell receptors are much less sensitive than are those of other animals is not true. It takes only one molecule of odorant to excite a human's olfactory receptor. The keen sense of smell of many animals is due to the fact that they have a greater number of receptors than humans.
3. The large difference thresholds for olfactory intensity reported in some experiments are due to the fact that it is difficult to precisely control the concentrations of the substances used as stimuli. When odorant concentrations are precisely controlled, the difference threshold for smell rivals the difference thresholds for vision and hearing.
4. When we have trouble identifying odors, this trouble is due not to a deficiency in our olfactory system but to an inability to retrieve the odor's name from our memory.
5. Smell has the potential of playing some role in human communication.
6. Many animals release chemicals called pheromones which, when sensed by other animals of the same species, trigger physiological or behavioral effects in these animals.
7. The receptors for smell are located in the olfactory mucosa. Contact of odorant molecules with the cilia of the receptors generates an electrical signal which travels to the olfactory bulb and then to higher olfactory centers.
8. Two of the problems of smell research are that a good classification scheme for odor quality has not yet been developed and that we do not yet know

exactly how the physical properties of odor molecules are linked to odor quality.

9. The stereochemical theory of odor postulates that a determinant of odor quality is a molecule's shape. There is some evidence for this theory, but there is also evidence that properties in addition to molecular shape also determine odor quality.

10. Most neurons respond to many different types of odorants. It is, therefore, unlikely that specificity coding operates in the olfactory system. There is, however, evidence that different odorants cause different spatial patterns of response in the sheet of receptors under the mucosa and in the olfactory bulb.

11. Different areas on the mucosa are sensitive to some odorants and are not as sensitive to others. This is called the regional sensitivity effect.

12. Different odorant molecules are attracted differently to the mucosa. Those that are strongly attracted stimulate receptors at the front of the mucosa more strongly, whereas molecules that are weakly attracted stimulate the receptors more uniformly across the mucosa. This is called the chromatographic effect.

13. Long-term exposure of animals to odorants causes degeneration of the olfactory bulb, with the pattern of degeneration being different for different odorants. The area that degenerates is the area that is *not* stimulated by the long-term odor exposure. Experiments in which rats are injected with radioactively labeled 2-deoxyglucose also indicate that different odorants result in different patterns of radioactivity in the olfactory bulb. In both the degeneration and the 2-DG experiments, there is a large area of overlap between the patterns for different odorants.

14. The results of both receptor and olfactory bulb experiments point to a much more diffuse type of coding in the olfactory system than in the other sensory systems.

15. A recently discovered olfactory center in the frontal lobe contains cells that each respond to fewer odorants than cells in other olfactory areas. This area may, therefore, represent a higher level of information processing in which detectors for specific odors are present.

Box

1. Although blind people have lower than normal sensitivity for odor detection, they are better at identifying odors than are sighted subjects.

Taste

1. The internal state of the organism influences food intake. A given stimulus can be pleasant or unpleasant depending upon signals from inside the body.

2. Many taste preferences are genetically determined. There is evidence that different people taste things differently and that some of these differences may be due to genetic differences between people.

3. Some differences in taste preferences may be due to people's past experiences with different foods.

4. Food preferences can be affected by a single pairing of food with sickness. This is called conditioned taste aversion.

5. Taste appears to play a major role in regulating the intake of substances like salt that are essential for survival.

6. The tongue contains four different kinds of papillae. Taste buds, each of which is made up of a number of taste cells, are found on these papillae. Fibers from the taste buds travel toward the brain in the chorda tympani nerve (for buds near the front of the tongue) or in the glossopharyngeal nerve (for buds near the back of the tongue).

7. Most taste researchers agree that there are four basic taste qualities: salty, sour, sweet, and bitter.

8. Water can be given a taste by first adapting the tongue to salty, sour, sweet, or bitter, and then flowing water over the tongue.

9. Specific physical and chemical properties are characteristic of each basic taste, but the exact properties involved have not yet been precisely determined.

10. According to specificity theory, different taste qualities are signaled by activity in specific nerve fibers. This method of signaling taste quality, which is called the labeled line theory, is supported by the finding that neurons that respond best to a particular taste quality tend to have similar response profiles.

11. According to across-fiber-pattern theory, taste quality is signaled by the pattern of activity in groups of nerve fibers. The results of cross adaptation experiments support this theory.

Box

1. The appearance of food affects peoples' attitudes about food and the color of taste solutions affects peoples' ability to make judgments about the taste of these solutions.

Study Questions

Olfaction

1. What is microsmatic? macrosmatic? (497)
2. Are the human's smell receptors less sensitive than those of other animals? Why are some animals more sensitive to odors than humans? (497)
3. What was Cain's finding regarding the variability of olfactory stimuli that are presented by placing a small amount of odorant on a cotton ball? (498)
4. What did Cain find when he presented stimuli using an olfactometer? (498)
5. If subjects are asked to identify a number of unfamiliar chemicals based on their smell, what percent of the chemicals will they identify correctly? (498)
6. If subjects are asked to identify a number of familiar substances based on their smell, what percent of these substances will they identify correctly? (498)
7. If, in 6 above, the substances are identified for the subjects when they are first presented, and the subjects are reminded of the correct identifications every time they make a mistake, what percentage will they eventually be able to identify correctly? (498)
8. Why do we have such a hard time identifying odors, according to Cain? (499)
9. Describe Russell's experiments in which he had subjects identify undershirts by their smell. (500)
10. What is menstrual synchrony? What mechanism has been suggested to explain this effect? (500)
11. What is a pheromone? a primer? a releaser? Give some examples of behaviors caused by primers and releasers? (501)
12. Does the sense of smell play any role in regulating the behavior of mammals? (501)
13. Does the sense of smell play an important role in regulating reproductive behavior in monkeys? (502)
14. Be able to label the following structures on a diagram of the olfactory system: receptors, olfactory mucosa, olfactory bulb. (502)
15. What is the first step in studying the sensory code in vision and hearing? Has it been possible to take that step for olfaction? (504)
16. Why do we say that we lack a specific language for odor quality? What problems face a person who wants to design a system for classifying odors? Are there any good odor classification systems? (504)
17. What is the stereochemical theory of odor quality? How well can we predict odor quality from the shapes and physical properties of odor molecules? (506)
18. Do olfactory receptors respond to one or to many odorants? (507)
19. What is the regional sensitivity effect? Describe experiments that provide evidence for this effect. (507)
20. What is the chromatographic effect? (509)
21. Describe Döving and Pinching's experiment. What are the two possible explanations for the degeneration observed in their experiment and which explanation is correct? (510)
22. Describe Stewart et al.'s 2-deoxyglucose experiments. How do the results of these experiments compare to the results of Döving and Pinching's experiments? What do the results of both experiments tell us about the nature of coding in the olfactory system? (511)
23. How did Tanabe show that the LPOF is important in olfaction? (512)

Box

1. Are blind or sighted people more sensitive to odors? Which group is better at identifying odors? (499)

Taste

1. What is alliesthesia? (513)
2. What is the evidence that different people taste things differently? What is taste blindness? the artichoke effect? (513)
3. Is there much experimental evidence that early experience with food results in permanent attachments to a particular food? Describe Moskowitz' experiment on early experience and food preference. (514)
4. What is conditioned taste aversion? How does conditioned taste aversion affect a food's taste? (514)
5. What are specified hungers? (516)
6. What are papillae? taste buds? Which papillae contain taste buds? Which parts of the tongue result in no taste sensations? (516)
7. What are the four basic tastes? Does a particular substance result in just one taste or in a combination of a number of tastes? (517)
8. What do we have to do to experience the taste of water? (518)
9. Are there specific physical and chemical properties that are characteristic of each taste? If so, which properties are associated with each taste quality? Compare our ability to correlate qualities with physical properties in taste and smell. (519)
10. What is the specificity, or labeled line, theory of taste coding? What evidence supports this theory? (519)
11. What is the across-fiber-pattern theory of taste coding? What evidence supports this theory? (521)

Box

1. How does the color of taste stimuli influence their taste? (515)

Glossary

Alliesthesia. "Changed sensation." Our reaction to a stimulus may be positive when we first experience it, but after repeated presentations our reaction may become more negative. (513)

Artichoke effect. Some people taste water as sweet after eating artichokes. (514)

Bruce effect. If a female mouse that has just mated is exposed to the smell of a strange male mouse within 24 hours, the female mouse will not become pregnant. (501)

Chromatographic effect. Different molecules distribute themselves differently on the surface of the olfactory mucosa. (509)

Conditioned taste aversion. An aversion to the taste of a food due to pairing of the food's taste with sickness. (515)

Cross adaptation. In taste, flowing one substance over the tongue affects a person's perception of another substance with the same quality. For example, adaptation with one salt might raise the threshold for detecting another salt. Adaptation across qualities, such as salt versus bitter, usually does not occur. (521)

Electroolfactogram. An electrical response recorded from the pooled activity of thousands of receptors in the olfactory mucosa. (509)

Gas chromatograph. A device that accurately measures the concentration of the vapor given off by a chemical stimulus. (498)

Labeled lines. In taste, the idea that different taste qualities are signaled by activity in specific nerve fibers. (519)

Lateral postero-orbital frontal cortex (LPOF). An area on the underside of the frontal lobe of the cortex that may be involved in processing olfactory information. (512)

Macrosmatic. Possessing a keen sense of smell. (497)

Menstrual synchrony. Women who live together often have menstrual periods that begin at approximately the same time. (500)

Microsmatic. Lacking a keen sense of smell. (497)

Odor prism. Henning's system for classifying odors. (504)

Olfactometer. A device that presents olfactory stimuli with great precision. (498)

Olfactory bulb. The structure that receives signals directly from the olfactory receptors. (502)

Papillae. Ridges and valleys on the tongue, some of which contain taste buds. There are four types of papillae: filiform, fungiform, foliate, and circumvallate. (516)

Phenyltiocarbamide (PTC). A substance that some people (*tasters*) can taste and others (*nontasters*) can't. (513)

Pheromone. A chemical released by an animal that causes specific physiological or behavioral reactions in another animal of the same species. (501)

Primer. A pheromone that triggers a chain of long-lasting physiological (usually hormonal) effects in an animal. (501)

Regional sensitivity effect. Different areas on the mucosa are sensitive to some odorants and are not as sensitive to others. (507)

Releaser. A pheromone that triggers an immediate reaction in another animal. (501)

Response profile. A graph that shows a neuron's response to each of the four basic taste qualities. (519)

Specific hunger. A genetically programmed taste preference that helps organisms seek out food that meets specific nutritional needs. (516)

Stereochemical theory of odor. The theory that there are different molecular shapes for different odor qualities. Some versions of this theory also propose that there are sites on the olfactory receptors which are shaped to accept only molecules with the correct shape. (506)

Taste blind. A person who is taste blind cannot taste PTC. (514)

Taste bud. A structure that contains a number of taste receptors. (517)

Water taste. Water can be given a taste by adapting the tongue to other substances. (518)

Psychophysical Methods

In this appendix we describe some psychophysical methods for measuring thresholds that have been in use since the beginnings of sensory psychology, and we also describe a method of measuring subjective magnitude above threshold that is much more recent. We begin by describing how we measure the absolute threshold.

MEASURING THE ABSOLUTE THRESHOLD

Absolute threshold is defined as the smallest amount of stimulus energy necessary for an observer to detect the stimulus. The idea of an absolute threshold

dates back to the early 1800s, when German philosopher J. F. Herbart suggested that for a mental event to be experienced it had to be stronger than some critical amount (Gescheider, 1976). This idea, which was developed further by Gustav Fechner in his book *Elements of Psychophysics* (1860) and by others after him, forms the basis of what has come to be called **classical threshold theory.** The basic idea underlying this theory is that at the absolute threshold there is a sharp transition between a state in which an observer cannot detect the stimulus (if the intensity is below the threshold) and in which the observer can detect the stimulus (if the intensity is above the threshold). This situation is shown in Figure A.1. According to this idea, an observer will never be able to detect a stimulus

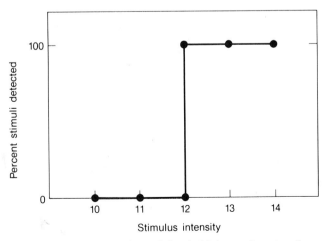

FIGURE A. 1 According to classical threshold theory there is a sharp step between an intensity at which an observer can't detect a stimulus (slightly below 12, in this case) and the intensity at which an observer can detect a stimulus (slightly above 12).

with an intensity of 10, 11, or just under 12, and will always be able to detect a stimulus with an intensity of 12 or greater; the absolute threshold would therefore be 12 in this case.

One way to think about classical threshold theory is to relate the threshold to activity in the nervous system. We know that there is always a level of nerve activity, called spontaneous activity, that exists even in the absence of any stimulation (see Chapter 2, p. 40). It would follow from classical threshold theory that we can detect a stimulus when its presentation causes some critical increase in neural activity above the spontaneous level. Results such as those plotted in Figure A.1 rarely occur, however. A more usual result is shown in Figure A.2. The transition between not detecting the stimulus and detecting it is usually gradual rather than abrupt. Classical threshold theory explains this result by saying that a sharp transition between nondetection and detection occurs only if all factors remain constant during the experiment but that in reality everything is not constant. For example, the level of spontaneous activity in the nervous system, the sensitivity of receptors that

pick up the stimulus, and the attention of the observer may all vary slightly with time. These variations cause slight shifts in the threshold so that the threshold is different at different points in time, and these variations cause the abrupt transition of Figure A.1 to become the gradual transition of Figure A.2.

In *Elements of Psychophysics,* Fechner described three methods of determining thresholds. These methods, which are known as the classical psychophysical methods, are the **method of constant stimuli,** the **method of limits,** and the **method of adjustment.**

Method of constant stimuli. To determine a threshold using the method of constant stimuli, it is first necessary to pick the stimuli to be presented to the observer. Usually five to nine stimuli are used, with the most intense being clearly above the threshold so that an observer detects it without fail and the least intense being clearly below the threshold so that an observer can never detect it. The stimuli between these two are of intermediate intensity so that they are detected on some presen-

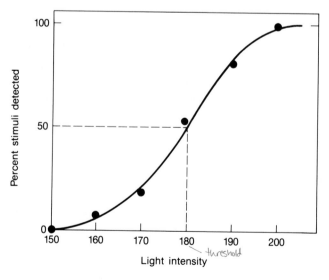

F I G U R E A. 2 Results of a hypothetical experiment in which the threshold for seeing a light is measured by the method of constant stimuli. The threshold, the intensity at which the light is seen on half of its presentations, as indicated by the dashed line, is 180 in this experiment.

tations and not on others. Each stimulus is presented a number of times in random order. The results for a hypothetical determination of the threshold for seeing a light are shown in Figure A.2. Each of the six light intensities is presented ten times *in random order*, and the percentage of times that each light is detected is plotted on the vertical axis. The results indicate that the light with an intensity of 150 is never detected, the light with an intensity of 200 is always detected, and lights with intensities in between are sometimes detected and sometimes not detected. The threshold is usually taken as the intensity that results in detection on half the trials, so in this case the threshold is an intensity of 180.

Method of limits. This method is similar to the method of constant stimuli since the experimenter presents different stimuli and asks the observer to indicate whether he or she can detect the stimulus. The major difference between the two methods is that in the method of constant stimuli the stimuli are presented in random order, whereas in the method of limits the stimuli are presented either in ascending or descending order. Table A.1 shows the results of such an experiment. On the first series of trials, the experimenter presents a light above threshold and the observer indicates by a "yes" response that the light is seen. This response is indicated by a "Y" at an intensity of 105 on the table. The experimenter then decreases the intensity and the observer makes another judgment. This continues until, at an intensity of 98, the observer indicates by an answer of "no" that the light is not seen. This change from "yes" at 99 to "no" at 98 is the "crossover" point, and the threshold value for this run is taken as the mean between 99 and 98, or 98.5. The procedure is then repeated in reverse, starting below the threshold and increasing the intensity until the subject says "yes." Then both the descending and ascending presentations are repeated a number of times. The threshold is calculated by determining the mean of the "crossover" values for each run, so in this experiment the threshold is 98.5.

It is particularly important, when using this method, that the stimuli be presented in both ascending and descending order. One reason for

TABLE A. 1

Intensity	1 ↓	2 ↑	3 ↓	4 ↑	5 ↓	6 ↓	7 ↓	8 ↑
105	Y						Y	
104	Y		Y		Y		Y	
103	Y		Y		Y		Y	
102	Y		Y		Y		Y	
101	Y		Y		Y		Y	Y
100	Y	Y	Y	Y	Y		Y	Y
99	Y	N	Y	N	Y	Y	Y	Y
98	N	N	Y	N	N	N	N	Y
97		N	N	N		N		N
96		N		N		N		N
95		N		N		N		N

Crossover → 98.5　99.5　97.5　99.5　98.5　98.5　98.5　97.5
values

Threshold = mean of crossovers = 98.5

this is that observers can develop response biases. For example, in descending series they may continue to say "yes" for one or two trials below the threshold because they said "yes" on the previous trials. A similar bias may occur during the ascending series, with observers continuing to say "no" for one or two trials above the threshold because they said "no" on the previous trials. But when both ascending and descending orders are used, these two biases will cancel out.

Method of adjustment. In this method, the intensity of the stimulus is slowly changed by either the observer or the experimenter until the observer says that he or she can just barely detect the stimulus. This just barely detectable intensity is then taken as the absolute threshold. When the observer adjusts the stimuli, this method has the advantage of giving the observer an active role in the proceedings, thereby maximizing the probability that he or she will stay awake during the entire experiment!

Which of these methods is usually used to measure thresholds? The answer depends on both the accuracy that is needed and the amount of time available. The method of constant stimuli is the most accurate method but takes the longest time, whereas the method of adjustment is the least accurate but is the fastest.

THE DIFFERENCE THRESHOLD

When measuring the absolute threshold we are interested in determining the minimum amount of stimulus energy that can be detected. When measuring the **difference threshold** we are interested in determining the minimum *difference* between two stimuli that can be detected. The pioneer in the study of the difference threshold was E. H. Weber who, in 1834, published the results of experiments in which he asked observers to lift a standard weight and a comparison weight and then judge which was heavier. By having observers compare a large number of different weights, Weber was able to determine the **difference threshold,** the smallest difference between two weights that could be reliably detected. He found that the size of the difference threshold, or **just noticeable difference (JND),** as it is also called, depends on the weight of the stimulus. For example, an observer can just notice the difference between a 100-gram standard weight and a 103-gram comparison weight, so the JND in this case is 3 grams. If, however, the weight of the standard is increased to 1,000 grams, the JND increases to 30 grams, so the comparison must be increased to 1,030 grams before the observer can distinguish it from the standard.

You can demonstrate to yourself that the JND gets larger as the stimulus gets larger, by doing a simple experiment with two boxes of wooden matches. Have a friend place 2 matches in one box (the standard) and 3 in the other (the comparison)

and, comparing the weights of the two boxes with your eyes closed, try to decide which box is heavier. After making this judgment, repeat this procedure; if you can't correctly judge which is heavier on three out of three trials, have your friend place another match in the comparison box and try again. Continue this procedure until you can consistently judge which box is heavier. If, for example, you can consistently tell that the comparison box is heavier when it contains six matches, then the JND equals four matches. Now repeat the above procedures but start with 20 matches in the standard box and 21 in the comparison. Since the JND gets larger as the weight of the standard gets larger, you should find that the JND for the 20-match standard is larger than the JND for the 2-match standard.

Weber found that the size of the JND follows a simple rule: the size of the JND is a constant fraction of the size of the stimulus. Expressed mathematically, this idea, which is called **Weber's law,** is $JND = KS$, where K is a constant called the *Weber fraction,* and S is the value of the standard stimulus. This equation is usually expressed in the form $K = JND/S$. Applying this equation to our example of lifted weights in the first paragraph, we find that for the 100-gram standard, $K = 3/100 = 0.03$, and for the 1,000-gram standard, $K = 30/1,000 = 0.03$. Thus, in this example, Weber's fraction (K) is constant.

Does Weber's fraction remain constant in actual experiments? Numerous investigators have tested Weber's law and found that it is true for most senses, as long as the stimulus intensity is not too close to the threshold. This is illustrated in Figure A.3, which shows that the Weber fraction for lifted weights is fairly constant for two different observers, as long as the weight of the standard is greater than about 50 grams (Engen, 1972; Gescheider, 1976).

MEASURING MAGNITUDE ABOVE THRESHOLD

So far we have been focusing on stimuli of such low intensity that they are difficult to distinguish from the background noise from other similar stim-

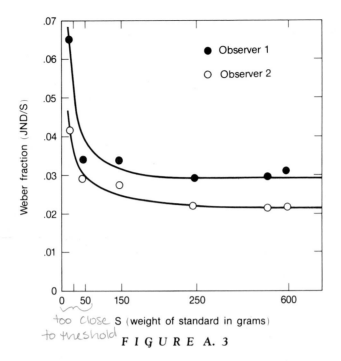

too close *to threshold* S (weight of standard in grams)

FIGURE A. 3

uli. But the vast majority of our experience takes place above threshold, when we can easily hear someone talking to us or can easily see what's around us. Thus, it is important to ask what the relationship is between above-threshold stimuli and our perception of the stimuli. Specifically, we will ask what the relationship is between the *intensity* of a stimulus and our *perception of the magnitude* of the stimulus. If we double the intensity of a light, does it look twice as bright? If we double the intensity of a tone, does it sound twice as loud? We will now describe two ways of answering this question, one proposed by Gustav Fechner, the other by S. S. Stevens.

Fechner's Law

Gustav Fechner derived a relationship between stimulus intensity and perceived magnitude by making the following two assumptions: (1) Weber's law, that the just noticeable difference (JND) is a constant fraction of the stimulus intensity, is valid; and (2) the JND is the basic unit of perceived magnitude, so that one JND is perceptually equal to another JND. It follows from these assumptions

that the perceived magnitude of a stimulus can be determined by starting at the threshold and adding up JNDs. Thus, a light with an intensity of 20 JNDs above threshold should appear twice as bright as a light with an intensity of 10 JNDs above threshold.

Based on his two assumptions, Fechner was able to derive the following mathematical relationship between perceived magnitude and stimulus intensity: $P = K \log I$. Perceived magnitude, P, equals a constant, K, times the logarithm of the physical intensity, I, of the stimulus. From this equation, which is called **Fechner's law,** we can determine whether doubling the intensity of a light makes it appear twice as bright. If we set $K = 1$ and $I = 10$, then $P = 1.0$ since the log of 10 equals 1.0. If we double the intensity to 20, $P = 1.3$ since the log of 20 equals 1.3. Thus, <u>according to Fechner's law, doubling the light's intensity does not double its brightness.</u>

Fechner's law, however, has been questioned for three reasons: First, the law is based on the assumption that Weber's law is correct, but we saw from Figure A.3 that Weber's law is correct only at medium and high stimulus intensities. Second,

Fechner's law is based on the assumption that the JND is the basic unit of measurement and that an intensity that is 20 JNDs above threshold should therefore result in a perceived magnitude twice as great as an intensity 10 JNDs above threshold. However, in 1936 S. S. Stevens showed that a sound 20 JNDs above threshold sounds much more than twice as loud as a sound 10 JNDs above threshold. Third, in 1957 Stevens proposed an alternate equation that describes the relationship between sensation and stimulus intensity for a wide range of senses more accurately than Fechner's law.

Stevens' Power Law

Stevens' equation grew from a technique, which he developed, called **magnitude estimation** (Stevens, 1957, 1961, 1962). This technique is very simple: The experimenter first presents a "standard" stimulus to the observer, let's say a light of moderate intensity, and assigns it a value of, say, 10; then lights of different intensities are presented, and the observer is asked to assign a number to each of these lights which is proportional to the brightness of the light. If the light appears twice as bright as the standard, it gets a 20, half as bright a 5, and so on. Thus, each light intensity has a brightness assigned to it by the observer.

The results of a magnitude estimation experiment on brightness are plotted in Figure A.4. This graph plots the means of the magnitude estimates of the brightness of a light for a number of observers versus the intensity of the light. You can see from this graph that doubling the intensity does not double the perceived brightness. Doubling the intensity causes only a small change in perceived brightness, particularly at higher intensities. This result is called **response compression.** As intensity is increased, the responses increase, but not as rapidly as the intensity. To double the brightness it is necessary to multiply the intensity by about nine.

Figure A.5 shows the results of magnitude estimation experiments for brightness, for the length of a line, and for the sensation caused by an electric shock presented to the finger. You can see that there are three different kinds of curves: (1) curves that bend down, such as the one for brightness, (2) curves that bend up, such as the one for elec-

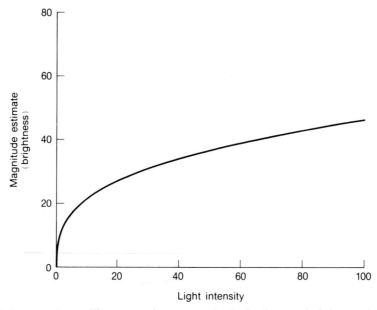

F I G U R E   A. 4   The magnitude estimates for the brightness of a light are plotted versus light intensity (adapted from Stevens, 1962).

tric shock, and (3) straight lines, such as the one for estimating line length. Curves that bend down show *response compression* (doubling the light intensity causes less than a doubling of the brightness). Curves that bend up show **response expansion** (doubling the strength of a shock causes more than a doubling of the sensation of being shocked). Straight lines are *linear* with a slope of close to one, so the magnitude of the response almost exactly matches increases in the stimulus (doubling the line length doubles the observer's estimate of the length of the line).

Should we conclude from the differences in the curves of Figure A.5 that the relationship between the intensity of a stimulus and our perception of its magnitude follows different rules for each sense? The answer to this question is that even though the curves of Figure A.5 look different, we can, in fact, find a common rule for all the senses. To find a common rule that can describe all the different curves of Figure A.5, we have to replot the curves by plotting the *logarithm* of the magnitude estimates versus the *logarithm* of the stimulus intensity. When we do this, all three curves

become straight lines, as shown in Figure A.6; functions that are straight lines on such a log-log plot are called **power functions** and are described by the equation $P = KS^n$. Perceived magnitude, P, equals a constant, K, times the stimulus intensity, S, raised to a power, n. This relationship is called **Stevens' power law.** The power n, the exponent of the power law, indicates the slope of the lines in Figure A.6. Remembering our discussion of the three types of curves in Figure A.5, we can see that the slope of the curve that shows response compression is less than 1.0, the slope of the linear curve[1] is about 1.0, and the slope of the curve that shows response expansion is greater than 1.0. Thus, the relationship between response magnitude and stimulus intensity is described by a power law for all senses, and the exponent of the power law indicates whether doubling the stimulus intensity causes more or less than a doubling of the response.

What do these exponents mean in terms of our experience? People other than photographers,

[1]The exponent for estimating line length is actually 1.1, but this is close enough to 1.0 so that the line in Figure A.6 is very close to being straight.

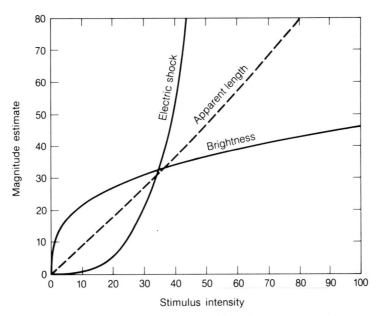

F I G U R E A. 5 Curves showing the relationship between perceived magnitude and stimulus intensity for electric shock, line length, and brightness (adapted from Stevens, 1962). The curve for brightness is the same one shown in Figure A.4.

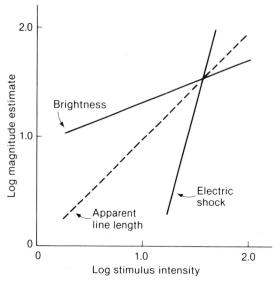

FIGURE A. 6   The three curves from Figure A.5 plotted on log-log coordinates. Taking the logarithm of the magnitude estimates and the logarithm of the stimulus intensity turns the curves into straight lines (adapted from Stevens, 1962).

artists, lighting engineers, and perceptual psychologists aren't that conscious of the actual values of light intensities in their surroundings, so most people are surprised when you tell them that you have to multiply light intensity by nine to double the brightness. But since we can be exposed to intensity ranges of 1 to 1,000 or more on a bright, sunny day, it makes sense that our perception of brightness should not span the same large range. If it did, we should probably be faced with a scene of such high contrasts and bright glare that looking at the scene would be difficult.

Estimating line lengths is something most people have had some experience with, due to exposure to rulers and other measuring instruments, and most people are fairly good at it. Try estimating the length of line B in Figure A.7, assuming that the length of line A is 10. (See the answer at the bottom of page 539 after making your estimate.) You probably came fairly close or overestimated slightly, as would be predicted by the exponent of 1.1 for estimating line length.

The exponent of 3.5 for shock seems compatible with our need to avoid potentially damaging stimuli. The rapid increase in pain for small increases in shock intensity serves to warn us of impending danger, and we therefore tend to withdraw even from weak shocks.

A

B

FIGURE A. 7   If the length of line A equals 10, what is the length of line B? (No fair measuring.)

The Signal Detection Procedure

IS THERE AN ABSOLUTE THRESHOLD?

In Appendix A we saw that various psychophysical methods can be used to determine an observer's absolute threshold. By using the method of constant stimuli, for example, we can randomly present tones of different intensities to a subject and determine the tone intensity to which the subject reports "I hear it" 50 percent of the time. But can the experimenter be confident that this tone intensity truly represents the subject's sensory threshold? For a number of reasons, which we will discuss below, the answer to this question is, "Maybe not." Many researchers feel that the idea of an *absolute* measure of sensitivity, called the threshold, which can be measured by using the classic psychophysical methods, is not valid. To understand the position of these researchers, let's consider a hypothetical experiment.

In our experiment we are going to use the method of constant stimuli to measure two subjects' thresholds for hearing a tone. To do this we pick five different tone intensities, present them in random order, and ask our subjects to say "yes" if they hear the tone and "no" if they don't hear it. Our first subject, Laurie, thinks about these instructions and decides that she wants to appear supersensitive to the tones; since she knows that tones are being presented on every trial, she will answer "yes" if there is even the faintest possibility that she hears the tone. We could call Laurie a liberal responder—she is more willing to say "Yes, I hear the tone" than to report that no tone was

present. Our second subject, Chris, is read the same instructions, but Chris is different from Laurie; she doesn't care about being supersensitive. In fact, Chris wants to be totally sure that she hears the tone before saying "yes." We could call Chris a conservative responder—she is not willing to report that she hears the tone unless it is very strong.

The results of this hypothetical experiment are shown in Figure B.1. Laurie gives many more "yes" responses than Chris and, therefore, ends up with a lower threshold. But given what we know about Laurie and Chris, should we conclude that Laurie is more sensitive to the tones than Chris? It could be that their actual sensitivity to the tones is exactly the same, but Laurie's apparently lower threshold is simply due to the fact that she is more willing to report that she heard a tone than is Chris. A way to describe this difference between the two subjects is that each has a different **response criterion.** Laurie's response criterion is low (she will say "yes" to almost anything), whereas Chris's response criterion is high (she says "yes" only when she is sure that she heard the signal). That factors other than the subject's sensitivity to the signal may influence the results of a psychophysical experiment has caused many researchers to doubt the validity of the absolute threshold, as determined by these psychophysical experiments, and to create new procedures based on a theory called **signal detection theory (SDT).**

In the next section we will describe the basic procedure of a signal detection experiment and will show how such an experiment can tell us whether Chris and Laurie are, in fact, equally sensitive to the tone even though their response criteria are

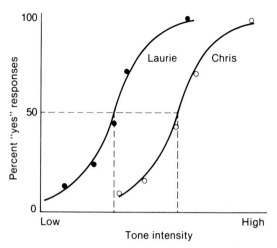

F I G U R E B. 1 Data from experiments in which the threshold for hearing a tone is determined for Laurie and Chris by using the method of constant stimuli. These data indicate that Laurie's threshold is lower than Chris's. But is Laurie really more sensitive to the tone than Chris, or does she just appear to be more sensitive because she is a more liberal responder?

very different. (If you are interested in understanding the *theory* on which these signal detection procedures are based, first read the section below and then turn to Appendix C.)

A SIGNAL DETECTION EXPERIMENT

Remember that in a psychophysical procedure such as the method of constant stimuli, at least five different tone intensities are presented, with a stimulus presented on every trial. In a signal detection experiment, however, we use only a single tone intensity—a low intensity that is difficult to hear—presenting this tone on some of the trials and no tone at all on the rest. So, a signal detection experiment differs from a classical psychophysical experiment in two ways: In a signal detection experiment (1) only one stimulus intensity is presented, and (2) on some of the trials no stimulus is presented.

Let's consider the results of such an experiment, using Laurie as our subject. We present the

tone for 100 trials and no tone for 100 trials, mixing the tone and no-tone trials at random. Laurie's results are as follows:

When tone is presented:

- Says "yes" on 90 trials. This is a correct response and, in signal detection terminology, is called a **hit.**
- Says "no" on 10 trials. This is an incorrect response and is called a **miss.**

When no tone is presented:

- Says "yes" on 40 trials. This is an incorrect response and it is called a **false alarm.**
- Says "no" on 60 trials. This is a correct response and is called a **correct rejection.**

These results are not that surprising, given that we know Laurie has a low criterion and likes to say "yes" a lot. This gives her a high hit rate of 90 percent but also causes her to say "yes" on many trials when no tone is presented at all, so her 90 percent hit rate is accompanied by a 40 percent false alarm rate. If we do a similar experiment on Chris, who has a higher criterion and therefore says "yes" much less often, we find that she has a lower hit rate (say, 60 percent) but also a lower false alarm rate (say, 10 percent). Note that although Laurie and Chris say "yes" on numerous trials on which no stimulus is presented, that result would not be predicted by classical threshold theory. Classical theory would say "no stimulus—no response," but that is clearly not the case here.

By adding a new wrinkle to our signal detection experiment, we can obtain another result that would not be predicted by classical threshold theory. Without changing the tone's intensity at all, we can cause Laurie and Chris to change their percentages of hits and false alarms. We do this by manipulating each subject's motivation by means of **payoffs.** Let's look at how payoffs might influence Chris's responding. Remember that Chris is a conservative responder who is hesitant to say "yes." But, being clever experimenters, we can make Chris say "yes" more frequently, by adding some financial inducements to the experiment. "Chris," we say, "we are going to reward you for making correct responses and are going to penalize you for making incorrect responses. For every hit, you will receive $100 and for every correct rejection you will receive $10; but you will lose $10 for every miss or false alarm." What would you do if you were in Chris's position? Being smart, you analyze the payoffs and realize that the way to make money is to say "yes" more. You can lose $10 if a "yes" response results in a false alarm, but this small loss is more than counterbalanced by the $100 you can win for a hit. While you don't decide to say "yes" on every trial—after all, you want to be honest with the experimenter about whether or not you heard the tone—you do decide to stop being so conservative. *You decide to change your criterion for saying "yes."* The results of this experiment are interesting. Chris becomes a more liberal responder and says "yes" a lot more, responding with 98 percent hits and 90 percent false alarms.

This result is plotted as data point L (for "liberal" response) in Figure B.2, a plot of the percentage of hits versus the percentage of false alarms. The solid curve going through point L is called a **receiver operating characteristic (ROC) curve.** We will see why the ROC curve is important in a moment, but first let's see how we determine the other points on the curve. Determining the other points on the ROC curve is simple: All we have to do is to change the payoffs. We can make Chris raise her criterion and therefore respond more conservatively, by means of the following payoffs:

Hit	Win $10
Correct Rejection	Win $100
False Alarm	Lose $10
Miss	Lose $10

This schedule of payoffs offers a great inducement to respond conservatively since there is a big reward for saying "no" when no tone is presented. Chris's criterion is therefore shifted to a much higher level, so Chris now returns to her conservative ways and says "yes" only if she is quite certain that a tone is presented; otherwise she says "no." The result of this new-found conservatism is a hit rate of only 10 percent and a minuscule false alarm rate of 1 percent, indicated by point C (for "conservative" response) on the ROC curve. We should

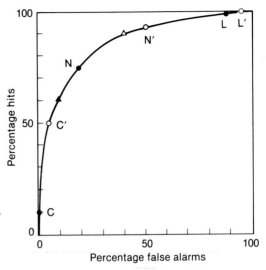

F I G U R E C. 2 The same probability distributions from Figure C.1, showing three criteria: liberal (L), neutral (N), and conservative (C). When a subject adopts a criterion, he or she uses the following **decision rule:** Respond "yes" (I detect the stimulus) if the perceptual effect is greater than the criterion; respond "no" (I do not detect a stimulus) if the perceptual effect is less than the criterion (see text for details).

note that although Chris hits on only 10 percent of the trials in which a tone is presented, she scores a phenomenal 99 percent correct rejections on trials in which a tone is not presented. (This follows from the fact that, if there are 100 trials in which no tone is presented, then correct rejections + false alarms = 100. Since there was one false alarm, there must be 99 correct rejections.)

Chris, by this time, is rich and decides to go buy the Datsun she's been dreaming about. (So far she's won $8,980 in the first experiment and $9,090 in the second experiment for a total of $18,070! To be sure you understand how the payoff system works, check this calculation yourself.) However, we point out that she may need a little extra cash to have air conditioning and a stereo tape deck installed in her car, so she agrees to stick around for one more experiment. We now use the following neutral schedule of payoffs:

Hit	Win $10
Correct Rejection	Win $10
False Alarm	Lose $10
Miss	Lose $10

and obtain point N on the ROC curve: 75 percent hits and 20 percent false alarms. Chris wins $1,000 more and becomes the proud owner of a Datsun, and we are the proud owners of the world's most expensive ROC curve. (Do not, at this point, go to the psychology department in search of the nearest signal detection experiment. In real life, the payoffs are quite a bit smaller than in our hypothetical example.)

Chris's ROC curve provides more evidence that factors other than sensitivity to stimulus determine the subject's response. Remember than in all the experiments we have described so far, the intensity of the tone has remained constant. The only thing we have changed is the subject's criterion, but in doing this we have succeeded in drastically changing the subject's responses.

But what does the ROC curve tell us in addition to demonstrating that subjects will change the way they respond to an unchanging stimulus? Remember, at the beginning of this discussion, we said that a signal detection experiment can tell us whether or not Chris and Laurie are equally sensitive to the tone. The beauty of signal detection theory is that the subject's sensitivity is indicated by the *shape* of the ROC curve, so if experiments on two subjects result in identical ROC curves, their sensitivities must be equal. (This conclusion is not obvious from our discussion so far. To understand why the shape of the ROC curve is related to the subject's sensitivity, look at Appendix C after finishing this section.) If we repeat the above experiments on Laurie, we get the following results:

Liberal Payoff:	Hits = 99 percent
	False Alarms = 95 percent
Neutral Payoff:	Hits = 92 percent
	False Alarms = 50 percent
Conservative Payoff:	Hits = 50 percent
	False Alarms = 6 percent

The data points for Laurie's results are shown by the open circles in Figure B.2. Note that although these points are different from Chris's, they fall on the same ROC curve as do Chris's. We also have plotted the data points for the first experiments we did on Laurie (open triangle) and Chris (filled triangle), before we introduced payoffs. These points also fall on the ROC curve.

That Chris and Laurie's data both fall on the same ROC curve indicates their equal sensitivity to the tones, thus confirming our suspicion that the method of constant stimuli misled us into thinking that Laurie is more sensitive, when the real reason for her apparently greater sensitivity is her lower criterion for saying "yes."

Before leaving the method of signal detection, let's look at an example of how this method was used in an experiment on the perception of pain. It has been hypothesized that members of non-Western ethnocultural groups are less sensitive to pain than are Westerners (Wolff & Langley, 1968). Crawford Clark and Susanne Bennett Clark (1980) decided to test this hypothesis while on a mountain-climbing trip in the Himalayas, which gave them access to two groups of subjects: (1) five English-speaking, college-educated mountain climbers ("Occidentals"), and (2) six Nepalese porters who accompanied the Occidentals on their climb. In the first part of the experiment, Clark and Clark used the method of limits to measure the responses of both groups of subjects to an electrical shock presented to the wrist and forearm. The results of these experiments are shown in Figure B.3. Note that the threshold intensity for just feeling the shock is the same for both groups but that the stimulus intensity for experiencing "faint pain" and "extreme pain" is much higher for the Nepalese porters. This result agrees with the hypothesis that non-Westerners are less sensitive to pain than are Westerners.

In the second part of the experiment, the method of signal detection showed, however, that there were actually no differences between the two groups of subjects. Apparently, both groups of subjects experienced the shocks in the same way, but the Nepalese porters took much higher shocks before reporting that they felt either faint pain or extreme pain. In signal detection language, we would say that the Nepalese had a higher criterion for reporting pain.

Although we won't go into the exact procedures used by Clark and Clark in the signal detection part of their experiment, it is important to note that signal detection procedures can be used without the elaborate payoffs that we described for Chris and Laurie. Much briefer procedures, which we won't describe here (but see Appendix C), can be used to determine whether differences in the responses of different subjects are due to differences in threshold or to differences in the subjects' response criteria.

What does signal detection theory tell us about functions such as the spectral sensitivity curve Figure 1.6, which was determined by one of the classical psychophysical methods? When the classical methods are used to determine functions such as the spectral sensitivity curve, it is usually assumed that the subject's criterion remains constant throughout the experiment, so that the function measured is due not to changes in the subject's criterion but to changes in the wavelength or some other physical property of the stimulus. This is a good assumption, since changing the wavelength of the stimulus probably has little or no effect on factors such as motivation, which would shift the subject's criterion. Furthermore, experiments such as the one for determining the spectral sensitivity curve usually employ highly practiced subjects who are trained to give stable results. Thus, even though

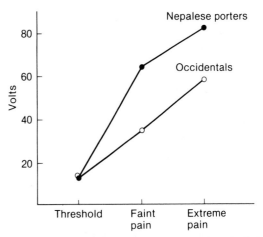

F I G U R E   B. 3   Data for the Clark and Clark (1980) experiment, which shows that the threshold for detecting a shock is the same for Western mountain climbers (Occidentals) and their native guides (Nepalese porters) but that the Nepalese porters take much higher levels of shock before reporting "faint pain" or "extreme pain." Is this result due to the fact that the Nepalese porters are less sensitive to the shocks, or does it simply mean that the porters are more conservative responders?

the idea of an "absolute threshold" may now be outmoded, many investigations using classical psychophysical methods under well-controlled conditions provide us with important information (like the spectral sensitivity curve) about the properties of sensory systems.

Answer to line estimation problem: Length of B = 25.

In this appendix, we will discuss the theoretical basis for the signal detection experiment described in Appendix B. Our purpose will be to explain the theoretical bases underlying two ideas: (1) the percentage of hits and false alarms depends on the subject's criterion, and (2) a subject's sensitivity to a stimulus is indicated by the shape of the subject's ROC curve. We will begin by describing two of the key concepts of signal detection theory (SDT): signal and noise. (See Swets, 1964.)

SIGNAL AND NOISE

To understand signal detection theory, we have to introduce the concepts of **signal** and **noise.** The signal is the stimulus presented to the subject. Thus, in the signal detection experiment of Appendix B, the signal is the tone. The noise is all the other stimuli in the environment, and, since the signal is usually very faint, noise can sometimes be mistaken for the signal. Seeing what appears to be a flash of light in a completely dark room is an example of visual noise. Seeing a flash of light when there is none is what we have been calling a false alarm, which, according to signal detection theory, is caused by the noise. In the experiment in Appendix B, hearing a tone on a trial in which no tone was presented is an example of auditory noise.

Let's now consider a typical signal detection experiment, in which a signal is presented on some trials and no signal is presented on the other trials. According to signal detection theory, rather than talk in terms of presenting a signal or no signal,

we talk about presenting signal plus noise (S + N) or noise (N). That is, the noise is always present, and on some trials we add a signal. Either condition can result in the perceptual effect of hearing a tone, with a false alarm resulting if the subject indicates that she heard a tone on a noise trial and a hit resulting if the subject indicates that she heard a tone on a signal-plus-noise trial. Now that we have defined signal and noise, we need to introduce the idea of probability distributions for noise and signal plus noise.

PROBABILITY DISTRIBUTIONS

Figure C.1 shows two probability distributions. The probability distribution on the left represents the probability that a given perceptual effect will be caused by noise (N), and the one on the right represents the probability that a given perceptual effect will be caused by signal plus noise (S + N). The key to understanding these distributions is to realize that "perceptual effect" is plotted on the horizontal axis. The perceptual effect is what the subject experiences on each trial; so, for an experiment in which the subject is asked to indicate whether or not a tone is present, the perceptual effect is the perceived loudness of the tone. Remember that in an SDT experiment the tone always has the same *intensity*. The *loudness* of the tone, however, can vary from trial to trial. The subject perceives different loudnesses on different trials, due either to trial-to-trial changes in attention or to the state of the subject's auditory system.

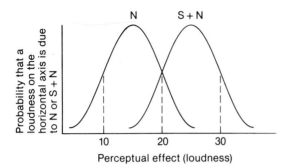

F I G U R E C. 1 Probability distributions for noise alone (N), on the left, and for signal plus noise (S + N), on the right. The probability that any given perceptual effect is caused by the noise (no signal is presented) or by the signal plus noise (signal is presented) can be determined by finding the value of the perceptual effect on the horizontal axis and extending a vertical line up from that value. The place where that line intersects the (N) and (S + N) distributions indicates the probability that the perceptual effect was caused by (N) or by (S + N).

The probability distributions tell us what the chances are that a given loudness of tone is due to (N) or to (S + N). For example, let's assume that a subject hears a tone with a loudness of 10 on one of the trials of a signal detection experiment. By extending a vertical dashed line up from 10 on the "perceptual effect" axis in Figure C.1, we see that the probability that a loudness of 10 is due to (S + N) is extremely low, since the distribution for (S + N) is almost zero at a loudness of 10. There is, however, a fairly high probability that a loudness of 10 is due to (N), since the (N) distribution is fairly high at this point.

Let's now assume that, on another trial, the subject hears a tone with a loudness of 20. The probability distributions in Figure C.1 indicate that when the tone's loudness is 20, it is equally probable that this loudness is due to (N) or to (S + N). We can also see from Figure C.1 that a tone with a perceived loudness of 30 would have a high probability of being caused by (S + N) and only a small probability of being caused by (N).

Now that we understand the curves of Figure C.1, we can see the problem the subject confronts.

On each trial, she has to decide whether no tone (N) was present or whether a tone (S + N) was present. However, the overlap in the probability distributions for (N) and (S + N) makes this judgment difficult. As we saw above, it is equally probable that a tone with a loudness of 20 is due to (N) or to (S + N). So, on a trial in which the subject hears a tone with a loudness of 20, how does she decide whether or not the signal was presented? According to signal detection theory, the decision the subject arrives at depends on the location of her criterion.

THE CRITERION

We can see how the criterion affects the subject's response by looking at Figure C.2. In this figure, we have labeled three different criteria: liberal (L), neutral (N), and conservative (C). Remember from our discussion in Appendix B that we can cause subjects to adopt these different criteria by means of different payoffs. The key to understanding these criteria is to remember that once the subject adopts a criterion, he or she uses the following rule to decide how to respond on a given trial: If the perceptual effect is greater than (to the right of) the criterion, say "yes, the tone was present"; if the perceptual effect is less than (to the left of) the criterion, say "no, the tone was not present." Let's consider how different criteria influence the subject's hits and false alarms.

Liberal Criterion

To determine how criterion L will affect the subject's hits and false alarms, let's consider what happens when we present (N) and when we present (S + N). (1) Present (N): Since most of the probability distribution for (N) falls to the right of the criterion, the chances are good that presenting (N) will result in a loudness to the right of the criterion. This means that the probability of saying "yes" when (N) is presented is high; therefore, the probability of a false alarm is high. (2) Present (S + N): Since the entire probability distribution for (S + N) falls to the right of the criterion, the chances are excellent that presenting (S + N) will result in a loudness to the right of the criterion. Thus, the probability of saying "yes" when the signal is presented is high; therefore, the probability of a hit is high. Since criterion L results in high false alarms and high hits, adopting that criterion will result in point L on the ROC curve in Figure C.4.

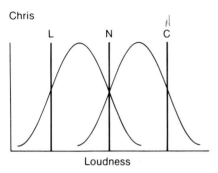

Chris

Loudness

F I G U R E   C. 2   The same probability distributions from Figure C.1, showing three criteria: liberal (L), neutral (N), and conservative (C). When a subject adopts a criterion, he or she uses the following **decision rule:** Respond "yes" (I detect the stimulus) if the perceptual effect is greater than the criterion; respond "no" (I do not detect a stimulus) if the perceptual effect is less than the criterion (see text for details).

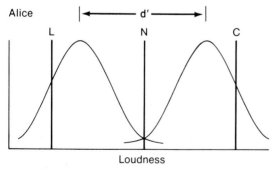

Alice

Loudness

F I G U R E   C. 3   Probability distributions for a subject who is extremely sensitive to the signal. The effect of increasing the subject's sensitivity is to move the (S + N) distribution to the right (see text for details).

Neutral Criterion

(1) Present (N): The subject will answer "yes" only rarely when (N) is presented, since only a small portion of the (N) distribution falls to the right of the criterion. The false alarm rate, therefore, will be fairly low. (2) Present (S + N): The subject will answer "yes" frequently when (S + N) is presented, since most of the (S + N) distribution falls to the right of the criterion. The hit rate, therefore, will be fairly high (but not as high as for the L criterion). Criterion N results in point N on the ROC curve in Figure C.4.

Conservative Criterion

(1) Present (N): False alarms will be very low, since none of the (N) curve falls to the right of the criterion. (2) Present (S + N): Hits will also be low, since only a small portion of the (S + N) curve falls to the right of the criterion. Criterion C results in point C on the ROC curve in Figure C.4.

You can see that when different criteria are applied to the probability distributions of signal detection theory, we generate the ROC curve in Figure C.4. But why are these probability distributions necessary? After all, in Appendix B we were able to explain how we got the ROC curve, simply on the basis of common sense. The reason the (N) and (S + N) distributions are important is that, according to signal detection theory, the subject's sensitivity to a stimulus is indicated by the distance (d′) between the peaks of the (N) and (S + N) distributions. With this fact in mind, we can show how the subject's sensitivity to a stimulus affects the shape of the ROC curve.

THE EFFECT OF SENSITIVITY ON THE ROC CURVE

We can understand how the subject's sensitivity to a stimulus affects the shape of the ROC curve by considering what the probability distributions would look like for Alice, a subject with supersensitive

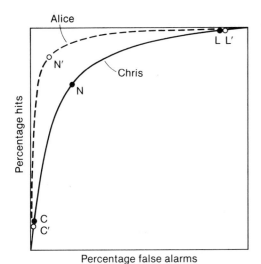

F I G U R E C. 4 ROC curves for Chris (solid) and Alice (dashed) (see text for details).

hearing. Alice's hearing is so good that a tone which is barely audible to Chris sounds very loud to Alice. If presentation of (S + N) causes Alice to hear a loud tone, this means that Alice's (S + N) distribution should be far to the right, as shown in Figure C.3. In signal detection terms, we would say that Alice's high sensitivity is indicated by the large separation (d') between the (N) and (S + N) probability distributions. To see how this greater separation between the probability distributions will affect Alice's ROC curve, let's see how she would respond when adopting liberal, neutral, and conservative criteria.

Liberal Criterion

(1) Present (N): high false alarms. (2) Present (S + N): high hits. The liberal criterion, therefore, results in point L' on the ROC curve of Figure C.4.

Neutral Criterion

(1) Present (N): low false alarms. It is important to note that Alice's false alarms for the neutral criterion will be lower than Chris's false alarms for the neutral criterion, because only a small portion

of Alice's (N) distribution falls to the right of the criterion. Compare Alice's situation to Figure C.2, in which some of Chris's (N) distribution is to the right of the neutral criterion. (2) Present (S + N): high hits. It is important to note that Alice's hits will be higher than Chris's, because all of Alice's (S + N) distribution falls to the right of the criterion. Compare Alice's situation to Figure C.2, in which not all of Chris's (S + N) distribution falls to the right of the neutral criterion. The neutral criterion, therefore, results in point N' on the ROC curve in Figure C.4.

Conservative Criterion

(1) Present (N): low false alarms. (2) Present (S + N): low hits. The conservative criterion, therefore, results in point C' on the ROC curve.

The difference between the two ROC curves in Figure C.4 is obvious. But before you conclude that the difference between these two ROC curves has anything to do with where we positioned Alice's L, N, and C criteria, see if you can get an ROC curve like Alice's from the two probability distributions of Figure C.2. You will find that no matter where you position the criteria, there is no way that you can get a point like point N' (with very high hits and very low false alarms) from the curves of Figure C.2. In order to achieve very high hits and very low false alarms, the two probability distributions must be spaced far apart, as in Figure C.3.

Thus, increasing the distance (d') between the (N) and (S + N) probability distributions changes the shape of the ROC curve. The greater the subject's sensitivity (d'), the more bowed is the ROC curve. In practice, d' can be determined by comparing the experimentally determined ROC curve to standard ROC curves (see Gescheider, 1976); or, d' can be calculated from the proportions of hits and false alarms that occur in an experiment, by using a mathematical procedure we will not discuss here. (Though we will not describe the mathematical procedure for calculating d', we should note that this procedure makes it possible to determine a subject's sensitivity by determining only one data point on an ROC curve.)

Contrast Perception and Fourier Analysis

The idea that we perceive different spatial frequencies by means of a number of channels, each of which responds to a narrow range of frequencies, has found favor among many (though not all) sensory psychologists and physiologists. Some of the researchers who subscribe to the idea of frequency channels feel that the visual system may use these channels to help carry out something called a Fourier analysis of the stimulus. In order to understand Fourier analysis, we need to introduce Fourier's theorem.

FOURIER'S THEOREM

Fourier's theorem was developed in the 1800s by French mathematician J. B. Fourier (pronounced Four-yay). Fourier's theorem states that any repeating waveform (such as a square wave) can be broken down into a number of sine-wave components. It also follows from Fourier's theorem that any waveform can be synthesized by adding together its sine-wave components. Rather than introduce the complex mathematical formulas that Fourier developed, we will illustrate how Fourier's theorem works, by showing how a square wave can be constructed from a number of sine waves.

Our goal is to synthesize a square wave from a number of sine waves. This process, which is called **Fourier synthesis,** is carried out as shown in Figure D.1.

1. Start with a sine wave, as shown in (a), with a frequency equal to that of the square wave we want to synthesize. This sine wave is called the *fundamental.*

2. Add to this sine wave another sine wave (b), with an amplitude equal to one-third the amplitude of the fundamental, and with a frequency three times the frequency of the fundamental. This sine wave is called the *third harmonic.*

3. When we add the fundamental (a) and the third harmonic (b) together, positioning the two sine waves so that the trough of the fundamental is lined up with one of the peaks of the third harmonic, as indicated by the dashed line, we get curve (c). Notice that curve (c) is beginning to look like a square wave.

4. Add to curve (c) a sine wave (d), with an amplitude equal to one-fifth the amplitude of the fundamental, and with a frequency five times the frequency of the fundamental. This sine wave is called the *fifth harmonic.*

5. When we add curves (c) and (d), we get curve (e), which looks closer to a square wave than curve (c).

To make our wave look even more like a square wave, we would add the seventh and ninth harmonics, and so on (you have probably noticed that to synthesize a square wave, we use only the odd harmonics). Every time we add a new harmonic, the result gets closer and closer to a square wave, until we eventually reach the square wave (f).

This demonstration illustrates Fourier's idea that a square wave is made up of a number of sine waves. But what does this have to do with contrast perception? To answer this question, let's consider an idea first proposed by Fergus Campbell (working with John Robson) in the 1960s.

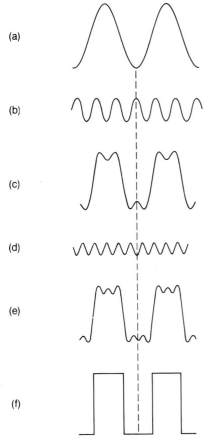

F I G U R E D. 1 Fourier synthesis of a square wave from a number of sine waves. Adding together the fundamental (a) and third harmonic (b) results in wave (c). Then adding the fifth harmonic (d) results in wave (e). The addition of each new harmonic brings the wave closer and closer to a square wave, until, after a few more harmonics are added, the square wave at (f) results. The dashed line is included to emphasize that these sine waves must be lined up correctly if a square wave is to result. For example, the peak of one of the waves of the third harmonic (b) must be lined up with the trough of the fundamental (a).

FERGUS CAMPBELL GIVES A TALK

One day in 1966, when I was a graduate student at Brown University, Fergus Campbell, a physiologist from the University of Cambridge, paid a visit

to the psychology department and gave a very interesting talk. He presented the thesis that the visual system performs an analysis on the light entering the eye. Campbell suggested that the visual system responds to a square-wave grating by responding to the spatial frequencies of its component sine waves. At the time, the idea that the visual system could perform such a mathematical analysis of the stimulus seemed rather far-fetched, but Campbell presented some persuasive evidence to back up his idea. This evidence, plus work by other researchers, has made the idea that the visual system performs a Fourier analysis on the stimulus seem more probable now than it seemed in 1966.

One experiment he talked about was subsequently described in a paper by Campbell and John Robson (1968) entitled "Application of Fourier Analysis to the Visibility of Gratings." This experiment involved two gratings, a square-wave grating and a sine-wave grating, each with frequencies of 26 cycles per degree. If the visual system performs a Fourier analysis on these two gratings, then the sine-wave grating would remain unchanged (since, when a sine wave is Fourier analyzed, you end up with the same sine wave); but the square wave would be broken down into sine waves with frequencies of 26 cycles per degree (the fundamental), 78 cycles per degree (the third harmonic), and 130 cycles per degree (the fifth harmonic), as shown in Figure D.2. (Thee are more harmonics than this, but, as you will see, they turn out to be irrelevant.)

Now, let's look at the contrast sensitivity function (CSF) of Figure 5.20 and consider how the visual system responds to each of the sine waves that make up our sine- and square-wave gratings. Since both gratings are well above threshold, the visual system has no trouble detecting the 26 cycles/degree sine-wave grating and the 26 cycles/degree fundamental of the square-wave grating. However, as you can see from the CSF, the visual system is totally insensitive to the square wave's third and fifth harmonics (78 and 130 cycles/degree). Thus, as far as the visual system is concerned, it sees only the 26 cycles/degree sine wave, which is the square-wave grating's fundamental. Campbell and Robson predicted, therefore, that the square-wave grating should look like the sine-wave grating, and this,

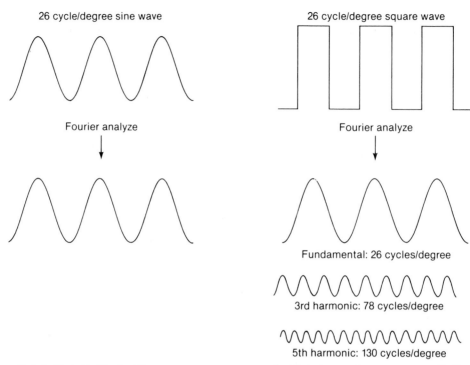

26 cycle/degree sine wave

26 cycle/degree square wave

Fourier analyze

Fourier analyze

Fundamental: 26 cycles/degree

3rd harmonic: 78 cycles/degree

5th harmonic: 130 cycles/degree

F I G U R E   D. 2   The sine-wave components of a 26-cycles-per-degree sine wave (left) and a 26-cycles-per-degree square wave (right), as determined by Fourier analysis. When we Fourier analyze the sine wave, we get the same sine wave. However, when we Fourier analyze the square wave, we get a number of sine waves; the fundamental (26 cycles/degree), the third harmonic (78 cycles/degree), and the fifth harmonic (130 cycles/degree) are shown here. If we were to add these harmonics together, plus the seventh and ninth harmonics, we would end up with a function closely approximating the square wave.

in fact, is what happened—the two were indistinguishable.

Our application of Fourier theory to visual gratings tells us that we should be able to tell the difference between the square-wave grating and the sine-wave grating only when some of the square wave's harmonics become visible. We can accomplish this by moving the two gratings closer to the observer. Since a grating's spatial frequency decreases as it is moved closer (see Figure 5.19), we can easily move the two gratings close enough to change their spatial frequencies from 26 cycles/degree to, say, 5 cycles/degree. When we do this, the fundamental of the square wave becomes 5 cycles per degree, the third harmonic becomes 15 cycles per degree, and the fifth harmonic becomes 25 cycles per de-

gree. Since the visual system will respond to frequencies of 15 and 25 cycles per degree, the square-wave grating now looks different from the sine-wave grating.

Since Campbell and Robson's experiments, other researchers (including Campbell and Robson) have provided further evidence which supports the idea that the visual system may perform a Fourier analysis on the stimulus. Therefore, some researchers have suggested that when an observer looks at a scene, the visual system uses Fourier analysis to break this scene down into its frequency components. According to this idea, just as we broke a square wave down into a number of sine waves of different frequencies, we also break a landscape down into sine waves of different frequencies, which are then signaled by the detectors, or channels, we described in Chapter 5. It is important to note here that, despite evidence that frequency-selective channels exist, it is by no means clear that the visual system actually uses these channels to perform a Fourier analysis on a whole scene; even if it does, we don't know whether, or how, the visual system uses this information to create perceptions. Thus, while we know that the spatial frequency of a stimulus definitely affects our perception, we are still uncertain as to the exact mechanism responsible for this effect.

Glossary

Absolute threshold. The minimum stimulus energy necessary for an observer to detect the stimulus. (527)

Adjustment, method of. A psychophysical method in which the experimenter or the observer slowly changes the stimulus until the observer detects the stimulus. (528)

Classical threshold theory. The idea that for a mental event to be experienced it has to be stronger than some critical amount. (527)

Constant stimuli, method of. A psychophysical method in which a number of stimuli with different intensities are presented repeatedly in random order. (528)

Correct rejection. In a signal detection experiment, saying "No, I don't detect a stimulus" on a trial in which the stimulus is not presented (a correct response). (536)

Decision rule. The rule usually adopted by subjects in signal detection experiments which states, "Respond 'yes' if the perceptual effect is greater than the response criterion. Respond 'no' if the effect is less than the response criterion." (541)

Difference threshold. The minimum difference between two stimuli that can be detected (530)

False alarm. In a signal detection experiment, saying "Yes, I detect the stimulus" on a trial in which the stimulus is not presented (an incorrect response). (536)

Fechner's law. A relationship between the physical intensity of a stimulus and perception of the subjective magnitude of the stimulus. According to Fechner, P (perception of magnitude) $= K$ (a constant) times the logarithm of S (the stimulus intensity). (531)

Fourier synthesis. The process of constructing a repeating waveform by adding the sine-wave components of the waveform (544)

Hit. In a signal detection experiment, saying "Yes, I detect a stimulus" on a trial in which the stimulus is present (a correct response). (536)

Just noticeable difference (JND). The smallest difference in intensity that results in a noticeable difference between two stimuli. (530)

Limits, method of. A psychophysical method in which the experimenter presents stimuli in alternating ascending and descending series. (528)

Magnitude estimation. A psychophysical method in which the subject assigns numbers to a stimulus that are proportional to the subjective magnitude of the stimulus. (532)

Miss. In a signal detection experiment, saying "No, I don't detect a stimulus" on a trial in which the stimulus is present (an incorrect response). (536)

Noise. All stimuli in the environment other than the signal. Noise can also be generated within a person's nervous system. The subject's perception of noise in a signal detection experiment sometimes causes the subject to mistakenly think a signal has been presented. (540)

Receiver operating characteristic (ROC) curve. A graph in which the results of a signal detection experiment are plotted as the proportion of hits versus the proportion of false alarms for a number of different response criteria. (537)

Response compression. When doubling the physical intensity of a stimulus less than doubles the subjective magnitude of the stimulus. (532)

Response criterion. In a signal detection experiment, the subjective magnitude of a stimulus above which the subject will indicate that the stimulus is present. (535)

Response expansion. When doubling the stimulus intensity more than doubles the perceived magnitude of the stimulus. (533)

Signal. The stimulus presented to a subject. (540)

Signal detection theory (SDT). States that a person's detection of a stimulus depends both on the subject's sensitivity to the stimulus and on the subject's response criterion. (535)

Stevens' power law. A relationship between the physical intensity of a stimulus and the perception of the subjective magnitude of the stimulus. (533)

Threshold. See Absolute threshold.

Weber's law. States that the just noticeable difference (JND) equals a constant (K), called the Weber fraction, times the size of the stimulus (S). This law is usually expressed in the form $K = JND/S$. (530)

In Chapter 13, we saw that the phonemes can be described by their place of articulation, manner of articulation, and voicing. The place of articulation, manner of articulation, and voicing are indicated below for all the consonants.

PLACE OF ARTICULATION

For English speakers, there are seven major places of articulation (Clark & Clark, 1977). These places, and the consonants associated with them, are:

1. Bilabial: the two lips together (*p, b, m, w*).

2. Labiodental: the bottom lip against the upper front teeth (*f, v*).

3. Dental: the tongue against the upper front teeth (θ, ð).

4. Alveolar: the tip of the tongue against the alveolar ridge (see Figure 13.3) (*t, d, s, z, n, l*).

5. Palatal: the tongue against the hard palate (*r, š, ž, č, ǰ, ẏ*).

6. Velar: the tongue against the velum (*k, g, ŋ*).

7. Glottal: the glottis in the throat (*h*).

MANNER OF ARTICULATION

The six major categories corresponding to different means of articulation are:

1. Stop (or plosive): complete closure at the point of articulation. For example, /p/ is produced by completely closing both lips and then releasing a slight rush of air (*p, b, t, d, k, g*).

2. Fricative: a constriction, but not complete closure, that sets up turbulence as air rushes through. Thus, to produce /f/, air is pushed between the upper teeth and lower lip (*f, v, θ, ð, š, ž, s, z, h*).

3. Affricate: complete closure, followed by the rushing of air through a constriction. For example, /c/ as in church (*č, ǰ*).

4. Nasal: the velum (see Figure 13.3) is lowered so that air passes through the nasal cavity. Try producing the sound /m/ while holding your nose shut. The pressure buildup you feel when you try this is caused by air being pushed into the nasal cavity (*m, n, ŋ*).

5. Lateral: the tongue is shaped so that the main opening is on the sides (*l*).

6. Semivowel: the tongue is shaped so that the main opening is in the middle (*w, r, y*).

These different manners of articulation produce different sounds, and these differences can be seen in the sound spectrogram. For example, stops are characterized by a brief silent period, followed by a "pop" or "explosion" when the rush of air is released. This silent period and rush of air are clearly illustrated in Figure 13.1 by an open space, followed by a sharp line, in the spectrogram patterns of the stops /k/ and /t/ of "cat." Fricatives, on the other hand, result in a long-duration, high-frequency noise, due to the turbulence as air rushes through the teeth, as illustrated by the pattern for the /s/ of "shoo."

VOICING

Voiced consonants: *b, d, g, v, z, ž, ǰ, m, n, ð, ŋ, l, r, y, w*.

Unvoiced consonants: *p, t, k, f, θ, s, š, h, č*.

PHONETIC FEATURES

We noted in Chapter 13 that each phoneme has its own set of phonetic features. Table E.1 indicates the phonetic features for the phonemes /d/, /t/, /m/, /w/, /f/, and /v/. If we were to include the rest of the phonemes, we would see, in fact, that no two phonemes have the same set of features.

T A B L E   E. 1 / *Phonetic Features of Six Phonemes*

	d	*t*	*m*	*w*	*f*	*v*
Place						
Alveolar	x	x				
Bilabial			x	x		
Labiodental					x	x
Manner						
Stop	x	x				
Fricative					x	x
Nasal			x			
Semivowel				x		
Voicing						
Voiced	x		x	x		x
Unvoiced		x			x	

References

The page number at the end of each reference keys it to its page in the text.

Abeles, M., and Goldstein, M. H. (1970). Functional architecture in cat primary auditory cortex: Columnar organization and organization according to depth. *Journal of Neurophysiology, 33,* 172–187. (433)

Abramov, I., Gordon, J., Hendrickson, A., Hainline, L., Dobson, V., & LaBossiere, E. (1982). The retina of the newborn human infant. *Science, 217,* 265–267. (325)

Adams, J. A., Maurer, D., & Davis, M. (1986). Newborns' discrimination of chromatic from achromatic stimuli. *Journal of Experimental Child Psychology, 41,* 267–281. (322)

Albers, J. (1975). *Interaction of color.* New Haven, CT: Yale University Press. (123)

Allen, T. W., Walker, K., Symonds, L., & Marcell, M. (1977). Intrasensory and intersensory perception of temporal sequences during infancy. *Developmental Psychology, 13,* 225–229. (336)

Ammons, C. H., Worchel, P., & Dallenbach, K. M. (1953). Facial vision: The perception of obstacles out of doors by blindfolded and blindfolded-deafened subjects. *American Journal of Psychology, 66,* 519–553. (384)

Amoore, J. E. (1970). *Molecular basis of odor.* Springfield, IL: Charles C. Thomas. (506, 507)

Amoore, J. E., Johnston, J. W., Jr., & Rubin, M. (1964). The stereochemical theory of odor. *Scientific American, 210*(2), 42–49. (502)

Anstis, S. (1980). The perception of apparent movement. *Proceedings of the Royal Society of London, 290B,* 153–168. (294)

Anstis, S. M., & Gregory, R. L. (1964). The aftereffect of seen motion: The role of retinal stimulation and eye movements. *Quarterly Journal of Experimental Psychology, 17,* 173–174. (299)

Arnheim, R. (1974). *Art and visual perception* (2nd ed.). Berkeley: University of California Press. (194)

Aslin, R. N. (1977). Development of binocular fixation in human infants. *Journal of Experimental Child Psychology, 23,* 133–150. (328)

Aslin, R. N. (1981). Experiential influences and sensitive periods of perceptual development: A unified model. In R. N. Aslin, J. Alberts, & M. J. Petersen (Eds.), *Development of perception* (Vol. 2, pp. 45–93). New York: Academic Press. (337)

Aslin, R. N., & Banks, M. S. (1978). Early experience in human: Evidence for a critical period in the development of binocular vision. In Sten-Schneider, H. Liebowitz, H. Pick, & H. Stevenson (Eds.), *Psychology: From basic research to practice.* New York: Plenum. (348, 349)

Aslin, R. N. & Pisoni, D. B. (1980). Some developmental processes in speech perception. In G. Yeni-Konishian, J. F. Kavanagh, & C. A. Ferguson (Eds.), *Child phonology, Vol. 2: Perception.* New York: Academic Press. (459)

Attneave, F., & Olson, R. K. (1971). Pitch as a medium: A new approach to psychophysical scaling. *American Journal of Psychology, 84,* 147–166. (436)

Aubert, H. (1886). Die Bewegungsempfindung. *Archiv fuer die Gesamte Physiologic des Menschen und der Tiere, 39,* 347–370. (278)

Awaya, S., Miyake, Y., Imayuni, Y., Shiose, Y., Kanda, T., & Komuro, K. (1973). Amblyopia in man, suggestive of stimulus deprivation amblyopia. *Japanese Journal of Ophthalmology, 17,* 69–82. (346)

Bach-y-Rita, P. (1972). *Brain mechanisms in sensory substitution.* New York: Academic Press. (470)

Bach-y-Rita, P., Collins, C. C., Saunders, F., White, B., & Scadden, L. (1969). Vision substitution by tactile image projection. *Nature, 221,* 963–964. (470)

Bach-y-Rita, P., Collins, C. C., Scadden, C., Holmlund, G. W., & Hart, B. K. (1970). Display techniques in a tactile vision substitution system. *Medical and Biological Illustration, 20,* 6–12. (470)

Backus, J. (1977). *The Acoustical foundations of music* (2nd ed.). New York: W. W. Norton. (409)

Baird, J. C. (1982). The moon illusion: II. A reference theory. *Journal of Experimental Psychology: General, 111,* 304–315. (259)

Baird, J. C., Wagner, M. (1982). The moon illusion: I. How high is the sky? *Journal of Experimental Psychology: General, 111,* 296–303. (259)

Banks, M. S. (1980). The development of visual accommodation during early infancy. *Child Development, 51,* 646–666. (327)

Banks, M. S. (1982). The development of spatial and temporal contrast sensitivity. *Current Eye Research, 2,* 191–198. (326)

Banks, M. S., Aslin, R. N., & Letson, R. D. (1975). Sensitive period for the development of human binocular vision. *Science, 190,* 675–677. (348)

Banks, M. S., & Salapatek, P. (1978). Acuity and contrast sensitivity in 1-, 2- and 3-month-old human infants. *Investigative Ophthalmology and Visual Science, 17,* 361–365. (324, 326)

Banks, M. S., & Salapatek, P. (1981). Infant pattern vision: A new approach based on the contrast sensitivity function. *Journal of Experimental Child Psychology, 31,* 1–45. (326)

Banks, W. P., & Prinzmetal, W. (1976). Configurational effects in visual information processing. *Perception and Psychophysics, 19,* 361–367. (211)

Barlow, H. B., Blakemore, C., & Pettigrew, J. D. (1967). The neural mechanism of binocular depth discrimination. *Journal of Physiology, 193,* 327–342. (243)

Barlow, H. B., & Brindley, G. S. (1963). Intraocular transfer of movement after-effects during pressure blinding of the stimulated eye. *Nature, 200,* 1347. (299)

Barlow, H. B., & Hill, R. M. (1963). Evidence for a physiological explanation of the waterfall illusion and figural after-effects. *Nature, 200,* 1345–1347. (299, 300)

Barlow, H. B., & Mollon, J. D. (Eds.) (1982). *The senses.* Cambridge, England: University of Cambridge Press.

Barrow, H. G., & Tannenbaum, J. M. (1986). Computational approaches to vision. In K. R. Boff, L. Kaufman, & J. P. Thomas (Eds.), *Handbook of perception and human performance* (Chapter 35). New York: Wiley. (189)

Bartoshuk, L. M. (1971). The chemical senses I. Taste. In J. W. Kling & L. A. Riggs (Eds.), *Experimental psychology* (3rd ed.). New York: Holt, Rinehart & Winston. (517)

Bartoshuk, L. M. (1978). Gustatory system. In R. B. Masterson (Ed.), *Handbook of behavioral neurobiology: Vol. 1. Sensory integration* (pp. 503–567). New York: Plenum. (520)

Bartoshuk, L. M. (1979). Bitter taste of saccharin: Related to the genetic ability to taste the bitter substance propylthiourial (PROP). *Science, 205,* 934–935. (514)

Bartoshuk, L. M. (1980, September). Separate worlds of taste. *Psychology Today,* pp. 48–56. (513, 514)

Bartoshuk, L. M. (1985). Chemical sensation: Taste. In R. L. Pollack & E. Kravitz (Eds.), *Nutrition in oral health and disease.* Philadelphia: Lea & Lebiger. (518)

Bartoshuk, L. M., Cain, W. S., & Pfaffmann, C. (1985). Taste and olfaction. In G. A. Kimble & K. Schlesinger (Eds.), *Topics in the history of psychology* (Vol. 1, pp. 221–260). Hillsdale, NJ: Erlbaum. (505, 506)

Batteau, D. W. (1967). The role of the pinna in human localization. *Proceedings of the Royal Society of London, 168B,* 158–180. (412)

Beauchamp, G. K. (1987). The human preference for excess salt. *American Scientist, 75,* 27–33. (516)

Beauchamp, G. K., Doty, R. L., Moulton, D. G., & Mugford, R. A. (1976). The pheromone concept in mammalian chemical communication: A critique. In R. L. Doty (Ed.), *Mammalian olfaction, reproductive processes, and behavior.* New York: Academic Press. (501)

Beauchamp, G. K., & Maller, O. (1977). The development of flavor preferences in humans: A review. In M. R. Kare & O. Maller (Eds.), *Chemical senses and nutrition* (pp. 291–311). New York: Academic Press. (514)

Beck, J. (1966). Effect of orientation and shape similarity in perceptual grouping. *Perception and Psychophysics, 1,* 300–302. (210)

Beck, J. (1972). *Surface color perception.* Ithaca: Cornell University Press. (196)

Beck, J. (1982). Textural segmentation. In J. Beck (Ed.), *Organization and representation in perception.* Hillsdale, NJ: Erlbaum. (215)

Beck, J., Hope, B., & Resenfeld, A. (Eds.). (1983). *Human and machine vision.* New York: Academic Press. (189)

Beck, P. W., Handwerker, H. O., & Zimmerman, M. (1974). Nervous outflow from the cat's foot during noxious radiant heat stimulation. *Brain Research, 67,* 373–386. (473, 478)

Beecher, H. K. (1972). The placebo effect as a non-specific force surrounding disease and the treatment of disease. In R. Janzen, W. D. Kerdel, A. Herz, C. Steichele, J. P. Payne, & R. A. P. Burt (Eds.), *Pain: basic principles, pharmacology, and therapy.* Stuttgart, West Germany: Georg Thiene. (487)

Beets, J. G. T. (1978). Odor and stimulant structure. In E. C. Carterette & M. P. Friedman (Eds.), *Handbook of perception* (Vol. 6A, pp. 245–255). New York: Academic Press. (507)

Beidler, L. M. (1978). Biophysics and chemistry of taste. In E. C. Carterette and M. P. Friedman (Eds.), *Handbook of perception* (Vol. 6A, pp. 21–49). New York: Academic Press. (518)

Békésy, G. von (1958). Funneling in the nervous system and its role in loudness and sensation intensity on the skin. *Journal of the Acoustical Society of America, 30,* 399–412. (479)

Békésy, G. von (1959). Neural funneling along the skin and between the inner and outer hair cells of the cochlea. *Journal of Experimental Child Psychology, 31,* 1236–1249. (479)

Békésy, G. von (1960). *Experiments in hearing.* New York: McGraw-Hill. (427, 429)

Békésy, G. von (1967). *Sensory inhibition.* Princeton: Princeton University Press. (479)

Berger, K. W. (1964). Some factors in the recognition of timbre. *Journal of the Acoustical Society of America, 36,* 1881–1891. (397)

Bernstein, I. (1978). Learned taste aversions in children receiving chemotherapy. *Science, 200,* 1302–1303. (516)

Berthenthal, B., Proffitt, D., Spetner, N., & Thomas, M. (1985). The development of sensitivity to biomechanical motions. *Child Development, 56,* 531–543. (335)

Bezold, W. von (1876). *The theory of color.* (American Ed.) Boston: Prang. (153)

Biederman, I. (1981). On the semantics of a glance at a scene. In M. Kubovy & J. Pomerantz (Eds.), *Perceptual organization.* Hillsdale, NJ: Erlbaum. (217)

Biederman, I. (1985). Human image understanding: Recent research and a theory. *Computer Vision, Graphics and Image Processing, 32,* 29–73. (218)

Biederman, I. (1987). Recognition-by-components: A theory of human image understanding. *Psychological Review, 94,* 115–147. (218, 219, 220, 221)

Blakemore, C. (1974). Developmental factors in the formation of feature extracting neurons. In F. G. Worden & F. O. Schmitt (Eds.), *The neurosciences, 3rd study program* (pp. 105–133). Cambridge, MA: MIT Press. (346)

Blakemore, C. (1976). The conditions required for the maintenance of binocularity in the kitten's visual cortex. *Journal of Physiology, 261,* 423–444. (346)

Blakemore, C. (1977). Genetic instructions and developmental plasticity in the kitten's visual cortex. *Philosophical Transactions of the Royal Society Series B 278,* 425–431. (346)

Blakemore, C., & Campbell, F. W. (1968). Adaptation to spatial stimuli. *Journal of Physiology, 200,* 11P–13P. (164)

Blakemore, C., & Cooper, G. F. (1970). Development of the brain depends on the visual environment. *Nature, 228,* 477–478. (342, 343)

Blakemore, C., & Mitchell, E. D. (1973). Environmental modification of the visual cortex and the neural basis of learning and memory. *Nature, 241,* 467–468. (344, 345)

Blakemore, C., & Sutton, P. (1969). Size adaptation: A new aftereffect. *Science, 166,* 245–247. (68)

Blakemore, C., & Tobin, E. A. (1972). Lateral inhibition between orientation detectors in the cat's visual cortex. *Experimental Brain Research, 15,* 439–440. (282)

Blakemore, C., & Van Sluyters, R. C. (1975). Innate and environmental factors in the development of the kitten's visual cortex. *Journal of Physiology, 248,* 663–716. (337)

Blank, D. L. (1974). Mechanism underlying the analysis of odorant quality at the level of the olfactory mucosa. II. Receptor selective sensitivity. *Annals of the New York Academy of Sciences, 237,* 91–101. (507)

Blasdel, G. G., Mitchell, D. E., Muir, D. W., & Pettigrew, J. D. (1977). A combined physiological and behavioral study of the effect of early visual experience with contours of a single orientation. *Journal of Physiology, 265,* 615–636. (19, 344)

Blumstein, S. E., & Stevens, K. N. (1979). Acoustic invariance in speech production: Evidence from measurements of the spectral characteristics of stop consonants. *Journal of the Acoustical Society of America, 66,* 1001–1017. (453)

Borg, G., Diamant, H., Strom, C., & Zotterman, Y. (1967). The relation between neural and perceptual intensity: A comparative study of neural and psychophysical responses to taste stimuli. *Journal of Physiology, 192,* 13–20. (57)

Boring, E. G. (1943). The moon illusion. *American Journal of Physics, 11,* 55–60. (257)

Boring, E. G. (1950). *A history of experimental psychology* (2nd ed.). New York: Appleton-Century-Crofts. (193)

Boring, E. G., & Holway, A. H. (1940a). The moon illusion and the angle of regard. *American Journal of Psychology, 53,* 109–116. (257, 258)

Boring, E. G., & Holway, A. H. (1940b). The apparent size of the moon as a function of the angle of regard: Further experiments. *American Journal of Psychology, 53,* 537–553. (257, 258)

Bornstein, M. H. (1976). Infants are trichromats. *Journal of Experimental Child Psychology, 21,* 425–445. (323)

Bowmaker, J. K., & Dartnall, H. J. A. (1980). Visual pigments of rods and cones in a human retina. *Journal of Physiology, 298,* 501–511. (83, 84)

Bowman, H. S., & Bedard, A. J. (1971). Observations of infrasound and subsonic disturbances related to severe weather. *Geophysical Journal Royal Astronomical Society, 26,* 215–242. (392)

Boynton, R. M. (1972). Color vision. In J. W. Kling & L. A. Riggs (Eds.), *Experimental psychology: Vol. 1. Sensation and perception* (3rd ed.) (pp. 315–368). New York: Holt, Rinehart & Winston. (135)

Boynton, R. M. (1979). *Human color vision.* New York: Holt, Rinehart & Winston. (135)

Braddick, O. J. (1974). A short range process in apparent motion. *Vision Research, 14,* 519–527. (291)

Braddick, O. J. (1980). Low level and high level processes in apparent motion. *Proceedings of the Royal Society, 290B,* 137–151. (298)

Bradley, A., & Freeman, R. D. (1982). Contrast sensitivity in children. *Vision Research, 22,* 953–959. (326)

Bregman, A. S., & Campbell, J. (1971). Primary auditory stream segregation and perception of order in rapid sequence of tones. *Journal of Experimental Psychology, 89,* 244–249. (404)

Bregman, A. S., & Rudnicky, A. I. (1975). Auditory segregation: Stream or streams? *Journal of Experimental Psychology: Human Perception and Performance, 1,* 263–267. (404, 405)

Brodatz, P. (1976). *Land, sea and sky. A photographic album for artists and designers.* New York: Dover. (265)

Brown, C. M. (1984). Computer vision and natural constraints. *Science, 224,* 1299–1305. (189)

Brown, J. F. (1931a). The visual perception of velocity. *Psychologische Forschung, 14,* 199–232. (278)

Brown, J. F. (1931b). The thresholds for visual velocity. *Psychologische Forschung, 14,* 249–268. (278, 279)

Brown, P. K., & Wald, G. (1964). Visual pigments in single rods and cones of the human retina. *Science, 144,* 45–52. (83, 126)

Bruce, C., Desimone, R., & Gross, C. G. (1981). Visual properties of neurons in a polysensory area in the superior temporal sulcus of the macaque. *Journal of Neurophysiology, 46,* 369–384. (94, 191)

Bruce, H. (1959). An exteroceptive block to pregnancy in the mouse. *Nature, 184,* 105. (501)

Brugge, J. F., & Merzenich, M. M. (1973). Responses of neurons in auditory cortex of the macaque monkey to monaural and binaural stimulation. *Journal of Neurophysiology, 36,* 1138–1158. (438)

Bryant, P. E., Jones, P., Claxton, U., & Perkins, G. M. (1972). Recognition of shapes across modalities by infants. *Nature, 240,* 303–304. (336)

Bugelski, B. R., & Alampay, D. A. (1961). The role of frequency in developing perceptual sets. *Canadian Journal of Psychology, 15,* 205–211. (17)

Buissert, P., & Imbert, M. (1976). Visual cortical cells: Their developmental properties in normal and dark reared kittens. *Journal of Physiology, 255,* 511–525. (337)

Burgess, P. R., & Perl, E. R. (1973). Cutaneous mechanoreceptors and nociceptors. In A. Iggo (Ed.), *Handbook of sensory physiology* (Vol. 2, pp. 29–78). Berlin: Springer-Verlag. (473, 476)

Burton, M. (1972). *The sixth sense of animals.* New York: Taplinger. (497)

Burzlaff, W. (1931). Methodologsche Beitrage zum Problem der Farbenhonstanz. *Zeitschrift fur Psychologie, 119,* 177–235. (173)

Buswell, G. T. (1935). *How people look at pictures.* Chicago: Chicago University Press. (24)

Butler, R. A., & Belendiuk, K. (1977). Spectral cues utilized in the localization of sound in the median sagittal plane. *Journal of the Acoustic Society of America, 61,* 1264–1269. (412)

Cabanac, M. (1971). Physiological role of pleasure. *Science, 173,* 1103–1107. (513)

Cabanac, M. (1979). Sensory pleasure. *Quarterly Review of Biology, 54,* 1–29. (513)

Cain, W. S. (1977). Differential sensitivity for smell: "Noise" at the nose. *Science, 195,* 796–798. (498)

Cain, W. S. (1978a). History of research on smell. In E. C. Carterette & M. P. Friedman (Eds.), *Handbook of Perception* (Vol. VIA, pp. 197–229). New York: Academic Press. (496)

Cain, W. S. (1978b). The odoriferous environment and the application of olfactory research. In E. C. Carterette & M. P. Friedman (Eds.), *Handbook of Perception* (Vol. VIA, pp. 277–304). New York: Academic Press. (496)

Cain, W. S. (1979). To know with the nose: Keys to odor identification. *Science, 203,* 467–470. (498)

Cain, W. S. (1980). Sensory attributes of cigarette smoking. *Banbury Rep. 3: A safe cigarette?* Cold Spring Harbor Laboratory, 239–249. (498, 499)

Cain, W. S. (1988). Olfaction. In R. A. Atkinson, R. J. Herrnstein, G. Lindzey, & R. D. Luce (Eds.), *Stevens' handbook of experimental psychology* (Vol. 1, perception and motivation, rev. ed.). New York: Wiley, 409–459. (496, 503, 506)

Campbell, F. W., & Robson, J. G. (1968). Application of Fourier analysis to the visibility of gratings. *Journal of Physiology, 197,* 551–566. (163)

Caron, A. J., Caron, R. F., & Carlson, V. R. (1979). Infant perception of the invariant shape of objects varying in slant. *Child Development, 50,* 716–721. (336)

Chapanis, A. (1947). The dark adaptation of the color anomalous. *Journal of General Physiology, 30,* 423–437. (81)

Chapanis, A. (1965). Color names for color space. *American Scientist, 53,* 327–346. (110)

Clark, H., & Clark, E. (1977). *Psychology and language.* New York: Harcourt Brace Jovanovich. (548)

Clark, W. C., & Clark, S. B. (1980). Pain responses in Nepalese porters. *Science, 209,* 410–412. (538, 539)

Clulow, F. W. (1972). *Color: Its principles and their applications.* New York: Morgan and Morgan. (113, 114, 115)

Cohen, W. (1957). Spatial and textual characteristics of the Ganzfeld. *American Journal of Psychology, 70,* 403–410. (159)

Coltheart, M. (1970). The effect of verbal size information upon visual judgements of absolute distance. *Perception and Psychophysics, 9,* 222–223. (235)

Conel, J. L. (1939). *The postnatal development of the cerebral cortex* (Vol. 1). Cambridge, MA: Harvard University Press. (325)

Conel, J. L. (1947). *The postnatal development of the cerebral cortex* (Vol. 3). Cambridge, MA: Harvard University Press. (325)

Conel, J. L. (1951). *The postnatal development of the cerebral cortex* (Vol. 4). Cambridge, MA: Harvard University Press. (325)

Contreras, R., & Frank, M. (1979). Sodium deprivation alters neural responses to gustatory stimuli. *Journal of General Physiology, 73,* 567–594. (521)

Cook, M., & Birch, R. (1984). Infant perception of the shapes of tilted plane forms. *Infant Behavior and Development, 7,* 389–402. (336)

Cook, R. K. (1969). Atmospheric sound propagation. *Proceedings of the National Academy of Sciences, 2,* 633–669. (392)

Costanzo, R. M., & Gardner, E. B. (1980). A quantitative analysis of responses of direction-sensitive neurons in somatosensory cortex of awake monkeys. *Journal of Neurophysiology, 43,* 1319–1341. (478)

Costanzo, R. M., & Gardner, E. B. (1981). Multiple-joint neurons in somatosensory cortex of awake monkeys. *Brain Research, 24,* 321–333. (485)

Cowey, A. (1982). Sensory and non-sensory visual disorders in man and monkey. *Proceedings of the Royal Society, 298B,* 3–13. (191)

Cranford, J. L. (1979). Auditory cortex lesions and interaural intensity and phase-angle discrimination in cats. *Journal of Neurophysiology, 42,* 1518–1526. (441)

Cranford, J. L., Igarashi, M., & Tramler, S. (1976). Effect of auditory neocortex ablation on pitch perception in the cat. *Journal of Neurophysiology, 39,* 143–154. (441)

Crawford, M. L. J., Smith, E. L., Harwerth, R. S., & von Noorden, G. K. (1984). Stereoblind monkeys have few binocular neurons. *Investiga-*

tive *Ophthalmology and Visual Sciences, 25,* 779–781. (341)

Crawford, M. L. J., & von Noorden, G. K. (1980). Optically induced concomitant strabismus in monkey. *Investigative Ophthalmology and Visual Science, 19,* 1105–1109. (340, 341)

Culler, E. A., Coakley, J. D., Lowy, K., & Gross, N. (1943). A revised frequency-map of the guinea-pig cochlea. *American Journal of Psychology, 56,* 475–500. (429)

Cutting, J. E. (1986). *Perception with an eye for motion.* Cambridge, MA: MIT Press. (269, 310)

Cutting, J. E., & Proffitt, D. R. (1981). Gait perception as an example of how we may perceive events. In R. D. Walk and H. L. Pick (Eds.), *Intersensory perception and sensory integration* (pp. 249–273). New York: Plenum. (306)

Cynader, M., Berman, N., & Hein, A. (1975). Cats raised in a one-directional world: Effects on receptive fields in visual cortex and superior colliculus. *Experimental Brain Research, 22,* 267–280. (345)

Cynader, M., Timney, B. N., & Mitchell, D. E. (1980). Period of susceptibility of kitten visual cortex to the effects of monocular deprivation extends beyond six months of age. *Brain Research, 191,* 545–550. (340)

Dallenbach, K. M. (1927). The temperature spots and end organs. *American Journal of Psychology, 39,* 402–427. (476)

Dallos, P., Billone, M. C., Durrant, J. D., Wang, C-Y, & Raynor, S. (1972). Cochlear inner and outer hair cells: Functional differences. *Science, 177,* 356–358. (423)

Daniel, P. M., & Whitteridge, D. (1961). The representation of the visual field on the cerebral cortex in monkeys. *Journal of Physiology, 159,* 203–221.

Dartnall, H. J. A., Bowmaker, J. K., & Mollon, J. D. (1983). Human visual pigments: Microspectrophotometric results from the eyes of seven persons. *Proceedings of the Royal Society, 220B.* 115–130. (126)

Delk, J. L., & Fillenbaum, S. (1965). Differences in perceived color as a function of characteristic color. *American Journal of Psychology, 78,* 290–293. (138)

DeLucia, P., & Hochberg, J. (1985). Illusions in the real world and in the mind's eye (Abs.). *Proceedings of the Eastern Psychological Association, 56,* 38. (260)

DeLucia, P., & Hochberg, J. (1986). Real-world geometrical illusions: Theoretical and practical implications (Abs.). *Proceedings of the Eastern Psychological Association, 57,* 62. (260)

deMonasterio, F. M., Scheir, S. J., & McCrane, E. P. (1981). Staining of blue-sensitive cones of the macaque retina by a fluorescent dye. *Science, 213,* 1278–1281. (127)

Derrington, A. M., Lennie, P., & Krauskopf, J. (1983). Chromatic response properties of parvocellular neurons in the macaque LGN. In J. D. Mollon & L. T. Sharpe (Eds.), *Colour vision* (pp. 245–251). London: Academic Press. (129)

Desor, J. A., & Beauchamp, G. K. (1974). The human capacity to transmit olfactory information. *Perception and Psychophysics, 16,* 551–556. (498)

Deutsch, D. (1973). Octave generalization of specific interference effects in memory for tonal pitch. *Perception and Psychophysics, 13,* 271–275. (394)

Deutsch, D. (1975). Two-channel listening to musical scales. *Journal of the Acoustical Society of America, 57.* (405, 406)

DeValois, R. L. (1960). Color vision mechanisms in monkey. *Journal of General Physiology, 43,* 115–128. (128)

DeValois. R. L., & Jacobs, G. H. (1968). Primate color vision. *Science, 162,* 533–540. (128, 136)

DeValois, R. L., & Jacobs, G. H. (1984). Neural mechanisms of color vision. In J. M. Brookhart & V. B. Mountcastle (Eds.), *Handbook of physiology, the nervous system III* (pp. 425–456). Bethesda, MD: American Physiological Society. (129, 130)

Devor, M. (1977). Central processing of odor signals: Lessons from adult and neonatal olfactory tract lesions. In D. Muller-Schwarze and M. M. Mozell (Eds.), *Chemical signals in vertebrates* (pp. 529–545). New York: Plenum. (501)

deVries, H., & Stuiver, M. (1961). The absolute sensitivity of the human sense of smell. In W. A. Rosenblith (Ed.), *Sensory communication.* Cambridge, MA: MIT Press. (497)

Diamond, I. T., & Neff, W. D. (1957). Ablation of temporal cortex and discrimination of auditory patterns. *Journal of Neurophysiology, 20,* 300–315. (442)

Dobelle, W. H. (1977). Current status of research on providing sight to the blind by electrical stimulation of the brain. *Journal of Visual Impairment and Blindness, 71,* 290–297. (51)

Dobelle, W. H. Mladejovsky, J. J., Evans, J. R., Roberts, T. S., & Girvin, J. P. (1976). "Braille" reading by a blind volunteer by visual cortex stimulation. *Nature, 259,* 111–112. (51)

Dobelle, W. H., Mladejovsky, M. J., & Girvin, J. P. (1974). Artificial vision for the blind: Electrical stimulation of visual cortex offers hope for a functional prosthesis. *Science, 183,* 440–444. (51)

Dobson, V., & Teller, D. (1978). Visual acuity in human infants. Review and comparison of behavioral and electrophysiological studies. *Vision Research, 18,* 1469–1483. (324)

Dodd, G. G., & Squirrell, D. J. (1980). Structure and mechanism in the mammalian olfactory system. *Symposium of the Zoology Society of London, 45,* 35–56. (497)

Doty, R. L., Green, P. A., Ram, C., & Yankell, S. L. (1982). Communication of gender from human breath odors: Relationship to perceived intensity and pleasantness. *Hormones & Behavior, 16,* 13–22. (500)

Döving, K. B., & Pinching, A. J. (1973). Selective degeneration of neurons in olfactory bulb following prolonged odor exposure. *Brain Research, 52,* 115–129. (510)

Dowling, J. E., & Boycott, B. B. (1966). Organization of the primate retina. *Proceedings of the Royal Society of London, 166B,* 80–111. (44)

Dowling, W. J. (1973a). The perception of interleaved melodies. *Cognitive Psychology, 5,* 322–337. (406)

Dowling, W. J. (1973b). Rhythmic groups and subjective chunks in memory for melodies. *Perception and Psychophysics, 14,* 37–40. (406)

Dowling, W. J., & Harwood, D. L. (1986). *Music cognition.* New York: Academic Press. (396, 403, 407)

Duclaux, R., & Kenshalo, D. R. (1980). Response characteristics of cutaneous warm fibers in the monkey. *Journal of Neurophysiology, 43,* 1–15. (473)

Duncker, D. K. (1929). Uber induzierte Bewegung (Ein Beitrag zur Theorie optisch wahrgenommener Bewegung). *Psychologische Forschung, 12,* 180–259. (Summary in W. D. Ellis [1938] *A sourcebook of Gestalt psychology.* London: Kegan Paul, Trench, Trubner.) (196, 295)

Duncker, D. K. (1939). The influence of past experience upon perceptual properties. *American Journal of Psychology, 52,* 255–265. (515)

Durlach, N. I., & Colburn, H. S. (1978). Binaural phenomena. In E. C. Carterette and M. P. Friedman (Eds.), *Handbook of perception* (Vol. 4, pp. 365–466). New York: Academic Press. (410)

Durrant, J., & Lovrinic, J. (1977). *Bases of haring science.* Baltimore, MD: Williams & Wilkins. (421, 422, 441, 442)

Eimas, P. D., & Corbit, J. D. (1973). Selective adaptation of linguistic feature detectors. *Cognitive Psychology, 4,* 99–109. (455, 456, 457)

Eimas, P. D., Siqueland, E. R., Jusczyk, P., & Vigorito, J. (1971). Speech perception in infants. *Science, 171,* 303–306. (458)

Elman, J. L., & McClelland, J. L. (1983). Exploiting lawful variability in the speech waveform. Paper presented at the Symposia on invariance and variability. Massachusetts Institute of Technology, Cambridge, Mass. (October, 1983). (454)

Emmert, E. (1881). Grossenverhaltnisse der Nachbilder. *Klinische Monatsblaetter fuer Augenheilkunde, 19,* 443–450. (250)

Engen, T. (1972). Psychophysics. In J. W. Kling & L. A. Riggs (Eds.), *Experimental psychology* (3rd ed.) (pp. 1–46). New York: Holt, Rinehart & Winston. (530)

Engen, T., & Pfaffman, C. (1960). Absolute judgements of odor quality. *Journal of Experimental Psychology, 59,* 214–219. (498)

Epstein, W. (1965). Nonrelational judgements of size and distance. *American Journal of Psychology, 78,* 120–123. (233)

Epstein, W. (1966). Perceived depth as a function of relative height under three background conditions. *Journal of Experimental Psychology, 72,* 335–338. (233)

Epstein, W. (1977). What are the prospects for a higher-order stimulus theory of perception? *Scandinavian Journal of Psychology, 18,* 164–171. (269)

Erickson, R. (1975). *Sound structure in music.* Berkeley: University of California Press. (389, 397)

Erickson, R. P. (1963). Sensory neural patterns and gustation. In Y. Zotterman (Ed.), *Olfaction and taste* (Vol. 1, pp. 205–213). Oxford: Pergamon. (54, 55, 521, 522)

Erickson, R. P. (1982). The across-fiber pattern theory: An organizing principle for molar neural function. In W. D. Neff (Ed.), *Contributions to sensory physiology* (Vol. 6, pp. 79–109). New York: Academic Press. (517)

Erickson, R. P. (1984). On the neural bases of behavior. *American Scientist, 72,* 233–241. (52, 54)

Evans, E. F. (1978). Place and time coding of frequency in the peripheral auditory system: Some physiological pros and cons. *Audiology, 17,* 369–420. (438)

Fagan, J. F. (1976). Infant's recognition of invariant features of faces. *Child development, 47,* 627–638. (320, 336)

Fantz, R. L. (1965). Visual perception from birth as shown by pattern selectivity. *Annals of the New York Academy of Sciences, 118,* 793–814. (332)

Fantz, R. L. , Fagan, J. F., & Miranda, S. B. (1975). Early visual selectivity. In L. B. Cohen & P. Salapatek (Eds.), *Infant perception: From sensation to cognition* (pp. 249–345). New York: Academic Press. (333, 334)

Fantz, R. L., Ordy, J. M., & Udelf, M. S. (1962). Maturation of pattern vision in infants during the first six months. *Journal of Comparative and Physiological Psychology, 55,* 907–917. (319)

Fechner, G. T. (1860). *Elemente der Psychophysik* (Vol. 1). Leipzig: Breitkopf and Harterl. H. E. Adler, D. H. Howes, & E. G. Boring (Trans.). New York: Holt, Rinehart & Winston. (528)

Fedderson, W. E., Sandel, T. T., Teas, D. C., & Jeffress, L. A. (1957). Localization of high frequency tones. *Journal of the Acoustical Society of America, 5,* 82–108. (409)

Fiorentini, A., & Maffei, L. (1973). Contrast in night vision. *Vision Research, 13,* 73–80.

Fitch, H., Halwes, T., Erickson, D., & Liberman, A. M. (1980). Perceptual equivalence of two acoustic cues for stop consonants. *Perception and Psychophysics, 27,* 343–350. (450)

Fletcher, H., & Munson, W. A. (1933). Loudness: Its definition, measurement, and calculation. *Journal of the Acoustical Society of America, 5,* 82–108. (391)

Fodor, J. A., & Pylyshyn, Z. W. (1981). How direct is visual perception? Some reflections of Gibson's "ecological approach." *Cognition, 9,* 139–196. (269)

Forecast. (1986). *Art of the eye: An exhibition on vision.* Minneapolis, MN: Forecast. (366, 370, 371)

Foulke, E. (1982). Reading braille. In W. Schiff, & E. Foulke (Eds.), *Tactual perception: A sourcebook.* Cambridge, England: Cambridge University Press. (490)

Fox, R., Lehmkuhle, S. W., & Westendorf, D. H. (1976). Falcon visual acuity. *Science, 192,* 263–265. (88)

Fox, R., & McDaniel, C. (1982). The perception of biological motion by human infants. *Science, 218,* 486–487. (335)

Fox, R., Aslin, R. N., Shea, S. L., & Dumais, S. T. (1980). Stereopsis in human infants. *Science, 207,* 323–324. (328, 329)

Frank, M. (1973). An analysis of hamster afferent taste nerve response functions. *Journal of General Physiology, 61,* 588–618. (520)

Franzen, O., & Lindblom, U. (1976). Coding of velocity of skin indentation in man and monkey. A perceptual-neurophysiological correlation. In Y. Zotterman (Ed.), *Sensory functions of the skin in primates* (pp. 55–65). Elmsford, NY: Pergamon. (58)

Freeman, R. D., & Pettigrew, J. D. (1973). Alterations of visual cortex from environmental asymmetries. *Nature, 246,* 359–360. (349)

Freeman, R. D., & Thibos, L. N. (1973). Electrophysiological evidence that abnormal early visual experience can modify the human brain. *Science, 180,* 876–878. (349)

Frey, M. von (1894). Beitrage zur Physiologie des Schmerzinns. *Berichte uber die Verhandlung der Koniglichen Sachsischen Gesellschaft der Wissenschaften zu Leipzig, Mathematisch-Physische Klasse, 46,* 185–196. (475)

Frey, M. von (1895). Beitrage zur Sinnesphysiologie der Haut. *Berichte uber die Verhandlung der Koniglichen Sachsischen Gesellschaft der Wissenschaften zu Leipzig, Mathematisch-Physische Klasse, 46,* 166–184. (475)

Friedman, M. B. (1975). Visual control of head movements during avian locomotion. *Nature, 225,* 67–69. (295)

Frishman, L. (1979). The velocity tuning of neurons in the lateral geniculate nucleus and retina of the cat. (Doctoral Dissertation, Department of Psychology, University of Pittsburgh). (282)

Gamble, A. E. McC. (1898). The applicability of Weber's law to smell. *American Journal of Psychology, 10,* 82–142. (498)

Garcia, J., Ervin, F. R., & Koelling, R. A. (1966). Learning with prolonged delay of reinforcement. *Psychonomic Science, 5,* 121–122. (515)

Garcia, J., Hawkins, W. G., & Rusiniak, K. W. (1974). Behavioral regulation of the Milieu Interne in man and rat. *Science, 185,* 824–831. (516)

Garcia, J., & Koelling, R. A. (1966). A relation of cue to consequence in avoidance learning. *Psychonomic Science, 4,* 123–124. (515)

Gardner, E. (1975). *Fundamentals of neurology* (6th ed.). New York: W. B. Saunders. (472)

Gardner, E. B., & Costanzo, R. H. (1981). Properties of kinesthetic neurons in somatosensory cortex of awake monkeys. *Brain Research, 214,* 301–319. (485)

Gardner, M. B., & Gardner, R. S. (1973). Problem of localization in the median plane: Effect of pinnae cavity occlusion. *Journal of the Acoustical Society of America, 53,* 400–408. (412)

Gelb, A. (1929). Die "Farbenkonstanz" der Sehding. *Handbook norm. path. Phys., 12,* 594–678. (176)

Geldard, F. A. (1972). *The human senses* (2nd ed.). New York: Wiley. (401, 513)

Gescheider, G. A. (1976). *Psychophysics: Method and theory.* Hillsdale, NJ: Erlbaum. (527, 530)

Getty, D. J., & Howard, J. H. (Ed.). (1981). *Auditory and visual pattern recognition.* Hillsdale, NJ: Erlbaum. (438)

Gibson, J. J. (1950). *The perception of the visual world.* Boston: Houghton Mifflin. (269)

Gibson, J. J. (1962). Observations on active touch. *Psychological Review, 69,* 477–491. (492)

Gibson, J. J. (1966). *The senses considered as perceptual systems.* Boston: Houghton Mifflin. (307)

Gibson, J. J. (1979). *The ecological approach to visual perception.* Boston: Houghton Mifflin. (25, 26, 69, 262)

Gilchrist, A. L. (1977). Perceived lightness depends on perceived spatial arrangement. *Science, 195,* 185–187. (181)

Gilchrist, A. L., Delman, S., & Jacobsen, A. (1983). The classification and integration of edges as critical to the perception of reflectance and illumination. *Perception and Psychophysics, 33,* 425–436. (177)

Gilinsky, A. S. (1965). The effect of attitude upon the perception of size. *American Journal of Psychology, 68,* 173–192. (253)

Ginsburg, A. (1983). Contrast perception in the human infant. Unpublished manuscript. (69, 326, 327)

Goldfoot, D. A., Essock-Vitale, S. M., Asa, C. S., Thornton, J. E., & Leshner, A. J. (1978). Anosmia in male rhesus does not alter copulatory activity with cycling females. *Science, 199,* 1095–1096. (502)

Goldstein, E. B. (1967). Early receptor potential of the isolated frog *(Rana pipiens)* retina. *Vision Research, 7,* 837–845.(xxi)

Goldstein, E. B. (1978). Cone pigment regeneration in frogs and humans. In J. Armington, J. Krauskopf, & B. Wooton (Eds.). *Visual psychophysics and physiology* (pp. 73–84). New York: Academic Press.(xxi)

Goldstein, E. B. (1979). Rotation of objects in pictures viewed at an angle: Evidence for different properties of two types of pictorial space. *Journal of Experimental Psychology: Human Perception and Performance, 5* 78–87.(xxi)

Goldstein, E. B. (1984). *Sensation and perception* (2nd ed.). Belmont, CA.: Wadsworth. (450)

Goldstein, E. B. (1987). Spatial layout, orientation relative to the observer, and perceived projection in pictures viewed at an angle. *Journal of Experimental Psychology: Human Perception and Performance, 13,* 256–266. (xxi)

Goldstein, E. B. (1988). Geometry or not geometry? Perceived orientation and spatial layout in pictures viewed at an angle. *Journal of Experimental Psychology: Human Perception and Performance, 14,* 312–314. (xxi)

Goldstein, J. L. (1978). Mechanisms of signal analysis and pattern perception in periodicity pitch. *Audiology, 17,* 421–445. (438)

Gombrich, E. H. (1960). *Art and illusion.* Princeton, NJ: Princeton University Press. (234)

Goodwin, M., Gooding, K. M., & Regnier, F. (1979). Sex pheromones in the dog. *Science, 203,* 559–561. (502)

Gossard, E. E., & Hooke, W. H. (1975). *Waves in the atmosphere.* Amsterdam: Elsevier. (392)

Graham, C. H. (1965). Perception of movement. In C. Graham (Ed.), *Vision and visual perception* (pp. 575–588). New York: Wiley. (288)

Graham, C. H., Sperling, H. G., Hsia, Y., & Coulson, A. H. (1961). The determination of some visual functions of a unilaterally color-blind subject: Methods and results. *Journal of Psychology, 51,* 3–32. (134)

Granrud, C. E. (1986). Binocular vision and spatial perception in 4- and 5-month-old infants. *Journal of Experimental Psychology: Human Perception and Performance, 12,* 36–49. (322)

Granrud, C. E. (1987). Visual size constancy in newborn infants. Paper presented at 1987 meeting of the Association for Research in Vision and Ophthalmology, Sarasota, Florida. (322)

Granrud, C. E., Artenbery, M. E., & Yonas, A. (1985). Size constancy in 3-month-old infants. Paper presented at the meeting of the Society for Research in Child Development, Toronto. (335)

Granrud, C. E., Haake, R. J., & Yonas, A. (1985). Infants' sensitivity to familiar size: The effect of memory on spatial perception. *Perception and Psychophysics, 37*, 459–466. (332)

Granrud, C. E., & Yonas, A. (1984). Infants' perception of pictorially specified interposition. *Journal of Experimental Child Psychology, 37*, 500–511. (332, 333)

Granrud, C. E., Yonas, A., & Opland, E. A. (1985). Infants' sensitivity to the depth cue of shading. *Perception and Psychophysics, 37*, 415–419. (332)

Granrud, C. E., Yonas, A., & Pettersen, L. (1984). A comparison of monocular and binocular depth perception in 5- and 7-month-old infants. *Journal of Experimental Child Psychology, 38*, 19–32. (322)

Green, D. G. (1968). The contrast sensitivity of the colour mechanisms of the human eye. *Journal of Physiology, 196*, 415–429. (127)

Green, D. M. (1976). *An introduction to hearing.* Hillsdale, NJ: Erlbaum. (410)

Gregory, R. L. (1966). *Eye and brain* (1st ed.). New York: McGraw-Hill. (250, 259)

Gregory, R. L. (1973a). *Eye and brain* (2nd ed.). New York: McGraw-Hill. (183, 212)

Gregory, R. L. (1973b). The confounded eye. In R. L. Gregory & E. H. Gombrich (Eds.), *Illusion in Nature and Art* (pp. 49–95). New York: Scribner's. (212)

Gregory, R. L., & Wallace, J. G. (1963). Recovery from early blindness: A case study. *Experimental Psychology Society Monograph, 2.* (347)

Grether, W. F. (1939). Color vision and color blindness in monkeys. *Comparative Psychology Monographs, 15*, 1–38. (136).

Griffin, D. R. (1969). The physiology and geophysics of bird navigation. *Quarterly Review of Biology, 44*, 255–276. (392)

Gross, C. G., & Mishkin, M. (1977). The neural basis of stimulus equivalence across retinal translation. In S. Harrad, R. W. Doty, L. Goldstein, J. Jaynes, & G. Kraulthamer (Eds.), *Lateralization of the nervous system* (pp. 109–122). New York: Academic Press. (191)

Gulick, W. L. (1971). *Hearing.* New York: Oxford University Press. (34, 421, 423)

Gyr, J. W. (1972). Is a theory of direct perception adequate? *Psychological Bulletin, 77*, 246–261. (283)

Hagen, M. A. (Ed.). (1979). *The perception of pictures* (Vols. 1 & 2). New York: Academic Press. (235)

Hagen, M. A. (1986). *Varieties of realism.* Cambridge, England: Cambridge University Press. (235)

Hall, E. T. (1966). *The Hidden Dimension.* Garden City, NY: Doubleday. (497)

Hall, J. L. (1965). Binaural interaction in the accessory sperior-olivary nucleus of the cat. *Journal of the Acoustical Society of America, 37*, 814–823. (438)

Hall, M. J., Bartoshuk, L. M., Cain, W. S., & Stevens, J. C. (1975). PTC taste blindness and the taste of caffeine. *Nature, 253*, 442–443. (514)

Hamilton, W. F., & Coleman, T. B. (1933). Trichromatic vision in the pigeon as illustrated by the spectral hue discrimination curve. *Journal of Comparative Psychology, 15*, 183–191. (136)

Hanson, A. R., & Riseman, E. M. (1978). *Computer vision systems.* New York: Academic Press. (189)

Harman, G. (1974). Epistemology. In E. C. Carterette & M. P. Friedman (Eds.), *Handbook of perception* Vol. 1, pp. 41–55. New York: Academic Press. (5)

Harris, L., Atkinson, J. & Braddick, O. (1976). Visual contrast sensitivity of a 6-month-old infant measured by the evoked potential. *Nature, 246*, 570–571. (324)

Hartline, H. K., Wagner, H. G., & Ratliff, F. (1956). Inhibition in the eye of Limulus. *Journal of General Physiology, 39*, 651–673. (149)

Heffner, H. (1978). Effect of auditory cortex ablation on the localization and discrimination of brief sounds. *Journal of Neurophysiology, 41*, 963–976. (441)

Heider, F., & Simmel, M. L. (1944). An experimental study of apparent behavior. *American Journal of Psychology, 57*, 243, 249. (307)

Heise, G. A., & Miller, G. A. (1951). An experimental study of auditory patterns. *American Journal of Psychology, 64*, 68–77. (403)

Held, R. (1965). Plasticity in sensory-motor systems. *Scientific American, 213*, 84–94. (330)

Held, R., Birch, E. E., & Gwiazda, J. (1980). Stereoacuity of human infants. *Proceedings of the National Academy of Sciences, 77*, 5572–5574. (330)

Held, R., & Hein, A. (1963). Movement produced stimulation in the development of visually guided behavior. *Journal of Comparative and Physiological Psychology, 56,* 872–876. (330)

Helmholtz, H. von (1852). On the theory of compound colors. *Philosophical Magazine, 4,* 519–534. (117)

Helmholtz, H. von (1954). *Die Lehre Von den Tonenpfindungen als physiologische Grundlege fur die Theorie der Musik* [On the sensations of tone as a physiological basis for the theory of music]. A. J. Ellis, Trans.). New York: Dover. (Original work published 1863) (427)

Helmholtz, H. von (1866/1911). *Treatise on physiological optics* (Vols. 2 & 3). Translated from the 3rd German ed. 1909–1911). (J. P. Southall, Ed. & Trans.). Rochester, NY: Optical Society of America. (236)

Helson, H. (1933). The fundamental propositions of Gestalt psychology. *Psychological Review, 40,* 13–32. (201)

Helson, H., Judd, D. B., & Wilson, M. (1956). Color rendition with fluorescent sources of illumination. *Illuminating Engineering, 51,* 329–346. (137)

Hendrickson, A. E., & Yuodelis, C. (1984). The morphological development of the human fovea. *Ophthalmology, 91,* 603–612. (325)

Hering, E. (1878). *Zur Lehre vom Lichtsinne.* Vienna: Gerold. (122, 123)

Hering, E. (1905). Grundzuge der Lehre vom Lichtsinn. In *Handbuck der gesammter Augenheilkunde* (Vol. 3, Chap. 13). Berlin. (123, 178)

Hering, E. (1964). *Outlines of a theory of the light sense.* (L. M. Hurvich & D. Jameson, Trans.). Cambridge, MA: Harvard University Press. (123)

Hirsch, H. V. B. (1972). Visual perception in cats after environmental surgery. *Experimental Brain Research, 15,* 405–423. (344)

Hirsch, H. V. B., & Spinelli, D. N. (1970). Visual experience modifies distribution of horizontally and vertically oriented receptive fields in cats. *Science, 168,* 869–871. (342)

Hirsch, H. V. B., & Spinelli, D. N. (1971). Modification of the distribution of receptive field orientations in cats by selective visual exposure during development. *Experimental Brain Research, 12,* 509–527. (342)

Hochberg, J. E. (1970). Attention, organization, and consciousness. In D. I. Mostofsky (Ed.), *Attention: Contemporary theory and analysis* (pp. 99–124). New York: Appleton-Century-Crofts. (23, 25)

Hochberg, J. E. (1971). Perception In J. W. Kling & L. A. Riggs (Eds.), *Experimental Psychology* (3rd ed.). (pp. 396–550). New York: Holt, Rinehart & Winston. (177, 201, 205, 230)

Hochberg, J. E. (1986). Representation of motion and space in video and cinematic displays. In K. R. Boff, L. Kaufman, & J. P. Thomas (Eds.), *Handbook of perception and human performance* (Chapter 22). New York: Wiley. (312)

Hochberg, J. E. (1987). Machines should not see as people do, but must know how people see. *Computer Vision, Graphics and Image Processing.* (260)

Hochberg, J. E., Triebel, W., & Seaman, G. (1951). Color adaptation under conditions of homogeneous visual stimulation (Ganzfeld). *Journal of Experimental Psychology, 41,* 153–159. (159)

Hodgkin, A. L., & Huxley, A. F. (1939). Action potentials recorded from inside a nerve fiber. *Nature, 144,* 710–711. (45)

Hohmann, A., & Creutzfeldt, O. D. (1975). Squint and the development of binocularity in humans. *Nature, 254,* 613–614. (349)

Holley, A., Duchamp, A., Revial, M. F., Juge, A., & Macleod, P. (1974). Qualitative and quantitative discrimination in the frog olfactory receptors: Analysis from electrophysiological data. *Annals of the New York Academy of Sciences, 237,* 102–114. (507)

Holst, E. von (1954). Relations between the central nervous system and the peripheral organs. *British Journal of Animal Behaviour, 2,* 89–94. (283)

Holway, A. H., & Boring, E. G. (1941). Determinants of apparent visual size with distance variant. *American Journal of Psychology, 54,* 21–37. (247, 250)

Hornung, D. E., Lansung, R. D., & Mozell, M. M. (1975). Distribution of butanol molecules along bullfrog olfactory mucosa. *Nature, 254,* 617–618. (509)

Hornung, D. E., & Mozell, M. M. (1977). Factors influencing the differential sorption of odorant molecules across the olfactory mucosa. *Journal of General Physiology, 69,* 343–361. (509)

Hornung, D. E., & Mozell, M. M. (1981). Accessibility of odorant molecules to the receptors. In R. H. Cagan & M. R. Kare (Eds.), *Biochemistry of taste and olfaction* (pp. 33–45). New York: Academic Press. (509, 510)

Houtsma, A. J. M., & Goldstein, J. L. (1972). Perception of musical intervals: Evidence for the central origin of the pitch of complex tones. *Journal of the Optical Society of America, 51,* 520–529. (437)

Howland, H., Boothe, R. G., & Kiorpes, L. (1981). Accommodative defocus does not limit development of acuity in infant *Macaca nemestrina* monkeys. *Science, 215,* 1409–1411. (327)

Hubel, D. H., & Wiesel, T. N. (1959). Receptive fields of single neurons in the cat's striate cortex. *Journal of Physiology, 148,* 574–591. (49, 93)

Hubel, D. H., & Wiesel, T. N. (1962). Receptive fields, binocular interaction and functional architecture in the cat's visual cortex. *Journal of Physiology, 160,* 106–154. (18)

Hubel, D. H., & Wiesel, T. N. (1963). Receptive fields of cells in striate cortex of very young, visually inexperienced kittens. *Journal of Neurophysiology, 26,* 994–1002. (337)

Hubel, D. H., & Wiesel, T. N. (1965a). Receptive fields and functional architecture in two nonstriate visual areas (18 & 19) of the cat. *Journal of Neurophysiology, 28,* 229–289. (93)

Hubel, D. H., & Wiesel, T. N. (1965b). Binocular interaction in striate cortex of kittens reared with artificial squint. *Journal of Neurophysiology, 28,* 1041–1059. (340)

Hubel, D. H., & Wiesel, T. N. (1961). Integrative action in the cat's lateral geniculate body. *Journal of Physiology, 155,* 385–398. (47)

Hubel, D. H., & Wiesel, T. N. (1970a). The period of susceptibility to the physiological effects of unilateral eye closure in kittens. *Journal of Physiology, 206,* 419–436. (340)

Hubel, D. H., & Wiesel, T. N. (1970b). Cells sensitive to binocular depth in area 18 of the macaque monkey cortex. *Nature, 225,* 41–42. (243)

Hubel, D. H., & Wiesel, T. N. (1974). Uniformity of monkey striate cortex: A parallel relationship between field size, scatter, and magnification factor. *Journal of Comparative Neurology, 158,* 295–306. (97)

Hubel, D. H., & Wiesel, T. N. (1977). Functional architecture of macaque monkey cortex. *Proc. R. Soc. Lond., 198,* 1–59.

Hubel, D. H., & Wiesel, T. N., & Stryker, M. P. (1978). Anatomical demonstration of orientation columns in macaque monkey. *Journal of Comparative Neurology, 177,* 361–379. (99)

Hurvich, L. (1981). *Color vision.* Sunderland, MA: Sinauer Associates. (112, 137)

Hurvich, L., & Jameson, D. (1957). An opponent-process theory of color vision. *Psychological Review, 64,* 384–404. (124, 135)

Hyvärinin, J., & Poranen, A. (1974). Functions of the association area 7 as revealed from cellular discharges in alert monkeys. *Brain, 97,* 673–692.

Hyvärinin, J., & Poranen, A. (1978). Movement-sensitive and direction and orientation-selective cutaneous receptive fields in the hand area of the postcentral gyrus in monkeys. *Journal of Physiology, 283,* 523–537. (478)

Iggo, A. I. (1982). Cutaneous sensory mechanisms. In H. B. Barlow & J. D. Mollon (Eds.), *The senses.* Cambridge, England: Cambridge University Press. (472, 474, 477)

Iggo, A. I., & Andres, K. H. (1982). Morphology of cutaneous receptors. *Annual Review of Neuroscience, 5,* 1–31. (474)

Imbert, M. (1979). Maturation of visual cortex with and without visual experience. In R. Freeman (Ed.), *Developmental neurobiology of vision* (pp. 43–50). New York: Plenum. (337)

Ittelson, W. H. (1952). *The Ames demonstrations in perception.* Princeton: Princeton University Press. (253)

Jacobson, A., & Gilchrist, A. (1988). The ratio principle holds over a million-to-one range of illumination. *Perception and Psychophysics, 43,* 1–6. (176)

Jameson, D. (1985). Opponent-colors theory in light of physiological findings. In D. Ottoson & S. Zeki (Eds.), *Central and peripheral mechanisms of color vision* (pp. 8–102). New York: Macmillan. (136)

Jenkins, J. J. (1985). Acoustic information for objects, plans and events. In W. H. Warren & R. E. Shaw (Eds.), *Persistence and change.* Hillsdale, NJ: Erlbaum. (382, 418)

Johansson, G. (1950). *Configurations in event perception.* Uppsala: Almquist and Wiskell. (301)

Johansson, G. (1975). Visual motion perception. *Scientific American, 232,* 76–89. (303)

Johansson, G. (1982). Visual space perception through motion. In M. Wertheimer, *Tutorials in motion perception.* (303)

Johansson, G. (1985). About event perception. In W. H. Warren Jr. & R. E. Shaw (Eds.), *Persistence and change* (pp. 29–59). Hillsdale, NJ: Erlbaum. (303, 305)

Johnson, K. O. (1983). Neural mechanisms of tactual form and texture discrimination. *Federation Proceedings, 42,* 2542–2547. (492)

Jones, K. R., Spear, P., & Tong, L. (1984). Critical periods for effects of monocular deprivation differences between striate and extrastriate cortex. *Journal of Neuroscience, 4,* 2543–2552. (340)

Judd, D. B., & Kelly, K. L. (1965). *The ISCC-NBS method of designating colors and a dictionary of color names.* U.S. National Bureau of Standards Circular 553 (2nd ed.). (111)

Judd, D. B., MacAdam, D. L., & Wyszecki, G. (1964). Spectral distribution of typical daylight as a function of correlated color temperature. *Journal of the Optical Society of America, 54,* 1031–1040. (112)

Julesz, B. (1971). *Foundations on cyclopean perception.* Chicago: University of Chicago Press. (244)

Julesz, B. (1978). Perceptual limits of texture discrimination and their implications to figure-ground separation. In E. Leeuwenberg & H. Buffart (Eds.), *Formal theories of perception* (pp. 205–216). New York: Wiley. (211)

Jusczyk, P. (1986). Speech perception. In K. R. Boff, L. Kaufman, & J. P. Thomas (Eds.), *Handbook of perception and human performance.* New York: Wiley. (450)

Kagan, J., Henker, B. A., Hen-Tov, A., Levine, J., & Lewis, M. (1966). Infant's differential reactions to familiar and distorted faces. *Child Development, 37,* 519–532. (334)

Kaiser, M. K., & Proffitt, D. R. (1987). Observers' sensitivity to dynamic anomalies in collisions. *Perception and Psychophysics, 42,* 275–280. (307)

Kaneko, A. (1970). Physiological and morphological identification of horizontal, bipolar and amacrine cells in goldfish retina. *Journal of Physiology, 207,* 623–633. (45)

Kanig, J. L. (1955). Mental impact of colors in food studied. *Food Field Reporter, 23,* 57. (515)

Kanizsa, G. (1955). Marzini quasi-percettivi in campi con stimolozione omogenea. *Rivista di Psicologia, 49,* 7–30. (194)

Kanizsa, G. (1979). *Organization in vision.* New York: Praeger. (205)

Kaplan, G. (1969). Kinetic disruption of optical texture: The perception of depth at an edge. *Perception and Psychophysics, 6,* 193–198. (239)

Karlson, P. & Luscher, M. (1959). "Pheronomes": A new term for a class of biologically active substances. *Nature, 183,* 55–56. (501)

Katz, D. (1935). *The world of colour.* London: Kegan Paul, Trenth & Trubner. (8)

Kauer, J. S. (1987). Coding in the olfactory system. In Finger and Silver (Eds.), *Neurobiology of taste and smell* (pp. 205–231). New York: Wiley. (496, 507)

Kauer, J. S., & Moulton, D. G. (1974). Responses of olfactory bulb neurons to odour stimulation of small nasal areas in the salamander. *Journal of Physiology, 243,* 717–737. (507, 508)

Kaufman, L., & Rock, I. (1962a). The moon illusion I. *Science, 136,* 953–961. (257)

Kaufman, L., & Rock, I. (1962b). The moon illusion. *Scientific American, 207,* 120–132. (257)

Kellman, P., & Spelke, E. (1983). Perception of partly occluded objects in infancy. *Cognitive Psychology, 15,* 483–524. (335)

Kellogg, W. N. (1962). Sonar system of the blind. *Science, 137,* 399–404. (384, 385)

Kenshalo, D. R. (1976). Correlations of temperature sensitivity in man and monkey, a first approximation. In Y. Zotterman (Ed.), *Sensory functions of the skin in primates, with special reference to man* (pp. 305–330). New York: Plenum. (473)

Kewley-Port, D. (1983). Time-varying features as correlates of place of articulation in stop consonants. *Journal of the Acoustical Society of America, 73,* 322–335. (453)

Kewley-Port, D., & Luce, P. A. (1984). Time-varying features of initial stop consonants in auditory running spectra: A first report. *Perception and Psychophysics, 35,* 353–360. (453, 454)

Kiang, N. Y. S. (1975). Stimulus representation in the discharge patterns of auditory neurons. In E. L. Eagles (Ed.), *The nervous system* (Vol. 3, pp. 81–96). New York: Raven. (424, 432, 448)

Kluender, K. R., Diehl, R. L., & Killeen, P. R. (1987). Japanese quail can learn phonetic categories. *Science, 237,* 1195–1197. (456)

Knibestol, M., & Vallbo, A. B. (1976). Stimulus-response functions of primary afferents and psychophysical intensity estimation of mechanical skin stimulation in the human hand. In Y. Zotterman (Ed.), *Sensory functions of the skin in primates, with special reference to man* (pp. 201–213). New York: Plenum. (58)

Knudsen, E. I., & Konishi, M. (1978a). Space and frequency are represented separately in auditory midbrain of the owl. *Journal of Neurophysiology, 41,* 870–883. (438, 440)

Knudsen, E. I., & Konishi, M. (1978b). Center-surround organization of auditory receptive fields in the owl. *Science, 202,* 778–780. (438, 440)

Koffka, K. (1935). *Principles of Gestalt psychology,* New York: Harcourt, Brace and World. (159)

Kolers, P. A. (1972). *Aspects of motion perception.* Elmsford, NY: Pergamon Press. (290)

Konishi, M. (1984). Spatial receptive fields in the auditory system. In L. Bolis, R. D. Keynes, & S. H. Maddrell (Eds.), *Comparative physiology of sensory systems.* Cambridge, England: Cambridge University Press. (441)

Kosambi, D. D. (1967). Living prehistory in India. *Scientific American, 216,* 105. (486)

Kozlowski, L., & Cutting, J. (1977). Recognizing the sex of a walker from a dynamic point-light display. *Perception and Psychophysics, 21,* 575–580. (306)

Krauskopf, J. (1963). Effect of retinal image stabilization in the appearance of heterochromatic targets. *Journal of the Optical Society of America, 53,* 741–743. (158)

Kreithen, M. L., & Quine, D. B. (1979). Infrasound detection by the homing pigeon: A behavioral audiogram. *Journal of Comparative Physiology, 129,* 1–4. (392)

Kris, J. von (1896). Uber die Funktion der Netzhautstabhen. *Zeitschrift fuer Psychologie, 9,* 81. (76)

Kruger, L. M. (1970). David Katz: Der Aufbau Der Tastwelt (The world of touch): A synopsis. *Perception and Psychophysics, 7,* 337–341. (492)

Kruger, L. S. (1982). A word-superiority effect with print and braille characters. *Perception and Psychophysics, 31,* 345–352. (491)

Kubovy, M. (1986). *The psychology of perspective and Renaissance art.* Cambridge, England: Cambridge University Press. (235)

Kuffler, S. W. (1953). Discharge patterns and functional organization of mammalian retina. *Journal of Neurophysiology, 16,* 37–68.

Kuhl, P. K. (1986). Theoretical contributions of tests on animals to the special-mechanisms debate in speech. *Experimental Biology, 45,* 233–265. (456)

Kunnapas, T. (1957). Experiments on figural dominance. *Journal of Experimental Psychology, 53,* 31–39. (206)

LaBarbera, J. D., Izard, C. E., Vietze, P., & Parisi, S. A. (1976). Four and six-month-old infant's visual responses to joy, anger, and neutral expressions. *Child Development, 47,* 535–538. (327)

Laing, D. G., & Panhuber, H. (1978). Neural and behavioral changes in rats following continuous exposure to an odor. *Journal of Comparative Physiology, 124,* 259–265. (511)

Laing, D. G., & Panhuber, H. (1980). Olfactory sensitivity of rats reared in an odorous or deodorized environment. *Physiology and Behavior, 25,* 555–558. (511)

Lashley, K. S. (1916). The color vision of birds. I. The spectrum of the domestic fowl. *Journal of Animal Behavior, 6,* 1–26. (136)

Lee, D. N. (1974). Visual information during locomotion. In R. B. MacLeod & H. L. Pick, Jr. (Eds.), *Perception: Essays in honor of J. J. Gibson* (pp. 250–267). Ithaca: Cornell University Press. (310)

Lee, D. N. (1976). A theory of visual control of braking based on information about time to collision. *Perception, 5,* 437–459. (311)

Lee, D. N. (1980). The optic flow field: The foundation of vision. *Transactions of the Royal Society, 290B,* 169–179. (309, 310)

Lee, D. N., & Aronson, E. (1974). Visual proprioceptive control of standing in human infants. *Perception and Psychophysics, 15,* 529–532. (308, 310)

Lee, D. N., Young, D. S., Reddish, P. E., Lough, S., & Clayton, T. M. H. (1983). Visual timing in hitting an accelerating ball. *Quarterly Journal of Experimental Psychology, 35A,* 333–346. (307)

LeGrand, Y. (1957). *Light, color and vision.* London: Chapman and Hall, Ltd. (126, 134)

Lele, P. P., & Weddell, G. (1956). The relationship between neurohistology and corneal sensibility. *Brain, 79,* 119–154. (476)

Lennie, P. (1980). Parallel visual pathways: A review. *Vision Research, 20,* 561–594. (89)

Lennie, P. (1984). Recent developments in the physiology of color vision. *Trends in Neuroscience, 7,* 243–248. (117)

Lerman, S. (1966). *Basic ophthalmology.* New York: McGraw-Hill. (360)

LeVay, S., Wiesel, T. N., & Hubel, D. H. (1980). The development of ocular dominance columns in normal and visually deprived monkeys. *Journal of Comparative Neurology, 191,* 1–51. (345)

Levine, J. (1955). Consensual pupillary reflex in birds. *Science, 122,* 690. (86)

Levine, J. M., & McBurney, D. H. (1983). The role of olfaction in social perception and behavior. In C. P. Herman, M. P. Zanna, & E. T. Higgins (Eds.), *Physical appearance, stigma, and social behavior: The Ontario Symposium* (Vol. 3). Hillsdale, NJ: Erlbaum. In press. (497, 506)

Lewis, E. R., Zeevi, Y. Y., & Werblin, F. S. (1969). Scanning electron microscopy of vertebrate visual receptors. *Brain Research, 15,* 559–562. (75)

Liberman, A. M., Cooper, F. S., Shankweiler, D. P., & Studdert-Kennedy, M. (1967). Perception of the speech code. *Psychological Review, 74,* 431–461. (449, 450, 455)

Liberman, A. M., & Mattingly, I. G. (1985). The motor theory of speech perception revisited. *Cognition, 21,* 1–26. (450)

Lichten, W., & Lurie, S. (1950). A new technique for the study of perceived size. *American Journal of Psychology, 63,* 280–282. (248)

Liebowitz, H. W., Shina, K., & Hennessy, H. R. (1972). Oculomotor adjustments and size constancy. *Perception and Psychophysics, 12,* 497–500. (229)

Liphovsky, S. (1977). The role of the chemical senses in nutrition. In M. R. Kare & O. Muller (Eds.), *The chemical senses and nutrition* (pp. 413–428). New York: Academic Press. (516)

Livingstone, M. S., & Hubel, D. H. (1984). Anatomy and physiology of a color system in the primate visual cortex. *Journal of Neuroscience, 4,* 309–356. (131)

Livingstone, M. S., & Hubel, D. H. (1987). Psychophysical evidence for separate channels for the perception of form, color, movement and depth. *Journal of Neuroscience, 7,* 3416–3468. (133)

Livingstone, M. & Hubel, D. H. (1988). Segregation of form, color, movement and depth: anatomy, physiology and perception. *Science, 240,* 740–749. (90, 133).

Loomis, J. M., & Lederman, S. J. (1986). *Tactual perception.* In K. R. Boff, L. Kaufman, & J. P. Thomas (Eds.), *Handbook of perception and human performance* (Chapter 31). New York: Wiley. (489)

Lowenstein, W. R. (1960). Biological transducers. *Scientific American, 203,* 98–108. (34)

Lowenstein, W. R., & Skalak, R. (1966). Mechanical transmission in a Pacinian corpuscle. An analysis and a theory. *Journal of Physiology, 182,* 346–378. (474, 475)

Luria, A. R. (1966). *Higher cortical functions in man.* New York: Basic Books. (190)

MacDonald, J., & McGurk, H. (1978). Visual influences on speech perception processes. *Perception and Psychophysics, 24,* 253–257. (457, 458)

Mach, E. (1914). *The analysis of sensations.* Republished 1959. New York: Dover. (147, 177)

MacKay-Sim, A., Shaman, P., & Moulton, D. (1982). Topographic coding of olfactory quality. Odorant-specific patterns of epithelial responsivity in the salamander. *Journal of Neurophysiology, 48,* 584–596. (509)

Maffei, L., & Fiorentini, A. (1973). The visual cortex as a spatial frequency analyzer. *Vision Research, 13,* 1255–1267. (164)

Marc, R. E., & Sperling, H. G. (1977). Chromatic organization of primate cones. *Science, 196,* 454–456. (126)

Marks, W. B. (1965). Visual pigments of single goldfish cones. *Journal of Physiology, 178,* 14–32. (136)

Marks, W. B., Dobelle, W. H., & MacNichol, E. F. (1964). Visual pigments of single primate cones. *Science, 143,* 1181–1183. (136)

Marr, D. (1976). Early processing of visual information. *Philosophical Transactions of the Royal Society of London, 275B,* 483–524. (220)

Marr, D. (1982). *Vision.* San Francisco: W. H. Freeman. (20, 220)

Marr, D., & Hildreth, E. (1980). Theory of edge detection. *Proceedings of the Royal Society, 207B,* 187–217. (220)

Marr, D., & Nishihara, H. K. (1978). Representation and recognition of the spatial organization of three-dimensional shapes. *Proceedings of the Royal Society, 200B,* 269–294. (220)

Matin, L., Picoult, E., Stevens, J., Edwards, M., & MacArthur, R. (1982). Oculoparalytic illusion: visual-field dependent spatial mislocations by humans partially paralyzed with curare. *Science, 216,* 198–201. (284)

Matthews, D. F. (1972). Response patterns of single neurons in the tortoise olfactory epithelium and olfactory bulb. *Journal of General Physiology, 60,* 166–180. (507, 508)

Maurer, D. (1985). Infants' perception of facedness. In T. Field & N. Fox (Eds.), *Social perception in infants.* Norwood, NJ: Ablex. (334)

Maurer, D., & Salapatek, P. (1976). Developmental changes in the scanning of faces by young infants. *Child Development, 47,* 523–527. (334)

Mayer, D. J. (1979). Endogeneous analgesia systems: Neural and behavioral mechanisms. In J. J. Bonica (Ed.), *Advances in pain research and therapy* (Vol. 3, pp. 385–410.) (489)

McArthur, D. J. (1982). Computer vision and perceptual psychology. *Psychological Bulletin, 92,* 283–309. (189)

McBurney, D. H. (1969). Effects of adaptation on human taste function. In C. Pfaffmann, (Ed.), *Olfaction and taste* (pp. 407–419). New York: Rockefeller University Press. (518)

McBurney, D. H., Levine, J. M., & Cavanaugh, P. H. (1977). Psychophysical and social ratings of human body odor. *Personality and Social Psychology Bulletin, 3,* 135–138. (500)

McBurney, D. H., & Shick, T. R. (1971). Taste and water taste of twenty-six compounds for man. *Perception and Psychophysics, 10,* 249–252. (518)

McClintock, M. K. (1971). Menstrual synchrony and suppression. *Nature, 229,* 244–245. (500)

McGurk, H., & MacDonald, T. (1976). Hearing lips and seeing voices. *Nature, 264,* 746–748. (458)

McKenzie, D. (1923). *Aromatics and the soul: A study of smells.* New York: Hoeber. (500)

McLeod, R. W., & Ross, H. E. (1983). Optic-flow and cognitive factors in time-to-collision estimates. *Perception, 12,* 417–423. (312)

Mello, N. K., & Peterson, N. J. (1964). Behavioral evidence for color discrimination in cats. *Journal of Neurophysiology, 27,* 323–333. (136)

Melzak, R. (1973). *The puzzle of pain.* New York: Basic Books. (486, 488)

Melzak, R., & Wall, P. D. (1965). Pain mechanisms: A new theory. *Science, 150,* 971–979. (487)

Merzenich, M. M., Knight, P. L., & Roth, G. L. (1973). Cochleotopic organization in cats. *Journal of Neurophysiology, 27,* 323–333.

Metzger, W. (1930). Optische Untensuchengen am Ganzfeld. II. Zur Phanomenologic des homogenen Ganzfelds. *Psychologische Forschung, 13,* 6–29. (159)

Meyer, D. R., & Anderson, R. A. (1965). Colour discrimination in cats. In CIBA Foundation Symposium, *Color vision* (pp. 324–344). London: Churchill. (136)

Michael, C. R. (1969). Retinal processing of visual images. *Scientific American, 220*(5), 104–114. (136)

Michael, C. R. (1978). Color vision mechanisms in monkey striate cortex: dual-opponent cells with concentric receptive fields. *Journal of Neurophysiology, 41,* 572–588. (130, 132)

Michael, C. R. (1983). Color processing in primate striate cortex. In J. D. Mollon & L. T. Sharpe (Eds.), *Colour vision* (pp. 277–289). New York: Academic Press. (130)

Michael, C. R. (1986). *Functional and morphological identification of double and single opponent color cells in layer IVCb of the monkey's striate cortex.* Paper presented at the meeting of the Society for Neuroscience. (133)

Michael, C. R. (1987). *Comparative studies of the color cells in layer IVCb and in the blobs of the monkey's striate cortex.* Paper presented at the meeting of the Society for Neuroscience. (133)

Michael, R. P., and Kaverne, E. B. (1968). Pheromones in the communication of sexual status in primates. *Nature, 218,* 746–749. (502)

Michael, R. P., Kaverne, E. B., & Bonsall, R. W. (1971). Pheromones: Isolation of male sex attractant from a female primate. *Science, 172,* 964–966. (502)

Michotte, A. (1963). *The perception of causality.* New York: Basic Books. (306, 307)

Middlebrooks, J. C., & Pettigrew, J. D. (1981). Functional classes of neurons in primary auditory cortex of the cat distinguished by sensitivity to sound location. *Journal of Neuroscience, 1,* 107–120. (441)

Miller, G. A., & Isard, S. (1963). Some perceptual consequences of linguistic rules. *Journal of Verbal Learning and Verbal Behavior, 2,* 212–228. (464)

Miller, J. D. (1974). Effects of noise on people. *Journal of the Acoustical Society of America, 56,* 729–764. (430)

Miller, J. D., Wier, C. C., Pastore, R., Kelly, W. J., & Dooling, R. J. (1976). Discrimination and labeling of noise-buzz sequences with varying noise-lead times: An example of categorical perception. *Journal of the Acoustical Society of America, 60,* 410–417. (456)

Mishkin, M. (1986). Two visual systems. Talk presented at Western Psychiatric Institute and Clinic, Pittsburgh, PA. January 24, 1986. (192)

Mishkin, M., Ungerleider, L. G., & Macko, K. A. (1983). Object vision and spatial vision: Two central pathways. *Trends in Neuroscience, 6,* 414–417. (192)

Mitchell, D. E., Reardon, J., & Muir, D. W. (1975). Interocular transfer of the motion aftereffect in normal and stereoblind observers. *Experimental Brain Research, 22,* 163–173. (348)

Mitchell, D. E., & Timney, B. (1984). Postnatal development of function in the mammalian visual system. In J. M. Brookhart and V. B. Mountcastle (Eds.), *Handbook of Physiology, The Nervous System III* (pp. 507–555). Bethesda, MD: American Physiological Society. (338, 342)

Mitchell, D. E., & Ware, C. (1974). Interocular transfer of a visual aftereffect in normal and stereoblind humans. *Journal of Physiology, 236,* 707–721. (299, 348)

Mitchell, D. E., & Wilkinson, F. (1974). The effect of early astigmatism on the visual resolution of gratings. *Journal of Physiology, 243,* 739–756. (349, 350)

Moskowitz, H. R., Kumraich, V., Sharma, H., Jacobs, L., & Sharma, S. D. (1975). Cross-cultural differences in simple taste preference. *Science, 190,* 1217–1218. (514)

Moulton, D. G. (1965). Differential sensitivity to odors. *Cold Spring Harbor Symposium on Quantitative Biology, 30,* 201–206. (507)

Moulton, D. G. (1977). Minimum odorant concentrations detectable by the dog and their implications for olfactory receptor sensitivity. In D. Miller-Schwarze & M. M. Mozell (Eds.), *Chemical signals in vertebrates* (pp. 455–464). New York: Plenum. (497)

Mountcastle, V. B., & Powell, T. P. S. (1959). Neural mechanisms subserving cutaneous sensibility, with special reference to the role of afferent inhibition in sensory perception and discrimination. *Bulletin of the Johns Hopkins Hospital, 105,* 201–232. (478)

Mozell, M. M. (1964). Olfactory discrimination: Electrophysiological spatiotemporal basis. *Science, 143,* 1336–1337. (509)

Mozell, M. M. (1966). The spatiotemporal analysis of odorants at the level of the olfactory receptor sheet. *Journal of General Physiology, 50,* 25–41. (509)

Mozell, M. M. (1970). Evidence for a chromatographic model of olfaction. *Journal of General Physiology, 56,* 46–63. (509)

Mozell, M. M., & Hornung, D. E. (1984). Initial events influencing olfactory analysis. In L. Bolis, R. D. Keynes, & S. H. Maddrell (Eds.), *Comparative physiology of sensory systems* (pp. 227–244). Cambridge, England: Cambridge University Press. (509)

Mozell, M. M., & Hornung, D. E. (1985). Peripheral mechanisms in the olfactory process. In D. W. Pfaff (Ed.), *Taste, olfaction and the central nervous system* (pp. 253–279). New York: Rockefeller University Press. (509)

Mozell, M. M., & Jagodowiez, M. (1973). Chromatographic separation of odorants by the nose: Retention times measured across *in vivo* olfactory mucosa. *Science, 181,* 1247–1249. (509)

Muir, D. W., & Mitchell, D. E. (1975). Behavioral defects in cats following early selected visual exposure to contours of a single orientation. *Brain Research, 85,* 459–477. (344)

Muller, J. (1842). *Elements of physiology.* (W. Baly, Trans.). London: Taylor and Walton. (52)

Murphy, C., & Cain, W. S. (1986). Odor identification: The blind are better. *Physiology and Behavior, 371,* 177–180. (499)

Murray, R. G., & Murray, A. (1970). The anatomy and ultrastructure of taste endings. In G. E. W. Wolstenholme & J. Knight (Eds.), *Taste and smell in vertebrates* (pp. 3–25). London: Churchill. (35, 517)

Nachman, M. (1963). Taste preferences for sodium salts by adrenalectomized rats. *Journal of Comparative and Physiological Psychology, 55,* 1124–1129. (516)

Nathan, P. W. (1976). The gate control theory of pain. *Brain, 99,* 123–158. (488)

Nathans, J., Thomas, D., & Hogness, D. S. (1986). Molecular genetics of human color vision: The genes encoding blue, green and red pigments. *Science, 232,* 193–202. (127)

Neff, W. D., Fisher, J. F., Diamond, I. T., & Yela, M. (1956). Role of auditory cortex in discrimination requiring localization of sound in space. *Journal of Neurophysiology, 19,* 500–512. (441)

Neisser, U. (1967). *Cognitive psychology.* NJ: Prentice-Hall. (214)

Nelson, R. J., Sur, M., Fellerman, D. J., & Kaas, J. H. (1980). Representations of the body surface in postcentral parietal cortex of macaca fasicularis. *Journal of Comparative Neurology, 192,* 611–643. (484)

Newton, I. (1704). *Optiks.* London: Smith and Walford. (139)

Nolan, C. Y., & Kederis, C. J. (1969). *Perceptual factors in braille word recognition.* New York: American Foundation for the Blind. (490)

O'Brien, V. (1958). Contour perception, illusion, and reality. *Journal of the Optical Society of America, 48*, 112–119. (155)

Olson, C. R., & Freeman, R. D. (1975). Progressive changes in kitten striate cortex during monocular vision. *Journal of Neurophysiology, 38*, 26–32. (340)

Olson, C. R., & Freeman, R. D. (1980). Profile of the sensitive period for monocular deprivation in kittens. *Experimental Brain Research, 39*, 17–21. (340)

Olson, C. R., & Pettigrew, J. D. (1974). Single units in visual cortex of kittens reared in stroboscopic illumination. *Brain Research, 70*, 189–204. (345)

Olson, H. F. (1967). *Music, physics and engineering* (2nd ed.). New York: Dover. (398)

Olson, R. R., & Attneave, F. (1970). What variables produce similarity grouping? *American Journal of Psychology, 83*, 1–21. (209, 210)

Oyama, T. (1960). Figure-ground dominance as a function of sector angle, brightness, hue, and orientation. *Journal of Experimental Psychology, 60*, 299–305. (206)

Palmer, S. E. (1975). The effects of contextual scenes on the identification of objects. *Memory and Cognition, 3*, 519–526. (26, 27)

Pangborn, R. M., & Hansen, B. (1963). The influence of color on discrimination of sweetness and sourness in pear-nectar. *American Journal of Psychology, 76*, 315–317. (515)

Pantle, A. J., & Picciano, L. (1976). A multistable movement display: Evidence for two separate motion systems in human vision. *Science, 193*, 500–502. (291, 292)

Pearlman, A. L., & Daw, N. (1970). Opponent color cells in the cat lateral geniculate nucleus. *Science, 167*, 84–86. (136)

Penfield, W., & Rasmussen, T. (1950). *The cerebral cortex of man.* New York: Macmillan. (483)

Peterson, M. A., & Hochberg, J. (1983). Opposed-set measurement procedure: A quantitative analysis of the role of local cues and intention in form perception. *Journal of Experimental Psychology: Human Perception and Performance, 9*, 183–193. (213)

Pettigrew, J. D. (1974). The effect of visual experience on the development of stimulus specificity by kitten cortical neurones. *Journal of Physiology, 237*, 49–74. (337, 338)

Pettigrew, J. D., & Freeman, R. D. (1973). Visual experience without lines: Effects on developing cortical neurons. *Science, 182*, 599–601. (345)

Pick, A. D., Thomas, M. L., & Pick, H. L. (1966). The role of grapheme-phoneme correspondences in the perception of braille. *Journal of Verbal Learning and Verbal Behavior, 5*, 298–300. (491)

Pinching, A. J., & Döving, K. B. (1974). Selective degeneration in rat olfactory bulb following exposure to different odors. *Brain Research, 82*, 195–204. (510)

Pirchio, M., Spinelli, D., Fiorentini, A., & Maffei, L. (1978). Infant contrast sensitivity evaluated by evoked potentials. *Brain Research, 141*, 179–184. (324, 326)

Pisoni, D. B. (1977). Identification and discrimination of the relative onset of two-component tones: Implications for voicing perception in stops. *Journal of the Acoustical Society of America, 61*, 1352–1361. (456)

Plomp, R., & Levelt, W. J. M. (1965). Tonal consonance and critical bandwith. *Journal of the Acoustical Society of America, 38*, 548–560. (400, 401)

Poggio, T. (1986). Vision by man and machine. *Scientific American*, 106–115. (189)

Pokorney, J., Graham, C. H., & Lanson, R. N. (1968). Effect of wavelength on foveal grating acuity. *Journal of the Optical Society of America, 58*, 1410–1414. (127)

Pollack, I., & Pickett, J. M. (1964a). The intelligibility of excerpts from conversational speech. *Language and Speech, 6*, 165–171. (461)

Pollack, I., & Pickett, J. M. (1964b). Intelligibility of excerpts from fluent speech: Auditory vs. structural context. *Journal of Verbal Learning and Verbal Behavior, 3*, 79–84. (461)

Pomerantz, J. R. (1981). Perceptual organization in information processing. In M. Kubovy & J. Pomerantz (Eds.), *Perceptual Organization.* Hillsdale, NJ: Erlbaum. (209)

Prinzmetal, W. (1981). Principles of feature integration in visual perception. *Perception and Psychophysics, 30*, 330–340. (216)

Prinzmetal, W., & Banks, W. P. (1977). Good continuation affects visual detection. *Perception and Psychophysics, 21*, 389–395. (210, 211)

Pritchard, R. M. (1961). Stabilized images on the retina. *Scientific American, 204*(6), 72–78. (157)

Proffitt, D. R., & Cutting, J. E. (1980). An invariant for wheel-generated motions and the logic of its determination. *Perception, 9,* 435–449. (301)

Proffitt, D. R., Cutting, J. E., & Stier, D. M. (1979). Perception of wheel-generated motions. *Journal of Experimental Psychology: Human Perception and Performance, 5,* 289–302. (196)

Proffitt, D. R., Gilden, D. L., Kaiser, M. K., & Whelan, S. M. (1988). The effect of configural orientation on perceived trajectory in apparent motion. *Perception and Psychophysics, 43,* 465–474. (290)

Purkinje, J. E. (1825). *Neurre Beitrage zur Kenntniss des Sehens in Subjectiver Hinsicht.* Berlin: Reimer. (82)

Ralls, K. (1971). Mammalian scent marking. *Science, 171,* 443–449. (501)

Ramachandran, V. S. (1981). *Perception of apparent motion: studies in the cognitive sciences 11.* Bulletin of the School of Social Sciences, University of California, Irvine. (293)

Ramachandran, V. S., Rao, V. M., & Vidyasagar, T. R. (1973). Apparent movement with subjective contours. *Vision Research, 13,* 1399–1401. (293, 298)

Ratliff, F. (1965). *Mach bands: Quantitative studies on neural networks in the retina.* New York: Holden-Day. (150)

Ratoosh, P. (1949). On interposition as a cue for the perception of relative distance. *Proceedings of the National Academy of Sciences, 35,* 257–259. (213)

Rauschecker, J. P., & Singer, W. (1981). The effects of early visual experience on the cats' visual cortex and their possible explanation by Hebb synapses. *Journal of Physiology, 310,* 215–239. (345, 346)

Ravin, J. G. (1985). Monet's cataracts. *Journal of the American Medical Association, 254,* 394–399. (366)

Rechtschaffen, A., & Mednick, S. A. (1955). The autokinetic word technique. *Journal of Abnormal and Social Psychology, 51,* 346. (298)

Reddy, D. R. (1976). Speech recognition by machine: A review. *Proceedings of the Institute of Electrical and Electronic Engineers, 64,* 501–531. (462)

Regal, D. M., Boothe, R., Teller, D. Y., & Sackett, G. B. (1976). Visual acuity and visual responsiveness in dark-reared monkeys. (*Macaca nemestrina*). *Vision Research, 16,* 523–530. (338)

Regan, D., & Cynader, M. (1979). Neurons in area 18 of cat visual cortex selectively sensitive to changing size: Nonlinear interactions between responses to two edges. *Vision Research, 19,* 699–711. (312)

Restle, F. (1970). Moon illusion explained on the basis of relative size. *Science, 167,* 1092–1096. (259)

Reynolds, D. V. (1969). Surgery in the rat during electrical analgesia induced by focal brain stimulation. *Science, 164,* 444–445. (488)

Rice, C. E. (1967). Human echolocation. *Science, 155,* 656–664. (384)

Riggs, L. A. (1965a). Light as a stimulus for vision. In C. Graham (Ed.), *Vision and visual perception.* New York: Wiley. (116)

Riggs, L. A. (1965b). Electrophysiology of vision. In C. Graham (Ed.), *Vision and visual perception.* New York: Wiley. (87)

Riggs, L. A. (1965c). Visual acuity. In C. Graham (Ed.), *Vision and visual perception.* New York: Wiley.

Risset, J. C. (1978). Musical acoustics. In E. C. Carterette and M. P. Friedman (Eds.), *Handbook of perception* Vol. 4 (pp. 521–564). New York: Academic Press. (403)

Risset, J. C., & Mathews, M. V. (1969). Analysis of musical instrument tones. *Physics Today, 22,* 23–30. (397, 399)

Roberts, M., & Summerfield, Q. (1981). Audiovisual adaptation in speech perception. *Perception and Psychophysics, 30,* 309–314. (456, 459)

Robinson, D. L., & Wurtz, R. (1976). Use of an extra-retinal signal by monkey superior colliculus neurons to distinguish real from self-induced stimulus movement. *Journal of Neurophysiology, 39,* 852–870. (286)

Robinson, J. O. (1972). *The psychology of visual illusion.* London: Hutchinson. (260)

Rock, I., & Kaufman, L. (1962). The moon illusion II. *Science, 136,* 1023–1031. (259)

Roederer, J. G. (1975). *Introduction to the physics and psychophysics of music,* 2nd ed. New York: Springer-Verlag. (401)

Rogel, M. (1978). A critical evaluation of the possibility of higher primate reproductive and sexual pheromones. *Psychological Bulletin, 85,* 810–830. (502)

Rolls, E. T. (1981). Processing beyond the inferior temporal cortex related to feeding, memory, and striatal function. In Y. Katsuki, R. Norgren, &

M. Sato (Eds.), *Brain mechanisms of sensation* (pp. 241–269). New York: Wiley. (191)

Rose, J. E., Brugge, J. F., Anderson, D. J., & Hind, J. E. (1967). Phase locked response to low frequency tones in single auditory nerve fibers of the squirrel monkey. *Journal of Neurophysiology, 30,* 769–793. (435)

Ross, H. E. (1974). *Behavior and perception in strange environments.* New York: Basic Books. (116)

Rozin, P. (1976). The selection of foods by rats, humans, and other animals. In J. S. Rosenblatt, R. A. Hinde, & C. Beer (Eds.), *Advances in the study of behavior.* New York: Academic Press. (516)

Rubin, E. (1915). *Synoplevede Figurer.* Copenhagen: Gyldendalske. (203)

Runeson, S. (1977). On the possibility of "smart" perceptual mechanisms. *Scandinavian Journal of Psychology, 18,* 172–179. (269)

Runeson, S., & Frykholm, G. (1981). Visual perception of lifted weights. *Journal of Experimental Psychology: Human Perception and Performance, 7,* 733–740. (306)

Rushton, W. A. H. (1961). Rhodopsin measurement and dark adaptation in a subject deficient in cone vision. *Journal of Physiology, 156,* 193–205. (78, 80)

Rushton, W. A. H. (1964). Colour blindness and cone pigments. *American Journal of Optometry and Archives of the American Academy of Optometry, 41,* 265–282. (135)

Russell, M. J. (1976). Human olfactory communication. *Nature, 260,* 520–522. (500)

Russell, M. J., Switz, G. M., & Thompson, K. (1980). Olfactory influence on the human menstrual cycle. *Pharmacology, Biochemistry and Behavior, 13,* 737–738. (500)

Rutherford, W. (1886). A new theory of hearing. *Journal of Anatomy and Physiology, 21,* 166–168. (433)

Sachs, M. B., Young, E. D., & Miller, M. I. (1981). Encoding of speech features in the auditory nerve. In R. Carlson & B. Grandstrom (Eds.), *The representation of speech in the peripheral auditory system* (pp. 115–130). New York: Elsevier. (460)

Sakata, H. & Iwamura, Y. (1978). Cortical processing of tactile information in the first somatosensory and parietal association areas in the monkey. In G. Gordon (Ed.), *Active touch* (pp. 55–72). Elmsford, NY: Pergamon. (480)

Sakata, H., Shibutani, H., & Kawano, K. (1977). Spatial selectivity of "visual" neurons in the pos-

terior parietal association cortex of the monkey. *Abstract, 27th International Congress of the Physiological Society.* (See Sakata and Iwamura, 1978). (296)

Salapatek, P. (1975). Pattern perception in early infancy. In L. B. Cohen & P. Salapatek (Eds.), *Infant perception: From sensation to cognition* (Vol. 1, pp. 133–248). New York: Academic Press. (333)

Salapatek, P., & Banks, M. S. (1978). Infant sensory assessment: Vision. In F. D. Minfie & L. L. Lloyd (Eds.), *Communicative and cognitive abilities: Early behavioral assessment* (pp. 61–106). Baltimore, MD: University Park Press. (326)

Salapatek, P., Bechtold, A. G., & Bushness, E. W. (1976). Infant visual acuity as a function of viewing distance. *Child Development, 47,* 860–863. (324)

Samuel, A. B. (1981). Phonemic restoration: Insights from a new methodology. *Journal of Experimental Psychology: General, 110,* 474–494. (465)

Sato, T. (1981). Neuronal mechanisms of pattern vision in the inferotemporal cortex of the monkey. In Y. Katsuki, R. Norgren, & M. Sato (Eds.), *Brain mechanisms of sensation* (pp. 129–139). New York: Wiley. (191)

Sato, M., Ogawa, H., & Yamashita, S. (1975). Response properties of macaque monkey chorda tympani fibers. *Journal of General Physiology, 66,* 781–810. (520)

Sawusch, J. R., & Jusczyk, P. (1981). Adaptation and contrast in the perception of voicing. *Journal of Experimental Psychology: Human Perception and Performance, 7,* 408–421. (460)

Scharf, B. (1975). Audition. In B. Scharf (Ed.), *Experimental sensory psychology,* (pp. 112–149). Glenview, IL: Scott, Foresman. (412)

Schiff, W., & Detwiler, M. L. (1979). Information used in judging impending collision. *Perception, 8,* 647–658. (312)

Schiffman, H. R. (1967). Size-estimation of familiar objects under informative and reduced conditions of viewing. *American Journal of Psychology, 80,* 229–235. (235)

Schubert, E. D. (1980). *Hearing: Its function and dysfunction.* Wien: Springer-Verlag. (420, 421, 422, 427)

Schultze, M. (1866). Aur Anatomie und Physiologie der Retina. *Arch. Mikroskop. Anat., 2,* 165–286. (75)

Schultze, M. (1872). Aur Anatomie und Physiologie der Retina. *Arch. Mikroskop. Anat.*, 2, 165–286. (75)

Schwartz, A. S., Perez, A. J., & Azulaz, A. (1975). Further analysis of active and passive touch in pattern discrimination. *Bulletin of the Psychonomic Society*, 6, 7–9. (492)

Schweitzer-Tong, D. (1976). Effect of adaptation on intensity-response relations in the dorsal lateral geniculate nucleus of the cat. Unpublished doctoral dissertation, Department of Psychology, University of Pittsburgh. (172)

Searle, C. L., Jacobson, J. Z., & Rayment, S. G. (1979). Stop consonant discrimination based on human audition. *Journal of the Acoustical Society of America*, 65, 799–809. (453)

Sechzer, J. A., & Brown, J. L. (1964). Color discrimination in the cat. *Science*, 144, 427–429. (136)

Sedgwick, H. A. (1973). The visible horizon: A potential source of visual information for the perception of size and distance. *Dissertation Abstracts International*, 34, 1301B–1302B. (269)

Sedgwick, H. A. (1983). Environment-centered representation of spatial layout: Available visual information from texture and perspective. In A. Rosenthal & J. Beck (Eds.), *Human and machine vision*, (pp. 425–458). New York: Academic Press. (269)

Sekuler, R., Hutman, L. P., & Owsley, C. J. (1980). Human ageing and spatial vision. *Science*, 209, 1255–1256. (166)

Shea, S. L., Fox, R., Aslin, R., & Dumais, S. T. (1980). Assessment of stereopsis in human infants. *Investigative Ophthalmology and Visual Science*, 19, 1400–1404. (328)

Shepard, R. N., & Zare, S. L. (1983). Path-guided apparent motion. *Science*, 220, 632–634. (291)

Sherif, M. (1935). A study of some social factors in perception. *Archives of Psychology*, 187, 1–60. (297)

Sherk, H., & Stryker, M. P. (1976). Quantitative study of cortical orientation selectivity in visually inexperienced kittens. *Journal of Neurophysiology*, 39, 63–70. (337)

Sherrick, C. E., & Cholewiak, R. W. (1986) Cutaneous sensitivity. In K. R. Boff, L. Kaufman, & J. P. Thomas (Eds.) *Handbook of perception and human performance* (Chapter 12). New York: Wiley. (488)

Shorey, H. H. (1977). Pheromones. In T. A. Sebeck (Ed.), *How animals communicate* (pp. 137–163). (501)

Slater, A. M., & Findlay, J. M. (1975). Binocular fixation in the newborn baby. *Journal of Experimental Child Psychology*, 20, 248–273. (328)

Slater, A., Morison, V., & Rose, D. (1984). Habituation in the newborn. *Infant Behavior and Development*, 7, 183–200. (320, 322)

Sloan, L. L., & Wollach, L. (1948). A case of unilateral deuteranopia. *Journal of the Optical Society of America*, 38, 502–509. (134)

Smith, D. (1974). Electrophysiological correlates of gustatory cross adaptation. *Chemical Senses*, 1 29–40. (522)

Smith, D., & Frank M. (1972). Cross adaptation between salts in the chorda tympani nerve of the rat. *Physiology and Behavior*, 8, 213–220. (521, 522)

Smith, D., Van Buskirk, R. L., Travers, J. B., & Bieber, S. L. (1983). Coding of taste stimuli by hamster brainstem neurons. *Journal of Neurophysiology*, 50, 541–558. (522)

Smith, E. L., Bennet, M. J., Harwerth, R. S., & Crawford, M. L. J. (1979). Binocularity in kittens reared with optically-induced squint. *Science*, 204, 875–877. (341)

Smith, K. R. (1947). The problem of stimulation deafness: II. Histological changes in the cochlea as a function of tonal frequency. *Journal of Experimental Psychology*, 37, 304–317. (430, 432)

Smith, K. R., & Wever, E. G. (1949). The problem of stimulation deafness: III. The functional and histological effects of high frequency stimulus. *Journal of Experimental Psychology*, 39, 238–241. (432)

Smith, P. C., & Smith, O. W. (1961). Ball throwing responses to photographically portrayed targets. *Journal of Experimental Psychology*, 62, 223–233. (241)

Stark, L., & Bridgeman, B. (1983). Role of corollary discharge in space constancy. *Perception and Psychophysics*, 34, 371–380. (285)

Stevens, J. K., Emerson, R. C., Gerstein, G. L., Kallos, T., Neufeld, G. R., Nichols, C. W., &

Rosenquist, A. C. (1976). Paralysis of the awake human. Visual perceptions. *Vision Research, 16,* 93–98. (284)

Stevens, K. N., & Blumstein, S. (1978). Invariant cues for place of articulation in stop consonants. *Journal of the Acoustical Society of America, 64,* 1358–1368. (453)

Stevens, K. N., & Blumstein, S. (1981). The seatch for invariant acoustic correlates of phonetic features. In P. D. Eimas & J. L. Miller (Eds.), *Perspectives on the study of speech.* Hillsdale, NJ: Erlbaum. (452, 453, 454)

Stevens, S. S. (1936). A scale for the measurement of a psychological magnitude: Loudness. *Psychological Review, 43,* 405–416. (532)

Stevens, S. S. (1957). On the psychophysical law. *Psychological Review, 64,* 153–181. (13, 532)

Stevens, S. S. (1961). To honor Fechner and repeal his law. *Science, 133,* 80–86. (532)

Stevens, S. S. (1962). The surprising simplicity of sensory metrics. *American Psychologist, 17,* 29–39. (56, 532, 534)

Stevens, S. S., & Volkman, J. (1940). The relation of pitch to frequency: A revised scale. *American Journal of Psychology, 53,* 329–353. (394)

Stewart, W. B., Kauer, J. S., & Shepherd, G. M. (1979). Functional organization of rat olfactory bulb analyzed by the 2-deoxyglucose method. *Journal of Comparative Neurology, 185,* 715–734. (511)

Stiles, W. S. (1953). Further studies of visual mechanisms by the two-color threshold method. *Coloquio sobre problemas opticos de la visión.* Madrid: Union Internationale de Physique Pure et Appliquée, 1, 65. (84)

Stone, H., & Bosley, J. J. (1965). Olfactory discrimination and Weber's law. *Perceptual Motor Skills, 20,* 657–665. (498)

Stone, J. (1965). A quantitative analysis of the distribution of ganglion cells in the cat's retina. *Journal of Comparative Neurology, 124,* 377–352. (98)

Stryker, M. P., Sherk, H., Leventhal, A. G., & Hirsch, H. B. (1978). Physiological consequences for the cat's visual cortex of effectively restricting early visual experience with oriented contours. *Journal of Neurophysiology, 41,* 896–909. (346)

Summerfield, Q. (1979). Use of visual information for phonetic perception. *Phonetica, 36,* 314–331. (458)

Supa, M., Cotzin, M., & Dallenbach, K. M. (1944). "Facial vision": The perception of obstacles by the blind. *American Journal of Psychology, 57,* 133–183. (384)

Svaetichin, G. (1956). Spectral response curves from single cones. *Acta Physiologica Scandinavica Supplementum, 134,* 17–46. (127, 136)

Swets, J. A. (1964). *Signal detection and recognition by human observers.* New York: Wiley. (540)

Takagi, S. F. (1980). Dual nervous systems for olfactory functions in mammals. In H. Van der Starre (Ed.), *Olfaction and Taste VII* (pp. 275–278). London: IRC Press. (503)

Tanabe, T., Iino, M., Oshima, Y., & Takagi, S. F. (1974). An olfactory area in the prefrontal lobe. *Brain Research, 80,* 127–130. (512)

Tanabe, T., Iino, M., & Takagi, S. F. (1975). Discrimination of odors in olfactory bulb, pyriform-amygdaloid areas and orbito-frontal cortex of the monkey. *Journal of Neurophysiology, 38,* 1284–1296. (503, 512)

Tansley, K. (1965). *Vision in vertebrates.* London: Chapman and Hall. (86, 87, 135, 136)

Tart, C. T. (1971). *On being stoned.* Palo Alto: Science and Behavior Books. (8)

Taylor, M. M., Lederman, S. J., & Gibson, R. H. (1973). Tactual perception of texture. In E. C. Carterette & M. P. Friedman (Eds.), *Handbook of perception* (Vol. 3). New York: Academic Press. (492)

Teller, D. Y., Morse, R., Borton, R., & Regal, D. (1974). Visual acuity for vertical and diagonal gratings in human infants. *Vision Research, 14,* 1433–1439. (324)

Ternus, J. (1926). Experimentelle Untersuchungen uber phanomenale Identitat. *Psychologiche Forschung, 7,* 81–136. (Summary in W. D. Ellis [1938] *A sourcebook of Gestalt psychology* (pp. 149–160). London: Kegan Paul, Trench, Trubner. (289)

Teuber, H. L. (1960). Perception. In J. Field, H. W. Magoun, & V. E. Hall (Eds.), *Handbook of physiology* (Section 1, Vol. 3). Washington, DC: American Physiological Society. (283)

Thouless, R. H. (1931). Phenomenal regression to the real object I. *British Journal of Psychology, 21,* 339–359. (262, 263)

Todd, J. T. (1981). Visual information about moving objects. *Journal of Experimental Psychology: Human Perception and Performance 7,* 795–810. (275)

Tomita, T., Kaneko, A., Murakami, M., & Paulter,

E. L. (1967). Spectral response curves of single cones in the carp. *Vision Research, 7,* 519–531. (136)

Tonndorf, J. (1960). Shearing motion in scala media of cochlear models. *Journal of the Acoustical Society of America, 32,* 238–244. (428)

Treisman, A. (1986). Features and objects in visual processing. *Scientific American, 255,* 114B–125. (194, 213, 217)

Treisman, A. (1987). Properties, parts, and objects. In K. R. Boff, L. Kaufman, & J. P. Thomas (Eds.), *Handbook of perception and human performance* (Chapter 35). New York: Wiley. (215)

Tretter, F., Cynader, M., & Singer, V. (1975). Modification of direction selectivity of neurons in the visual cortex of kittens. *Brain Research, 84,* 143–149. (345)

Trevor-Roper, P. (1970). *The world through blunted sight.* Indianapolis, In: Bobbs-Merrill. (349)

Ullman, S. (1980). Against direct perception. *Behavioral and Brain Sciences, 3,* 373–415. (269)

Vallbo, A. B., & Hagbarth, K. E. (1967). Impulses recorded with microelectrodes in human muscle nerves during stimulation of mechanoreceptors and voluntary contractions. *Electoencephalography and Clinical Neurophysiology, 23,* 392. (58)

Vallbo, A. B., & Hagbarth, K. E. (1968). Activity from skin mechanoreceptors recorded percutaneously in awake human subjects. *Experimental Neurology, 21,* 270–289. (58)

Vallbo, A. B., & Johansson, R. (1976). Skin mechanoreceptors in the human hand: Neural and Psychophysical thresholds. In Y. Zotterman (Ed.), *Sensory functions of the skin in primates, with special reference to man.* New York: Plenum. (58)

Vallbo, A. B., & Johansson, R. S. (1978). The tactile sensory innervation of the glabrous skin of the human hand. In G. Gordon (Ed.), *Active touch* (pp. 29–54). New York: Oxford University Press. (482)

Valvo, A. (1968). Behavior patterns and visual rehabilitation after early and long lasting blindness. *American Journal of Ophthalmology, 65,* 19–23. (347)

Van Sluyters, R. C., & Blakemore, C. (1973). Experimental creation of unusual properties in visual cortex of kittens. *Nature, 246,* 506–508. (345)

Verheijen, F. J. (1961). A single afterimage method demonstrating the involutnary multi-directional eye movements during fixation. *Optica Acta, 8,* 309–311. (157)

von Noorden, G. K. (1973). Experimental amblyopia in monkeys. Further behavioral observations and clinical corrections. *Investigative Ophthalmology and Visual Science, 12,* 721–726. (338)

von Noorden, G. K., & Maumanee, A. E. (1968). Clinical observations on stimulus deprivation amblyopia *(amblyopia ex anopsia). American Journal of Ophthalmology, 65,* 220–224. (346)

Wald, G. (1964). The receptors of human color vision. *Science, 145,* 1007–1017. (81)

Wald, G., & Brown, P. K. (1958). Human rhodopsin. *Science, 127,* 222–226. (81, 82)

Wald, G., & Brown, P. K. (1965). Human color vision and color blindness. *Cold Spring Harbor Symposia on Quantitative Biology, 30,* 345–359. (83)

Wallach, H. (1959). The perception of motion. *Scientific American, 201*(1), 59–60. (296)

Wallach, H. (1963). The perception of neutral colors. *Scientific American, 208*(1), 107–116. (176)

Wallach, H., Newman, E. B., & Rosenzweig, M. R. (1949). The precedence effect in sound localization. *American Journal of Psychology, 62,* 315–336. (410)

Wallach, H., & O'Connell, D. N. (1953). The kinetic depth effect. *Journal of Experimental Psychology, 45,* 205–217. (301)

Walley, A. C., Pisoni, D. B., & Aslin, R. N. (1981). The role of early experience in the development of speech perception. In R. N. Aslin, J. Alberts, & M. J. Petersen (Eds.), *The development of perception: Psychobiological perspectives* (pp. 219–235). New York: Academic Press. (459)

Walls, G. L. (1942). *The vertebrate eye.* Reprinted in 1967. New York: Hafner. (274)

Ward, W. D., & Glorig, A. (1961). A case of firecracker induced hearing loss. *Laryngoscope, 71,* 1590–1596. (430)

Ware, C., & Mitchell, D. E. (1974). On interocular transfer of various visual aftereffects in normal and stereoblind observers. *Vision Research, 14,* 731–735. (348)

Warren, R. M. (1970). Perceptual restoration of missing speech sounds. *Science, 167,* 392–393. (465)

Warren, R. M., Obuseck, C. J., & Acroff, J. M. (1972). Auditory induction of absent sounds. *Science, 176,* 1149. (406)

Warren, W. H., & Shaw, R. E. (1985). *Persistence and change.* Hillsdale, NJ: Erlbaum. (301)

Warrington, E. B. (1982). Neurophysiological studies of object recognition. *Proceedings of the Royal Society, 298B,* 15–33. (190)

Watkins, C. R., & Mayer, D. J. (1982). Organization of endogenous opiate and nonopiate pain control systems. *Science, 176,* 1149. (301, 489)

Weber, E. H. (1834). *De pulsu, resorptione, auditu et tactu: Annotationes anatomical et physiological.* Leipzig: Koehler. (530)

Webster's new collegiate dictionary. (1956). Springfield, MA: Merriam. (110)

Weinstein, S. (1968). Intensive and extensive aspects of tactile sensitivity and a function of body part, sex, and laterality. In D. R. Kenshalo (Ed.), *The skin senses* (pp. 195–218). Springfield, IL: Thomas. (481)

Weisenberg, M. (1977). Pain and pain control. *Psychological Bulletin, 84,* 1008–1044. (487)

Weisstein, N., & Wong, E. (1986). Figure-ground organization and the spatial and temporal responses of the visual system. In E. C. Schwab & H. C. Nusbaum (Eds.), *Pattern recognition by humans and machines* (Vol. 2). New York: Academic Press. (211)

Werner, G., & Mountcastle, V. B. (1965). Neural activity in mechanoreceptive cutaneous afferents: Stimulus-response relations, Weber functions, and information transmission. *Journal of Neurophysiology, 28,* 369–397. (57)

Werner, J. S., & Wooten, B. R. (1979). Human infant color vision and color perception. *Infant Behavior and Development, 2,* 241–274. (323)

Wertheimer, M. (1912). Experimentelle Stuidien uber das Sehen von Beuegung. *Zeitschrift fuer Psychologie, 61,* 161–265. (22, 193, 288, 290)

Wever, E. G. (1949). *Theory of hearing.* New York: Wiley. (425, 434)

White, B. W., Saunders, F. A., Scadden, L., Bachy-Rita, P., & Collins, C. (1970). Seeing with the skin. *Perception and Psychophysics, 7,* 23–27. (470)

White, C. W., & Montgomery, D. A. (1976). Memory colours in afterimages: A bicentennial demonstration. *Perception and Psychophysics, 19,* 371–374. (138, 139)

White, J. (1968). *The birth and rebirth of pictorial space* (2nd ed.). London: Faber and Faber. (235)

Whitfield, I. C. (1978). The neural code. In E. C. Carterette & M. P. Friedman (Eds.), *Handbook of perception* (Vol. 4, pp. 163–183). New York: Academic Press.

Whitfield, I. C. (1979). The object of the sensory cortex. *Brain Behavior and Evolution, 16,* 129–154. (442)

Whitfield, I. C. (1980). Auditory cortex and the pitch of complex tones. *Journal of the Acoustical Society of America, 67,* 644–647. (482, 442)

Whitfield, I. C., & Evans, E. F. (1965). Responses of auditory neurons to stimuli of changing frequency. *Journal of Neurophysiology, 28,* 655–672. (442)

Whitsel, B. L., Roppolo, J. R., & Werner, G. (1972). Cortical information processing of stimulus motion on primate skin. *Journal of Neurophysiology, 35,* 691–717. (478)

Wiesel, T. N., & Hubel, D. H. (1963). Single cell responses in stirate cortex of kittens deprived of vision in one eye. *Journal of Neurophysiology, 26,* 1003–1017. (339)

Wiesel, T. N., & Hubel, D. H. (1974). Ordered arrangements of orientation columns in monkeys lacking visual experience. *Journal of Comparative Neurology, 158,* 307–318. (337)

Wightman, F. L. (1973). Pitch and stimulus fine structure. *Journal of the Acoustical Society of America, 54,* 397–406. (438)

Wilson, E. O. (1963). Pheromones. *Scientific American, 208*(5), 100–114. (501)

Winston, P. H. (1975). *The psychology of computer vision.* New York: McGraw-Hill. (189)

Wittreich, W. J. (1959). Visual perception and personality. *Scientific American, 200*(4), 56–60. (254)

Wolff, B. B., & Langley, S. (1968). *American Anthropologist, 70,* 494. (538)

Wong, E., & Weisstein, N. (1983). Sharp targets are detected better against a figure and blurred targets are detected better against a background. *Journal of Experimental Psychology: Human Perception and Performance, 9,* 194–202. (211)

Woodhouse, J. M., & Barlow, H. B. (1982). Spatial and temporal resolution and analysis. In H. B. Barlow & J. D. Mollon (Eds.), *The senses* (pp. 133–163). Cambridge, England: University of Cambridge Press. (89)

Woodworth, R. S. (1938). *Experimental psychology.* New York: Holt, Rinehart & Winston. (505)

Woolsey, C. N., Marshall, W. H., & Bard, P. (1942). Representation of cutaneous tactile sensibility in the cerebral cortex of the monkey as indicated by evoked potentials. *Bulletin of the Johns Hopkins Hospital, 70,* 399–441. (483)

Wyszecki, G., & Stiles, W. S. (1967). *Color science: Concepts and methods, quantitative data and formulas.* New York: Wiley. (112)

Yager, D., & Thorpe, S. (1970). Investigation of goldfish color vision. In W. C. Stebbens (Ed.), *Animal psychophysics* (pp. 259–275). New York: Appleton-Century-Crofts. (136)

Yarbus, D. L. (1967). *Eye movements and vision.* New York: Plenum Press. (24)

Yonas, A., Granrud, C. E., Arterberry, M. E., & Hanson, B. L. (1986). Infants' distance from linear perspective and texture gradients. *Infant Behavior and Development, 9,* 247–256. (332)

Yonas, A., Pettersen, L., & Granrud, C. E. (1982). Infant's sensitivity to familiar size as information for distance. *Child Development, 53,* 1285–1290. (332)

Young, T. (1801). On the theory of light and colours. *Philosophical Transactions of the Royal Society of London, 92,* 12–48. (117)

Young-Browne, G., Rosenfield, H. M., & Horowitz, F. D. (1977). Infant discrimination of facial expression. *Child Development, 48,* 555–562. (329)

Yuodelis, C., & Hendrickson, A. (1986). A qualitative and quantitative analysis of the human fovea during development. *Vision Research, 26,* 847–855. (325)

Zatorre, R. J., & Halpern, A. R. (1979). Identification, discrimination, and selective adaptation of simultaneous musical intervals. *Perception and Psychophysics, 26,* 384–395. (456)

Zeki, S. M. (1977). Colour coding in the superior temporal sulcus of rhesus monkey visual cortex. *Proceedings of the Royal Society, 197B,* 195–223. (130)

Zeki, S. M. (1978). Functional specialization in the visual cortex of the rhesus monkey. *Nature, 274,* 423. (281)

Zihl, J., von Cramon, D., & Mai, N. (1983). Selective disturbance of movement vision after bilateral brain damage. *Brain, 106,* 313–340. (281)

Zimmerman, M. (1979). Peripheral and central nervous mechanisms of nociception, pain, and pain therapy: Facts and hypotheses. In J. J. Bonica, J. D. Liebeskind, & D. G. Albe-Fessard (Eds.), *Advances in pain research and therapy* (Vol. 3, pp. 3–32). New York: Raven. (473)

Zotterman, Y. (1956). Species differences in the water taste. *Acta Physiologica Scandinavica, 37,* 60–70. (518)

Zwicker, E., Flottorp, S., & Stevens, S. S. (1957). Critical bandwidth in loudness summation. *Journal of the Acoustical Society of America, 29,* 548–557. (400)

Author Index

Subject Index

Illustration Credits

Complete citations of journal articles appear in the References section. Photographs other than those credited here are the work of the author.

Chapter 1 *Figs. 1.5 and 1.6:* Adapted from "The Receptors of Human Color Vision" by G. Wald, *Science, 145,* pp. 1007–1017, September 4, 1964. Copyright 1964 by the American Association for the Advancement of Science. Used by permission. *Fig. 1.9:* Adapted from S. S. Stevens, 1962, *American Psychologist, 17,* pp. 29–39. Copyright 1962 by the American Psychological Association. Reprinted by permission. *Fig. 1.10:* From A. Chapanis, 1947, *Journal of General Physiology, 30,* pp. 423–437. Used by permission. *Figs. 1.13, 1.17, and 1.18:* From B. R. Bugelski and D. A. Alampay, 1961, *Canadian Journal of Psychology, 15,* 205–211. *Fig. 1.19:* The Bettmann Archive. *Fig. 1.24:* From *How People Look at Pictures* by G. T. Buswell. University of Chicago Press, 1935. Used by permission. *Fig. 1.26:* Courtesy of Eleanor J. Gibson. *Fig. 1.29:* From "Perceptual Organization in Information Processing" by M. Kubovy and J. Pomerantz (eds.), in *Perceptual Organization,* 1981, p. 158. Used by permission.

Chapter 2 *Fig. 2.2:* From "Biological Transducers" by W. R. Lowenstein, *Scientific American, 203.* Copyright © 1960 by Scientific American, Inc. All rights reserved. Used by permission. *Fig. 2.3:* From *Hearing: Physiology and Psychophysics* by W. Lawrence Gulick. Copyright © 1971 by Oxford University Press, Inc. Reprinted by permission. *Fig. 2.5:* Adapted from "The Anatomy and Ultrastructure of Taste Endings" by R. G. and A. Murray in G.E.W. Wolstenholme and J. Knight (eds.), *Taste and Smell in Vertebrates,* J & A Churchill, 1970. Used by permission. *Fig. 2.17:* Adapted from J. E. Dowling and B. B. Boycott, 1966, *Proceedings of the Royal Society of London, 166,* Series B, pp. 80–111. Used by permission. *Fig. 2.20:* Adapted from "Integrative Action in the Cat's Lateral Geniculate Body" by D. H. Hubel and T. N. Wiesel, 1961, *Journal of Physiology, 155,* pp. 385–398. Used by permission of Cambridge University Press. *Fig. 2.23:* Adapted from "Receptive Fields of Single Neurons in the Cat's Striate Cortex" by D. H. Hubel and T. N. Wiesel, 1959, *Journal of Physiology, 148,* pp. 574–591. Used by permission of Cambridge University Press. *Fig. 2.29:* From "Sensory Neural Patterns and Gustation" by R. R. Erikson in Y. Zotterman (ed.), *Olfaction and Taste,* Vol. 1, pp. 205–213. Pergamon Press Ltd., 1963. Used by permission. *Fig. 2.30:* Adapted from S. S. Stevens,

1962, *American Psychologist, 17,* pp. 29–39. Copyright 1962 by the American Psychological Association. Reprinted by permission. *Fig. 2.32:* From "The Relation Between Neural and Perceptual Intensity: A Comparative Study of Neural and Psychophysical Responses to Taste Stimuli" by G. Borg, H. Diamant, C. Strom, and Y. Zotterman, 1967, *Journal of Physiology, 192,* pp. 13–20. Used by permission of Cambridge University Press. *Fig. 2.33:* From "Stimulus-Response Functions of Primary Afferents in Psychophysical Intensity Estimation of Mechanical Skin in the Human Hand" by M. Knibestol and A. B. Vallbo in Y. Zotterman (ed.), *Sensory Functions of the Skin in Primates,* pp. 201–213. Plenum Publishing, 1976. Used by permission. *Box 2.1:* From "Physiological and Morphological Identification of Horizontal, Bipolar and Amacrine Cells in Goldfish Retina" by A. Kaneko, 1970, *Journal of Physiology, 207,* pp. 623–633. Used by permission of Cambridge University Press. *Box 2.2:* Figure from W. H. Dobelle, 1977, *Journal of Visual Impairment and Blindness, 71,* pp. 290–297. Used by permission.

Chapter 3 *Fig. 3.4:* From "Size Adaptation: A New Aftereffect" by C. Blakemore and P. Sutton, *Science,* Vol. 166, pp. 245–247, October 10, 1969. Copyright 1969 by the American Association for the Advancement of Science. Used by permission. *Fig. 3.12:* Adapted from *Human Information Processing,* Second Edition by P. H. Norman and D. A. Lindsay. Academic Press, 1977. Used by permission. *Fig. 3.22:* From "Human Rhodopsin" by G. Wald and P. K. Brown, *Science,* Vol. 127, pp. 222–226, January 31, 1958 and "The Receptors of Human Color Vision" by G. Wald, *Science,* Vol. 145, pp. 1007–1017, September 4, 1964. Copyright 1964 by the American Association for the Advancement of Science. Used by permission. *Fig. 3.23:* From A. Chapanis, 1947, *Journal of General Physiology, 30,* pp. 423–437. Used by permission. *Fig. 3.24:* From "Human Color Vision and Color Blindness" by G. Wald and P. K. Brown, *Cold Spring Harbor Symposia on Quantitative Biology, 30,* pp. 345–359. Cold Spring Harbor Laboratory, 1965. Used by permission. *Fig. 3.27:* From "Visual Acuity" by L. A. Riggs in C. Graham (ed.), *Vision and Visual Perception.* Copyright © 1965 by John Wiley & Sons, Inc. Reprinted by permission of John Wiley & Sons, Inc. *Fig. 3.35:* From "Receptive Fields of Single Neurons in the Cat's Striate Cortex" by D. H. Hubel and T. N. Wiesel, 1959, *Journal of Physiology, 148,* pp. 574–591. Used by permission of Cambridge University Press. *Fig. 3.36:* From D. H. Hubel and T. N. Wiesel, 1965, *Journal of Neurophysiology, 28,* pp. 229–289. Used by permission. *Fig. 3.37:* From "Visual Properties of Neurons in a Polysensor Area in the Superior Temporal Sulcus of the Macaque" by C. Bruce, R. Desimone, and C. G. Gross, 1981. *Journal of Neurophysiology*, 46, pp. 369–384. Used by permission of the American Physiological Society.

Chapter 4 *Figs. 4.3, 4.4 and 4.5:* Adapted from F. W. Clulow, *Color: Its Principles and Their Applications*. Morgan and Morgan, 1972. Used by permission. *Figs. 4.15, 4.16, and 4.17:* From L. Hurvich and D. Jameson, 1957, *Psychological Review*, 64, pp. 384–404. Copyright 1957 by the American Psychological Association. Reprinted by permission. *Fig. 4.19:* From G. Svaetichin, 1956, *Acta Physiologica Scandinavica Supplementum*, *134*, pp. 17–46. Used by permission. *Fig. 4.20:* From "Primate Color Vision" by R. L. DeValois and G. H. Jacobs, *Science*, Vol. 162, pp. 533–540, November 1, 1968. Copyright 1968 by the American Association for the Advancement of Science. Used by permission. *Figs. 4.24 and 4.25:* From "Color Vision Mechanisms in Monkey Striate Cortex: Dual-opponent Cells with Concentric Receptive Fields" by C. R. Michael, 1978, *Journal of Neurophysiology*, 41, pp. 572–588. Used by permission of the American Physiological Society. *Fig. 4.29:* From "Memory Colours in Afterimages: A Bicentennial Demonstration" by C. W. White and D. A. Montgomery, 1976. *Perception and Psychophysics*, 19, pp. 371–374. Reprinted by permission of the Psychonomic Society, Inc.

Chapter 5 *Fig. 5.6:* Adapted from *Mach Banas: Quantitative Studies of Neural Networks in the Retina* by F. Ratliff. Holden-Day, 1965. Used by permission. *Fig. 5.14:* From F. J. Verheijen, 1961, *Optica Acta*, 8, pp. 309–311. Used by permission. *Fig. 5.15:* From "Stabilized Images on the Retina" by R. M. Pritchard, *Scientific American*, *204*. Copyright © 1961 by Scientific American, Inc. All rights reserved. Used by permission. *Fig. 5.20:* From "Application of Fourier Analysis to the Visibility of Gratings" by F. W. Campbell and J. G. Robson, 1968, *Journal of Physiology*, 197, pp. 551–556. Used by permission. *Fig. 5.21:* From "On the Existence of Neurons in the Human Visual System Selectively Sensitive to the Orientation and Size of the Retinal Image" by C. Blakemore and F. W. Campbell, 1969, *Journal of Physiology*, 203, pp. 237–260. Used by permission. *Fig. 5.23:* From "The Visual Cortex as a Spatial Frequency Analyzer" by L. Maffei and A. Fiorentini, 1973, *Vision Research*, 13, pp. 1255–1267. Reprinted by permission of Pergamon Journals, Ltd. *Fig. 5.24:* From "Size Adaptation: A New Aftereffect" by C. Blakemore and P. Sutton, *Science*,

Vol. 166, pp. 245–247, October 10, 1969. Copyright 1969 by the American Association for the Advancement of Science. Used by permission. *Fig. 5.26: Requiem* (detail), pastel and acrylic, by Tom McDonald, 1982. Reproduced with permission. *Fig. 5.32:* Adapted from "Effect of Adaptation on Intensity—Response Relations in the Dorsal Lateral Geniculate Nucleus of the Cat" by D. Schweitzer-Tong. Doctoral dissertation, University of Pittsburgh, 1976. Used by permission. *Fig. 5.38:* From *Experimental Psychology*, Third Edition, edited by J. W. Kling and Lorrin A. Riggs. Copyright 1938, 1954. © 1971 by Holt, Rinehart and Winston, Inc. Reprinted by permission of Holt, Rinehart and Winston. *Fig. 5.42: Corfu: Lights and Shadows* by John Singer Sargent, American 1856–1925, painted in 1909, Hayden Collection. Courtesy, Museum of Fine Arts, Boston. *Figs. 5.46 and 5.47:* From "Perceived Lightness Depends on Perceived Spatial Arrangement" by A. L. Gilchrist, 1977, *Science*, 195, pp. 185–187. Copyright 1977 by the American Association for the Advancement of Science. *Fig. 5.48: Sunlight in a Cafeteria* by Edward Hopper, Yale University Art Gallery, bequest of Stephen Carlton Clark. Used by permission. *Box 5.1:* Collection of the Metropolitan Museum of Art, Harris Brisbane Dick Fund, 1917. Used by permission.

Chapter 6 *Figs. 6.4 and 6.5: From Art and Visual Perception* (2nd ed.) by R. Arnheim. University of California Press, 1974. Used by permission. *Fig. 6.7: Carapace* by Diane Sloan. Collection of the Oakland Museum, gift of Mr. Joseph Chowning. Used by permission. *Fig. 6.8:* Reprinted from Jacob Beck: *Surface Color Perception*. Copyright © 1972 by Cornell University. Used by permission of the publisher, Cornell University Press. *Fig. 6.14:* Photo by Randy Choura. *Fig. 6.15:* Photo by Randy Choura. Dancers: Brian Bloomquist and Laura Desiree. *Fig. 6.17: The Great Bridge at Rouem* by Pissarro. Museum of Art, Carnegie Institute. Pittsburgh, Pennsylvania. Used by permission. *Fig. 6.20:* Photo by Randy Choura. Dancers: Alexander Nagiba and Henry Stevens. *Fig. 6.21: The Forest Has Eyes* by Bev Doolittle © 1984 The Greenwich Workshop, Trumbull, CT. Used by permission. *Fig. 6.23: Pintos* by Bev Doolittle © 1979 The Greenwich Workshop, Trumbull, CT. Used by permission. *Fig. 6.25:* From *Experimental Psychology*, Third Edition, edited by J. W. Kling and Lorrin A. Riggs. Copyright 1938, 1954, © 1971 by Holt, Rinehart and Winston, Inc. Reprinted by permission of Holt, Rinehart and Winston. *Fig. 6.26:* From *Organization in Vision* by Gaetano Kanizsa. Copyright 1979 by Gaetano Kanizsa. Reprinted by permission. *Fig. 6.30: Two Indian Horses* by Bev Doolittle © 1985 The Greenwich Workshop, Trumbull, CT. Used by permission. *Fig. 6.36:* From "Effect of Orientation and Shape Similarity in Perceptual Grouping" by Jacob Beck, 1966, *Perception and Psychophysics, 1,* pp. 300–302. Used by permission. *Fig. 6.37:* From "What Variables Produce Similarity Grouping?" by R. R. Olson and F. Attneave, 1970, *American Journal of Psychology, 83,* pp. 1–21. Copyright 1970 by the American Psychological Association. Used by permission. *Fig. 6.38:* From "Good Continuation Affects Visual Detection" by W. Prinzmetal and W. P. Banks, 1977, *Perception and Psychophysics, 21,* pp. 389–395. Used by permission. *Fig. 6.39:* From "Configurational Effects in Visual Information Processing" by W. P. Banks and W. Prinzmetal, 1976, *Perception and Psychophysics, 19,* pp. 361–367. Used by permission. *Fig. 6.47:* From "Principles of Feature Integration in Visual Perception" by William Prinzmetal, 1981, *Perception and Psychophysics, 30,* pp. 330–340. Used by permission. *Fig. 6.48:* From "On the Semantics of a Glance at a Scene" by I. Biederman in *Perceptual Organization,* M. Kubovy and J. Pomerantz (eds.), 1981. Used by permission. *Figs. 6.51, 6.52, 6.53, and 6.55:* From "Recognition-by-components: A Theory of Human Image Understanding" by Irving Biederman, 1987, *Psychological Review, 94,* pp. 115–147. Used by permission. *Box 6.1:* Figure from *Higher Cortical Functions in Man* by Aleksandr Romanovich Luria, translated from the Russian by Basil Haigh. © 1966 by Consultants Bureau Enterprises, Inc. and Basic Books, Inc., Publishers, New York. Used by permission. *Box 6.2:* From "Object Vision and Spatial Vision: Two Central Pathways" by M. Mishkin, L. G. Ungerleider, and K. A. Macko, 1983, *Trends in Neuroscience, 6,* pp. 414–417. Used by permission.

Chapter 7   *Fig. 7.3: Place des Lices, St. Tropez* (1893) by Paul Signac. Museum of Art, Carnegie Institute, Pittsburgh, Pennsylvania. Used by permission. *Fig. 7.5:* Reproduced by special permission of *Playboy* Magazine; copyright © 1971 by Playboy. *Fig. 7.7:* Photo courtesy of University of Pittsburgh, Office of University Relations. *Fig. 7.11: A Street with Various Buildings, Colonnades, and an Arch, c.* 1500, artist unknown, School of Donate Brumante. Museum of Art, Carnegie Institute. Pittsburgh, Pennsylvania. Used by permission. *Fig. 7.14:* Stereogram by Mike Chikris, 1977. Used by permission. *Fig. 7.20:* D. H. Hubel and T. N. Wiesel, 1970, *Nature,* 225, pp. 41–42. Used by permission. *Figs. 7.25 and 7.26:* Adapted from "Determinants of Actual Visual Size with Distance Variant" by A. H. Holway and E. G. Boring, 1941, *American Journal of Psychology,* 54, pp. 21–37. Used by permission

of the University of Illinois Press. *Figs. 7.32 and 7.33:* Tony Tye/*Pittsburgh Post-Gazette.* Used by permission. *Fig. 7.43:* Photograph courtesy of Philip Brodatz. *Fig. 7.44: Vega-Nor* (1969) by Victor Vasarely. Albright-Knox Art Gallery, Buffalo, New York. Gift of Seymour H. Knox, 1969. Used by permission. *Box 7.2:* Figure from *Foundations of Cyclopean Perception* by B. Julesz. University of Chicago Press, 1971. Used by permission. *Box 7.4:* From "Phenomenal Regression to the Real Object. I" by R. H. Thouless, 1931, *British Journal of Psychology, 21,* pp. 339–359. Used by permission of Cambridge University Press.

Chapter 8   *Fig. 8.11:* From C. Blakemore and E. A. Tobin, 1972, *Experimental Brain Research, 15,* pp. 439–440. Used by permission. *Fig. 8.12:* Adapted from "The Velocity Tuning of Neurons in the Lateral Geniculate Nucleus and Retina of the Cat" by L. Frishman. Doctoral dissertation, University of Pittsburgh, 1979. Used by permission. *Fig. 8.13:* From "Perception" by H. L. Teuber in J. Field, H. W. Magoun, and V. E. Hall (eds.), *Handbook of Physiology,* Section 1, Neurophysiology, Vol. 3, pp. 1595–1668. American Physiological Society, 1960. Used by permission. *Fig. 8.26:* From "Apparent Movement with Subjective Contours" by V. S. Ramachandran, V. M. Rao, and T. R. Vidyasagar, 1973, *Vision Research, 13,* pp. 1399–1401. Used by permission. *Fig. 8.29:* Courtesy of Mark Friedman. *Fig. 8.34:* From H. B. Barlow and R. M. Hill, 1963, *Nature, 200,* pp. 1345–1347. Used by permission. *Fig. 8.35:* From *The Intelligent Eye* by R. L. Gregory. McGraw-Hill, 1970. Used by permission. *Fig. 8.44:* From "A Biomechanical Invariant for Gait Perception" by J. E. Cutting, D. R. Proffitt, and L. T. Kozlowski, 1978, *JEP:HPP, 4,* pp. 357–372. Copyright 1978 by the American Psychological Association. By permission of the author. *Fig. 8.46:* From F. Heider and M. L. Simmel, 1944, *American Journal of Psychology, 57,* pp. 243–249. Used by permission of the University of Illinois Press. *Fig. 8.47:* From "Visual Proprioceptive Control of Standing in Human Infants" by D. N. Lee and E. Aronson, 1974, *Perception and Psychophysics, 15,* pp. 529–532. Used by permission of the Psychonomic Society, Inc. *Fig. 8.50:* From "The Optic Flow Field: The Foundation of Vision" by D. N. Lee, 1980, *Transactions of the Royal Society, 290B,* pp. 169–179. *Box 8.2:* From *Aspects of Motion Perception* by P. A. Kolers, Pergamon Press, Ltd., 1971. Used by permission.

Chapter 9   *Fig. 9.7:* Adapted from "Visual Acuity for Vertical and Diagonal Gratings in Human Infants" by

D. Teller, R. Morse, R. Borton, and D. Regal, 1974, *Vision Research, 14*, pp. 1433–1439. Copyright 1974, Pergamon Press, Ltd. Used by permission. *Fig. 9.8*: From "Infant Contrast Sensitivity Evaluated by Evoked Potentials" by M. Pirchio, D. Spinelli, A. Fiorentini, and L. Maffei, *Brain Research, 141*, pp. 179–184. Used by permission. *Fig. 9.9*: From *The Postnatal Development of the Cerebral Cortex*, Vol. 1, 1939 and Vol. 3, 1947, and *The Postnatal Development of the Human Cerebral Cortex*, Vol. 4, 1951 by J. L. Conel, Harvard University Press. Used by permission. *Fig. 9.14*: From "Assessment of Stereopsis in Human Infants" by S. L. Shea, R. Fox, R. Aslin, and S. T. Dumais, 1980. *Investigative Ophthalmology and Visual Science, 19*, pp. 1400–1404. Used by permission of the C. V. Mosby Company. *Fig. 9.15*: From "Stereoacuity of Human Infants" by R. Held, E. E. Birch, and J. Gwiazda, 1980, *Proceedings of the National Academy of Sciences, 77*, pp. 5572–5574. Used by permission. *Fig. 9.16*: From "Infants' Perception of Pictorially Specified Interposition" by E. E. Granrud and A. Yonas, 1984, *Journal of Experimental Child Psychology, 37*, pp. 500–511. Used by permission. *Fig. 9.17*: From "Infants' Sensitivity to Familiar Size: The Effect of Memory on Spatial Perception" by C. E. Granrud, R. J. Haake, and A. Yonas, 1985, *Perception and Psychophysics, 37*, pp. 459–466. Used by permission. *Fig. 9.18*: From "Pattern Perception in Early Infancy" by P. Salapatek in L. B. Cohen and P. Salapatek (eds.), *Infant Perception: From Sensation to Cognition*, Vol. 1, Academic Press, 1975. Used by permission. *Fig. 9.21*: From "Infant's Recognition of Invariant Features of Faces" by J. F. Fagan, 1976, *Child Development, 47*, pp. 627–638. Copyright 1976 by the Society for Research in Child Development. Used by permission. *Fig. 9.25*: From C. R. Olson and R. D. Freeman, 1975, *Journal of Neurophysiology, 38*, pp. 26–32. Used by permission. *Figs. 9.27 and 9.28*: From "Optically Induced Concomitant Strabismus in the Monkey" by M. L. J. Crawford, 1980, *Investigative Ophthalmology and Visual Science, 19*, pp. 1105–1109. Used by permission of the C. V. Mosby Company. *Fig. 9.30*: From C. Blakemore and G. F. Cooper, 1970, *Nature, 228*, pp. 477–478. Used by permission. *Fig. 9.31*: From H. V. B. Hirsch and D. N. Spinelli, 1971, *Experimental Brain Research, 12*, pp. 509–527. Used by permission. *Fig. 9.32*: From C. Blakemore and G. F. Cooper, 1970, *Nature, 228*, pp. 477–478. Used by permission. *Fig. 9.33*: From C. Blakemore and E. Mitchell, 1973, *Nature, 241*, pp. 467–468. Used by permission. *Fig. 9.36*: From "Sensitive Period for the Development of Human Binocular Vision" by M. S. Banks, R. N. Aslin, and R. D. Letson, 1975, *Science, 190*, pp. 675–677. Used by permission.

Fig. 9.37: From *The World Through Blunted Sight* by P. Trevor-Roper, Bobbs-Merrill, 1970. Used by permission. *Fig. 9.38*: From "The Effect of Early Astigmatism on the Visual Resolution of Gratings" by D. E. Mitchell and F. Wilkinson, 1974, *Journal of Physiology, 243*, pp. 739–756. Used by permission of Cambridge University Press. *Box. 9.1*: Figure from R. Held and A. Hein, 1963, *Journal of Comparative and Physiological Psychology, 56*, pp. 872–876. Copyright 1963 by the American Psychological Association. Reprinted by permission.

Chapter 10 *Box 10.2*: Mary Solbrig, *Our Home*, 1985. Courtesy of Forecast Public Artspace Productions of Minneapolis. *Box 10.3*: (Left) Scott Nelson, *Glance #2,672,493*, 1985. (Right) Carmello Ganello, *Retinal Detachment*, 1985. Courtesy of Forecast Public Artspace Productions of Minneapolis.

Chapter 11 *Fig. 11.11*: From "The Relation of Pitch to Frequency: A Revised Scale" by S. S. Stevens and J. Volkman, 1940, *American Journal of Psychology, 53*, pp. 329–353. Used by permission. *Box 11.1*: Figure from "Sonar System of the Blind" by W. N. Kellogg, *Science*, Vol. 137, pp. 399–404, August 10, 1962. Copyright 1962 by the American Association for the Advancement of Science. Used by permission. *Box 11.2*: Figure from "The Sensory World of the Homing Pigeon" by M. L. Kreithen in A. M. Granda and J. H. Maxwell, *Neural Mechanisms of Behavior in the Pigeon*, 1979. Used by permission of Plenum Publishing.

Chapter 12 *Fig. 12.2*: From *Human Information Processing* (2nd ed.) by P. H. Lindsay and D. A. Norman. Academic Press, Inc., 1977. Used by permission. *Fig. 12.3*: From *Hearing: Physiology and Psychophysics* by W. Lawrence Gulick. Copyright © 1971 by Oxford University Press, Inc. Used by permission. *Fig. 12.6*: From "Disorders of Human Communication," Vol. 1, by E. D. Schubert, *Hearing: Its Function and Dysfunction*, p. 15, Wien, New York: Springer, 1980. Used by permission. *Fig. 12.10*: From "Hearing: Physiology and Psychophysics" by W. Lawrence Gulick. Copyright © 1971 by Oxford University Press, Inc. Used by permission. *Fig. 12.16*: From "Disorders of Human Communication," Vol. 1, by E. D. Schubert, *Hearing: Its Function and Dysfunction*, p. 18, Wien, New York: Springer, 1980. Used by permission. *Fig. 12.17*: From J. Tonndorf, 1960, *Journal of the Acoustical Society of America, 32*, pp. 238–244. Used by permission. *Figs. 12.18 and 12.19*: From *Experiments in Hearing* by G. von Békésy. McGraw-Hill, 1960. Used by permission. *Fig. 12.20*: From "A Revised Frequency

Map of the Guinea Pig Cochlea" by E. A. Culler, J. D. Coakley, K. Lowy, and N. Gross, 1943, *American Journal of Psychology*, 56, pp. 475–500. Used by permission of the University of Illinois Press. *Fig. 12.22:* From "Stimulus Representation in the Discharge Patterns of Auditory Neurons" by N. Y. S. Kiang in E. L. Eagles (ed.), *The Nervous System*, Vol. 3. Raven Press, New York, 1975. Used by permission. *Fig. 12.23:* From M. M. Merzenich, P. L. Knight, and G. L. Roth, 1973, *Brain Research*, 63, pp. 343–346. Used by permission. *Fig. 12.31:* From E. I. Knudsen and M. Konishi, 1978, *Journal of Neurophysiology*, 41, pp. 870–883. Used by permission. *Fig. 12.32:* From "A Neural Map of Auditory Space in the Owl" by E. I. Knudsen and M. Konishi, 1978, *Science*, 200, pp. 795–797. Used by permission. *Box. 12.1:* Figure from "A Case of Firecracker Induced Hearing Loss" by W. D. Ward and A. Glorig, *Laryngoscope*, 71, pp. 1590–1596, 1961. Used by permission.

Chapter 13 *Fig. 13.1:* From "Stimulus Representation in the Discharge Patterns of Auditory Neurons" by N.Y.S. Kiang in E. L. Eagles (ed.), *The Nervous System*, Vol. 3. Raven Press, New York, 1975. Used by permission. *Fig. 13.3:* From *Psychology and Language: An Introduction to Psycholinguistics* by Herbert H. Clark and E. V. Clark, © 1977 by Harcourt Brace Jovanovich, Inc. Reproduced by permission of the publisher. *Fig. 13.6:* From "Time-varying Features of Initial Stop Consonants in Auditory Running Spectra: A First Report" by D. Kewley-Port and P. A. Luce, 1984, *Perception and Psychophysics*, 35, pp. 353–360. Used by permission of the Psychonomic Society, Inc. *Fig. 13.7:* Courtesy of Ronald A. Cole, Carnegie-Mellon University, Pittsburgh. *Fig. 13.8:* From P. D. Eimas and J. D. Corbit, 1973, *Cognitive Psychology*, 4, pp. 99–109. Used by permission of Academic Press, Inc. *Figs. 13.11 and 13.12:* Courtesy of Ronald A. Cole, Carnegie-Mellon University, Pittsburgh. *Box 13.1:* Figure from "Speech Perception in Infants" by P. D. Eimas, E. R. Siqueland, P. Jusczyk, and J. Vigorito, *Science*, Vol. 171, pp. 303–306, January 22, 1971. Copyright 1971 by the American Association for the Advancement of Science. Used by permission. *Fig. 13.13:* © 1988 Archie Comic Publications, Inc.

Chapter 14 *Fig. 14.1:* From *Living Images* by G. Shih and R. Kessell. Jones and Bartlett Publishers, Inc., 1982. Used by permission. *Fig. 14.2:* From *Fundamentals of Neurology* (6th ed.) by E. Gardner. W. B. Saunders Company, 1975. Used by permission. *Fig. 14.4:* From D. R. Kenshalo in Y. Zotterman (ed.) *Sensory Functions of the Skin in Primates*, p. 309. Plenum Publishing, 1976. Used

by permission. *Fig. 14.5:* From "Nervous Outflow from the Cat's Foot During Noxious Radiant Heat Stimulation" by P. W. Beck, *Brain Research*, 67, pp. 373–386. Used by permission. *Fig. 14.6:* From W. R. Lowenstein, "Biological Transducers," *Scientific American*, 203, August 1960. Used by permission. *Fig. 14.7:* From "Mechanical Transmission in a Pacinian Corpuscle: An Analysis and a Theory" by W. R. Lowenstein and R. Skalak, 1966, *Journal of Physiology*, 182, pp. 346–378. Used by permission of Cambridge University Press. *Figs. 14.12 and 14.13:* From "Movement-Sensitive and Direction and Orientation Selective Cutaneous Receptive Fields in the Hand Area of the Postcentral Gyrus in Monkeys" by J. Hyvärinen and A. Poranen, 1978, *Journal of Physiology*, 283, pp. 523–537. Used by permission of Cambridge University Press. *Figs. 14.14 and 14.15:* From "Cortical Processing of Tactile Information in the First Somatosensory and Parietal Association Areas in the Monkey" by H. Sakata and Y. Iwamura in G. Gordon (ed.), *Active Touch*, pp. 55–72. Pergamon Press Ltd., 1978. Used by permission. *Figs. 14.17 and 14.18:* From "The Tactile Sensory Innervation of the Glabrous Skin of the Human Hand" by A. B. Vallbo and R. S. Johanssen in G. Gordon (ed.), *Active Touch*, pp. 29–54. Pergamon Press Ltd., 1978. Used by permission. *Fig. 14.20:* Adapted from "Living Prehistory in India" by Nalini D. Kosambi, 1967, *Scientific American*, Vol. 105, pp. 110–111. Used by permission. *Box 14.1:* Figure from B. W. White, F. A. Saunders, L. Scadden, P. Bach-y-Rita, and C. Collins, 1970, *Perception and Psychophysics*, 7, pp. 23–27. Used by permission. *Box 14.3:* From "Multiple-joint Neurons in Somatosensory Cortex of Awake Monkeys" by R. M. Costanzo and E. P. Gardner, 1981, *Brain Research*, 214, pp. 321–333.

Chapter 15 *Fig. 15.1:* From "The Stereochemical Theory of Odor by J. E. Amoore, J. W. Johnston, Jr., and M. Rubin, *Scientific American*, 210. Copyright © 1964 by Scientific American, Inc. All rights reserved. Used by permission. *Figs. 15.3 and 15.4:* From *Experimental Psychology* by Robert S. Woodworth. Copyright 1938 by Henry Holt and Company, Inc., renewed © 1966 by Mrs. Greta Woodworth Herron, Svenson Woodworth, William Woodworth, and Virginia Woodworth. Reprinted by permission of Holt, Rinehart and Winston, and Mrs. Greta Woodworth Herron, Svenson Woodworth, William Woodworth, and Virginia Woodworth. *Fig. 15.5:* From "The Stereochemical Theory of Odor" by J. E. Amoore, J. W. Johnston, Jr., and M. Rubin, *Scientific American*, 210. Copyright © 1964 by Scientific American, Inc. All rights reserved. Used by permission. *Fig.*